THE UNITED STATES NAVY

THE
UNITED STATES NAVY

200 YEARS

Edward L. Beach

Captain, U.S.N. (Ret.)

HENRY HOLT AND COMPANY
New York

Library of Congress Cataloging in Publication Data
Beach, Edward Latimer, 1918–
The United States Navy : 200 years.
Bibliography: p. 523
Includes index.
1. United States.   Navy—History.   2. United
States—History, Naval.   I. Title.
VA55.B36   1986   359'.00973   85–8617
3 5 7 9 10 8 6 4 2

ISBN 0-8050-0476-9

Designer: Jacqueline Schuman
Printed in the United States of America

ISBN 0-8050-0476-9

This book can be dedicated only to our navy itself,
and to all the men and women who have been in it,
and of it, since the beginning—
and most especially to the one whose name I bear.

A Grateful Salute to Bill Dunne

William M. P. Dunne, my research assistant for the first part of this book, deserves a more prestigious title. He has been far more than a mere assistant. A sometime race-car driver, yachtsman, and now a yacht broker, Bill underwent practical training in wooden boat construction in recent years, as a result of which he developed a deep, all-consuming interest in the wind-powered, wooden warships that figured in our early history. An early schoolboy interest in history thus bloomed into a passion, and he became a habitué of the widely seperated sources of information about them. He spent three years in England studying the plans and records available at the National Maritime Museum, Greenwich, and the Public Records Office, Kew. Following this he researched the files existing between Portsmouth, New Hampshire, and Charleston, South Carolina, turning up information that, in some cases, had been buried since the day it was compiled or written. His continued immersion in the smallest details of these ships has produced much new information about their design and construction. Much of the history of our navy of that era was a direct outgrowth of the way its ships were built—as is now clear.

Bill's contribution has been to bring these structural details forward with lucid explanations. I owe him a great deal, as will be clearly seen in the pages to follow. He knows more about the ships of that long ago but not forgotten time than anyone in my experience. I want to state this unequivocally, and salute him enthusiastically.

Contents

Contents

Pictures fall between pp. 160–177 and pp. 368–385.

Acknowledgments

Second only to Bill Dunne's professional assistance, my family, in particular my beloved wife, Ingrid, has been my anchor to windward. She has scrutinized every line herein and has made her own direct contributions in terms of conciseness, thoughtfulness, composition, and readability. She has been steadily encouraging at all times, most specially when I have been so deeply submerged that it seemed there was no way at all to the surface and its life-giving fresh air.

Among the institutions that helped with this book, the Navy Department Library stands preeminent—not only for assisting with research but also in providing day-to-day support in the thousands of mundane questions that arose in a work of this nature. Founded by Commodore Dudley Knox early this century in what is now the Indian Treaty Room of the President's Old Executive Offices Building (formerly the State, War and Navy Building), alongside the White House, this library has grown to true professional stature and is becoming world-known as the repository of the papers and collections of naval officers searching for a place where the work of a lifetime can be preserved. It has, of course, had its vicissitudes but, manned by an inspired group of professionals and at last moved to enlarged quarters in the historic Washington Navy Yard, it is becoming importantly felt in historical circles. Stan Kalkus, John Vajda, and Barbara Lynch of the library staff are deeply involved in their jobs and gave willingly of their time and research talents. They helped me far above and beyond the call of duty. It is a pleasure to say so publicly.

In addition, I owe much to Chuck Haberlein and Aggie Hoover, and the "yellow dog" group of naval aficionados Chuck has founded, not only for photographic research but also for their informal enthusiasm. They will see more of me, for I intend to become a sometime yellow dog myself. I am also grateful to my old friend, Louis Smaus, who loaned me his collection of stereo views of old ships of the turn of this century, some of which are reproduced in this book (and are being copied by Chuck to add to the navy's wide collection under his charge).

Nor can I fail to mention Mary and Vance Gordon who, some five years ago, twice invited me to their home in Colorado but forbade any visiting between breakfast and dinner, so that their home was a retreat for uninterrupted work. And I am also very appreciative of the interest and assistance of Jack Kane, Director of Naval History, and his thoughtfully motivated assistants, Dean Allard and Bill Dudley.

Finally, I must give a great deal of credit—as is evident from perusal of the bibliography—to the files of two world-renowned magazines, the *Naval Institute Proceedings* and *American Heritage*. Both organizations are imbued with the same philosophy I have tried to express here: a love for our country's organization and its institutions, and a passion to present the facts, and what came from them, truly in all their nuances of meaning.

Naturally, all inferences and derivations from the story recounted on these pages are my own. No one else bears any responsibility for them, except my father, gone these four decades and more—and for him I gladly carry it all.

Edward L. Beach
Captain, U.S. Navy
Washington, D.C.
August 1985

Author's Note

There are essentially two views of history: that which one has studied, and that which one has experienced. It is not possible to combine the two. To critics who will say that World War II is sparsely covered, even though it is called our Armageddon at sea and even though I served through it, the only answer is that this book is not a history but a progress. Those expecting the usual view of history, in which some attempt is made to tell all the operational details of events, will be disappointed.

What follows is the progression of events that led us to, and through, World War II. It is the story of naval officers who cared mightily about their country, and the navy they chose as the means of their contribution to it. Sadly, not all of them, nor all the anecdotes, could be covered. They are too many, including nearly the whole of our naval officer corps; and the events are legion. The development of our navy, nevertheless, is a continuous story of dedicated people. This book is my version of the pivotal events that shaped it.

A Very Personal Preface

There was a sense of Armageddon at sea in 1942, a feeling that the great test for which our navy had been created had at last arrived. Not merely the "greatest" of all its testings, but the culmination of its entire history, of everything that had gone before. It was this for which all the wars, campaigns, battles, and, particularly, all the work it had done and all the development it had undergone had been but preliminaries.

We could sense it. It was palpable. This was what we had built our navy for. In the unfathomable all-knowing wisdom of instinctive mind, this was the conflict toward which the United States Navy had been targeted.

George Washington, commanding the Continental Army, began our navy on his own authority by commissioning a few small ships to support his soldiers on the trackless flank to the east. A few years later, he ended the Revolutionary War by brilliant coordination with fortuitously available sea power: the French fleet came up from the West Indies at his urgent plea, cutting Cornwallis off from rendezvous with his own navy and enabling Washington to force his surrender at Yorktown.

Our navy subsequently fought France, England a second time, Mexico, Spain, and Germany. It also fought a fierce war with itself, and the War Between the States could be called a four-year battle. But our naval history before World War II was largely one of growth and development, with only sporadic fighting. During the Revolution, John Paul Jones's epic battle with HMS *Serapis* gave us our first big victory at sea; there were three well-fought frigate duels during the quasi-war with France in 1798; and there was a series of brilliant single-ship battles—and two with small fleets on our lakes—in the War of 1812. In the Spanish-American War, there were two squadron battles against totally outclassed Spanish forces. Until 1941, our country was at war for only some twenty years, of which there was a real shooting war in only about eleven. And the time spent in actual naval battle would add up to only about 56 hours. The rest of our navy's time was spent in training. But considering the payoff that began in 1941, those years were well spent.

As tyranny spread in the 1930s, the free world came under intolerable threat, and at the end of that decade, Europe exploded into general war. As it had in the Great War of 1914–1918, the Atlantic Ocean gave safe haven to German submarines, which ranged it freely, doing tremendous damage to our allies of that earlier war. The Germans called this the "happy time," because they sank ships with virtual impunity. It was not a happy time for England or France, and, a little over two years after the war began, on a Sunday morning while we were still technically at peace, our own surprised battle line lay crushed into the smelly mud and oil of Pearl Harbor, and we knew the biggest and most dangerous thing that could happen had happened: war on both sides of our water-bounded nation, on two fronts at once, in both of the huge oceans that had protected our hemisphere so long. War against two powerful, ruthless foes.

We had had training and preparation for at least part of this war, for the prospect of having to fight Japan had for years loomed large in the curriculum of the Naval War College at Newport, Rhode Island. In the naval war games played there, Japan was known as Orange, and the general war plan made there was known as the Orange Plan. But our preparation for war with Japan was both too much and not enough.

Much of our training had been directed at the wrong things. We trained too much on the premise that Japan would fight according to the European Marquess of Queensberry rule book. Even as we drew up our war plan, we assumed Japan would fight the sort of war we would, were we in her shoes. We reveled in what history taught us: for example, that the key to control of the sea is to keep your own fleet concentrated, bring the enemy fleet to battle, and defeat it. Control of the sea, a term coined by our great naval theorist of the turn of the century, Alfred Thayer Mahan, meant essentially that no enemy force could plan on using it, for fear of being met by ours. All our accepted war plans envisaged the climactic fleet battle, typified by 1916's Jutland, in which great opposing fleets of ships would come together in a titanic, decisive struggle. (We misread history and misinterpreted Mahan, for such a battle had not taken place since Trafalgar. At Jutland, though the great columns of battleships assembled, they were not in action for any significant time. Jutland was actually a battle-cruiser skirmish, and was not decisive because neither fleet was eliminated.) Jutland was thoroughly studied at the naval colleges of England and the United States, where students and instructors alike were captured by the grandeur of the tremendous battle that nearly happened. Except for our naval aviators, we mostly missed the signs of change that were already evident. As it turned out, the war at sea that we found ourselves fighting in 1941 bore far more resemblance to the preliminary high-speed battle-cruiser action of Jutland—which did take place—than to the crunching engagement between great iron fortresses that both fleets had expected, and which did not occur.

In the slow-moving days of sail when all ships had to use the same wind, there was validity to the concept of actually "controlling" the sea. Judicious stationing of the battle line, with scouting ships that kept information flowing to the fleet commander, could prevent a nation's enemies from transporting the resources of war by sea and would thus contribute to, if not ensure, their defeat—provided the enemy navy was ineffective or had been neutralized. Or, that navy could be forced to deliver itself to battle, after which total control could no longer be disputed. This Horatio Nelson did at Trafalgar, decisively confining Napoleon to the continent of Europe by denying him the sea, and incidentally confirming himself as a hero to the English people. Because of his thorough study of this period, Mahan became a hero to the English people as well, and consequently to our navy, too. But because Mahan's work was so well done that his principles were accepted as law, we became too ready to accept rationalization of the past as projection of the future. His fame as an intellectual made it easy for lackluster minds of high rank to dispose of argument by quoting him, whether appropriately or not. Mahan would have been horrified, and in fact several times said as much.

Thus we sought and achieved perfection in an outmoded form of naval warfare, one that differed only slightly from the glorious past. We saw columns of great armored steel ships, fueled by oil instead of the wind or coal, refighting the Battles of Trafalgar and Jutland, and (except for small groups of far-seeing officers—most of them fliers) we ignored the changes wrought by time and technology. Basically, only a small group of naval aviators recognized that fleet actions such as these would never take place again.

None of our preparation had adequately visualized the situation we would encounter. Our planners had dealt with some of the technological innovations—submarines and aircraft, for example—but had crammed them into an outmoded strategy instead of permitting them to achieve what they could best do. Both were programmed into the role of "fleet scout," with aircraft given the additional function of spotting main battery gunfire. Both were foreordained to act as adjuncts to the great fleet battle, the replay of magnificent combats of the past, while we lulled ourselves into believing the problems were static and that we had solved them. We believed training in the weapons of 1915 would remain useful in 1941. We trained so that we could win the Battle of Jutland were it to be fought again. As late as 1941, we still had not seen, let alone applied, the lessons of battle already so evident in Europe, so painfully learned by those fighting there since 1939. Our sword was old and out-of-date; we had kept its blade and scabbard shining, but we had neglected to reshape its cutting edge.

Training was the shibboleth to which we all subscribed. Along the line, competition between ships and units had been instituted as a means to improve training, and by 1941, winning was more important than anything else. Upon it hung prizes and promotion—not to mention that indefinable "ship's spirit" that denied the impossible. Many were the stratagems devised to improve one's score, including demonstrations that unsatisfactory equipment could be used despite failure by others. Thus, machine guns that rusted in minutes on exposure to sea air, and hence were of no value whatever to naval warfare, were overhauled just before practice firings and afterward repacked in heavy grease—making them unusable—until cleaned and overhauled for the next practice. Undependable diesels were maintained by working engine-room crews day and night, sometimes until they dropped in warm corners for a few moments of sleep, all in the name of making a poorly designed engine perform so that the ship would not "get a bad name."

Similarly, depth-charge attacks were graded on the excellence of the charts prepared afterward, in which a perfect score was achieved if all the little circles depicting "lethal radius" touched each other: that is, the submarine could not pass between them, ergo it must have been "sunk." Such results required only a little skill with a drawing pen. Similarly, ship engineers routinely squirreled away extra fuel in their tanks during noncompetitive periods, so that during engineering competition it could be doled out as necessary to indicate less fuel used than was in fact the case, and thus show operational economy for the judging period. One battleship won the engineering "E" (for Excellence) by cutting off virtually all internal heat, lights, and power, and drastically reducing fresh-water consumption, becoming practically uninhabitable in the process. A gunnery "E" was once awarded because the ship was given a slight list, by judicious use of fuel, exactly equal to the precalculated elevation required of the guns, which could therefore be fired at a faster rate. Performance was the criterion by which careers rose and fell; practice always had to be successful, regardless of what was tested. Torpedo readiness tests, for example, were always preceded by a thorough overhaul of the torpedo to be fired, regardless of whether such a test accurately represented probable wartime conditions. In extreme cases, actual "gundecking" took place (a "gundecked" report was composed on the gundeck and sometimes bore little relation to the real task and data involved).

Those who raised voices against such practices (and there were many) were usually put down as being too lazy to engage in real competition. The payoff was in results, regardless of usefulness or applicability to improved efficiency, and the fervor was analogous to the hysteria over college football.

Despite this, our overall training, our morale, our feel for what we were doing, our loyalty to our organization and to the country, were high. Our ships, products of a design and engineering tradition dating from the Revolutionary War, were top quality, although many, unfortunately, were no longer new. They were, however, pridefully maintained—and what they could do, they did well. The sad thing was that the crews serving them did not know their limitations in modern technology, while those who did know, or should have known—the high-ranking officers and politicians—permitted the pressures of the times, the demand for economy in the face of a not-yet-ended Great Depression, to blind them to experiences already well documented in the war in Europe. But in loyalty, intelligence, determination, and perseverance, our men could not be faulted. And the delight of those fortunate enough to receive new equipment or serve in a new ship could not be greater.

Demonstrably, during its history our navy has served our country well, even though it was, and is, a society of its own, a private mini-society within the greater American society. Could anyone have expected anything different of ships that stay at sea for months at a time? Or of men accustomed and trained to act as concerted units, with a single voice and a single direction? Of course our navy is authoritarian, but as a consequence it has held together in face of extreme pressures, in combat and otherwise. Its officer corps believes in strict ideals of conduct, loyalty up and down, responsibility, and self-abnegation. So, in the main, do its enlisted men. Through two centuries of history it has built up a standard of efficiency, technical knowledge, resiliency, and professionalism. It was this that sustained it during the terrible trials of the first years of World War II.

This standard still exists, carefully nurtured by those who believe in it, passed along to those coming after. It is the tradition into which I was born, the pattern to which I was raised. My earliest memories are of the navy, even though they are in truth only of my father telling me about it. The first stories I remember reading were of the navy, and they were history, not children's storybooks. Lying on my stomach on our living room rug, I literally read Father's copies of James Fenimore Cooper's and Edgar Maclay's naval histories to pieces, for I was less than understanding in my treatment of books and bindings in those days. Father's own books, which I discovered at the age of about seven, complete in special author's bindings, received the same treatment. So did a number of fine picture books he had acquired somewhere. Some of these books stand on my library shelves today, professionally and beautifully rebound as penance for my heedless younger days, and one of the picture books, which I thought I had completely destroyed and thus lost forever, has recently reappeared, in the form of an undamaged copy from a friend who understood how much I would value it.

My father entered the U.S. Naval Academy in 1884, served until retirement in 1922, and died in 1943. I went to Annapolis in 1935 and was on continuous active service until the end of 1966. Both my father and I loved the navy, wrote books and articles about it, served on the board of the U.S. Naval Institute (an independent navy-oriented organization that publishes the highly regarded monthly *Proceedings*), and read naval history as a special area of personal interest. My first knowledge of our navy thus came in fact at Father's knee, when I was about six years old and he was already a retired captain. As a youngster I built wooden models of our entire battle fleet, with his help as to numbers of stacks and masts (made with big nails), and great guns (small nails)—and such other obvious distinguishing features as clipper bows. My models would not have been acclaimed among the ship-modeling fraternity (most of them ended up as firewood and it was well they did), but in the summer of my seventh year there were some great evening naval battles fought on our large front porch.

To my mind and heart, Father never left the navy, nor have I, though his days at sea were over when I knew him, and so, now, are mine. In the sense in which I write, we already compass together just about half the entire period of our navy's existence. It is not an unworthy point of pride. He bequeathed his understanding of our navy, and his appreciation for it, to me. I am the inheritor of all his history, all his writings (including a few unpublished manuscripts), and everything he knew or felt about the sea service of our country. I have always felt myself to be a continuation of him, a surrogate extension. It has been an abiding emotion in my personal makeup.

In 1898 my father fought at Manila Bay as a junior officer, and in 1918 he commanded the flagship of the American Battle Squadron of the British Grand Fleet, based in Scapa Flow, Scotland. But the second battle of the great fleets, after the disappointing Jutland in 1916, never took place, and he watched the surrender of the German High Seas Fleet from the bridge of his battlewagon, with his crew at battle stations just in case.

I came along at about this time, and by 1941, with only two years of commissioned service in the navy, felt within myself a strange ambivalence: on the one hand youth and inexperience, on the other the excitement of the challenge brought by the most serious crisis of our time. Would we—would I—be able to master this greatest of all tests? How would my father's junior officers, now pretty well running things, react to my puny contributions? Would they even be aware of them? Could anything I did make any difference to the war?

Somehow I felt strangely left behind, almost an outsider looking on. My logical place, it seemed to me, should have been with the officers my father had helped train, who would be in the forefront of the battle—but I had been born late in Father's life, and they were all oldsters to me. Except in the sense of being welcomed as my father's son, I was beneath their notice, not truly worthy in my own right.

In the crucible of the war years, this lack of confidence, while natural enough perhaps, could not last long. I found my niche, and have the glad feeling that I did contribute to the winning of the war. So, in a reverse sort of way, did my father. The submarine of which I was executive officer was within a day of going on patrol when news came that he had died; I could not go home right then, although I did after we got back. I expressed my grief in the only way I could think of, a childish way, but it made me feel better. I quietly penciled his name on the warheads of our torpedoes. One of our chiefs saw me do it, but he knew what had happened, and he must have guessed from the look on my face that I was best left alone.

Being my father's son has also produced warm rewards. "I knew your dad," senior officers have said to me. "I served in the old *Neversink* with him." Or, amazingly often, "I entered the navy because of your father's books." My favorite such yarn concerns Admiral Nimitz. It was not long after the war, and he was Chief of Naval Operations. I was a lieutenant commander, the most junior member of the inspection party the admiral was taking with him on a long propeller-driven aircraft flight to California. Some hours after we had taken off, the admiral's aide came forward to us in the steerage with the news that the CNO wanted to play cribbage; as the most junior person present, his aide said, it was my duty to oblige him. Never questioning the process by which I had been selected, and blessing Father's foresight in teaching me the game, I moved aft to the admiral's cabin, apologized for not being very good at cards, and settled in to keep my wits about me and do the best I could. Partly with the help of some extraordinary cribs, I won the first game handily. In fact, I nearly skunked the old man, but somehow he managed to peg just enough holes to escape that ignominy. During the game, I thought he handled the cards rather slowly for the inveterate cribbage player I had assumed he must be, and I could not help noticing that his ring finger was missing from his left hand. His Naval Academy ring was on his right hand. The gap in his left hand where a finger should have been was constantly before my eyes; gradually memory stirred, and at last I got up the courage to say, "Admiral, excuse me for asking a personal question, but I can't help noticing that you have lost a finger. When I was a small boy, a naval officer came to see my dad, and he was missing that same finger. I was fascinated and kept asking him about it. He said it had been torn off in a machinery accident in a submarine, and when I asked if it hurt a lot he said no, not right then, but it sure hurt a lot later. Could this have been you?"

There was a little smile on Admiral Nimitz's face. "I was just wondering if you'd remember," he said. "Your father gave me some good advice that day. You were pretty young, but you said you wanted to go to Annapolis, and I see you made it.''

It was his turn to deal. This time, he shuffled the cards much more quickly. I cut, and he dealt them out for the second game. But my winning streak had ended.

I retired from active duty in our navy in December 1966, more than 31 years after I entered the Naval Academy. It has been a long and satisfying career during which great things happened in and to our navy, and I would not exchange my time in it for anything I can think of. Dad used to say the same thing. Looking back on our combined naval service, I see many high points and very few low ones. Father served through some of our navy's most formative years and commanded five of its finest ships. I served through its period of majority, when it won the widest ranging, hardest fought, and most important war of human history. I have served in nine important ships and was skipper of five, one of them a nuclear-powered submarine. Nothing can equal that thrill. But all those old ships have long been broken up for scrap, except for one currently in mothballs and one on everlasting duty station off the coast of Japan.

I see this recital of our navy's development as part of the debt I owe my father, and that he and I owe to our long-dead shipmates and to the living ones as well. To them, as to my father and me, and to all those who have served in our navy, there has been an undefinable smell of adventure, of having a hand in great matters. The navy is many things, of course; but most of all it is a taut, idealistic group of men who live a life different from the more comfortable norm, who have been subjected to stresses their shore-bound brothers never felt, never saw, never thought of. As a result, they speak a different language.

This is not what one might call a complete or a ''proper'' history. My objective has been to describe some of the ships, people, and events that, together, contributed to the growth of our navy, with some judgment of the importance of each. There are events and individuals left out of this account that some may feel should have been included. Though many battles are described, others are barely mentioned, or not at all, because they do not fit into my conceptualization of the development of our navy. I have tried to describe this as it has seemed to those serving in it, but these pages can reflect only my own personal outlook, perceptions, and evaluations. I have listed my references at the end of this book; the story, the heroes, and what they accomplished are there for anyone with the interest to read about them, after which he can be free to make up his own mind. This is the story I have lived with all my life.

I am a naval officer, not a historian, although I have read history, particularly naval history, since childhood. This book is far from an operational history of our navy, nor is it, speaking in the sense that histories are supposed to be chronological and even-handed, organized in the usual way. There are many diverse threads running through it, but in my opinion all stem from the same fundamental baseline, a continuity of innovation running through our history that, forced by the times, has led us steadily to the position of preeminence we now occupy. I shall not try to tell everything that happened at a particular time, nor name all the great names, but I do hope to take each of the primary themes of our navy's history and pursue it to its conclusion, showing how it added to, or was detrimental to, our readiness for the Armageddon at sea that came in World War II. What I seek to delineate, from the outlook of one of its own members peering through time at the men, influences, and events that have shaped it, is this single grand progression which so clearly underlies everything. This thread, fumblingly followed at some times, brilliantly pursued at others, brought our navy on line during World War II and made possible our victory. The navy had its faults then, and no doubt has them now; but the whole was and is much greater than all its faults put together.

There have been great changes in the world in the past half century. More, probably, than in any other similar length of time. Our navy has adjusted to the changes as they have occurred; of recent years it has actually led them, instead of following after. To remain as a viable force it has had to, for the age of electronics and computers is upon us. Even though he frequently predicted massive improvements in the way it would do its business, my father would be dumbfounded could he see our navy today.

It is part of the human condition that we shall always try to anticipate what the future will bring. Our navy has its own ideals, prejudices, traditions, and deep-set problems, some of them dating back to World War II and even earlier. It is facing new, equally deep problems in the world, in our own population, and in our national intent. Unexpected changes in technology, politics, or diplomacy will affect it. We all have the right to try to influence the outcome, and an idea of what has gone before—how we in the navy perceive our heritage—can help such efforts land closer to the mark.

A subtle function of citizenry is to steer our government, and through it, to steer our navy. Since the navy's purpose, simply stated, is to provide for use of the sea in the common defense, it is meet that as many people as possible be aware of whence our navy sprang, how it got where it is today, and what at least one of its members, conditioned by his own personal history, sees as its immediate future.

THE UNITED STATES NAVY

1

Trees, the Establishment, and Our Revolution

Some things must always have seemed mysterious to anyone reading about our early naval history. How was it possible for a barely organized revolutionary confederacy to build such a large navy in the very short time it did? A review of the characteristics of the ships we built shows them to have been fully the equals of their contemporaries anywhere, including in particular those of the veteran, professional, battle-experienced British navy. How did we manage to design such fine ships? And having built them, where did we get naval crews able not only to sail them but also to handle the heavy ordnance they carried?

From these, the ancillary questions: How did we employ our Continental Navy? What did it accomplish, beyond supplying the British navy with good ships via capture? Other than as a bad example, did it have any effect on the new navy founded in 1794? Why was it so ineffective—and why do we sweep it under the rug today? We call John Paul Jones the father of the U.S. Navy and revere his shrine at the Naval Academy at Annapolis, Maryland; yet we hold that our navy was founded in 1794, two years after Jones's death in Paris. Why does the Continental Navy not figure in what we consider to be the history of the navy that won World War II in two oceans at one and the same time?

It remains sadly true that, beyond a certain small amount of harassment of British supply lines, the accomplishments of our Continental Navy were almost nil. It did give us our first naval hero, John Paul Jones, who won two of its few victories during the Revolutionary War, one of them quite extraordinary. It also gave us Nicholas Biddle, who bequeathed us our first shining legacy in the way he died, and could have done much more had he lived. And it boasted a few other excellent commanders: Lambert Wickes, remembered as one of the best, whose brief career ended late in 1777 when his ship foundered in a storm; Gustavus Conyngham, said to have made "the most spectacular [commerce-destroying] cruise of the war"; John Barry, who survived to become the senior captain of the new navy created by an Act of Congress in 1794; John Young, commander of the sloop of war *Saratoga*, an aggressive skipper who might have gone much further had he survived (but the *Saratoga* disappeared in a squall on March 18, 1781, before the startled eyes of the prize crew she had just put aboard a captured enemy merchantman); John Manly, apparently competent enough, who, after a good record in a much smaller cruiser, was given the beautiful and fast 32-gun frigate *Hancock*, but, deserted in action by his consort (whose skipper was cashiered), was captured by superior force early in the war. And that was about all, except for a nearly unbroken litany of failures or disasters. And except for the ships themselves.

Magnificent stands of timber were among the natural resources that instantly struck the early explorers of North America. Tall straight yellow pines and firs, fit to mast and spar His Majesty's ships, needing only to be carried to England to end dependence on the uncertain supply from the Baltic area and on her own rapidly dwindling forests. So said all the reports to the British Admiralty. Then, early in the colonial period, the live oak tree, found only along the coast of North America from the Virginia capes to the Rio Grande—with a small stand in Cuba's western end and one or two in Mexico—began to become famous among shipbuilders. Timber was one of the incentives for colonization, and early reports enthusiastically touted the special values of ships built of the newfound American oak. (The trees, of the beech family, were first classified in 1696.) An attempt was made to grow an experimental group of them in England during the first part of the eighteenth century, but the climate was too rigorous.

Despite the tremendous difficulty of getting the huge live oak timbers out of the inhospitable terrain in which they grew, they quickly became favorite building material among the colonial shipwrights. Growing in sandy or marshy soil close to the sea, the trees seemed to thrive on being pelted with sand and salt water during storms and were essentially impervious to most of the insects and blights that affected many other types. The wood was tremendously heavy—heavier than water—and very strong. It was very difficult to cut or work when green, but became so much harder after seasoning that it would dull the tools used by average craftsmen. New techniques to handle it had to be developed; this amounted to rough shaping while still green, then seasoning in salt water for an appreciable time, and finally storing in specially constructed huts or sheds—after which the wood was said to last a hundred years without deterioration. The branches typically grew into gnarled and curved shapes, highly favored by shipwrights for futtocks, knees, stems, frames, and stern posts. Live oak had only the single disadvantage that the trunks of the trees did not grow straight but instead in short, sturdy, twisted shapes, the better to support extremely heavy branches, which tended to grow horizontally relatively close to the ground. For this reason it was not suitable to be made into planking for decks or the sides of ships, but other wood was available for these uses, and the delight of the shipwrights was in the great strength of structure they could devise from the many intricate shapes they got from the knobby pieces the live oak offered so profusely. Finally, because of the extraordinary durability of the wood, ships built of it had very long lives of useful employment.

Yellow pine and cedar were also highly valued woods in short supply in Europe. The pine, tall and straight and extremely strong, was ideal for masts, deck planking, and spars. (It is noteworthy that when under repair, ships regularly had sections of their wood replaced, but never the live oak, which simply grew stronger and harder with age.) Many other specially useful woods abounded in the American forests. During the early colonial days, wood of various kinds was the most valuable product of the American continent. To England especially, always in chronic need of good wood for her ships, the American forests were a treasure.

England and France had both already virtually denuded their own forests of the types of wood preferred for shipbuilding, although France was in marginally better condition than England. Her naval ministry had caused far-seeing timber conservation measures to be instituted during previous centuries. Surprisingly, while England had more reason than France to be concerned over maritime timber stock— she had fewer and smaller forests and larger investments in merchantmen and warships—her several attempts to establish some sort of conservation had been failures. In the sixteenth century, English oak was already precious for the hulls of ships, and yellow pine for their spars and decks. The English Crown held the right to preempt entire private forests to stock the shipyards, but in practice the king's agents merely went through them, reserving the best trees by marking them with ''the king's broad arrow.'' Farsighted naval administrators like Samuel Pepys caused groves of the most useful trees to be planted. He employed expert foresters to maintain them and bend the young trees into the specialized shapes needed for the important strength members of large seagoing hulls, but he never saw the harvest of his slow-growing crop, and none of England's various efforts at reforestation ever produced effective results. Ship-quality timber had become scarce in England as early as the Spanish Armada. During the early colonial period in America, Britain was importing huge quantities of timber from the Baltic countries; her agents were going deep into Sweden, Russia, and Prussia to select and purchase trees that could be dragged to nearby rivers, floated to the sea, and loaded into ships for transport.

Some of the blame for this failure can perhaps be laid to the individualism that was one of the characteristics of Britons. Orders from the king's ministers were continually circumvented. Forestry programs that took upward of one hundred years to produce mature trees almost always were forgotten or disregarded in the interests of expediency. In England, timber conservation was simply too long-range.

In the seventeenth century the demand for wood for the British navy was insatiable, never really fulfilled. In time of war, its lack was a never-ending source of anxiety. Gradually, as domestic supplies diminished and competition with other countries for suitable timber grew, the high cost of transporting man-of-war-grade wood from the virgin forests across the Atlantic became less of an obstacle.

There was even a way around the deprecatory attitude of English shipbuilders, who insisted on the superiority of English workmanship and their favorite materials, English oak and European yellow pine, over just about all else—including live oak from America. As always, economics was everything. To commercial shippers, it soon became evident that a ship could be built in the colonies, loaded with cargo, and sailed on her maiden voyage toward Europe more profitably than if she were brought over as timber. The seventeenth century consequently saw the growth of shipbuilding facilities in the New World rivaling those in mother England. Grudgingly, English shipbuilders began to accept the idea that ships with hulls built of the extremely long-lived and slow-to-rot American live oak were very durable. Colonial-built ships, in spite of disparagement by "home" competitors, gradually developed a reputation for being of good quality, and master shipbuilders flourished in the colonies. Like their counterparts in England, they held their own trade secrets closely, and were not above a little close dealing when it came to profit. They became adept at pre-empting choice pieces of timber for their own needs, and were not above manipulating the stocks of American timber theoretically selected by the king's agent for his navy yards in England, so that exchanges of timber took place to their advantage. It soon became a concern to English shipbuilders that the best live oak would seldom if ever leave colonial shores except in the form of an already constructed ship.

Thus, during the eighteenth century, many merchant ships were built in the New World. As for warships, sub-rosa effort seems to have been made to keep their construction a monopoly of the home shipbuilders in England. This may have been deliberate policy on the part of the British Admiralty, from which one might guess war with the colonies had been considered a future possibility. While many small warships were produced in America—schooners and sloops well suited to the shallow colonial coastal waters—only four of the larger classes of warship, none over 50 guns, were built. Nevertheless, in spite of British efforts to maintain a monopoly on warship building, all builders were well acquainted with the differences between merchant-men and men-of-war. The structural features principally involved stronger decks to carry more guns (all ships carried some guns as a matter of course), thicker sides with much heavier frames, and mini-mum spacing between frames. In effect, they were armored in wood, and the harder the wood used, the better. Commonly, men-of-war also had more interior decks and much more crew-berthing space (obvious requirements). Their other desirable features, such as speed, maneu-verability, and combat ability in blowing weather, were matters of professional masting, rigging, and hull design—as applicable to mer-chant ships as to warships (and to racing sailboats today). Because men-of-war always had much bigger crews, they were, however, able to handle taller masts, larger sails, and, in general, more stressful situ-ations. For this reason, warships were naturally much faster sailers than merchantmen. But a builder of good merchant ships could learn to build good warships; there were no secrets involved—and in America, unlike Europe, there was no shortage of the huge timbers required, or of suitable wood of all kinds.

The top layout man, or designer, of the shipyard was almost always the master shipbuilder himself, a craftsman who took great personal pride in his work. Seldom, however, was he a qualified draftsman. He knew what a ship should look like, and his reputation as a builder rode on each one. Each ship was an individual creation. Such men tended to insist on their own ways and their own designs, and usually needed only a set of specifications from which to estimate costs and building time; after this, they were on their own. For this reason, ships built in different yards to the same plans often differed consider-ably from each other. Such generally invisible but nonetheless signifi-cant matters as shape of bows, location and shape of midsection, amount of deadrise, drag (greater depth aft) or "rockering" (a slight curve, similar to rocking chair runners) of the keel, and the relation of all these to the center of sail area were entirely in the builder's province. The underwater lines, which had everything to do with speed and performance, were his private monopoly. The weight and density of seawater made even small changes in such factors of enormous significance, though not easily discerned by uninitiated observers. Shipbuilders gained wealth and prominence if their ships were faster or could carry more cargo or were stiffer in a blow than ships of the same class built by others, and quite naturally they tended to keep their special design secrets to themselves.

Shipbuilders and their idiosyncrasies were as highly regarded in England as in the colonies, but the British navy faced the necessity of maintaining large numbers of ships, many of them on far distant stations. Unnecessary differences in ships of the same class therefore created severe problems in the supply system. Accordingly, to achieve standardization, in 1706 the first "establishment" was decreed. Under this system, England classed her men-of-war in descending order, from "first rate," 100 guns or more, intended for a fleet flagship, to "sixth rate," fewer than 30 guns. The size and characteristics of each rate were fixed and, correspondingly, the complicated supply lines were made more manageable. The establishment was revised several times, but the system and nomenclature persisted.

Initially, when guns were essentially all the same type, differing only in bore and weight, the size of a ship was accurately reflected in her gun rating. But it was natural for a skipper, proud of his command and wishing to add to her capability and his reputation, to add extra guns where space seemed to exist and rearrange his primary and secondary batteries to suit his own ideas. Some went much further. Both John Paul Jones and Charles Stewart (of later War of 1812 renown) relocated the masts in their ships to improve their sailing qualities—in both cases with noted success. A few extra light guns could easily be added to most ships; indeed, their sides were usually pierced with extra gunports to allow shifting of guns if desired, and the only bar to the addition of more was their scarcity (generally, guns were the most valuable equipment aboard) and the effect of the additional weight on the ship's speed. Thus the *Randolph*, rated as a 32-gun frigate, actually carried 36 guns. Later the *Alliance* and *Confederacy*, originally rated as 32s but in reality often carrying upward of 40 guns of various calibers, were upgraded to 36-gun ships to describe their actual size more accurately.

In the colonies, the few ships built for the British navy were intended to conform to the establishment, but because plans had to come from a long distance, and reference to the designer for resolution of problems was not easy, colonial shipbuilders exercised more independence than those of the mother country. France and Spain, of course, built to their own systems and paid no attention to England's establishment. The drive for economy and standardization therefore resulted in the English ships being smaller and more compact than those built in foreign shipyards, including American yards, and for this reason one often sees reference in British writings to the greater size and desirability of captured warships. The fact seems to be that despite additional supply problems, to the commanders of British fleets chronically in need of more ships, and to the officers eager to command them, an occasional mild anachronism built across the Atlantic, or a larger one, a captured French or Spanish man-of-war, was generally a popular addition to the ships available. Chief among the establishment's effects, so far as America was concerned, was that it stultified design of English warships; and the central point is that this was very well understood by colonial shipbuilders—John Wharton and his younger partner Joshua Humphreys in particular. To them, the sort of ship needed by a weak navy that could not compete in quantity but only in the quality of its ships was obvious; not only would they advise building bigger and faster ships, with more guns; they would also urge maximum utilization of the fabled live oak, regardless of how difficult and time-consuming it might be to get the wood out of the forbidding Southern swampland. It is unsure whether Wharton or Humphreys first fixed on this concept; most likely it was the older man, from the depth of his experience. It is, however, certain that Humphreys adopted the philosophy wholeheartedly, for it governed his entire career.

Late in 1775, the Continental Congress of the rebelling colonies became convinced of the need for a navy and created a Marine Committee of the Congress to see to it. The committee system remained in being for the duration of our war for independence, endeavoring to perform the functions of what we would today call a "navy department." The technical effect was that the Congress theoretically ran the navy's day-to-day business, issued cruising and operational orders, made personnel assignments, gave promotions, and handed command of ships to the officers it liked best. But no committee, especially one of the Congress, could give such a mandate the full-time attention it had to have to function successfully. In the outcome, the committee's work was for three years done single-handedly by financier Robert Morris, who sometimes, for expediency to get the thing accomplished, advanced his own funds, much of which was never reimbursed. It was an impossible job. He had to deal with not only a difficult group of opinionated captains, but also cantankerous and sometimes fearful Congressional overseers. He did his best, but he was swamped in bottomless detail, with no help.

It was largely due to this committee's unfamiliarity with the requirements for successful command at sea that the record of the Continental Navy is so poor. It had additional problems with funding its own directives, and its inability to handle the officers to whom it awarded naval rank, especially the captains, compounded its difficulties. Pierre Landais, the cashiered French naval officer who was given the newest and best frigate of the Continental Navy, the *Alliance*, in which he demonstrated not only his incompetency but his actual insanity under stress, was one of the results.

The Marine Committee must, however, be given credit for beginning its duties energetically at the outset of the war. A small squadron of converted merchantmen was quickly assembled and placed under command of Esek Hopkins, a merchant skipper of high commercial and personal reputation, though unfortunately with little or no naval experience. In December of that same year the committee persuaded Congress to appropriate funds for the construction of thirteen quality frigates, ranging in size from 24 to 32 guns. Not much is known of the inception of their design, other than that they were excellent ships, but there is a report that Humphreys submitted a sheaf of plans to the committee for its study, and it must be believed these were influential to some degree at least. The committee commissioned plans to be drawn—by whom it is is not clear, though because of the location of their shipyard in the seat of government, the weight of what evidence there is leans to Wharton and Humphreys. After approval, laboriously hand-drawn copies were made for each of the designated building yards, an extremely time-consuming process that in itself ensured the ships could not be built to them unless an inordinately long delay were acceptable, which it was not. None of the "official" plans for any of the ships can be found today except for the *Randolph*, built by Wharton and Humphreys in Philadelphia. The best information we have of the rest comes from those captured and examined by the Royal Navy.

Here, however, is a most valuable source of information. The British Admiralty habitually "admeasured" captured warships it took into its navy, carefully "took off the lines," and drew a set of plans of each one. The procedure gave the Admiralty basic facts from which to gauge proper manning, supply, and repair factors needed for effective utilization of such new acquisitions. More than half of the new Continental frigates were captured and added to the British navy, and the resulting Admiralty draughts are the only sets of plans representing the ships as actually built. Although the Continental Congress commissioned naval architects to design the three classes of frigates it had ordered, the three-month delivery date specified by the anxious legislature was totally unrealistic. In the event, the shipbuilders concerned leaped into the breach. More than likely, most already had general ideas, if not plans drawn, for their own "dream" ships. They began to build the best ships they could within the general parameters they had been given, recognizing the new nation's need (and their own need for work), and figuring to conform as closely as they could to the plans if and when they finally arrived. The surviving plans, located in the Admiralty Draughts Collection at Greenwich, England, dramatically show the resulting differences.

Randolph, the only ship whose official American plans have been found, was a 32-gun frigate built in Philadelphia under almost daily view of the Congress. Logically, it is likely her plans arrived first and were followed most closely. It is also likely that young Humphreys and the older Wharton, already known for the excellence of their ship-yard's products, were consulted by the Marine Committee in laying the plans out. Everything known about the two men indicates they would have recommended the new ships be superior to the most powerful British frigates on the American station—their 32-gun class—and that all the available live oak in the various shipyards be utilized in their construction. The *Randolph*'s plans show her to be about 20 percent bigger, and 20 percent heavier, than theoretically comparable British 32s. *Raleigh* and *Hancock*, also 32s, were quickly captured by the British navy, and their English draughts confirm this comparison. All three were markedly superior to British ships of equal rating, judging by such factors as length, beam, size of frames and planking, height of masts, depth of hold, and height of main battery guns above water. By all contemporary reports, they were also faster. They appear to have been handsome, well-built vessels. Of the three, *Hancock* was the greatest departure from England's establishment of the time for 32-gun frigates, being another 10 percent bigger than *Randolph* or *Raleigh*.

The plans of the 28-gun *Virginia* show her to have been similarly advanced over the establishment standard. As for our three 24s, the Royal Navy thought they were more properly 28-gun ships and rated them accordingly after their capture.

That none of these fine frigates can be said to have served the Continental Navy well—or even satisfactorily, with the single exception of *Randolph*—was not the fault of the ships or the Congress, which seems to have had a good appreciation of the purpose of its little navy and got the ships it wanted. Of the thirteen ships ordered, two were never completed. Two were scuttled, not yet ready for sea when British forces captured Philadelphia. Another was set afire and burned by her own crew. One blew up in battle. The remaining seven were captured and taken into the British navy. As the war went on, numerous other ships were built or purchased for the Continental Navy. In all, fifty-three ships served in it at one time or another, but at the close of the war only two were left in service. A third had just been completed but was not yet in operation. All others had been lost in one way or another.

The *Hancock*, a 32-gun frigate built in Newburyport, Massachusetts, has excited interested speculation whenever her name and history have come up. She was quickly captured and rechristened *Iris* in the Royal Navy, where she immediately made a reputation for being fast and handy. She could serve her guns in weather that might force a lesser ship to keep her gundeck ports closed. She was weatherly in all sea and wind conditions and was also commodious and comfortable. In the service of Great Britain she was a favorite ship, known for bringing in much prize money.

A study of *Hancock*'s British-drawn plans tells us why. She was larger in all respects than her sister 32s in the Continental Navy, and very much larger than her contemporaries in the Royal Navy. *Hancock*'s builder, Jonathon Greenleaf, had her well along by the time the Congress's official plans and supervising inspectors finally arrived in Newburyport in February 1776. The inspectors found the new ship so near completion they no doubt felt it would be counterproductive to complain about her deviations from the plans they had just delivered. When completed, she turned out to be 80 tons greater in displacement than any of the other Continental 32s, and about 30 percent bigger than the establishment in vogue for English men-of-war of the same class. She served England virtually the entire war, with fine results, and after capture by France late in 1781, finished her career in that navy (where she was equally popular).

One thing the *Hancock* did accomplish for her original owners: after the war for independence, when former Continental Navy officers considered what had gone right and what wrong, her superb potential came up repeatedly. She was a better ship than her contemporaries, and better than British warships of the next larger class. One British officer effusively described her as "the finest and fastest frigate in the world." Even before her capture, this was recognized in the Continental Navy, and in 1778 we built two more, *Alliance* and *Confederacy*, very much like her—on the same model and with the same ideas, but 200 tons bigger yet. Had we been able to match these three innovative ships with more commanders like Nicholas Biddle, John Paul Jones, John Young, and John Barry (both Jones and Barry later did command the *Alliance*, Barry with distinction at the end of the war), the Continental Navy might have rendered a better account of itself.

How much of the fault lay with the Continental Navy's crews? All accounts from all sources agree that enlisted men who shipped "before the mast" were pretty much alike, regardless of which navy—or which merchant ship of which country—they served in. Rough-hewn characters, they were uneducated in the usual sense but adept and fearless with masts, yards, sails, and rigging. With minimum training they could serve anywhere. Although there were of course various specialties in all crews (gunner, carpenter, sailmaker, cook, master-at-arms, boatswain), all were accustomed to the hundreds of brute-strength operations necessary to handle sail, hoist and lower boats, load and unload cargo, drop, lift, and secure an anchor for sea, or serve the guns.

Men of the sea were known as a special breed who should be avoided on land if possible, unless one made one's living from them. They knocked about from port to port, jumping ship when the fancy moved them—though sharp-eyed merchant skippers often left them behind to avoid paying their meager wages. Many had been criminals, released into the custody of a flint-eyed captain or mate. All were expected to become impossibly drunk as soon as they got ashore and to awaken in brothel basements, slum halls, or filthy alleys minus what money they might have had. They were preyed on by everyone. Many a rooming-house keeper augmented his income by delivering groups of them, insensible from drink, a knock on the head, or some cheap drug, to merchant ships awaiting crews before setting forth on long voyages. The skippers of such ships, having made arrangements with the "crimp" (as the rooming-house keepers were known), would pay an agreed-on fee per man delivered on board; when the seaman came to, he had a terribly aching head and was again a virtual prisoner in a ship bound for an unknown destination. In addition, he was in debt for the fee paid for him to the crimp. Looked down upon and abused wherever he was, the sailor tended to be hard to handle even when sober.

Nationality was not a matter of great importance, nor was language. Crews were literally international. Shipboard vocabulary was small and specialized. One quickly "learned the ropes" involved with the various sailing evolutions (this is where the term originated), which was all one needed to avoid instant punishment by boot or lash.

Royal Navy skippers had a better way than merchantmen to enlist crews, one that was legal: impressment. Although occasionally used by other navies, impressment reached its zenith in the chronically crew-hungry British navy. A party of armed men, under a junior officer, would comb the streets of harbor towns to kidnap able-bodied seamen for service. Occasionally there were horror stories of men being snatched from the bosom of their weeping families, but these were often invented to dramatize the social injustice, and sometimes in fact staged. For the most part, press gangs preyed on the known waterfront dives and crimp houses and on merchant ships themselves, suspecting them to be manned in excess of minimum needs by sailors hoping—and even paying—to escape another period of forced and risky servitude in a warship.

And with some amusement and incredulity, though little sympathy, one can imagine the logistic problem faced by the crimp, who had to (1) keep the confidence of his guests; (2) pose as willing to help them after they had run out of money, or he had stolen it; (3) conceal them when press gangs were about; (4) surreptitiously conclude deals with merchant skippers; (5) get the selected men insensible at the right time; and finally (6) furtively deliver them into the right boat without anyone being the wiser—neither town authorities, the British navy, nor customers still able to pay. It took an ingenious, thoroughly devious type to be a successful crimp—and not wind up at the bottom of the harbor with a sailor's knot cinched tightly around his neck and a weight at the other end of the line!

Because of the manner in which many, if not most, of its crew had been enlisted, a warship preparing for a cruise habitually anchored well away from shore and kept its crew members captive on board. Only trusted seamen—and then only under close supervision of officers—would be allowed on shore to obtain supplies or to form press gangs. Human nature and the male animal being what they are, one should not be surprised to find that the most aggressive press gang personnel were, not infrequently, men whose own naval service had begun in just the same way.

By operation of all these factors, sailors of one nationality not infrequently found themselves serving aboard warships of another country. During war, they might be forced to fight against their own land. Some unusually thoughtful commanders would, in such circumstances, excuse men from their battle stations. Generally, however, concerns of this nature never occurred to the officers, and this angle of their involuntary servitude apparently bothered only a few of the men. They were, after all, completely incarcerated within their own wooden walls, very little aware of what might be going on outside. Besides, there were always so many other and more pressing causes for misery.

It is to the officers—in particular the ship commanders—that we must look for the failure of our Continental Navy. Officers were a very different group from their men. In England, second sons of nobility often were appointed midshipmen in the navy. In America, despite general (not total) absence of a noble class, there was nevertheless great social separation based on wealth, education, and occupation. Congress used this primary criterion to select its naval officers, considering naval experience less important than social and political standing. In this it followed the example of England, but that country had developed over the years a tradition of naval apprenticeship (midshipman status) followed by obligatory performance that caused the system to function. In the revolting colonies there were all the trappings of jealously guarded "gentility," but very little naval tradition. An inexperienced young man might do well with the right guidance, but in the case of a ship commander it was too much to expect that mere social or political status in themselves could confer the requisite command qualities. Although many of the Continental Navy skippers had had merchant service—which in those days of piracy on the high seas meant they were accustomed to the possibility of combat—most of them had no real understanding of the demands of a regular naval service. It can also be suspected that some of the very best qualified chose to become privateers instead of entering the navy, for it was here that fortunes could be made.

As might be expected, much the same situation held with regard to the army, but there, two other and very fortunate factors intervened: the selection of George Washington as overall commander was the best appointment Congress ever made; and the army was virtually always under the near observation of the Congress and the public, whereas once at sea, the navy was beyond the influence of either.

Washington had held colonial rank in the British army. In similar fashion, a few of the Continental or state naval officers had received their early experience in the Royal Navy.* Some had been entered as midshipmen at extraordinarily youthful ages (reputedly, in one case at age three, but he remained on leave of absence) in order to begin accumulating the seniority so important to high rank in later years. In any case, while there are a number of candidates for the title of father of the United States Navy, the true mother was the navy of England. Not only did our shipbuilding capabilities and techniques come initially from there, so did our early regulations, our naval tactics, some of our officers, our system of organization, and most of our old traditions. To this day, the officers and men of either navy feel at home aboard the ships of the other. In 1776 it was totally and completely due to the British navy that our rebel colonies, in those groping early days, were able to take to the sea at all, and the tradition has lasted.

Nicholas Biddle, scion of the famous Philadelphia family and later captain of the *Randolph*, was one such officer trained in the Royal Navy. During his service, one of his messmates was the young Horatio Nelson, later England's greatest fighting admiral. Ships being very small, the quarters confining, and the voyages long, the two ambitious young men doubtless had numerous opportunities to exchange ideas

---

*George Washington's idolized sixteen-years-older half brother, Lawrence, served for a time with a British naval expedition in the Caribbean but returned home with tuberculosis and died soon after. Had he not had this misfortune, he might have remained in the British navy. He so revered his commander, Admiral "Old Grog" Vernon (though there is little evidence of direct contact), that he named his home, which he later willed to George, in his honor. Mount Vernon it was throughout the Revolutionary War, and Mount Vernon it remains.

When he was sixteen years old George also accepted an appointment as midshipman in the Royal Navy. His bags were packed, but an emotional leave-taking from his difficult mother caused her to become ill. Contritely, George unpacked his luggage, she quickly recovered her health—and one is left to ponder the consequences had he been slightly less filial.

about whatever such men discuss when time stretches ahead interminably. Nelson's interests have been well documented by his armies of biographers. He and Biddle, and whoever else of similar persuasion there might have been on board, must have spent hours on the professional topics of the day. They may have argued about impressment. One visualizes youthful agreement that daring commanders were an indispensable condition for victory, that opportunities must be seized quickly, that personal honor, ship's honor, and national honor must be preserved at all costs.

All this is but speculation, but it cannot be too wide of the mark, given conditions aboard ship and the facts we do have. The careers and even the fates of the two men were similar. Both were killed in a moment of supreme daring, in combat, on the quarterdecks of their ships. One was at the climax of a glorious naval career, the other, twenty years younger, at the very beginning.

When news of the Boston Tea Party reached Biddle in 1774, he recognized that the ten-year march of worsening relations with England was leading to war. Apparently, he had given long thought to what he should do once war appeared inevitable. Almost surely, he received private estimates of the situation from family members in Philadelphia. The upshot was that he resigned his appointment, returned home, and was involved in the struggle from the beginning. Initially employed in the Pennsylvania state navy with gunboats in the Delaware River, he applied for a commission when the Continental Navy was formed and was appointed commander of the brig *Andrew Doria* (sometimes correctly rendered *Andrea Doria*). With this small vessel, he achieved considerable success as a commerce raider. Once, for a short time, responsibility for the entire tiny navy devolved upon him. Among the officers thus placed under his command was John Paul Jones, then skipper of the slightly smaller sloop *Providence*.

Biddle had something in common with Jones, although being in different ships they must have had few opportunities for leisurely discussion. But as far as operations went, they saw eye to eye. Biddle's orders to Jones were classic: get to sea as quickly as possible, and do as much damage to the enemy's commerce as he could. Then Biddle took his own ship to sea with the same purpose. Under the energetic command of the two strong-minded professionals, both small warships turned in extremely successful cruises, capturing numerous supply ships intended for British troops. Late in 1776, Biddle received notice that he had been named to command the recently launched *Randolph*, fitting out in Philadelphia, the first to be completed of the new fleet of thirteen frigates. He got his handsome ship to sea early in 1777, but then encountered severe misfortune. The first bad weather she ran into, really only a minor blow, snapped out her two tallest masts; her splintered stumps gave evidence of the cause—both were riddled with rot.

Charleston, South Carolina, was the haven Biddle sought for refit, and it is probable that his sojourn in that charming city was the happiest period of the young captain's life. The whole political, military, and social fabric of the city turned inside out for the handsome Biddle and his crew. New masts were procured and installed; the ship was cleaned, fumigated, and painted. While the various difficulties he experienced—lightning that twice destroyed new masts and a persistent lack of manpower—held him in port longer than his patriotic spirit felt comfortable with, the delay worked for him personally, since he also became engaged to be married. Despite all this, he sailed on two cruises from Charleston.

The first was very successful in terms of damage to enemy commerce and prize money to his crew. During his second stay in Charleston he had *Randolph* careened to clean her bottom, which had become sufficiently foul to affect her speed. In the process something went wrong; she overset and sank at the careening dock, requiring still more time until she could be righted, pumped out, and cleaned. Early in 1778, accompanied by a small fleet of South Carolina state warships, he took his ship out on another commerce-destroying mission, which was to become her last cruise. After a month of moderate success, he encountered the old 64-gun ship of the line *Yarmouth*, considerably more than twice *Randolph*'s strength because of her heavier guns. Biddle's ship was new, however, and very well trained, and he refused to shun battle. Instead, he drove directly into a furious night engagement. Reports from *Randolph*'s consorts indicate she was doing very well in the unequal contest, outshooting her adversary four broadsides to one and doing sufficient damage that it was visible in spite of the darkness, when unaccountably *Randolph*'s magazine exploded and blew her into small pieces.

Four days later, still engaged in repairing the considerable damage she herself had suffered, *Yarmouth* cruised through the area of battle and found four survivors floating on a piece of wreckage; but Nicholas Biddle was not one of them.

It is hard to imagine the relatively small *Randolph* in fact beating her much bigger adversary—older and probably decrepit though *Yarmouth* must have been—yet had the god of luck been looking her way it is conceivable she might have. Being new, handy, well trained, and much faster on all points of sailing, she had every advantage save the very important ones of thicker sides and greater firepower. But she was built of oak, which must have given Biddle some confidence in her ability to absorb damage—as apparently she did, up to the fatal explosion.

The detonation of *Randolph*'s munitions cannot be easily or satisfactorily explained and ought not to have uncritical acceptance. Danger of a magazine explosion is such a well-known hazard in warships that the most stringent safeguards are routinely employed. There have been extremely few instances of this happening, and none at all in battle, except as a result of something like a fire or other preliminary injury. The supposition in the *Randolph*'s case has been that a lucky shot struck a magazine, but this is hardly likely given its protected location, well below the waterline. Suicidal carelessness on someone's part, perhaps? One is also tempted to wonder if the flooding that occurred while the ship was careened could have been the proximate cause of the fatal explosion. There are hints that water may have gotten into some of *Randolph*'s gunpowder through the mishap, requiring that it be dried before she got under way that last time; if true, this should have been viewed very seriously. Once wet, gunpowder becomes notoriously unstable and remains unstable thereafter, even if later dried. If someone, from zeal for economy or some other reason, dried wet gunpowder and returned it to the unfortunate ship, the possibility of being to blame for the catastrophe must point to him, for the feverish activity of battle would have created multiple chances of disturbing it enough to set it off.

What is important is that Biddle, a fighter of the stamp of John Paul Jones but less flamboyant a seeker after glory, would have held an equally heroic stature had he lived. And, totally unlike Jones in motivation and character, he would have been a force to reckon with during the future shaping of our navy. Very likely, he would have risen to a truly commanding position, and some of the history of our Continental Navy during those confused days might have been prouder. He was only twenty-seven when he died.

It was a tragedy also from the historical point of view that Nicholas Biddle died so young. Had he lived there might have been some tradition of consequence to build on. There was no one else to take his place. John Paul Jones, never really an American, died in Paris in 1792, less than ten years after the close of the Revolution. John Barry, an excellent skipper, died of heart disease in 1803 at the age of fifty-eight, at the head of the new navy list, but he had suffered for several years from progressive heart failure, and, some say, senility. The only other who might have made a difference had he been spared was John Young of the *Saratoga*. The history of our navy of this period is full of ineptitude, incompetence, and suspected insanity—not to mention at least two instances in which outright cowardice was imputed.

All in all, the Continental Congress and the thirteen colonies had very little to show for their initial efforts to create a viable navy. Some state navy ships turned in creditable performances—for example, the Pennsylvania cruiser *Hyder Ali*, under Joshua Barney, which captured the British *General Monk* in the Delaware River in 1782. But the status of these small navies was more that of temporary militia than of full-fledged navies. Indeed, although conclusive facts are lacking, it is probable that the greatest damage to British supply lines and to their maritime commerce in general was done by privateers. One of the most successful was commanded by a young skipper named Thomas Truxtun, who brought in so much greatly needed equipment and supplies that he received the personal praise of General Washington. In all, some two thousand American privateers are estimated to have operated at one time or another during the Revolution. Captures of British ships numbered more than three thousand.

Although they kept for personal profit everything they were able to capture, frequently selling it to Washington's suppliers for use by the Continental Army, privateers or ships holding letters of marque were not pirates. They were officially commissioned by competent authority of the time, possessed a license authorizing combatant status, and were required to conform to the rules of warfare in all respects. A letter of marque authorized a cargo-carrying ship to arm itself and capture merchantmen of the other side. A privateering license was issued to a ship frankly fitted out as a private warship, with no pretense of carrying a cargo herself. In practice, the two licenses produced the same result: harm to the enemy and diversion of supplies from his side to one's own. Should such ships be captured, as many were, their licenses entitled their crews to treatment as legitimate prisoners of war, instead of ordinary pirates. Since pirates were bandits who preyed on merchant ships of any country and usually murdered their victims, in the eighteenth century the distinction between privateer and pirate was very clear.

Perhaps to confirm the lackluster quality of our service, the single supremely successful sea operation of our Revolutionary War was carried out by the French navy in an extraordinary, long-distance supporting campaign initiated by George Washington. French admirals de Barras and his superior, de Grasse, urgently summoned at Washington's request by General Rochambeau, sailed respectively from Newport, Rhode Island, and Antigua in the Caribbean to rendezvous in Chesapeake Bay. The first to arrive was de Grasse. In the meantime, the British army under Cornwallis had occupied Yorktown and begun fortifying the place while awaiting relief by the British fleet based in the Hudson River. Cornwallis had been led to the peninsula between the York and James rivers in chase of the retreating Lafayette and Nathanael Greene and their French and revolutionary troops. Greene, considered by some students as second only to Washington as a military strategist, had artfully withdrawn just fast enough to lead Cornwallis into the trap, inflicting serious casualties on him along the way. When Greene turned on him, as planned, the only escape from a suddenly newly aggressive Continental Army was by sea. De Grasse, bringing his entire force from the West Indies station, arrived while Washington and Rochambeau, by a series of forced marches, were moving their armies into the York peninsula to augment Greene's strength. The story may be apocryphal, but when he learned of the arrival of the French fleet, Washington, normally of monumental reserve, is recorded as waving his hat wildly in one hand and his handkerchief in the other as he excitedly greeted Rochambeau's arrival in the operational area.

The British fleet, based at New York and Barbados, had learned of the French scheme to combine their two fleets and did the same. But the British in Barbados did not expect the entire French fleet to sail from Antigua, missed contact with it during the northward voyage, and rendezvoused with the other squadron in New York harbor. Once the two British fleets had combined and again got under way, they finally arrived off the entrance to Chesapeake Bay to find de Grasse already there with his whole fleet, instead of only part of it. His Newport reinforcements had not yet arrived, but his twenty-four ships were far superior to the twelve the British were expecting. They had only nineteen, and the disparity in force concerned them greatly, unaware as they were of the difficulties being faced by de Grasse (ships revictualing, crews ashore getting water, landing parties cooperating with Lafayette, boats plying all over the area).

The battle that ensued was actually something of a comedy of errors, but fortunately for the American rebels, the English admiral made the more serious ones. When the British hove into sight, de Grasse immediately ordered his fleet out of port to meet them, and his ships straggled out in considerable confusion, in some cases leaving substantial portions of their crews ashore. Instead of falling upon them as they cleared the capes, Graves, the British admiral, allowed them to come out and form a semblance of a line of battle—and then, through confusion in signals, the British failed to engage properly. Part of their fleet, in fact, did not engage at all. The Battle of the Virginia Capes, which began off the entrance to Chesapeake Bay, between Cape Henry and Cape Charles, was inconclusive on the first day (September 5, 1781), and lasted technically a total of five days, during which the two fleets remained in sight of each other without actually fighting. Then, favored by a shift in the wind, de Grasse put about and returned to Chesapeake Bay to find de Barras waiting for him with twelve more ships of the line, while the discomfited British returned to New York and left Cornwallis to his fate at Yorktown.

The surrender of Cornwallis ended the combat phase of our revolution against the English Crown, but our navy had nothing to do with this far-reaching event. It had by this time been swept from the seas, many of its ships taken into the British navy, with the rest destroyed to prevent capture or sunk. Only two remained in service in 1782: *Alliance* and *Hague*. The just-built *Bourbon* had no crew and had not yet been commissioned. She and *Hague* were sold shortly after the end of the war. *Alliance*, our favorite ship, was retained until 1785, at which time the navy was disestablished and she was sold into the merchant service.

Her final fate was ignominious. After several years in merchant service to the Far East, she was converted to a towed barge (not an unusual disposition for strong ships past economical repair) and was at last abandoned in the Delaware River. Her hulk is supposed to have continued to exist somewhere along the muddy banks of the Delaware, and according to one account her old timbers could be seen as late as 1901. Even at that late date, a determined effort could have taken some of her measurements and reconstructed others.

It is a pity this was not done, for it would be significant if *Alliance* turned out, as strongly suspected, to be the progenitor of the six fine frigates Congress authorized in 1794. Then *Hancock* would be, too, and we would know exactly where our naval direction began to take its very special shape.

2

The Yankee Race Horse, Truxtun, and Finally Preble

During the decade following the surrender of Cornwallis and the confirmation of our independence by the peace treaty of 1783, the new nation was fully occupied with the structure of its government and consolidation of its new position in the North American continent. Not surprisingly, little thought was given to naval matters. An ally's navy had helped us corner Cornwallis at an important time; doubtless that ally would help again, if necessary. Our own navy had been useless, so far as the conduct and outcome of the Revolutionary War were concerned. And besides, a navy was very expensive—much more so than an army—because of constant heavy upkeep charges for maintenance of ships. Continental currency was at a nadir. "Not worth a continental" was a popular epithet. The new nation was nearly bankrupt.

The army, with the help of the French navy, had won the war with England and might be needed again: Canada, on our northern border, might yet wish to break away from England, or in some other way involve us in war, and warlike Indians were still everywhere. Provision was made for its continuance. Without expensive equipment comparable to the navy's investment in ships, the army was cheaper by far. The country was accustomed to generals: Washington, revered by all, had been one. Admirals provoked fear—fear of creation of a navy elite that might somehow subvert our newly won liberties—and this lay in the background of the national disaffection. Our navy had little claim to national loyalty and few influential supporters who understood its proper function.

In 1789, a new Congress, a new chief executive, and a new United States were inaugurated. Fittingly, the President was George Washington, the former general remembered for his Cincinnatus-like self-abnegation when his subordinate officers suggested creating a monarchy with him at its head. The problems immediately besetting his administration included that of the so-called Barbary pirates.

Situated on the African coast, the Barbary states—Morocco, Tunis, Algiers, and Tripoli—bordered the Mediterranean Sea. Their rulers nominally owed allegiance and annual tribute to the ruler of the Ottoman Empire, the Sultan of Turkey. As practical fact they were independent of all control except their own. They purchased freedom of action from their Sultan by providing him with revenue; and to raise money for him and for themselves, they robbed or extracted tribute from travelers falling into their clutches. Considering themselves at war with all infidels, they had invented a system of "declaring war" whenever tribute was not equal to their needs. In practice, this meant that their corsairs captured American merchantmen whenever they were in the mood, and took the unfortunate ships and crews into whichever Barbary state happened at the time to be dissatisfied with the latest tribute received. Most such captures took place in the Mediterranean Sea, but some of the corsairs were large ships that did not hesitate to venture into the Atlantic Ocean in search of victims.

Prior to our independence from England, the broad sails of the Royal Navy sheltered American colonial merchant ships from the rapacious North African corsairs. England paid a modest tribute, but at the same time kept a squadron on station in the Mediterranean to enforce the safe conducts guaranteed by the many treaties the Barbary states had signed. England was not alone; the Portuguese navy guarded the Straits of Gibraltar, and the Swedes were accustomed to maintaining a small squadron of frigates in the Mediterranean for the same purpose. So did the French. By 1785, the Barbary states had begun to capture American ships and demand gifts and tribute from the new nation as the price for tolerating its ships in the Mediterranean Sea. No longer shielded by the British navy and with no navy of our own, the United States had to pay tribute. Congress authorized money for the purpose as part of the annual appropriation. Every year more was demanded, complicated by rivalry among the Barbary states as to which received the largest tribute, and punctuated by occasional capture of a merchantman to emphasize their power.

The common fate of the captured personnel, whether passengers or crew, was imprisonment pending ransom, or sometimes some combination of imprisonment and slavery. The ships and cargoes were sold to profit the dey or bashaw involved, and could be bought back by their original owners, although this was seldom feasible.

A nation that submissively kept up with the constantly escalating demands of the Barbary rulers could expect its ships to be allowed to proceed unmolested; but, given the time and distance involved, this was not always certain. Nations that did not pay or had not paid quickly enough or had in some other way fallen out of favor found their merchants attacked, their goods and ships seized, their people killed or enslaved. It was a simple system, and it kept the beys and bashaws (Dey of Algiers, Bey of Tunis, Bashaw of Tripoli, and Emperor of Morocco)—and the decadent Sultan of the Ottoman Empire—in funds. Most seafaring nations kept up the payments as a matter of course, as the easiest and cheapest way out of a difficult situation, but some of them, notably Britain, played a much cooler game.

England's trade by sea was vital to her survival. In furtherance of her maritime traffic she had developed the world's most powerful fleet, and during the seventeenth and eighteenth centuries had used it continually. The nations of Europe, all with trade ambitions similar to hers, were of course her main rivals. Keeping them in check was a huge international chess game in which foreign policy, power on land

and sea (but increasingly on the sea), the diplomatic finesse of her ministers, and her far-flung intelligence system all played their special roles. Although England's huge navy could have totally subdued the Barbary states' piratical proclivities at any time, as part of her overall strategy she saw no need to make the seas safer for her rivals. Instead, at the same time as her cruisers regularly impressed the Barbary rulers with the instant and severe retribution that would follow any interference with ships flying the colors of Great Britain, she saw to it that they realized this protection no longer extended to ships flying the American flag.

Diplomatic protests were of little comfort to an imprisoned crew and passengers, nor to the owners of the hijacked ship and cargo. Once taken, only ransom could free any of these. Vociferous and frequent protests from American merchant shippers gradually brought Congress and the administration to realize that it must somehow replace the protective umbrella of England's fleet.

Whatever form of government the newly independent states of America adopted was immaterial to the Barbary states, and most likely not even known to them; but on the other side of the Atlantic, inauguration of the United States, in 1789, made two crucial differences. The new Congress was charged to ''provide for the common defense,'' and the new president was a man accustomed to forthright action in the discharge of his duties. To the general who had on his own created the first Continental naval force, sometimes called ''Washington's navy,'' and had in fact once thought he might enter the Royal Navy, it became evident that only an active force at sea could place effective pressure on the Barbary states, and that it would have to be our own navy. In 1794, therefore, Congress passed an act directing construction of six frigates of the finest quality, four to be rated as 44-gun ships, two to be only slightly smaller, initially rated as 36s. Washington immediately signed commissions for six captains in the new navy, each officer being assigned to supervise construction of his own ship.

The captains were ranked in order of their commissions, and by this reckoning John Barry, holding commission number 1 and superintending construction of the frigate later to be named *United States*, came by the title father of the U.S. Navy, so loved by the Hibernian Society of Philadelphia, of which he was a member.

Samuel Nicholson, skipper of one of the original thirteen Continental frigates, was ranked number 2 and was given charge of the *Constitution*. Silas Talbot, a former officer of the Continental Army who had distinguished himself in some actions on the water, was number 3. Joshua Barney, skipper of the *Hyder Ali* in her victorious engagement with the *General Monk*, was ranked captain number 4; and Richard Dale, Jones's first lieutenant in the battle with the *Serapis* off Flamborough Head in 1779, was named number 5.

Most important for our navy, a merchant ship captain who had merited the praise of General George Washington, Thomas Truxtun, was given the sixth and last slot. Of the original six, he was the only one who had had no service during the Revolution in either the Continental Navy or one of the state navies. He had, however, been pressed into the British navy during an altercation with Spain (which was finally amicably settled), and so impressed his captain that the latter actively encouraged the young Truxtun to accept a midshipman's warrant. Instead, he returned to the colonial merchant service, where his industry and skill caused him to rise rapidly in rank. In the first years of the Revolutionary War he served in a privateer in several actions, and later, although still a very young man, commanded one himself. By the end of the war, aged only twenty-seven, he had achieved a notable reputation for success in combat against superior odds.

Unfortunately, Washington's advisers had done inadequate research into the problems of seniority among the officers named, and these appointments laid the grounds for quarrels over precedence that made for years of acrimony and dissatisfaction. Barney declined his appointment because Talbot had been ranked ahead of him, and accepted instead a commission as a commodore in the French navy, with the proviso that he would never be required to serve where he might find himself arraigned against his own country. (He rejoined the U.S. Navy in 1812 and is especially remembered for his part in the defense of Washington, D.C., when it was captured and burned by the British in 1814.) Dale, number 5 on the original list, was also upset over

Talbot and, with his prospective ship in hiatus, asked for a furlough to make a merchant voyage to India. (He took over a large, well-built merchantman, the *Ganges*, and disappeared for a time.) But the most serious problem came with Truxtun, and it would rob the navy of its best officer several years later.

In the event, construction of the six ships was halted temporarily in 1796 when a treaty was signed with Algiers, then the most militant of the Barbary states. In short order, however, the pro-navy faction in Congress was able to muster the votes to continue work on the three ships most advanced (then designated frigates A, B, and E, afterward named the *Constitution*, *United States*, and *Constellation*). Ultimately, work was resumed on the last three ships, frigates C, D, and F, later known as *President*, *Chesapeake*, and *Congress*.

Considerably more is known about the planning and intentions behind the building of these six ships than about their predecessors of the Continental Navy. There was something very special about them that was not an accident of design. It was, on the contrary, deliberate and it harked back to the earlier days of the *Hancock*, *Confederacy*, and *Alliance*. The best-known name concerned with the design of the new ships is Joshua Humphreys, by 1794 a master shipbuilder of Philadelphia.

Humphreys had had nearly twenty years to think over the ideas he contributed to the Marine Committee's plans for the Continental Navy's thirteen frigates, and it is apparent that he improved his earlier premises in only one significant way. The largest and best of the original thirteen were the 32s, among them the *Randolph* and *Hancock*. Later came the *Alliance* and *Confederacy*. By 1794, he held that a weak nation like the United States should not only build superior frigates, it should build ships able to meet even a ship of the line on reasonably equal terms. Possibly he had in mind Biddle's action in the *Randolph* against the *Yarmouth*, and the reports concerning the near equality of the battle until the fatal explosion in Biddle's ship. In any case, he strenuously held out for a new class of frigate, the 44-gun ship, keel length as long as a 74 of the current British establishment, sides just as thick, masted and sparred accordingly, with frames of the wonderful live oak that grew only in American forests and was superior to any shipbuilding material the world over. Inspection of the legislation by which Congress authorized these ships is instructive, because it prescribes the wood to be used with such intimate detail that a master shipbuilder must have prepared it—or at least sat at the author's elbow. Beyond much doubt, this man was Joshua Humphreys.

Josiah Fox and William Doughty are also names to be remembered for our early ships. Both were initially employed by Humphreys as draftsmen, worked for him for several years, and received his recommendations for employment by the navy as its needs expanded. Fox left a large file of correspondence, preserved at the Peabody Museum at Salem, Massachusetts, from which it is apparent that he had his own strong ideas about ship design, basically more conservative than those of his superior. However, he loyally carried out the directions he received from his employer, not injecting his own ideas into the ships he drew on the mould loft floors until he had achieved personal independence. Doughty appears to have been more of a craftsman than an innovator, and in later years designed his own ships for the navy. Joshua's son, Samuel, did the same. Summing it up, to the older man, Joshua Humphreys, and probably to John Wharton, his predecessor at the Philadelphia shipyard, clearly belongs the credit for the innovative designs of the ships our navy built in those formative years.

Fox was originally trained in English shipyards, and his meticulous work shows this influence. After some years in the employ of Humphreys, he was sent in 1795 by the navy (on Humphreys's recommendation) to the Gosport Yard at Norfolk, Virginia, as assistant naval constructor for frigate D, the 44-gun ship to be built there. (Though she would finally be christened *Chesapeake*, there is some evidence that one of the names considered for her may have been *Revolution*, which has some parallel with those selected for the other five ships.) Her keel, a duplicate of those of the other 44s, was laid in December 1795, but early in 1796 the work was stopped, and Fox was sent to Portsmouth, New Hampshire, to design and supervise construction of the frigate *Crescent*, rated at 36 guns, intended for presentation as tribute to the Dey of Algiers. This ship was deliberately designed to be as small as possible, given her rate, and Fox, never enamored of Humphreys's big ships, was in the element he liked best. *Crescent* was a tiny jewel of a ship, 40 feet shorter than the *Constellation*, which at this time was still rated as a 36. She was in fact considerably smaller than the 36-gun *Alliance* of the old Continental Navy. Launched in 1797, *not* built of live oak, she was completed late that year.

In April 1798, in face of the growing difficulties with France, the navy was separated from the War Department and a new cabinet office created. In July the new navy secretary, Benjamin Stoddert, sent Fox back to Gosport as a naval constructor with a large increase in pay. Stoddert simultaneously ordered that work begin again on the three big frigates that had been laid aside two years earlier, and directed Fox to complete frigate D within twelve months.

Originally slated to be one of the 44s, this ship was the last to be constructed. Some of the stored stock of live oak timber that had been assembled for her had already gone to Baltimore for use in frigate E, the *Constellation*, that frigate being further along and pushed hard by two most energetic characters, her captain, Thomas Truxtun, and her builder, David Stodder. When the treaty with Algiers caused the work to be stopped, frigate D's keel, sized for a 44, had simply lain at Norfolk (the Gosport yard at Portsmouth, Virginia) in the weather for two years. When Fox returned there in 1798, he found there was insufficient live oak timber to build her to the plans of a 44. Stoddert, in the meantime, had made it plain that he wanted the ship in the water in the shortest possible time; so Fox proposed a smaller ship, Stoddert approved, and Fox in effect designed his own frigate. For some reason, perhaps a simple error, he always referred to her in correspondence as the "*Congress*, 44," until corrected by Secretary Stoddert. When completed, frigate D was slightly smaller than frigates E and F, the *Constellation* and *Congress*. All three of them, however, were pierced for six or more additional guns, as were the 44s. D was proportionally "beamier" than E or F—that is, her length-to-beam ratio was less, and for all her career she was known as a dull sailer, as were all Fox's frigates. Apparently she had one special good quality, rather commodious quarters for her commander or a squadron commander.

Apprised of the differences in specifications of the ships, Stoddert directed *Chesapeake* be rerated as a 36, *Constellation* and *Congress* as 38s, and at about the same time wrote to Fox specifically informing him that the new ship was to be named *Chesapeake*, not *Congress*.

George Washington himself is supposed to have selected the names of the first three ships, the *United States*, *Constitution*, and *Constellation*, from a list proposed to him. John Adams, who became president in 1797, selected the names for the *President* and *Congress*. Only the *Chesapeake*, the last and least, memorialized geography instead of a feature of the new government. She was the last built and smallest, was changed in plan so that she differed from the others, and in general seems to have been treated as an afterthought throughout her building period. So it was with her name; it was assigned some time after those of the others, and no one appears to have thought of the discrepancy. She must have been launched on a Friday, for ill fortune struck her hard. All ships have accidents from time to time, but in some ships every accident is considered the work of a malevolent star, some evil spirit of bad luck hovering over her. Such was the case with *Chesapeake*, even though operationally she seems to have been liked as a flagship, and her career was in many ways not unsuccessful. But she was flagship for Richard V. Morris during the Mediterranean command from which he was recalled and dismissed, and she was to figure in two notorious misfortunes to the U.S. Navy. Her reputation as a bad-luck ship was thereby sealed, and it may all have begun because, of the six original ships, she was the runt of the litter.

The *Constitution*, *United States*, and *Constellation*, the first three completed, achieved the most fame and were always considered to be lucky ships. When William Bainbridge, often referred to as an unlucky officer, was given the *Constitution* in 1812, the opinion freely circulated that "his bad star would be in conflict with his ship's good one"—and when she received more battle injury under his command than at any other time, it was wisely opined by those who knew of such things that hers had won, but it had been a hard struggle. Of the last three, *President* was the fastest and possibly the best built. She was a favorite ship for most of her career. But she contributed little during the War of 1812, partly because during most of the war she was commanded by the personally tough but militarily nonaggressive John Rodgers. Not until late 1814 did she have an opportunity, under another commander, to make a mark on our history, but through a series of mishaps this became a debacle. In 1815, actually after conclusion of peace with England, she was captured by a British squadron. Of the other two, the *Congress* and *Chesapeake* both did well in commerce raiding, but the former did not distinguish herself in any other way, and *Chesapeake* moved into a spectacular disaster. Thus, the last three ships have generally been thought of as unlucky.

Specifications for the new frigates are revealing when compared with those for the British establishment. Our 44s were 20 feet longer, 5 feet wider, and 250 tons heavier—roughly 20 percent superior to the principal class of cruising frigates of that time in the British navy. Their scantlings equaled those of 74-gun ships of the line, to the point where British apologists for defeats in 1812–13, William James in particular, called them ''disguised 74s.'' This was, in fact, precisely Humphreys's intention, as expressed in a letter of January 1793. Their sides were as shot resistant as those of British 74s—perhaps more so because of the extraordinary hardness of live oak—but the ships were properly called frigates since they had only a single gundeck. In addition, they were fast, thanks to their towering masts and generally fine lines, much faster than any line-of-battle ship and also faster than the few extra-large frigates England possessed. The British navy had plenty of opportunity to observe them before the War of 1812, and did, in fact, recognize that their design had achieved, as in the case of the Continental Navy, exactly what the Congress had ordered: a better ship of the class, perfectly suited to the problem facing an inferior navy. In a later day and age they might have been called ''pocket battleships.'' Despite disparaging comments attributed to Englishmen about ''a few fir-built frigates,'' a more considered opinion was rendered in 1803 by Admiral Horatio Nelson of the Royal Navy, who said, ''I see trouble for Britain in those big frigates from across the sea.''

Being individually superior in all categories to their adversaries, they should have been able to win their battles, and in fact did so. So should the ships of the old Continental Navy, especially *Hancock*. The difference was in the quality of their officers, and for this we have initially to thank Thomas Truxtun.

It was supremely fortunate for our navy that Truxtun was first to sea in *Constellation*, and that he had about six months to get his ship trained as his perfectionist mind demanded. When the Algerian treaty of 1796 stopped our initial impetus to build a new navy, shipbuilding funds were reduced and construction severely curtailed. Three of the six captains named construction superintendent of their ships were, however, asked to continue in service to see to their well-being, and the most active such person during this period was Truxtun. Among other efforts, he wrote a personal plea to President Washington to order the work to be continued on his ship. Washington obtained funding from Congress and directed that progress continue on the three that were furthest along; in 1797 Truxtun's was the second of the new frigates to take the water, the only one launched without mishap, and in 1798 the first to sea.

The Barbary pirates were not, of course, the only foreign policy problem faced by Washington's administration. As the eighteenth century drew to a close, great trouble was growing on the European continent. Radical social revolution, brewing for a long time, burst out in France in 1789. The initial reaction of Americans was that the time seemed ripe for radical change. Democracy, introduced with such success in their own country, was a new way and its time had come, or so they thought. Human rights, the hunger for land of one's own, for freedom of choice based on personal bent and ability, for release from the bondage of a system in which the privileged classes had been taught that their franchise was an inalienable right of birth—these were at the base of revolution in the English colonies in 1775, and in France only fourteen years later. It seemed to many at the time that the two upheavals were essentially the same.

But there was in fact a tremendous difference, for in America the temperament of the people was different, and there were not the pressures that existed in France: there was plenty of land; although a privileged class had been brought from England, it faced much the same problems as everyone else; since there was more elbow room and less oppression, class hatreds were less virulent. Those who thought democracy would develop in France in the same way it had in America were finally disabused when reports began to be heard of wholesale killings of men, women, and even children, simply because they belonged to the clergy, or the aristocracy, or had supported them—or were somehow connected with those who had. Even makers of French lace were guillotined, because lace was a luxury of the nobility!

In the former English colonies, the advent of independence and democracy was essentially a political change. Separation of religion from government was one of its axioms, but religion itself was supported, not subjected to vengeance. The nobility was excised, but only institutionally. Its members were not harmed. Many of them, in fact, conformed to the new system and created new careers under the new strictures. Significantly, no other nations existed cheek by jowl with the new democracy, so that only in the Canadian colonies was there an old system that might feel threatened by the proximity of the new. In Europe the unprincipled excesses in France, and the expressed intent to bring the same social revolution to her neighbors, struck fear into the governments of all nearby countries and led to defensive pacts even before the outbreak of war. In spite of French support during our war for independence only a few years previously and our still less than totally amicable relations with Britain, it became impossible for the United States to associate herself with the new radical regime in France.

Thus a second problem to engage Washington's administration— which swiftly became more urgent than the Barbary states imbroglio he had inherited from the Continental Confederacy—was what policy to adopt toward our extraordinarily transformed erstwhile ally. Although the radical stage of the French Revolution had essentially ended in 1795, one of its results was almost uninterrupted warfare between England and France from 1792 to 1815. The United States was trying to maintain trade with both of the warring powers, and each side strove mightily to block any trade with its adversary. By consequence, in

1798 we engaged in the quasi-war with France, and in 1812 a declared war with Great Britain. So far as our relations with France in 1798, it made things no easier to reflect that of all those who had led that country into cooperation with the revolting colonies—nobility and clergy, politicians, admirals, diplomats and generals, army and navy officers of lower ranks, members of their families—nearly all, with a few exceptions, had been officially murdered in the most sanguinary and brutal way. Americans could not accept this cold-blooded proceeding as the right of any ruling class, or any leaders.

Unlike most wars, which can be dated specifically from a declaration that a state of war exists, the quasi-war with France had no clear-cut beginning. The war in Europe that was foreseen as an outgrowth of the French Revolution broke out in 1792, and in an amazingly short time the free-running French soldiers, undrilled and unseasoned, fighting with verve instead of mechanical precision, were defeating the professional armies of the monarchies surrounding the new French Republic. Despite representations from France, notably by the offensive Citizen Genêt, President Washington and the Congress held that our alliance with the France of Louis XVI did not require the United States to enter the new war in Europe. In the meantime, John Jay, in England, negotiated a treaty by which British merchant ships were again permitted to enter United States ports. The new French government reacted irately, holding that American neutrality actually benefited England. It directed its warships to capture our merchantmen, and by 1796 many such warlike acts had occurred.

Disenchantment with French democracy was compounded by incendiary incidents like the XYZ Affair, in which French representatives W, X, Y, and Z, acting under instructions from French Foreign Minister Talleyrand, demanded bribes as their price for beginning the negotiations for which President Adams had sent three envoys to their country. In January 1798, France directed its naval vessels and privateers to seize neutral ships carrying anything of English origin—an order aimed squarely at the huge American merchant marine, which she claimed was British in another form. This led Adams to create the Navy Department (April 30, 1798), and to direct emergency completion of the remaining three of the six frigates begun four years earlier. In May, Adams ordered the first three frigates, already very near completion, and the few ships of war we had been able to convert from merchant vessels, to seize French privateers. (The *Ganges*, now purchased by the navy, hastily converted into a warship, and still commanded by Richard Dale, was the first to go to sea.) In July, Congress abrogated the treaty of alliance with France. The quasi-war may be considered to have begun with these actions, although French ships had already captured some American warships and the first capture of a French privateer, *Le Croyable*, built in Baltimore that same year, by Stephen Decatur, Sr., in the *Delaware*, had already taken place.

Thomas Truxtun consequently recruited and organized his crew under threat of hostilities, actually an advantage to a person of his combative makeup. He had been half owner and commander of a tiny merchant sloop in 1775, and as a privateer commander during the Revolution had made so many captures that he earned Washington's praise for "being as a regiment." Following the war, he became master of a packet in the transatlantic trade (the *London Packet*, in which he carried Benjamin Franklin home from France), after which he made voyages to China and India. His reputation for good navigation, meticulous responsibility, and instant reaction when anything threatened his ship, his passengers, or the cargo entrusted to him, continued to grow. Widely known as a thoroughly trustworthy merchant skipper who never lacked for persons to invest money in his voyages, he brought his ship in to Philadelphia from his last merchant voyage in 1794, and a few months later was appointed Supervisor of Construction of frigate E, which was being built at Baltimore.

All accounts of Truxtun as captain of *Constellation* make the same point: after about six months of shakedown, during which he physically left his ship only three times, she was superbly trained, organized to perfection, ready to meet any situation that he or anyone could imagine possible. Happily—but considering her antecedents not surprisingly—she was also the sort of speedy powerhouse that John Paul Jones had in mind when he said, "I want nothing to do with a ship that will not sail fast, for I mean to go in harm's way."

Constellation was already being called the Baltimore Race Horse by her proud builders and crew (in the Civil War it was changed to Yankee Race Horse). During the same training period, Truxtun wrote a set of ship's regulations that is still viewed as a model for the time. He devised a system of signaling using flags by day and lights at night. He collaborated with four other captains in recommending Articles for the Government of the Navy to Stoddert. (This was the first attempt to set forth a code of military law, as distinct from shipboard regulations. It later became known as Navy Courts and Boards, or Rocks and Shoals, the navy bible of law, and following passage of the Unification Act of 1947 was combined with the army Articles of War to give us the present Uniform Code of Military Justice.) Not satisfied with these two beginnings, he also set forth strict instructions on the etiquette he required to be observed at all times on board ship. A disciplinarian, even a martinet, he nevertheless found it necessary only once to flog a crew member, a marine private whom he thought guilty of planning a mutiny.* This amounts to surprising abstinence for the eighteenth century (his favorite punishment was to "stop the grog").

In comparison with modern conditions, life in Truxtun's *Constellation* was difficult, not to say tough. In the context of the times, however, she would probably qualify as a happy ship, despite a thoroughly autocratic commanding officer. She was well run, efficient, well trained, and well commanded. Her crew knew exactly what was expected of them and what would be done for them. She was the epitome of a taut ship in the best sense of the word.

The proof of everything was in two brilliant battles *Constellation* fought. In the first, early in 1799, she captured the French frigate *L'In-*

---

*Mutiny was a dread word. The British fleet had just mutinied at Spithead and the Nore because of intolerable conditions on board. The crews were largely impressed, usually under the most illegal and not infrequently inhuman circumstances. When ships were "paid off," their crews often were not paid at all. Sometimes they were simply turned en masse into another ship about to depart on another long and dangerous voyage. The first mutinies were respectfully and honorably conducted by sailors driven beyond endurance. Later, not surprisingly, they turned uglier, especially when the Admiralty took heavy revenge in terms of hangings and floggings. A notorious case had occurred in the Caribbean: the crew of the British frigate *Hermione* had risen in revolt against a sadistic captain, killed him and most of the other officers, and then turned their ship over to the Spanish authorities.

surgente, of the same rate but smaller (and recently, but no longer, under command of Joshua Barney). This battle was the first payoff of Humphreys's design concepts. A year later she nearly sank the older, more heavily armed *La Vengeance*, being robbed of complete victory only by the loss of her mainmast at a critical moment (but nevertheless, the navy and the American public considered the action as a total victory for Truxtun and the *Constellation*). These were the first victories by any American ship since John Paul Jones captured the *Serapis* twenty years earlier, the first ever by a top-grade unit of our navy, built in America. It was also clear to everyone, and especially clear in the navy, that these victories were due in no small part to the training Truxtun had given her crew.

History records that Truxtun rendered service to the infant U.S. Navy of inestimable and lasting value. He was the first out in a time of emergency at sea, and his success was the result of discipline and shipboard morale of extraordinary intensity. He is supposed several times to have said, "We have an infant navy to foster and to organize, and it must be done." Whether these were his exact words is not important—he was not good at epigrams—but they do express his outlook. He was a superb organizer and an equally good motivator. While not all of Truxtun's officers received his wholehearted approval—of some he disapproved heartily—others, the ones he liked most, went on to outstanding careers in our navy. He was innovative, ingenious, and broad in outlook as to what was needed not only in his own ship but also in the entire navy—as illustrated by his regulations, his signal book, his rules on shipboard behavior, and his participation in the first Articles for the Government of the Navy. That he also fought his ship skillfully was obvious from his victories. That he beat two first-class enemy war vessels with her, in the very first ship our new navy sent to sea, confirmed the navy's dedication to the twin principles of organization and training that have been its hallmark ever since. This was Thomas Truxtun's gift to the United States Navy.

Unfortunately for his personal history, he suffered from a disability that affects some men after they attain fame. Honors were heaped on him by an exultant Congress, Lloyds of London (England was also at war with France), the delighted navy secretary, and the country as a whole. He was the hero of the time, sought out for innumerable festivities, wildly praised by everyone. As his ego grew, his understanding of others waned. He antagonized nearly everyone, including Ben Stoddert, John Adams's secretary of the navy, who nonetheless remained his admiring friend, and Robert Smith, whom he had treated arrogantly and who was not an admirer at all. Twice, in pique, he resigned from the navy. The first time it was because of a mixup over precedence in the list of captains. At the time, Truxtun had for two years been third on the list, behind only Barry and Nicholson, but suddenly President Adams, importuned by Talbot, restored Talbot to the list ahead of Truxtun. Truxtun, surprised and indignant, promptly resigned. The combined efforts of Secretary Stoddert, Charles Biddle (older brother of the dead Nicholas and now a power in Philadelphia), and former President Washington, along with the prospect of further action against the French, led him to withdraw the letter of resignation on condition that he would never be subject to Talbot's orders, an assurance Stoddert was delighted to grant.

He actually had more excuse the second time, but Jefferson was now President, and Robert Smith, whom he had once offended, was secretary of the navy. Truxtun had returned from another cruise in ill health, suffering from a nagging fever (probably malaria) that wore him down and remained in his system. He had been home for some months, still not fully recovered, when, early in 1802, Smith asked him to take the Squadron of Training and Observation to the Mediterranean to relieve Dale, who had had the post for a year. This he agreed to do, providing he could have a flag captain to command his flagship, *Chesapeake*. It was a reasonable request; Hugh Campbell, a junior captain, was so ordered—and then could not take the post because of illness. Apparently no one else was available. Truxtun requested a senior lieutenant for the job, but given the great reduction of the navy that had taken place under the Jefferson administration, none could be found. Truxtun had labored incessantly to ready the *Chesapeake* for the duty, and in the process had unduly exercised his own notoriously short-fused temper. Deciding to bring the matter to a head, he wrote

Secretary Smith to the effect that "if this cannot be done I must beg leave to quit the service."

Whether, when he wrote this fatal letter, the doughty commodore meant to resign from the navy, or only from the service in the Mediterranean upon which he was bound, has never been determined for sure. Smith was perhaps already tired of catering to Truxtun's demands, though it is clear that he had not really done very much to help him. He was a member of the anti-navy party, the Democratic-Republicans, who were opposed to the navy in all possible ways. Perhaps Smith sensed an opportunity to get even for the slight of years ago (Truxtun had apparently snubbed him in Baltimore while getting the *Constellation* ready for sea): he peremptorily sent for Richard Morris to take over the squadron, and bluntly answered Truxtun's letter by accepting it as a definite resignation from the naval service. Truxtun was only forty-seven years old.

Using his political office for the purpose of revenge amounted to serious misconduct on the part of Smith, for which history has severely censured him. The damage to the country was mitigated only by the fact that the navy had another officer, also destined to be buffeted by a rigid seniority system that put pure length of service ahead of demonstrated capability, waiting in the wings for the call that would soon come as a result: Edward Preble. Had Truxtun gone to the Mediterranean, there can be no doubt that he would have performed far more successfully than Richard V. Morris, who went in his place. As it was, because of Smith's meanness of spirit, the country had to wait another year before the situation in the Mediterranean Sea began to be more to its liking.

Truxtun's sparkling victories brought about two important consequences, as a result of which he, too, has sometimes been called father of our navy. First, he generated wild enthusiasm for it. Careers on the sea began to shine more brightly. Various localities took up drives to raise funds to construct ships for the navy. Congress had concentrated on building the large frigates, but there seemed always a dearth of the smaller ships needed to produce well-rounded squadrons. In the newly created naval euphoria, local pride found expression by building ships and giving them to the government. Important cities naturally built big ships, named after themselves (*New York, Philadelphia, Boston*), while smaller municipalities subscribed the fast little ships for which they were in many cases justly famous. Congress, too, was not unaffected. More funds were voted, and within the space of a very few years, shortly after the turn of the nineteenth century, the United States possessed a really formidable navy where, only a few years before, there had been nothing at all.*

The second effect of Truxtun's successes was a growing bellicosity toward the Barbary pirates, who seemed, in spite of tribute regularly delivered, to be growing ever more quick to find a pretext to capture American merchantmen, or to inflict some other indignity on our ships or people. Very possibly these incidents were beginning to receive wider publicity at this period because of the public's greater receptivity. The lack of the British naval umbrella began to be remarked upon. A large segment of the population was greatly concerned with the free use of the sea for the commercial benefits now so valuable to it. To all this should be added the influence of those persons most affected by expansion of the navy, its own officer corps. In the simplest terms, the United States was beginning to flex its naval muscles, and we liked what we saw and felt.

To the alarm of the advocates of a strong navy, however, coincident with settlement of the quarrel with France,** the Federalist party lost the election of 1800. During that campaign Jefferson's party, the Democratic-Republicans, had made no secret of its intention to enact a massive reduction in the navy. Fearing they meant its total abolition, as in 1785, Adams's outgoing Navy Secretary, Stoddert, managed to

---

*For this, Secretary Stoddert deserves much credit: when he took office he found a navy with only three ships, just nearing completion. When he left office there were more than fifty. In the process, he neglected his own affairs and impoverished himself, but Benjamin Stoddert richly deserves the thanks of the nation.

**In 1800 a treaty was finally negotiated with France, more or less coincident with one of the temporary truces (perhaps more accurately described as periods of reduced hostilities) between England and France. France was so anxious to regulate matters with America that even before the treaty had been formally ratified, her government sent instructions placing it into effect to her forces in the West Indies. French depredations on our commerce died down late in 1800, and our squadrons were directed to cease fire early in the next year.

get the Peace Establishment Act through Congress, preserving what he could of the navy he had so successfully built up. After Jefferson's inauguration on March 4, 1801, the anti-navy group began enthusiastically reducing the navy to the smallest possible size. All but thirteen ships were sold, and the remainder laid up "in ordinary" (the 1801 equivalent of mothballs)—under preservation, with skeleton crews. All personnel except the minimum number were discharged. This drastic action was viewed with dismay by the Federalists, the seafaring communities, notably in New England, and the active-duty officers.

The high quality of that navy had been proved. It had hardly begun to amass a tradition, but at last there were some good beginnings after the Continental Navy's dismal record. Now that it appeared finally to be coming into its own, political expediency seemed about to destroy it once more. Feelings in the service ran high—and then the Barbary states themselves came to our rescue, with the incident of the *George Washington* in Algiers.

Washington had died in 1799, less than three years after leaving the presidency. In 1800 a ship-sloop (a purchased merchantman armed with 32 guns) named in his honor happened to be the one selected to carry the usual load of tribute to the Dey of Algiers. The ship, commanded by William Bainbridge, had been excessively delayed in arriving and had been awaited with impatience. She was, nevertheless, courteously received and promptly drawn into the inner harbor, under the guns of the fort guarding it. Her cargo of tribute was inspected and deemed acceptable. Then, with the ship completely at the mercy of the Algerian fortress, Bainbridge was blandly informed that it would be most convenient for all concerned if he were to carry the annual payment due the Sultan of Turkey from Algiers to Constantinople, and furthermore would he please fly the Algerian flag during the mission! Caught by surprise, helpless under the guns of the fort, Bainbridge was forced to make the voyage. It was however very successful in the diplomatic sense, for Bainbridge was given high honors by the Sultan (who until his arrival had not even known of the existence of the United States) and presented with a "firman," or passport of high privilege. Returning to Algiers, *George Washington* was carefully anchored out of range of the fort, and the document silenced demands for a second trip. The Dey then declared war on France; so the American commander used the firman to guarantee safe conduct for the French consul, his staff, and their families, and actually transported them in his crowded ship to a place of safety, an act for which he received the official thanks of the French government. (This occurred before termination of the hostilities with France and may have had a bearing on the willingness of France to negotiate the end of the quasi-war.) When Bainbridge brought his ship back to the United States he delivered a furious report of the incident, ending with the words—bombastic today but appropriate for the times—''The next time I am directed to deliver tribute, I hope it will be through the mouths of cannon!''

Bainbridge's account of his forced mission was widely disseminated. It aroused national indignation, intensified, of course, by the insult to the memory of the first president and the national colors. Although Jefferson had ordered the navy reduced upon entering office, he was not entirely the man of peaceful inaction he has been painted. Realizing the role of England's navy in the Mediterranean Sea, he determined to utilize what remained of his navy in the same way. He had, however, little understanding of the requirements such a mission would demand of the U.S. forces that might be sent. Richard Dale, back on the navy list as a senior captain, was given the first squadron, but by modern standards his orders totally lacked comprehension of the problems he would face once on station. He was enjoined to take no overt action, to operate only as a ''squadron of observation,'' to give none of the Barbary states excuse for additional excesses or demands, and not to keep any of his personnel in service longer than their agreed upon enlistment of one year.

Dale strove to fulfill his instructions, but his imagination was not up to the task of accomplishing the real desires of the administration: somehow to overawe the Barbary states, and their freebooting corsairs, without using force. He spent his entire year shifting men about between his ships in order to send home those with the least time left to serve. After a year, in which transit time both ways across the Atlantic

Ocean had to be included, he obeyed orders and sailed his flagship back to the United States, having demonstrated only that instructions to ships at sea must be clear and bear relation to the realities, and that a single-year enlistment was unworkable for a European cruise with weeks or months of transit time in both directions. Dale's cruise in the Mediterranean was his last service to the navy, for shortly afterward he submitted his resignation.

Command of the second squadron was offered to Truxtun, but it was at this moment that he went too far with Secretary Robert Smith and found himself out of the navy. His replacement, Richard V. Morris, was a nonaggressive person who must have been Truxtun's opposite in nearly every measure. It is not known from whom the reports of his lack of activity emanated once he arrived in the Mediterranean, though very likely some can be laid at the door of our consul in Tunis, a former Revolutionary army captain and soldier of fortune named William Eaton. Eaton wanted to start a rebellion against the Bashaw of Tripoli in favor of his brother, who had been ousted by a coup. He got nowhere with Morris and returned to Washington fuming with frustration. Secretary Smith evidently heard other reports of Morris's dilatory conduct from personal letters that some of the officers in the squadron had sent home. Firebrands Henry Wadsworth (uncle of Henry Wadsworth Longfellow) and David Porter, in letters home referred in disparaging terms to the Commodore's pregnant wife, who lived aboard the flagship *Chesapeake* (though permitted, this was never accepted as good practice). The *Chesapeake* was herself criticized for never coming near the coast of Tripoli, a state of war then technically existing. In any case, Morris was summarily recalled to face a court of inquiry, as a result of which President Jefferson dismissed him from the navy—unfairly since Morris had had no opportunity to defend himself.

His relief, with his "broad command pennant" (a blue pennant with a single star, flown by a captain commanding a squadron) fluttering from one of the *Constitution*'s masts, was Edward Preble. In a very broad sense, Truxtun's real replacement had finally arrived.

Preble was already a sick man, almost certainly with abdominal cancer (he died of it in 1807), and he had a violent temper that probably was aggravated by his illness. However, during his short command tour in the Mediterranean he was at least part of the time in a period of remission, and he benefited from the mild climate. It would be nice—even dramatic—to be able to say that Preble had served with Truxtun and therefore was bringing with him some of the older man's ideas and outlook, for there seemed to be no uncertainty in his concept of what the situation demanded, any more than there was in Truxtun's. However, in a close society like the navy it was not necessary then, nor is it now, for one person to have served intimately with another to absorb what the latter has to offer in the common endeavor. It is often enough, sometimes better, to have had contact only through third parties—particularly in the case of two strongly opinionated men like these, who would almost surely have clashed bitterly unless the junior, Preble, were able totally to subordinate himself. Whatever Preble may have thought about Truxtun (it is certain he must have had strong opinions), from near two centuries of hindsight one can only say they were very much alike.

Edward Preble was a dynamic leader, determined to carry the peculiar type of war waged by the Barbary states to the very gates of their citadels, and in this he excelled over those who came before and after him. He was also adept, as Truxtun had been, at bringing out the capabilities of his subordinates, many of whom afterward served with the greatest distinction. It is here, in fact, that the source for much of Preble's fame arises. Preble's young skippers, whom he called "boys," grew to fame in the War of 1812. In the process they established a naval tradition we still revere. Historians now claim, with justice, not only that they were outstanding as young officers, but that it was Preble's leadership, and the example he showed in himself, which brought out their latent qualities.

In the Mediterranean, the sporadic hostilities lasted from the late eighteenth century until 1815, but only Preble, in 1803–04, drove them into history. The principal incidents of his tenure are part of our naval heritage: Tripoli, demanding greater tribute, had declared war in 1801 by chopping down the flagpole of our consulate. At the very beginning of Preble's command tour, Bainbridge, after the *George Washington* now commanding the fine 36-gun subscription frigate *Philadelphia* (a near sister to *Chesapeake*, and also built by Fox), ran her aground in the harbor of Tripoli. Second in importance only to the *Constitution* in Preble's small squadron, and the only other ship of significant force, the *Philadelphia* could not be got off the shoal and was forced to surrender. The ship was refloated at high water the next day and moored off the fort where her crew were already imprisoned. She was a fabulous prize of war; the aghast Preble moved at once to blockade her. Neutralizing her permanently was a bigger problem, but it was all put right a few months later when young Stephen Decatur, Jr., son of the man who in 1798 had made the first capture of an enemy ship during the quasi-war with France, entered the harbor at night in a captured ketch christened *Intrepid* for the occasion, boarded *Philadelphia* by surprise, set her afire, and got clean away without loss of a man of his crew.

In contrast to the relative inaction of other commodores sent to the Mediterranean, Preble's gunboat attacks on Tripoli, his bombardment of the forts opposed to him, and the aggressive way he kept his ships at sea and on patrol to inhibit depredations by Barbary corsairs delighted Congress and his countrymen. All this, and more, he did on his own, making up his strategy and campaigns as the situations developed. The sketchy records also indicate he had a few bad moments from his cancer, but his energy never flagged.

By the seniority system Preble was one of the junior captains in the navy, in spite of the fact he was also one of the oldest—it was all according to date of rank, not age, experience, or ability—and when Robert Smith decided to send him the reinforcements he had asked for, it was an automatic part of the package that the senior officer of the new detachment would be superior to him. Unavoidably, Preble would be superseded in command. It is now believed his hurry to take some severe, dramatic action against Tripoli in final hope of gaining release of the *Philadelphia* crew caused him to make his one large error in judgment. (It may also have been due, in part, to physical unease from his illness.) He assented to Richard Somers's scheme to sail the little

Intrepid, loaded with explosives, into the harbor of Tripoli and there blow her up in the midst of the Bashaw's fleet of freebooters. (Lieutenant Somers was skipper of the schooner *Nautilus*, and a long-time crony of Decatur's.) Probably discovered during her approach, the vessel blew up early, doing little or no damage to the enemy but, of course, killing everyone on board. In retrospect, it was counterproductive, an action Preble should never have authorized. The failed attempt strengthened the Bashaw's position and caused him to raise his ransom demands.

It was not at any time the intent of Congress to recognize the wars declared by any of the Barbary states as "real" wars in the sense wars with England or France would have been. Congress wanted only to teach them a lesson, as England had already done and would do again. That is, if their corsairs behaved suspiciously, they should be captured or driven from the sea. Their seacoasts were to be patrolled, or kept under threat of patrol. American merchantmen were convoyed, or protected by blockading the nearest piratical base while they passed. Under extreme provocation, they were protected by bombardment, or threat thereof. As the orders to the commanders of the successive squadrons made clear, our purpose was not at that time to abolish the ancient system of tribute (regardless of how much we disliked it), but to keep it within bounds, as the English were doing, and at the same time to safeguard our merchant shipping from spur-of-the-moment capture. To do so it was necessary to keep the Barbary rulers and their corsairs in fear of reprisal, for this was the only language they understood.

Preble did not accomplish all of this, but he succeeded best of all our commanders. Not until 1815 did anyone do better. It is customary to hold that it was for this that he has been given a place in our historical escutcheon, and a cursory review may make this seem a fair judgment. But there are sometimes subliminal ways, often wholly beyond the appreciation or understanding of those most intimately involved, in which needed things are done—and Preble's contribution was of this subtle order. His campaign in the waters before Tripoli and the other Barbary states did not bring a cessation of hostilities, but it was the means through which his real contribution was made. It is hardly likely he ever understood what it really was; but to his amazement, on his return to the United States he discovered that somehow his countrymen did. Subconsciously they had wanted action, not wordy arguments and the payment of tribute, and action he had produced. They wanted to be proud of their nation and their navy, not ashamed. Preble was the only man who had done this for them, it had been fully publicized at home, and he was a hero!

For our navy had faltered badly in its beginning, during the Continental period. This is the main reason why some historians now insist the United States Navy did not exist until 1794. Such arguments are based on technicalities. Our navy began in the Revolutionary War, then was set aside for ten years. In 1794 it was revived briefly, then set aside again. It was nearly set aside a third time when Thomas Jefferson became president. Its great good fortune was not only to have superior ships (the navy of 1775 had good ships too), but also to have Thomas Truxtun to command the first ship of the new group to get to sea, and Edward Preble to stop the third move to eliminate it. He did this by giving the nation a reason to admire the navy. Beyond this, he started the young men who would be our commanders in the War of 1812 on the road to the competence they would need.

Truxtun reached heights of fame in America that had previously been equaled only by John Paul Jones. But Jones had mostly been fitted out in France, and lived more in Paris than in his adopted country. (Napoleon is supposed to have said, during one of his tirades against the ineffectiveness of his navy, "If Jones had lived, then *France* might have had an admiral!") Truxtun and the *Constellation* and everything about them were American. For the first time there was an authentic naval hero of our own, not an adopted foreigner, and his ship was also our own, not a foreign-built one. But Truxtun, poorly advised, faded too soon. Had Preble not picked up his mantle of personal leadership, operational competence, and dynamic pursuit of national objectives—all supremely important to our navy at this time—there would almost surely have been another period of naval doldrums. We would not have trained our future skippers in the art of successful war at sea. We would, instead, have continued to reproduce the unimaginative officers of which our service was already too full, officers expert at dealing with the small difficulties that are particularly the lot of the seaman but unable to see beyond their own limited horizons. In 1812 they would have been overawed by the great navy of Britain, as their immediate predecessors were only a generation before.

Had we not had Truxtun and Preble, and particularly had we not had Preble, we could not have been ready for the War of 1812. As events demonstrated, we were, even so, perilously near to reverting back, once again, to the old, comfortable, conservative but unready days. There were still many bad habits of thought and leadership to overcome.

3

The Beginning of the War of 1812

During most of June 1807, the United States frigate *Chesapeake* lay in Hampton Roads, off Norfolk, preparing for an Atlantic voyage to Gibraltar and the Mediterranean Sea. She was assigned as the flagship of Captain James Barron, who already wore the courtesy rank of commodore by virtue of his orders to take the place of the recently returned Commodore John Rodgers on the Mediterranean station. In nominal command of the ship, Master Commandant Charles Gordon spent the entire time on board supervising the loading of stores, provisions, equipment, and ammunition. The ship was expected to be overseas for at least two years, and there was much in the way of spares she would need; the more she could bring with her, the better. She would also be carrying Dr. John Bullus, prospective U.S. Navy agent in the Mediterranean, and his wife, children, and servants, as well as the wife of a Marine Corps captain assigned to the *Chesapeake*, the furniture of the two households, and a group of Sicilian musicians and their families and belongings en route home.

The war in Europe was at full head. Napoleon was still in the flush of his amazing military victories. Even the loss of his combined French and Spanish fleets at Trafalgar had yet to hurt his power in central Europe, and the British navy was still hard pressed to maintain the blockade of his ports. Because of the war, the American squadron in the Mediterranean Sea and the few American consuls or "agents" stationed in the area had great difficulty providing local supplies for the ships or themselves. What could be purchased was usually expensive and of low quality. For the sake of economy, it had become customary to load warships bound for Mediterranean duty with whatever the government desired to send over, often to the detriment—and sometimes the total elimination—of their military capabilities on the way across. This special service extended also to the transportation of diplomatic passengers, including their families. One frigate, the *John Adams*, had arrived at Gibraltar with her main battery guns stowed below in order to free deck space for passengers and their personal belongings. *Chesapeake*, a relatively roomy vessel, was being loaded in accordance with this custom. Gordon did not put her guns in the hold, but he had them triced up for heavy weather, securely lashed out of the way. None were free even for the possibility of firing a salute, for which, however, he would be ready during the passage upon entry into Gibraltar. Some of the broadside battery would also be got ready at the same time against the possibility of meeting with a particularly intrepid corsair, though it could hardly be imagined that any corsair would dare take on an American ship of war, especially one the size of the *Chesapeake*. Gordon's job was to get her over in the best possible form, with the least difficulty to any of the important passengers and the least harm to the cargo expected by equally important persons awaiting her arrival in Europe. For none of this did Barron have any responsibility, beyond the implicit one of having authorized the specially unready condition of the ship during her Atlantic transit—which he could not very well avoid, inasmuch as her extra cargo and passengers had been directed by the navy secretary himself. It was Gordon's job to see to it that all was in proper condition upon arrival on station. Barron's job would be that of handling the problems of the station itself. Withal Gordon, his flag-captain, was far too junior to command a ship as important as the *Chesapeake* on his own. By the naval custom of centuries he shared this responsibility with Barron, his immediate superior.

There is no counterpart to Gordon's position in our modern navy, for he was not "commanding" in the sense the word is used today. It might be accurate to characterize him in modern parlance as somewhere between commanding officer and executive officer, in that he was totally responsible to Barron for all details involving the ship herself. An independent captain was, and still is, also responsible for everything the ship does, or fails to do. For the *Chesapeake*, in the year 1807, all that was in Barron's purview.

James Barron and his older brother Samuel were members of a naval and maritime family. Samuel had served in the Virginia state navy, of which his father had been the commodore, and had been the first skipper of the *Chesapeake*. James, who had served in the merchant service for a time, entered the U.S. Navy in 1798 with the rank of lieutenant aboard the new frigate *United States*, with Captain John Barry. That same year he distinguished himself in saving the frigate from severe damage in a heavy gale, for which he received Barry's praise and official thanks. Stephen Decatur, Jr., was a midshipman aboard the same ship, and the records show that Decatur and Barron were very good friends, the younger man eagerly learning from the tutelage of the older. Later, Barron was flag-captain for Barry, and subsequently for Richard Dale in the *President*. At age thirty-eight, he was at the pinnacle of his career with his own flag-captain, assigned as commodore of the United States Squadron in the Mediterranean, the post made famous only a few years before by Edward Preble. His was a situation to be envied, and Barron took full pleasure in it.

There was, however, one fly in Barron's soup. The man he was technically to relieve was Commodore John Rodgers, a dour argumentative person with whom he had had a particularly unpleasant falling out, culminating in challenges to a duel. The duel never took place, partly because several high personages, among them the secretary of the navy, took it on themselves to keep the men apart. Rodgers had made a great point of his indignation at being kept from satisfying his honor; by contrast, Barron made no noticeable protest. The situation was noted throughout the navy, to Barron's discredit. It was whispered darkly that he "would not stand fire," that though a skillful enough seaman, he did not have the backbone to stand up against Rodgers. No more devastating comment could be made. And now he was destined to sail across the ocean to take his archenemy's place on a foreign station. No doubt both he and the secretary were secretly relieved that in accordance with the most recent orders to reduce the active-duty strength of the navy, Rodgers had already brought most of his squadron home.

Modern naval commanders would doubtless find fault with Barron's methods of preparation for his important post, but aside from whatever thought he may have given Rodgers, these methods were not far different from those of his contemporaries—except Preble, who sailed in complete readiness and had occasion to prove it. Barron saw only a long voyage in prospect; there would be ample time to shake the crew down en route to Gibraltar; by the time he got his ship on station, he and Gordon would have seen to it that her crew was well trained. In the meantime, a long absence from family and friends was in prospect. The town of Hampton, bordering on Hampton Roads, was his home. Barron had last been employed at sea in 1802, and now, five years later, there were many details to arrange before he could leave for another protracted period. His friends and neighbors, delighted in the distinction that had come to him, offered much social life. Surrounded by well-wishers, he allowed himself, as a distinguished commander about to undertake a prestigious and difficult assignment, a pleasant send-off period. During the entire preparation of his flagship, Barron visited on board the *Chesapeake* only twice—on neither occasion for long.

Nor did he concern himself with any problems his flagship might be having. These were the responsibility of his flag-captain, Gordon. He was not even disturbed by the fact—later widely reported to *Chesapeake*'s detriment—that she had been unable to fire the customary salute to George Washington's grave as she passed Mount Vernon on her way down the Potomac River. (In justice to Barron, he might have been totally unaware of this at the time, for although it was brought up later, Gordon probably did not report it to him.) The ship, laid up for nearly four years in the Washington Navy Yard, had been hurried out from there by pressure from the secretary, who had become disturbed at the lengthy time taken to get her ready. Her departure had been consequently attended with some confusion. Nonetheless, the salute could have been handled with a little forethought. It had already become traditional, although our first president had been dead only eight years—and the lack of readiness for a totally predictable situation presaged the much more serious unreadiness soon to be demonstrated at great cost. But the salute was Gordon's problem, not Barron's. So far as is known, Gordon, a relative by marriage to, and protégé of, Secretary of the Treasury Gallatin, was not in any way taken to task for the dereliction. It doubtless would have been forgotten were it not for the events that followed shortly afterward.

While *Chesapeake* was outfitting in Washington, the British minister had complained to the State Department that four deserters from HBMS *Melampus*, 74, had enlisted among the *Chesapeake*'s crew and, in accordance with accepted normal procedures, he asked they be returned. The matter was referred to Barron, who delegated investigation to Gordon. After inquiry, Gordon reported that the men had indeed deserted from the Royal Navy, but that all were American citizens, born in America and impressed into the British navy from an American merchantman on the high seas. They had simply availed themselves of the chance to get away from their enslavement. The British minister in Washington was satisfied, but Vice Admiral Berkeley, R.N., commanding the North American station at Halifax, was not. In the meantime, *Chesapeake* moved to Norfolk, and while she lay there, five more deserters from another British warship, *Halifax*, enlisted aboard. One of them, Radford or Ratford by name, had been recognized on a Norfolk street and had publicly insulted the British officer who spotted him. Of these five, all but Radford deserted *Chesapeake* before she departed Norfolk. But Radford remained, and the British wanted him on two counts: desertion, and insolence to a British naval officer, the second being the more serious. Berkeley therefore sent a written order to all his ships on the American station that, on falling in with the *Chesapeake*, they were to require a search for deserters. HBMS *Leopard*, 50, carried the order to his ships in Lynhaven Roads, at the mouth of Chesapeake Bay, where a British squadron lay at anchor blockading two French ships that had taken refuge in American waters.

Upon many previous occasions, unpleasant incidents involving U.S. merchant ships had grown out of Britain's insistence on the right of impressment. The British navy had been using press gangs in British seaports to man its ships for many years. Prior to the Revolution, press gangs were occasionally sent ashore in the colonies. Pressing seamen from merchantmen at sea was a standard practice too, and British men-of-war had not hesitated to take "excess men" off their own or colonial merchant ships. After American independence, they could no longer send press gangs ashore in the former colonial ports, but the British navy still maintained that all merchant ships at sea were obligated to lower their sails on sighting a British warship and permit it to muster the crew in search of British nationals. Since there were virtually no United States warships about, ships of the former colonies generally found it expedient to comply, much as they had before independence; and although there was always a difference of opinion regarding how many men a ship needed to work her, she could usually rely on being left with enough, though barely enough, to do the job. But the British considered any man once an Englishman to be still subject to the crown. Thus, anyone born before independence was still subject to impressment. Circumstances being as they were, moreover, a man's protestations that he had been born after 1776 were often ignored by boarding officers intent on their own needs, and immediate force was stronger than legal niceties. It was a common complaint of merchant skippers that their best sailors were always deemed British and hauled away.

In defense, British diplomats cited the international quality of most crews, the uncertain nationality of many seamen (as well as their own law that English subjects could not renounce their responsibilities as citizens by taking up citizenship in another country), the war emergency faced by England, and the undisputed fact that the British navy was the only thing between England and the armies of Napoleon. In the view of the United States, this last point, though freely admitted, was irrelevant. To British naval officers it was irrelevant too; they had been taught they had the right—and there was no question they had the power to enforce their will—and so far as merchant ships of their own or other countries were concerned, they would exercise both right and power to the point of total arrogance.

Not content with impressing men from merchant ships, however, the British navy had three times tried and twice succeeded in taking men from American warships. The first episode occurred in 1798, when the U.S. sloop of war *Baltimore*, a converted merchantman commanded by one Isaac Phillips, fell in with a British squadron. Despite Phillips's protests that he was an American naval officer and his ship a regular warship of the United States Navy, he could not show commission papers, having been hurried to sea before they were ready. While Phillips was on board the senior British ship explaining this awkward situation to its commander, a boarding party, unbeknownst to him, was mustering his crew. Fifty-five of them were then taken aboard the British ship. After interrogation, fifty men were returned a few hours later, but five were impressed.*

When Phillips's report of the incident reached Washington, he was immediately dismissed from the naval service, with neither trial nor opportunity to defend himself. The indignant secretary of the navy went on to inform all commanders that "It is the positive command of the President . . . to resist to the utmost of your power" in any future similar situation, and specifically, to "surrender your ship before you surrender your people." In 1799, the British frigate *Surprise* encountered our converted merchantman *Ganges*, now commanded by

---

*Interestingly, some days earlier a British privateer had come alongside the *Baltimore* at night under the impression she was a merchantman, hoping by a surprise attack to gain a quick and easy prize. Its skipper's embarrassment at his mistake was understandable, but this was compounded when Phillips coolly turned the situation to his own advantage by impressing some men from the privateer's crew. It was one of the few instances of impressment in reverse that has been recorded. There is a possibility the British were aware of Phillips's action, which would explain their sending a boat with a boarding party to the *Baltimore* at the same time as he, in his boat, was en route to them. One can also surmise that the impressed privateers lost no time making their plight known to the British boarding officer, which would explain his reason for bringing such a large number from *Baltimore*'s crew back with him. Records do not show whether the five men finally impressed had been members of the privateer's crew, nor whether they were returned to the privateer or simply taken into the British navy.

Thomas Tingey, and demanded "all Englishmen aboard." In response, Tingey beat to quarters, and the English did not pursue the matter further.

The second instance of impressment from a public vessel of the United States occurred in 1806. In 1803, the Jefferson administration became enamored of the infamous "gunboat theory," the idea that many small ships were superior to a large one with the same number and size of guns. The aghast professional opinion that such cockleshells could in no circumstances equal the value and performance of the ship they reputedly replaced did not avail against the theory; the gunboats were undeniably cheaper to build and needed many fewer personnel. To the theorists, whose motive was really to eliminate the navy, a battle between a group of gunboats and an opposing frigate of equal force would inevitably result to the advantage of the gunboats, which could attack from all sides, whereas the frigate would have to concentrate on only the few gunboats that happened to be within reach of her broadside. No consideration was given to the fact that in blowing weather the big ship would be the faster; that she could overhaul one gunboat after another, blow it out of the water with only a partial broadside, or literally run it down and smash it under her keel; that she could keep the sea in heavy weather that would swamp the gunboats; that coordination of simultaneous action by such a large number of small boats was an impossibility; that even assembling them all was problematic; or that they were useful only in calm weather in shallow water. It was a cheap solution appealing to those whose eyes were turned away from the sea. Preble, hero of the war against the Barbary pirates, had just returned from the Mediterranean urgently recommending that the navy build many gunboats, the lack of which had been his major problem. This played directly into the hands of those who wanted to abolish the big ships, and they used it to the hilt. In 1805, Congress directed construction of numerous gunboats: small schooners or luggers of various types, 50 to 70 feet in length, one or two heavy guns, a crew of about forty men and three officers, the senior being a lieutenant. Some 50 had been built by 1806, and over 100 more were on order. All told, before the craze ran itself out, 177 were constructed. These little boats, hardly fit to weather a storm at sea, were expected to cross the Atlantic Ocean to reinforce the squadron in the Mediterranean. Some did.

In 1806, James Lawrence, a lieutenant commanding *Gunboat Number 6*, two guns, sailed her to Gibraltar. In the harbor, in his capacity as commander of a U.S. man-of-war, he called upon Admiral Lord Collingwood, Nelson's successor after the fatal Battle of Trafalgar. Collingwood's flagship was HBMS *Dreadnaught*, first rate, 96 guns, a behemoth of the time. While Lawrence was aboard *Dreadnaught*, three of his men seized the opportunity to jump into a British boat and claim they had deserted from the British navy and now wished to return to it, apparently having had enough of the life in a 60-foot gunboat. They were brought aboard the *Dreadnaught*, where Collingwood, to give him credit, thoughtfully listened to the young American skipper's strong protest before gravely rendering the decision that "there was nothing to be done about it." Nor would he accept surrender of *Gunboat Number 6*. Instead, he put the anguished Lawrence back in her and, so far as he was concerned, that was the end of the matter.

Lawrence wrote a full report of the incident to Commodore Rodgers, then commanding the American squadron, who forwarded it to the Navy Department with his own strong endorsement. And it was noteworthy that neither the commodore nor the secretary of the navy thought there was anything more the gunboat under Lawrence's command could or should have done against the 96-gun British flagship. It was only too obvious that Collingwood had felt Lawrence to be faintly ridiculous with his two-gun boat and had treated him gently, as one might a child. The whole affair was simply swept under the rug and forgotten, except perhaps by Lawrence, who seems to have been a spirited soul with an almost mystical sense of personal honor, and possibly by the British, who concluded that American naval vessels could be insulted freely, as they proceeded to do again a year later.

Surprisingly, the acrimonious official atmosphere over impressment from merchantmen seems not to have extended into personal relationships between officers of the two navies. Among the senior officers, a certain spirit of sociability and good fellowship apparently existed along with the natural professional rivalry that might be expected. In its bases in the West Indies, the Royal Navy gave willing support to the United States Navy during the quasi-war with France (of course, France was a common enemy) and (with slightly less justification) it did the same at its bases in the Mediterranean Sea—notably Gibraltar, Port Mahon, and Malta—during the Barbary wars.*

Not surprisingly, American traders did not welcome British naval vessels into their home ports during the period prior to the War of 1812. Although the British no longer sent press gangs ashore, impressment at sea was a constant possibility, and it was feared they might follow American merchant ships to sea, where they could work their will on them. In 1806, however, when two French warships sought refuge from bad weather in Norfolk, a superior British blockading force anchored in Lynhaven Roads, just inside the entrance to Chesapeake Bay. There they remained into 1807, joined in June by a ship bearing a name destined to become very well known to American history: *Leopard*. The presence of British men-of-war in the bay was tolerated since they punctiliously carried out the diplomatic niceties, kept their crews and junior officers on board ship, and avoided giving offense in any way. During their few excursions into Norfolk, the senior British officers were accepted as additions to the social scene, even though, by 1807, more than six thousand of our men had been forced into the British navy against their will and contrary to American law.

As the *Chesapeake* made her final preparations for getting under way, Barron thought his explanation regarding the four men from the *Melampus* had been accepted by England through her minister, David Erskine. The five from the *Halifax* had not even been the subject of

---

*There appears to have been a spirit of good-natured rivalry between skippers as to the professional qualities of their respective ships and navies, extending even to wagers over the outcome of possible battles between them. No record exists that any senior British naval officer of this time ever implied, much less said, that the American navy would not fight and indeed did not know how—which words, or similar ones, resulted in one of the only recorded duels between junior officers of the two navies prior to the War of 1812 (there were numerous duels afterward). In this instance, Midshipman Joseph Bainbridge (younger brother of William) challenged the private secretary of the governor of Malta, a Mr. Cochrane, and shot him dead. Stephen Decatur acted as Joseph's second, and the duel caused much notoriety at the time. Both Bainbridge and Decatur were immediately sent back to the United States to avoid prosecution for murder.

inquiry by Erskine, and in any case, four of them had deserted again. Only Radford, enlisted under the name of Wilson, was still on board, not a very serious matter. Barron could not conceive of anything happening other than a diplomatic protest. The *Baltimore* affair had taken place in 1798; the *Gunboat Number 6* incident was really a trivial business. This was now 1807, and the *Chesapeake* was a fully recognized major warship of the United States Navy. All these nuisances would be behind him once his ship finally got a fair breeze and pointed her bows toward Gibraltar. That *Chesapeake* was crowded with extra passengers and stores was not unusual, any more than that her gundeck was so cluttered with unstowed gear of all kinds that her guns could not be reached to be made ready for use without extensive shifting about and re-stowing. The transatlantic voyage was really merely a ferry trip and, given the season, hopefully pleasant, with good weather. Barron did not expect to have any duties to perform until the ship reached Gibraltar—and then only to fire appropriate salutes and obey diplomatic protocol. Except for unsettled conditions in the Mediterranean, the United States was at peace. No action would take place until arrival on station. He foresaw no problems, did not think about possible special contingencies, expected to enjoy a nice voyage.

Late in June, all preparations were complete. Barron bade his family good-bye and went off to the ship he had hardly visited during the preparation period. The fair breeze Barron and Gordon awaited came on the morning of 22 June. *Chesapeake* hove up her anchor and set sail, anticipating only the usual organizational turmoil attendant upon at last getting under way for a long deployment.

As *Chesapeake* approached Lynhaven Roads, her officers saw signals being exchanged among the British ships anchored there. There was nothing unusual in that—they were still carrying on their year-long blockade of the two French ships inside Chesapeake Bay. HBMS *Leopard* hove up her anchor and stood out, preceding *Chesapeake* through the capes. No bother. The ships did not interfere with each other. Doubtless the *Leopard* was bound for the British naval station at Halifax and would soon stand off to the north.

But *Leopard* did not turn north. She sailed ahead of the *Chesa-*

peake for several hours on an easterly course and, early in the afternoon, by now several miles beyond the three-mile limit, came about and ranged up within speaking distance.

"I have a message for you," hailed the British captain. "Request you heave to and receive my boat."

The very moment the British ship changed course Barron should have recognized her action as out of the ordinary. Even more unusual was the request to receive a message hours after both ships had left the same port. However, Barron was not on his guard (as all other U.S. warships ever after would be). He conceived of no problem from the other ship's approach, saw no objection to letting her close while his own ship made no other preparations than to receive her boat punctiliously. Niceties were commonplace between senior officers of the two navies. The boat, seen to be carrying a lieutenant in full regalia in her stern sheets, was taken alongside with the honors befitting a foreign man-of-war. The British lieutenant asked if he could speak privately with the American commodore. In Barron's cabin, he produced Admiral Berkeley's order that the *Chesapeake* be searched for deserters; the lieutenant also presented a written request from his captain that *Chesapeake*'s commander muster his crew for him so that he could ascertain by inspection and interrogation whether there were in fact, as had been reported, four British subjects among them. Astonished at the message, Barron was for the first time uneasy, but he remained closeted in his cabin while he discussed the unprecedented request at length with the British lieutenant and with Dr. Bullus, his senior passenger. After lengthy discussion, Barron wrote a brief reply that he could under no circumstances permit inspection of his crew by officers of a foreign nation and asked the lieutenant to convey his regrets back to his commanding officer.

At this point Barron still could conceive of no further action other than an unpleasant message in response. Possibly there would be some diplomatic repercussions. But while he was closeted in his cabin the officers of the *Chesapeake*, to their amazement, saw the *Leopard* come close aboard, with gunports open, tompionless gun muzzles staring at them, the tense faces of her crew at action stations peering out the ports along their gun barrels. A group of officers accosted Gordon, insisting he report their concern to the commodore and ask that Barron order the ship prepared for action. Quietly, Gordon went to Barron's cabin with the suggestion, but Barron held back, stalling for time until the British emissary had entered his boat and departed. As he later described his purpose, he did not wish to make any untoward move that might offend the *Leopard*. After the boat was clear, he directed that the crew go quietly to quarters, without drums or the customary rattle so as not to alert the British.

The English captain, Humphries by name, was well aware of the unready state of the American ship, and the lieutenant he had sent to her confirmed it. The *Leopard* was an older ship than *Chesapeake*, slightly smaller, with a marginally smaller broadside. With scantlings originally intended for a 44-gun frigate, the American ship was more damage resistant. Waiting for the *Chesapeake* to get organized was not in Humphries's plan. He brought his ship closer. "I have orders to remove British deserters from your ship, sir!" he hailed.

No response from the *Chesapeake*. At Barron's direction, Gordon had hauled in his sheets and braced his yards around to the wind. The American frigate was gathering way through the water.

"Heave to, or I shall fire!" bellowed the Englishman.

"I cannot understand you!" shouted Barron. *Leopard* had more sail set, was fore-reaching slightly on the *Chesapeake*. Suddenly there was the bang of a cannon. Unbelievably, a splash rose in the sea forward of *Chesapeake*'s bows.

"Heave to!" again shouted the *Leopard*'s captain. Another shot flew across *Chesapeake*'s bow.

There was a turmoil on the decks of the hapless American ship. A shot across the bow was reserved for merchant ships! Across the bow of a warship, it was an insult no self-respecting man-of-war could tolerate! But *Chesapeake*'s crew, who had hardly ever been mustered on their stations, let alone drilled in their duties, were slow in getting there. Much extra impedimenta lay around the guns, themselves triced up with special lashings in case of bad weather. The gun captains, who had not been ready to fire a salute when they passed Mount Vernon, were no more ready now, for although the magazine was hurriedly opened and a few charges somehow rousted up, there were no loaded powder horns to prime them with and no matches burning in the gun tubs—or to be found. The guns could not be fired.

In the midst of the feverish preparations, there was a thunderous crash. A full broadside! At point-blank range, the whole side of the *Leopard* erupted with flame, smoke, and shot. Cannonballs crashed into *Chesapeake*'s unresisting hull. A hailstorm of splinters arose, compounding the damage. Shrieks and groans from the wounded. Bursts of profane rage from others. But the *Chesapeake*'s guns were silent. Never had a ship been more unready.

Barron, standing helpless on the quarterdeck, began bellowing. "Return the fire!" he shouted, as if his order could accomplish a miracle in place of prior preparation. "Open fire! My God, will no one do his duty?" Flying splinters struck him in the leg; he staggered, grasped a wooden stanchion to steady himself. "Will no one do his duty?" he shouted again.

A second broadside crashed aboard, then a third, and a fourth. More men were wounded, four altogether were killed. More shrieks, more enraged curses. Blood flowed on the decks. Had this been a regular battle, the damage thus far received would have been considered no more than might be expected, since the enemy would, supposedly, have been receiving some hurt also. Under the special circumstances, it was pure horror, the *Chesapeake* like a sitting duck, incapable of doing anything to stop it, and all about, confusion that was now uncontrolled and beyond remedy.

According to some accounts, Barron became incoherent, continuing to command his unready forces to return the fire. Finally, a lone gun fired a single shot, the only gun fired by the *Chesapeake* during the entire miserable action. Lieutenant William Henry Allen, a fiery young man who later took a leading part as an unfriendly witness in Barron's court-martial, fired the gun personally by—tradition has it—seizing a red-hot coal from the galley in his bare hands and rushing it to the gun. Since there is nowhere mention or record of any injury to his hands, it is likely that he used a pincers or similar instrument.

After a number of broadsides, seven according to most reports, *Leopard* ceased fire. "Heave to!" her skipper demanded again. "Stand by to receive my boat!"

Despairingly, Barron directed Gordon to have the yards braced aback. Owing to damage received aloft, this was not an easy maneuver—particularly with a demoralized and disheartened crew—but it was done. The same lieutenant returned. Pointedly ignoring Barron's statement that he had surrendered his ship, he directed that the crew be mustered, selected three whom he identified as having deserted from the *Melampus*, searched the ship for Radford, found him where the terror-stricken man had hidden, and unceremoniously departed. The *Leopard* filled her sails and stood back into Chesapeake Bay, where she anchored that same evening with her captives manacled on board. Her squadron mates, having already recalled their personnel—thus demonstrating they knew what *Leopard* was about from the beginning—made room for her in their midst, so that she lay surrounded on all sides.

When the *Chesapeake* abjectly crept back into Hampton Roads the next morning, the fury of the inhabitants of Norfolk became dangerous. A British lieutenant sent ashore with papers for the English consul (a report destined for Berkeley in Halifax) was mobbed and would have been killed had not local authorities intervened.

Berkeley ordered the captives brought immediately to Halifax for trial, and began writing a detailed and defensive report for the British Admiralty. Meanwhile, Captain Thomas Hardy, who less than two years before had been flag-captain for Nelson at Trafalgar, succeeded to command of the squadron blockading the French men-of-war. More sensitive to the situation in the United States than his superior, he took his ships from Lynhaven Roads and conducted his blockading duties from sea, beyond immediate sight of land. He also directed them to avoid unnecessary offense to American ships of war; and he sent the *Leopard* to Bermuda, off the American station, never to return to a port of the United States.

It was well the *Leopard* was so wisely disposed of, for more than one American skipper of a big man-of-war vowed to attack her and take her, war or no war, if ever he had the fortune to encounter her. Such bombastic fantasies were understandable, if not realistic, but some difficult incidents, like the near lynching of the British lieutenant, were bound to occur, though none was of the gravity of the insult to the *Chesapeake*. So far as is known, no ship of the navy of Great Britain bearing the name *Leopard* ever returned to our shores.

President Jefferson was by now in a quandary. The grossness of the incident was maddening. There were cries for war everywhere, most particularly in seacoast towns and throughout New England, since it was they who had most felt the effects of impressment. Both houses of Congress were enraged. Jefferson tried to defuse the issue by pressing for the Embargo Act, which prohibited all trade by sea with any nation and was finally enacted in December. But this act added fuel to the national anger and was unpopular on all sides. To shipowners it caused financial loss. To those most affected by impressment, the seamen, it stopped their livelihood entirely. To naval officers itching to redress the insult, it was pusillanimous. As Jefferson left office it was replaced by the Nonintercourse Act, which prohibited trade only with the "aggressors," meaning England and France. This act lasted only one year and was replaced with a simple prohibition against the entry of any armed ship of the belligerent powers into American ports.

The repercussions of the *Chesapeake-Leopard* affair, however, lasted many years. Strong diplomatic protests were made to England. Negotiations, complicated by a continuing accumulation of exacerbating incidents, dragged on inconclusively.

Barron was court-martialed aboard his former flagship, which had been diverted from the Mediterranean assignment and given to Stephen Decatur, whose orders were to bring her back to a state of high morale and fighting efficiency. Decatur, having officially asked in writing to be excused from acting in the court-martial on the grounds of prejudice against Barron, was required nevertheless to sit as one of its members. John Rodgers, despite the well-known circumstances of his intent to duel with Barron, was ordered as its president. Both officers were Barron's avowed enemies and participated in its verdict: "guilty of neglecting, on the probability of an engagement, to clear his ship for action." The sentence was five years' suspension from duty, beginning at once; since the court's verdict was not rendered until 1808, this meant Barron was suspended until 1813.

The sea being Barron's only means of livelihood, he went into merchant service, was in Europe when war with England broke out, and made no effort to return to duty either in 1812, when the war began, or a year later, when his suspension expired. He did not, in fact, return until 1818, long after the end of the war. No doubt the bitter feelings he held prevented any such move, although there may have been more to it—in 1820 he fought Decatur in a duel over the matter, and when both men were lying wounded on the ground Barron was reported to have told the dying Decatur that he could not return because he had been in a debtor's prison in England. There is no proof of the truth of this, and it is of little consequence. Probably he believed there were enough ambitious officers seeking a chance for glory, his erstwhile friend Decatur among them, so that no matter how sincere, his efforts would be brushed aside.

This was most likely true, in view of the number of captains looking for commands during the war, and most likely it was also true that ambition and personality were deeply embedded in the proceedings of the court-martial. Review of the record raises significant questions as to the fairness of its conduct. Many currents were flowing, involving many different people and many different motives, some of them political. These converged to fix sole blame on James Barron, who, though not directly *Chesapeake*'s commanding officer, was clearly the senior officer present and in charge of the ship. He had behaved indecisively (Lieutenant Allen privately said he had been cowardly, and used nearly as direct language in his official court statements), and was to blame, therefore, for the worst debacle in the entire history of our navy.

Charles Gordon, technically the real skipper but too junior in rank and too inexperienced to have been entrusted with such an important ship on his own, was saved by his political connections. In contrast to Barron's lengthy ordeal, which included both a court of inquiry and a later court-martial, Gordon, in his own obligatory court-martial, was quickly tried and quickly acquitted.

Barron himself seems to have come to the conclusion that the fault lay in incompetent and cowardly subordinates, on whom he tried to lay the entire blame. One may legitimately entertain the belief that he was a man of poor command ability who should never have been entrusted with high responsibility in the first place. Certainly he did not have the broad perceptions demanded by the situation in which he found himself. And he would hardly have been able to deal with the complex political and naval interaction intrinsic to being commander of the Mediterranean Squadron. It is likely that most officers of the navy of the time, particularly after the example of Preble, were aware of Barron's innate shortcomings and felt strongly that he was not suited to the assignment. This was practically the universal opinion of the officers of his ship.

Barron was, in fact, a perfect example of the error inherent in the traditional navy system of selection to command through seniority alone. A minisociety with traditions inherited from England but imperfectly understood, the navy's system of organization and succession to command rewarded only seniority in rank. Accomplishment, moral courage, and daring were recognized by superficial "decorations," but the real rewards of service came with longevity. Thus, good leaders often were held back in deference to the seniority rights of superiors who were, all the same, of poorer quality. Only in warlike conditions do such situations adjust themselves, and even then not until after sad experience. In the more ordinary conditions of peace, there is the tendency to perpetuate mediocrity, the certainty of succession, despite general awareness of the deficiencies of those in command. Thus, the unease that may have attended Barron's appointment would have been called jealousy by his adherents, while contrary-minded advisers of the navy secretary would be pacified by the fact we were at peace and hence it was unlikely Barron would face any serious test. Somehow he would muddle through what problems he did encounter. But when Barron so signally failed, the system turned on him and made him the sacrificial goat. This is not to suggest that there was a concerted plot against Barron. It was merely the way human nature operated—and to a large degree still does.

Decatur commanded the *Chesapeake* for two years. As a member of the navy's officer corps with a bright individual reputation to uphold, he felt his own personal honor had been impugned, in addition to that of the navy, by the *Chesapeake-Leopard* affair. In this he was not alone, for his crew felt the same. Appealing to their sense of having been wronged as fighting men, he used some unusual stratagems to keep their disgrace always before them and, promising revenge, he succeeded in reestablishing morale of a high order. For one thing, *Chesapeake* did not return gun salutes or render passing honors because ''a ship without honor can render none.'' He also drilled his gun crews rigorously and constantly assured them that if a British man-of-war so much as looked askance at their ship, the instant response would repay any repetition of the blood insult she had received. As for *Leopard*, he promised that if she should ever appear again on *Chesapeake*'s horizon he would attack her forthwith. With his crew spoiling for a fight, he cruised the area between Norfolk and Maine enforcing the unpopular embargo, but he never fell in with British ships in a situation making possible fulfillment of the boast.

If Decatur and *Chesapeake* had no chance for revenge, the *President–Little Belt* affair of 1811, superficially similar to that between the *Chesapeake* and *Leopard*, was interpreted at the time as being a fitting answer. But the incident is more accurately an illustration of the feelings between the two navies on the eve of the War of 1812. John Rodgers, commanding the 44-gun *President*, was hastily ordered to sea by Secretary of the Navy Paul Hamilton on receipt of news that the British frigate *Guerriere* had impressed a man named Diggio, a native of Maine, from an American merchant brig off the port of New York. A few days later, about forty-five miles outside of Chesapeake Bay, Rodgers sighted a British warship. It initially approached aggressively and then, evidently realizing the *President* was not a simple merchantman, turned to avoid contact. Rodgers pursued all afternoon. Finally, after nightfall, the superior sailing qualities of the *President* got her within speaking distance. The stranger refused to identify herself when Rodgers hailed. Instead, she demanded Rodgers identify himself first. The acrimony continued through several hails until a shot was fired—from which ship cannot today be determined, since the official report of each claimed it came from the other. But Rodgers was no Barron. His ship was in all respects ready, and *President* launched a devastating broadside. *Little Belt*, also at action stations, responded immediately. The night action continued for a quarter of an hour, during which Rodgers and his officers realized the ship they were engaging was much smaller than their own. Firing finally ceased, more or less by mutual consent, and this time the stranger answered *President*'s hail with the information that she was HM Ship Sloop *Little Belt*, 18 guns, and had suffered considerable damage. Rodgers remained nearby until daylight, sent a boat to offer assistance, which was declined, confirmed that the other ship was in no danger of sinking, though "much cut up, alow and aloft," and then, like *Leopard*, sailed away. It cannot have failed to cross Rodgers's mind to demand *Little Belt*'s crew be mustered for inspection (he had been president of Barron's court-martial, and could have duplicated the *Leopard*'s procedure in every detail). But he resisted the temptation.

The causes of the War of 1812 are among the more complex in our history, being in fact a gradual escalation of incidents none of which— not even the *Chesapeake-Leopard* affair—triggered war of itself. Under the emotions of the day, had Rodgers decided to treat *Little Belt* exactly as *Chesapeake* had been treated, he might have brought on the war a year sooner. Likewise, had Decatur had his wish for another encounter with *Leopard* in 1807, there might have been war then, or another quasi-war similar to the one with France. On the other hand, a more determined reaction, contrary to bringing on a war that came anyway, might actually have prevented it by forcing the British navy to act with greater restraint, and thus eliminating or reducing the pace of events that led toward June 1812.*

Finally coming to understand its culpability in the *Chesapeake* affair, the British government decided on conciliation. In mid-1812, emissaries from England arrived in Washington empowered to settle the issue and make such amends as were practicable. It was, of course, too late, since war had already been declared. Of the four kidnapped seamen, Radford, who had insulted an officer, had already been hanged. One of the other three, who were all by this time acknowledged by Britain to be Americans, had died. In July, the other two were formally returned to the *Chesapeake*, now lying in Boston harbor under command of William Bainbridge. The first shots of the War of 1812 had already been fired, and so the men were brought into the harbor under a

---

*Interestingly, British Admiralty records list the *Little Belt* as "captured" by the *President*. She was in fact sold out of the service later that same year.

flag of truce. The British had the courtesy, at least, of returning the abductees on board the very ship from which they had been taken; the nicety might have been even better observed had they been returned by the captain who had commanded the *Leopard*, and better yet if they had been brought into Boston by the *Leopard* herself. But this display of regret was too much for the British authorities. The delegation was received by Bainbridge, who made a short speech of welcome to the two seamen and sent them forward to their old stations. Then he invited the British officers to lunch! "Compensation" was also paid to the U.S. government for damage to its frigate. There is no indication anyone on either side thought compensation or indemnity might be due the two survivors of the incident, who apparently were simply put back into *Chesapeake*'s crew, or to either of the two men who had died.

But all this, of course, was too late. Frontier skirmishes with the Indians, supposedly incited by the British, fueled the flame of war. A large segment of the population sympathized with the "war hawks," a short-lived political grouping that was all its name implied. Others felt Canada should have been included in the territories ceded in 1783. The country was in the midst of a presidential campaign, and James Madison, elected our fourth president in 1808, was running for reelection. Underlying all this was the issue of impressment: every occurrence was an insult to our nationhood and to the ideals on which the country had been founded. Our navy itched for revenge, itched to prove its quality. It was a classic case, though institutionalized, of the son fighting his own father.

War was declared in June 1812, and fortune smiled on the U.S. Navy from the beginning. In July, contact with a British naval force was made by the *Constitution*, commanded by Isaac Hull, one of Preble's young skippers of nine years earlier. Hull was en route from Annapolis to New York, where he was to join the squadron being assembled by the navy's senior officer at sea, Commodore John Rodgers. The ships he met off New Jersey, which he first took for Rodgers's squadron, turned out to be the British fleet instead. A sixty-six-hour chase ensued, nearly all of it in very light winds, sometimes in a flat calm. Both sides displayed consummately fine seamanship: taking advantage of every puff of air, wetting down the sails to hold the wind better, kedging (hauling the anchors as far ahead as possible by boat, then winding the ship up to them with her capstan), and towing by the ship's boats. Hull picked up his boats on the run whenever a cat's-paw of breeze put a little way on his ship—a tricky maneuver demanding great coordination—and it gained him a little distance. In the British fleet, all the boats were put to towing one of their number, the 38-gun *Shannon*, in hopes of getting her near enough to cripple and thus slow the *Constitution*. But the luck of the ship held, assisted by some stage-managing by Hull.

Heavy clouds gathering in the sultry sky indicated the probability of a sudden storm. The *Constitution* waited until the last minute, and then, just before the squall struck, began precipitately hauling in her sails. The British assumed, as Hull hoped they would, that he would never do this while trying to escape them unless convinced that very severe weather was due—and they all imitated his actions. In a short time all British ships had snugged down for very heavy weather. Hull had only pretended to do so. The storm broke with much rain and heavy wind, but as soon as his pursuers were blotted out of sight Hull spread all the canvas he dared carry. With her heavy build and tall masts, *Constitution* was on her best point of sailing, bowling along "full and bye" with everything set and drawing—and when the squall passed, the British were far astern.

During the encounter, Hull had pumped his fresh water overboard to lighten his ship. He now had no recourse but to continue to the nearest port, which was Boston.

Even before the war began, there had been two differing concepts of how our naval operations should be carried out. Secretary of the Navy Hamilton had asked all his senior captains for recommendations. Rodgers strongly held that a squadron should be formed of as many ships as could be got together, with himself in command, to cruise off the coast of England and in particular to intercept the British East India convoy. Decatur, Bainbridge, and Charles Stewart, commanding the *Constellation* in Norfolk, recommended instead that ships go to sea singly or in very small squadrons, twos or threes, on independent commerce-raiding missions. Many years later, Alfred Thayer Mahan would write that Rodgers's plan was "the most consonant with sound military views." In fact, although both schemes were aimed at damaging Britain's commerce, Rodgers's plan accomplished the least while the individual independent cruises did England the most damage. From hindsight, the reason is easy to ascribe: success of the concentration of force depended on the judgment and initiative of one man only. Individual cruises held far more openings for initiative, for seizing the moment of opportunity, with far less at stake in case of failure.

Had Rodgers been brought to a decisive action by a large British force, he might have lost the war for the United States right then. The moment England knew the whole U.S. naval force was at sea in a single fleet, she would have deployed several superior fleets to search it out. The whole British navy would have seen that fleet as an opportunity for fame and glory, as a chance for the repetition of Trafalgar. Concentration of the American fleet would have assured its ultimate destruction by an eager British navy. Capture of any of the single ships would not have had that effect.

Like so many others, Hamilton was awed by Rodgers's presence, but he tried to have it both ways. Rodgers was given his large squadron, but provision was also made allowing some latitude for individual cruises. Rodgers sailed many thousands of miles, but opportunity eluded him; there were those even then who thought it was actually the other way around, that he eluded opportunity because he could never seize the chances that did come his way and showed too much circumspection, not to say caution, in always overestimating the strength of the enemy ships he sighted, and avoiding encounter. In simple fact, Rodgers was a perfect example of the man of strong overbearing personality who sweeps all before him on the strength of his presentation, but who is better in the board room than on the quarterdeck. Selection of the right commanders is one of the most difficult of requirements, never satisfactorily solved. Stewart, Decatur, even Hull might have proved to be effective commanders of such a fleet. Not Isaac Chauncey (later commander on the Great Lakes), Bainbridge, or Rodgers. John Rodgers's four long cruises kept the ships in his squadron from more effective employment, and we were lucky they were not met by one of the stronger forces sent out to find them.

Hull brought *Constitution* into Boston on Sunday, 26 July, in urgent need of provisions and water (he had been at sea a full week after his near miraculous escape, subsisting on rainwater and what little remained in his water casks). The only orders he had were to join Rodgers, who had sailed from New York on 21 June, but he had no idea where Rodgers might now be. With no hope of finding the squadron he was to join, he began to prepare for what nearly all the skippers of that day wanted, a long independent cruise. It is probable that, like many military commanders, he had cultivated his own private grapevine and had foreknowledge of orders on their way to him. This story has been so often repeated that it is the perception, whatever the facts. What can be confirmed is that he stayed in Boston barely long enough to provision; he had no access to funds for this, and Mr. William Gray, of Salem, underwrote the entire cost as a patriotic gesture. On 1 August, less than a week after his arrival, Hull was at sea once more, thus missing by a few hours Secretary of the Navy Hamilton's order turning his ship over to his friend, Bainbridge, and holding her in port for the time being. In mid-August, about 700 miles east of Boston, he fell in with the 38-gun frigate *Guerriere*, Richard Dacres commanding. The chance for fame and glory had arrived, and Hull was ready.

Dacres is supposed to have boasted that *Guerriere* was superior to any American frigate, and to have issued one of the unofficial challenges so popular then, proposing to meet the 44-gun *President*, "or any other American frigate of equal force, for a few minutes' *tête-à-tête*." In the professional rivalry that existed between the two navies before outbreak of war, it was the general understanding that somewhere a hat had been bet on the outcome of the first such battle, and most British and American frigate captains had adopted the wager as their own.

Dacres's ship, *Guerriere*, was a captured French frigate—big for her rate as all French ships were, but not the equal of *Constitution*, which was a ship half again heavier with more and bigger guns. In Dacres's view, however, the odds were not too long, and in any case the honor of Horatio Nelson's navy, victorious always at sea, impelled him to accept combat even though he had the smaller ship. He could not have avoided it in any case, for *Constitution* had caught him alone in an empty sea, was definitely the faster, and therefore held the option of battle. This was just as Joshua Humphreys had planned. Hull and Dacres might be compared to medieval knights. Both were mindful of the colors they wore on their helmets, the history of the past few years, and the decision at sea both sides yearned for. They entered the lists gladly.

At first a few preliminaries, as the two ships approached, tried a few long-range shots, and maneuvered for the advantage. Then the invitation to combat: *Guerriere* shortened sail to her "fighting canvas"—jib, topsails, and spanker—and held off on an easy tack with the wind over her port quarter. There were two traditional British battle tactics: preferred was the yardarm-to-yardarm action, in which the contest was decided by the efficiency of the gun crews and the ability of England's strong ships to absorb punishment. She built the ships of her establishment with this in mind. Their stout hulls were shorter, their guns closer together and handier, English gun crews better trained. They drilled for proficiency, with the objective of being able to fire "three broadsides to the enemy's two," as a British historian of Nelson's time wrote.

The alternative was to run the other ship aboard, heavy wooden hull crashing into heavy wooden hull, and grapple. Then would come abandonment to the exulting fury of hand-to-hand combat on the decks of the enemy ship, finally to end with the enemy crew confined below decks under guarded hatch gratings, while someone had the glory of hauling down the enemy flag. Sails, it was generally held, were solely for the purpose of bringing a ship into action. Once that had been accomplished, they were useful for keeping her steady, and not much else. The "wooden walls of England," with their gun crews working enthusiastically behind them, or spewing forth their hordes of fierce battlers, would reach the decision of the day.

This was how Dacres had been indoctrinated, and how he expected the fight to develop. The British navy had not, however, developed any standard to which all ships had to adhere. Each captain was expected to uphold the honor of the navy and train his own crew. Although it was generally accepted that Captain Philip Broke, skipper of

the *Shannon*, was especially interested in gunnery and had some unusual ideas about how to fight his ship, for anyone to reflect upon the
capabilities of any other frigate of equal force was tantamount to invit-
ing challenge to a duel. Personal honor could permit no such invidious
comparisons. But Dacres's crew had not been trained the way Broke's
had; he had concentrated more on the appearance of efficiency, had a
tidy, neat ship, even showing a bit of spit and polish. If and when it
came to battle, Dacres was confident his ship would be the equal of any
other anywhere. Hull had much the same training, but was freer of the
dogma because there was less of the tradition of success. His navy had
engaged in only three frigate actions during the past fourteen years, all
in the quasi-war with France, and all victorious. When it had last
fought the British navy, more than twenty-five years before, it had lost
all its ships but two. And only five years ago had occurred the shameful episode of the *Chesapeake*. Against the Royal Navy it had no history of victory.

Overhauling the waiting *Guerriere* rapidly, Hull also shortened
sail, though to a lesser extent than Dacres. At the same time, he forbade his crew to open fire until he gave the order. Then he drove his
ship close aboard, "within biscuit shot"—the distance one could flip a
spinning ship's biscuit, as the saying went.

Foot by foot, rapidly, *Constitution* moved into the slot alongside
Guerriere. Aboard Dacres's ship it was already obvious that this was
no unprepared *Chesapeake*. Both crews were silent, eyeing each other
nervously through the gunports as the faster moving *Constitution*
closed the distance, fingering their gunlocks, matches, and recoil
breechings, ready with reloads, standing by. The officers, behaving
according to tradition, affected not to see the drama of the situation,
pretended nonchalance, ostentatiously marched on their stations with
complete disregard for the storm of iron and flying wooden splinters
soon to be unleashed. The creak of rigging, the noise of water passing
between the two hulls, the rumble of a last-minute adjustment of a
gun—in the silence, these familiar sounds came loudly, took on new
meaning. Everyone present, in both ships, knew that the battle about to
begin would be different, somehow, from any that had taken place

before. Some must have understood that history was about to be made.

Dacres had ordered his gunners to "fire as you bear," meaning that as the opposing ship came up alongside, the first gun in his ship to see the enemy ship in its sights—in this instance the aftermost gun on the port side—would fire, then the next, and so on in succession. As the second gun was firing the first would already have recoiled. Its crew would begin sponging out, reloading, and readying for a second shot as quickly as possible. The broadside thus delivered was in effect a ripple of gunfire from aft forward, not lacking in power for all that. It tended naturally to concentrate on *Constitution*'s forward parts, and it had the advantage that the first gun to be fired would often have its second shot off well before the last gun in line had been able to fire at all. In the best of all worlds, a "continuous sheet of flame" would burst from the side of a ship as the successive guns fired again and again.

Hull, however, wished to demonstrate with one devastating blow the crushing power of his own broadside. The psychological effect would be great, and it would also silence forevermore the carping criticisms of American frigates. He had therefore ordered his battery to remain silent until he himself gave the order to open fire. The result was that as *Constitution* gained on *Guerriere*, her relative speed decreasing as she braced around her main yards and backed her biggest sails, she had to endure, in total silence, repeated hits from the enemy's guns. One by one, *Guerriere*'s 18-pounders roared out, and one by one they struck home, ripping planking, parting rigging, throwing into the air their quotas of splinters, killing or wounding unlucky men. This period lasted probably only a few minutes, but to judge from contemporary accounts, it seemed agonizingly long.

Finally, *Constitution* ranged fairly alongside, in the position Hull wanted (incidentally the position Dacres wanted him in also). Hull, a rotund, short man who had to stand on a box the better to see over the high bulwarks and hammock nettings of his ship, reached up a clenched fist, swung it down in a mighty arc, bellowed "Fire!" at the top of his lungs. The gesture cost him a pair of pants. In accordance with naval tradition, he had donned his best uniform for the occasion, one that had been tailored for his form a number of years earlier. Through a not unusual fact of life, his breeches were no longer as strong as they had been in his younger days, and the internal pressure was greater. They burst in back, from knee to waist, as his body bent double to lend emphasis to the commanding sweep of his arm.

Under the circumstances, no one noticed. *Constitution*'s broadside of 24-pound shot, fired with the heavy powder charges of the long guns in her main battery, was delivered almost as a single explosion. Her hull, masts, rigging—the entire fabric of the ship—shook with the force of the simultaneous blast; but the hurricane of iron that swept *Guerriere*'s decks was death's scythe itself. No former French frigate—nor any English frigate—had been built to stand up against such a broadside. What *Guerriere* received, at this disastrous moment, was 736 pounds of heavy metal, fired at point-blank range. The below-deck carnage was terrific. Several guns, struck fair on their muzzles, were dismounted, their crews killed or wounded; a great number of men were lacerated by flying splinters, some impaled to the deck or to the opposite side of the ship by huge chunks of jagged timber driven completely through their bodies. Many were grievously injured by the flying cannonballs themselves, or by a ricocheting piece of sharp-edged shrapnel, spalled off a damaged gun at the point where a spinning 24-pound cannonball smashed into it. The upper decks, the forecastle, and the quarterdeck with their connecting gangways, suffered slightly less physical damage, since *Constitution*'s spar-deck guns were carronades, fired with a smaller charge of gunpowder than her main battery, but here guns were dismounted too. Some of the American frigate's spar-deck guns had been loaded with what was known as "dismantling shot"—cannonballs or iron bars linked together by short pieces of chain—others with grape and canister. These, flung across the short space between ships with a lethal whirl and a shotgunlike spray of lethal pellets, played havoc with rigging and personnel.

Dacres was staggered at the destruction. He could hear the groans, the shrieks of the badly injured, the despairing murmurs of men with suddenly shattered bodies who knew now they must die. And he recognized the momentary cessation of *Guerriere*'s fire for what it was: the shock, the unbelieving shock, attendant upon the terrible blow just received. Joshua Humphreys had predicted exactly this effect in January 1793.

Whether Dacres perceived it rationally, no one can say; but in that incomprehensible instant he knew that his ship was outclassed, already beaten. More of this would sink her outright. There was only one hope left: the hand-to-hand action made most famous of all by Lord Nelson. Typical of the English bulldog Dacres had been taught to be, he shouted "Boarders away!" and ordered the helm thrown down. Obediently, the English frigate swung to port, toward her antagonist—just as another thunderous sheet of smoke and flame erupted from the other's side. Again a hail of iron, clouds of wooden and iron fragments flying about, screams of the wounded, more whistling sounds as laboring lungs tried to suck air into destroyed and rapidly dying bodies. More disaster: a 24-pound ball had struck the mizzenmast, tearing off a huge splinter close to the deck. Many of the shrouds and stays had already been cut by the first broadside; more were sliced by the second at the same time the wood itself was injured. There was noticeable swaying in the great stick. With that wound it probably could not stand even if all the guys and braces were still intact, and now nothing could save it. "Stand clear of the mizzen!" shouted Dacres's sailing master.

The mizzenmast was no longer swaying, it was falling. One by one its wood fibers stretched, then broke off near the deck. It leaned forward toward the taller mainmast. Like a fainting woman losing touch with her surroundings, all its controls, its connecting stays with the mainmast, went suddenly slack. The big timber's base snapped clean off; a roll of the ship shrugged it off to port. Shrouds and braces broke in succession as the strain came on them. For a short time some of the lines bracing it to the mainmast held, then they, too, gave way. Sails askew, everything still in place but not right because of the sudden loss of control, the mast crashed into the sea, smashing a part of *Guerriere*'s port quarter as it fell. Now it acted as a rudder, bumping alongside, swinging the bowsprit of the suddenly unmanageable frigate into her antagonist's rigging. In response to Dacres's order, his men with cutlasses and boarding pikes, the officers with swords and pistols, had gathered on the forecastle. He hurried forward to join them. *Constitution*'s broadsides were no longer simultaneous, as her gunners vied with one another in reloading and firing. Successive hammer blows were smashing into *Guerriere*'s hull. Boarding over the bow must be accomplished soon, for she could not stand such punishment for long. But, facing Dacres's men across the heaving sea, behind the bulwarks of the other ship, an equal horde of men, likewise armed with cutlass and pike, stood ready for them.

Nor were the fighting tops of either ship silent. Sharp-shooting marines stationed there were fulfilling their duties, as they had been trained. Intersecting fusillades of musket fire poured down into the two massed groups of seamen. Men and officers were falling, the latter, more conspicuous though much fewer numerically, suffering the higher losses. Dacres felt a blow in the back of his shoulder, and knew he had been hit by a bullet. There was no pain—it was just a blow to the back. But now he could not raise his arm. He tried to grasp his sword; his hand was slippery with blood, would not function properly. *Guerriere*'s way was falling off—though no longer on the quarterdeck, Dacres could sense it. Someone was trying to pass a line to lash the two ships together, someone else was heaving a grappling iron, but both were having difficulty. The Americans seemed to be preparing to board in their turn, but they, too, were suffering injury from the British marines. One of their officers leaped on the ship's gunwale, sword in hand, then doubled over, clutching his abdomen. Another jumped to take his place; a splash of red appeared on his forehead as something heavy slammed his head backward. He disappeared. *Constitution*'s mainmast had been braced around again; its sails filled, she began moving ahead. *Guerriere*'s bowsprit was passing across the enemy's rigging. It intersected with a particularly heavy shroud just as her bow plunged into a sea. The heavy spar, guided by the shroud into perpendicular contact with *Constitution*'s heavy bulwark, snapped clean.

Now there would be no chance to board, on either side. *Guerriere*'s sails were backing, the wreckage on her port quarter having turned her farther into the wind than intended. The destruction on deck made sail handling nearly impossible. All her after sails were gone, and now so were the headsails. Her foremast had been sprung days before; it had been braced with three small spars made fast to it with many windings and lashings. Now the weakened mast had lost all of its support from forward. The ship was rolling. All her foresails were bellied flat aback. The vertical outline of the mast showed through them. A sharp crack, cries of warning. The huge vertical spar—actually three of the biggest spars in the ship, attached one above the other and reaching 143 feet into the air, its base a solid 3 feet in diameter—cracked in two at the weak point. A tremendous spike of splintered wood remained upright where it stood, but the spars used to "fish" it were out of line, their lashings pulled apart in many places. One of them was broken. The entire structure, with yards, sails, hundreds of feet of line and rigging, swayed to starboard, and fell majestically over the side. The upper portions of the mainmast, the main topmast and main topgallant mast, secured to the foremast with many lines of their own, broke off and came down also.

Suddenly rolling violently now that she had no sails to steady her, *Guerriere* dragged around to the right. The great encumbrances on her port quarter and starboard bow bumped and thudded heavily against her sides. She could not stand this very long. Her sides would be beaten in if the wreckage could not be got clear. Automatically, some of her men began to cut away the lines still holding the wreckage. The *Constitution* shot ahead. Her guns fell silent.

Dacres was not yet finished. Most of his battery and most of his crew were still effective. *Guerriere*'s starboard side had not yet been in action. At Trafalgar, Nelson's ships had continued to capture other ships after nearly all their spars had been shot away. If he could somehow regain control of his ship it might yet be possible to get *Constitution* alongside, and this time the worth of English gunners might be better requited. He directed one gang of men to work on freeing her from the wreckage of her masts, a second gang to bring such order as was possible to the shambles on the gundeck, and a third to rig some jury headsail. The lower mainmast was still standing. Its big mainyard and the still furled main course were undamaged. With frenzied activity, lines were spliced and knotted, a storm jib set on the stump of the bowsprit, and the main course spread. *Guerriere*'s violent rolling eased noticeably, and then the *Constitution* was observed approaching once more.

The obvious move was to swing *Guerriere* so that her uninjured starboard side could be the one in action. Her helm was put up, her single yard braced around, and slowly the wounded frigate began to open her fresh battery to the advancing American. *Constitution* seemed not to notice, sailed serenely onward as if to come alongside once more. Dacres's gundeck, despite the holocaust just endured, was once again ready, its gunners waiting for the opportunity to pay back some of the damage inflicted on them. But, without warning, the other ship's bow fell off the wind. Hoarse shouts could be heard from her decks. All of her yards on all three masts were precipitately swung to the other tack, her helm went full starboard, and she steered directly across the British frigate's bow, every gun in her uninjured broadside aimed squarely at *Guerriere*'s sparsely armed bow. In a sailing man-of-war, the bow and stern were the weak points. Everyone on board knew what was to come. *Constitution* was taking the classic position for a raking broadside. There was no way to prevent it, not with only a single mast and only two sails, while their enemy's rigging appeared intact. Grudgingly, Dacres admitted the inevitable correctness of the American maneuver, even while he dreaded its results.

When the *Constitution* was directly athwart his hawse, her port battery trained on his hapless bow, she released another of her fantastic broadsides. Again the air was full of fury. Twenty-six cannon, most of them long 24-pounders, the rest 32-pound carronades, swept the length of *Guerriere*'s decks. Her bow was battered in. The stump of her mainmast collapsed, taking with it all hope of getting sail on the ship. Once again there was a mass of wreckage alongside, smashing against the hull in steady plank-starting thumps, adding continuous damage to that taken from the guns. *Guerriere* fell into the trough of the sea, again rolling wildly, totally unmanageable. There was no possibility left for steadying sail. The sea, not heavy, was a regular march of medium-size waves from the northeast. Her formerly steady decks began sweeping through great ninety-degree arcs, forty-five degrees to either side, with a sharp snap thanks to the heavy ballast needed to stabilize her under sail. With every insane roll, gunports and the shattered timbers around them were plunged under water. The sea poured through the submerged ports, through the gaping and splintered holes where shot had entered, mixed with the blood, the gory remains of men, the sand sprinkled to help maintain footing, loose gear of all kinds. The gundeck, particularly, was already slippery beyond the capacity of sand to cope, especially with the violent motion. Uninjured men were unable to keep their feet. The wounded and dead simply slid in the bloody puddles until they came up on something. Dacres knew he was beaten.

The American ship stood off once more, wore around, came back, this time heading for her antagonist's stern. There was no pretense of coming alongside. It would have made no difference: *Guerriere* could not maneuver. No gun could have been loaded or fired in face of her violent motion, and if it could, there would be no telling where the shot would fly. Nothing could be done. Only the English colors, now attached to a light pole lashed upright on the quarterdeck, still spoke defiance. Dacres braced himself to receive the next raking broadside. It might be all that was needed to sink his ship—but, to his surprise, *Constitution* did not fire. She stood on, wore again, and backed her mainsails, killing her way completely. For long minutes she paused in the middle distance.

Hoping, though hardly believing, that his enemy had for some reason decided to terminate the now grossly unequal contest, that perhaps some other British ship, attracted by the sound of gunfire, was approaching, Dacres watched her carefully, encouraged somehow by the sight of his own ensign still flying in the freshening wind. If indeed someone was approaching, if Dacres could be left in peace, even now, with all the damage, it might be possible to get up some kind of a small jury mast, and some sail, cope with the worst of the damage, and make his way to Halifax for the assistance his ship so badly needed. But for this, he must have time, and peace, and have them quickly. In his bones he knew the *Guerriere* was sinking.

There were men in *Constitution*'s rigging. A bustle, not much, on her deck. He understood these signs. She was repairing what little damage she might have received to her rigging. And, in a short time, around came her yards, the sails filled, and she approached once more. Dacres watched her come with a kind of hopeless horror. Should the American subject him even once more to one of those horrible broadsides, his ship must surely sink. Yet, the British navy did not surrender. No frigate the size of *Guerriere* had ever surrendered, in any manner, to an American ship. John Paul Jones, some thirty years before, was more of a fluke than the only exception, for Jones was a Scot, his ship and most of his crew Frenchmen, and in the battle with the *Serapis* he had had an entire squadron. No, Dacres would not do it now. He would not surrender to an American fir-built frigate with sides of pine boards! It would be better to go down fighting the hopeless battle to the end. Spiritlessly, he watched his enemy come on. She was being well handled—he'd grant her that. She backed the sails on her mainmast, again killed her way, lay right across his stern. She could fire with impunity, could hold target practice. Every shot would hit home, each one of them in a vital spot. Dacres nerved himself to take it. There was nothing else to do.

But the American did not fire. Instead, there came a hail, through a speaking trumpet, and Dacres thought he recognized the voice. In any case, he recognized the forceful point of the brief message. In her present position, *Constitution* could blow *Guerriere* out of the water, or sink her at leisure. There was nothing whatever he could do about it. "Have you struck?" asked the hollow voice, its lower register emphasized by the trumpet cone. It sounded strangely monotonous in timbre.

The inevitable, the unthinkable, was on him. Dacres bowed his head. His career would be finished, but his crew, and he, would continue to live. He was still young. Perhaps, in some unforeseen, unimagined way, he might yet be able to live down the disgrace of being the first, and no doubt the only, Royal Navy captain ever to surrender his ship to an American. Perhaps some of the officers in the American navy with whom he had been friendly on the American station before the outbreak of war could help to make things easier for him. But the biggest thing in his mind was the disgrace, the inevitable court-martial.

This he had to measure against the need of his crew for help. The groans of the wounded had not ceased. Many of them were where they had fallen, or where they had huddled out of the way of their hurrying comrades, clear of the guns on the gun carriages that, with the violent motion of the ship, now were rolling forth and back on their wooden wheels to the limits of their tethers. There was a rising stench, from wounds and vomit. His own wound was beginning to hurt badly. There was no more fight left in his ship, or in himself.

To his quartermaster, standing nearby with eyes that were large and eloquent, he made a motion with his good hand. The man hurried over to the flagstaff, steadied himself against the wreckage and the tangled line, slowly pulled down the ensign, and rolled it up.

Once the colors were down, things moved with kaleidoscopic swiftness. A boat came alongside. Men jumped out, moved unbelievingly across the heaving deck. An officer, staggering against the rapid roll, approached Dacres and saluted. "Captain Hull's compliments, sir," he said. "Our ship is the *Constitution*, 44. He would be pleased if you would permit me to convey you on board."

"My men need help," said Dacres slowly. He was no longer in command, could not refuse the courteously worded summons. Hull! He had met him! A short, stocky man, several years older than himself. Reputed to be a good seaman. So now he commanded one of those big American frigates that were supposed to be too big, and too poorly built, to be effective. Those broadsides had been effective enough! What was the lieutenant saying? He concentrated on listening.

"I've brought our surgeon with me, and he'll do all he can. When we return to my ship, we'll send some of his mates over to help also."

"You can't deprive your own wounded to help us," began Dacres, and suddenly he understood the impulsive, immediate embarrassment behind the lieutenant's reply, as if he had just realized the import of his own words.

"Oh, we're all right, sir. Our men are already taken care of."

The remainder of the story of this first encounter ends on a pleasanter note, though like so many of the unofficial tales it may be apocryphal, or it may have occurred at a different time and place, or even more than once. No matter, really, since the story is more important for what it conveys than for its specifics. Stepping aboard the victorious *Constitution*, Dacres saluted the colors and then the officer with torn pants standing at the gangway to meet him: a man wearing the epaulets of a captain, who returned both salutes. Still in something of a daze at the disaster that had befallen him, the pain in his shoulder more acute with every motion, Dacres fumbled with the scabbard clips of his sword, handed sword and scabbard over to his antagonist. Hull took it in his left hand and, looking Dacres directly in the eye, saluted a third time. He handed the sword back. "I shall not take your sword, sir," he is supposed to have said. "You have so well defended it that I cannot. But I *will* take that hat!"

The battle once over, the two crews turned to as a team to make the best they could out of the disaster that had overtaken the *Guerriere*. The medical people worked as one. So did the boatswains and gunners and quartermasters. Boat after boat plied back and forth between the drifting, rolling British hulk and the stable American. The wounded were transferred first, made as comfortable as the rough conditions on board the American frigate permitted. The dead were gathered together, each on board his own ship, and consigned to the sea at nightfall with minimum though poignant ceremony. Next morning, inspection of *Guerriere* convinced Hull that bringing her into port as a prize of war was not practicable. She had been too badly damaged. His carpenter had discovered too much rot in her shattered frames and planking. Water was gaining in her sounding wells faster than the pumps could discharge it overboard. Her motion became logier as water gained in her bilges—making the necessary work easier at the same time it proved she had not much longer to live. After all possible useful equipment and personal gear was removed, she was set afire in the afternoon of the day after the battle, and shortly thereafter, the fire having been set with a train to her magazine, the defeated ship was seen to blow up.

Isaac Hull had fulfilled his life's ambition. His place in naval history was secure. His older brother had just died, leaving Isaac with a family of orphans to help support, and his uncle, General William Hull, had disgraced himself the previous week by surrendering Detroit's Fort Dearborn to a greatly inferior British force. On return to Boston, Hull asked for leave to attend to his family affairs and proposed he be relieved by Bainbridge as Hamilton had originally planned. He also sent the *Guerriere*'s biggest flag to Washington for delivery to the secretary of the navy.

Hull's action in precipitately going to sea under an old set of orders, probably aware that a new set that would have prevented him from leaving Boston were on their way, must be viewed more leniently than the same insubordination would be seen today. In 1812, the British navy was considered invincible, and this extended psychologically on an individual basis to her ships of war, and their skippers, also. Truxtun's two brilliant victories were over the French, not the English. Except for that extraordinary maverick John Paul Jones, all other encounters between major units of our navy and England's had been disastrous, even humiliating. The administration rightly was concerned to move with caution, not expose its navy too fast, nor too much, until sure of its capabilities against this greatest of all possible foes. But it had not, on the other hand, fully appreciated what Joshua Humphreys and those other early designers had accomplished.

Our naval professionals, wearing the mantle of Preble, knew their ships were more powerful than the comparable ones of England, and notably faster also. And since the infamous affair with the *Leopard*, they had honed their combat powers. Not only Hull but all our captains felt confident of their ability to take any British frigate they might encounter in single combat; and because of the speed and ease of handling of their ships, they felt equally confident they could escape from more powerful force when necessary. Hull had proved this to be true, and at exactly the right time.

The demonstration that our naval officers were right, the irrefutable proof that, properly handled, our ships and our crews could stand up under fire and do the job for which they had been created, was the *Constitution*'s legacy to this country. More to the point, however, hers was only the first of many.

Fame and glory mean different things in different times. John Paul Jones exhibited no false modesty about his objectives. He sought glory, as his own letters and words have made clear. But the glory he sought also benefited his adopted country. Similarly, what might appear vainglorious in the modern context was appropriate and patriotic in 1812. An individual given to the self-deprecation expected today would have been thought to have a poor opinion of himself then. What the United States needed, in 1812, both at sea and ashore, was success: victory, proof that our cause had strength behind it, that our soldiers and sailors were worthy of the nation's confidence, that in the contest we were facing there was a chance for our side. Hull's victory, although over an inferior ship, was due to superiority in detail, beginning with the very design of the ship with which he won it, whose performance won her the affectionate nickname of Old Ironsides. It brought glory to him, his ship, and his crew, of course, but it also restored popular regard for our navy to the peak it had briefly enjoyed with Truxtun and Preble. The country badly needed encouragement at the moment, for the war otherwise had begun very poorly. Had Hull not gone to sea and met *Guerriere* in August, Decatur with the *United States* might not have been able to meet *Macedonian* in October, and Bainbridge might well not have been on the coast of Brazil to meet and conquer *Java* in December. Perhaps the story of that war at sea might have been very different, even a repetition of 1775–1783, and equally difficult to explain today.

4

Victories on the High Seas

In 1812 our navy was so small that all the officers of command rank knew one another well. They were not, however, always on the best of terms. Personal ambitions, professional jealousies, and even festering hatreds took their toll. In the British navy, one of Nelson's purposes in dubbing his captains "a band of brothers" had been to build up mutual esteem and confidence. He aimed to inculcate full awareness of his intentions as their commander, including ample opportunity to discuss all phases of the current operation. If necessary they would be thereby able to act without specific instructions and with no doubts as to what they were expected to accomplish. He delighted in such epigrams as, "When in doubt, no captain can go very far wrong if he lays his ship alongside that of an enemy," and he publicly praised his subordinates whenever he could. His extraordinary leadership qualities welded together a group that was indeed stronger than the sum of its several parts. This was not true of the United States Navy then, though it would become so later.

Of all the U.S. Navy's early leaders, only Preble is given credit for a concept similar to Nelson's, but he had less opportunity than Nelson, and certainly not as much time. Nelson also enjoyed the benefits of centuries of naval tradition as part of the greatest naval power in the world. The navy in which Preble served had existed only a few years and had suffered many defeats—although, as noted, most recently Truxtun had given it two very important victories. All Preble's officers were to distinguish themselves, and all were to trace their success to his inspiration, but they never learned to lay aside the personal rivalries that bedeviled our navy of those days. Success was ours in the War of 1812—at least in its early stages—but the cohesive synergistic power of a unified, unselfishly motivated force still lay years away. Nevertheless, it was a singular thing that at this time and place in history the ambitions of a small interlocking band of naval iconoclasts should have been so precisely suited to what their country needed most.

Among them, Stephen Decatur was the most glamorous. Son of a successful frigate captain of the same name who had served during the Revolution and the quasi-war with France, and who many felt had been wrongly discharged during the naval reduction of 1801,* he had aspired to a naval career since early boyhood. A leader among his fellows, combative by nature, quick with his fists as a youth and as a young man, he was just what the Congress was looking for when it sought officers for the renewed navy of 1798. Contemporary descriptions say he was slightly above average height, sallow of complexion, slender of build, and extremely active physically. His personal supply of adrenaline must have been far greater than the average. Although his formal schooling was less than his parents appear to have desired, he had a facility with words that marked him as superior to his brother officers. He was something of a ladies' man, a heroic figure toward whom romantic young women and matronly hostesses alike gravitated. No one in the naval service could equal the ease with which he moved in political and social circles. Nor could anyone rival his feats of dar-

---

*One of the most effective officers of the time, he asked for leave of absence after three years at sea. Apparently in the process he displeased Acting Secretary of the Navy Samuel Smith, who responded by removing him from command of his ship, the *Philadelphia*. A few months later Samuel's brother Robert became secretary and wrote to the senior Decatur that his services would no longer be needed.

ing at sea. Fully aware of the image he cast, he also enjoyed playing to it.

Already marked among his fellows because of the burning of the captured *Philadelphia* in Tripoli harbor and his hand-to-hand combats aboard Tripolitan gunboats, Decatur had also the special confidence of Jefferson's secretary of the navy, Robert Smith (Truxtun's nemesis in 1802), who, in 1807, personally selected him to take over the *Chesapeake* after the *Leopard* debacle. Two years later, the new navy secretary in Madison's administration, Paul Hamilton, assigned him to the big *United States*, then completing a two-year refit at the Washington Navy Yard, with orders to get her ready for sea. Most of *Chesapeake*'s crew went with Decatur to his new and greater command, gladly abandoning the lesser ship to her unlucky reputation and the necessity of yet another reorganization. When war began in 1812, Decatur, like Hull, was ready with his powerful frigate, and both were directed to join John Rodgers's first squadron. The *Constitution*, as related, met a British squadron and barely escaped, getting into Boston to find Rodgers was already gone to sea from New York. The *United States*, however, participated in the first of Rodgers's four unproductive voyages and returned to Boston empty-handed, just in time to cheer Hull in the *Constitution* for the first victory of the war.

Decatur's thirsty spirit must have envied the honors being given his friend, and he jumped with alacrity at Hamilton's new proposal, that each of the big 44s, now all in Boston, become flagship of a small three-ship squadron. Decatur's included his old ship, *Chesapeake*, and the brig *Argus*, but only *United States* and *Argus* were ready to sail. The *Constitution*, which required refit, was held in port, but the other two squadrons, under Rodgers and Decatur, sailed together, early in October, separating after a few days, and a few days later, contrary to Hamilton's desires, Decatur directed the *Argus* to proceed independently. He himself went to cruise between the Canary Islands and the Azores, where he knew British frigates were often stationed. Late in the month his hopes were fulfilled when he sighted the sails of HMS *Macedonian*, 38, a new British frigate launched only two years previously. Her commander, John Carden, was also looking for an antagonist, having been informed that the U.S. frigate *Essex*, well known to carry an unusual armament of heavy short-range guns (all carronades, except for a small battery of light "long" guns on the quarterdeck), had been seen cruising in the area. Taking the powerful *United States* for the smaller *Essex* was a fatal misjudgment on Carden's part, though the right identification would not have dissuaded him from accepting battle or have changed its outcome. But knowing whom he was about to fight would definitely have changed his tactics. Unlike Dacres, Carden decided to keep the range open, cut up *Essex* with his long 18-pounders, and then close for the decisive yardarm-to-yardarm finale.

This might have worked for *Essex*, were *Macedonian* lucky enough quickly to damage her rigging and sails; for *Essex*, renowned as one of the fastest of the American frigates, undoubtedly would have tried to close immediately to get her heavy but short-ranged main battery into action. The British captain planned to counter this with a barrage of canister and dismantling shot aimed high so as to damage *Essex* aloft. But he found himself opposed by a skipper who showed no hurry about getting into close quarters. Worse, the enemy's heavy round shot was coming aboard and smashing his ship long before the grape and canister with which he had ordered his spar-deck guns loaded—or, for that matter, the longer-ranged 18-pounders on his gundeck—could even reach his opponent. Early in the engagement Carden changed his estimate of his adversary, but it was already too late. The *United States*'s heavy 24-pound shot, fired from long-barreled main deck guns that, to a large extent, were manned by gunners who still remembered their humiliation in the *Chesapeake* only five years earlier, were taking out his masts stick by stick and knocking great holes in the sides of his suffering ship.

Among the members of the *Chesapeake* crew serving with Decatur in the *United States* was William Henry Allen (he of the red-hot coal for *Chesapeake*'s only reply to *Leopard*), now first lieutenant of the *United States*. Not only because of the lesson of *Chesapeake*'s unreadiness but also because they strongly believed in them, skipper and first lieutenant were addicted to gunnery drills. And the heritage of the *Chesapeake* debacle had caused their crew to like the drills also. They went at them with gusto. Decatur and Allen had developed confidence in the excellence of their gunners, as their crew had in their own abilities and in their commanders.

Some of Decatur's detractors later insinuated that he might have lacked courage in not driving right alongside, as Hull had, for the traditional yardarm-to-yardarm battle, but no objective facts support this. Carden himself had planned not to do so, and the tradition was mainly purveyed by the very partisan British historian William James in his flawed account of that war. Though Decatur was undeniably a romantic, such sentiments do not obligate one to fight a sea battle foolishly, nor sacrifice life needlessly. With superb gunnery—virtually every shot hit the target—Decatur's gunners cut up the *Macedonian*, instead of the other way around.*

Once aware of his error, Carden doggedly tried to bring his ship into close range, but his own scheme of battle had already worked against him. Nearly all his standing rigging was shot away, but with only the stump of his mainmast left, he still tried to crawl toward his foe. The *United States*, practically undamaged, sailed around him at will. Finally, Carden held a desperate council of war with his officers. His first lieutenant adamantly held out for continuing the hopeless fight; the others argued this would be useless self-destruction. Accepting the inevitable, Carden lowered his flag, feeling, like Dacres, that he had betrayed his trust as a captain in the British navy.

Like Hull, Decatur treated his captives magnanimously. By some accounts, it was he, not Hull, who claimed the hat when his defeated enemy offered his sword. More to the point, though he had been beaten in the race for the first victory, there was one way he could better Hull's accomplishment. The *Macedonian* was a new and strong ship. She could be made seaworthy again, could be brought into port as a prize of war. Giving up his projected cruise on the ground that bringing in a prize of this magnitude for the first time was a worthy substitute, he escorted the beaten frigate to New London, Connecticut, which he reached without event on 4 December. Decatur then showed

---

*It should be noted that the sides of Decatur's ship were said to be the hardest of the three big sisters (which might have been the reason *Constitution*'s proud crew beat their rival to claim the sobriquet of Old Ironsides as soon as they had a legitimate excuse).

his special talent. On landing, he discovered that a great naval ball was to be given in Washington in honor of Hull and the officers of the *Constitution*. It was to be climaxed by formal presentation of the flag of the beaten *Guerriere* to Dolley Madison, wife of the President. One of Decatur's officers was Archibald Hamilton, the son of the secretary of the navy, and this was too good a chance to miss. The young officer was directed to proceed to Washington immediately, by the fastest possible conveyance, bearing Decatur's official report and the biggest flag found aboard the *Macedonian*. No doubt there were also some specific instructions from Decatur, delivered by direct word of mouth, concerning the time of his arrival and his exact behavior.

Lieutenant Hamilton arrived in Washington the evening of the great ball. According to an account in *Niles' Weekly Register*, "about nine o'clock a rumor was spread through the assembly that Lieutenant Hamilton, the son of the Secretary of the Navy, had reached the house, the bearer of despatches from Commodore Decatur and the colors of the *Macedonian*. He was escorted to the festive hall [and] the flag of the *Macedonian* was borne into the hall by Captains Hull and Stewart."

The drama was spectacular. Around the big battle flag of the *Guerriere* were the President of the United States and the First Lady, the entire cabinet, the cream of Washington society and of the navy, all in their finest evening dress. The navy and the *Constitution* and her crew were the toast of the evening. Then there came a bustle at the door. Captain Charles Stewart, skipper of the *Constellation*, then under blockade at Norfolk, was called. He returned, beckoned to Hull. Both disappeared, and in a moment in came a young man, weary, dusty, smelling of horse and human sweat, his hair tousled, his eyes bloodshot with the strain of four days on the road, dressed in traveling clothes but with a naval jacket under his doublet. With a fond look toward his parents, he strode past them, bowed proudly before the President. Behind him, on the shoulders of Decatur's two old friends, was a huge rolled-up package, which they spread out on the floor before the popular wife of the President.

It was another British battle flag, equal in size to that of the *Guer-*

riere. The navy's stock at that delirious moment could not have been higher. Nor could that of Stephen Decatur.

Decatur, had he lived beyond 1820, might well have become a political figure, and even our first naval president, for he had the quality and the image. That he did not live longer was another legacy of the unlucky *Chesapeake*. Archie Hamilton was less fortunate still. He had only two years and one month left.

The naval officers of 1812 were very right in one thing: the time to meet British ships at sea in reasonably equal contests was immediate. If the victories they felt certain of were indeed forthcoming, the uplifting effect on the country, and on its navy, would be electric. Whatever the criticisms, Decatur was right in cutting short his cruise to bring in the captured *Macedonian*, for the real need of the country was the psychological stature this war gave it—not the conquest of Canada or any of the other putative possibilities of a victorious war with England. There were those who contended that the greatest navy in the world, heir to the memory of the nearly deified Nelson, could not be defeated by our little one, even with the help of a vicious, transcendentally important war in Europe. Our inferiority, after all, was on the order of 60 to 1, although it could be argued that measured in the types of ships most suited to a distant cruising war, English superiority was not quite this great. Her individual ships could be beaten, her vaunted total command of the sea punctured, if an opponent were sufficiently innovative to put higher quality on the firing line, where it counted most. Some of the more thoughtful recognized that if the optimistic predictions of many American victories were to be borne out, England would ultimately be forced to increase her naval presence, and the weight of numbers, if nothing else, would be telling. But in the meantime, the quality of the American navy would be proved, the gnawing feeling of inferiority done away with, the growth of national consciousness speeded. Absent actual invasion and threat of territorial loss, such an outcome could prove to be the most important of all. The legacy of Biddle and *Randolph*, the promise of the *Hancock*, the unrealized potential of our earlier navy, the deadly insult to our flag in the *Chesapeake*—all—would be requited at last.

By such considerations is history really determined. These early victories provided the strongest possible encouragement for our side, and have had influences extending to the modern navy today. In deepest truth, the War of 1812 was the fruition of the legacies of Truxtun and Preble, and therefore, in all but the material and statistical ways, it marks the time when our navy actually began to exist. In this sense, the United States Navy was not founded by act of the Continental legislature, nor by the 1794 or 1798 Acts of later Congresses. It was founded over a period of forty years by a relatively large number of men, all of whom had faith in the value of what they were doing.

Having taken over the *Constitution* from Hull, William Bainbridge met the 38-gun frigate *Java* off the coast of Brazil late in December. The action was not a tactical repetition of the two earlier battles, but the result was the same. *Java*, totally dismasted, was set afire and blown up after a desperate resistance. Her commander, Lambert, died of his wounds.

The reputation Bainbridge carried into the fight was of a skilled seaman and good ship handler who was prone to bad luck. He had been captured by superior forces during the quasi-war; he was skipper of the *George Washington* when that ship was forced by Algiers to carry tribute to Istanbul; in 1803 he ran the *Philadelphia* aground, dooming himself and crew to nearly two years in prison. Those who put stock in such matters were wont to say the battle with *Java* was a conflict in the stars, and that Old Ironsides' good star was able to overcome her skipper's unlucky one.

In fact, Bainbridge appears to have been something of a schemer. He clearly maneuvered to get command of the best ship of our navy, and he sought the glory that only a successful battle at sea could give him. Finding the opportunity, however, he fought his ship skillfully and well. Initially closing for the traditional yardarm-to-yardarm exchange of gunfire, his heavier guns demolished *Java*'s masts and rigging. Thereafter the British frigate could not maneuver, and the *Constitution*—despite being forced to handle her rudder by relieving tackles two decks below because a shot had smashed her steering wheel—nimbly danced about her enemy, pouring in heavy broadsides. Still, this was her hardest battle, her most costly victory in terms of casualties. Both the superstitious and the nonsuperstitious were satisfied.

Afterward, *Java*'s uninjured wheel was installed on *Constitution*'s quarterdeck, where tradition says it remained many years—though no one knows where it is now. James Fenimore Cooper tells the story of a British officer, visiting on board some years after the war, who commented that the steering wheel was the only thing aboard whose workmanship failed to measure up to the high standard of the rest of the frigate—and was told, with the smugness exhibited by some of our people of *that* day, that the wheel was a trophy of the victory over the *Java*. Cooper tells the story with delight, but he wrote in 1839, and had probably read William James. Attitudes were different then.

Hornet, an 18-gun sloop of war (or ship-sloop, in the terminology of the day) commanded by James Lawrence, the same who, commanding Gunboat Number 6, could not contend with Collingwood in the 96-gun *Dreadnaught*, had left Boston in company with the *Constitution*. Sailing in a broad zigzag twice across the Atlantic together, first to the Azores and then to the coast of South America, the two American vessels found the British *Bonne Citoyenne*, 20 guns, in harbor at Bahia, Brazil. A blockade was promptly instituted. Lawrence sent in a challenge to the captain of the *Bonne Citoyenne*, with Bainbridge's guarantee not to interfere. The British captain, Greene by name, would not rise to the bait because his ship was loaded with gold and silver, and he felt Bainbridge might be tempted to break his word if Lawrence were beaten. *Constitution* then departed, leaving *Hornet* to blockade alone, returned victorious over *Java*, sailed away again— and still *Bonne Citoyenne* refused to come out and fight. Instead, her skipper summoned help from Rio de Janeiro. *Hornet* had been on blockade more than a month when the tables were turned by the arrival of the British 74-gun line-of-battle ship *Montagu*. Fleeing in frustration, angrily calling Greene a coward, Lawrence finally got the fight he sought: he sank HM Brig *Peacock*, 18, in twelve minutes. The decisive little action took place within sight of another British naval brig of the same size and armament, *L'Espiegle*, which watched it all and made no effort to assist her comrade.

When *Hornet* arrived in New York with her prisoners (who were effusive over the magnanimous way in which they had been treated*), it would not have been surprising if the populace had become sated with the succession of naval victories. The fact was the opposite: the series of successes by the navy provided a welcome antidote to the dour reports of defeats on land. The campaign to conquer Canada, entered into with the conviction that that huge state would be an easy conquest and might even leap at the chance to join its former brethren to the south, had encountered only reversals. Canadian and British troops, helped by Indian allies (prominently Tecumseh, a brilliant Shawnee leader, and his half-brother, the Prophet), were actually threatening to take back some of the territory ceded after the Revolution and establish an Indian buffer state south of the Canadian border. Fear of even more serious losses on land was beginning to generate second thoughts about the war so blithely begun only a year before. It is not too much to say that our navy's successes, more than any other single influence, kept the nation together at this critical time.

In New York, James Lawrence was given parades, medals, honors. Most important to him, he had so pleased Bainbridge during their months of cruising in company that his superior lobbied strenuously for Lawrence to succeed him in command of *Constitution*. That ship, now twice victorious, was fast becoming the navy's favorite. Bainbridge felt Lawrence had special claims to consideration, which he carefully enumerated. Giving him the navy's best command would be only proper, he wrote. But whatever his new protégé's rightful claims, Bainbridge's motives for supporting him so strongly must certainly have included the fact that, in the naval hierarchy, Lawrence was relatively young and junior in rank, so that he posed no threat to Bainbridge's own ambitions.

---

*One of the injured British seamen, suffering complications from his wound and about to undergo his second amputation, refused to consent to the operation unless Lawrence agreed to adopt his small son—who had been in the *Peacock* and was a popular prisoner of war aboard the *Hornet*—in the event he did not survive. Lawrence promised, the second amputation was performed, and the man survived.

But there was a new secretary of the navy in Washington, a man just beginning to learn about the touchy and divergent personalities of his captains. On 4 May 1813 William Jones wrote Lawrence that he would assign him to the *Constitution*. On 6 May he wrote that he had just received a request for relief by the *Chesapeake*'s captain on the grounds of illness. That ship being nearly ready for sea, he desired Lawrence to take her out and carry out the already issued orders to her previous skipper for another commerce-raiding cruise. At the same time, although he did not mention it to Lawrence, he decided to give the renowned *Constitution* to Charles Stewart of the *Constellation*, still impossibly blockaded in Norfolk. Stewart had done a magnificent job of defending her against a series of British forays, and now it was proper that he should be given something better.

Although *Chesapeake* was known as an unlucky ship, Samuel Evans, Lawrence's predecessor, had brought her back to Boston in good condition after a fine commerce-destroying cruise in which she alone captured more prizes than the entire squadron under Rodgers. One of them was laden with specie, gold, and silver and when disposed of in prize court brought an extraordinary price. None of this did much to debunk the superstitions. But the accident that befell one of *Chesapeake*'s masts as she entered port, killing a crewman, and an excessive delay in paying the crew's share of the prize money from the cruise (because of the specie-laden prize, this was an imposing sum that the men, about to be sent forth once more, felt they should have before departure) were instant *prima facie* proof of the ship's evil star.

Ships are more susceptible to superstitions than any other of man's inanimate creations. Experienced naval leaders of today know that the only way to destroy such a chain of self-confirming defeatism, once started, is by a dramatic interruption, a change big enough and forceful enough to bestow a totally new character on its object, the ship. Pragmatic leadership, in such a case, usually requires making a "clean break" with the past. Decatur did this for the *Chesapeake*, for a time, with the navy secretary's understanding support. But he left her too soon; the only light in that ship's bleak history seems to have been the period when he had her prepped for a renewal of the *Leopard* encounter of 1807. But she was not given the opportunity to retrieve the intangible honor whose loss hung so heavily over her, and when Decatur took her crew—or most of it—to the *United States*, the cloud gathered over her once more.

Had Paul Hamilton still been secretary of the navy in June 1813, his known sensitivity to the intangible factors involved might have impelled him to give Lawrence some special attention and advice: for example, to use Decatur's approach, concentrate on welding his new crew, along with those of the *Hornet* he might have brought with him, into a well-oiled and well-coordinated fighting machine, then convert the unhappy past into spiritual strength by aiming *Chesapeake* for a battle of vengeance. This would not have been out of line—as events had already shown, individual ship victories were the tonic the navy and the country needed. Lawrence might even have sent a formal challenge to HBMS *Leopard*, wherever she might then have been, recognizing that—whether or not *Leopard* ever received it—merely sending the challenge would have immeasurably benefited the *Chesapeake*'s morale, and therefore her fighting ability. This would have been true despite Decatur's taking so many of the 1807 crew with him, for, in a ship, the present crew inherits the history—a phenomenon familiar to all men of the sea.

But Hamilton was no longer navy secretary. A known alcoholic, described as almost insensibly drunk at the great ball when his son brought in the *Macedonian*'s colors to be spread at the feet of Dolley Madison, he had finally been asked to resign, and William Jones, a successful businessman, replaced him. Jones was a conscientious man who had not yet developed a sense of the many discordant lines of force for whose guidance he now held responsibility. He expected to run the navy like the efficient business he had just left. He had no time for controversies with dissatisfied captains. The *Chesapeake* was an excellent ship. All she needed was someone with the ability to get the best from her and end that silly superstition about her unlucky star. Lawrence was known as an excellent leader. He was one of the most popular officers in the navy. His triumphant cruise in *Hornet* was the culmination of years of service that had stamped him as a man second only to Decatur in his ability to inspire enthusiasm among his crew.

Jones gave *Chesapeake* to him with the expectation of good results and had directed him to get her to sea as soon as possible, specifically to carry out the carefully drafted orders already sent to Evans. It probably did not occur to Jones that he might owe some form of special attention to the disappointed Lawrence. He felt no further responsibility. Lawrence now had his chance, a big ship under him, and it was up to him to make good.

The *Hornet* had returned to New York late in March 1813, and on 20 May Lawrence took command of the *Chesapeake* in Boston. There had been no word of any kind from Jones, only the standing order that *Chesapeake* get under way on another commerce-destroying cruise as soon as ready for sea. A very sensitive man, Lawrence is reported to have had an almost religious sense of duty. Whatever his initial protests about the *Chesapeake*, he had been ordered to get her to sea at once; he would do so. But the port of Boston was blockaded by a single British frigate standing off the harbor. If the Navy Department could not understand the significance of that lone British ship, it was clear enough to all naval officers. Commerce-destroying cruise or not, the challenge she represented could not be denied.

The *Bonne Citoyenne* had had support from her superiors in not going out to meet the *Hornet*. Her cargo was too valuable to be risked. *Chesapeake*, by contrast, had only her honor (and his). He must have discussed the situation with his friends, Bainbridge and Hull, but there is no record of what consideration or advice they may have given. As the event developed, it was probably bad advice. He resolved to disobey his orders and accept the invitation to combat with the *Shannon*. Hull and Bainbridge must have been in agreement.

Lawrence had a year of drill and exercise with little *Hornet* before taking her into combat; when he got his opportunity, against a nominally equal (but not nearly so well trained) *Peacock*, his ship and crew were devastatingly superior. When he set out to sea in *Chesapeake*, he had been in command for only ten days. During the ten days he had drilled his men routinely. But not all of them were aboard until a day or so before he sailed. However, *Chesapeake* was by no means the unorganized ship she had been in 1807; Augustus Ludlow, her young first lieutenant, wrote his older brother (a former naval officer) that he had never seen her so well prepared for battle. But she was not a team, and she had no team spirit.

Lawrence had had no opportunity to shake his men down into a smoothly functioning man-of-war's crew. History commonly says his defeat came about because his crew was not well trained, yet there is much more to this than simple training in handling guns or sails. His men had done this all their adult lives, but they had never done it together. To function at its best, a team, or crew, must live together and work together. They must come to know one another, respect one another, and support one another. Books have been written about the intangibles of how teams work, how the invisible tendons of morale hold them together during difficulty, how the strength of the whole is greater than the sum of its parts. No one really knows how this works, but all athletic coaches, and all sports fans, recognize its importance. Whether Lawrence thought about his disadvantage in this area is not known. There is record of his unease during a walk in one of Boston's parks the night before he got under way, although the story is contradicted on the grounds that no captain would have gone ashore on such a night. One wonders whether he might not then have sensed that all was not as right with his ship as he would have liked. But by this time he felt bound to go.

Built by France, captured by the British, her captain declared a coward by Lawrence, *Bonne Citoyenne* had the last laugh; just six months after the confrontation at Bahia, James Lawrence was in the identical situation, and it cost him his new ship and his life.

History records that a veritable fleet of spectator craft followed *Chesapeake* to sea on the fateful 1 June 1813, and that among the spectators, in the largest private schooner, were Captains Hull and Bainbridge, off to a sporting event. It is to wonder at the extraordinary blindness of the human spirit, when it wills itself not to see.

Captain Philip Broke was no stranger just arrived on the American coast. He had been there since before the war, and had been in command of the *Shannon* since she had been built, in 1806. So far as the British Admiralty was concerned, he was one of their "expensive" skippers; his ship regularly requisitioned more supplies of ammunition than any of its fellows, for, entirely contrary to Nelson's famous dictum, "Get so close you *can't* miss!," Broke had the peculiar idea that British gunners and marine sharpshooters could be improved by frequently shooting at targets. In the Admiralty's view, he unnecessarily used up a lot of ammunition in this expensive pastime, but he was the senior officer afloat on the American station and was therefore to be humored. And undeniably, he had produced one of the top British frigates; on this there was no argument.

Blockading Boston, Broke could see the masts of the *Chesapeake* from his quarterdeck. The British Secret Service had made him aware that Lawrence, the victor over *Peacock*, had taken over the much more powerful *Chesapeake*. Like all British officers, Broke had been alarmed by the unbroken string of American victories. In at least some of the cases he felt he knew the cause, even though the code of the Royal Navy forbade any such insinuation against the efficiency of brother officers as suggesting that their crews needed more training and their officers some ingenuity. So far as he was concerned, what other skippers did was their business. His business was being ready for battle, and he had long ago resolved that *Shannon* would be different. Of course, were *Shannon* to come up against one of the big 44s, she would probably be outmatched, though even for this eventuality he had a few tricks up his sleeve. But *Chesapeake*, the smallest of the big American frigates, was not much bigger than his own ship. She was fitting out practically under his nose, was clearly intending to get to sea—and it was his duty to stop her. More than this, she presented an opportunity for fame and glory.

The Admiralty had already issued an order forbidding the standard-size British 38-gun frigates to take on the big American ones. The lesson had sunk in that the Americans were thoroughly professional, both in ship construction and in the way they fought. Whether Broke had yet received this order is not clear. Whatever the case, he was not at the moment obeying it, for no other British ship patrolled the entrance to Boston harbor. Perhaps he felt the order did not apply to the *Chesapeake*, for she was not a 44, nor even as big as the two American 38s, the *Constellation* and *Congress*. Rated at 36 guns, she was the only ship of her class in the U.S. Navy, a few tons larger than his own *Shannon*, rated by the Royal Navy as a 38. She was made to order for him, and for this reason he had sent his consort, *Tenedos*, away. And he brought his own ship close in, in full view of the shore, his very presence challenging Lawrence to come out. Also, he tried a little psychological warfare, whether he thought of it as such or not, for he sent a letter via a released merchant skipper, offering to meet at an agreed-on location if Lawrence wished first to get his ship to sea for a short shakedown. The letter was extremely carefully drafted. Broke had obviously given it much thought. Although as events turned out Lawrence never received it, in his campaign to bring the *Chesapeake* to battle on his own terms, Broke could not have played his cards better.

The day Broke's letter might have arrived, Lawrence completed his preparations, said good-bye to his pregnant wife and his daughter, moved his ship into the outer harbor, anchored, and fired a single gun. This was done in broad daylight, in full sight of Broke and his crew. The symbolism of the days of chivalry was clear. There were those who placed great store by it, who held the quixotic idea that the captains of ships of war were knights who had taken their lances and their chargers to sea. How rational-minded men could risk not only themselves but everything they had been brought up to cherish on a quixotic replay of an outmoded form of combat raises eyebrows today, and one can come up with but one explanation: the clear-seeing ones gave lip service to the idea because it was the fashion, but they were as hardheaded as they knew how to be when it came to what counted. This, from the long view, is the true description of Philip Broke. His letter was only part of his campaign to bring about the battle he sought. He could feel himself succeeding, knew precisely the meaning of Lawrence's move into the outer harbor, fully understood why Lawrence had fired his gun. Broke answered at once. It was the promise he had so avidly sought.

The challenge of *Shannon*'s daily presence, full of meaning as it was, was being accepted. *Chesapeake* was coming out. Both captains were punctiliously observing all the rules of chivalry as they were thought to apply to warships. On the practical side, each skipper was responsible for his own preparation. Broke had had years to train his ship, and he had had over a month to work out exactly how he would deal with his adversary. He played his dual role—chivalrous knight and master of detailed preparedness—to perfection. No one could have been more ready than he, no ship more rehearsed than HBM frigate *Shannon*.

One can imagine the talks in the wardrooms of both frigates that night, the fevered discussions among their crews: Broke and Lawrence reviewing their preparations, issuing final instructions, haranguing their crews in the time-honored tradition. Wills and last testaments were written, letters written home. Among the crews, instructions as to disposition of personal effects were handed to friends.

Next day, with *Chesapeake* anchored a few miles away in plain sight, obviously completing last-minute arrangements, Broke had his officers to lunch on the quarterdeck. He made them a speech, drank wine (beautiful metaphor) with them. They all shook hands solemnly, and he quietly gave the orders to make ready for battle. They were ready, as ready as could be. They had prepared faithfully; they were ready to use all the equipment with which their ship was fitted to the very best of their ability, and with some carefully planned innovations besides, known only to themselves. They knew that the honor of the British navy, in a very special way, would rest on them that day.

In *Chesapeake* the situation was the opposite. While the disposition of contemporary American writers (and later ones too) was to emphasize her unreadiness, that of British writers was to comment on how evenly matched the two ships were, in contrast to the three lost battles against the big 44s. The more accurate comparison was that although the ships were evenly matched, and *Chesapeake*'s condition was truly not too much different from that of other ships of either navy on the eve of deployment, there was no way in which she could be considered a match for *Shannon* in readiness. Bad Luck *Chesapeake* was fated to enter upon the climactic incident of her career minus the opportunity afforded most ships for the crew to get to know one another in the intangible way any team must to do its best, and she was pitted against the very best the Royal Navy had to offer. All those who have sought to explain the outcome of the battle simply in terms of mechanical training, or failure of some small cog in the organization (such as the bugler who could not be found to sound the call for repelling boarders), have missed this crucial difference.

Broke had a very carefully thought out battle plan. He had had ample cause to consider what had happened to his friends who had the misfortune to come up against U.S. frigates. The Nelsonian fighting spirit by itself was not enough, for the Americans seemed to have an equal supply of this quality, and their ships, once condemned as too big and too unwieldy, had proved to be just the opposite. He had studied the effect of British gunfire against the tough American hulls, as compared to what happened to the sides of British frigates. Live oak was much tougher than anyone had been willing to credit, and it was beginning to be suspected (as was indeed true) that the sides of the big 44s were considerably thicker than the sides of comparable British ships. How would he, in *Shannon*, as good a ship of her class as could be found, cope with a ship like *Constitution* if he came up on her? Assuming nearly equal gunnery capability, a long-range cannonade, as tried by Carden in the *Macedonian*, would certainly be more damaging to *Shannon* than to the enemy. There was no victory to be found that way. Better results could be had if he could achieve strategic surprise, but how to do this against an alert enemy? Maybe catch her as she came out of port, overwhelm her in an intense, very close-range action that would culminate in boarding and hand-to-hand fighting. He laid his plans accordingly, even painstakingly reenacted Lawrence's role at Bahia. Courtesy of the British Secret Service, he knew his man. He was not at all surprised to see *Chesapeake* move to the outer harbor and begin obvious preparations to meet him next day. It was precisely what Lawrence thought *Bonne Citoyenne* ought to have done.

One of Broke's precepts, drilled into the marines who manned his fighting tops, was that every man at the helm, and every officer, not to mention anyone else identifiable as holding a critically important position, was to be shot as quickly as possible. So far as he was concerned, he had discharged the responsibilities of noblesse oblige by writing to Lawrence, even though it now seemed hardly likely Lawrence had had time to receive his letter. Any more chivalry would be ridiculous foolishness. The idea that enemy leaders were somehow not to be deliberately aimed at made no sense at all. An enemy's officers were the key to his effectiveness. "Kill them," he said time after time, "and the ship is ours."

In analyzing the maneuvers of the two ships, the question has been raised as to why Broke merely shortened sail with his head to the southeast to await Lawrence's approach from the west. In so doing, he gave Lawrence the weather gauge; that is, he let him approach downwind. Broke would be firing into the wind, and the smoke from the broadsides of both ships would drift over his own. Generally this was undesirable, since it obscured the target for one's own gunners. But it would also leave *Chesapeake*'s decks clear for the trained sharpshooters (with rifles instead of the standard muskets) in *Shannon*'s tops, while Broke's own decks would be shrouded in smoke and could not be seen from the *Chesapeake*.

The only thing left to chance, so far as Broke was concerned, was whether his enemy would choose to come to close quarters; but he had placed himself to give the maximum invitation for Lawrence to do so. He had also arranged the hottest possible reception for him. In addition to her main battery of cannon and the expert riflemen in her fighting tops, two cannon had been carefully placed on *Shannon*'s forecastle, one a 32-pound carronade loaded with antipersonnel grape and canister to sweep the enemy ship's forecastle, the other a long 9-pounder on a raised swivel that could be elevated to the unusual angle of thirty-three degrees—and loaded with dismantling shot to knock down *Chesapeake*'s headsails. A similar huge improvised shotgun was located on *Shannon*'s quarterdeck, aimed at *Chesapeake*'s quarterdeck, as was another elevated long 9 with dismantling shot intended for the enemy's spanker, her main steering sail. No exception can be taken to any of these innovative provisions. They are recited here only to show the refinements possible when there is plenty of time to prepare. None of them even occurred to Lawrence. In any case, he had his hands full getting his new ship and crew organized in the normal way.

But no other commander of any ship during the entire War of 1812 was deliberately sought out and shot as a specific part of the battle plan. James Lawrence, and all his officers, with one exception, were shot at least twice.

By contrast to Broke, Lawrence had only an improvised plan of maneuver. It has been suggested that he hoped to blanket *Shannon*'s sails from windward as his ship came up and then luff across her bow for a raking broadside. This theory is belied by the manner in which he handled *Chesapeake*, bringing her right alongside at the extremely close range of forty yards and then shivering his own sails to cut his speed. He expressly sacrificed all advantage he might have had in position or maneuvering (the weather gauge, which might have allowed him to open the action with a raking broadside) to let the cannon alone decide the contest. But Broke felt no similar compulsion to abandon any of the special arrangements he had prepared.

The details of the battle illustrate the importance of thorough readiness and the folly of fighting as the enemy wishes. *Chesapeake* got under way at noon, with the *Shannon* in sight awaiting her. Both ships sailed off shore until about four, when Lawrence had another gun fired as a signal that it was time to engage, and Broke shortened sail to await him. Gallantly, but stupidly, Lawrence came right alongside, very close aboard. For a few minutes a furious and equal cannonade took place, during which *Shannon*'s lighter hull timbers suffered more than the heavier scantlings of her adversary.

But Broke had indoctrinated his crew well. "Fire into her quarters, gundeck to gundeck, maintop to maintop," he had said over and over again. "Kill the men and the ship is ours." With the first broadside, the specially prepared and aimed pivot gun on *Shannon*'s forecastle took off *Chesapeake*'s headsails. The one aft similarly shot away the brails on the spanker and flung it, untended, to the wind. These were the control sails without which a square rigger can neither steer nor maneuver. Every man on the helm was shot by the sharpshooters Broke had so long and carefully trained. The relief helmsmen who ran to replace them, as their battle stations prescribed, were instantly shot also. Within moments there was no one at the wheel, for to approach it brought an immediate fusillade. Instantly the *Chesapeake* was unmanageable; and there was no one to manage her—for every officer on deck had also been shot. Lawrence, wounded in the thigh, struggled to keep his feet but was shot again, this time through the body. James Fenimore Cooper, who states the facts without understanding their real portent, notes merely that "Mr. Broome, the marine officer, Mr. Ballard, the acting fourth lieutenant, and the boatswain, were mortally wounded. Mr. White, the [sailing] master, was killed; and Mr. Ludlow, the first lieutenant, was twice wounded by grape and musketry." Ludlow, the twenty-one-year-old second-in-command, was in fact mortally wounded at the same time as his captain. Acting third lieutenant William Cox, a midshipman of the *Hornet* who had followed Lawrence to the *Chesapeake*, at the call for boarders came up from his post on the gundeck. Aghast at the carnage, shocked at the wounds received by his beloved skipper, he helped take below the semi-conscious Lawrence, who kept feverishly repeating, "Don't give up the ship!" But nothing could be done for him.

In the meantime, the uncommanded *Chesapeake* came up into the wind. Her double steering wheels spinning madly under the action of the sea on the rudder two decks below, she drifted backward into contact with the nearby enemy. Broke was ready; with the *Chesapeake* right alongside, her main deck totally exposed, the huge improvised shotguns were fired at point-blank range. The effect was terrible. Virtually everyone on the deck was downed, the upper (spar) deck swept clean. Seeing their opportunity, the British boarded, and in a furious hand-to-hand combat against disorganized though (for a short time) fierce resistance, they swept the spar deck and replaced the American flag with their own. This was accomplished some four minutes after they first stepped aboard, in the very best Nelsonian tradition. When Acting Lieutenant Cox attempted to come topside after getting Lawrence below, the hatch openings were already blocked by hastily thrown over gratings and guarded by armed British sailors and marines. The ship was in the hands of the enemy only fifteen minutes after the beginning of the action, only three minutes longer than it took the *Hornet* to conquer the *Peacock* (some accounts give only twelve minutes, exactly the same time)—and, although he did not know it, through the disability of everyone senior to him, Cox was now in command!

From beginning to end the battle was a debacle for the American side, although apparently the gundeck, behind its thick oaken walls, did good work for a time. Measured in total killed and wounded, the battle was by far the most sanguinary naval battle of the war. Casualties were severe in both ships. Out of a crew of 340 men, the *Chesapeake* had 48 killed, including nearly all her officers, and 98 wounded, including all her remaining officers but one. Only the *Essex*, in her heroic but hopeless battle against two enemy ships a year later, suffered more deaths (but fewer wounded). *Shannon*, decisively victorious, had about 30 dead and 56 wounded out of a slightly smaller crew. Historians differ on the number (some say she had 43 dead), but all agree she had more casualties than any other victorious ship on either side. By comparison, of the beaten British frigates *Guerriere* had 15 killed, *Macedonian*, 36, and *Java*, officially at least, 22. (*Java* carried a detachment of troops bound for India, for whom casualty figures were never fixed with certainty.) In February 1815, however, when *Constitution* fought *Cyane* and *Levant*, the combined death toll of the two British ships was 50. Possibly Charles Stewart, *Constitution*'s captain in this brilliant engagement, took a leaf out of Broke's book, though since the battle was fought at night it is more likely the heavy toll was simply due to the thinner sides of the smaller British ships.

One of the severely wounded in the *Shannon* was Philip Broke himself, who received a bad saber cut on his head while leading his boarding party. The wound left him unconscious for several days and nearly cost him his life (and did, in fact, force him to be invalided home and eventually retired). Perhaps to this happenstance—as well as to the previous indoctrination that only Broke could have reversed had he been able, once victory had been attained—can be attributed the bad behavior of the British crew after the battle. There had been up to this time five single-ship actions, all won by the Americans, and in all five instances the British accounts were full of praise for the thoughtful treatment they had received from the victors—from the high-minded Lawrence in *Hornet*, particularly. *Chesapeake* was the first British naval victory, and there was no reciprocity. Ship and crew were looted of clothing, side arms, money, and nautical instruments. The surviving midshipmen were locked into a small room. Lawrence was given medical care but scant courtesy while he lay dying aboard the frigate he had commanded such a short time. His captors had taken over everything on board the ship, and even refused to return his wife's letters to him. By account of the officers and crew of the beaten ship, the British lieutenants in charge, and their prize crew, "behaved with brutality." It was not until the two ships arrived in Halifax that magnanimity in victory was finally restored. Lawrence, Ludlow, and the other dead officers were buried with full military honors, and later returned to Boston under flag of truce—and it is possible that a certain degree of shame attached itself to at least some members of the Royal Navy, for when Decatur was taken, a year and a half later, his captors could not do enough for him and his crew.

As might be imagined, English public opinion went wild with delight when the news of the *Shannon*'s quick and uncompromising victory was received. Britons had become accustomed to an almost unblemished line of victories at sea. They could not understand, and had become vociferously restive about, the long string of bad news about the "little war" with the United States. Now, at last, British strength, stamina, and sea power had again come to the fore, had again, as under Nelson, been conclusively demonstrated. Broke became an instant national hero, and was knighted. It was an honor much deserved, for his victory was very much needed.

Lawrence's duty, by contrast, had been to get to sea and do as much damage to the interests of Great Britain as possible. He had actually disobeyed his orders, choosing instead to expend everything he had against a force that, on the plane of the metaphysical, if not the material, was infinitely superior to his own. He had been beaten before he got under way. The contrast to Hull's superficially similar situation was absolute. With all due respect to an American naval hero, an admirable character on the personal level, the man who, dying of his wounds, gave us the naval motto, "Don't give up the ship!"—Lawrence deserved to be beaten. In the process he did more for the morale of England than anyone else in the entire war, even including the man who killed him and who became Sir Philip Broke, Baronet, by consequence.

Probably had there been two British frigates on guard, Lawrence would have had no hesitancy in trying to evade them, as all other commanders had done. But one, of equal force, was a challenge he could not avoid. He felt bound to fight, but no one has yet been able to suggest how he could have thought he might win.

He egregiously failed in his duty to prepare his ship for combat, though not in the ordinary sense. Modern football is the best analogy, for being up for a contest is well known as having more·importance than anything else in the preparatory phase. *Chesapeake* could have beaten *Shannon* had Lawrence played the cards dealt to him as well as Broke played his, for she was in truth a better armored ship. Even his poignant last words, feverishly and obsessively repeated during the four days it took him to die from his wounds, are hardly a battle cry, though, thanks to Oliver Hazard Perry, we have made them into one.

And, in the meantime, with enough ships available and the growing myth about American invincibility at sea effectively blown away, England's Admiralty got down to business with the job at hand across the Atlantic. Regardless of the requirements of the war still going on with Napoleon, sufficient forces also had to be provided to the Halifax station. A tight blockade of all U.S. ports had to be instituted. Special types of frigates had to be built, or improvised by "razeeing" * 74-gun battleships, to match the big 44s of the *Constitution* class. Smaller frigates—the 38s mounting 18-pound cannon in the main battery instead of *Constitution*'s 24-pounders—were forbidden to engage except in pairs. As had in fact been anticipated, the net of sea power was thrown and drawn. But before this was done, the United States Navy had proved it had a place on the sea.

The subsequent histories of the *Chesapeake* and *Shannon* are of passing interest. *Chesapeake* was "purchased" into the British navy (the term means that her value was estimated and that that amount was paid to her captors as "prize money," in a manner analogous to actual sale of a captured merchant ship and cargo), but her reputation as a

---

*From the French word *raser*, "to shave." A *vaisseau rasé* ("razay") was a "shaved (or razed) ship," thus one with the top deck shaved off. The English corruption of the word, both in spelling and pronunciation, entered into their nautical vocabulary to designate a large warship that had had her upper deck and guns removed, thus greatly lightening her and also reducing the height of her sides. "Razeeing" a 74-gun ship of the line would convert her into a very heavy frigate, usually with the same masts and spars as before the operation. With the right combination, the modified ship would be both fast and powerful and, because of her lower sides, could sail closer to the wind than before.

bad-luck ship persisted, contrary to the experience with most captured men-of-war (e.g., *Hancock*). Perhaps *Chesapeake*'s selection, while still in Halifax, as the place to hold the court-martial of Captain Edward Grafton for running the old *Leopard* aground and losing her, added to that perception. But it may also be viewed as someone's attempt to lay the ghost of the disgraceful 1807 incident. (Whatever the reason, all other British courts-martial of that period on the American station were held aboard the flagship, the *San Domingo*.) Late in 1814 the *Chesapeake* sailed for England, but on arrival ran aground in Plymouth Sound, and her skipper was promptly relieved of command. Then sent to Capetown, South Africa, she learned of peace with the United States in mid-May 1815. She was finally broken up in 1820. The excellent timbers in her hull were used in the construction of a flour mill in Wickham, England, not far from Portsmouth, where they can be seen today.

Surprisingly, *Shannon*, built in 1806 and therefore six years younger than her antagonist, had a shorter life span. There is no record of any further active service after the battle, and England's Public Record Office shows she was permanently put out of service in November 1813, though she served sometime later as a receiving ship. Broke was therefore her only commander. While making significant deductions from this bare fact is a risky business, it may be that she had suffered so much from the close-range fire of the American frigate as to be beyond economical repair. According to information at hand, her sides at their thickest point were fifteen inches thick, and for much of her length only eleven inches thick. *Chesapeake*, at comparable locations, measured nineteen and seventeen inches. *Chesapeake*'s "armor," in other words, was between 27 and 55 percent thicker than *Shannon*'s, and in addition was made of extremely hard live oak, which had weathered since 1795. Had she been as well handled as her design and construction deserved, she should have been able to atone for her dereliction in 1807.

Poor William Cox also suffered from his ship's bad star. Of all the officers, he was the only one unhurt. His regular station was on the gundeck, and he actually fired the last gun from *Chesapeake* into the British frigate's hull. This, in fact, took place after the American ensign had been hauled down by members of the British boarding party, although Cox had no means of knowing it. The other thing he did not know was that because the five officers senior to him had been shot, he had, by navy regulations, succeeded to command. Public opinion, having become accustomed to victory, demanded a scapegoat. So Cox was tried by general court-martial and sentenced ''to be cashiered with a perpetual incapacity to serve in the Navy of the United States.'' The rest of poor Cox's life, until 1874, was lived under the shadow of this unjust sentence. Even the young Theodore Roosevelt, in his otherwise excellent history of the War of 1812, says, ''utterly demoralized by the aspect of affairs [Cox] basely ran below without staying to rally the men.''

To Cox's descendants, Roosevelt's book was the final indignity. The family began a campaign that lasted until 1952, when a joint resolution of Congress, supported by two successive directors of naval history, authorized the President ''to issue the late William S. Cox a commission as a third lieutenant, effective the date of his death.'' There was no demand for back pay or damages, hence the strange date selected. His family wanted only to clear his name, and in this they succeeded. May his scarred spirit rest a little more easily.

5

The War on the Lakes and Finale on the Seas

Among the dreams of the more ambitious revolutionists at the beginning of the War for Independence was that of carrying Canada along with us, making the whole of the English portion of the North American continent, down to the possessions of Spain and France, into a single unified confederation of newly independent states. From a purely military point of view, this move would have protected the northern flank against British attack. But the idea was frustrated on the last day of 1775—and, as it turned out, for all time—by the defeat of Generals Richard Montgomery and Benedict Arnold before Quebec (the highly regarded Montgomery lost his life in the assault).

After the conclusion of the Revolution, great numbers of still loyal British subjects emigrated to Canada. Many of them had been wrongfully evicted from their property and were understandably bitter. Many arrived by foot, their cattle pulling canvas-covered wagons much like those used three-quarters of a century later in our march to the West. The welcome influx of these new settlers is still celebrated in Canada with pageant and festivity.

During the years following, despite the clearly demonstrated disaffection of the new Canadians for their former homeland and the equally proved loyalty to the English Crown of those who had been long established north of the St. Lawrence River, the idea persisted in the United States that most Canadians would like nothing better than to become part of the new republic to the south. This was, in fact, an underlying cause of the War of 1812, among certain "war hawks," at least. Had our early military expeditions into Canada been better organized and led, Canada might indeed have been conquered, for a time. But it is difficult to conceive of England accepting a second insult in the North American continent so soon after the one administered by George Washington's Continental Army. At the minimum, the War of 1812 would have lasted far longer; and, with the release of pressure in Europe after the downfall of Napoleon, there is the strong possibility such an enlarged war might have terminated less favorably for the United States than it in fact did.

In the event, the citizens of Canada gave strong support to the Crown in the new war. The Canadian port of Halifax, in Nova Scotia, was the primary fleet operating base, the headquarters of the North American station, and St. John's, Newfoundland, was an important convoy staging and operational base. Many Canadians joined British army forces to repel the inept invasion efforts from the south (typically, however, British army officers considered Canadian troops to be totally ineffective). When our army on the Canadian border met with decisive defeat, the security of our northern border against counterinvasion from Canada became of primary concern to President Madison and his administration. There was fear the British might descend the Lake Champlain–Lake George–Hudson River waterway, as had been tried twice during the Revolution; and there was even greater fear for the safety of the interconnected inland seas of fresh water to the west, the Great Lakes, since the poor performance of our army had changed them from an avenue of possible entry into Canada into a route for a reverse invasion from the north.

Congress, too, could study the maps. Following General William Hull's pusillanimous surrender to inferior force at Fort Dearborn shortly after war was declared, it appropriated money to prepare naval defenses on the Great Lakes and formally asked the Navy Department to assign an experienced sea officer to the post. On the last day of August 1812, Navy Secretary Hamilton accordingly ordered Captain Isaac Chauncey to take command of the two most threatened lakes, Ontario and Erie. Hamilton also had the inspiration, or excellent advice, to support Chauncey with the services of Henry Eckford, a renowned shipbuilder. "Forty ship-carpenters [*sic*] left New York in the first week of September, and more followed immediately," according to the *Commercial Advertiser* of New York, bringing with them huge stocks of cordage, canvas, oakum for caulking seams, and builder's stores of all kinds. At about the same time the first contingent of officers and men, laden with guns, munitions, and other naval equipment, left New York for Lake Ontario. Others came at various times, as needed, from Boston, Portsmouth (New Hampshire), and New London. As the threat from the north became more serious, Hamilton even directed ships to be laid up to provide the necessary nucleus of trained personnel, selecting, of course, those that were blockaded by the British, and making the shifts in utmost secrecy so that the enemy would continue to expend effort in blockading inoperative ships.

In the selection of Eckford, the navy secretary could not have done better. At Sackett's Harbor, the designated naval base on the south shore of Lake Ontario, there was a fine basin for anchoring ships in deep water and a magnificent stand of growing timber. At once, Eckford set his men simultaneously to lay out the launching ways, select the shipbuilding area, construct roads for bringing in supplies, build fortifications and habitations for themselves, and mark trees for cutting according to the schedules he put forth. His first ship, the *Madison*, named for the president, was launched late in November 1812. Only nine weeks before, her timbers had been growing in the forest.

At about this time it became evident that the British did indeed have plans for a naval campaign on the Great Lakes, for Captain Sir James Yeo, R.N. (who had recently lost his 32-gun frigate *Southampton* on a reef in the West Indies, along with a captured prize, the brig

Vixen of Preble's old Mediterranean squadron), arrived at Kingston, on the opposite shore of Ontario, and began constructing a small fleet. So far as their naval policies were concerned, the two opposing commodores were cut from the same cloth. Yeo had one advantage: he got his basic ship structures—frames, stern posts, transoms, and similar complicated pieces, all prefabricated—and the shipwrights to put them together, from England. Like Chauncey, however, for the rest of his shipbuilding material he had to look for green timber in the Canadian forest. Chauncey's strength lay in the prodigious Henry Eckford. During the entire War of 1812, the rival commanders settled down to the most unusual, and for the times and conditions extraordinary, of building races.

There were, to be sure, several minor skirmishes, but one side or the other always avoided decisive battle. The plain fact was that the commodore with the biggest ship in operation simply took command of the lake, sailed his accumulated fleet upon it—and retired when his opponent commissioned a bigger one. The drain on United States naval resources for men, guns, cordage, and canvas was tremendous. So, too, was that on England—or Canada.

In justice, it can be said that both sides fully appreciated the possible results of an adverse decision at arms, and could not bring themselves to risk all on the uncertain dice of battle. When peace came, Yeo had in the water and "at sea" a fleet of a dozen ships of all sizes, ranging from the small schooners he had at the beginning of the campaign to (according to unverifiable sources) a regular 74 and a huge ship of the line pierced (having gunports) for 112 guns! Eckford was building two battleships variously described as carrying from 102 to 120 guns each, and Chauncey (according to James Fenimore Cooper's *Naval History*) "would have taken the lake, as soon as navigation opened, with 2 sail of the line, 2 frigates, 2 corvettes, 4 brigs, and as many small craft as the service could possibly have required."

Henry Eckford, the shipbuilding genius, undertook to launch Chauncey's two big line-of-battle ships within sixty days of the time he began to work on them, "the timber then standing in the forest." He had been engaged only twenty-nine days with the first, the *New Or-*

leans, when word of peace arrived. The great battleship, with some 80 gunports visible on two covered gundecks (the uppermost deck with another 20 to 40 ports was never built), stood on her stocks until 1884, a tremendous solitary sentinel over Lake Ontario (only 193 miles long and 53 miles maximum width). She was thoroughly photographed during the three-quarters of a century of her existence, but she never tasted the water. Her only claim to fame—an excellent one at that—was that she had been "run up" to this condition in less than a month.

The lake warships had no need for long cruising range. Since they rarely remained "at sea" for more than a few days at a time, living quarters on board were minimal. They required no water at all, the water of the lakes being fresh and totally potable, and little in the way of provisions. No one expected them to have to last more than a few years at most—so green timbers, of almost any quality so long as they possessed requisite strength, would do. There was no problem in transporting the timber to the building site and not much in storing it, for the trees were marked in advance, cut as needed, and often laid right into the hulls. While strong gales sometimes swept the Great Lakes, Ontario was the smallest and most sheltered; there was far less "fetch" for large waves to build up in its restricted waters, and sea-keeping (or lake-keeping) qualities could be minimized. The ships could devote more of their displacement to armament and required less depth of hold for stores. To have adequate stability in a strong breeze, greater proportionate beam compensated for shallow draft and less deep-lying ballast. Through all these factors, a ship's nominal gun rating—the standard size and power measure of the time—was skewed upward. (The *Superior*, Chauncey's biggest operational ship, rated a 60-gun frigate by most accounts, was lengthened on the stocks, before launch, in response to false reports of the size of Yeo's latest ship.* She is conceded to have been of about the same displacement, but actually longer and beamier, than the high-seas-capable *Constitution*, rated as a

---

*An unusual footnote to the history of this period: both Yeo and Chauncey evidently had fairly clear ideas of some of the uses of propaganda, or "disinformation," as it might today be called. There is evidence that each deliberately misled the other as to the size and power of his ships in commission and as to the strength and degree of advancement of the new ones being built.

44, and she carried bigger guns as well as more of them.) There are no positive details about Yeo's 112-gun *St. Lawrence*; but for sixty-nine years the 120-gun *New Orleans* gave silent testimony to the fact that she would have been nearly as big as Nelson's revered *Victory*.

The U.S. crews were to a large degree obtained from seagoing warships rendered inoperational through blockade. The lake warships were cheaper to build and operate than comparable ships intended for the open sea, not only in provisions and water storage but also in all sorts of general construction details. From the point of view of the sailor accustomed to long voyages and consequent privations on the oceans, lake warships could not sail far from home, never stayed under way more than a few days at a time, never were out of sight of land, got back to port frequently, and since icing closed the lakes to navigation for part of each year, seldom if ever faced freezing winter storms. Creature comforts, for crews accustomed to privation no matter where they served, could be reduced to the barest necessities. Arming them, however, was a major difficulty: the guns had to be transported overland through largely virgin country, which necessitated cutting new roads, at least at first, as they progressed.

One wonders why Congress, or the secretary of the navy, stood for the extraordinary expense, particularly when one considers that the biggest ships in our navy during the entire War of 1812 were in the smallest of the Great Lakes, restricted in their total area of action to a few thousand square miles of deep water. Although Henry Eckford was adept at improvisation and eschewed all frills in their construction, the huge ships were still a tremendous drain in funds and manpower. The answer is that, as the war dragged on, both sides began to appreciate the dimensions of the vacuum that existed in the Northwest Territories and the extraordinary importance of the Great Lakes. Since transportation overland was primitive, whichever side held navigational control of the lakes could, almost automatically, assure victory in any trial by arms. Pressures were thus increased, the ship carpenters on both sides became performing prodigies, and the arms race fed on itself.

On balance, it seems that Canada and the United States may have profited from the lack of fighting. Although nothing of a conclusive nature happened on Lake Ontario, from a larger point of view one might today say that Yeo and Chauncey, through their mutual lack of determined aggressiveness, really served the best interests of both sides. They kept each other in check and the feared border war did not develop. Despite history's thirst for battles and, indeed, in spite of the hard battle fought on the other side of Niagara Falls in Lake Erie, their unwitting contribution to the history of the two neighboring nations was to confirm a border destined to become a classic of nonbelligerent inviolability.

On the other hand, Oliver Hazard Perry, aged only twenty-seven, walked into a very different situation. In 1812 General (and future president) William Henry Harrison, commanding U. S. Army forces in the Northwest Territories, began his campaign to frustrate British establishment of an Indian buffer state south of the Great Lakes. Harrison was under heavy pressure to restore the U.S. Army's prestige, which had suffered severely from General Hull's debacle at Fort Dearborn. Early on, he recognized how dependent he was for success on control of Lake Erie, and consequently urgently asked that Chauncey set up a naval force there for that purpose. Chauncey, recognizing his responsibility but wishing to preserve the strength of his fleet on Lake Ontario, sent the contentious Lieutenant Jesse D. Elliott as provisional commander of the Lake Erie forces, with the brothers Adam and Noah Brown to build a small fleet for him.

In their reputation as shipbuilders, the Brown brothers were second to none, not even the redoubtable Henry Eckford, and their selection for the crucially important post at Presque Isle (now Erie, Pennsylvania) was no accident. Within days of their arrival they had begun building two large and powerful war brigs. Soon afterward, Master Commandant Perry reported to Chauncey for duty and was sent by him to supersede Elliott at Lake Erie. Chauncey's motives for displacing his original appointee are not clear. Elliott was Perry's senior in age, but Perry was senior in naval rank. Perry's service reputation was that of an enthusiastically competent officer who always gave a good account of himself. Elliott, by contrast, was considered an egotistical malcontent by all who knew him. Men serving under him were often on the brink of open insubordination and would go to nearly any length to place themselves under some other master. There is no evidence as to Chauncey's thinking, however; one can only attempt to place one's self in his position. Perhaps, knowing—or at least sensing—Perry's superior fitness for the post, and relying on his seniority in rank to answer Elliott's predictable anger, the commodore simply hoped the move would seem a normal one for a military organization. True to the character he showed throughout his life, however, Elliott felt himself displaced from his rightful deserts, refused to stay at Erie, and returned to Lake Ontario. There, probably hoping to assuage Elliott's clamorous ego, Chauncey gave him command of the flagship, *Madison*. Not long afterward, nonetheless, Chauncey found occasion again to rid himself of a troublesome subordinate and sent him back to Perry as second-in-command. Sadly, he thereby also laid the seed for one of our navy's great tragedies.

Like many other younger officers of the navy, Perry had been a close friend and admirer of James Lawrence, whom he felt to be the outstanding officer of his grade. The shock of his death in battle grieved all his contemporaries. With a small fleet at his disposition, Perry named one of the two new brigs *Lawrence*, and took her as his flagship. Her identical sister, *Niagara*, he assigned to the jealous Elliott. He also had made an embroidered personal banner, emblazoned with the last words of the dying Lawrence, "Don't give up the ship!" It was under this standard, on 10 September 1813, that Perry won victory and fame.

Each of the little fleets contained two relatively large vessels, which bore the brunt of the fighting. Altogether, the American flotilla contained nine ships, or, more properly, two brigs of 20 guns each, a schooner of 4 guns, and six boats mounting one or two guns each. The British squadron had six vessels in all, but of a more homogeneous style: two three-masted "ships" with 19 and 17 guns respectively, a large schooner of 13 guns, a brig of 10 guns, and two boats with one gun each. During the battle *Niagara* (according to Elliott) was held out of action by light contrary winds. Her sister ship, *Lawrence*, slightly larger and heavier than the largest enemy ship, fought the entire British

fleet almost single-handed and was virtually destroyed in the process.*
By lagging behind, Elliott had opened his distance from the *Lawrence*,
so that he was soon in the lead of two-thirds of Perry's squadron,
which, following Elliott, remained likewise out of what developed into
a most unequal battle. When *Lawrence* had been reduced to a sinking
hulk and was virtually out of ammunition as well, Perry rolled up his
banner, had himself rowed over to his totally undamaged number-two
ship, and sent Elliott to "bring up" the rest of his little squadron.
Casualties in the *Lawrence* had been enormous. More than three-
quarters of her crew were dead or wounded. Doubtless, Elliott was
astounded to see his superior, totally uninjured, climbing upon his as
yet unbloodied deck, but history does record that he went without protest on his mission to round up the other stragglers. Under Perry,
Niagara's unfavorable wind immediately became favorable; entry of
an entirely fresh ship into the fray brought about a decision, and the
young commodore was soon able to send his famous message to General Harrison: "We have met the enemy and they are ours."**

---

*After the battle, Elliott, well aware that his lack of support in the engagement on Lake Erie
might be interpreted to his discredit, begged Perry for favorable mention in his official report. In
the euphoria of victory, Perry acquiesced. But in the navy, Elliott was not admired. A story began
to circulate that he had behaved in a cowardly manner and had failed to do his duty, even that he
wished for Perry's death so that he, Elliott, could succeed to command. He consequently continually demanded more testimonials from an increasingly reluctant Perry. In due course the
interchanges between the two young men became acrimonious, and eventually Elliott, looking for
an ally, fastened on James Barron, himself a figure of controversy after his court-martial for the
disgraceful *Chesapeake-Leopard* affair, and obsessed with jealous hate for Decatur as a principal
cause of his misery.

**The *Lawrence* was so damaged as to be hardly worth repair, although the evidence is that this
was done nevertheless, perhaps as a sentimental gesture. She had endured one of the most severe
battles and suffered the most severe casualty rate of any conflict in the entire war. She and her
sister ship *Niagara* remained in service until 1820, then were deliberately sunk in the lake in order
to preserve their hulls in the cold and organism-free fresh water. Considerable deterioration
nevertheless took place in *Niagara*—they might not have been sunk deeply enough. *Lawrence*
was raised in 1876 and her splinters sold for souvenirs at the Philadelphia Centennial Exposition.
In 1913, *Niagara* was raised and restored for the Perry centennial, subsequently again neglected,
and finally fully restored in 1963. Today she is mounted on concrete blocks in Erie, Pennsylvania, near her building site. Whether the ship is exactly as first constructed in 1813 cannot be
stated with certainty, but, regardless, the impression on the visitor is that she was clearly built for
one purpose only. Broad of beam, shallow of draft, nearly devoid of interior accommodations,
she mounted an extraordinarily heavy gun battery. In contrast to seagoing men-of-war, which
normally had high bulwarks, partly as a protection against weather, she provided practically no
protection to her crew. The high casualty rate in the identical *Lawrence* is no mystery; it is clear
that Elliott might indeed have had reason to expect Perry's injury or death, and one is left to
wonder what might have been the consequences to history.

General Harrison's delighted reply was to the effect that since Perry had been so instrumental in setting the stage for victory on land he had earned the right to see it to a finish. Thus Perry, on horseback, was a member of Harrison's staff in the final battle of the campaign. The Battle of the Thames took place on October 5 on the Canadian side of the Lakes. In it the British troops fled, and Chief Tecumseh of the Federated Indian Tribes was killed heroically defending their rear. From all accounts, Tecumseh must have been a truly extraordinary man. When the outnumbered British troops were routed, he personally held his Indian troops together in a desperate action to cover their flight and only his death ended the battle. With him died the powerful Indian federation he had put together.

The second fleet or squadron action of the War of 1812 also occurred on an inland fresh water lake: Lake Champlain. Thomas MacDonough had already earned the service reputation of being a fierce fighter. From a rather mild-mannered and deeply religious midshipman, he had developed into a veritable firebomb in battle, and there can be little doubt that his selection to command on that crucially important lake came because he could be depended on to fight with every ounce of his being. By good fortune, he had a year and a half to get ready.

Study of the topography of the Lake Champlain–Hudson River defile quickly makes clear its military importance during the early period of our country. It lent itself to dependable maintenance of a large force between the St. Lawrence and Hudson rivers. Except for two short portages over land, such a force could be supported entirely by water, and from either end. Two rivers, the Richelieu flowing north into the St. Lawrence and the Hudson flowing south into the Atlantic, plus two long and narrow lakes, Champlain and George, occupy the lowlands between the north- and south-oriented chains of mountains in New York and Vermont. To any army tactician, this natural configuration gave potential to separate New England from the rest of the United States. Given that area's known affinity for England, in both the Revolution and the War of 1812 this would have been of tremendous strategic importance to England, and in both wars Great Britain made an effort to do just that.

Any British advance along this line, whether up the Hudson or down from Canada, automatically constituted a threat of the highest degree, to be blocked at all cost. In 1776, General Sir Guy Carleton was stopped by Benedict Arnold's fleet of scratch boats in Lake Champlain (one of these, named *Philadelphia*, in appearance but a huge rowboat, may today be seen at the Smithsonian Museum of American History). A second attempt in 1777 by a British army under General Burgoyne was defeated at Saratoga, a short distance south of Lake George. In the War of 1812, as soon as our army failed in the attempt to invade Canada it became a certainty that the British would, sooner or later, repeat the attempt to split the United States into two parts.

MacDonough's fleet on Lake Champlain was, like Perry's on Lake Erie, a small one. In 1814, however, the British began preparations in earnest to renew the old strategy. MacDonough urgently presented his needs to the secretary of the navy, William Jones, who may be considered to have learned something about handling his officers since the debacle with James Lawrence the previous year. Jones deployed the forces available to him with excellent judgment. Henry Eckford, then engaged in building the heavy frigate *Superior* for Isaac Chauncey, was directed to divert his energies sufficiently to design a powerful, quickly built lake cruiser for MacDonough. Drawing heavily upon the plans he had already made for Chauncey's ships, Eckford produced the design of a very strong 26-gun sloop of war, a three-masted no-frills warship with armament on only one deck. Noah Brown, one of the builders of Perry's two big brigs in Lake Erie, was directed to move to Lake Champlain to build the ship, which he launched forty days after cutting the first tree. Intended only for battle, like all the lake warships, the ungainly looking vessel became MacDonough's flagship; he named her *Saratoga* in recognition of the important battle of 1777, which many historians feel turned the tide of victory in our war for independence.

Sir George Prevost, the British general in charge of the campaign for the Lake Champlain waterway, was generously supplied with seasoned troops from Wellington's victorious veterans in Europe. Clearly an all-out effort was planned. But General Prevost was a very cautious man. Beginning the campaign in 1814, he insisted on undisputed control of Lake Champlain before he would march his army southward. The British navy did its best, sending from England frames, timbers, and the necessary builders to construct a shallow-draft, fresh-water frigate rated at 36 guns, and assigning the highly thought of Captain George Downie to the task. Downie had no Eckford or Brown to help him; building a ship of this size in the conditions he faced involved delays and problems, as might be expected. Winter was nearing; Prevost would not move, was peevishly exhorting him to expedite. Finally, the ship, named *Confiance*, was complete. Caving in to Prevost's importuning, Downie started southward down the long narrow lake before he had fully organized or trained his crew, while Prevost paralleled his movement along the lake shore. *Confiance* had, in fact, been launched only seventeen days before.

It was the story of the *Chesapeake* over again, with General Prevost probably once fully competent but by 1814 acting as if senescence had struck him. Like Lawrence, Downie should have insisted on adequate preparation and training before taking his ship (and in this case her consorts) into battle.

MacDonough had, of course, kept himself fully advised as to the movements to the north and had carefully prepared his plan of battle. The British army would have to advance along the shore of the lake, for immediately inland of the shore road lay steep hills. Forced to march close to the water, it could not avoid being exposed to the fire of ships moored close-in. MacDonough sought a position where his guns could command both the army's only possible route and the lake approach by which Downie's fleet would have to come. A shallow bay off the town of Plattsburgh provided the perfect spot. He could cover the entire entrance with his little fleet, and therefore, contrary to usual naval doctrine, he determined to fight at anchor. No matter what happened (except his own total defeat), there would be no opportunity— not even the short one sometimes found between maneuvers—for the enemy army to get through the land blockade that MacDonough had set up from the lake.

In preparation for the battle, the American commander anchored his ships by bow and stern, and took the special precaution of having underwater ''springs''—extra cables to the anchors—laid out on both sides from their bows and quarters. By heaving in on some cables and paying out others, he could turn his ships completely around at their anchorages without use of sails. In nautical terminology, he prepared to "wind" (rhymes with *mind*) his ships. Thus if his engaged sides suffered too heavily, he had the option of continuing to fight with the other sides, in effect with new ships.

The battle, in September 1814, was a disaster for the British forces and for Downie personally. As MacDonough had anticipated, Prevost marched south along the west coast of Lake Champlain while Downie sailed in concert offshore. When the cautious British general encountered the threat of MacDonough's ships, he halted for Downie to clear away the difficulty. But MacDonough had anchored his ships so closely together and so near to the land ahead and astern that there was no way for the British fleet to get inshore of them to interpose between MacDonough and Prevost's threatened army. Downie decided the most appropriate way to fight a squadron anchored in this situation was to anchor also, and this he proceeded to do.

For a while, the cannonading was essentially even, with both flagships taking considerable damage. The ships' dimensions were essentially the same, but the *Saratoga* had a lighter broadside. What really mattered was that *Confiance* was a brand-new ship, far from shaken down, while MacDonough's flagship had been in commission since the previous April, with opportunity for training and for building fighting morale. Like Broke in *Shannon*, MacDonough had carefully and thoroughly planned for the battle he expected. In this case it was Downie, like poor Lawrence, who relied on expediency alone. Like the *Chesapeake-Shannon* debacle, there could have been no other outcome of the fight.

Simple bad luck also struck the British. Shortly after the battle began, one of the *Saratoga*'s shot struck the muzzle of a cannon behind which the English commander happened to be standing. The heavy blow drove the huge piece of iron off its carriage and into Downie's groin, pinning him to the deck with its weight and causing him intense suffering until he died. (The gun, with the fatal dent on its muzzle, can be seen at the U.S. Naval Academy at Annapolis.) The battle was continued by Downie's second-in-command, but he, too, was forced to rely on expediency alone against a man who had tried to prepare for every eventuality. When all *Saratoga*'s engaged broadside guns had been disabled and her bulwarks shattered, MacDonough used his ace in the hole: he "wound" ship, presenting an entirely fresh broadside to the nearly as badly damaged *Confiance*. The British ship's first lieutenant, valiantly attempting to exercise the command that had devolved upon him, attempted a similar maneuver. But *Confiance* was already under fire when she came to anchor; there had been no time to lay out spring lines with the care shown by MacDonough. The British flagship was able to come only halfway around, where she hung in irons, exposed to raking fire from what amounted to a new enemy. A few more broadsides from the rejuvenated *Saratoga* ended the battle.

When General Prevost realized that the British fleet had lost and the American squadron now totally controlled the lake, he turned his army about and marched precipitately back to the north, in his haste leaving behind great quantities of equipment, as well as British strategic hopes.

The Battle of Lake Champlain took place exactly a year and a day after Perry's victory on Lake Erie. MacDonough made no attempt to match Perry's stirring message to General Harrison, but he had won two victories in one: over the British squadron, under Downie, and over an army of Wellington's veterans, now led by a general with much less drive. It was the last big naval battle of the war, the biggest, by most comparisons, and strategically probably the most important. News of the outcome had a massive effect on the peace negotiations then going on in Ghent, Belgium. The British emissaries had been intransigent in their demands, the American ones less sure of themselves, for the latest news had been only of the successes being achieved by British arms. That all changed when the results of the Battle of Lake Champlain were made known. The treaty ending the war was signed on 24 December 1814, and ratified by the U.S. Senate the following February, but before it could take effect, three more battles took place. Two were naval—one a victory and one a defeat—and the other was a great victory on land, with naval overtones. Two of them had unusual preludes.

The victory at sea was Old Ironsides' third, and in the minds of most naval officers her greatest. Certainly it fixed her for all time in the affections of her country. The *Constitution*, under command of the highly regarded Charles Stewart, had needed a large refit after Bainbridge's long cruise and the battle with *Java*. Stewart was consequently not able to get her to sea until the last day of 1813. He cruised to the West Indies, made several captures, pursued but failed to catch the frigate *Pique*, 36, which eluded him at night, and returned to the Boston area on 3 April 1814, where the blockading squadron chased him into Marblehead. He lay under the guns of Fort Pickering, off Salem, until 24 April, when he was finally able to get his ship back to Boston. The adroitness of his control of his ship, the manner in which he always seemed one step ahead of his problems, have caused him actually to be credited with extrasensory perception. Once in Boston, he calmly readied for another cruise and then awaited the opportunity to break out, maintaining full readiness to get under way at virtually a moment's notice. The chance did not come until 17 December, when a winter gale blew the blockaders off their post. When they regained it, their bird had flown.

By this time in the war, the Royal Navy had constructed several big frigates expressly to match *Constitution* and her heavy sisters. Stewart knew a squadron of them would be scouring the seas for him as soon as the British became aware that the nemesis of *Guerriere* and *Java* was again on the loose. He consequently shifted his cruising area in ways intended to keep them guessing as to his location. On 9 February 1815 he "spoke" a ship (closed and hailed, exchanging news and pleasantries), thus learning of the peace treaty signed in Ghent on Christmas Eve. This was confirmed the next day by another ship. Stewart was of course aware that the peace was not effective until it could be ratified by both governments; he continued his cruise, and off the Azores on 19 February added to his growing reputation for supernatural prescience by announcing that *Constitution* would be in action within twenty-four hours.

Shortly after noon the next day, the *Cyane* and *Levant*, one a small frigate and the other a new ship-sloop, were sighted some distance apart although evidently proceeding in company. The *Constitution* squared off in chase and brought the two to action at nightfall. It was the apotheosis of single-ship combat and seamanship, so far as Stewart was concerned, exciting admiration on the part of all students of naval warfare. Not only did *Constitution* engage two enemies simultaneously, she raked both of them several times and yet avoided being raked herself—unheard of when two maneuverable ships fought a single enemy. Tactically, it has always been considered our most professional naval engagement of the war, one in which Charles Stewart's consummate seamanship, superb ship-handling ability, and tactical skill were demonstrated in a manner never to be equaled in our navy. At one point he sailed between the two enemy ships, firing raking broadsides from both sides and then, under cover of the darkness and smoke, "threw her main and mizzen topsails, with topgallant sails set, flat aback, shook all forward, let fly her jib sheet, and backed swiftly astern"*—between them a second time, raking them both again. Stewart was all his life known as a highly competent ship handler, as this action well proved to be true.

Both ships were captured and discovered to mount between them 53 guns, one more than carried by the *Constitution*, with a total broadside weight marginally greater than hers. Most of the guns, however, were short-ranged 32-pound carronades. The combined tonnage of the British warships, by British measurement, was 1,004 tons, one-third less than that of the *Constitution*.

After the battle, Stewart took the three ships to Porto Praya (now Praia) in the Cape Verde Islands, where by misfortune the fleet searching for the *Constitution* since it left Boston appeared the next day, the tops of their masts being sighted above a low fog. Stewart's quick reactions were never more evident; sure the British would not observe the neutrality of the Portuguese harbor, he instantly got his little flotilla under way and headed to sea. During the ensuing chase he directed them to separate, and all three big British frigates followed the little *Levant* back to Porto Praya, where, just as he had predicted, they

---

*This quotation is taken from Cooper's naval history, which he wrote with the assistance of Isaac Chauncey. There can be little question that the technical language came from someone well versed in handling large square-riggers, or that it expresses great professional admiration of Stewart.

opened fire. *Levant* was forced to surrender, but *Constitution* and *Cyane* escaped scot-free.

There are some indications that both captured British captains knew of the Treaty of Ghent, and most likely Sir George Collier, commanding the British squadron, knew of it also. No matter—everyone involved fought anyway, almost as if for the sheer joy of fighting. But one must remember that official confirmations traveled slowly in 1815. The U.S. Senate ratified the treaty of peace on 17 February, but the last shots of that war were fired on the last day of June (five months after Congress, at the bidding of President Madison, had recognized that a new war existed with Algiers and two weeks after Decatur's new squadron had blasted and captured the Algerian 44-gun frigate *Mashouda*). Stewart reached America in his grand old ship in May to the plaudits of his countrymen. Serving on active duty until 1861 (at age eighty-three), he lived to become the grand old man of the navy. In 1859 Congress had created the special rank of Senior Flag-Officer for him, and in 1862, after he had retired, made him a rear admiral on the retired list. Although he never wore that rank while on active duty, he was officially the first U.S. Navy rear admiral.* He was once proposed for nomination for the presidency, and died in 1869, at the age of ninety-one.

Of the other naval battle, the defeat, its prelude can be seen today in one of the more artistic drawings depicting the period. It is a watercolor entitled *Christmas Guests Arriving on the Flagship, 1814* and it shows a group of handsomely uniformed officers receiving several attractive, beautifully clothed ladies on the quarterdeck of their ship. The weather is clear and cold. The ladies are properly bundled against the chill, but enough is revealed of their pretty faces, the lovely dresses under their outer garments, and a fashionable ankle stepping down from the gangway, to give an impression of some of the pleasanter aspects of life during those otherwise grim but nevertheless romantic

---

*Our first rear admiral on active duty was David Glasgow Farragut, appointed in July 1862 in consequence of his capture of New Orleans. He subsequently was promoted to vice admiral and finally full admiral. Unlike Stewart, he actually served at sea in those ranks.

days. The ship is the *President*, flagship of Commodore Stephen Decatur, at anchor in New York harbor. It is Christmas Day, 1814. None of the figures shown is directly identifiable, the scene having been intended not for portraits but to describe a mood and show the clothing. The artist might well have painted it from life, for the deck setting, the cordage and rigging, the proportions of bulwark, deck, cannon, are all impeccable. This is, of course, pure conjecture, but one can imagine him sitting out of the way, unnoticed, swathed in a great boat cloak because of the cold, sketching as the women came aboard in their finery and as the officers of the ship, so straight and tall, so relaxed and happy, helped them down from the bow and received them on deck. Lieutenant Archibald Hamilton, who brought the *Macedonian*'s ensign to the ball in Washington that wonderful night in 1812, could have been one of them. Another might be Lieutenant Fitz Henry Babbitt, also doomed.

One of them, indeed, might be the commodore himself, though this drives the fantasy rather hard. But what is hardest of all to contemplate is that the war had already ended, on that very day, though no one here depicted would know it for weeks, and that authentic representation or not, two of the handsome young officers would be dead in less than a month.

Decatur had been blockaded in the Thames River, upstream of New London, Connecticut, since his triumphant return in the *United States* leading the battle-torn *Macedonian* into harbor. John Rodgers, in *President*, the fastest and most favored of the big 44s, was similarly blockaded in New York. Rodgers, slated for command of the new *Guerriere* then under construction at Philadelphia, had commanded the *President* for four years. There was no hope of evading the blockade off New London, but there seemed a possibility of doing so from New York. Gladly, Decatur accepted the suggested shift to the *President*. Taking some of his old crew and officers with him, he left a corporal's guard in the *United States* and *Macedonian*, set up fortifications at Gales Ferry to block British forays up the Thames River, and moved to New York. If he could get to sea in his new command and outrun or evade the blockading squadron, the speedy *President* might yet make her mark on history and join her illustrious sisters in the victor's circle. More important still to Decatur was the prospect of being the only frigate captain to bring in two prizes like the *Macedonian*. If he could bring off this coup, his stature would be unequaled in our infant navy.

So must he have thought. As usual, there was much training of the crew, much preparation for the anticipated voyage. Decatur would not make the mistake of the lamented Lawrence, but there was time, too, for pleasures, such as having friends and loved ones aboard for Christmas dinner.

On 14 January 1815, a northeast storm drove the blockading British ships temporarily off their station, and Decatur felt this was the best opportunity he would have to get *President* free. Commercial pilots, men well acquainted with New York harbor and its channels, had been employed to see the ship safely over the bar and on her way. The weather was clear though cold, the sea choppy, the wind strong. Visibility was excellent. Marker boats had been put out with shielded lights to mark the channel. Nevertheless, the pilots drove the laden frigate hard aground. For an hour and a half she pounded on the sand and gravel bar, doing severe damage to her bottom, in fact breaking the ship's keel. The sudden stop when she struck, and the heavy shaking experienced as she pounded on the reef, also ''sprung'' (split, or cracked) her masts. The aghast Decatur and his crew tried all the traditional remedies for the fix their ship was in. Lightening ship by pumping overboard the precious fresh water and jettisoning provisions and nonvital equipment, they tried first to back her off and return to the safety of her anchorage. But the wind, favoring departure, only drove *President* harder aground. Decatur ''sallied'' ship (had his nearly 500-man crew run in unison from side to side to rock her) and did everything except jettison ammunition. Finally, with the tide rising, he concentrated on driving over the bar, and in this, after hours of grinding agony and much damage, he was at last successful.

But he had lost hours of critically important time. To Decatur's dismay—though it was not unexpected considering the battering the ship had received—the *President*'s speed had suffered. But now there was no help for it. He was at sea and had to make the best of the

situation. Estimating that the weather would have driven the blockaders to the south, he squared off to run to the eastward along the Long
Island coast, hoping to get clear before they were able to return. It was
a vain hope, for the British commander had been well aware that Decatur was waiting for a chance to get away and correctly estimated the
course he would take had he seized the opportunity of the recent storm.

Even so, the four ships of the English squadron would have been
too late had it not been for Decatur's misadventure on the bar. The
President was sighted running under full sail close to Long Island and
instantly recognized for what she was. Despite her broken bottom,
however, she was still a fast ship. She might have been able to stay far
enough ahead through daylight that, during the next night, she could
hope to give the three farthest enemy ships the slip; but the nearest one,
Endymion, was a fast and powerful frigate with a main battery of 24-
pounders instead of the 18s in *Guerriere*, *Macedonian*, and *Java*. She
was larger than they, too, though not as big as the *President*. Her
commander was Henry Hope, older brother of *Macedonian*'s first lieutenant who, two and a half years before, had vainly urged John Carden
to fight to the death rather than surrender. For Hope, in a loose sense,
the tables were now turned; his was the only blockading ship able to
overhaul the fleeing American frigate, and he made the most of his
opportunity, staying on *President*'s quarter to pound her with his big
guns, but giving her no chance to respond in kind. After enduring a
long cannonade to which he was unable to reply, Decatur turned and
took on his antagonist broadside to broadside, succeeded in his objective of crippling her masts and sails, and then tried to make off again.
But it was not to be; two other British ships had been able to come up,
and after receiving several broadsides from the *Pomone*, with the *Tenedos* in threatening position and the much larger *Majestic* in the offing,
Decatur surrendered.

Decatur has been criticized for not having taken on the *Pomone*.
Conceivably he might have disabled her with a few of his heavy broadsides, and then turned on the *Tenedos* (both of these were 18-pounder
frigates). It was clear he would have had no trouble outsailing the
Majestic. Even today it is possible to wonder why he did not try. But
he and his crew had been thirty-six hours on their feet, under the most

grievous strain, and had already suffered heavy losses in killed and wounded. Lieutenants Hamilton and Babbitt were dead. Decatur himself was wounded in two places. The weather was freezing, with snow flurries. It is easy to say he should have fought on; probably he should, for he might indeed have inflicted more damage on the British, and just possibly have got clear with his damaged ship. But the fact was he and his crew were completely played out, exhausted, and disheartened. *President* had been run to earth by a superior force and could not have done much more, or tried much harder, than she did. She would have escaped scot-free, without detection, if her pilots had not put her ashore, and here lies the question that has never been answered, nor, so far as is known, investigated. With the given capabilities of the British Secret Service, is it beyond imagining that those pilots, or whoever placed the marker boats, made a less than honest mistake?

Decatur and his forlorn crew were taken to Bermuda, given every courtesy, and promptly exchanged for British prisoners of equivalent rank and value. In contrast with the unsympathetic treatment of Lawrence, the British commander went out of his way to assure Decatur's wife of his safety and to facilitate exchange of correspondence between them. The *President*, a legitimate prize of war even though captured after peace had been signed, was retained for the British navy. In dry dock, however, her hull was found so badly damaged from having been aground that, after the customary "taking off lines," she was scrapped, and a new ship of the same design, also named *President*, constructed in her place. It was this *President* that Herman Melville describes as racing the old *United States* in his book *White Jacket*.

When Decatur returned to the United States, far from being criticized he found his stock higher than ever. He was promptly given the new *Guerriere* in place of Rodgers (now heading the newly created Board of Naval Commissioners), along with a squadron of fast frigates and smaller support ships, and ordered back to the Mediterranean Sea. Eight days after the treaty of peace with England had been ratified, President Madison asked Congress to declare war on Algiers, which had been particularly unfriendly during the recently concluded conflict. This was done on 2 March 1815. Less than three weeks later, Decatur, still recovering from his defeat in the *President* and wild with eagerness for battle to "vindicate his honor," set forth on his mission; he met and demolished the *Mashouda* on 17 June; on the thirtieth, on the decks of the *Guerriere*, he dictated an uncompromising peace treaty with Algiers. In the process, he made a bitter enemy of William Bainbridge, who thought he had earned the right, and was preparing, to enter the Mediterranean with a much bigger fleet. But Bainbridge had been delayed by problems with his new flagship, our first line-of-battle ship, the *Independence*. To him therefore fell the ignominy of following after Decatur had skimmed the cream of the venture—and this, from the man who only eleven years previously had also gained glory at his expense by burning the *Philadelphia* after Bainbridge had run her aground and surrendered her, the older man could not stand.

Of the second victory, the Battle of New Orleans, which took place on 8 January 1815, the consequences were significant. But it is its prelude that concerns us here. This consisted of an attack on an American privateer, the *General Armstrong*, a 9-gun brig with a crew of ninety men, which had anchored in the port of Fayal, in the Azores, on 26 September 1814. Her skipper, Samuel Reid, was an officer of the navy who, "wearying of service in blockaded frigates," as he put it, had obtained leave of absence to go privateering. The accumulated depredations of privateers during the two wars with Great Britain did far more damage to her trade—the lifeblood of England—than did the exploits of our navy. Reid, who commanded the *General Armstrong* for four extremely profitable cruises, was one of the best.

The day *General Armstrong* arrived in Fayal, three British warships took station off the port and began preparing to attack her. It was obvious that Fayal's neutrality would not dissuade them from their purpose; so Reid ran his little ship close into shallow water where the deep-draft ships of the enemy could not follow, and made strenuous defensive preparations. The attack came that very night. It was repulsed with heavy losses. Despite protest from the Portuguese governor, the British commander resolved upon a second attack the next night. This he made with overwhelming force, estimated at twelve boats and four hundred men—only to meet with another costly defeat. Next morning the smallest of the three British men-of-war took station as near to the *Armstrong* as she could, opened fire, and was herself repulsed by the accurately aimed fire of the privateer's only heavy gun, a pivot-mounted long 24. However, the British ship inflicted enough damage that Reid now recognized his position as hopeless. He thereupon scuttled the *Armstrong* and got ashore to safety with his men, having had 2 killed and 7 wounded. By contrast, the British lost 120 killed and more than that number severely wounded.

The *Armstrong*'s spirited defense won national acclaim for Sam Reid, but the most important result was more immediate. The British squadron had been designated to augment General Pakenham and Admiral Sir Alexander Cochrane in their planned assault on New Orleans. The losses at Fayal slowed the arrival of these reinforcements, causing still further delay in the British campaign against that important Southern city. No less a figure than Andrew Jackson himself, after the victory at New Orleans that put him on the path to the White House, wrote, "If there had been no battle of Fayal . . . there would have been no battle of New Orleans." What Jackson meant was that had the British attack taken place as originally scheduled, in November 1814, he would not have had enough time to ready his defenses, and would not have been able to contest capture of the city.

It is also appropriate to note that Jackson could not have been successful had not his right flank, to the south, been anchored by naval forces in the Mississippi River under Master Commandant Daniel T. Patterson, whose services he strongly praised.

The British had recently burned Washington and unsuccessfully attacked Baltimore. Now New Orleans was the target, and the American defenders had learned something from the debacle at Washington and the successful defense of Baltimore. Patterson had a small fleet (two sloops and a number of the Jefferson gunboats) and, although initially in disagreement with Jackson over where the British would attempt their landing,* cooperated with him with verve and ingenuity.

---

*Jackson believed the British would first attack Mobile, considerably to the east of New Orleans. Patterson strongly disagreed, pointing to the logic of their landing in a position to threaten the bigger city much more quickly, and even accurately predicting the route the invading force would take. He was fortunately able to convince Jackson, who moved his force from Mobile to New Orleans only six days before Admiral Cochrane's fleet anchored in the nearby sound.

The defense of New Orleans was a model of joint operations between inspired army and navy commanders.

Author's comment: This recital of the events of the War of 1812 has omitted many of the cruises and operations which ought normally to be included in a proper history. As noted, however, this is not a "proper" history. It is the story of our navy and how it grew into what it is today. Many may dispute my selection of the shaping influences, and one case omitted from the text certainly deserves this special footnote. This is the cruise of the *Essex*, 32, Captain David Porter. Still armed with a main battery of carronades instead of long guns, she departed the United States in October 1812 with orders to rendezvous with Bainbridge in the *Constitution* and cruise under the latter's command as commodore. It was another instance of a planned squadron that never materialized. Failing to make contact with Bainbridge, Porter rounded Cape Horn, entered the Pacific, and began capturing British whaling ships. He engaged in this occupation for the whole of 1813, supporting himself entirely from the stores of his prizes and in the process becoming commodore of a nice little squadron of the best captured ships. He totally destroyed the British whaling industry in the South Pacific—a neat blow against England, though without effect on either the outcome of the war or our subsequent naval development. This did, however, demonstrate what an imaginatively handled raider could do with a large radius of action in an unprotected area: a lesson used by the Confederate Navy's raiders half a century later, by German raiders of both world wars—and by submarines as well.

While the *Essex*'s short guns doubtless provided a dividend in extra space during this long cruise, surely much appreciated by her crew, they were a detriment contributing to her capture when HMS *Phoebe*, 36, and *Cherub*, 18, trapped her against the coast of Chile with speed impaired through loss of her main topmast. Well aware of the particular deficiency in his antagonist's main battery, Captain Hillyar of *Phoebe* stationed his ships at long range and pounded *Essex* to pieces. It was not chivalrous, but it was his duty. The defense put up by the *Essex* was tremendous, as was the damage she endured before hauling down her flag.

The War of 1812 passed into history with the Treaty of Ghent, signed in that city on Christmas Eve, 1814—although the news did not reach the United States until February. When thoughtful persons scrutinized the provisions of the treaty, however, they were puzzled to find no mention of the causes of the war or their resolution. The fact was, the reasons the United States had declared war were no longer operative after the defeat of Napoleon and his exile to Elba. England, suffering terrific strain under the threat from France, had been forced to ignore temporarily many of her own cherished beliefs concerning the rights of her own citizens, and had not matured enough to understand the arrogance of her behavior as seen by others—most especially by a newly independent country, hardly yet free from old antagonisms, and far from mature itself.

In America and Canada, as well as in England, however, there was general satisfaction at the outcome. The question of Canada had been settled for all time; moreover, it was the last time arms of any kind were used on that extraordinarily long border until, by mutual consent, the Great Lakes were used for training during World War II. England's urgencies over European commerce were ended with the end of Napoleon's "empire," and some of her citizens may even have dimly perceived how important to their own future a free and powerful United States would become only a century later. And as for the newly independent nation in America, in her "second war for independence" (not an inappropriate title), the United States had proved its mettle. After a very poor beginning, she had reestablished the ability of her army to campaign, and give battle, on equal terms with the best Europe had to send against it. The navy had tested itself against the British navy, and had shown itself able to defeat the standard of the world. Most important, the United States had established itself as a power to be reckoned with whenever her interests appeared to be importantly concerned.

After being disestablished in 1785, placed under a "great reduction" (the Peace Establishment Act) in 1801, and surviving the Jefferson administration's poorly considered "gunboat policy" of 1806, the United States Navy was at last firmly established as an indispensable necessity for the nation. A three-man Board of Naval Commissioners, comprised of its most highly regarded officers, was established to provide the navy secretary with professional advice for the conduct of its affairs. Most important of all, it had attained public understanding and approbation, and for a few years held almost as high a place in the public esteem as the Royal Navy of Great Britain held in the eyes of loyal subjects of their king.

It was well it did so, for the events of the next several years greatly reduced that esteem. Had it not been for the reservoir of pride built up by the successes of the second war with England, these events might well have nearly destroyed it a fourth time.

6

The Slow Advent of Steam

The period between the War of 1812 and the Civil War has been described as a lackluster time when our navy did some cruising and a little exploring, and fought the advent of steam propulsion because it hated to soil its clean white sails with smoke from a dirty stack. Not quite. It was a very busy and useful time, during which the U.S. Navy participated in the location and founding of Liberia, had its only mutiny, blew up two cabinet members and a senator, invented the beer-bottle-shaped gun, fought in the Mexican War, explored the Arctic Ocean and the Antarctic continent, opened up Japan, and twice captured California. The effects of the Industrial Revolution were tremendously important to navies, naval ships, and the techniques of sea power. Our navy also had a few interesting adventures—some apocryphal, some even comic—and indeed did take a long time to accept steam as being here to stay. There is a grain of truth to that indictment, though not to the idea that our navy was opposed to powering its ships that way. The facts were far more subtle, for the argument was not over steam at all.

After 1815, one thing was clear to everyone, in and out of the navy: the fourth emergency in four decades had just terminated. The prestige of our navy was at its height. It had fully recovered the acclaim of the Truxtun and Preble years, and had indeed gone far beyond that. For the first time, the American navy did not have to face the burning question of whether it should continue to exist. This, at least, had been settled for the foreseeable future. Never mind that the War of 1812 seemed to have settled little else; it had, in fact, settled a great deal. Indecisive in all other ways, the War of 1812 was the greatest single factor in preparing the United States Navy for the destiny that awaited it.

Not unnaturally, the heroes of that sailing-ship war saw no other evolution than more of the same, better in degree but otherwise unchanged. After 1815 a period of stagnation set in, most obviously shown by the ships they built, even though some of them could rightly be called masterpieces of warship design. For years, we built copies of the *Constitution*. As a frigate there could be no better. She became the standard and we built many more ships like her, as well as bigger ones. The *Ohio*, a large and beautiful 74-gun ship of the line, designed and built by the redoubtable Henry Eckford in 1820, was for years considered the epitome of wooden battleships. Nearly as big as Nelson's *Victory*, she was an excellent sailer, was said to "handle like a frigate," was stable in the wind, and carried her guns well clear of the sea. She was the favorite command in our navy; seagoing officers of all navies praised her. In the War of 1812, she would have been magnificent.

But the world had passed her by. It had passed beyond all these great ships. By 1840, we were building and operating them only as monuments to past glories. For example, though memorialized in dramatic paintings, *Ohio* served in all only six years under way. The remainder of her time was spent as a receiving ship (moored at a navy yard to provide housing for transient crews) or "in ordinary" (preservation status). So it was with all her sisters, including the biggest sailing warship ever built for the U.S. Navy, the huge *Pennsylvania*, built for 120 guns (pierced for 132) and a crew of eleven hundred men. A colossal waste of shipbuilding talent and money, her sailing career lasted only a week—the time it took her to sail from the Philadelphia Navy Yard, where she was built, to the Norfolk Navy Yard, where she spent her life slowly rotting away until set afire in 1861 by retreating Union forces.

Equally archaic and far more deadly to the navy was the still extant tradition of the code duello. Probably the most sensational incidents in the navy of this period were two duels—one that took the life of the widely admired Stephen Decatur, and the other, planned by the same pair of malcontents who had plotted against Decatur, that did not take place. If it had, it would probably have cost the life of another popular naval hero, Oliver Hazard Perry—but he eluded his enemies by dying of yellow fever while on an expedition to South America. Jesse Elliott, the malcontent of the Battle of Lake Erie, had determined to kill Perry in a duel to avenge his wounded pride. Seeking support, in 1818 he allied himself with James Barron, the disgraced skipper of the *Chesapeake* in 1807. There is reason to believe that Elliott was the prime mover of the entire affair; that his motive in pushing Barron into a duel he really did not want was to create a parallel to his own intended duel with Perry. A century and a half later, Barron looks more like an object of pity than the villain he made of himself in 1820,* and it is the opinion today that Jesse Elliott is the man to blame for the resulting tragedy.

Elliott and Barron agreed to act as seconds for each other in the duels they desired to initiate, the reluctant Barron egged on by his captious friend. It is, however, true that some of the letters Decatur wrote to Barron in response to the latter's own intemperate correspondence (in which the fine hand of Jesse Elliott is evident) are worded in inflammatory language, as if Decatur felt Barron lacked personal courage. Barron might have quietly bowed his head to one more indignity—he had received many since 1807—had not the vindictive Elliott been at his elbow. But it is also evident that Decatur was trying to

---

* A review of the details of the *Chesapeake* debacle and the court-martial testimony indicates that, although he certainly deserved much—perhaps most—of the blame, there were others worthy of censure who were protected, and Barron did not receive a fair trial.

avoid a duel while, step by step, Barron's letters finally elicited the commitment he wanted.

Decatur was then one of the three naval commissioners, the other two being John Rodgers and David Porter. He asked each of his colleagues, separately, to be his second (the necessary go-between to arrange the details), and both not only refused but attempted to dissuade him. But this was too late, for by this time he had agreed to meet Barron. There is nevertheless a hint, though only the barest, that Porter or Rodgers might have still entertained hopes of somehow preventing the duel from taking place. Both had argued with Decatur that his honor did not require it. By protocol, his second had to be a peer, and by refusing him they may have hoped to buy time to begin the delicate counternegotiations necessary to break the inexorable chain of events. Rodgers cannot have failed to remember how seniors had prevented the duel between himself and Barron, thirteen years earlier.

But if either had harbored such ideas, Elliott undoubtedly thought of them too. It was then that Bainbridge, who reputedly had not spoken a single word to Decatur since being upstaged by him in the Mediterranean during the war with Algiers in 1815—he had snubbed him on every possible occasion since—suddenly sought him out to volunteer to act as his second for the on-coming duel.* Decatur, needing someone and glad to believe Bainbridge's bitterness was at last ended, accepted. After that, things moved very rapidly. There is no other indication that Bainbridge ever forgave Decatur, and both seconds wished to expedite the duel.

Whether or not Elliott prompted Bainbridge's involvement at this point, these two men arranged all the details privately. Neither one, apparently, held much if any consultation with his principal. The seconds agreed to the extremely short range of eight paces, selected a meadow in Bladensburg, Maryland, just beyond the borders of the

---

*Arranging a duel was not easy to accomplish. They were unlawful. All participants, including seconds and the doctors customarily present, were subject to arrest on charges of murder, attempted murder, or being an accessory. However, these penalties were seldom enforced when high-ranking persons were involved. In the Decatur-Barron duel, as with the Hamilton-Burr encounter, there was not even the hint of official investigation.

District of Columbia, and saw to it that the duel took place at dawn on a cold and bleak day of March 1820—even though, at the last minute, both principals appeared willing to patch up the quarrel. Decatur and Barron both fell to the ground wounded. Elliott, proving the truth of the Lake Erie rumors of his lack of personal courage, left Barron lying where he had fallen, leaped into the carriage in which they had arrived together, and fled. Unbeknownst to all participants, Porter and Rodgers had secretly—and separately—journeyed to the dueling ground on horseback (thus proving their culpable knowledge of the duel). After the shots were heard, Porter approached the tragic group, saw both principals lying on the wet ground, and witnessed Elliott's furtive departure. Indignant, Porter ran back to his hidden horse, pursued the carriage containing Barron's fleeing second, caught up with him a couple of miles away, and using language itself worthy of a challenge, forced Elliott to return to the dueling ground to assist his wounded principal. Decatur, aged only forty-one, died several hours later in his beautiful house facing Lafayette Square in Washington, D.C.* His widow, Susan, never recovered from the shock of awakening in an empty bed and shortly thereafter having a group of men bring her mortally wounded husband home to die. She moved from Washington to Georgetown (then a separate city) and lived the life of a recluse for forty years, bitterly denouncing the navy that had robbed her of both husband and the political future they had aspired to.

James Barron remained on active duty in the navy where, because his first commission was dated in 1799, he ranked over everyone except Rodgers. He was never given another sea command (some say Susan Decatur had extracted a promise from President James Monroe to this effect), but this amounted to little compared to his being elevated to the position of second-highest officer in the navy. In 1838, when Rodgers died, he became the senior ranking officer.

To the country at large, the death of Decatur came as a shock second only to the similar death of Alexander Hamilton at the hands of

---

*The house, designed by famous architect Benjamin Latrobe, is now the property of the National Trust for Historic Preservation.

Aaron Burr, then its vice-president, sixteen years earlier. But there was a much longer lasting and more debilitating effect, so far as the navy of the United States was concerned. It was not simply that Decatur, the most popular and heroic naval hero, had been killed, or that Perry, equally heroic and almost equally popular, had been marked for the same fate, by the same malcontents.

The navy, as an institution, had condoned the whole disgraceful proceedings. Several highly placed officers had been well aware of the impending duel but had not prevented it, contrary to law though it was; Bainbridge and Elliott, the two high-ranking seconds, had actually facilitated it. Worse, Barron and Elliott not only got off scot-free of any official action—they retained full official respect and authority. Barron retired from active service in 1848, at the age of seventy-nine. Elliott, sixteen years younger, served until his death at age sixty. For more than twenty years, both discredited officers had charge of the lives and well-being of younger officers and men. The notoriety both malcontents had earned shadowed them through the remainder of their long naval careers, but this was unofficial, and in the public perception not nearly equal to the honors they received daily through their elevated rank. No one could understand or respect an institution able to countenance such a travesty. The discredit brought on the navy was subtle but long lasting, one of the reasons for the miasma of distrust of naval officers (contrary to our army's experience) that plagued it until recent years.

The period between 1815 and 1860 was also a time of complacency as the heroes of the famous naval war rested on past laurels. For ambitious younger officers in search of new distinction, the only career examples lay in the techniques of glory-seeking. But for them there were to be no opportunities like the quasi-war with France, the Barbary wars, or the War of 1812. The aura of the commander at sea was slow in fading, and the younger officers succeeding to command responsibilities felt keenly the lack of opportunity for renown. Numerous letters and books attest to this. So do several little-heralded incidents.

In 1842, Commodore Thomas ap Catesby Jones, in command of the U.S. Pacific squadron, was incorrectly informed that war had begun between our country and Mexico. Accordingly, he proceeded to Monterey, the capital of California, fired off a few cannon as a show of force (they were taken as a salute), and then summoned the Mexican governor to surrender. The governor demurred, claiming he had not heard of the war but, faced with superior force, yielded gracefully. Only two days later, poor Jones, learning that the rumor of war was false, had to restore the captured territory. There was no battle, no loss of life, and no injury to anyone. The incident was passed off with the best of good humor and gentlemanly behavior by all concerned. Nevertheless, the U.S. government felt obliged to have its senior representative in California relieved of his command for the premature action. So Jones's career was the only casualty. (The real war with Mexico began four years later, in 1846.)

Another off-the-target incident happened in 1858, near Tientsin, China. An American commodore, Josiah Tattnall, found himself standing idly by while a combined British and French force attacking Chinese forts appeared in danger of defeat if not annihilation. Having been the beneficiary of professional courtesies on the part of the British admiral, and finally unable to stand aloof, Tattnall moved to the succor of his friends, bringing in both British and American reinforcements. Later, asked to justify his action, he simply said, "Blood is thicker than water"—and thus created for himself a sobriquet that has endured. "Blood is thicker than water" Tattnall he will always be (but the U.S. government was not amused).

Despite these and other incidents, much serious work was going on in the navy between 1815 and 1860. Technological innovations brought about by the Industrial Revolution were coming one on the heels of another. It was a time of ferment, with many looking forward, others hanging on to the old things (sometimes beyond a logical limit), and all trying to adjust to new and as yet not fully accepted ideas. Withal, the navy was responsible at the same time for maintaining the readiness for action that had become its watchword since the debacle of the *Chesapeake* (no ship of our navy, for example, ever again went to sea in the condition she did in 1807). And, of course, this was the era that introduced steam.

More than one person has noted that Robert Fulton had his *Cler-*

mont in steady operation up and down the Hudson River during the entire War of 1812. Indeed, *Clermont's* first trials took place in 1807. Why, then, with the proved ability of steam to move ships against wind and tide, did no steamship figure in that war? (Actually, *Clermont* did, in her own way; she was the most dependable source of supplies for MacDonough's fleet on Lake Champlain.) The answer lay in another consideration: range. The *Clermont* took on firewood for her boilers at either end of her two-hundred-mile route between New York City and Albany. For her, replenishment was not a problem. But the *Constitution's* famous battles took place, successively, off Boston, near the coast of Brazil, and near the Azores. The *President's* second voyage covered some twelve thousand miles, and penetrated north of the Arctic Circle; during the War of 1812 she traveled more than thirty thousand miles. Likewise, the famous cruise of the *Essex* covered the entire southern Pacific Ocean. These three vessels logged thousands of miles at no cost except use of sailcloth and muscle power, neither of which could be said to have been "expended." No steamer could have done as much. The entire storage capacity of the frigates was devoted to water, provisions, and ammunition, and their cruising ranges were limited only by their ability to replenish these critical items. Not until the introduction of nuclear power did ships feel a comparable freedom from logistic supply lines. The low-powered, inefficient, space-consuming steam engines of that day would have been more impediment than help, except in battle.

During the closing months of the War of 1812, there was, however, one steamship in the United States Navy. She was designed and built by none other than Robert Fulton, still smarting over his treatment at the hands of the British navy a decade previous, when he had tried to interest it in his idea for a submarine. This steamship, upon which Fulton bestowed the name *Demologos*, was the final inventive effort of this engineering genius. To practicing naval officers, she was not a success. Very much aware of the vulnerability of *Clermont's* side-mounted paddle wheels, Fulton gave *Demologos* a single wheel mounted midway between two big catamaranlike hulls, with the result that although the ship could move, slowly, she could not steer. Had her engine been sufficiently powerful to give her a respectable speed, she might have been able to control her direction of movement to some degree. But ships need more than the ability merely to steer while moving; they must also be able to maneuver in confined waters—as anyone who has ever handled a boat or ship will understand. A skilled seaman prided himself on being able to cast head or stern in whatever direction he desired regardless of the direction of the wind, and felt powerless only when the wind failed him entirely. Fulton's ship, a tremendously heavy craft with sides three feet thick and an extremely powerful broadside battery, had been designed for harbor defense only and was short and ungainly. It had not been thought necessary to fit her with masts and sails, but her engine and single paddle wheel were actually useful only as a sort of auxiliary power. Normal movement and maneuver were performed by pulling boats and hawsers, or by using capstans to kedge to previously laid out anchors.

Demologos was, in short, useless as a ship of war. She never left New York City, where she was built. She might conceivably have rendered a good account of herself had New York been attacked, though it is hard to envision a warship possessed of any sort of motive power permitting herself to be brought to action by as unwieldy a monster as Fulton's creation proved to be. Fulton died at the end of the war, in 1815, and *Demologos* was renamed *Fulton* in his honor. She remained a curiosity in New York harbor, never moving from it, nor, finally, even from her moorings. In 1829 she caught fire and blew up.

Steamships were seen as having other disadvantages for naval service. Wood, as fuel for boiler fireboxes, occupied entirely too much space for practical use. Coal was much more promising. But since coal also had to be carried in large quantities at the expense of other supplies, it greatly reduced action radius—even for a ship fitted with masts and sails. Paddle wheels reduced the number of guns a ship could carry in her broadside batteries, were extremely vulnerable to gunfire, and would be damaged if another ship laid herself alongside in the traditional fleet action (but the new guns were already demonstrating that the traditional battle alongside was a thing of the past). Danger from fire, always a terror in a wooden ship, was multiplied many times in a ship with numerous fireboxes under her boilers. Boilers could explode if damaged by accident or enemy action. Since engine and boilers were especially susceptible to damage in battle, ideally they should be out of reach of shell fire, entirely below the waterline; this necessitated totally new concepts of ship arrangement and design. And the boilers required distilled water of high quality, far more pure than water for drinking or cooking. No ship could carry enough water to keep them supplied; there had to be provision for making it directly from the sea. Automatically there developed an inflexible need for a dependable distilling apparatus.

It was also true that soot from the stack soiled beautifully scrubbed decks and white canvas sails (no sails were white very long after being put in service, but soot-stained sails were worse, and had to be scrubbed twice as often). And the constant need to replenish the supply of coal in the bunkers laid a new difficulty upon the already hard life of a sailor: "coaling" ship, loading coal into her bunkers, was a terribly dirty job, after which everything on board had to be scrubbed to remove the fine-grained coal dust, black and pervasive, that infiltrated everywhere.

None of these difficulties detracted, however, from the fully appreciated fact that in battle a ship with no dependence on the wind had an inestimable advantage. The problem was only how to capitalize on the potentials of steam at the least cost to needed capabilities already existing.

Demologos, or *Fulton*, was only the first. Two years later, while the *Fulton* was still being visited by curious civilians and astute naval designers alike, the navy list for 1817 shows Congressional authorization for two large steam frigates. Among those who devoted years of his professional life and much of his energy to getting steam power into the navy was Matthew Calbraith Perry, a younger brother of Oliver Hazard of Lake Erie fame. He was the first commander of the *Fulton II*, a fast, successful, though rather small and unarmed side-wheel steamer. Following this duty, Perry was put in charge of completing the *Mississippi*. She and her sister ship, the steam frigate *Missouri*, were fast and powerful, adding to the navy's reputation for good design. *Mississippi* would later serve as Perry's own flagship in the "opening up" of Japan in 1854.

These two big frigates had huge paddle wheels on either beam, each operated by its own engine, and were therefore very maneuverable in close quarters and at slow speeds. An unavoidable deficiency in their gunnery capabilities was that guns could not be mounted in the center of their broadsides, in the areas of the wheels. However, the wheels were protected from the elements and from gunfire by heavy sheathing; while not completely proof against collision or battle damage, they were far better protected than the paddle wheels of peaceful merchant ships. And the machinery inside their big wooden hulls, which had to be at least partly above the waterline simply to operate the great wheels, was given an added measure of protection by building the coal bunkers around it, so that the coal also served as armor.

The *Missouri* had a short history and her end, which deserves description, was most dramatic. On her maiden Atlantic voyage, she had just anchored in Gibraltar harbor and was coaling at night when she caught fire through inexcusable carelessness in handling turpentine. There was culpable negligence, and her fire-fighting measures were poorly executed. The ship was totally destroyed in the spectacular fire, which was witnessed by all the denizens of the Rock as well as by half a dozen warships of other nations anchored there. Among the spectators were some artists, so that numerous drawings, sketches, and paintings of the scene survive. Best known is the often reproduced lithograph by Edmund Fry, now in the Mariner's Museum at Newport News, Virginia. Titled *The Burning of the United States Steam Frigate* Missouri *at Gibraltar, August 26th 1843*, it depicts the doomed ship at the height of the conflagration, showing "the falling of the mainmast and the explosion of the last gun, which occurred at the same moment." The ship is listing to port, illuminated by flames reaching high along her burning masts and spurting from her ports while smoke billows hundreds of feet into the dark night. A number of boats with sailors sitting in orderly rows are clustered around her—none too close, for the heat must have been tremendous and the boats had to be a safe distance away when the fire reached the big warship's magazine.

Crouched on the very tip of the spanker boom is a strange figure, huddled in fear, what appears to be a lone member of her crew who had not been able to escape, a human being in desperate travail—and yet not human. It is Bess, a young female bear, shamblingly affectionate, beloved of *Missouri*'s crew, almost human in her clumsy attempts to adapt to a way of life for which she was totally unsuited. But poor terrified Bess had panicked. Her accustomed sleeping place was high on one of the ship's masts, and no one had thought of her while there was still some semblance of order and discipline on board. Afterward it was too late. Crazed with fear, she crawled out on the spanker boom, as far from the fearful fire as she could, and there awaited her doom. Entreaties from the men in the boats were to no avail—the bear would not budge from her trembling perch, and the boats finally had to be ordered away. Poor Bess died when the magazines exploded. The painting has caught a poignant scene; but so human was the terror of the bear that, not knowing of its presence as mascot, most viewers today see only a tiny, ungainly crew member huddled on the end of the boom and wonder why he was there and not in one of the boats.

The two big frigates were not the only approach to the use of steam. There were other designs, some of them not so well thought through. One, intended to remove some of the known disadvantages of side-wheel steamers, proposed to place the paddle wheels in horizontal slots in the hull, well below the waterline and rotating about a vertical axis. The ship built as an experiment was fortunately small, so that no large loss (except to the designer's pride) was incurred when the new wheels proved entirely useless. The paddle wheels had to be small to fit through a reasonably narrow slot above the turn of the bilge, and this robbed them of some effectiveness. They lost more, however, from the water column pushed through the slots in the reverse direction, and one wonders why this did not occur to anyone beforehand.

Another new idea was the "Stevens battery." This craft was the brainchild of wealthy Edwin Augustus Stevens of New York City and Hoboken. The Stevens family (including a father and an older brother) held many patents in railroading and steam engineering. For a time they competed with Robert Fulton in steamboats and ferry lines, and during the War of 1812 Edwin's father, John Stevens, designed and strenuously advocated a sort of floating and rotating fort, plated with iron, in which, as the floating fort turned on its axis, the guns bore on an enemy in sequence. A somewhat similar idea had been proposed for some of the gunboats of 1803–1808, in that the two guns were to be installed on a rotating platform, facing in opposite directions, so that the recoil of firing one of them would turn the platform and bring the other gun on target.

In the 1840s, with war expected against Mexico, Edwin Stevens proposed an invulnerable warship, built of iron, powered by steam, and armored by the sea itself. One design, seriously enough considered to have a sketch printed in a newspaper, evidently contemplated partial submergence in battle (an idea proposed many times by persons unfamiliar with the vital function of reserve buoyancy in a man-of-war). The drawing shows the ship, or "battery"—as the Stevens brothers referred to her—with only smokestack, conning station, and guns visible, the gun crews standing up to their waists in water. Presumably this version was intended to fight only in tropical climes.

Stevens, though he lacked the practical experience to separate the feasible from the infeasible, had ideas that were full of originality—some of them far ahead of their time and some ludicrous today. In 1843 Congress contracted with him to build one of the versions of his battery, but despite heavy investments and sincere perseverance over many years, the ship was never finished. The partially completed hull lay moribund on its ways in Hoboken for a number of years. It enjoyed a brief spurt of interest in 1861, when it was apparent that Confederate conversion of the half-burned hulk of the *Merrimack* into an ironclad warship would require an answer in kind, and again in 1865, when George B. McClellan, the former general of the Army of the Potomac and unsuccessful Democratic candidate for president, took on the job of bringing her to completion. So far as is known, no naval person of reputation or competence was ever involved with her, and the only interest in the "Stevens battery" today is that so much should have been expended for what was so unprofessional a scheme. More profoundly, it was an example of the new ferment in engineering produced by the Industrial Revolution, in which anyone with money and access to a machine shop could expect to build whatever he had a mind to. It well illustrated the consequences when politically powerful persons take action without really knowing whereof they are dealing.

In contrast to this attitude, the opposite existed also: what might be defined as unthinking conservative prejudice against things out of the ordinary. The response to the screw propeller is a case in point. Although it had been experimented with for many years (Leonardo da Vinci designed one to operate, helicopterlike, in air, and David Bushnell's Revolutionary War *Turtle*—the first-known operational war-submarine, which, however, failed in its one attempt to sink a British warship—had one for propulsion and another for depth control), there were those who refused to believe the screw propeller could actually work. The benefits of steam propulsion, first proved with paddle wheels, had a second evolutionary development to go through.

Paddle wheels had several advantages over the screw propeller: they were on either side of the ship, and if turned by separate engines—as nearly all were, at least, in warships—gave it fantastic maneuverability. Some of the warship tactics prior to the age of sail began to appear useful again. In a closely confined battle in a harbor (where nearly all battles in the days of galleys were fought and some were yet to be again), speedy maneuverability was invaluable. The propeller, on the other hand, pushed only from the stern, and thus did not lend itself to maneuverability in confined waters. There was the additional question of whether a ship could steer at all with the source of propulsion just in front of its rudder, as appeared to be the only practicable arrangement, and there was concern over possibly dangerous leakage. Paddle-wheel shafts projected through the hull well above the waterline, where there could be no leak, while the screw propeller created an important leakage problem in the large loose-fitting hole its shaft required below the waterline. Moreover, the paddle blades could easily be lifted clear of the water while the ship was under sail, whereas a propeller created heavy drag and could be demounted only with great difficulty (some later ships habitually did this, however, while others were fitted with a two-bladed propeller that could be locked in the vertical position behind the sternpost, where its drag was least).

But on the other hand, the propeller had the undeniable advantage of reduced vulnerability. Furthermore, it removed an ungainly impediment to fully one-third of a ship's potential broadside battery. And there was no question that it lent itself to a handsomer design.

To the Royal Navy of Great Britain belongs the credit for settling most of the controversy over the respective merits of the paddle wheel and screw propeller. Conservative to the core, it first demanded proof, by a working model, that a propeller could drive a boat. John Ericsson, who had attained the rank of captain in the Swedish army engineering corps, arrived in England in 1826 with an overpowering ego and a head full of engineering innovations. Learning of the Royal Navy's interest, he built and demonstrated such a model. The navy then commissioned the inventor to build a screw-propelled tugboat, and Ericsson spent most of the next five years designing and building it. In 1837, Ericsson became acquainted with Robert F. Stockton, a wealthy American naval officer then on leave in England. When, despite successful tests, England refused Ericsson's new tugboat, Stockton purchased it for his own family's company and prevailed upon Ericsson to leave England's crusty conservatism for America—where Stockton claimed he had enough influence with the Navy Department to cause a warship to be built according to Stockton's own design.

But although England muffed the chance to capitalize on Ericsson's undoubted genius, his screw propeller, upon which he claimed to have made patentable improvements by building an attached circular shroud around it, had nevertheless made an impact upon the Admiralty. England began to build her own screw-propelled warship, the little brig *Rattler*, and launched her the same year Stockton's screw-propelled *Princeton* took the water in Philadelphia. But another century was to pass before the particular advantages of Ericsson's shrouded propeller were to become known and put to use.

In 1843, however, the British navy was not yet fully convinced that a flower-shaped contraption with twisted petals could drive a ship as well as two great wheels that so effectively—and tirelessly—took the place of hundreds of oarsmen. A dramatic trial was therefore ordered. In Portsmouth harbor, in 1845, the paddle-wheel steamer *Alecto* was attached with strong cables stern to stern to the *Rattler*. Both ships had about the same horsepower, the *Alecto* being rated slightly the more powerful. At the agreed signal, the two ships cast loose their moorings in the center of the harbor and started their engines. Water churned astern of *Rattler*, its cause invisible; *Alecto*'s paddle wheels began driving two frothing rivers of water astern, one on either side. The ships had been secured close to each other. Their propulsion turbulences met, joined in little whirlpools. And then, plainly to be seen by thousands, the *Alecto* began to move backward, the *Rattler* ahead. For upward of an hour, the funnels of both little ships belching black smoke as their sweating firemen threw more and yet more coal into the fireboxes, *Rattler* dragged *Alecto* around the harbor while the latter's paddle wheels frothed futilely, churned up the water, and did no good at all. Moreover, *Rattler* seemed to have no difficulty in steering, whereas *Alecto* was being towed backward, totally immobilized, as though she were a barge. That it was not a matter of *Rattler* possessing unsuspected greater horsepower, that more power to *Alecto*'s paddles would not have affected the result, was proved by the fact that everyone saw the paddles turning in the ahead direction, at full speed—and yet she went backward.

No more conclusive demonstration could have been given. The British navy, and thousands of ordinary citizens, had witnessed it. All the navies of the world had watched too, in the person of their representatives or vicariously—it mattered not. None needed to evaluate the decision: it was obvious to all who could see, or read about it. The propeller was clearly the more efficient instrument. Its special problems, such as sealing the passage where its driving shaft went through the stern of the ship while still allowing it to turn freely, or developing new maneuvering and steering techniques, would have to be discovered and solved, somehow accommodated, so that its advantages could be seized upon. Paddle wheels, and the disadvantages they had brought with them, had had their brief day and could now be done away with. The way for steam was clear.

If the years from 1815 to 1860 may with justice be called the period of naval exploration of new technology, it was also an age of naval exploration of new geography. Navies, it was clear, were better suited to such exploration than any other of a country's agencies, and the size of the world was shrinking rapidly. In our navy, in the euphoria following the naval successes of the recent war with England, numerous distant voyages were undertaken. Some were altruistic ventures, impelled by forces that sometimes bore little relation to the results sought, or achieved. Others had a dual purpose, one military, the other scientific. Such a voyage was the *Alligator*'s cruise in the suppression of the slave trade in 1821. She was directed at the same time to investigate possible sites for establishment of a homeland for slaves returned from the United States under the auspices of the American Colonization Society, a member of which made the cruise. *Alligator* was commanded by Robert F. Stockton, and he succeeded in both objectives, for Liberia was in this way located, explored, and founded.

In 1828 Congress began to consider an "Exploring Expedition" and finally authorized one in 1836, appropriating $150,000 for its expenses. But that body had apparently no specific idea of what the expedition should accomplish, other than increasing the sum of human knowledge. It was, in truth, an expression of the greater self-confidence of the country, a development of the national growth, and a reaction to Charles Darwin's recent voyage in HMS *Beagle*, as well as to the earlier explorations of Captain James Cook. Nor were the scientific personnel assigned or volunteering of much assistance, since they immediately engaged in arguments over accommodations for themselves and their equipment, and over their privileges on board. After several commanders had given up and asked to be relieved, the expedition was turned over to Lieutenant Charles Wilkes, himself of a strong scientific bent. The result of his odyssey, which lasted from 1838 to 1842 and included a lengthy cruise along the coast of Antarctica, was the accumulation of many boxes of plants and shells from sea floors and beaches and a series of continual scientific observations of the earth's gravity and climate. In addition, there was a lengthy narrative of three thousand pages composed by the redoubtable Wilkes himself. Some of the things he brought back are visible to this day in the United States Botanical Gardens, in the Smithsonian Institution, and in many private hands (for whom, according to Wilkes, they had been stolen).

During this period, the navy was also both an arm and an avenue of diplomacy. News, cargoes, passengers, diplomatic maneuvers of all sorts, traveled slowly. The world was adjusted to the time scale of a horse or a sailing ship. This was simply the time it took, and all things behaved accordingly. In Europe, perhaps, an inspired rider on a fast horse could go from one capital to another in short order; for America, far removed geographically, a long sea voyage was the only means of communication with the outside world. U.S. naval officers in consequence found themselves in the forefront of our State Department's negotiations with other countries; if not involved in substance, they were nevertheless concerned with transmitting information—or, not infrequently, carrying the messengers, and sometimes protecting them. Often they were the only American officials present and therefore also had to be statesmen—and frequently the force they commanded was important in the negotiations as well.

The situation cut both ways, of course. The senior naval officer on the scene took action in accordance with his carefully written instructions and his best judgment, as the circumstances required. If he had correctly understood and properly applied the national policy, his report would receive support and even praise. Should he err, or should the position in Washington have changed, the administration could disavow him as overzealous or misinformed and, if necessary, discipline him—as had been done when Jones prematurely captured Monterey.

In 1854 the U.S. Navy achieved its greatest diplomatic success. Commodore Matthew Calbraith Perry, with a powerful fleet of steam and sailing ships and bearing an official letter from the President of the United States to the Emperor of Japan, anchored in Tokyo Bay in 1853 and opened negotiations aimed at securing a treaty of amity and commerce with that hitherto reclusive nation. His success at the second meeting, in 1854, was based on thorough study of the customs of Japan and careful preparation to meet the Japanese in terms they could appreciate.

During this same period, the ships of our navy in the Far East were also occupied in protecting the merchant ships of the West (not only our own but those of England, France, and other European nations as well, sometimes in concert with their war vessels and sometimes not) from bandits and pirates in Southeast Asia and China proper. Some pitched battles took place, although in general the obvious superior power of the warships and their landing parties simply overawed the native forces and bloodshed was avoided. Information about these operations, when it got back to the shogun then ruling Japan, facilitated the negotiations with that country.

In 1846, following a series of incidents—not least of which was the revolt of Texas from Mexico in 1835 and its admission to the Union ten years later—the war with Mexico began. In terms of territorial acquisition, this war was the most successful our country has engaged in—but it was against a weak and poorly organized country with endemic problems beyond its ability to resolve. When the war came, Mexico's culture was a hundred years' older than that of the United States, but she could offer no competition, except in the purely personal courage of her citizens and warriors.

The Mexican War, consequently, was a series of victorious expeditions on land and a few desperately fought battles. At sea there were no engagements, because Mexico had no navy with which to contest its control. When the United States decided to support General Zachary Taylor's army, invading Mexico from the north, with a flanking invasion from the east, an amphibious landing was directed at Veracruz. Commodore David Conner, the naval commander on the scene, set a standard for meticulous planning for which he is still remembered; it has since been considered the epitome of such an operation. There was no opposition to the landing, but this only partly obscured the fact that the landing forces were well prepared to handle anything that might have developed. Conner's dispositions were thoroughly studied by the U.S. Marines, particularly in the period between World Wars I and II, and provided a precedent for the amphibious landings in the Second World War.

The main functions of the U.S. Navy, completely commanding the sea on both sides of Mexico, were to support the activities of the army invading from the gulf, to blockade and capture Mexican ports to prevent logistic support from reaching their own armies, and to patrol against the possibility of Mexican raiders preying on American commerce (in the event, there were none, although for a time Mexico hoped to commission privateers in Cuba). Most important for the future of the United States, its navy (with the help of a small army contingent) captured the huge California tract that now comprises the states of California, Nevada, and Utah, most of Arizona, and parts of Colorado, New Mexico, and Wyoming.

The principal figure in the conquest of California was Commodore Robert F. Stockton, fresh from what had become a disastrous relationship with John Ericsson. He had been ordered as junior commodore, second in command to Commodore J. D. Sloat on the Pacific station, but when the inactive and sick Sloat was invalided home, Stockton took over with energy, coordinating army, navy, and marines in a brilliantly executed war of tactical movement, skillfully using the mobility of his ships to transport the tiny available force up and down the long west coast of the continent. In the end, the immense territory, with its extraordinary wealth, was captured with a handful of men. But unfortunately for Stockton, a dispute over command arose in the army that culminated in a haughty refusal to obey orders and a court-martial in which, although he had had nothing to do with the quarrel, Stockton found himself testifying as the officer under whose jurisdiction the breach of army protocol occurred. In this role, his personal qualities were less praiseworthy than his leadership in direct military matters.

Perhaps Stockton had learned something from his experience with John Ericsson. In California, he accomplished a very great deal for his country, and for this he should receive credit. He and Sloat and the two foremost army commanders, Frémont and Kearny (whose quarrel caused the court-martial), are today remembered in California by roads, towns, and cities bearing their names.

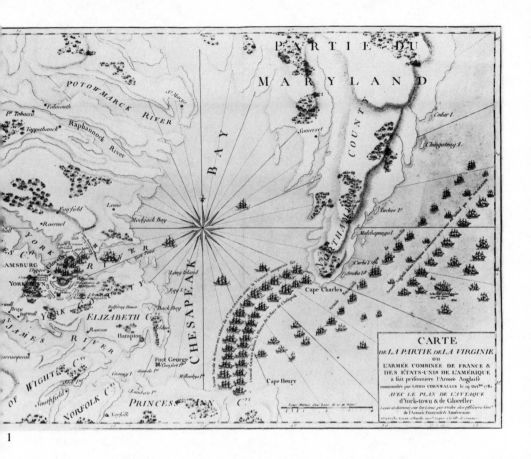

1

1. A fanciful French depiction of the Battle of the Virginia Capes—"The Pivot Upon Which Everything Turned," 5 September 1781—drawn late in the same year. Needless to say, the battle at sea in no way resembled this idealized drawing, but the plight of Cornwallis is well illustrated. *(The Library of Congress)*

3

2

2. The popular concept of what a battle at sea ought to be—a mass of wooden ships pounding each other into oblivion, but only because this was how the British navy idealized it. (The painting, by W.L. Wyllie, was done in 1905.) Except for de Grasse's victory at the Virginia Capes, no such naval battle ever figured in our history, and very few in England's. Jutland, 111 years later, called the second Trafalgar, was not the decisive victory England had hoped for.

3. HMS *Shannon* leading the captured USS *Chesapeake* into Halifax, 6 June 1813. The English artist exaggerated perspective to portray the *Chesapeake* as considerably the larger ship when in fact the two were nearly the same size. Note the stripes in the American flag. *(The Beverly Robinson Collection, U.S. Naval Academy Museum)*

4

4. *The Battle of Lake Erie*, by William H. Powell. This huge painting, which hangs in the Capitol, shows Oliver Hazard Perry shifting his flag from the badly damaged *Lawrence* to the uninjured *Niagara*. With the exception of the nearby port quarter of the *Lawrence*, most of the details shown are not accurate. (Count the stripes in the U.S. flag, and inspect the next photograph.)

5. In 1820, the *Niagara* was deliberately sunk for preservation in the fresh water of Lake Erie. Nearly one hundred years later, she was raised and restored, and is shown here as she looked at the Perry Centennial in 1913. Subsequently rebuilt again, she is now on exhibit in Erie, Pennsylvania.

6. The *New Orleans*, the biggest ship on either side during the War of 1812, was "run up" to this astonishing condition in twenty-nine days, but was never launched. The ship's upper gundeck, with another row of gunports, was never built. This photograph was taken in 1884.

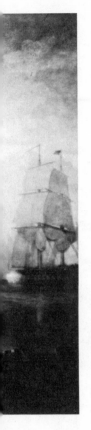

5

6

7

7. Artist's concept of the *Constitution* in combat with the *Cyane* and *Levant* in February 1815. The *Constitution* has just passed between the two enemy ships, firing heavy broadsides from both sides. Now she is about to swing her foreyards to port, "shake all forward, let fly the jib sheet"—and set all sails aback to back down between them again. *(Painting by Carlton T. Chapman)*

8. Robert Fulton's preliminary design (drawn in 1813) for the first steam man-of-war, the USS *Demologos* (later renamed *Fulton*). Designed with a catamaran hull, her engines were on one side and her boilers on the other. The paddle wheel is ridiculously undersized, and the ship, as shown, is clearly impractical.

Demologos

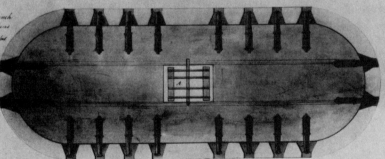

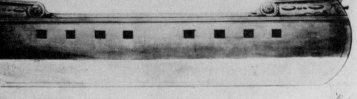

8

9

9. Lithograph showing the explosion of the Peacemaker in 1844. Most of those standing on the gun's left side were killed, mowed down by a huge piece of iron. Captain Stockton and those on the right side of the gun were essentially uninjured. *(By N. Currier)*

10. Like his cousin Theodore, Franklin D. Roosevelt had a passion for ships and the navy. The *Monitor* and *Merrimack* were not the first ironclad warships, but they were the first to be tested in combat and hence signaled the end of wooden fleets. This dramatic painting of the famous battle between the two ironclads, by J.O. Davidson, is from FDR's personal collection.

11

11. John Ericsson, Swedish-born designer of the USS *Princeton*, the Oregon Gun (or Orator), and the USS *Monitor*. The *Monitor* became the model for an entire new class of warship that eventually grew into the modern battleship. Ericsson was a very difficult man, but a genius.

12. Dr. Oscar Parkes of England made the study of battleships his consuming interest. In his watercolor of the USS *Miantonomoh*, one of Ericsson's "seagoing monitors" (the one in which Assistant Navy Secretary Gustavus Fox voyaged to Europe), the beginning of battleship design is clearly evident.

13. The end of the *Tecumseh*. The "torpedo" she detonated separated the hull plates on her port side forward. Having virtually no reserve buoyancy, she sank with extraordinary speed, capsizing in the process. In this drawing from *Harper's Weekly*, men are shown frantically squeezing free through her turret gunports. They had only seconds, and most of her crew went down with her.

14. At Mobile Bay, all the wooden Union ships rammed the *Tennessee*, damaging themselves more than the Confederate ship, but hoping to "bear her down" by their weight. This reasonably accurate drawing shows the ironclad listing and the Union *Lackawanna* riding up on her slanting casemate. Had *Lackawanna* struck her on her low-lying forecastle, *Tennessee*'s bow would likely have been driven under far enough to dip her forward gunports and sink her (as *Merrimack* barely avoided when the sinking *Cumberland* was impaled on her ram).

15. Surrender of the *Tennessee*, surrounded by Farragut's fleet. Of the three surviving Northern monitors, only one was effective: the *Chickasaw*, shown at lower right having just blown away *Tennessee*'s steering chains. The other two had severe operational problems with their turrets. *(Painting by J.O. Davidson)*

Lackawanna butting Ram

Capt. J.B. Marchand.

14

16

17

18

16. The USS *New Ironsides*, whose construction was begun in response to reports about the conversion of the *Merrimack*, was not completed until after the emergency in Hampton Roads. She was a very powerful ship and considered a great success. Although usually depicted with masts and billowing sails, she served most of her time without them, as show here.

17. After capture at Mobile Bay, CSS *Tennessee*, the most powerful of the Confederate "rams," was repaired and taken into the Union Navy service. Her Union crew liked her, in spite of her feeble engines. She was sold for scrap immediately after the war.

18. Admiral David G. Farragut, photographed by Matthew Brady in 1863.

19

20

19. Benjamin Franklin Isherwood's masterpiece, USS *Wampanoag*, from an old glass-plate negative. Once Gideon Welles left office, she was renamed *Florida* in 1869. Her yards have been sent down and she is high in the water with no colors flying—evidence that she is out of commission. Compare with the photo below.

20. After our Civil War, while all European navies were building iron warships with powerful engines, we reverted to wooden hulls and small engines. The *Trenton*, launched in 1876, was rated a first-class war steamer—but her only function was to show the flag. In 1889, she was destroyed at Samoa by a ferocious hurricane; for many years thereafter, her figurehead, a handsomely carved eagle, was on display at the U.S. Naval Academy.

7
Mutiny?

In 1842, there occurred another incident that is consistently deemphasized but that nevertheless had important long-range effects. This was the so-called mutiny aboard the brig *Somers*. The *Somers*, named for Richard Somers, who died when our converted bomb-ketch *Intrepid* exploded prematurely in Tripoli harbor, was a tiny 290-ton training ship. Her crew during the voyage in which the "mutiny" occurred consisted almost entirely of young trainees: apprentice sailors and midshipmen. She also carried a small leavening of experienced officers and enlisted hands, and her captain was a sanctimonious prig by the name of Alexander Slidell Mackenzie, whose wife was a member of the famous Perry family.

An article of faith among followers of the maritime professions is contained in the old saying, "The best place for a young man is at sea." It followed that the environment of a ship at sea was where navy midshipmen and apprentice seamen should receive their training, and the system in vogue until 1842 amounted simply to assigning them to cruising ships where they would be exposed to what they were expected to learn. The popular term for this, still in use, was "the school of the ship." Training at sea has unquestioned merit, honored by annual cruises of some kind by nearly all maritime training institutions. In 1842, the idea that all instruction of midshipmen or apprentice seamen, even in academic subjects like mathematics or physics, should take place aboard ship and preferably under way, was virtually a form of religion. Nevertheless, it had drawbacks.

Aboard ship, officers and petty officers often could not or did not give adequate time to instructing their charges. Although there were outstanding exceptions, they were frequently poor teachers with neither interest nor training in the role. In an attempt to improve the education of the navy's future officers, schoolmasters were assigned to the bigger ships and shore installations, and regular study times were prescribed for the midshipmen or young officers preparing for their examinations. Subjects taught were usually left entirely to the particular inclinations of a ship's schoolmaster, sometimes with her commander's overview and approval. Conscientious schoolmasters generally tried to teach navigation, astronomy, and mathematics, with occasionally something more frivolous, such as English or literature, thrown in. The cramped conditions on board ship were not conducive to study, but even had they been, a single schoolmaster could not effectively cover all the possible subjects, nor, aboard ship, was he usually accorded the rank and prestige necessary to command the serious attention of his students. Invariably he found himself competing with the ship's own needs, which were always more immediate and usually more interesting. Many otherwise motivated schoolmasters were unequal to the special challenges of instructing in an active ship; almost uniformly, whenever they are mentioned in accounts of service in those times, the reference is disparaging.

When a ship was in port was the most difficult of all, for the midshipmen, boys of high school age for the most part, were hard to handle at best. If a ship were to be in harbor for a lengthy period, her crew and officers were frequently reduced and there was neither anything for the midshipmen to do nor anyone to supervise them. The schoolmaster's authority derived from that of the captain; unless he were an exceptional individual and had his captain's full support, he might lose his young charges entirely. There was, fortunately, one such exceptional teacher. William Chauvenet, a graduate of Yale, entered the schoolmaster system in 1841 and quickly impressed everyone who encountered him. In 1842, aged only twenty-two, he took over a school to help senior midshipmen prepare for the examinations for lieutenant. Schools of this type were originally informal—set up aboard ship or ashore, anywhere they were needed. Buildings ashore were far better suited to such use, and over the years some of them took on a form of permanence. The one run by Chauvenet was in the Philadelphia Naval Asylum, an institution for old and indigent sailors. From this it became known as "the asylum school." Chauvenet began immediately to agitate for a real naval school, with a curriculum, faculty, and regular classes. By good fortune, Commodore James Biddle, of the same Philadelphia family that had produced Nicholas thirty-three years earlier, was then serving as governor of the asylum. Biddle, recognizing the importance of Chauvenet's proposals, supported him enthusiastically.

For enlisted men, training in basic shipboard skills was expected to be automatic through their daily duties. Midshipmen were required to learn these skills as well. But all shipboard functions required supervision by someone skilled in doing them. Danger was always present in a sailing ship, for yards and sails were massive, forever in movement, and continually in need of attention; ground tackle—anchors and their associated cables, chains, and hoisting gear—was likewise cumbersome and generally slippery with slime; lines in running and standing rigging were in constant use and often under heavy tension—an unnoticed weakness could, and often did, cause an accident. Yet speed of execution was nearly always necessary, or at any rate demanded by impatient officers intent upon demonstrating efficiency. To a busy ship and crew, the presence of raw recruits was often a hindrance, seldom a help.

There were many criticisms of the system, both from those who begrudged the resulting loss of efficiency and from those who felt the trainees, both midshipmen and enlisted apprentices, were not receiving the attention they should. There was growing pressure for establishment of a true naval academy for future officers (the army had established such a school at West Point years before) and a preliminary training school for enlisted men, where recruits could be better indoctrinated with basic skills before they went aboard ship. Nevertheless, the adherents of the school of the ship continued to win the day in Congress, where new ideas always stumbled over the additional expense invariably accompanying them. In 1841, however, a small experiment had been authorized. In addition to the schools in regular ships, there would be a training ship, a small one of course, expressly designed for and assigned to the initial training of newly recruited sailors and midshipmen. The *Somers* was the result. She was built for that purpose, but in addition, since she was not intended to engage in battle, her designer, Samuel Humphreys (son of Joshua), apparently felt he could indulge his fancy for low and racy lines and make her very fast, almost like a yacht. She was fitted with guns, since they would be needed for training, but her thin sides were not expected to encounter serious gunfire. *Somers*, in truth, could have been described as a large toy. She was launched in 1842, and Commander Mackenzie, the navy's most literarily inclined officer and also something of a preacher and moralist, was assigned to command.

He seemed an obvious choice. The brig was too small to harbor a schoolmaster, logical though it might have been to include one aboard. There was no spare space in her to use for schooling in any case. However, Mackenzie could be trusted to give much attention to improvement of the minds of his young charges. As a writer of books, he would be sure to insist that midshipmen study tomes devoted to navigation, seamanship, and gunnery, and also that they improve their minds by reading some of the classics he would select for them. His known pedantry would be usefully employed supervising the practical training of the teenage boys, many fresh from the farm and recruited as apprentice seamen, in marlinspike seamanship (splicing and reeving ropes, called "line") operating ground tackle, handling small boats, working the sails, and operating the ship's small broadside guns. With nearly everyone aboard new to naval service, his evangelistic streak would also be put to good use: he could be expected to see to their proper moral uplifting. This last point was considered very important.

The *Somers*'s tiny hull, 103 feet between perpendiculars and 25 feet extreme beam, could not have been designed with much thought to what a school ship should be. The "tween decks" dimension (floor to overhead) of her one covered deck, the berth deck, was only 4 feet 10 inches. Her crew would have to stoop lower than in any other ship of our navy, except in the *Somers*'s near identical sister, *Bainbridge*. She had been built for the large complement, considering her small size, of ninety-eight persons, in keeping with her mission as a school ship. Of these, the two commissioned officers in her planned complement (one of them the captain), the three warrant officers, and fourteen seaman billets could be counted as experienced. There were also to be seventy-two apprentices cooped up in her, sleeping in hammocks from closely spaced hooks in a part of the berth deck, and seven midshipmen. The midshipmen's berth, also graced by the 4-foot 10-inch overhead, measured 8 by 14 feet. Here the seven youths were to sleep, take their meals, and keep all their equipment.

Almost immediately there was a complication. A ship exclusively devoted to training would relieve the cruising ships of much of the nuisance of instructing ignorant sailors and stupid midshipmen, and give the ships more space for other purposes. Nearly all seized the opportunity to divest themselves of an unpopular duty. Recruits and midshipmen were assigned to the *Somers* with no apparent regard for her extremely limited space, so that before setting forth on his first cruise, Mackenzie protested at the excessive number of persons detailed to his tiny craft. No one paid attention. When the *Somers* finally got under way, she was literally bulging with more than 120 men aboard, most of them young trainees.

No vessel could have been less appropriate for training new navy men, whether destined for the quarterdeck or "before the mast." She was too heavily sparred, too shallow of draft, too slender of hull. She was fast, but also very tender, easily listed over by a strong breeze. She had no reserve for awkwardness in handling sail, or in trimming ship, or any other of the many functions in which an unhandy crew of apprentices might be less than expert. Skill was required to sail her, and continual vigilance against sudden disaster. Many a better-found ship had foundered, sometimes even despite adequate warning of bad weather. Mackenzie was concerned about this, and he was right to be so. Four years later she did indeed capsize and sink, with heavy loss of life, and in 1863 so did her sister, *Bainbridge*.

In 1842, Mackenzie had already celebrated his thirty-ninth birthday and had served twenty-five years in the navy. At that age, Stephen Decatur's career had been nearing its end; he was twenty-four when he leaped to fame from the burning *Philadelphia*, and thirty-three when his big *United States* captured the *Macedonian*. Oliver Perry, Mackenzie's brother-in-law, commanding a squadron, had won the Battle of Lake Erie when he was only twenty-eight. At thirty-one, John Rodgers had commanded all U.S. naval forces in the Mediterranean. In contrast, Mackenzie, at thirty-nine, commanded only a small school ship.

Mackenzie was a friend and occasional visitor of Washington Irving, by whom he was much influenced, and who had assisted him in the promotion of his first book, written after a lengthy furlough in Europe, *A Year in Spain*. By 1842 he had published six books, three of them biographies (of John Paul Jones, Stephen Decatur, and Oliver Hazard Perry). None of his writings was enduringly important, but to a navy composed of persons not noted for literary accomplishment and easily awed by a bound book and the speaking acquaintance of Washington Irving, they were uncritically accepted as brilliant. As it happened, the last month of 1842 and the first half of 1843 became the period of Mackenzie's greatest output, consisting entirely of self-justification for hanging three members of his crew because he believed they were plotting to convert their swift little school ship into a pirate corsair.

It was, in fact, simple murder, an act of panic by an unstable man who had no business being autocrat of his own little kingdom in a ship of the U.S. Navy. Yet such was his ability at presenting the facts to his own advantage that even though one of his victims was the son of Secretary of War John Canfield Spencer, and even though Spencer vowed to avenge his son's death by seeing to it that Mackenzie was tried in civilian court for first-degree murder, the guilty captain got off scot-free, acquitted by a navy general court-martial of all charges. No official notice was taken of the eleven more "mutineers" he brought back under arrest in the *Somers*, some in irons. Despite the fact that their "confederates" had been hanged for the crime of mutiny, or planning to mutiny, not one was even brought to trial. In dribs and drabs, they were all simply released and allowed to return home, the obligated time remaining on their enlistments forgotten. The charges under which they had been manacled for weeks and jailed for months in New York were never vacated, nor any lesser ones brought. In today's more legally sophisticated society, they could have sued for false arrest.

There was, however, an unlooked for result. Everyone in the naval service—and to a greater extent yet, the body politic of the country—was uneasily aware there was something radically wrong with an organization that could justify high-handed action like Mackenzie's. The new school-ship program, barely begun, came under intense scrutiny, as did the older system of sending midshipmen and recruits to sea to learn by doing. As discussed later in this chapter, a radical change was indicated, and the upshot was the founding in 1845 of the United States Naval Academy.

The sordid details: Philip Spencer, the eighteen-year-old son of the New York politician who was Tyler's secretary of war, had long been in rebellion against his father. He did poorly in school, was slovenly in his person, was almost never without a cigar in his mouth, and hated constructive activity or authority of any kind. He drank to excess (though evidently he could hold liquor well) and insulted his elders whenever he thought he might do so without punitive consequences. He was either cross-eyed or walleyed, a physical affliction that may have been one of the root causes of his personality disorder.

With little understanding or sympathy for his troubled son, his father thought to straighten him out by procuring him an appointment as midshipman in the navy. This was less than successful; Midshipman

Spencer had already been turned out of two ships as unsuitable for naval service when Secretary of the Navy Abel P. Upshur, acting on the personal request of his colleague, reversed the most recent dismissal and sent young Philip to the new school ship. No doubt both cabinet officers believed that if anyone could wean him from his debauched habits, the *Somers*'s schoolmaster-preacher-skipper, over a period of time, would be able to do so.

But the concatenation of circumstances worked exactly in the opposite direction. Spencer's last-minute arrival crowded the tiny midshipmen's quarters unbearably. Spurned by his messmates because of his antisocial appearance and behavior, the young misfit found companionship among the enlisted men of the crew, thus breaking another taboo. The apprentices were flattered that an officer, even an unprepossessing one, should find them interesting; the older hands gave him lip service in return for surreptitious handouts of food, tobacco, and liquor—some from the midshipmen's mess, some that the well-heeled lad purchased ashore. Philip Spencer might have become a writer of adventure stories had he lived, for he apparently had a good imagination and evidently indulged himself and his audiences with fantasies about turning pirate. Unfortunately for him, one crew member reported what he had heard. Mackenzie had Spencer seized and searched. A paper with Greek characters in his handwriting was found concealed in his neckerchief, supposedly listing those to be killed and those who would join him in his piratical adventure.

The *Somers* was homeward bound. She had crossed the Atlantic twice, touching first at Madeira and then at Monrovia, capital of the newly created Free Liberia, and now she was within a week of reaching her next port, St. Thomas, Virgin Islands, still one of the avenues for the illegal importation of slaves to the New World. The last known case of piracy on the high seas had occurred ten years before, but the illegal slave trade still existed and, by international agreement, all ships in the slave trade were defined as pirates.

The accusation by a crew member trying to curry favor, when added to Spencer's Greek paper, was enough for the humorless and credulous Mackenzie. Deciding that he and his loyal crew members were in mortal danger, he clapped the hapless midshipman in hand and leg irons and put him under guard on the quarterdeck. (There was nowhere he could be confined in the packed spaces below.) Soon Mackenzie had two other unpopular crew members in irons also, and within a couple of days a number of others: four more at first, finally a total of eleven, were added. During the next four days, as the *Somers* steadily approached St. Thomas, Mackenzie directed his executive officer and the others in the wardroom to consider the situation and give their opinion as to the action he should take. After a number of recommendations that did not satisfy him, he received what he subconsciously must have wanted to hear: Spencer and the other ringleaders constituted a danger to the ship and should be put to death. They were hanged immediately.

Two days later the rakish training brig entered the lovely harbor of St. Thomas, then a Danish dependency. Tarrying only long enough to take aboard fresh provisions and water, she got under way as quickly as possible, bound for New York.

Historian Samuel Eliot Morison has given as his opinion that Mackenzie was justified in directing the executions, but this conclusion cannot stand inspection. By naval regulation (and tradition too), only the highest naval court, a general court-martial, has power to award the death penalty, and even then it cannot be carried out until approved at the highest level. This was the rule in 1842, and it is the rule today. After a half century, our code of naval law was thoroughly established. A mere captain of a ship could not (in 1842, any more than now) order a general court-martial. He could—and may still—order lesser courts-martial, each rigidly limited as to offenses that may be tried and punishments that can be awarded. In 1842, as today, only flag officers were empowered to order general courts-martial. (Nowadays, the proceedings and verdicts must be reviewed by the officer ordering the court, who may not be a member, and forwarded for review up the chain of command until they arrive before the judge advocate of the navy, its highest-ranking law officer.) Mackenzie, only a commander in rank, ordered no court of any kind. He directed his officers to "advise" him, sent them back repeatedly until they said what he wanted to hear, permitted the accused men no opportunity to defend themselves, and after rendering the fatal judgment allowed them only ten minutes, later extended to an hour, to make their peace with God.

Summary executions have taken place during war, particularly in the case of spies and traitors, but whenever possible due form of trial has always been carried out. Even pirates were brought in for trial if at all possible.*

In the *Somers* case there was no war, and no lack of facilities at her captain's disposal. There was an American consul in St. Thomas, with the customary consular powers. The prisoners, still in irons if the captain felt it necessary, could have been turned over to him for further transport, under charges, to New York or any other port. In his defense, Mackenzie made much of his fears that his disaffected crew would rise and take the ship during those last two days, but this is in fact a measure of the hysteria that gripped him. The charge of planned mutiny was never proved, nor was it ever tried, either aboard the *Somers* or later, when the remaining eleven unexecuted accused could have been brought before a court in New York City. To this day there are only the suspicions of a paranoid captain, based on garrulous talk by a lonely misfit as reported by a favor-currying member of the crew, that a mutinous plot existed.

Even had there been, it seems hardly credible that the officers and loyal members of the crew, with access to the ship's arms chest, could not have held control against many times their number of fearful and demoralized youths, up to 14 of whom were already in chains. The far more likely scenario is that the whole crew was terrified, and had good reason to be.

Whatever rationale may be offered for Mackenzie's conduct, the fact remains that Midshipman Spencer, Boatswain's Mate Samuel Cromwell, and Seaman Small were hanged in contravention of their rights under the laws and Constitution of their country, without due

---

*Piracy is generally considered to have ended in 1834 with the execution of one Captain Gibert, but his sentence was preceded by a full trial in Boston.

process, without the knowledge that their execution was being debated or that a "trial" was being held—without an opportunity to speak even as witnesses in their own defense. And once the decision had been taken, they were killed with cruel speed.

The *Somers* continued to New York with eleven prisoners manacled on deck, and on arrival her skipper sent off the first of several reports to Secretary of the Navy Upshur. When news of the executions came out, initial reaction was favorable to Mackenzie; but as reporters pried more deeply it began to shift against him. From here on it is difficult to assess exactly what took place, and why. Much was kept secret, passed only by word of mouth, with no records kept. Secretary of War Spencer was of course outraged. He had never understood Philip, nor made much of an effort to help him; but his being hanged for mutiny was a different matter. What occurred in Washington in the private councils that must have taken place between the two cabinet members can only be guessed at. What is clear is that Upshur defended his skipper and the navy, that a dispute of grand proportions erupted between the two politicians, that the skipper of the *Somers* never admitted there was ever any question whatever of the absolute probity and rightfulness of his action nor of the compassionate feelings with which, as he described the moment, he painfully gave the dreadfully difficult orders. And after official investigation by a court of inquiry and trial by general court-martial, all of which lasted dreary months, Mackenzie was exonerated of all wrongdoing.

The press behaved as might have been expected, eagerly following the story and developments in the court-martial so long as there was public interest. A short time after the initially favorable press reports, a spirited defense of the three unfortunates had appeared in a Washington newspaper, signed only by the letter S., which stated their side of the case and generated a great deal of interest. The popular guess of the time was that its author could only have been Philip Spencer's father. Though conclusive proof does not exist, the intimate knowledge the writer had of the case, and of Philip Spencer personally, could hardly have been possessed by anyone else. As the press began to delve more deeply into the matter, James Gordon Bennett of the *New*

York Herald wrote scathing editorials. James Fenimore Cooper angrily denounced Mackenzie in letters and articles. And Commander Mackenzie, as soon as the chill began to descend, asked for an official court of inquiry.

This court, acting in much the same way as a civilian grand jury, after examination of all the evidence and circumstances gave as its verdict that there was no cause for further action against Mackenzie.

In the meantime, Cromwell's young widow, Margaret, had become associated with Secretary Spencer in an effort to bring Mackenzie before a civilian judge on charges of murder. Charges were actually preferred, but, citing the possibility of double jeopardy, the judge before whom they were placed refused to admit them while the court of inquiry was still in session. Several weeks later, however, once the naval court of inquiry had found no basis for prosecution, there were four days during which civilian charges could again have been filed. None was.

On the fourth day, in disregard of the verdict of the court of inquiry, Navy Secretary Upshur nevertheless ordered a general court-martial and directed that charges be preferred. With his signature to this order, the rule against double jeopardy stood again between Mackenzie and civilian justice.

A few editorialists, chief among them Bennett and Cooper, publicly excoriated Mackenzie before and during his trial and denounced the results of the court-martial when they were given out. The verdict rendered was perhaps what one might have predicted, given the composition of the court and the high-level advice it may have received— although it is only speculation that such advice was ever given, or that the members of the court would so have betrayed their sworn oaths. But it is not guessing to state that the navy's top officials wished to sweep everything under the rug for fear of public reaction, that the members of the court shared this desire, and that all of them had the wit not to do this hurriedly. Strangely, in the face of these circumstances, nowhere was a rationale found for the indecisive action of the new principals in the affair: the secretary of war, John Spencer, and Mrs. Margaret Cromwell, a recent bride and now suddenly a widow.

In fact, Margaret Cromwell and Secretary Spencer had had several meetings. A former judge experienced in military legal procedures through his service as the army's chief, Spencer well knew how and when to bring charges before a civil court. Without question, he was well aware of the four-day hiatus during which he could have re-filed the charges of murder. What is inexplicable is why he—and the widow—neglected this opportunity and so precipitously abandoned their campaign to clear his son's and her husband's names (not to mention that of Seaman Small, who seems to have had no one taking his part). Speculation suggests a plausible answer, but, not surprisingly, there is no hard evidence.

That the two bereaved persons did not pursue the matter, while an opportunity they could not have failed to recognize lay before them, can lead to but a single conclusion. Not only must they have felt there was nothing to be gained, no rehabilitation of the dead or vengeance upon their killer, but not improbably there was something more that might yet be lost. There are only two possibilities, both of which could have been operative at the same time. One can imagine Secretary Spencer reviewing all he could find out about his son's last days. He was well aware that his son was a troubled youth, that at times he behaved strangely. He would have found out that his son consorted more with the enlisted men than with his fellow midshipmen and superiors, that he patronized them with gifts and hard drink, and perhaps with something more: strange drugs. There comes down to us the account of an excursion on shore in Liberia, from which young Spencer returned in a very different mood, approaching euphoria, from that in which he began it. Secretary Spencer would have found out that his son had varying moods on board as well.

Not much was known of mind-altering drugs in 1842, beyond the fact that they existed. Typically, there was much misinformation as to their effects, but one thing had already changed greatly. They no longer had their earlier social acceptance. They were becoming viewed as responsible for aberrant behavior, as addictive, and as responsible for many awful permanent effects. The case against drugs had only begun to be compiled, but social reaction was already severe. Drug users were held in utmost scorn, fear, and condemnation: lost souls whose families bent every effort to keep the dread affliction secret and whose friends avoided them. To John Spencer, even the unsubstantiated suggestion of drug abuse by his son would have been personally devastating, politically very damaging, and at the same time awfully believable. Drugs could explain all of Philip's abandoned behavior, but the cost to his family, in particular to his father, would have been very high.

The secretary of war would also have discovered that his son was disliked, distrusted, and—I speculate—he may have been suspected of being "queer." There may well have been a suggestion of perversion, an accusation extremely easy to make and, by the clandestine nature of both accusation and alleged behavior, extremely hard to defend against. The merest whisper of it was enough to make one a pariah. Society was adamantly unforgiving. Reaction, even to mere rumor, was horrified and spontaneous. Neither wife nor father could wish such accusations to become public property.

Today, historians and psychologists alike accept—given the conditions that were known to have existed in ships of the time—that sexual deviation must have been far more common than anywhere admitted. Philip Spencer's continued association with members of the crew, to the exclusion of his own peers, might easily have brought this suspicion, justified or not, upon him. The merest hint of such a calamitous accusation would have been sufficient to demolish utterly both the father and the wife, and nothing else could have had such extraordinary effect. But there had to be a credible, powerful source for the suggestion, one whose hinted concern could not be ignored. There was but one man who could fill these qualifications, only one man to whom Spencer would have to listen: his colleague in President Tyler's cabinet, Abel Upshur, the Secretary of the Navy. It is not generally known that he was the older brother of one of Mackenzie's close friends— thus establishing a perfect conduit for informal communication. It is only speculation to infer that the dread insinuation was made. But something obviously happened to cause Spencer to stay his obvious move. In the meantime, to ensure that the case would remain within naval jurisdiction in case of a later stiffening of his colleague's will, Upshur hastened nevertheless to hale Mackenzie before the most powerful naval court, where he would be subject to legal jurisdiction but, through the double jeopardy rule, safe from civilian processes of law.

He may even have assured Secretary Spencer that the navy court would prosecute Mackenzie to the full extent of naval law, certainly as stringent as applicable civilian statutes, but if so, Upshur then came close to actually breaking his word. The man he ordered as president of the court-martial was Matthew Perry, Mackenzie's other brother-in-law. Perry permitted the accused the widest latitude in conducting his defense, which he dramatically did, in uniform, while the prosecutor was hindered at nearly every turn. The voluminous proceedings took months. The court's final verdict on each of the several charges preferred was not guilty. Three days later, in the tiny wardroom of the *Somers*, the brig's doctor, who had reluctantly gone along with Mackenzie's demand for a death sentence, committed suicide. No doubt he was in despair, but no explanation has ever been offered.

Noteworthy in naval court-martial proceedings is that they can adjudge a higher level of acquittal than civilian courts are allowed: over and above a verdict of not guilty, they can "most fully and most honorably acquit." This higher degree of innocence was, and is still, sometimes adjudged when the court feels it necessary totally to absolve the accused of any suspicion whatsoever. But Alexander Mackenzie's court-martial, despite the pressures upon it, could not bring itself to approve his action to this degree. It had done enough for him. The navy's dirty linen would not be further exposed to public view. The embattled skipper was simply found not guilty. Nothing was said about being "most fully and most honorably acquitted." All the same, it was enough.

Many of the facts about the "mutiny" in the *Somers* must forever remain in the realm of speculation. Historians whose training permits them only to record what is provable often rail at their inability to state more than what they can prove by reference to some established fact. Persons desirous of concealing something, or controlling history's later reports on events within their interest, know this well. The *Somers* is a case in point.

With Mackenzie's less-than-full acquittal he was nonetheless protected from further legal action. He was safe from all but the slow verdict of the society and the service to which he had caused such devastating damage. Secretary Spencer came to realize he had been tricked and was so angry with Secretary Upshur that they nearly came to blows at a cabinet meeting and had to be separated by other members. Mackenzie continued writing, remained always totally convinced of the rightness of his decision aboard the *Somers*, but had no further impact on the navy.*

In the quiet recesses of thoughtful consideration there can sometimes be the ground swell of what might be called a psychic reaction. The nation, and more to the point the navy, knew that three men had been summarily hanged without any of the protections guaranteed by the Constitution and by law. The man who killed them had been judicially protected by two successive naval courts, which seemed partisan, to say the least. Murderer or not, he had been held above the law.

In public opinion the navy had already suffered a great deal from the support it gave James Barron after his murder by duel of the popular Stephen Decatur—support that extended to keeping him in service in positions of responsibility and trust. Barron was now the senior officer on active duty, in charge of a naval station. There, judging by the *Somers* case, he could inflict death upon anyone he chose, and would be defended and even exonerated by the navy. His friend, Jesse Elliott, whose intent to kill the navy's other young hero, Oliver Hazard Perry, was well known, was also still responsible for the well-being of hundreds of young officers and sailors. Nor was it lost to public perception that despite the high rank and honor given to both, neither

---

*Our destroyers numbers 17, 175, and 614 have been christened *Mackenzie*, but they were named after his son, Lieutenant Commander Alexander Slidell Mackenzie, Jr., who was born in 1842 and was killed in action in Formosa in 1867. The official *Dictionary of American Fighting Ships*, contrary to usual custom in such cases and despite the identical name, does not list the senior Mackenzie as one of those whom the ship honors.

Barron nor Elliott had behaved admirably during the War of 1812, and, according to well-substantiated reports (but passed clandestinely, for fear of Elliott's revenge), Elliott had cravenly run away from the fatal dueling ground at Bladensburg.

The navy was fast gaining the reputation of being a law unto itself, in which the officer class lived and acted by tradition and rules foreign to the rest of the population.

Things seemingly could not have gotten much worse, but the ultimate apostasy took place only a year later, when the great gun on the *Princeton*'s forecastle killed two members of the cabinet, one of them Abel Upshur, now elevated to the State Department portfolio. Others were Upshur's successor as secretary of the navy; the father of President Tyler's fiancée (and possible future United States senator); a promising diplomat; and four other persons—and came close to taking the life of the President. In 1815, the navy was one of the objects of the nation's greatest pride. Only thirty years later it had sunk to a nadir of national regard. It was clearly headed for the most precarious of times, but by great good fortune there were some farsighted men in positions of authority.

James K. Polk became president in 1845, succeeding John Tyler, who had not been nominated for a second term. His secretary of the navy was George Bancroft, who was already much concerned over what he had been hearing about the service now under his charge. For forty years the army had had an academy for its cadets located at West Point, site of a famous Hudson River fort. There, among other things inculcated into impressionable minds, high and idealistic principles of probity and honor were fostered. Proposals for a similar navy establishment had always been overturned because of the cost, on the grounds that in any case the school of the ship produced the best training for young men of the navy, whether officers or enlisted.

The *Somers* had demonstrated, however, nearly all the bad features of such a system of training and none of the possible good ones. Principal among its faults was that the ship would be at sea, out of touch with the land, or the country, for long periods during which it would be entirely subject to a man over whom there could be no supervision whatsoever. Whether he was a good teacher and schoolmaster or a poor one, while the ship was at sea there was no way his absolute control over his little school could be monitored. Even under the best of circumstances, operation of the ship must always take precedence over simple schooling. In a sense this was endemic to all ships at sea, any of which might by misfortune have a poor or stupid captain, or one who became so under stress. But a naval ethic that would support capital punishment on suspicion alone was unsupportable under any rationalization. Naval officers had to have a better understanding of their duties and responsibilities than this.

Bancroft came into office with determination to set up a naval academy on the lines of the one at West Point. With the willing acquiescence of Secretary of War William L. Marcy—whose son (schoolmaster William Chauvenet's enthusiastic assistant at the Philadelphia Naval Asylum) was a "passed midshipman" in the navy— Bancroft took over old Fort Severn at Annapolis, Maryland, for the site and quietly moved the residue of all the various schools and schoolmasters into it.* Chauvenet, who had ceaselessly campaigned for a better educational system and was noted already for his energy and brilliance as a teacher, was appointed to head its faculty. The

---

*Mindful of the difficulty in getting Congress to fund the establishment of a naval academy (several previous proposals had been defeated), Bancroft resolved to set it up in a series of small steps, each carefully planned to be within his statutory authority. Initially, for example, no new faculty was appointed; the old schoolmaster system was simply changed, the schoolmasters ordered to Annapolis instead of to various ships and stations. All the shore-based schools, including the Asylum School, were terminated, and any midshipmen in attendance were ordered to Annapolis. The academy was in place before anyone except Bancroft's advisers (many of them prominent officers) was aware it existed.

During this period there were several strong moral reform movements in American society as a whole, some of them quite militant, such as the abolitionist wing of the antislavery movement. Prohibition of alcoholic beverages was another popular reform movement. As a moral evangelist, Mackenzie had much company, probably most among the abolitionists. One of the basic purposes behind foundation of the Naval Academy was to get midshipmen away from grog, then routinely served aboard ship (it was abolished in the U.S. Navy in 1862), and all the other "bad influences" reputed to exist in men-of-war. Franklin Buchanan, its first superintendent, was noted for his moral rectitude, and this was one of the reasons for his selection.

Another story about the founding of the Naval Academy relates that Bancroft himself, as acting secretary of war, officially signed over Fort Severn to the navy on a day when Marcy was temporarily absent. The deal had nevertheless been made, and Marcy was in full accord. One might even speculate that the signing detail was deliberately set up.

establishment of the "Naval School" was announced in 1845. Its first class graduated the following year.

Today, at the Naval Academy at Annapolis, the spot where old Fort Severn stood can be found only on old maps of the grounds. It is well removed from the water now, for much heavy fill has been placed around it during succeeding years. The fort itself, a nondescript round structure, is long gone. In its place stands a looming granite building of great size and sprawl: Bancroft Hall, the midshipmen's dormitory, largest in the world, housing more than four thousand young men and women. Not far away is a new academic building named Chauvenet Hall.

To start developing continuity, tradition, patriotism, honor, and idealism, Bancroft needed the right superintendent. For this post he picked the most outstanding man he could find, Commander Franklin Buchanan, a well-known and highly thought of officer from Maryland.

Buchanan was not, however, to make his mark on naval history through supervising a school, even one as important as the U.S. Naval Academy. Fate had a much more dramatic role, on a much broader and more highly colored tapestry, destined for him. But he would have to wait some fifteen years longer.

8

The Gun and the Ship

In November 1839 the steamer *Great Western* landed in New York after a stormy passage from England, and among the debarking passengers was a stocky, powerfully built, onetime artillery captain in the Swedish army, holder of a degree in engineering from Sweden's prestigious University of Lund. After thirteen years in England as a steamship propulsion designer and engineering consultant, John Ericsson had chosen the United States as the mold in which his future would be shaped. Now thirty-six, Ericsson was already known as a man of boundless energy, a meticulous designer who spent hours over his drawing board and, so it was said, sometimes was there all night, curling up in his clothes alongside it for a few hours of sleep before going back to it in the morning. He had also developed a reputation for obstinacy and controversy.

Ericsson had met Robert F. Stockton in 1837. Born in 1795, Stockton had been a junior officer during the War of 1812. He thirsted for the combat reputation that might have been his had he been only a few years older, or had the war lasted longer. In this he was by no means alone. All of his contemporaries felt the same. Our navy of this period was being run almost exclusively by the successful frigate captains of 1812, many of whom were not many years older than he and most of whom were still in excellent health. The system by which an officer could aspire to higher rank depended entirely upon the creation of a vacancy above him, generally through death. There was no mandatory retirement system. Even superannuated officers manifestly not able to cope with the rigors of naval life often could not be persuaded to retire. Instead, encouraged by personal friends and family, they sometimes remained on the navy list into their dotage—and in so doing blocked advancement of everyone junior to them.

For years, Stockton had chafed at the situation. The navy had expanded in the aftermath of the War of 1812, but that was over. Now, if anything, it was retrenching slightly. There seemed no opportunity for advancement even remotely similar to that enjoyed by men who had had the good fortune to be born a little earlier. But Stockton was unique among his contemporaries in possessing the means of doing something about his disappointment.

Sharing Mackenzie's ambition and frustrations, but far ahead of him in position and wealth, Stockton found a different solution. Both men compensated in unusual ways, and it was fortunate, in the long run, that there was only one of each—for each brought incalculable damage to the naval service.

Stockton happened to be one of the most politically influential citizens of the state of New Jersey. Grandfather Richard Stockton was a signer of the Declaration of Independence. His father, also Richard, had served in the U.S. Senate from 1796 to 1799. The city of Princeton was built on land originally granted to the Stockton family in early colonial days. By 1837, Robert had involved himself in state and national politics to a degree that astonished his fellow officers in the navy (and that today would not be permitted). He had not hesitated to take long leaves of absence without pay from active duty in order to perform political work, had cultivated friendships among senators and governors, and had rendered financial support where it seemed needed.

In his methods of operation he was more like European or South American nobility than a regular naval officer of the United States and he had not the slightest idea of the dislike he thereby aroused among his less-endowed peers in the navy. Now in his early forties, still holding the rank of lieutenant (the next higher rank was captain), Stockton entered into direct rebellion. He had joined the navy to achieve fame and reputation, both important to the American aristocracy in which he moved. To a man of his temperament and wealth, the prospect of being doomed to mediocrity was not to be accepted. His trip to England, made while on leave of absence from the navy, had the deliberate intent of finding something in the industrial ferment in that country with which to support his effort to become the construction supervisor, and in command when ready for sea, of the soon to be built steam frigate *Missouri*.

Years previously, the navy had authorized construction of two big steam frigates, to be named *Mississippi* and *Missouri*, but no important work had been done on them until recently, when Matthew Perry was given an unusual set of orders, much of which he had actually written himself. He was to supervise building and then command for a short time the little *Fulton II* to try out the most recent ideas for steam propulsion. Then he was to become construction superintendent for the first of the two great steam frigates, the *Mississippi*. The other frigate had not yet been assigned. Could Stockton but have that ship put under his charge, to put into her his own new ideas, some original development to make her efficient, fast, powerful, and innovative, obviously better than her sister, his future would be assured.

So, at any rate, he believed. He had not studied steam engineering as Perry had, but would soon make that up by getting the right professional assistance, hiring the man himself if necessary. He had ample financial and political resources at his disposal. He needed only to put together a plausible proposal that his friends in the government and Congress could legitimately support. To a person in his position, this was not an impossible thought.

The U.S. consul at Liverpool, Francis B. Ogden, who had some background in metallurgy, had received assistance from Stockton in obtaining his diplomatic post. Apprised of the purpose of Stockton's voyage to England, he repaid part of his debt by arranging a meeting with the controversial but generally well regarded Ericsson. Ericsson's credentials were impressive, and so was his performance. Once he had satisfied himself as to Stockton's bona fides, new ideas burst from his eager mind with overlapping speed. And for Stockton, Ericsson was the answer to his dreams. He set himself to convince the Swede to throw his lot in with the new nation across the Atlantic, under his sponsorship. It was a move to which Ericsson was not averse.

To Ericsson, a vista of opportunity opened with Stockton's statement—not totally implausible for the time—that the U.S. government was about to authorize him to build a frigate for its navy in accordance with his own ideas. In many long conversations, Ericsson and Stockton, each with his own motives, explored what they thought a warship of the new age ought to be. Stockton told Ericsson that he possessed the political power to have him designated the designer and builder of the ship, with himself, Stockton, in charge of the project. There was not yet an effective steam-powered warship in the United States Navy, despite the fact that foreign navies had been building them for years. That Stockton expected to command the new ship impressed Ericsson not at all. That he himself was to have a free hand in her design and construction impressed him greatly. The time, both men felt, was propitious.

Perry got the little *Fulton II* into the water the same year Stockton and Ericsson met, and was beginning to make plans for construction of the first of the two big frigates originally projected in 1817, the *Mississippi*. Stockton, now ready to make his move, preceded Ericsson to America to set the necessary events in motion to get the second ship for himself.

Along with a complete set of preliminary plans for the great new warship, the self-confident Swede had arranged to have shipped to America considerable equipment he had already built or purchased to go into her. Foremost among this was a huge gun he had had forged and given its first proof-tests in England. Stockton and he had agreed it was to be the prototype for guns to be built in America for the *Mis-*

souri's main battery. Despite later claims by Ericsson's biographer that the gun was entirely designed and fabricated according to Ericsson's direction, there is evidence that Stockton, Ericsson, and Ogden discussed it at length. Central to their concern was to arm the new ship in a novel and invincible way, with the biggest guns in any ship, able to fire either solid shot of unprecedented weight or the lighter explosive shell of the same diameter to unprecedented range and with unprecedented accuracy. A ship so armed would be the most fearsome warship on the sea, able to command immediate surrender from any ship not able to race away. She should, therefore, be fast under sail or steam, with powerful engines located entirely below the waterline, where enemy shot that might penetrate the hull could not reach them.

To fire the heavy shot, the guns would have to be much heavier and far stronger than any guns heretofore built. The three men explored the options. Cast bronze guns lacked the strength to contain the powerful propellant charge required. The malleable metal would deform under each successive firing, no matter how large the gun, and would anyway be totally prohibitive in size and weight. Cast steel guns had the strength if uniformity of the metal could be assured, but they were prone to catastrophic explosions, which there was no way to predict. Wrought iron was the strongest and most dependable metal known, but despite many attempts, no large gun made of wrought iron had survived proof-testing. Small guns, rifles, and pistols had been successfully made of wrought iron for years, but no large cannon had. On the other hand, large forgings for propeller shafts and other heavy machinery were common. The problem lay in the manufacturing process. To forge a large shaft, many heavy wrought-iron bars were laid side by side under a tremendously heavy, machine-operated hammer, heated to a red heat, and then welded together by repeated hammer blows. The result was a long shaft with great longitudinal or twisting strength, but with little strength in the transverse direction, where it depended entirely on perfect welds. To construct a wrought-iron gun it would be necessary to lay up a short, tremendously thick, solid shaft and then bore it out to the desired diameter. This had been tried already, but the propellant charge on firing tended to separate the welds, and all such guns had failed by coming apart. However, Ericsson was sure he could overcome this difficulty, and the decision was made to have a wrought-iron gun forged at the best English foundry, the Mersey Iron Works, and bored to a 12-inch caliber. Ericsson designed the gun and pre-scribed its initial testing. It was shipped to America in 1841.

Proof-firings carried out in America, again under Ericsson, re-sulted in a small crack through which water seeped during the standard water-pressure tests. Ericsson thereupon had two bands, or hoops, forged in different sizes, with the strength lines around instead of lengthwise (this was possible given their large circumferences), and had their inner and outer surfaces precisely machined to carefully cal-culated dimensions. When expanded by heat, the bands were posi-tioned around the cold breech in sequence, one on top of the other, and allowed to cool slowly. In cooling they gripped it with tremendous force, thus employing all their tensile strength to prevent the possibil-ity of explosion. Many further firings confirmed the success of this innovation. After well over a hundred proof-firings, the gun was cer-tified for use.

Stockton's assurances to the contrary, however, the navy did not reward his enterprise by assigning him to the second big steam frigate. The *Missouri*, it was decided, would be a duplicate of the *Mississippi*, and she was given to someone else. Nor did a third ship in the 1839 program, the strange little ship with the submerged horizontal paddle wheels, go to him either.

Stockton pulled out all the political stops, engaging all the power and influence of his formidable family. Congressional allies and recip-ients of previous favors were marshaled. But the navy proved un-usually lethargic. There was little enthusiasm in it for Stockton's project. It did not help that his enemies looked jealously at the naked power he was displaying. A favorable decision was slow in coming. Ericsson had become distinctly restive, even suspicious that Stockton's power was not all he had claimed, when the long promised Congres-sional action came at last, in 1841. A political debt was paid: Stockton had actively assisted William Henry Harrison and John Tyler in their campaign for the presidency and vice presidency, and when Harrison died one month after taking office, Stockton turned all his political savoir faire to the support of Tyler's succession to the presidency. It was a difficult situation for Tyler, since he was the first vice president to become president in this manner, and although a former governor of Virginia and U.S. senator, he had been almost an unknown in the campaign. In gratitude, Tyler offered Stockton the post of secretary of the navy, but Stockton asked instead for approval of his project as it now stood, to build an entirely new ship, as yet unauthorized, in which he could incorporate all the new ideas teeming in his and Ericsson's brains. With Tyler's strong help, the thing was done.

The authorization as finally passed by the Congress, however, was not to build a 3,000-ton ship of the first class, but a much smaller one, a 700-ton corvette (a sloop of war with all guns on a single deck, exposed to the weather). By unprecedented act of Congress, however, she was Stockton's—and Ericsson's—to design and build as they desired.

Although the allowed size of their ship was a disappointment, now that they had the desired authority Stockton and Ericsson devoted all their energies to designing and building the most innovative, most powerful, fastest, and most nearly invulnerable ship in the U.S. Navy. She would change the basic design of all warships, make all nations sit up and take notice. Totally revolutionary in concept and design, she would be the ship the Lords of the Admiralty in Whitehall could have had five years earlier. Her sides, while made of wood, would be far thicker than the sides of a normal corvette. She would have the screw propeller, not yet accepted by England, and engines of a new design by Ericsson, small enough to lie in the bottom of the ship completely below the waterline, fast enough to be directly connected to the propeller shaft, and with a minimum number of vulnerable moving parts. Her furnaces would have air blowers so that a tall stack for draft would be unnecessary. She would burn anthracite coal, thus be virtually smokeless. The smokestack or chimney would in fact be telescopic and could be lowered at any time to conceal her character as a steamer. By coming into being on the other side of the Atlantic she would salt the wound Ericsson was by this time eager to inflict on his erstwhile friends in England, who had so cavalierly refused to accept his steam tug even after it had so completely proved itself.

The new ship was to be named *Princeton*, chosen by Stockton to honor his family seat. To Ericsson this mattered not at all. What mattered was that he had carte blanche to embody in her all his ideas and theories. To this, Stockton (now at last a captain) had firmly agreed. For armament, *Princeton* would have to be restricted to what her light corvette hull could carry; she would be made more effective, however, by a simple range-finding device (which Ericsson had already invented) and by his equally innovative automatic firing lock that fired all guns in a broadside simultaneously at the proper elevation. Furthermore, she would have two big swivel guns capable of being fired to either side, one mounted on the forecastle, the other in the center of the quarterdeck aft. One of them was to be the great gun Ericsson had already built, which he called the Orator because it was intended to speak with authority. Despite the new ship's small size, with this gun—the largest and most powerful gun ever made, able to shoot a 225-pound solid shot virtually in any direction—the *Princeton* would be able to knock out any battleship in the world long before the larger ship could get her own battery in range. For both Stockton and Ericsson, she would be a convincing demonstration of their theories of what a technologically modern warship could and should be.

The accounts of her construction stating that *Princeton*'s hull was of iron, and that she was therefore the first iron warship, are not correct. Her hull was of white oak, though considerably more heavily built than was usual for a corvette. Her innovations lay in propulsion, fire control, protection of her machinery and gun power, as well as the ability, with draft for combustion provided by her air blowers (the forerunner of forced draft), to steam without making smoke or giving any outward evidence of her machinery. With her sails furled as well, she could move as if by magic. Ericsson was the designer and inventor; Stockton the promoter and patron, or, to use his own title for himself, the "projector." The arrangement seemed ideal, since each man got what he wanted. Had Captain Stockton been willing to leave it at this, the navy and the nation would have benefited.

But two such widely diverse characters as Ericsson and Stockton could not long pull in the same harness. Disagreement no doubt began in small irritations, but it became important and long-lasting, and it began over the gun. The Orator was not merely an oversize but otherwise ordinary ship's cannon. It was a massive wrought-iron gun, many times the size and weight of the largest ever made (except for the famous cannon now standing at Edinburgh Castle, in Scotland, and one or two slightly smaller but equally unsuccessful ones on display in old castles in Sweden). Designed to use a 50-pound charge of black powder, the Orator could throw a 225-pound shot a distance of five miles or more, much farther than any other gun had ever been able to reach. The original idea had been to arm the big *Missouri* entirely with such guns.

But the *Princeton* was not large enough to carry an entire battery of Orators. She could carry only one, which would be mounted on her forecastle on a pivot so that it could be fired in any direction, and a lesser pivot gun, probably firing a 64-pound shot, would be mounted on her quarterdeck. But if the second pivot gun could also fire a long-ranged 225-pound shot, the little ship's battle capability would be effectively doubled. Stockton was already restive with Ericsson's dominance over all technical decisions. This one, being over a naval gun, in his opinion was clearly within his own expertise; without consulting Ericsson, he contracted with a New York firm for a new gun. It was to be of the same bore and caliber as the Orator, like it made of wrought iron, but with external thickness hammer-welded on to the breech instead of shrunk on. It would fire the same huge projectiles. To ensure adequate strength, the captain directed that it be made much heavier in the breech than Ericsson's gun, twelve inches greater in external diameter, and of course several tons heavier. Crucially important, however, was the fact that it had no shrunk-on bands. The extra metal welded around the breech by hammer blows had all the faults of previous wrought-iron guns: little strength with which to resist the transverse bursting power of the propellant charge. Then Stockton added insult to injury by forcing Ericsson to supervise boring the 12-inch diameter hole down the center of the great gun-tube.

It was now late in 1842. The Navy Bureau of Ordnance and Hydrography had been created a few months earlier, with Captain William Crane, years senior to Stockton, in charge. It is evident that he tried to do his duty, but his responsibilities and authority were as yet ill defined. He had heard that Stockton had turned down the post of secretary of the navy under President Tyler, but obviously he still enjoyed the President's full support and approbation. Crane knew as well that Stockton had also been given a free hand by Congress to build and outfit the *Princeton*. Already Stockton had haughtily informed Crane that he would proceed "any way I may see fit considering my entire responsibility in the matter." Stockton had his way in whatever he wanted; he was a formidable adversary, one whom it would be damaging to confront, a man of high temper and tremendous influence, which he would not hesitate to use. In another incident, also associated with the *Princeton*, Crane's own superior had feared to contest him. Still, Crane was clearly uneasy over the great guns being built for the new ship and over the uncontrolled procedures employed in their tests. He asked the opinions of other ordnance experts in both the navy and the army as to the safety of such big wrought-iron guns and received prophetically discouraging answers: The experience to date had been all bad.

In the meantime, Daniel Webster had resigned as secretary of state, Abel P. Upshur relinquished the navy portfolio and took his place, and David Henshaw, a new navy secretary destined not to be confirmed by the Senate, took the post. Upshur's departure robbed Crane of the best support he had in his new office, but he nevertheless prevailed on Henshaw to direct Stockton to prove the new gun before the Navy Department would pay for it. Obediently, Stockton towed the gun to sea aboard a wooden barge, fired five shots with gradually increased powder charges, and reported the gun fully proof-tested. He then ceremoniously hoisted it on board the *Princeton* and baptized it Peacemaker with champagne.

To Ericsson, who had nursed the Orator through upward of 150 firings in a sandbank at the Sandy Hook proving ground, the tests placed on the Peacemaker were a travesty. The gun, described glowingly as "the largest mass of iron that had up to that time been brought under the forging hammer," and "beyond comparison the most extraordinary forged work ever executed," had been superficially forged and poorly tested. No determined action had been taken to counteract the possibility of some concealed weakness in the metal. Peacemaker was more than half again as heavy as the Orator—as though the extra iron could take the place of Ericsson's carefully thought out solutions to the age-old problem of bursting—and this, to the Swede, was if anything more dangerous than if the gun had been made too light. Thin wrought iron might stretch—elasticity was one of its properties—but the very thickness of such a big casting guaranteed that if any stretch whatever took place the outer circumference would begin to crack.

Ericsson was also forced to make changes in the design of the ship to accommodate the greatly increased weight of the new gun, which was moreover to be located high, where it would affect stability, and—a small but significant thing—placed on the forecastle, traditionally the location of most honor. Ericsson's gun would go aft, on the quarterdeck, in place of the 64-pounder originally slated to be mounted there. Stockton was adamant. He refused to listen to any so-called scientific argument. *Princeton* was his ship, his creation, and he needed no foreign inventor to tell him how to deal with shipboard guns. It was the first serious conflict the two had had, and in Stockton's eyes, control over his own project was at stake. Citing the loudly voiced claims that American wrought iron was superior to any in the world (better even than that of Sweden), that forging such a gun was now well within the capacity of American industry (as the New York company had assured him), and that, on principle, an American warship should carry guns made in America, he flatly insisted on having his way, and angrily refused to listen to further discussion. Beaten at last, Ericsson lapsed into silence.*

---

* No one in 1843 fully understood the behavior of metals under stress, nor the molecular results of the forging process, but Ericsson's engineering mind had hit upon what became the standard means for opposing explosive force by metals in tension. (British development followed a variation of the technique: thin red-hot strips of iron or steel wound around the gun barrels; British guns were therefore described as wire-wound.)

Intent upon asserting himself over his difficult partner, Stockton had made the classic mistake of closing his mind to the voice of truth. Ericsson's opinion that the Peacemaker had not been properly designed or proofed, and therefore was unsafe, did not change. It would burst one day, and men would probably be killed. Then he would be proved right. In the meantime there was nothing he could do about it. Given the circumstances, his silence is understandable. Nevertheless, as subsequent events were to show, he should have continued to protest and would likely have found allies in the rest of the navy.

For there were other protests over the two new guns, from a different quarter, the operating forces. When their unprecedented size became known, captains and gunnery experts who had held ordnance posts on board ship—possibly urged by Crane, who was looking for help anywhere he could find it—voiced concerns regarding the ability of the small *Princeton* to stand their tremendous recoil. The time-honored way of taking up recoil aboard ship was by gun-tackle (pronounced "take-ul"): ropes fastened to the gun's breech and passed through blocks (large pulleys) attached to the ship's bulwarks on both sides. When the gun was about to be discharged its crew first set their backs to resist the recoil by sheer muscle power, allowing it to roll back just enough to be in loading position. After it had been reloaded, the gun crew hauled it back into firing position with the same gun-tackle and prepared to resist the next recoil.

The questions now raised related only to how the pieces were to be handled. The two guns, especially the Peacemaker, were the heaviest ever planned for use on board ship, and their propellant charges were likewise much heavier than any heretofore employed. No gun's crew could possibly stand their tremendous recoil, or, for that matter, man-handle them back into firing position. On the contrary, it was feared when the great guns were fired they might tear the blocks and securing eyes in the ship's light bulwarks clean off her.

Captain Stockton was ready for the question. He did not propose to have the gun's crew hold the Peacemaker at all, he explained, nor reeve the breeching tackle to the ship's bulwarks. He claimed he had calculated the dynamic force of the recoil and devised a friction recoil mechanism that would make the piece easier to serve than "an ordinary thirty-two pound carronade."

The friction recoil mechanism, forerunner of those used today for big guns, and all the mathematical calculations, were, like nearly everything else aboard, entirely Ericsson's.

The ease with which Stockton's gun had been introduced into his dream-ship reinforced his own self-confidence, as well as his rivalry with Ericsson. It also caused him to harbor some other thoughts. Was not the ship in her entirety his also? Had he not conceived her, fighting Congress and the Navy Department to procure the authorization for her? And was it not he, at great personal expense, including a trip to Europe to meet him, who had brought Ericsson to America to work on her? Ericsson claimed "partnership," but there was no written agreement to that effect. The Swede made much of the innovations with which the ship abounded, but Stockton had suggested many of them, or at least they had come about through common discussion. True, Ericsson had drawn the designs for them, but he was only an engineer and that was his job. With little difficulty, Stockton convinced himself that his was the real driving force behind the *Princeton*. It was his prestige and influence that built her, not the Swede's. Ericsson was nothing more than a hired hand who, despite his pretensions, was not an associate. He was quarrelsome, brusque to the point of rudeness. Many of the best workmen would have long since quit over the way Ericsson treated them had not Stockton himself smoothed over the rough spots and convinced them to see the job through. Ericsson was a man he would long ago have dropped, were it not for his undeniable usefulness. So went Stockton's rationale.

In justice to Stockton, it should be noted that Ericsson had few endearing qualities beyond his prodigious ability to work, and his ego knew the bounds of neither modesty nor reticence. There is no indication that Stockton from the outset planned to euchre Ericsson of his share of the professional or financial rewards of their project. The years of their close association combined with their difficult personalities to produce a slow eroding of goodwill and confidence on both sides. But Stockton was a man of the world, a ranking member of the aristocracy of the United States, accustomed to the exercise of his political prerogatives (for which his peers in the navy already distrusted him). No doubt he viewed the absence of binding documents setting forth the mutual obligations and rights of "projector" and inventor as advantageous to himself. Certainly, the closer *Princeton* came to completion, the less was his need of the difficult Swede.

By contrast, Ericsson's power lay only in his great working and intellectual capacities. His engineering reputation, greater in his own mind than in either England or Sweden, had not yet been established in America. Without a political or social base in his new country, without American educational credentials, he was totally dependent on the success of the *Princeton*. He was terribly vulnerable—a fact that should have grown upon him as his relations with his employer deteriorated. But he was not equipped to deal with—nor even to understand—the human factors of his situation. He had always forced his will on those around him and even now could not understand how to deal with someone else equally imperious. Nor could he realize that the greatest impediment to his attainment of the status he sought—first in his own country, later in England, and now in America—was that same self-seeking immovability of mind.

He sought to insulate himself against the increasingly divisive atmosphere in which he labored by throwing himself ever more fully into the job of getting the little warship ready. Stockton had far too many naval and political matters occupying his mind to spend all his time with the construction and outfitting details of his new ship. Traditionally, captains left such details to their subordinates. On the other hand, the *Princeton* was Ericsson's whole life; she consumed his every waking moment. Incessantly, he supervised everything, earning himself both praise from the workmen for his ready availability and quick decisions, and anger for the roughshod, domineering manner with which he treated everyone. To Ericsson, oblivious of all this, it was a happy period; at least, it was so whenever Captain Stockton was away. Whatever he felt the *Princeton* needed, he simply drew on his drawing board and commanded be done. Virtually everything in her that was innovative was his, from armament to engine. The ship would be perfect; the U.S. Navy—and therefore the world—would recognize it and give him the credit he deserved. Then he would no longer need Stockton.

Of these two difficult characters, both easy to fault, one would have to judge Stockton as the less admirable. Far more sophisticated than the Swede, he began to see that the more credit Ericsson got for the new ship, the less there would be for himself. And as the *Princeton* began her first trials, his sense of fairness deserted him. The ambitious naval officer could see nothing to be gained by continuing to avow Ericsson's aid. He determined to cut Ericsson out of the pattern.

The first evidence of the direction in which Stockton's mind was tending occurred in a highly publicized race with the renowned paddle-wheel steamer *Great Western*, the same ship that had brought Ericsson to New York four years earlier. After several carefully manufactured exploits in which the *Princeton* towed various large ships and barges some distance to prove the efficiency of her engines and her huge 14-foot-diameter "water wheel," Stockton went to sea well behind the *Great Western*, overtook her, circled completely around her, and then ran her out of sight in his wake. The Swedish inventor had been aboard for the earlier trials, during which he occupied himself with seeing to the proper operation of his precious engines, but, on the pretext they no longer needed such close attention, he was left behind during the race with the *Great Western*. Ericsson may have acquiesced in missing the trial with the famous Atlantic liner. Far more serious was the omission of any mention of his name in a report Stockton wrote in February 1844 as *Princeton* was being made ready for a voyage down the coast to Chesapeake Bay and up the Potomac to Washington, D.C. In arranging the trip and the demonstration of her capabilities, which he planned as public proof of her fighting power and careful design (and his own personal triumph as well), Stockton sent a written report to the secretary of the navy describing with detailed enthusiasm the innovative features with which his new ship abounded. The unusual engines, the "water wheel," the telescopic chimney, the forced-draft blowers for use with the stack down, the range finder, the automatic firing locks for the guns, all were proudly described. Special emphasis was given to the two tremendous pivot guns: the Peacemaker on the bow and a similar one, originally called the Orator but which he now called the Oregon gun, on the quarterdeck, able to fire a 225-pound shot in almost any direction. His report concluded, "The improvements in the arts of war, adopted in the *Princeton*, may be productive of more important results than anything that has occurred since the invention of gunpowder." Copies of the multipage document were given to the press and circulated in Congress.

Mentioned nowhere was John Ericsson, who was responsible for nearly every one of the *Princeton*'s innovative features. The man who designed and supervised construction of the low, semicylindrical, "vibrating lever" engines, the innovative fire control system (the first of its kind), the strange-looking propeller in a cutaway place before the rudder, the first of *Princeton*'s huge pivot guns, which constituted her main battery—the man who even more than Stockton had lived and breathed nothing but the *Princeton* for four years was completely ignored.

The final phase of shipbuilding is nearly always one of tension, given the fast approaching deadlines and the concern by everyone for successful completion of a myriad of interconnected tasks. Many a good skipper and honest builder have come to odds here after months of common effort. From the professional naval officer's point of view, it is the time for the breaking of the umbilical cord if the ship is ever to get to sea. In the builder's, it is a time when the natural impatience of skippers must be fought to get the job done right. In the case of the *Princeton*, Ericsson was far more than her builder; he also, with much justice, felt himself literally her inventor. The shadow of Stockton's report lay heavily over the final preparations. The last few days in New York cannot have been pleasant.

It had been previously agreed that Ericsson should travel in the new ship from New York to Washington, see for himself the reaction of the navy and members of Congress, and be recognized for his contributions. Then he would return overland to New York while Stockton went on to the next leg of the shakedown cruise. Despite the full-blown animosity now existing between him and his partner, the cantankerous Swede apparently had no idea that Stockton might resort to "the cut direct" to avoid sharing the limelight in Washington with him.

Stockton was not without duplicity and a certain meanness of spirit. He may even have relished what he proceeded to do. Under the strained circumstances, Ericsson might better have taken himself, with all his gear, on board the ship the night before.

On the appointed morning Ericsson, accompanied by several suitcases of personal luggage, arrived on the dock at the foot of Wall Street, where he was to await a boat to bring him on board the departing *Princeton*—but there was no boat. He stood there alone, in plain sight of the ship, saw her anchor come up, a small plume of smoke from her anthracite-fired boilers, a bustle of water astern. Perhaps Stockton had decided to bring the *Princeton* herself alongside the dock—but no! Grandly, but without slowing, the beautiful new sloop of war swept past the pier upon which stood the lonely, bulky figure of her inventor. Plainly visible on her quarterdeck, alongside the massive Orator (now always referred to as the Oregon gun), stood Captain Stockton; but he took no notice of Ericsson, or of the pier head on which he stood, was intent on something more important in another direction. As the stern of the lovely little ship on which he had lavished so much effort disappeared downstream, the spurned engineer returned to his sparse lodgings blind with hatred for Stockton and everything connected with the United States Navy.

From the moment *Princeton* moored at the Washington Navy Yard, Captain Robert F. Stockton was the toast of the capital city. It was undeniably his hour, or more literally his fortnight. Day after day parties of congressmen, high government officials, naval officers on duty in the Navy Department, and prominent local personages came aboard to be shown through the new ship. Several times, groups were taken for short trips down the Potomac River, treated to ship exercises and, once past Mount Vernon, to gun-firing exhibitions. A sumptuous repast was served on the return trip in the specially decorated officers' and crew's berthing areas, where partitioning curtains could be pulled aside to create a large dining space. A very wealthy man, proud and happy with his new creation, the captain spent his own money lavishly to provide the best of all things. In the twentieth-century vernacular, he went first class all the way.

The high point of each excursion came midway of each trip, at its farthest extension downstream, when the thunderous voice of the great Peacemaker, mounted on the forecastle, belched a tremendous blast of gunpowder, and its huge smooth throat vomited the largest shot ever fired. Possibly because the shock of firing might disturb the dining arrangements immediately beneath it, the Oregon gun was discharged not even once.

On 17 February 1844, President John Tyler repaid some of his political debt to Stockton by coming aboard, with his cabinet and members of the Senate, for one of these exhibition trips. On the twentieth, the House of Representatives had its turn, and a fragment of a letter of that date from one congressman to a newspaper in Ohio paints the following florid portrait:

> When the Queen of Sheba visited King Solomon, who, it was said, was somewhat partial to ladies, she declared upon her sacred honour that not the half had been told her of the power and glory and gallantry of the illustrious philosopher-king, the mighty successor of the minstrel-monarch of the Golden City of Zion; so it is impossible to tell you the half that we saw and heard and enjoyed in the excursion given to the House of Representatives by Captain Stockton of the steam-frigate Princeton, this day. We found the Princeton armed with twelve 42-pounders and two tremendous pieces of ten tons' weight each, (of wrought iron, carrying a ball of two hundred and thirty pounds for two miles with the precision of a rifle), all on the upper deck. The two great guns are fixed at the bow and stern of the ship and are called the "Peacemaker" and the "Oregon." These two "bursters" are as bright as Aunt Peggy's pewter plates on Saturday evening, shining all in a row on the top shelf of the kitchen cupboard. When the ship was fairly underway, Captain Stockton, mounting one of the guns, said, "Now, gentlemen of the House of Representatives, fellow citizens and shipmates, we are going to give a salute to the wisdom of this mighty republic (God bless her!) in Congress assembled. Stand firm and you will see how it feels!" In rapid succession the pieces were fired, the ship thrilling and the distant hills reverberating with the thunderpeals. The instantaneous combustion of forty pounds of gunpowder in a discharge from the "Peacemaker" closed the round of twenty-six guns. The deck of the ship was enveloped in smoke. We came near to falling over the venerable Ex-President Adams in the mo-

mentary darkness. Captain Stockton's voice rose high amid the din of the battle. ''It's nothing but honest gunpowder, gentlemen; it has a strong smell of the Declaration of Independence, but it's none the worse for that. That's the kind of music when negotiations fail. It has a little the ring of the earthquake, but it tells handsomely of salt water.'' Someone asked Mr. Speaker Jones what was the main question before the House. The Speaker promptly rejoined that ''the main question was the Navy, and that it had been carried by the casting vote of the 'Peacemaker.' ''

On 28 February another excursion was planned, this time with ladies. When the *Princeton* got under way, in addition to the ship's normal complement there were 150 female and 200 male guests aboard. Again among them was President Tyler, this time accompanied by his fiancée, Miss Julia Gardiner, her sister, and their father, Colonel David Gardiner of Long Island, a New York state senator who aspired to appointment to the United States Senate. Also on board were Secretary of State Abel P. Upshur, Senator Thomas Hart Benton, an elderly woman named Dolley Madison, and Thomas W. Gilmer (newly appointed secretary of the navy in Henshaw's place) and his wife, Ann Elizabeth. Tyler, in his written account of the terrible event to follow, recorded Mrs. Gilmer as having all day had such a premonition of disaster that she hardly could bear to leave her husband's side.

At 1:00 P.M.—1300 hours—of a brisk but clear day, *Princeton* weighed anchor and started off on the familiar trip down the Potomac. This was to be the last, and finest, of the demonstrations. Stockton had ordered the most lavish of all his collations. The triumph in Washington had been complete. Congress and the U.S. Navy were in the hollow of his hand. His place in the navy and in the history of the United States was secure.

Four hours later, her bell tolling, the *Princeton* crept upstream and anchored off Alexandria. A big section of her starboard bow bulwark was missing, her bowsprit was damaged, black soot covered her once immaculate forecastle. In the center of the desolation, still on its rotatable carriage, stood the Peacemaker, but with a horrible difference. All of its breech was gone, as was part of the barrel forward of it, up to the trunions. The heavy iron gun carriage with Ericsson's patented recoil mechanism was bent and covered with soot, but it still supported what remained of the huge gun, now a ridiculous tube of heavy iron open from one end to the other. Its muzzle sagged almost to the forecastle deck in the destroyed gun carriage, looking as though it were aimed to shoot a hole right through the deck and out the side of the ship. But half of the Peacemaker was gone, The jagged broken end where the breech had been was raised into clear and devastating view. One could see through the heavy iron tube from end to end.

At its last discharge, unplanned but specially requested by Secretary of the Navy Gilmer, the Peacemaker's tremendous iron breech had split into two parts and broken entirely off the gun's barrel. Part of it lay where it had fallen, beside an ugly gash in the once beautifully scrubbed deck, but the larger portion was gone, lost in the river, along with twenty feet of the ship's starboard bow bulwark. Most tragic sight of all, eight motionless forms lay near the gangway, wrapped in hastily commandeered canvas hammocks and covered with the ensign of the United States. They had been standing a few feet to the left of the gun when it was discharged and the lethal piece of wrought iron, weighing a couple of tons, had mowed them down.

In the first boat to come alongside a number of injured were sent to the nearest hospital. In another, President Tyler personally carried a fainting Julia Gardiner ashore, sent her and her equally distraught sister to their home, and returned to the ship. That he—and perhaps she—were still alive was because she was cold and wanted to remain below when the gun was discharged, and he had stayed with her. Secretary Gilmer's request for the gun to be fired again had been, as he expressed it, "in order to allow some of the guests, who had not been able to get close enough previously, to see it better." History does not record whom he had in mind, but there is the supposition it may have been I. More, John Tyler's devoted black personal servant, who for the first time was enabled to get near enough to see. Now he was dead, and so were the secretary of state, and the secretary of the navy, and Senator Gardiner of New York, who never would see his daughter become the First Lady or put "USS" after his name to indicate membership in the United States Senate. Also dead were Virgil Maxcy, the recent U.S. chargé d'affaires at The Hague, Commodore Beverly Kennon, chief of the Bureau of Construction, Equipment and Repairs, whose 29-year-old widow lived 67 more years with the memory of that awful day, and two members of the gun crew. Ann Gilmer was in uncontrollable hysterics, the object of dumb, astonished commiseration by all.

Ericsson's private opinion that Stockton's gun would sooner or later burst had been devastatingly confirmed. But even he was hard put to explain why it had exploded under only a half-weight charge, 25 pounds, instead of the normal 50 to which it had been tested. Perhaps there had been an unsuspected crack growing under all the polish lavished on the gun. Witnesses reported a "ring of red fire" that came out all around the forward part of its huge breech, where the principal break occurred. Deaths occurred not from the explosion, which only singed hair, hurt eardrums, and knocked a few people off their footing, but from the relatively slow passage of a piece of wrought iron weighing more than 4,000 pounds through the place where they stood; or, in the case of Secretary of State Upshur, from being struck in the head by a smaller piece of iron that had already torn through the body of Secretary Gilmer. Standing alongside her husband, Mrs. Gilmer was not injured, nor was anyone on the right side of the gun, though their clothes were soiled by smoke and soot. Senator Benton was knocked momentarily unconscious but was not seriously hurt. A young woman seated to his right was knocked down, not hurt, but More, immediately on Benton's left, was killed.

The person nearest the gun was Stockton himself, standing alongside it but to the right with one foot resting on the gun carriage. Badly singed, his fine uniform ruined, and by one account bleeding badly from one ear, he quickly recovered and took charge of the situation, doing what could be done for the dying, taking care of the injured, directing navigation of the now mournful ship upstream to Alexandria, sending a message for boats and ambulances as soon as signal communication could be established. By all accounts, his behavior in the extremity, and that of his officers and crew, was of a high, competent order.

By Tyler's direction the dead lay in state in the East Room of the

White House until their common funeral, three days later. All were in closed caskets with their faces visible through glass except for I. More. The navy directed that until further notice no guns were to be fired with greater than half-weight powder charges, and convened a court of inquiry. It also directed Captain Crane of the Bureau of Ordnance and Hydrography to begin a full-scale investigation into the causes of gun explosions, of which the histories of all navies were far too full.

In question was the entire process of what went on inside a gun when it was fired, for although the Peacemaker had used a half-weight charge for its last and fatal firing, it had already withstood a full-weight proof charge with no apparent damage. And why had it given way so uniformly around the breech? There was already much to answer for in unexplained burstings, and now there were the deaths of five important people, two of them cabinet officials. Gilmer's successor as navy secretary, John Mason, directed the inquiry be given maximum priority.

In the meantime, through the House Naval Affairs Committee, Congress had begun its own investigation. Vigorously preparing Stockton's defense, his counsel, or perhaps the embattled captain himself, asked Ericsson to come to Washington to testify that all proper precautions and proof tests had been complied with. But this the contentious engineer and inventor could not do. Feeling himself at last in a position to deal a blow of his own, Ericsson wrote a short letter declining to render any assistance whatsoever. But again he underestimated his man. The fact was that upon reflection Stockton by no means wanted Ericsson in Washington to show how much he had had to do with the design and construction of the *Princeton*. Nor was he anxious for Ericsson to have the opportunity to expose his unorthodox procurement and proof-testing methods as the slipshod performances they actually were. It had been necessary to ask for Ericsson's testimony, but by his unfeeling response Stockton was both relieved in mind and given an excuse for his now pathological hatred of his former colleague.

Possibly Ericsson expected to be subpoenaed; but he had passed his opportunity by, for the politically powerful Stockton saw to it that the Swede's expressed declination to come to Washington to testify was scrupulously honored. Ericsson's brilliance did not extend to understanding even rudimentary political matters. There was no subpoena issued.

In a message to Congress on the day after the explosion, President Tyler expressed his personal grief over the terrible loss of life and extolled the *Princeton* and "the merits of her brave and distinguished commander and projector." Stockton, during the next few days, having now grounds to consider himself done a grave injury, made the most of them. Ericsson's refusal to come to Washington provided ample opportunity for innuendo if not direct blame for the entire fiasco. The "ingenious mechanic," he let it be known, feared responsibility for the failure of the Peacemaker: after all, had it not been built to his design? And had he not approved the results of the tests? Had not Stockton the right to place confidence in his judgment, and had it not been Ericsson's duty, regardless of the now revealed personal animosity, to have checked and certified the Peacemaker before allowing it on board? The proof of it all, of course, was that he had avoided coming to Washington to testify.

Both investigations into the accident ended, predictably, with no decision as to its cause. Stockton was not only exonerated of any guilt or responsibility, but praised for his handling of the traumatic incident. The House Naval Affairs Committee, however, was objective in at least part of its conclusions. While upholding the finding of the naval court of inquiry, it pointed out that the Peacemaker had been procured in an irregular manner, and that for any similar situation henceforth, the full approval of the Navy Bureau of Ordnance and Hydrography should be required before any such experimental weapons were installed.

In the meantime, President Tyler endeavored once more to assist his friend by using his authority to cause an order to be placed with the Mersey Iron Works in Liverpool, which had built Ericsson's original gun, to manufacture another gun on the plans of the Peacemaker. It was his intent to have this gun mounted in the *Princeton* in place of the one destroyed. Stockton, now alert to the desirability of putting responsibility elsewhere, asked for proofing instructions from Crane, but the bureau chief, now more confident, refused on the grounds that his bureau had not designed it. The gun was nevertheless delivered and paid for, but except for a single proof round, it was never fired nor put in service. After many years at the Brooklyn Navy Yard, it now stands near the restored Commandant's House in the grounds of the Washington Navy Yard in the District of Columbia, a near perfect replica of the most disastrously misdesigned weapon our navy has ever had.

Ericsson, officially only a hired person (although there were many who had some idea of the highly visible inventor's actual contribution to the *Princeton*), was nowhere mentioned in either of the investigations. Under the difficult and embarrassing circumstances, it was easier for all to think of him as a mere employee, bearing no actual responsibility. Ironically, however, when he wrote to ask the Navy Department for payment for his two years of labor on the *Princeton* and the patents he had freely given, the secretary referred the matter to Stockton. This gave Stockton the opportunity to deny that there had ever been any agreement for pay, or even for repayment of out-of-pocket expenses such as those for construction of the firing locks and range-finding device. On the contrary, he stated, Ericsson had been allowed to work on the vessel as a personal act of favor and kindness of his own, which he now regretted. Thereafter, except when forced to do so, Stockton studiously avoided either word or thought of John Ericsson. Nowhere in any of his papers is the Swede's name mentioned. Nor is his name anywhere to be found in Stockton's "biography," which is considered politically inspired and was almost certainly written under his supervision, if not largely by himself.

Not one to give up easily, Ericsson presented his accounting in a memorial addressed to Congress, and finally, after numerous hearings and the introduction of two bills which failed to pass, the U.S. Court of Claims rendered a decision in his favor. As we have seen, Stockton went on to win battle renown, of a sort, in California, where his contribution was decisive. He acted as provisional governor of the newly captured territory for a short time, and then installed John C. Frémont of the army in his place. Returning home, he resigned from the navy. Shortly afterward the New Jersey legislature chose him for appoint-

ment to the United States Senate, where he served from 1851 to 1853.*
There may or may not be any connection between his service in the
senate and Congress's failure ever to vote the money to satisfy
Ericsson's claim, which in the sum of $13,390, not counting accrued
interest, is still outstanding as an unpaid debt of the United States.

Despite Stockton's effort to submerge Ericsson's contribution, a
large residue of knowledgeable opinion persisted that the Swedish engineer deserved recognition for much of it, probably most of it, and
that the Peacemaker debacle had been no fault of his. He was rewarded
with a growing reputation, though not with the instant high acclaim he
had hoped for. He remained in New York City, now his home, though
he never sent to England for his wife and small son. He continued to be
active as an engineer and inventor and retained his interest in warships
as concentrated examples of engineering design and talent. Some years
prior to the outbreak of America's Civil War, he proposed to England
and France a design for an invulnerable warship, built entirely of iron,
powered by steam and driven by a large shrouded screw propeller, and
mounting two very powerful guns in a rotatable armored casing. Neither nation expressed interest at the time.

Despite her short life, the *Princeton* left behind her more legacies
than perhaps any other ship of her era. She was the first screw-
propelled ship of war. She may well have also been the most innovative warship ever built, a worthy follow-on to the tradition begun by
the *Constitution* and her sisters—or even earlier than they, by the *Hancock*, *Alliance*, and *Confederacy*. Stockton's boast that she could have
defeated any other warship of the era was probably accurate. Her ma-

---

*There appears also to have been much deep professional jealousy in the navy over Stockton's
wealth, political influence, and the manner in which he used both. When he resigned, no time was
lost in condemning the *Princeton* as being "rotted beyond repair," and having her broken up in a
scrap yard. When Stockton became a senator, however, the navy suddenly perceived it desirable
to have the ship rebuilt, with the original (that is to say, Ericsson's) machinery. But she was not
the same. An indignant Senator Stockton denounced the new ship from the floor of the Senate as
"this abortion of which we have heard so much lately . . . from being the first ship in the country,
she is now the scorn of all seamen and all engineers." In none of this, of course, did Stockton
mention his former associate in any way. Parenthetically, he may have been right. The new
Princeton was never considered a useful or effective ship, and in her turn was broken up after an
unusually short time in active service. No one knows today what became of the remarkable
engines Ericsson designed for the first ship of that name. When the second *Princeton* was broken
up, they disappeared.

chinery was dependable, at least in the hands of persons who knew how to operate it; her armament was the most powerful ever placed aboard any ship. But the disaster threw a shadow over all her contributions, as though they had never existed, and she became, instead, the cause of consuming distrust by John Ericsson for the U.S. Navy and everyone serving in it. Nevertheless, seventeen years later, when he was again approached by the United States Navy with an urgent plea for emergency assistance, it was he who gave our navy the means of staving off a terrible defeat that might have resulted in the destruction of the Union.

In the long range, the *Princeton* disaster brought about a policy determination by the House Naval Affairs Committee that the navy Bureau of Ordnance and Hydrography should henceforth carry the sole responsibility for proof-testing of naval weapons, that uniform and rigorous standards should be instituted, and that no weapons were to be placed in service until all applicable proof-firings, inspections, and safety measures had been carried out. It caused issuance of a long-lasting naval directive that no guns were to be fired with more than half their designed powder charges. And it strongly reinforced, if it did not in fact begin, the tradition in our navy that it is not desirable for officers to be politically powerful in their own right.

The explosion on the *Princeton*'s forecastle thus nipped in the very bud, only two decades after it might have started, a potential to which the rising star of Stephen Decatur had given birth. Decatur made few fundamental political mistakes in his career, except for the fatal one of fighting a duel with James Barron. Contrariwise, Decatur's nearest counterpart in the political arena, Stockton, entered it with advantages of wealth and position virtually unrivaled in our naval history—but can be faulted at almost every juncture. After him, after the *Princeton*, some naval officers held political ambitions within the navy itself, but hardly any looked beyond it into national politics. One and a third centuries were to pass before an officer of the so-called regular navy (as opposed to those holding reserve commissions for wartime service only) achieved the high office to which Decatur, and conceivably Stockton had he been unflawed, might have aspired. (Stewart turned down a proposal by the Whig party that he run for nomination for president.) A very few have achieved office of the second rank, the cabinet or a seat in Congress. By contrast, there have been numerous cases where officers of the army have reached such positions; and, George Washington aside, beginning with Andrew Jackson a number of them have attained the highest office our nation has to offer.

The only concrete souvenir of this entire extraordinary episode, with its repercussions so far into the future, is the gun christened Orator by its designer. Never fired except during proof tests, it now reposes, bearing a small bronze plaque but otherwise unmarked and unknown, at the U.S. Naval Academy at Annapolis in a tiny grassy triangle near Worden Field, the parade grounds. The plaque contains the only surviving expression of Stockton's small-minded vindictiveness toward Ericsson. It calls the great wrought-iron tube with its two shrunk-on hoops the Oregon gun.

9

Iron Ships and Shell Guns

John Dahlgren's experiments in ordnance began slowly, but he had the methodical approach typical of a Swede (he was of Swedish parentage but born in the United States) and shared the confidence the discoveries of the Industrial Revolution had instilled in nearly all inventors and engineers. He was a regular naval officer qualified to command at sea, however, not an egocentric engineer like Ericsson. Nevertheless, he is not remembered for commanding ships or fleets, but for his work in the design of naval guns. What he accomplished is quickly told, but the doing took years and put his name indelibly on a certain type of gun. It was an enduring contribution.

Like all naval officers of all navies, Dahlgren had long been appalled at the tendency of guns to burst occasionally, nearly always with no warning. Sometimes a crack in the barrel might cause a gun to be put aside, especially if the crack seemed to be enlarging during successive firings. Some cracks were only on the surface, incidental to the casting process, and if they did not grow wider were not considered dangerous. Other cracks, however, might be totally hidden deep within the metal. Still others were sometimes inadvertently concealed by the mixture of tallow and lampblack used by gun crews to keep their pieces polished for inspection. And sometimes, despite the vigilance of ordnance inspectors, a gun that had failed the standard proof-tests was inadvertently placed on board a ship. Whatever the cause of the defect, whether concealed cracking under repeated firing, poor-quality metal, or wrong procedure, the outcome was always and tragically the same. The gun would be fired—possibly a number of times safely—and then it would be fired for the last time. Instantly, everyone in the vicinity would recognize that it did not sound the same—it had fired with a louder, flatter voice. Black smoke, instead of issuing from its muzzle, would cover the area around it. Silence would descend, as though sharply damped by this sinister fog, and there would be no movement beneath it. But then, slowly, the cries of the injured would rise above the bustle of their fellows, some in an increasing crescendo of agony, others in the defeated moans of the dying. A catastrophic eruption of shrapnel of varying size, all of it lethal, would have wreaked destruction on all around it. The voice of that gun would nevermore be heard, nor would the voices of those who had been standing near it.

Captains were normally responsible for the guns on board their ships, including their acceptance for naval use and their location. Within the limits of logic and the design of their ships, their ideas controlled the armament they took to sea.* They put the various types of guns where their own training and experience showed them to be of the most use, although the design of the ship generally dictated most such decisions.

No captain deliberately took aboard a faulty gun, but errors were made. One of the most publicized such mistakes occurred aboard John Paul Jones's flagship, *Bonhomme Richard*. In an effort to increase her fighting power, Jones put six long 18s in her "gunroom," well aft and

---

*The notable exception to this was the *Essex* of 1812, with her all-carronade battery against which David Porter unavailingly protested. During his famous raider cruise in the South Pacific, Porter shifted guns among his captured ships according to where he thought they might best be used, but he never found any suitable to augment the short-ranged battery in the *Essex*.

immediately below the ship's gundeck, and cut six new gunports on each side, so that all six guns, the heaviest on board, could be fought at once in either direction. But outfitting his ship was difficult under the chaotic conditions then obtaining in France; unable to procure the new, proof-tested guns he had been promised, he finally accepted six old condemned ones. It was a grave error, for at the first broadside in his epic battle with HMS *Serapis*, two of the six burst, causing heavy casualties. The survivors deserted the remaining guns, with the result that Jones's potentially best gun battery was useless during the entire battle. He forced *Serapis* to surrender despite this deficiency, but his victory was due to sheer power of will, as history has well recognized.

Another gun explosion with important consequences occurred in the *President*, early in the War of 1812, while chasing the British 36-gun frigate *Belvidera*. One of the big American frigate's bow chasers burst while Commodore John Rodgers, her captain, was standing alongside. Several men were killed, more were wounded, and the commodore's leg was broken. The setback proved to be the margin of *Belvidera's* narrow escape. Three years later, during the first days of the second Barbary States war, Stephen Decatur's new flagship, the just completed *Guerriere*, went into action for the first time only to have one of her main battery 24-pounders burst, killing or wounding some thirty of her crew.

The bursting of Stockton's Peacemaker aboard the *Princeton* was of the same pattern. Here, the fault clearly lay in the gun's construction, which was of an experimental nature, and in careless proof-firings. The high status of the Peacemaker's victims, however, galvanized naval authorities into action. Because of Dahlgren's known scientific interest in gunnery and his service reputation for tenacious pursuit of his objectives, the then recently formed Bureau of Ordnance and Hydrography, with authority enhanced because of the explosion, selected him to carry out the searching investigation mandated by the accident. It was an excellent choice.

As cursory inspection of guns of that period shows, there was already a body of empirical information about the need for greater strength in certain parts of guns. The most common cracking that occurred consisted of spalling off small pieces at the tip of the muzzle. (On firing, small bits of iron would fly off in all directions outside the gunport; no one would be injured, and often the gun would be continued in action.) In the effort to minimize this propensity, virtually all cannon were designed with increased thickness of metal at the mouth, giving them their well-known belled appearance. It was of course understood that the force of the powder charge was greatest at the instant of detonation and tapered off as the shot, or cannonball, traveled the length of the bore. In recognition of this, guns were always thickest at the breech end. But no one really knew how thick their walls should be. Most guns therefore merely tapered uniformly from breech to muzzle, except for the small belling found by experience to be necessary at that point. There were no scientific studies of what actually happened inside the gun when the propellant charge was set off. Dahlgren, already long interested in the problem, set himself to measure precisely the shape of the pressure wave when a ship's gun was fired.

He had, or would construct, the principal tool he needed, a pressure gauge—numbers of gauges—which could accurately record the high pressures he expected to measure. On an experimental gun, holes were drilled through the side of the barrel a few inches apart for its entire length, and the pressure gauges installed. When Dahlgren ordered the gun fired, he received, for the first time by anyone, a true indication of the pressures at each station along the bore. The results of the first test were astonishing. The pressure wave in the firing chamber was several times higher than predicted, dropped dramatically as the projectile moved down the bore to the muzzle, and definitely did not increase as the cannonball exited. The experiment was repeated with different guns, different lengths of bore and more sophisticated gauges, always with similar results.

Several fixes, or improvements, immediately suggested themselves. The drop in pressure as the shot traveled down the bore was so precipitous that the principal function served by the longer barrel of the "long guns" was only to guide the ball a little farther before releasing it to free flight. If a powder charge could be devised that detonated slightly more slowly than the black powder in common use—only microseconds slower—there would be a lower initial shock in the firing chamber and a more sustained push down the bore behind the projectile. By juggling the amount and detonating speed of a new propellant charge, it would be possible to reduce the necessary size and weight of the gun and still increase the initial velocity with which the ball left the gun. This would, of course, correspondingly increase the range it could reach. Still more to the point, very greatly increased ranges and much heavier shot became feasible, now that gun design was better understood.

All Dahlgren's initial experiments were carried out at the Washington Navy Yard, where he could fire his test cannon down the Anacostia River. Observations of the fall of shot from both sides of the river gave him the range achieved in his various trials. He discovered, for example, that by careful variation of the percentage of saltpeter in an ordinary propellant charge of black powder (the standard of centuries), he could vary the speed of its detonation. A long-range solution would require new chemicals and new manufacturing techniques, but the simple change he had already made was an immediate contribution. However, it was obvious that his laboratory in the navy yard, in the middle of a densely populated area, was not suitable for the work he knew would be required. Much more room was needed, for one thing, far away from other activities, so that guns and armor plate could be tested to destruction. Only in this way could the empirical data so necessary for the investigation be assembled. He therefore prevailed upon the Bureau of Ordnance to set up another laboratory at Indianhead, Maryland. He was crossing the threshold of a new field of scientific inquiry, and he knew that years might be necessary to produce the precisely calibrated results he anticipated. This powder factory, as it is now called, greatly changed and expanded over the years, is still in existence.

Dahlgren's immediate objective, however, was the relatively straightforward but not at all simple one of preventing big guns from exploding. Discovery of much higher than expected pressures in the firing chamber at the instant of firing showed the cause, and Ericsson's forged wrought-iron gun, with transverse-forged hoops, had given a hint of a successful solution, for it had withstood many proof-firings. But no wrought-iron guns had ever successfully been put into regular service; the Oregon gun (John Ericsson's Orator) would perhaps have been the first, but its mate, the wrought-iron Peacemaker, had failed in the most catastrophic way. After that, the U.S. Navy wanted nothing more to do with such guns, President Tyler's faith in Stockton notwithstanding. Dahlgren realized from the outset that his new guns would have to be cast, that wrought iron, theoretically stronger, would be unacceptable, and that a great increase in iron around the breech, tapering in an entirely different way toward the muzzle, would be necessary.

His consideration therefore turned on how to prevent the huge castings he projected from cracking, particularly on the outside, where the laws of physics stipulated that most cracks would almost surely begin. This led to experiments on the properties of metals in various forms and culminated in development of a new, heretofore untried procedure for casting large iron objects: very slow cooling from the outside in. By keeping the interior of the gun molten while the exterior slowly solidified, carefully controlling the temperature throughout in accordance with his experimental findings, Dahlgren was able to cast a gun much bigger in exterior diameter than even the ill-fated Peacemaker or the duplicate ordered by Tyler, while at the same time essentially repeating Ericsson's feat of getting maximum homogeneous strength.

As for the problem encountered at the tip of the muzzle, this was found to be caused by simple shock-wave effect, resulting from the abrupt change when the speeding shot left the gun. Dahlgren's solution, annealing the metal at the tip of the muzzle, eliminated need for belling (Ericsson had also believed this was not needed). But tradition dies hard; while most of Dahlgren's guns were made without bells, some still had them, more or less as a style item. To Dahlgren this was no longer of importance. What was important was that his new guns, though less beautiful than the old, were far more effective.

The U.S. Navy was not, of course, the only outfit in the decade before our Civil War that was interested in large-caliber guns. Our army had been for years, and so, too, were European military organizations. For the record, it needs to be noted that a Captain Rodman in our Army Corps of Engineers came to much the same conclusions as Dahlgren, and in some quarters is believed to have been the first to utilize the progressive-cooling technique. In fact, they complemented each other. Both services had the same interest in safe guns, and the two officers exchanged information freely. Some sources have tried to distinguish between the two service ordnance experts by giving Rodman credit for the casting principle and Dahlgren credit for the bottle-shaped gun, but this is splitting hairs. The Rodman and Dahlgren guns, and their manufacturing processes, were essentially interchangeable.

But once Dahlgren had discovered what happened inside a gun, and how to make it stronger, he had to go further. An early idea in gunnery, used in siege warfare for centuries, had been to fire explosive shells, or ''bombs,'' into enemy fortifications, such as walled cities. The shells were simply hollow spheres, filled with gunpowder and fused. They were, of course, much lighter than the older solid shot. Being also spherical, they otherwise resembled them (except for the hole where the fuse was inserted), but were usually of greater diameter. To fire them successfully, care had to be taken not to collapse them under too heavy a propellant charge. Consequently a technique was developed of lobbing them with a small charge in a high arc, and this resulted in specialized types of cannon: howitzers (in the army) or mortars on board ship.

Specialized ships, ''bomb ketches,'' designed for use against coastal forts or cities and carrying large mortars fixed in elevation (range was controlled by varying the firing charge), had long been in existence but could not be used at sea. They required smooth water for accurate placement of their steeply descending shells, hence were useful only in very confined bays or harbors. Standard shipboard guns customarily were fired almost horizontally, necessitating only proper timing as a ship rolled. For somewhat analogous reasons, armies on land tended to use shells only for siege work. At the end of the eighteenth century, however, the possibilities inherent in explosive shells began to interest army officers, and field guns were specially designed to fire them. They interested naval officers as well. Stephen Decatur, for one, experimented with them in 1811, reportedly announcing that in the interest of fair play he would not use them in the event of war with England. The first successful shell gun was apparently built by the U.S. Army and adapted for France by a General Paixhans, after whom, with not unprecedented illogic, the guns were named. (Paixhans himself credited the design to our army, and Robert Fulton intended to mount four of them in *Demologos*.) Shortly after the conclusion of the War of 1812, the so-called Paixhans gun was accepted into the arsenal of naval weapons. More lightly built than regular naval guns but with a large diameter bore, Paixhans guns could not stand the propellant charge for solid shot and hence were restricted to shells only. Ships of this period were given a mixed armament of shell guns and regular cannon.*

In the early nineteenth century there were also numerous attempts to increase range and accuracy by imparting spin to the projectile. The principle was already employed in small arms, pistols, and rifles, but there had been less success in designing a big rifled gun, one with a bore of several inches. The problem lay in the inherent difficulty in loading a rifled muzzle-loader, since it was necessary for the projectile to grip the rifling. A British firm manufactured guns with a hexagonal bore, requiring projectiles carefully machined to fit, but not until just before our Civil War was there a dependable rifled cannon in our navy, and this, of course, could not use the traditional spherical solid shot that had been the mainstay of naval gunnery for so many centuries.

Dahlgren was a practical naval officer. He had successfully dealt with the need to make an immediate correction to gun design, and was well aware that no one wanted anything more to do with monsters as big as the Peacemaker. Merely getting the 225-pound shot into its muzzle was a major operation. A 125-pound solid ball might be manageable, however, and was certainly heavier—and therefore more destructive to an enemy—than the 64-pound shot that had heretofore been about the maximum. Now that the actual pressures involved had been discovered and a slower burning powder devised, safe operations

---

*Since the weight of shells varied widely, it coincidentally became the custom to identify guns by the diameter, or caliber of their bore, in inches or metric measure, instead of the older designation by weight of solid shot. Much thought was also given to development of a gun that could fire either shells or solid shot.

of shipboard guns could be depended on. If Dahlgren could eliminate the necessity of carrying two different types of guns, one for solid shot and one for shells, and make one gun serve both purposes merely by varying the propellant charge, he could simplify armaments and increase versatility at the same time. It became a challenge that seemed eminently do-able. Not only would he make his new guns much safer than guns had been in the past, but he would design them to use heavier charges, fire heavier cannonballs and the lighter, more fragile shells as well, and shoot much farther than any gun had shot before—with the exception of the two doomed guns of the *Princeton*. And even those, as his gunpowder tests and gun designs continued to show, he would soon outrange.

He went further. Mindful of his suspicions about the possible cause of the Peacemaker's explosion,* he carefully calculated the pressures for half and full charges, and the ranges to be expected. He then issued precise instructions for loading each charge, including placement of wadding and location of the ball. His guns, he swore, would not burst so long as his instructions were followed. Every one of the new guns was officially tested, approved, and issued by the Bureau of Ordnance and Hydrography. Even its location on board ship was specified, and this much of captains' privileges was now lost to them. As might be expected, in due course Dahlgren became chief of the bureau for which he had worked so successfully.

The new guns had one major difficulty: they were so much heavier than their predecessors that a ship built to carry the old guns could not support the new. Or, if her beams and deck timbers could be adequately reinforced, the ship as a whole could not carry anything like the same number of guns as before. On the positive side, the new

---

*The Franklin Institute of Philadelphia (not to be confused with the Franklin Mint) made a careful study of the recovered parts of the Peacemaker immediately after the disaster, and concluded that the gun had come apart principally along the lines of faulty hammer welds, with some fracture of metal contributing. It ventured no opinion as to the proximate cause, other than that the gun had been fired, but there may have been significance in the burst under a half-weight charge. Under certain circumstances of loading, this might have been equivalent to ramming the shot only halfway down the bore, which always gave erratic pressure conditions, sometimes with extraordinary peaks. What Dahlgren may have surmised as to the exact cause of the explosion is, of course, entirely speculative, but it is significant that he devoted so much effort to calculating the pressures with reduced charges.

guns—already called Dahlgren guns—discharged bigger projectiles, with far greater initial velocity, thus achieving more range and greater destruction than ever before (always excepting the two originally aboard the *Princeton*).

The navy's reaction was prompt. New ships were designed to capitalize on the new guns and the best of the old ships were modified to handle them. Not much change was made to the old *Constitution* and *United States*, and some of their newer sister ships: they were simply fitted with fewer, though heavier, guns, but some of the later ones underwent extensive rebuilding. The new steam frigates *Mississippi* and *Missouri* had been designed in anticipation of heavier ordnance, although only the *Mississippi* remained, but numbers of newer and heavier ships, with screw propellers instead of side-mounted paddle wheels, were being built. To a considerable degree, the ferment in armament required changes also in the planned loading of the gun-decks of these newest ships, but their structure, at least, had been designed with the far greater weight of ordnance in mind.*

As the pressures that would result in our Civil War began to grow, the U.S. Navy (which became the Union Navy) had developed dependable ordnance of extremely long range, able to fire extraordinarily heavy solid shot, as well as the lighter shells, from the same cannon. It had also built or converted the ships necessary to carry them, foremost among which was a new class of very powerful wooden frigates, twice the displacement of the venerable *Constitution*, half again as long, propelled both by steam engines driving a propeller and by a standard suit of sails. (They were very similar to the heavy frigate Stockton and Ericsson originally planned.) The armament of these new ships is given as fourteen 8-inch, two 10-inch, and twenty-four 9-inch guns,

---

*Inexplicably, however, despite the proven tests and clearly increased safety of Dahlgren's new guns, the Navy Department did not rescind the order relative to half-weight charges in practice or action. Perhaps Dahlgren should not have made such a point of certifying safety for the smaller charges: they may have seemed a good economy measure to navy bureaucrats and the Congress. Perhaps it was inertia, since for the time being there was no emergency to make things move along. Possibly there was a residue of bitterness, not to say trepidation, over the disaster that resulted from going too far, too fast with the huge guns in the *Princeton*. Whatever the reason, the order remained in effect for eighteen years, long after Dahlgren guns had become standard, and it cost the navy a dearly needed victory in battle at a critically important time.

for a total of forty. For comparison, *Constitution* normally carried thirty long 24-pounders (approximately 5-inch bore) on her gundeck and twenty or more smaller guns on her spar deck.

Among them, fate was to designate for historical memory the Atlantic Fleet flagship *Minnesota*, perhaps the best of that group, and to an enduring place in naval lore, her weakly engined twin sister, the *Merrimack*.

Among the converted ships was one destined for luster in our naval history, the *Cumberland*, originally built as a 44-gun frigate of the basic Humphreys design, laid down in 1825 but not completed until 1842. A brand-new frigate of the first class, she was an immediate candidate for strengthening and rebuilding to carry the heavy Dahlgren guns. Her conversion was completed in 1856, and in the process she was reduced in rate, though not in size, to a 24-gun sloop of war.*

During the same period, much was happening in European navies as well. Though it would be some years before our country took up the European habit of keeping observers aboard the naval ships of friendly foreign countries engaged in war, many studious naval officers kept themselves well informed about contemporary technological developments and actual battle performance. One engagement that was especially noteworthy was the Battle of Sinope, which occurred late in 1853.

Sinope, a small harbor on the northern coast of Asia Minor, was once Turkey's principal harbor on the Black Sea. Other than being the birthplace of Diogenes, however, it had few claims to fame before this battle, which was to change the shape of navies and naval tactics.

A Turkish squadron of seven frigates and some other smaller ships,

---

*The old *Constellation* was also revamped. Famous for her two victories under Thomas Truxtun during the quasi-war with France, this fine frigate was greatly modified in 1853–1854 to carry the new guns. Like the *Cumberland*, she came out of the Norfolk Navy Yard rigged to carry twenty-four heavy guns on her covered gundeck and none at all on the spar deck above. She was also lengthened 12 feet, and her stern was rebuilt into a round shape to provide a greater field of fire for her after guns. In this new form, now largely returned to her original frigate configuration with guns on her spar deck, she still exists in Baltimore, afloat in the inner harbor, not far from where Truxtun launched her in 1797.

all armed with traditional solid shot, was found at anchor off Sinope by a Russian fleet of six heavy ships of the line, armed with large shell guns. Under cover of fog, the Russians approached undetected and began a process of total annihilation. One small Turkish ship escaped; all others were sunk. The Russians suffered 37 killed and 229 injured—and killed 2,960 Turks. Victory by the Russians occasioned no surprise, since their fleet was much the superior; what hit the world's navies with something like severe shock was the huge disparity in losses. The Turks fought bravely, but their solid shot, except in a few cases, did not penetrate the heavy sides of the Russian battleships. In the meantime, the Turkish ships were completely demolished: sunk, set afire, blown to bits. There was no escape, and the Russians were without pity, even shooting men as they were drowning.

The difference between the fleets lay not in Russian superiority—estimated by naval experts as two to one—but in the way the Russian ships were armed. Their fleet was fitted with French and English shell guns, the projectiles of which exploded after impact. Unlike solid shot, which simply penetrated, showering wooden splinters everywhere—or, as in the case of tough Old Ironsides, merely making a dent without going through—when the lighter shell hit it usually stuck in the enemy's side, at least momentarily. Then, a split second later, it exploded, shattering timbers over a wide area and blowing a huge hole, doing far more damage than a solid cannonball. If a shell in any way got inside the enemy ship before exploding, the casualties were enormous.

All the navies of the world realized instantly what some of their forward-looking officers had been preaching for years: the wooden ship could no longer be considered a viable man-of-war—at least, not in close action. Lacking in aesthetic appeal or not, iron sides were needed to stop iron projectiles. The old yardarm-to-yardarm engagements glorified by hundreds of years of naval warfare were over. Henceforth, Horatio Nelson's famous dictum, "Get so close you *can't* miss!," would have to be disregarded. Battles would have to be maneuvering battles at relatively long ranges, in which a few good hits would be decisive, and accuracy of gunfire far more important, than the old measures of numbers of guns and "weight of broadside." Henceforth, "blowing a ship out of the water" was a plausible possibility, instead of implausible semantics. And henceforth, the battle between guns and armor was joined.

But if these were the long-range results of Sinope, a more immediate effect was the Crimean War, into which it led directly. In this war, the function of the English navy amounted principally to protecting the transportation of supplies, but there were also some bombardments carried out in support of troops. In a number of cases, the bombardments were against enemy forts, which not surprisingly reacted by shooting back. A basic principle of naval warfare has always been to stay out of range of forts on land. Not only was it impossible to sink a fort, in most cases a fort's guns were bigger than any that a ship could carry and were often situated high on promontories, in commanding locations. They usually had also had ample opportunity to construct a fire-control grid of the surrounding area and could hit a target far more accurately than could a newly arrived ship.

Forts were armored with masonry—stone or brick—anywhere from 10 to 50 feet thick. Bringing ships of the Royal Navy into action against Russian forts in the Crimea seemed a foolhardy idea, but the British navy felt a great need to do something more than merely convoy supplies, and Commander Cowper P. Coles, R.N., made a proposal that was accepted. The Coles rafts, as they were called, were heavy-timbered affairs covered with armor plate. Each carried a single large-caliber gun, fixed in train, inside a protective armored gunhouse. Abaft the gunhouse was a little boiler with a tall stack, a small supply of coal, and a small steam-driven winch. The rafts were towed into position at night, within range of the fort targeted for bombardment, and held there by three and sometimes four lines to outlying anchors. Heaving in or slacking appropriate lines caused the gun to traverse in train (swing right and left), permitting an effective bombardment, while enemy shot and shell, if they hit the tiny target at all, bounced harmlessly clear.

As it turned out, since England and France were allied in a common effort against Russia, shipyards of both navies produced the armored rafts. Apparently, those built in France were the more successful. But this was inconsequential. The lesson of the Coles rafts was an obvious one, immensely important in light of the Turkish experience at Sinope: iron armor, if properly disposed, could render a raft (and therefore, a ship) impervious to the heaviest shot and shell fire. Feverish calculations among the navies of Europe resulted. Rafts were simple things, solid beneath the armor plating, very low to the water. A ship with a crew was something very different. It had to be hollow, to provide accommodations and necessary supplies, and it might have to engage in battle after a long voyage with much bad weather. Could a wooden ship bear the weight? How was the armor to be attached? Corrosion had not been a problem with the rafts, built with no expectation of service longer than a few weeks or months, but ships should last for years. How could the side armor be protected from corrosion, especially where it rested against the side of the ship and could not be reached for regular preservation measures—and what would be the effect of corrosion on the wood?

Most importantly, a raft's armor lay flat on deck (except for that around the gunhouse), presenting a type of target very different from the vertical side of an opposing ship. If necessary to stop a leak, a shot hole through a ship's wooden side could be plugged temporarily from the inside during battle by planks and braces, but how to plug the jagged inside edges of a hole through iron armor? Could a ship as heavy as a first rate (the biggest wooden battleship) be sailed and maneuvered effectively if she were required to carry additional tons of armor? Could wooden frames and keel, even of the highest quality, stand the added strain in bad weather?

Answers had to be found and would be, but much careful evaluation of good and bad ideas and much experimentation lay ahead. England and France quickly emerged as the primary contenders for the honor of first solving the many problems—and, incidentally, of having the foremost navy of Europe. The celebrated French naval constructor, Dupuy de Lome, won the race in 1859 with the first ironclad warship, *La Gloire*. In other respects a standard sailing ship of the line with auxiliary steam power (though her bow was atypically ugly, not like that of the usual sailing vessel, and the size of her sailing rig seemed somewhat small for her hull), *La Gloire* had her entire sides, from bow to stern, encased in iron 4 inches thick, backed by 17 inches of teak and oak.

No solid shot from any gun then known could penetrate those formidable sides. No shell could punch through or stick in them while the charge exploded; all ordnance of the time simply shattered on impact or bounced off. De Lome, just named *directeur du matériel* of the French navy (a post he held for a third of a century), had also made a point of equipping his masterpiece with powerful and dependable engines, viewing her more as a steamship with auxiliary sail power than the other way around. She was, in short, the epitome of good warship design; immune to any gunfire, faster under steam than any other comparable ship, and with a longer cruising range as well. She was a sensation to all the navies of the world, and to none more than France's ally in the recent war in the Crimea. The French navy immediately ordered a number of identical or nearly identical ships, and the British began to build their first.

England's Royal Navy was, in fact, aghast. It had been left at the starting gate. Its boast—and policy—of being superior to the combined strength of any two other navies in Europe had been dramatically challenged. Combat against *La Gloire* was impossible to contemplate. Dupuy de Lome had put his country far in the lead—a situation totally unacceptable to the heirs of Horatio Nelson's tradition of victory at sea.

With a ship of their ancient foe demonstrating her invulnerability in test after test, continually breaking records for speed and endurance at sea, the balance of power, as perceived in England, was severely strained. *La Gloire* had become the cynosure of all naval eyes in Europe. At the same time, several international crises increased the general feelings of insecurity of the English. The people demanded their government take action in face of the possible threat, and in response, HMS *Warrior* was built and got to sea on trials in 1861, only two years after the Admiralty placed the order. About half again as big as *La Gloire*, the British ship was built entirely of iron, with an additional thickness of armor over only the "vital" portions of her hull. She was considered an ironclad in the terminology of the day, but in fact she was the progenitor of all armored fighting ships up to and including the largest battleships of World War II.

Unable to predict the future, the Royal Navy felt only that *Warrior* was a step beyond the wooden-hulled *La Gloire* in warship design. And when *Black Prince*, *Warrior*'s twin, came along a year later, the Admiralty believed England's naval supremacy had been reasserted.*

Whether directly involved or not, naval officers of all countries deeply interested in their profession were consumed with curiosity as to how the new ships would behave—indeed, how they were to be used—in combat. Despite the experiences in Sinope and the Crimea, some British officers still held strenuously to the wooden ships. Their arguments were considered and thoughtful if not in tune with the times, and tradition played a large part in them: the navy of Nelson should not lightly be cast aside; spirit is to matériel as ten to one; wooden sides, properly built of the best wood, could stop shot or shell as well as iron; British sailors always fought best at close quarters, in the old traditional way, culminating by boarding and a ferocious hand-to-hand fight, as proved by Trafalgar.

In 1862, when *Warrior* entered service, Trafalgar was fifty-seven years into history. Such arguments were blind to the extraordinary changes in navies that had taken place since that battle.

Change, especially in long-established institutions, always creates opposition, but one had only to cite the advent of machinery suitable to

---

*These two ships caused a problem in the British navy that today would be considered of no consequence whatever. Although incomparably more powerful than anything else on the navy list, they mounted guns on only two decks and therefore were frigates, not ships of the line of battle. Some old line post-captains were said to fear loss of prestige if they accepted command of a ship of a lesser rate than their rank demanded, while ambitious junior captains used the same argument to press their own claims to the assignment. The Admiralty, however, was unmoved by these notions, and when the new *Warrior* became operational, all dissension disappeared. She and *Black Prince* turned out, like *La Gloire*, to be what designers of ships dream about: enormously successful for their mission. Despite their size, they were handy (although they required a larger turning circle than expected). They sailed well, their engines behaved well, and their gun batteries were strong enough to sink any other ship in the world—including *La Gloire*—with a single broadside. So their officers and crews believed. The two ships served the Royal Navy many years and were the progenitors of a long line of following designs. HMS *Warrior* still exists and is currently under restoration as a national monument in England.

drive ships at considerable speed and the great improvement in ordnance to prove that opposition to the new order was pure nostalgia. To those fond of citing the age of *Victory*, Nelson's flagship at Trafalgar (forty years), as proof of the immutability of the principles of war on the sea, the answer was that while ships and tactics had not changed much between the Spanish Armada and Nelson's famous victory, they had changed a very great deal since then. Tellingly, either *La Gloire* or *Warrior* could blow *Victory* out of the water—most likely receiving no damage whatever in return.

Yet even this insight could not sufficiently anticipate what the machine age had wrought. A century ago, the time element for innovation had already contracted to a fraction of its former length. Today it is a fraction of a fraction: most things affecting the decisions of man are obsolescent while still in the design stage, even before construction is begun. In nothing is this so important as in matters affecting a nation's ability to maintain itself in an avaricious and competitive world. *La Gloire*, invulnerable when built, enjoyed that status only two years. Replicated sections of her armored sides, impenetrable in 1859, were defeated on her own navy's proving ground in 1861 by a new rifled gun under development. Both she and *Warrior* had long since been set aside by the time they reached *Victory*'s age at Trafalgar. By then, Britain was about to build the new and revolutionary battleship *Dreadnought*; World War I—the Great War—with submarines and aircraft, was about to begin.

The process of rapid obsolescence of arms is much faster today.

In 1860, the navies of Europe were on the threshold of the Iron Age. England and France were the principal competitors, with Spain, Russia, and Holland eagerly watching and planning their own moves. At issue was the growing realization that a massive change in naval orientation was in the works. But it was still theoretical. Naval tactics and strategy had been affected in theory; tests at sea and on proving grounds showed the superiority of the new ships and weapons, but they had not been put to the test of combat. The imponderables had not been tried. If it was true that "spirit is to matériel as ten to one"—a concept still held today among nearly all military forces—there was still much to be learned. The American Civil War gave promise of providing the first test in battle, and the European powers sent as many observers to the armies and navies of both Union and Confederate forces as could be accommodated.*

European alertness to prospective modernization of navies did not, however, greatly infect the United States Navy of 1860. Perhaps only the expatriated Swede John Ericsson, still biding his time in New York City, still smarting from his experience of sixteen years previously, had a concept big enough for the changes that were to come.

---

*Meanwhile, Cowper Coles had been far from idle. Since the close of the Crimean War he had continued to mine the same lode that had brought him his initial notice. His armored rafts had been an expedient, a quick solution to an immediate problem. Traversing their guns by hauling or veering anchor cables was slow, imprecise, and dangerous to the crews who had to expose themselves on deck in the process. An armored, rotatable gunhouse would be far better, one that could be turned by machinery while the ship on which it was mounted remained stationary. Such a system would be faster and more accurate; it would also protect the gun's crew. He visualized ships with not one but several such rotatable gunhouses, rumbling around to whatever bearing an enemy might lie on. Indefatigably, he submitted new schemes to the Admiralty, which authorized him to try many of them out. It also tried to maintain secrecy, but for centuries the navies of Europe had employed the same basic tools interchangeably, usually via capture. Confidentiality of naval technology had never been important, and even England's traditional astuteness was not equal to keeping the security she would have liked. All the European navies awaited the results of Coles's experiments, for great change was in the air.

10

The Race Between the Ironclads

Irreconcilable differences underlay our Civil War, deeply embedded in economic, social, moral, and political issues of long standing. Its immediate genesis, however, lay not in the institution of slavery, nor in the somewhat recondite principle of states' rights, but in a dispute over real estate and equipment. This is not to say that if a certain army major had been less obstinate there might have been no Civil War at all, but it is worth specifying that the actual fighting began over owner-ship of federal property located within the boundaries of the seceded states. The man who ignited the conflagration was Major Robert An-derson, who was commanding a tiny detachment of sixty-nine men and nine officers of the United States Army in Charleston, South Carolina.

Summoned by South Carolina to surrender the federal property un-der his command when the state seceded, Anderson refused. Events moved slowly, if implacably, until, determined to be faithful to his trust, on the day after Christmas 1860 Anderson unexpectedly evacu-ated his mainland forts. He moved his force to Fort Sumter, isolated by water in the entrance to Charleston harbor and therefore the most defensible of the positions he commanded. South Carolina reacted angrily, terming the move a "change of the status quo and therefore a breach of faith," and promptly occupied all the installations he had abandoned. Weeks passed. Anderson had seen to it that Sumter was well stocked with supplies and ammunition, but since receipt of provisions and reinforcements was blocked (though dependents and mail were allowed free movement), he could not hold out indefinitely. In January of the next year, desirous of sending him supplies and reinforcements but fearing to use the navy in the volatile Charleston atmosphere, President James Buchanan sent them in the merchant ship *Star of the West*, which was met by gunfire on attempting to enter the harbor. Although the guns were sporadically fired and poorly aimed, her skipper put about without further attempt to complete his mission.

Nothing more was done by either side; the South Carolina authorities evidently believed time was working for them. When Abraham Lincoln took office, however, an energetic effort (though in hindsight poorly organized) was started to reinforce posts like Fort Sumter at Charleston and Fort Pickens at Pensacola. The expected imminent arrival of a new relief expedition brought on the bombardment of Fort Sumter on 12 April 1861. This took place five weeks after Lincoln's inauguration, but four months after South Carolina adopted the ordinance of secession from the Union. As the first shot from Fort Johnson curved over the Sumter parade ground, all hope for peaceful settlement of the dispute disappeared and the war was on.

Lincoln's administration, recognizing from the beginning the tremendous vulnerability of the nation's capital, sandwiched as it was between the two slave-holding states of Maryland and Virginia, bent every possible effort to keep both in the Union. In both states the situation was touch and go, and in both the final test came in April in the aftermath of the attack on Fort Sumter. The nearest boundary of Virginia, teetering on the razor's edge of secession, was only the width of the Potomac River from the Capitol Building and the White House. Beyond it, ceded back to Virginia in 1846, lay Arlington County, the southern third of the original 100 square miles selected for the seat of the federal government. Had the retrocession not taken place, the home of Robert E. Lee, now the centerpiece of Arlington Cemetery, would have remained within the District of Columbia instead of becoming (again) part of Virginia, and Lee might have accepted command of the Union armies—an imponderable of history. But Fort Sumter surrendered on 13 April, Lincoln called for 75,000 volunteer troops to meet the emergency, the Confederacy viewed this as a warlike act when "all we want is to be left in peace," as President Jefferson Davis put it, and on 17 April the Virginia legislature passed an ordinance of secession. Her own western counties thereupon invoked the same right of secession and formed the state of West Virginia, which remained loyal to the Union.

In Maryland there were riots on the streets of Baltimore when federal troops attempted to pass through on their way to the defense of Washington. Its capital, Annapolis, site of the recently established Naval Academy, was full of Union troops, some bivouacked on the academy grounds within only a few hundred yards of the state capitol. For this reason, the Maryland legislature was convened on 22 April, in Frederick instead of in Annapolis, to consider the ordinance of secessin; it failed by a very few votes. Had it not, the U.S. government would have then had to move northward, perhaps back to Philadelphia, its original site, and might have stayed there. Lincoln might even have had to abandon all hope of holding the Union together.

The great prize in Virginia, so far as the U.S. Navy was concerned, was the big navy yard at Norfolk. Originally known as the Gosport Yard, this biggest of the navy's shore installations lay across the Elizabeth River from Norfolk, adjoining the town of Portsmouth. Recognized by all as holding far more practical value than the symbolic importance of Sumter, the Norfolk Navy Yard was under the uncertain command of Captain Charles McCauley, an aged and indecisive veteran of fifty-two years' service who, though once a very highly thought-of officer, was now nearing seventy years of age and had apparently become something of an alcoholic. In March and April 1861 the Norfolk Navy Yard contained a higher percentage of the Union Navy's strength than any other yard, including not only important ships but also supplies of all sorts—not the least of which was the navy's biggest single stock of the new Dahlgren guns. Placing an infirm officer in this choice post was an example of one of the worst evils of the simple seniority system then controlling duty assignments.

In March, as unrest increased in Virginia and the state moved relentlessly closer toward secession, Lincoln's secretary of the navy, Gideon Welles, went to great lengths to avoid confrontation in any area where security of navy installations might be involved. Some places in the interior of the South, mainly army posts, had already been surrendered, and the precedent was well established that seceding states would demand title to all government installations within their borders, including all supplies and equipment. President Buchanan had not actively fought this idea, and many forts and some navy yards in the first states to secede had been tamely given up on demand (in a number of cases their senior officers "went south" also). However, Lincoln insisted that secession did not absolve officers from their oaths to protect and defend the federal property entrusted to them, whatever their own personal loyalties. As might be expected, the seceding states took the position that the passage of an ordinance of secession released "all officers, civil and military . . . from any and all oaths they may have taken to support the Constitution of the United States of America [which are hereafter] inoperative and void, and of no effect."

Some of the more hot-blooded interpreters of these ordinances went on to propose that Southern officers in charge of federal installations or ships of its navy bring these over with them to their new government. In the case of a landlocked army fort in the middle of Texas, for example, there was not much else that could be done—although supinely handing over equipment and supplies that could be transported into safe territory created much indignation on the part of loyal army officers. It was noteworthy, however, that despite considerable acrimony over title to government supplies and sometimes very bitter local differences, there were few if any restrictions put on individuals who chose to return to the North from such surrendered positions.

In the case of ships, their mobility created a very different set of considerations: did a commanding officer have the right—much less the obligation—to sail his ship into a Confederate port and turn her over to Confederate authorities at the same time as he personally transferred his own loyalties? Or, if his ship was in a Southern port at the time he decided to "go south," did he still have the obligation to save her for the North? In either case, what about his crew?

So far as operational ships were concerned, the record shows that all officers scrupulously honored their responsibilities to the federal government. Some commanders did bring their ships into Northern or neutral harbors and then resigned their commissions in order to serve the South. Northern warships and merchantmen not removed from Southern harbors were taken over by civilian authorities, but not through any connivance of their officers. The ability of the ships to move on their own power was the key. If they could move, they were saved for the Union or, if merchantmen, for their owners, whether Northern or Southern shipping firms.

Norfolk Navy Yard, containing massive ship-overhaul and ordnance facilities, had been in continual use by the navy since revolutionary times. It lay within a mile of the confluence of the James River and Hampton Roads and their debouchment into Chesapeake Bay. Only a few miles to the north, where the York River also joined the Bay, lay Old Point Comfort and Fort Monroe, both solidly in the hands of the Union. Beyond all this was the wide body of Chesapeake Bay, forming an inland sea bordered on the north by the still loyal state of Maryland. The yard's easy accessibility from the bay might make its defense possible, particularly if troops were brought in quickly and strongly supported by naval vessels, but the best assurance of its continued availability to the Union Navy was if the ordinance of secession then under debate at Richmond failed. Federal government policy, designed by James Buchanan, had been to permit no situation to develop that might strengthen the position of prosecession forces. But Virginia's radical secessionists loudly trumpeted that once the ordinance was passed, the navy yard and everything in it—including all the ships moored there, mobile or not—belonged to the state of Virginia. They added a new twist by insisting the situation as of the time the secession ordinance was introduced must remain inviolate; that until the secession issue was resolved, everything should remain frozen, in the status quo—which term had now assumed special meaning for them, in fact a slogan of the time. Though Virginia was still part of the Union while its legislature was debating, they held that the possibility of secession barred the North from any move to save federal property within its boundaries.

From Secretary of the Navy Welles's point of view, any attempt to remove anything of value from the Norfolk Navy Yard would add to the pressures favoring secession. Initially, he therefore directed McCauley to avoid adding fuel to the flames. And as the situation grew more tense, he continued to move very slowly for fear of worsening it.

The most important of the ships in the Gosport yard was the fine new steam frigate *Merrimack*, one of six big sisters built only five years before, and known for having the poorest engines of the lot. Recently returned from a cruise during which she had experienced considerable engine trouble, she had been sent to Norfolk for a thorough machinery overhaul. Early in April, recognizing the possible effect of the Sumter relief expedition on Virginia's secessionist movement, Benjamin Isherwood, thirty-nine, newly appointed engineer-in-chief of the navy, urgently recommended that Welles have *Merrimack* removed from the threatened yard. He made his point well; the ship was much too valuable to be allowed to remain immobilized where she might be seized by a seceding Virginia. Now concerned, Welles directed McCauley to have the ship readied for immediate departure. McCauley's reply, believed to have been suggested by Southern sympathizers on his staff, was that a minimum of four weeks would be required to put her engines back in working order and that the ship could not be moved sooner. Isherwood stood his ground, saying she could be made ready within a week. The now thoroughly alarmed Welles directed him to proceed at once to Norfolk and take over the repairs. Commander James D. Alden, who traced his lineage back to Priscilla and John and was qualified to command at sea (Isherwood, an "engineering duty only" officer, could not, by statute, be so qualified), was sent with him to take command and bring the ship out as soon as the engineer-in-chief was able to get her engines functioning.

Arriving at the yard on 14 April, Isherwood accomplished a miracle. Working around the clock, somehow simultaneously driving and inspiring the workmen he had managed to assemble, he had the *Merrimack*'s engines repaired and tested, and the ship ready to get under way, in two and a half days. Late on the afternoon of the seventeenth he reported to Captain McCauley that the *Merrimack* was ready to go. But despite Isherwood's earnest expostulations, the doddering old man saw no need for precipitate action and finally peremptorily directed that steam not be raised on her until next morning. He gave no reason for this, but Isherwood believed (and so reported to Welles later) that he was drunk. In any event, as commandant of the yard he had ultimate charge of the ship, and his mind was closed to all attempts to make him change it.

Isherwood determined to take the maximum action possible within the limits of McCauley's order. Shortly after midnight on the eighteenth, he had fires lighted under the *Merrimack*'s boilers and was impatiently waiting in the commandant's office when McCauley arrived (despite the emergency not until 0900) to report that all was in readiness to cast off. To his consternation, McCauley now demurred that he had not yet determined to send the ship away from Norfolk. In Isherwood's judgment, as he later reported to Welles, McCauley was already intoxicated as well as nearly senile. Whatever his condition, he obstinately and finally vehemently refused to let the ship leave the yard. The only recourse left to the desperate engineer was the appeal he immediately made to Commander Alden to take her out on his own. But while Alden had the requisite status as a line officer, he was not equal to the emergency and refused to act in disobedience to a superior, even though the problem was plain and a greater superior, the secretary of the navy, had directed he move the ship.

Merrimack was on the point of departure: steam up, engines turning over slowly, chains and cables to the pier removed. In naval jargon she was "singled up" with men and axes ready to cut the remaining lines holding her to the pier. She could have been under way at a moment's notice and could have been safe in Hampton Roads within an hour. The despairing Isherwood, seeing time running out and fully aware of the possible consequences should the Confederacy take over the ship he had been sent to save, seriously considered ordering the cables cut and himself somehow navigating the tall-masted wooden ship out into the bay. Such action would, however, have been in unprecedented disregard of all naval regulations governing the conduct and responsibilities of staff officers. As a staff, not a line, officer, no engineer could do such a thing, even under the secretary of the navy's direct order; most especially not in defiance of a senior line officer's categorical command to the contrary. In later years, Isherwood pointed out that had he succeeded he would have had only "the saving of a fine warship" to explain his action, while he would simultaneously have prevented from happening all the later events that would have constituted his only defense for doing so.

When Secretary Welles received the report from Isherwood and Alden, both of whom returned immediately to Washington, he was outraged. Isherwood had been right in his concern and had been exemplary in his duty. Alden, by contrast, had abjectly failed—and in the meanwhile, precisely at this time, Virginia had passed its ordinance of secession. Without doubt, at that very moment plans were being laid to take over the Norfolk Navy Yard. Instantly Welles dispatched Commodore Hiram Paulding, a line officer a few years junior in service to McCauley but by virtue of holding the post of special assistant to President Lincoln clearly his senior in rank, to relieve McCauley summarily of his command and at least save the ships. Paulding departed immediately in the steam sloop *Pawnee* for the overnight voyage from the Washington Navy Yard to the Norfolk yard. Pausing only long enough to take aboard Union soldiers from Fort Monroe, the *Pawnee* steamed up the Elizabeth River on 20 April practically at the same moment that McCauley, boozily realizing the enormity of his dereliction, ordered all the useful ships in the yard scuttled. As Paulding arrived he saw the *Merrimack*'s masts begin to tilt as she settled on the bottom.

The navy yard gates were of course locked and guarded. A mob of angry secessionists was gathering beyond the walls, and there were threats of overrunning the yard. Probably much of this was exaggeration for the benefit of McCauley and Paulding, both of whom also believed false reports of Confederate troop train arrivals in Norfolk. There was nothing now that could be done for the *Merrimack* and the other ships, and under the circumstances it seemed defense of the yard itself was impossible (later postmortems disagree on this point; perhaps a determined resistance, with more help from the soldiers at Fort Monroe, might have saved it).

Believing the stories about the arrival of troop trains, however, time pressure upon Paulding was tremendous; some of the panic that had immobilized McCauley infected him also. He could see no other alternative than to destroy the navy yard immediately. When the men with him set about doing this, the crowd outside the gates redoubled its menace, and the work of destruction was not well done. Despite stories in the Northern press of great fires raging out of control within the navy yard, the crowds outside the wall rushed in as soon as the Union forces withdrew, put out the important fires, and extinguished the fuse laid to explosives intended to destroy the dry dock. The fires set in the ships, excepting that in the portion of the *Merrimack* above water, were allowed to burn. All the ships—including the huge receiving ship *Pennsylvania*, the biggest sailing warship ever built for the U.S. Navy, moored there since her maiden voyage—burned to the water's edge. In the *Merrimack*, however, the flames were quickly confined to only her upper deck and rigging, and the main part of the ship was saved.

The only ship Paulding was able to save was the sloop-of-war *Cumberland*, which lay at anchor in the Elizabeth River and was thus somewhat removed from the chaotic navy yard. The greatest loss, according to all Civil War historians, was the guns, numbering, according to Paulding's report, "nearly 3,000 of various sizes, 300 of them being Dahlgren guns of the latest type." The figures are not corroborated by all sources (some have them divided by half), but they do give an indication of the extent of the damage.

Far more visible in terms of history to follow, however, was the loss of the *Merrimack*.

Although requiring extensive repair, she was still incomparably the most powerful warship possessed by the South. In May her great hull was pumped out and placed in the yard's undamaged dry dock, while Confederate Secretary of the Navy Stephen R. Mallory of Florida (who had been chairman of the Naval Affairs Committee while serving in the U.S. Senate) debated the question of how best she could be employed. Sometime previously, Chief Engineer John L. Porter had submitted a model of an ironclad warship of his own original design, not based on the partly burned hulk of the *Merrimack*. Mallory himself made the decision to undertake the conversion, and it was he who decided that when converted the former Union frigate should bear a new name symbolic of the new life she was to begin: *Virginia.** He directed that work proceed on her with the greatest urgency: Porter was to design and superintend the hull work, Lieutenant John M. Brooke was to procure and install her armor and armament, and Chief Engineer William P. Williamson was to superintend refitting her old and undependable engines. Mallory needed no other ideas than his own as to how the extraordinary ship was to be used after the conversion; as head of the Naval Affairs Committee, he had been well aware of the ironclad warships being built for European powers and of the theoretical arguments over their most effective use. If the truth were known, it was probably he as much as anyone who conceived of building an ironclad navy for the South. Now the immediate chance was at hand: a conversion instead of a new ship, but quicker because of it. He seized the first opportunity to put some of these ideas into practice. Many purposes would be served, but the great imperative was to get her ready. As he wrote to the Confederate Congress, "as time is of the first consequence in this enterprise I have not hesitated to commence the work and to ask Congress for the necessary appropriation." It was a massive undertaking for the Confederacy, where there was virtually no manufacturing capability for the iron plates needed, nor for casting engine parts or making guns.

There was no such thing as secrecy, either, whether of operational plans or forces available (what professionals call "the order of battle"). The Confederate plans for the *Merrimack* were immediately known to the North, which received a flow of reports on the progress of the conversion. Although no ship of the U.S. Navy had yet been equipped with iron armor, Union and Confederate navies both already knew what iron sides could do for a ship of war.

---

* All Confederate documents thereafter referred to the ship as the *Virginia*. The North continued to call her *Merrimack* (often misspelled without the terminal letter *k*). To avoid confusion, she will here be called by her original name, except when quoting a Southern document. Although later there was competition for credit for the idea of converting *Merrimack* to an ironclad, it appears that Lieutenant John M. Brooke, a member of the second class to graduate from the Naval Academy at Annapolis, probably was the first to suggest it. He did this immediately after the ship was seized, in a letter to Mallory.

Lack of resources forced Mallory into a single basic design of iron-clad, whether a conversion or newly built; but he nonetheless moved rapidly and effectively within the lesser capabilities of the South. On the other hand, Gideon Welles, by background a newsman with little inherent knowledge of naval matters, continued to move slowly despite his position as chief of a functioning, operating navy that should have had an appreciation of the realities and given him better advice. Instead, his first priority was to find more wooden ships to implement the Union's blockade strategy. Not until July, after continual urging by Assistant to the Secretary Gustavus V. Fox (a former naval lieutenant, Fox's position was later called assistant secretary—a semantic change that greatly gratified him) and by Isherwood and numerous members of Congress, did he ask Congress to create an Ironclad Board. And only in early August was the measure approved.

Though unavoidably late in beginning their duties, the board's members—Commander Charles Davis and Commodores Joseph Smith and Hiram Paulding—wasted no time. Their report was ready a month later and recommended immediate construction of three types of ironclad vessel. The largest, which would obviously take longest to build, was a casemate ship carrying a broadside of heavy guns. Named *New Ironsides*, she performed well when completed, but would never have been ready to meet the converted *Merrimack*. The second, *Galena*, too lightly armored for combat with shore batteries, was generally classed as a failure. The third, John Ericsson's *Monitor*, has however been called "the most influential American innovation in naval design in the nineteenth century," and "perhaps the most original design in the entire history of naval architecture."

It was fortunate that the Ironclad Board contained Commodore Joseph Smith, for he was apparently the only U.S. naval officer who was able to earn the respect and friendship of John Ericsson. In getting Ericsson's cooperation, he had the help of New Haven shipbuilder Cornelius S. Bushnell, who was instrumental in reversing the inventor's antipathy for the navy that had treated him so shabbily seventeen years previously. The story is told that when Bushnell visited Ericsson in New York to seek his professional advice on the design of the *Ga-*

lena (for which Bushnell had received the contract), the Swede announced he had long resolved to have nothing further to do with the U.S. Navy. But when Bushnell pressed him, Ericsson went into another room and returned with a model of the little ship with a rotating gunhouse that he had proposed to Napoleon III. Bushnell immediately asked to bring the model to Secretary Welles, whom he evidently knew well, pointing out to Ericsson the tremendous urgency of being able to meet the *Merrimack* when she came out of Norfolk and reminding him of the fame that awaited if his ship proved to be what he claimed. Ericsson could not resist the flattery, combined as it was with the temptation to his engineering mind. He later boasted that his preliminary design for the *Monitor* was accepted four hours after being submitted, and while clerks were writing up the formal contract (which this time he insisted on), the iron plates for the *Monitor*'s keel were already being drawn through the rolling mill.

Pointing to the great urgency animating the members of the Ironclad Board, the contract specified that the *Monitor* be completed in a hundred working days. As with the *Princeton*, Ericsson threw himself into the work; this time he was not working for an ambitious self-aggrandizing glory-seeker whom he did not know how to handle. This time it was the United States Navy that had given him a contract. The Swedish inventor made the most of it, in the process demonstrating once again the totally dedicated performance Stockton had disdained as being that of "an ingenious mechanic." There never was a detailed design for the new ship, except the one Ericsson no doubt carried in his head. Yet, during the one hundred days, he drew more than one hundred detailed plans for various parts of her. Nearly everything was new and untried. It was said that when the ship was complete she contained more than forty patentable innovations. Ericsson supervised the entire project, subcontracting major parts to other firms. He was as irascible as ever, but he was in his element. Quickly he became Welles's and Fox's only hope to meet the *Merrimack* on anything like equal terms, for the Ironclad Board's most ambitious project, *New Ironsides*, could not be ready for many months, and it was becoming clear that Bushnell's lightly armored *Galena* could not match her. Concern from

Washington that there be no delay in getting his ship ready only increased Ericsson's drive, sending him, when necessary, back to sleeping beside his drawing board. In addition, he was the troubleshooter. Whenever something went wrong, as it did occasionally, he would dive into the affected space and design corrective measures on the spot. Whatever he wanted was done instantly, with the full weight of the Union Navy Department backing him up. He was never happier.

Contrariwise, the Union Navy Department was probably never unhappier, for it was receiving reports, nearly on a daily basis, of progress on the *Merrimack*. It was soon clear that much too much time had been lost, that even having Ericsson's supposedly quickly built craft ready in time was almost an impossibility. *Merrimack* was expected out of Norfolk early in February 1862. Welles and his assistant secretary were entering into a state of panic. It had been hoped the *Monitor* could leave New York about the middle of February, but one delay after another intervened while Fox, in particular, sent telegram after telegram entreating Ericsson to hurry.

In Norfolk, Lieutenant Catesby ap Roger Jones, forty-one-year-old nephew of the commodore who prematurely captured California in 1842, was in charge of getting the *Merrimack* ready. He drove the men under his control without mercy, seven days a week, and they responded with equal fervor. Everyone in Norfolk—in Virginia—knew that the survival of the Confederacy depended on breaking the Union blockade of Southern ports. Everyone also had heard that the North was building not one but three ships to counter the converted *Merrimack*. If the South could get their ship into action first, she would probably be able to destroy the entire Northern fleet in Hampton Roads, or at least certainly drive it away. And once that fleet was decisively defeated, the blockade broken, there might be support from Europe.

As *Merrimack*'s designated executive officer, Jones was in charge of organizing and training the crew, outfitting the ship, and, in fact, readying everything that pertained to her fighting efficiency. The Confederate Navy was organized exactly like its parent, the Union Navy, but with a crucial difference: of bureaucratic red tape there was none, for there was neither the time nor the personnel to develop any. Jones therefore had more authority than his counterparts in the Union Navy, and so did Porter, Williamson, and Brooke, the three staff corps officers who also labored over the ship. All four operated, in effect, out of their hip pockets, making decisions on the spot without reference to anyone, secure in the knowledge that they had Mallory's backing whenever they found it expeditious to cut a corner. Even so, their work moved forward very slowly because there was practically no heavy industry in the South. By December 1861, they knew for sure they were in a building race with John Ericsson.

Like the North, the Confederacy had kept itself well informed of what was going on in the territory of their enemy. This was easy to do. On neither side was it ordinarily necessary to resort to organized spying or undercover work, for there were many Southern sympathizers in the North (and vice versa), and there was no controlling the press. One had merely to obtain copies of newspapers to discover everything that was going on or planned. The North knew the South was desperate to win the maritime victory that might give it a quick and relatively painless separation from the Union. The South knew the North knew this. And both sides knew almost to the minute the state of construction and readiness of the other's first ironclad warship.

Franklin Buchanan, first Superintendent of the Naval Academy at Annapolis, had been selected for the post at the age of forty-five by Secretary Bancroft as the officer most fitted to imbue young midshipmen with the ideals of honor, patriotism, rectitude, and professional competence that the navy needed. He had the service reputation of being quick to make up his mind, quick to take action, and quick to anger. He was a dynamic leader and a determined fighter. In 1845 these qualities recommended him to Bancroft. Subsequently, he commanded a ship during the war with Mexico, and participated in Matthew Calbraith Perry's expedition to Japan in command of another, in 1853. By 1860, now sixty years old, he was in command of the Washington Navy Yard.

As a citizen of Maryland, with his ancestral home on the Eastern Shore of that state, he expected secession. Characteristically impetuous, however, he wrote his letter of resignation from the navy before Maryland acted. As can be imagined, there was great tension in the Navy Department at this time. No one knew who was loyal and who was planning to resign. Buchanan's resignation was dated 22 April, only days after Virginia's secession, the same day Maryland's legislature met in Frederick to consider a similar ordinance. He personally delivered it to Secretary Welles, discussed his reasons at length, and saw it endorsed, "You are hereby detached from the command of the Navy Yard at Washington. . . . Your resignation is yet under consideration."

Two weeks later, as it became evident that Maryland was not going to secede, Buchanan wrote again to Welles, asking to rescind his hasty action, and on the same day sent a more personal letter to the head of the Bureau of Details (assignments) to the same effect, citing the last official word he had received that his resignation was "yet under consideration." Exactly what was in Welles's mind at this point has been the subject of some speculation, the most obvious deduction being that he had greatly hardened his position since Buchanan's first letter. Prior to the inauguration of Lincoln, resignations from officers whose states had seceded were accepted as a matter of course, without prejudice. Welles came to the navy secretariat with the department in turmoil. The army was in no less a state of upset, and doubtless the matter of resignations received much discussion within Lincoln's cabinet as well as privately by the two secretaries and the President himself. Almost surely Lincoln's own imprint, probably orally expressed, was incorporated into the policy as developed.

The third week of April 1861 became a watershed, culminating in the loss of the navy's best repair facility, the Norfolk Navy Yard. Many resignations were submitted at just this time, and there was a great deal of emotion, since good friends were separating in the knowledge that when next they met they might be trying to kill each other. An affecting story at the Naval Academy tells of a midshipman assembly to embark them aboard the old *Constitution* for transfer to Newport, Rhode Island, for the duration of the war. Twenty resigning Southern midshipmen fell in for the last time to take their leave of their friends and classmates. Many, on both sides, were in tears.

No impediment was put in the way of these departures, but the situation was changing rapidly.

All evidence indicates that on Buchanan's initial visit to deliver his resignation, the navy secretary listened courteously to his extensive explanations. Had the former Naval Academy superintendent asked reconsideration within a day or two, Welles might have been sympathetic. But two weeks later, the secretary had reached the decision that some drastic and prominent action was necessary to keep the trickle of resignations from becoming a destructive flood. Buchanan's second letter may have served to remind him that this bit of unfinished business provided a candidate for the hard line by which he intended to keep others in the service. Whatever his unspoken motives, his action on receiving it was uncompromising. By return mail, Buchanan was curtly informed that "By direction of the President your name has been stricken from the roles of the navy."

This wording, amounting to outright dismissal from the naval service without recourse, hit the proud and hot-tempered Buchanan where it hurt the most. Already forced to grovel for reinstatement, in his view he had been ground into the dust. The voluminous letters he wrote to relatives and friends, justifying his action by hyperbolic protestations of his loyalty to flag and principle, citing his record of forty-six years of faithful service, and yet announcing that he regretted having attempted to rescind his resignation because "nothing could induce me to remain in that navy [whose flag had become] the emblem of tyranny and a military despotism," are ample index to his state of mind.

The fuming old commodore puttered around his estate near Easton, Maryland, until he could stand the inactivity no more. Executing legal bills of sale of all his personal and real property to his wife, daughters, and son, he left Maryland, made his way to Richmond, Virginia, and early in September offered his services to the Confederacy. He was commissioned a captain, Confederate States Navy, and was initially employed in erecting gun battery emplacements to block river access to the Confederate capital at Richmond.

Thus Buchanan became one of the few high-ranking military officers to "go south" while his state remained in the Union.* Buchanan's first assignments in the Confederate Navy were a series of odd jobs, as might be expected, but he asked unceasingly for duty afloat. It is a reasonable assumption that one of his motives was to assuage his anger against the old navy he felt had treated him so poorly.

From S. R. Mallory, Secretary of the Navy
To Captain Franklin Buchanan, C.S. Navy
Navy Yard, Norfolk, Virginia

C.S. Navy Department
Richmond, February 24, 1862

Sir: You are hereby detached from the Office of Orders and Detail and will proceed to Norfolk and report to Flag-Officer Forrest for the command of the Naval Defenses, James River.

You will hoist your flag on the *Virginia*, or any other vessel of your squadron, which will, for the moment, embrace the *Virginia*, *Patrick Henry*, *Jamestown*, *Teaser*, *Raleigh*, and *Beaufort*.

The *Virginia* is a novelty in naval construction, is untried, and her powers unknown, and the Department will not give specific orders as to her attack upon the enemy. Her powers as a ram are regarded as very formidable, and it is hoped you will be able to test them.

Like the bayonet charge of infantry, this mode of attack, while the most distinctive, will commend itself to you in the present scarcity of ammunition. It is one also that may be rendered destructive at night against the enemy at anchor.

Even without the guns the ship would be formidable as a ram.

Could you pass Old Point and make a dashing cruise on the Potomac as far as Washington, its effects upon the public mind would be important to the cause.

The condition of our country, and the painful reverses we have just suffered, demand our utmost exertions, and convinced as I am

---

*Another was Rafael Semmes, also of Maryland but not quite so high ranking, who was to achieve lasting fame with the commerce raider *Alabama*. On the opposite side of the coin, a number of others, notably David G. Farragut, remained loyal to the Union despite the defection of their states and heavy pressure from their families. Midshipman Robley D. Evans, from Virginia, the later, "Fighting Bob" Evans, describes in his autobiography how he had to convince the Navy Department that the resignation submitted for him by his mother should not have resulted in his summary discharge. In his case, at least, he was promptly reappointed.

that the opportunity and the means of striking a decided blow for our Navy are now for the first time presented, I congratulate you upon it, and know that your judgement and gallantry will meet all just expectations.

Action—prompt and successful action—now would be of serious importance to our cause, and with my earnest wishes for your success, and for the happiness of yourself, officers and crew,

I am, very respectfully, your obedient servant,

S. R. Mallory
Secretary of the Navy

Catesby Jones and the crew he had assembled for the rebuilt *Merrimack* expected things to start popping the moment their new skipper arrived, and they were not disappointed. Buchanan reported on board 4 March 1862. His first move was to convene his officers and men and read his orders to them. Next, he set out upon a thorough inspection of the ship. Lastly, he ordered all the navy yard workmen, except those engaged in jobs vital to *Merrimack*'s operational capability, to leave her.

"This vessel is about to face the enemy," he somewhat pompously declared, "just as soon as I can get her there!" In vain Commodore Forrest, the Confederate yard commandant, protested that she was not yet quite ready, that some of the armor plate for her sides below the waterline had not yet arrived, and that there had not been time to attach all the gunport shutters.

"I mean to try her against the enemy, sir! There will be time to complete the shutters and armor after we have proved her in action!" Buchanan was in possession of information that no one else had. The *Monitor*, unbelievably, had been completed and might even at that moment be en route to Norfolk! In a few days she might be shelling the navy yard and attempting to destroy the *Merrimack* at her dock. Though small, *Monitor* would be *Merrimack*'s most dangerous adversary, and he knew the hated Gideon Welles and his subservient federal Navy Department were placing their entire hope of beating his new ship in her. The *Merrimack* might be able to whip the *Monitor* because of her greater size and greater number of guns if she could meet her on even terms. But the *Merrimack* had a more important mission to perform than merely fighting another ship. The Confederate Navy Department expected her to drive the blockading Union fleet—that noxious assemblage of outmoded wooden ships—out of Chesapeake Bay. This would eliminate the threat from General George B. McClellan's Army of the Potomac and give Richmond a free access to the sea down the James River. Once this was done, *Merrimack* would fight anyone. The *Monitor*'s arrival before the Union fleet was dispersed might just make it impossible to carry out Secretary Mallory's plans.

Buchanan well appreciated that his flagship was not seaworthy in the accepted sense—although this was apparently lost on nonsailors—because her highest watertight deck, upon which all her guns were mounted, was barely above the waterline. In combat, for protection against enemy guns, the ship was ballasted down so that her bow and stern, extending some forty feet forward and aft of the iron casemate, would be two feet below the surface. This left the deck within the casemate approximately one foot above the waterline—and this volume represented her entire reserve of buoyancy. It could, presumably, be made essentially watertight, although there must have been numerous places—such as in the vicinity of the smokestack and around necessary access hatches—where watertight integrity was at best marginal. Thus she was kept afloat by the small amount of buoyancy measured by the freeboard between the water and the bottom of her gunports. She had, moreover, no transverse watertight bulkheads. Should any appreciable amount of water accumulate in her bilges, it would run to the bow or stern, whichever was the lower. This is now called "free-surface effect," and obviously once it began to weigh one end down lower, more water would collect in the low spot and the downward tilt would be accentuated. A ship with small reserve buoyancy would inevitably sink the moment water, even in small volume, began to enter her hull.* In the case of the *Merrimack*, watertight integrity of the casemate, which looked like a huge iron roof floating

---

*Monitors also suffered from small reserve buoyancy. The *Monitor* herself sank in a moderate storm a few months later, when her pumps were unable to keep up with the amount of water that found its way below decks. And the monitor *Weehauwken* sank with heavy loss of life while at anchor in Charleston harbor, when waves rolled up on her low-lying bow and poured for only a few seconds through an open hatch. The principles of buoyancy were not yet well known.

on the water, ceased at the gunports. Their shutters, designed to keep out enemy fire, were not yet all in place, and in any case, they were of only marginal use against entry of seawater. If a few seas were to slosh in, or a sizable leak develop from battle damage, the *Merrimack* would sink immediately.

But it might not be necessary to go to sea or even up the Chesapeake, let alone the Potomac River, which in any case was too shallow to float the deep-draft *Merrimack*. Mallory and Buchanan held the vision of a crushing defeat inflicted on the most important and powerful part of the Northern fleet, right in its anchorage in Hampton Roads. This was possible, if only the powerful *Merrimack* could get into action before arrival of the federal ironclad. It would open fantastic psychological and diplomatic possibilities, extending even to recognition by Great Britain. It might so discourage the North that a settlement involving the Confederacy's continued independence could be reached with Lincoln.

To Buchanan, there was another incentive. Welles's injustice in refusing to permit him to recall his resignation rankled deep. Personal vindication, revenge for the affront, justification for the fact that he now fought against all he had once supported, including his own state—these were among his emotions, inextricably bound together with the larger and more formal motives he overtly protested.

It was a case of the congruence of personal and official requirements. Buchanan could not—would not—wait. Every day brought the *Monitor* nearer. True, inability to keep military secrets, common to both sides, gave possibility that the Union gunners already knew that *Merrimack*'s armor at the waterline had not been finished, that this was the place to aim at. For a certainty, every day's delay increased that possibility. He would have liked to await complete readiness, but the iron plates and bars were very slow in coming, and every day's delay increased the likelihood that *Merrimack*'s first battle would be against the formidable *Monitor*, instead of against the wooden ships already in his sights across the Roads. Another month, the present estimate, would be much too long. The big chance was now or maybe never. He fixed *Merrimack*'s maiden voyage for the night of 6 March, two days after taking command.

To get down the Elizabeth River at night and into Hampton Roads required lights in the channel. But all navigational lights had been removed, and some obstructions placed in it. A boat was therefore sent out on the fifth, under supervision of one of the pilots, to place temporary lights where required for guidance. Buchanan had directed that no one should leave the ship on Thursday the sixth, and had intended to call all hands together for a "before the battle" speech. Late that afternoon, however, Chief Pilot William Parrish sought him out.

Exactly what words passed between Buchanan and his pilot were never recorded, but considering the timing, the conversation must have been one of more than usual tension. The pilot announced he would not take responsibility for bringing the *Merrimack* down the Elizabeth River during darkness. He feared unmarked shoals, swift current, and possible inaccuracies in the locations of the block ships the Confederates had sunk in the river. Parrish was a civilian, hired by the navy because of his special knowledge, but not subject to naval laws or discipline. His entire training had been never to assume any risk whatever, whether to a ship or to himself. Moral courage he might have had; speaking to Buchanan under these circumstances would imply as much. There were those who afterward questioned if he had enough of the other kind. It is clear, in any case, that combat was not something he looked forward to.

In spite of his own desires, the ironclad's skipper was forced to acquiesce. He told Parrish to be ready to go at daybreak, but the pilot would have none of this either. With *Merrimack* drawing 23 feet, he said, she could clear the bar at the mouth of the Elizabeth only at high tide, at about two in the afternoon. Buchanan was forced to accept this judgment. If he disregarded his senior pilot's advice and thereby damaged the *Merrimack* to the detriment of his new country's interests, he would merit the condemnation of the entire Confederacy. Yet there could not be many more days before the *Monitor* would be in Hampton Roads. Buchanan was furious, but there was nothing he could do.

Tense and irritated, Buchanan stamped around his ship in futility. Finally he forced himself to turn in. His officers and most of the crew stayed up nearly the entire night supervising last-minute preparations. With dawn of the seventh, however, came further disappointment:

lowering clouds, strong winds, some rain. Under these conditions the pilots said they could not be responsible for getting the ship over the bar or back in again. There was some right on their side, and Buchanan was forced to agree. Once more a delay.

The eighth dawned a bright sunlit day. No wind, no storm clouds. The pilots, under strong pressure from a skipper now approaching rage, agreed to get the ship over the bar on the flooding tide a few minutes after eleven. With a growl from a restive Buchanan, *Merrimack* cleared her moorings and headed downstream. With her went the gunboats *Beaufort* and *Raleigh*. As soon as they saw her move, *Jamestown, Patrick Henry*, and *Teaser* came down from their station in the James River where they had been waiting. In order more easily to deflect enemy shot, the massive bulk of the ironclad had been liberally slushed down with tallow and wax. She glistened monstrously in the noonday sun. Shortly after noon the two doomed Union sailing warships saw the enemy they had been waiting for.

Part of Commodore Louis Goldsborough's strategy, as flag-officer commanding the Norfolk blockading squadron, was to keep the Confederate forces in the James River from having access to those in the Elizabeth. He accomplished this by keeping the *Congress* and *Cumberland*, sailers only and therefore among his less mobile ships, anchored in a narrow part of the channel between the two rivers. The channel passed close to Newport News; so the two sailing ships were also supported by the Union gun emplacements at that point. It was well understood that the *Congress* and *Cumberland* together could not match *Merrimack* in her new guise, any more than they could have before her conversion. However, the new ordnance pieces mounted by the *Cumberland*, though fewer in number, were the same as those of *Minnesota* and *Roanoke*, and had proved able to penetrate more than four inches of iron armor. The rifled pivot guns of all three ships had a long range and as good accuracy as any guns the Confederates might have. *Congress*, a few years older than *Cumberland*, had not yet been converted to carry the new guns and consequently, though she carried a greater number, they were of an older and less powerful type. Goldsborough was most concerned about the dependence of these two fine though antiquated ships on the wind alone for motive power, and had asked Welles for assignment of a pair of tugs to attach to them exclusively to move them when and if necessary. No tugs had yet been provided, but in Washington there were already beginning to be second thoughts about the advisability of exposing the defenseless *Congress* so close to the point where the converted *Merrimack* would first be seen. During the last week in January, Welles directed Goldsborough to send the *Congress* to Boston once he thought she could be spared from her station in Hampton Roads. Like all official correspondence of the time, the letter bearing this instruction was painstakingly copied by a clerk in beautiful penmanship on excellent quality lined paper, and sent by regular courier. Dated 24 January 1862, it ended, in accordance with the formula of the times: "I am, respectfully, your most obedient servant, Gideon Welles."

The letter arrived while Flag-Officer Goldsborough, commanding at Hampton Roads, was away at Roanoke Island with an expedition to capture the place. Temporary command had devolved upon the senior officer present, Captain John Marston, skipper of the steam frigate *Roanoke*, which, unfortunately, had a broken propeller shaft and, like the *Cumberland* and *Congress*, could move only by sail power. The letter Marston wrote to Welles in reply, likewise transcribed in beautiful penmanship by a yeoman trained in the art, said:

USS *Roanoke*
Hampton Roads, January 28, 1862
Sir: Your letter of the 24th instant, relative to the *Congress* going to Boston is at hand; but as long as the *Merrimack* is held as a rod over us I would by no means recommend that she should leave this place.
Very respectfully, your obedient servant,
John Marston

Work on the *Monitor* had been going forward rapidly. She was launched 97 days after her keel was laid, 101 days after the contract was let, and she went into commission 26 days later, on 25 February. The race was nearing the finish line.

In the meantime, other things also were being arranged. Ericsson's revolutionary "battery" would need a skipper and crew:

From Commodore Joseph Smith to Lieutenant John L. Worden:
(Private)   January 11, 1862
    My Dear Sir: I have only time to say I have named you for the command of the battery under contract with Captain Ericsson, now nearly ready at New York.
    This vessel is an experiment. I believe you are the right sort of officer to put in command of her.

Yours, truly, in haste,
Jos. Smith

The best personal description of Lieutenant Worden is found in a letter from Paymaster William F. Keeler of the *Monitor* to his wife, recently discovered and published by the U.S. Naval Institute. "He is quite tall, thin and effeminate looking, not withstanding a long [black] beard hanging down his breast—he is white and delicate, probably from long confinement, and never was a lady the possessor of a smaller or more delicate hand, but if I am not much mistaken he will not hesitate to submit our iron sides to as severe a test as the most warlike could desire. He is a perfect gentleman in manner." Keeler's mention of "long confinement" referred to Worden's recent imprisonment in Montgomery, Alabama. Prior to the beginning of hostilities, he had been sent as a courier by rail with dispatches for Fort Pickens and the Union fleet off Pensacola concerning their imminent reinforcement, and had been arrested as his train passed through Alabama. He had memorized and destroyed the messages, however, and since none were found he was allowed to proceed. On his return through Alabama he was again arrested on charge of violating his parole, and kept in solitary confinement until regularly exchanged in November 1861. The confinement was in part an effort to force him to reveal whatever information he was bringing North with him; partly, it was out of undisguised anger over the successful defense of Fort Pickens against the Confederate attempt to capture it—which, as it happened, took place the day after the reinforcements arrived.

John Worden at age forty-three had served twenty-eight years in the navy but had attained only the rank of lieutenant, owing to the slow creation of vacancies and consequent slow promotion during the pre-war years. Nevertheless, he was known as a very effective officer. It had already become the custom to find noncombat assignments for the superannuated officers with which both the army and navy were encumbered, in order to employ resilient younger ones in the more demanding situations. Thus Worden received what turned out to be the most important single ship command the navy had to offer. He reported to New York as prospective skipper of the *Monitor* on 16 January 1862, three days after receipt of his orders. On the thirtieth, his new ship was launched.

Assistant Secretary of the Navy Fox to Ericsson (telegram):

> NAVY DEPARTMENT, JANUARY 30, 1862
> I CONGRATULATE YOU AND TRUST SHE WILL BE A SUCCESS. HURRY HER FOR SEA, AS THE MERRIMACK IS NEARLY READY AT NORFOLK AND WE WISH TO SEND HER THERE.
>
> G. V. FOX

On 2 February, Captain G. J. Van Brunt, commanding officer of the flagship *Minnesota*, wrote to Goldsborough, still at Roanoke Island. The portion of his letter relating to the trial soon to be undergone by the Union fleet gives a good picture of the confused situation, but even so one wonders how Goldsborough could content himself with being absent on a relatively unimportant expedition when it was apparent to many that an engagement of some kind might be imminent.

> The *Merrimack* is, without doubt, out of dock and almost ready for a move. I am anxiously expecting her and believe I am ready, but I have doubts about her venturing out of Elizabeth River. I understand they have been putting down moorings for her about a mile inside Sewell's Point, and should not be surprised if she was only used for harbor defense, as I am told she floats with her roofing 2 feet under water, and that, in consequence, she can carry no battery. She is exceedingly crank and would be unsafe if she happened to get across the tides and might turn turtle.
>
> Your old friend and messmate,
> G. J. Van Brunt

Captain Van Brunt, and perhaps others of the blockading fleet, had read with interest and not a little relief certain accounts in Norfolk newspapers to the effect that the big new ironclad had proved a failure. Welles and Fox were in receipt of better information, and it does not appear they were at any time unaware of the true circumstances regarding their antagonist. The same cannot be said of the senior officers at Hampton Roads, however. Leaving the two sailing warships, *Cumberland* and *Congress*, at anchor without ready means of moving, and virtually without support, at the place where the *Merrimack* must inevitably first attack, cannot strike anyone as a sensible disposition of forces.

From Captain Marston to Secretary Welles:

> USS *Roanoke*
> Hampton Roads, February 12, 1862
>
> Sir: I learn from a man (a Russian) sent on board of me this day by General Wool, and who was at work in the Norfolk navy yard as late as Monday, the 10th, that it is still the intention of the rebels to bring the *Merrimack* down into these waters. That vessel is to be taken out of the dock next Monday, but when she will be ready my informant could not say, but probably soon, as everything—provisions, stores, etc.—were being put into her while she was in dock. This man says that the editorial in the Day Book was put in to deceive us, and that the *Merrimack* is not a failure.
>
> I have deemed it my duty to give you this information, and, trusting that we shall be able to give the rebels a warm reception, I remain,
>
> Very respectfully, your obedient servant,
> John Marston

With *Monitor* nearing completion, official orders for her employment were required. In accordance with long-standing custom, these were in letter form. It had been years, however, since such orders came directly from the secretary of the navy. For the *Monitor*, however, there was a letter from Secretary Welles to Lieutenant Worden:*

---

* It had become customary that newly commissioned ships should receive their initial orders from the command under whose authority they had been built or placed in commission. But from this moment on, in the case of the *Monitor*, Secretary Welles took direct control of the ship, transmitting orders and advice directly to her skipper by whatever means seemed appropriate. Worden,

Navy Department, February 20, 1862
Sir: Proceed with the U.S.S. *Monitor*, under your command, to Hampton Roads, Virginia, and on your arrival there report by letter to the Department. Commodore Paulding has been instructed to charter a vessel to accompany the *Monitor* provided none of our vessels are going south about the time she sails. Transmit to the Department a muster roll of the crew and a separate list of the officers of the *Monitor* before sailing from New York

I am, respectfully, your obedient servant,
Gideon Welles

Things were moving in Hampton Roads, too. Captain Marston wrote the following to Secretary Welles:

USS *Roanoke*, Hampton Roads
February 21, 1862
Sir: By a dispatch which I received late last evening from General Wool, I learn that the *Merrimack* will positively attack Newport News within five days, acting in conjunction with the *Jamestown* and *Yorktown* from James River, and that the attack will be at night. I can only regret that the *Roanoke* should be without an engine, and has a deficiency of 180 men in her crew; but you may be assured we shall do our best.

Very respectfully, your obedient servant,
John Marston

Assistant Secretary Fox to John Ericsson (telegram):

WASHINGTON, D.C., FEBRUARY 21, 1862
IT IS VERY IMPORTANT THAT YOU SHOULD SAY EXACTLY THE DAY THE MONITOR CAN BE AT HAMPTON ROADS. CONSULT WITH COMMODORE PAULDING.

G. V. FOX

From Chief Engineer Stimers to Commodore Smith:

New York, February 26, 1862
Sir: The *Monitor* would have gone to sea this morning, but was

---

for his part, recognized the special circumstances by occasional reports directly to the secretary, bypassing the chain of command. There is no record that anyone protested, for all realized the urgencies of the situation did not admit of institutionalized procedure.

detained for her ammunition. At dusk this evening, however, the last shell was snugly stored, and we sail at daylight in the morning, unless the weather prove unfavorable.

The draft of water, taken at the extremes of upper vessel, is: Forward, 9 feet 2 inches; aft, 10 feet 5 inches. . . . She has 80 tons of coal in the bunkers, which will lighten the stern as it comes out, and I consider it advisable that she shall always trim by the stern at sea, as when a sea breaks over the bow it has to sustain the superincumbent weight of the wave while it rolls across, which, of course, depresses it, and if we trimmed to an even keel in smooth water we would always be down by the head when underway in rough weather. . . .

> I am, very respectfully, your obedient servant,
> Alban C. Stimers

From Lieutenant Worden to Secretary Welles:

> U.S.S. *Monitor*
> New York
> February 27, 1862

Sir: I have the honor to report that the U.S.S. *Monitor*, under my command, left the navy yard this morning to proceed to sea. In going down the East River she steered so badly that I deemed it advisable not to proceed farther with her. I therefore returned, and am now at anchor off the navy yard.

Chief Engineer Stimers will immediately call on Mr. Ericsson to ascertain from him what he proposes to do to remedy the defect in her steering apparatus.

> Respectfully, your obedient servant,
> John L. Worden

Paymaster Keeler wrote a much more dramatic version of this incident to his wife:

> New York, Feb. 28, 1862

Here I am at anchor in Bridsey's Store. When I last wrote you everything was hurry & confusion on board expecting to start immediately. Powder, shot, shell, grape & canister were taken aboard in abundance & I have made as I suppose my last visit ashore as we were under sailing orders & were to leave the same day, but our preparations were so numerous we were delayed till the next morning (yesterday), when our hawsers were cast loose & we were on our way to Hampton Roads in the midst of a terrible snow storm. We ran first to the New York side then to Brooklyn & so back & forth across the river, first to one side then to the other, like a drunken man on a side walk, till we brought up against the gas works with a shock that nearly took us from our feet. We found she would not answer her rudder at all & it was of no use to go further, so we took a tow back to the Yard & am now waiting for alterations in her steering apparatus, which we hope will be completed by tomorrow night so that we hope to try once more either Sunday or Monday morning—All are getting impatient & want to get alongside the *Merrimac*—still I should not be at all surprised if we met with further delays & eventually were obliged to have a new rudder. . . .

The urgency of the situation had begun to tell on everyone. Welles knew that the *Merrimack* was due out within a matter of days. So was the *Monitor*, but she had a distance of four hundred miles to travel. The *Monitor* had to be finished; but she also had to be ready for combat. Welles could not wait upon telegraph or letters. The delay even in delivery of telegrams might amount to several hours. Fox therefore traveled to New York with instructions to make decisions on the spot.

From Lieutenant Worden to Assistant Secretary Fox (telegram):

> NEW YORK, MARCH 1, 1862
>
> YOUR DISPATCH IS JUST RECEIVED. CAPTAIN ERICSSON WILL HAVE COMPLETED CHANGES IN THE STEERING GEAR TOMORROW, AND WE MAKE A TRIAL TRIP ON MONDAY MORNING.
>
> WORDEN

Monday was the third. Fox arrived in New York in time to be aboard the *Monitor* during the trial of the rudder. On the fourth, he went out again to witness the trial of *Monitor*'s guns, and was forced to sit by while a derangement in the friction recoil system was repaired. Too practical a man not to welcome the accident at a time when the builder was readily available to make repairs, Fox nevertheless found it difficult to contain his impatience over the additional delay. He used the time to some advantage by having Commodore Paulding, now commandant of the New York Navy Yard, issue the orders detaching the *Monitor*, and by telegraphing Welles that the ship would be on her way on the fifth.

The tension over the *Merrimack* had built up in Washington. Exaggerated claims as to her prowess had been made almost daily in Southern newspapers, and equally exaggerated estimates were prevalent among Northern authorities. At the same time, it had become recognized that the little *Monitor* was the only ship in the Union navy that could meet her on any terms of possible near equality—and she was totally untried. Despite Ericsson's confidence in her, few others shared his claim that his two 11-inch guns in their rotating iron house could equal the *Merrimack*'s eight 9-inch Dahlgren guns on her broadsides and the two rifled 7-inch pivoting guns commanding her bow and stern arcs. Everyone in the government had his own ideas about how the *Monitor* should be used, and did not hesitate to express them. Welles had good reason to fear the effect of all the unsolicited advice upon the men in Hampton Roads, and the absence of Fox left him uneasy. On 4 March he sent the following to Marston:

> Sir: . . . Do not allow the *Monitor* to go under fire of the enemy's batteries, except for some pressing emergency, until further orders from the Department. Her commander should exercise his men at the guns, and in all respects prepare for serious work.
> I am, respectfully, your obedient servant,
> Gideon Welles

Welles had been having political troubles over the *Merrimack* as well. Through the new secretary of war, Edwin Stanton, General McClellan, commander of the Army of the Potomac, demanded assurance that the navy would protect his flanks on the Potomac River. Stanton had the idea that his cabinet precedence over Welles meant also that the navy was somehow subordinate to him, and proceeded to send a number of orders directly to Captain Marston at Hampton Roads, to

Commander Dahlgren at the Washington Navy Yard, and to others. Had he known how to reach Worden, he would have sent him orders to report to General McClellan for duty. Welles was fearful that Worden might receive ill-advised orders to engage in some activity that might endanger the safety of his supremely valuable ship. Recognizing the effect Stanton was beginning to have on Lincoln and unable to convince them that the *Merrimack* drew too much water to hazard the lengthy Potomac River passage (which had a limiting draft of approximately twenty feet), Welles was finally forced to agree to have Worden bring his little ship to Washington for protection of the capital.

Perhaps the *Minnesota* and the others could keep the *Merrimack* occupied for a time; it was hardly believable that four powerful ships could not deal with one, even one with armored sides. And once the *Monitor* was in the Potomac, she could be sent down to join the fight at any time. The big thing was to get her into the action area, where her presence would prove a powerful deterrent to Confederate adventurism. So went the rationale for this illogical order. It had become a cabinet decision, which Welles was forced to honor.

Here, however, under maximum pressure from all sides, the navy secretary displayed his Connecticut shrewdness. Recognizing the unpredictable character of McClellan—leading to the probability that, not aware of other orders, or not caring to inform himself, McClellan might attempt to control the *Monitor* directly—Welles sent his next message in army cipher, via Major General Dix at Baltimore to Major General Wool at Old Point Comfort, with the request that it be sent out to the *Roanoke* by boat. As a cabinet officer, his orders would take precedence over those of any general, and he had taken the precaution, by using army code and the "via" procedure, of making them known to the army officers commanding in the communication chain. This would effectively prevent McClellan from issuing contradictory directions under the guise of ignorance. Now the only persons who would dare to send orders of any kind to Worden or Marston would be Stanton or Lincoln. Of the President he had no fears on this score, and he would keep a close eye on the secretary of war. He sent his message on 5 March, and made it very simple:

FOR CAPTAIN JOHN MARSTON: DIRECT LIEUTENANT COMMANDING *
JOHN L. WORDEN, OF THE MONITOR, TO PROCEED IMMEDIATELY TO
WASHINGTON WITH HIS VESSEL.

GIDEON WELLES, SECRETARY OF THE NAVY

Fox had informed Welles by telegram on the fourth that the *Monitor* would in all probability leave New York on the fifth. But on the fifth he was forced to add another day. Welles then sent the following telegram to Commodore Paulding:

NAVY DEPARTMENT, MARCH 6, 1862
LET THE MONITOR COME DIRECT TO WASHINGTON, ANCHORING BE-
LOW ALEXANDRIA.

GIDEON WELLES

But Welles could hardly contain himself. All his senses were jangling. Reports from Norfolk were that the *Merrimack* was on the point of leaving the yard, that she was about to attack the Union fleet. Goldsborough was still away from his post. Marston, although a good man, was merely a substitute, and in a disabled ship at that. Fox, whose knowledge about the navy had been of tremendous support and encouragement, was not in Washington. Welles was being assailed on all sides with advice and demands for information. He was afraid of what McClellan, or someone else usurping authority, might try to do in the misguided intention of "helping." He dared not let the *Monitor* get away from his immediate control. He sent another telegram to Paulding on the same day, and tried to camouflage his anxiety by adding a second, unrelated inquiry about another ship:

NAVY DEPARTMENT, MARCH 6, 1862
PLEASE TELEGRAPH AS SOON AS THE MONITOR LEAVES. WHAT VES-
SELS DID YOU SEND AFTER THE VERMONT?

GIDEON WELLES

---

* Although Worden had not been "promoted"—he was still officially a lieutenant—the commissioning of the *Monitor* took place on 25 February. He was from that moment a lieutenant *commanding* a man-of-war, and automatically took that title, along with a pay increase. By custom, as with the courtesy rank of commodore, once an officer had attained command he retained the title and rank, and could expect to be assigned thereafter to comparable responsibilities. The telegram from Welles was his first official acknowledgment of Worden's new status. The present lieutenant commander rank is, of course, derived from the older custom.

Paulding tried but was unable to carry out the secretary's instructions regarding the *Monitor*'s destination. She had gotten clear of New York at last, and though he pursued her with a tug, he was unable to catch her or attract her attention. But on the following day, the seventh, a welcome letter arrived at the Navy Department. Captain Marston had accurately read between the lines. No instructions received through the army or any other means, if not from Welles, would be honored.

From Captain Marston to Secretary Welles:

> U.S.S. *Roanoke*
> Hampton Roads, March 6, 1862
> Sir: I have the honor to acknowledge receipt of your letter of the 4th instant. . . .
> The *Monitor* will be sent to Washington immediately on her arrival at this place, in accordance with your telegraphic despatch through General Dix.

Shortly thereafter came another, made unnecessary because Gustavus Fox, who had seen Worden off, was now back at his desk in Washington.

From Lieutenant Commanding Worden to Secretary Welles:

> U.S.S. *Monitor*
> off New York Harbor, March 6, 1862
> Sir: By the pilot I have the honor to report that we passed the bar at 4 P.M., the steamers *Currituck* and *Sachem* and tug *Seth Low* in company. The weather is favorable. In order to reach Hampton Roads as soon as possible, whilst the fine weather lasts, I have been taken in tow by the tug.

There was much to do in Washington on Friday, 7 March. Having visited the *Monitor* and gained a firsthand acquaintance of her power, Fox had, by extension, an impression of the power of the ship she was to meet. It was obvious that no ship without equal armor could survive in combat against either. Each had only to approach her enemy close aboard. As had been amply proved at Sinope and by Dahlgren's firing tests, at close range the *Monitor*'s 11-inch smoothbore cannons would shatter a wooden opponent's sides with ease. So, obviously, could the

Merrimack's guns. Naval combat had entered a new phase: as guns had improved over the past few years, ships in combat tended to fight at longer ranges compatible with their own survival. Armor changed all that; an armored ship could approach within feet of an opponent in total safety to herself. At such short range, her guns could not miss, nor could wooden timbers of any thickness stand against them.

Fox came back to Washington convinced that the *Cumberland* and *Congress*, exposed in Hampton Roads as they were, were helpless against the *Merrimack* and in dire danger. In the meantime, a letter from Captain Marston had announced the arrival of the sailing frigate *St. Lawrence*, a duplicate of the *Congress*. She, too, was now anchored as a target in Hampton Roads. The fleet flagship *Minnesota* and her consort *Roanoke*, much bigger and more heavily built ships, were nearly as vulnerable—particularly *Roanoke*, without use of her engine. Keeping them in this position was suicidal, and it gave the *Merrimack* a magnificent target. If the Union fleet in Hampton Roads were to be eliminated—and without the *Monitor* Fox saw this as a strong possibility—the effect on the Union's prospects might be close to catastrophic. His analysis agreed in every detail with that of his opponents, Mallory and Buchanan. How to prevent it from becoming a reality?

First, of course, was to convince Welles, no longer a difficult thing to do. *Merrimack* was clearly poised for action. She had been seen at a fitting-out pier, and Northern sympathizers in Norfolk reported the dismissal of the workmen, albeit some were still aboard finishing some last-minute items. If all went well with the *Monitor*, she should arrive on Sunday, 9 March. Far better for the *Merrimack* to have free run of the James River and Hampton Roads until then. Doubtless Secretary of War Stanton would protest mightily at the possible embarrassment of General Wool; General McClellan, if he behaved according to pattern, would delay the start of his peninsula campaign still longer. But the *Monitor* would surely arrive on Sunday. The *Merrimack* would not enjoy her superiority in lower Chesapeake Bay more than a day or two. Then the *Monitor*'s presence would redress the odds and protect Washington from the dreaded foray up the Potomac; if necessary, she could seek a battle. The most likely scenario would simply be that her mere presence would hold the status quo long enough for General McClellan to begin his long-delayed campaign.

From Secretary Welles to Captain Marston (telegram):

> NAVY DEPARTMENT, MARCH 7, 1862
>
> SEND THE ST. LAWRENCE, CONGRESS AND CUMBERLAND INTO THE POTOMAC RIVER. LET THE DISPOSITION OF THE REMAINDER OF THE VESSELS AT HAMPTON ROADS BE MADE ACCORDING TO YOUR BEST JUDGEMENT AFTER CONSULTATION WITH GENERAL WOOL. USE STEAM TO TOW THEM UP. I WILL ALSO TRY AND SEND A COUPLE OF STEAMERS FROM BALTIMORE TO ASSIST.
>
> GIDEON WELLES

From Assistant Secretary Fox to Lieutenant Parker, Navy Yard, Washington (telegram):

> NAVY DEPARTMENT, MARCH 7, 1862
>
> IS THE TELEGRAM TO CAPTAIN MARSTON RECEIVED AND UNDERSTOOD, AND WILL IT GO TONIGHT?
>
> G. V. FOX

From Fox to F. S. Corkran, Naval Officer of Customs, Baltimore (telegram):

> NAVY DEPARTMENT, MARCH 7, 1862
>
> CAN YOU CHARTER AND SEND A COUPLE OF STEAMERS TO OLD POINT TO ASSIST IN TOWING TWO OR THREE SAILING VESSELS INTO THE POTOMAC? DO SO, IF POSSIBLE, ON THE BEST TERMS.
>
> G. V. FOX

It was a long and worried night in Washington. Worden was fully aware of the need for speed and could be depended on to make the best time possible. It could hardly be conceived, however, that news of his departure from New York had not been flashed by telegraph to Richmond. No doubt, despite the problems they, too, must be facing with the *Merrimack*, the Confederates would try strenuously to get their ship out before the *Monitor* could arrive. Saturday, 8 March, was bound to be a crucial day.

That morning, Fox came to the department with an idea. He would go to Old Point Comfort himself, see to the necessary arrangements, and make any required adjustments on the spot. Both he and Welles were concerned that Flag-Officer Goldsborough was not present. It would be well for Fox to be there. There would have not yet been time to move the endangered ships. That, too, Fox could handle on the spot.

It must parenthetically be suggested that had Goldsborough been in Hampton Roads, Fox would have thought of some other reason why his own presence was required as well. He had earned the confidence of his superior, the idea suited the personalities of both, and in any case the assistant secretary, a former naval officer himself, could not have kept away from the scene of the impending conflict.

From Secretary Welles to Captain Marston (telegram):

> NAVY DEPARTMENT, MARCH 8, 1862
>
> THE ASSISTANT SECRETARY WILL BE AT OLD POINT BY THE BALTI-MORE BOAT OF THIS EVE. DO NOT MOVE THE SHIPS UNTIL FURTHER ORDERS, WHICH HE WILL CARRY.
>
> GIDEON WELLES

From Assistant Secretary Fox to F. S. Corkran, Baltimore (telegram):

> NAVY DEPARTMENT, MARCH 8, 1862
>
> WAIT FURTHER INSTRUCTIONS. I GO TO OLD POINT IN THE 3 PM TRAIN.
>
> G. V. FOX

From Assistant Secretary Fox to Moor N. Falls, Baltimore (telegram):

> NAVY DEPARTMENT, MARCH 8, 1862
>
> I MUST GO TO OLD POINT BY THE 3 PM TRAIN. TWO OR THREE FRIENDS. DONT LET THE OLD POINT BOAT GO.
>
> G. V. FOX

Fox was referring to the 3 P.M. train from Washington to Baltimore. The normal way to travel between Washington and Norfolk was by the overnight steamer from Baltimore. He would arrive early on the morning of the ninth, carrying with him Welles's full delegation of authority.

But time had already run out for the ships in Hampton Roads.

While Fox was in the train en route to Baltimore, the *Cumberland* was sunk and the *Congress* set afire, from which she would explode in a fantastic display of pyrotechnics after nightfall. The Union fleet flagship *Minnesota*, helplessly aground, had been heavily damaged, not only by the *Merrimack* but also by the *Merrimack*'s consorts, who had been able to fire upon her with impunity while her attention was taken by the menacing ironclad. The *Roanoke* and *St. Lawrence* had likewise run aground and were unable to assist the flagship. Hampton Roads was a shambles.

The Union fleet in Chesapeake Bay had suffered a stunning defeat. The ironclad *Merrimack* had single-handedly turned the tide of the war. The Army of the Potomac, the soldiers at Newport News, all the Union soldiers stationed in the grand old fort at Old Point, had witnessed the debacle. When he arrived on the scene the next morning, Fox knew he was looking at a national disaster, alleviated only by whatever might result from arrival of the *Monitor*, several hours earlier.

11

Battles Between Ironclad Ships; War in the Inland Waters and at Sea

Saturday, 8 March 1862, was washday in the Union fleet in Hampton Roads. The rigging of all the ships anchored there was festooned with the drying clothing of their crews. A few minutes before noon, the smoke of three ships was noted rising from behind the land in the back reaches of the Elizabeth River and this was reported to Lieutenant George Morris, executive officer of the *Cumberland*. Commander Radford, her skipper, had been summoned to the *Roanoke* to sit on a court of inquiry. Morris was temporarily in command. Next junior to him was Lieutenant Thomas Selfridge, *Cumberland*'s gunnery officer. For a wooden sloop of war, their ship was a powerful unit, much more so than the *Congress* or *St. Lawrence*, but less powerful than the *Minnesota* or *Roanoke*. Her principal deficiency, however, was that she lacked an engine. As to her battery, she carried only half as many guns as prior to her conversion, but they were of the Dahlgren type, very heavy smoothbores. On her forecastle she had her best piece of ordnance, a long rifled cannon with great accuracy and long range, mounted to permit being trained in any direction. Nearly all her guns could shoot either solid shot or the lighter explosive shells. Selfridge had taken pride that his ship and his gunnery department were "on point," as it were, of any prospective action. The rifled cannon was a very special piece. If it came to a contest with the *Merrimack* or any other ship armored to resist gunfire, it was to this gun that he looked to penetrate the iron and equalize the odds. And, he had trained his crews hard.

Cumberland was third strongest of the Union warships, but only the *Minnesota* had a steam engine. All the others could move only under sail or with the assistance of tugs, which were far too few and too vulnerable to be of much use in combat. The tugs and additional steamers so desperately ordered at the last minute by Welles and Fox had not arrived. There was no wind, no way to move. *Cumberland* would have to fight at anchor. Parenthetically, one wonders what the Union commanders could have been thinking of when they convened a court of inquiry on a day the Navy Department in Washington was nearly frantic with the signs of imminent movement by the *Merrimack*. It was almost as though they could not lay aside their rituals, even in the face of signals that one of the life-and-death struggles of the Civil War was about to take place. Had Buchanan and Mallory succeeded in their grand design, the course taken by the war might have been very different. Significantly, no one today knows nor cares what the court of inquiry was about, or who were the interested parties.

As the officers trained their long glasses on the smoke in the Elizabeth River, in the direction of the old Norfolk Navy Yard, they also noted two other ships in the James River, which had evidently come down during the night. Smoke was rising from them too! Aboard *Cumberland* there was an unnatural stillness. The normal clatter and bustle of a busy crew on a relaxed routine had ceased. Men who had a moment earlier been occupied in a hundred little tasks of ship's or personal upkeep stopped what they were doing. All activity had come to an end. A portentous quiet lay upon them. Everyone sat, or stood, where he had been, alertly upright, listening, watching, anxious to know if this was to be the day they had feared. If so, many of them would be dead before nightfall. The silent question roared out of a hundred suddenly dry throats: *"Is it the Merrimack?"*

Morris made his movements very deliberate. He could feel the flesh on the back of his hands twitch, and the soles of his feet within their uniform shoes suddenly perspired. Carefully he pitched his voice. Clear. Loud. Exaggeratedly formal, in accordance with tradition. Confident, although he did not feel confident, or even sure he was not announcing his own death.

"Mr. Selfridge, will you have the ship cleared for action, if you please." It was then exactly forty minutes after noon.

At about the same time, Chief Engineer Ramsay of the *Merrimack* made a report to Buchanan that he was never to make again: their ship's engines were behaving well. Before "going south," Ramsay had been assistant engineer of the old Union frigate. He was back at his old job—but now in charge—and his words actually were more wish than fact. After their lengthy and careful overhaul, the engines and boilers, for a very short time, were performing at their best.

Buchanan was still standing on top of *Merrimack*'s casemate, rubbing his hands together, feeling with his palms the brisk air of the ship's passage. For March, it was a beautiful day; not too chilly, though certainly not warm. There was no breeze to assist the maneuverability of the Union ships. A flat calm lay on the waters of Hampton Roads, much different from the day before. His chief engineer's report pleased him immensely. There was no sign of the *Monitor*, although there had been a rumor that she had left New York two days before. Perhaps he had beaten her! There was much to do, and his opportunity lay directly before him. His new ship had it within her to become Queen of Chesapeake Bay, and he aimed to cause it to happen.

For a considerable time, Buchanan, Catesby Jones, and one or two others still kept to the exposed upper deck, disdaining for the time being the cramped conical pilothouse on the forward end of the ship's iron casemate. Where they stood the deck was about twenty feet wide, constructed of iron bars formed into a large grating. Under their feet they could see the men of the guns' crews gathered in knots around their pieces. Just forward of them was the cast-steel pilothouse, its tip waist-high. Halfway to the stern rose the great iron smokestack, braced with guy-wires, standing vertically and menacingly in the middle of the deck. All the way aft, at the stern of the casemate and atop a tall flagstaff, floated a large Confederate flag.

Beneath them the black sides of the casemate, gleaming under a coat of heavy grease, fell away sharply to water. Heavy black cannon muzzles protruded through ten of the fourteen gunports. The heat of the boilers and engines below came up through the grating, warming the men topside. Despite the cold March air in Hampton Roads, it must already be hot inside the casemate. It would be much hotter soon.

In the meantime, *Cumberland* had put up a flaghoist to alert the ships around the bend in Hampton Roads. After an interval, the gunboat *Mount Vernon*, coaling in the Roads, repeated the signal. Several minutes later, getting no response from the two big ships near Old Point Comfort, *Mount Vernon* fired a gun to attract their attention. This had the desired result. Black smoke belched from the stacks of both *Minnesota* and *Roanoke*, although since the *Roanoke*'s engine was not operational, fires under her boilers affected morale only. No orders had been given not to light them, most likely for exactly this reason. The three tugs available were hastily summoned alongside the big ships, one to the flagship and two to the otherwise immobile *Roanoke*.

The *Merrimack* drew so much water that she had to remain in the middle of the Elizabeth River channel until after she had passed Sewell's Point, site of the present Norfolk Naval Operating Base. Then she entered the broader navigable waters of the Roads. Slightly to starboard and dead ahead lay the *Minnesota*, *Roanoke*, and *St. Lawrence*, anchored in a row off Old Point Comfort and Fortress Monroe. As the Confederate ironclad passed from the Elizabeth River channel into the wider reaches of the waters joining Hampton Roads and Chesapeake Bay, *Cumberland* and *Congress*, anchored well off to port in the James River, disappeared behind Newport News Point. In the center of Hampton Roads and almost due west of the exit from the Elizabeth River channel lay a banana-shaped reef called Middle Ground, so located that ships of deep draft had to pass either north or south of it. Buchanan thus had his choice of continuing directly ahead and slightly to the right to attack the hurriedly preparing Union flagship and her consorts, or turning sharp left, passing above or below Middle Ground

Reef, to make for the two weaker ships anchored off Newport News in the James River.

By such decisions are the lives and deaths of men shaped. Buchanan had already decided to attack the *Cumberland* and *Congress* first, inasmuch as they blocked the James River and egress of two small vessels of his squadron, *Patrick Henry* and *Jamestown*. But as the officers of the two sailing ships watched, their formidable enemy passed out of sight beyond Newport News Point headed toward the three ships near Fort Monroe. For a few heart-stopping minutes they felt a reprieve from danger, but then the heavy smoke of the big menacing ironclad seemed to remain in one place. And shortly afterward, it could be seen coming their way. Buchanan had put his helm hard to starboard, rudder to the left, was passing Middle Ground Reef by the north channel, and soon appeared once again around Newport News Point, followed by the two smaller steamers that had come down the Elizabeth River with him.

It had been, of course, a fatal error for the Union forces to divide their strength, even by the small distance separating Old Point Comfort and Newport News. This presented Buchanan with two small enemy squadrons which he could attack individually: the dream of every fleet commander. As he proceeded to take advantage of the opportunity, *Minnesota*, *Roanoke*, and *St. Lawrence* desperately got up their anchors to come to the assistance of their two threatened comrades, but it was too late.

All this time, an equally desperate *Monitor* was struggling southward from New York. Thursday the sixth had been a good day at sea, but the seventh had been miserable. The same storm that kept the *Merrimack* from going out when Buchanan originally intended had gone eastward off the coast of New Jersey, where it struck the low-lying little *Monitor* with a fury intensified by the long "fetch" over sea, unhindered by intervening land masses. Large waves rolled unimpeded across the little craft's low flat deck, inundated her tiny pilothouse (which had to be covered with a tarpaulin), and burst in cascades of spray against the great round turret. Much water worked under the base of the turret, and quantities more leaked in through various other openings. As the day wore on the weather worsened to the point where waves came aboard that were higher than the temporary ventilation intake ducts (four feet high above the deck) and, indeed, higher than the six-foot temporary smoke pipes fitted to carry away the little ship's stack gases. Water poured down both intakes and exhausts, dampened the coal, nearly drowned the boiler fires, and so wet the belts driving the ventilation blowers that they stretched and began to slip on the driving pulleys. The *Monitor*'s interior was consequently filled with noxious gases. Many of her engineering people passed out at their posts, and for a time it appeared as if her crew might have to abandon ship. A full-fledged emergency faced Worden and his men, some of them so ill from seasickness and the gases of combustion they had been breathing that they were thought to be dying (one was believed dead when pulled out of the engine room). But the distance from New York to Cape Charles was short, the storm was short-lived, and the emergency, which at one time had *Monitor*'s ensign inverted as a sign of distress to her escorts, came finally under control. Next day, Saturday the eighth, at about the time the *Merrimack* appeared to the Union fleet, the *Monitor* had Cape Charles in sight and was nearing the entrance to Chesapeake Bay. A little after 4:00 P.M. she cast off the tow, steamed between the capes into the bay, and began to hear heavy gunfire in the distance.

The heavy Union frigates had attempted to go to the assistance of their fellows under attack off Newport News, but with little success. The 18-foot shoal line runs nearly directly between Old Point Comfort and Newport News, and perhaps for fear of exposing themselves too much to the *Merrimack* if she should turn upon them, the skippers of *Minnesota*, *Roanoke*, and *St. Lawrence* hugged the shallow water too closely with the result that all three ran aground. Only the *Minnesota*, with her own motive power, came close enough to the location of the battle to become actively engaged, though not until after her two consorts to the west had been destroyed.

The battle was not a battle but a massacre, so far as *Cumberland*

and *Congress* were concerned. Rightly judging the recently renovated *Cumberland* as the most dangerous, Buchanan made for her first, firing at the *Congress* at convenience only. The sloop of war fought back desperately, earning much credit from all observers on both sides. Her pivot gun fully proved up to the heavy expectations placed on it, breaking off the muzzles of two of the ironclad's guns and raising havoc with her topsides in general. Unfortunately for the North, the vulnerability of *Merrimack*'s waterline, to which the planned armor had not yet been fixed, had been a secret well kept. The *Cumberland* aimed at her antagonist's gunports when she realized she could not penetrate her armor, and it never occurred to anyone to aim lower, where an accurate shot would have penetrated and probably sunk her. The *Cumberland* caused nearly all the casualties sustained by the *Merrimack* during her two days in action: two killed and a number wounded.

At the same time, the Confederate ironclad had been inflicting horrendous damage on the Union ship. At point-blank range, her powerful guns tore her opponent apart. Shot after shot went completely through both sides of the doomed sloop of war. The greatest damage, however, was inflicted by the *Merrimack*'s ram, which smashed a hole in her side "big enough to drive a horse and cart through." *Cumberland* began to sink, her weight bearing down upon the Confederate ram's submerged bow, depressing it to a worrisome extent. Additional submergence did not increase displacement until the rounded forward portion of the *Merrimack*'s shield began to go more deeply into the water—some distance aft of where the sinking ship's weight was applied. According to all reports, the water rose up the side of the shield to within only inches of the lower edges of the gunports. Had it overflowed and poured into the interior, nothing could have saved the pride of the Confederate Navy from going down with her first victim.

But this was not to be. Aware of the danger, Buchanan was backing at full speed to pull clear. In the process the two ships swung alongside each other, causing the *Merrimack* to wrench her ram out of the wooden ship's side with a prying motion instead of backing it out directly as had been Buchanan's intention. The 1,500-pound piece of wrought iron, inadequately fastened, was ripped off her bows and broken in the process. The sloop of war began to sink rapidly, still firing the guns that had not yet submerged. She went down with her flag flying, to the plaudits of friend and foe alike; and when she fetched up in fifty-three feet of water, the upper portions of her masts remained above the surface, still flying it.

Now it was the turn of the *Congress*. But that ship had set her fore topsail and cut her anchor cable; what little wind there was drifted her into the mud near Newport News Point. The *Merrimack*, of greater draft than the obsolescent frigate, could not follow, but she was able to lie within gun range and pound *Congress* to pieces. Lieutenant Joseph Smith, her former second-in-command and newly appointed skipper (son of the commodore on the Ironclad Board), was killed at this time, and command devolved upon his executive officer, Lieutenant Austin Pendergrast. Still aboard, after some three weeks awaiting transportation to his next duty assignment, was Joseph Smith's immediate predecessor in command, Commander William Smith, who by this circumstance was the senior officer on board the ship.

It is evident William was not the man Joseph was. Pendergrast consulted with his old skipper, and the two men decided to give up the fight. Buchanan directed the gunboat *Beaufort* to go alongside and receive the surrender. (When old Commodore Smith heard that his son's ship had surrendered, his sorrowful comment was, "Then Joe's dead!")

The situation was clearly a confused one. When the *Beaufort* came alongside, Commander Smith and Lieutenant Pendergrast came down the side of the taller *Congress* and declared they had surrendered. The commander of the *Beaufort* directed them to return aboard the *Congress* and get their swords in order to make the surrender in proper form. This they did, although Pendergrast returned with an ordinary ship's cutlass instead of the more appropriate officer's dress sword, which he either did not have or could not find in his hurry. But in the meantime the troops at Newport News Point, watching the goings-on with understandable interest, found they could reach the Confederate ships with rifle fire and opened what was described as "a tremendous barrage." This had the effect of frustrating the surrender, since Buchanan's forces could not take possession without suffering casualties. Smith and Pendergrast, according to the Confederate report, asked to return to the *Congress* to supervise transfer and protection of the wounded; then, along with most of their crew, they seized the opportunity to escape in one of the boats or (this is not clear) perhaps by swimming to the shore.

The real point at issue was the collision between the realities of the situation and the romantic notions about naval chivalry to which Buchanan adhered. His attitude may be summarized as that, the *Congress* having surrendered, he should have been allowed to take possession without molestation by troops on shore. They, of course, could not know what was going on aboard the ships, nor would the knowledge have dissuaded them from firing in any case. Finding their enemy unable to consummate the surrender, Smith and Pendergrast felt no obligation to insist on becoming prisoners. Buchanan considered them totally dishonorable in not returning.

Much grist was thereby created for the mills of partisan historians, who wrote lengthy dissertations on the rights and wrongs of the actions taken. Buchanan, as might be expected, exploded in a towering rage. He snatched up a rifle and began shooting at the *Congress* and at the militiamen ashore. He also ordered that fire be reopened on the hapless frigate with red-hot shot in order to set her afire. But the doughty commodore paid for his histrionics: a rifle bullet from the shore struck him in the upper thigh, injuring the femoral artery and disabling him. Command of the *Merrimack* now fell to Lieutenant Catesby Jones. The *Congress* burned for several hours, finally exploding about midnight. The little *Monitor* arrived in time to see her tragic final fireworks.

One of the Confederate objectives was of course the opening up of the James River to traffic from Norfolk. Of immediate benefit was the juncture Buchanan's force was able to make with the two ships sent from Richmond to join in the battle. Although the Union forces could count more guns, he now had quite as many ships under his command as were under the absent Goldsborough—and one of them was the most powerful ship yet to fight on either side.

Not unnoticed by the Confederate officers, nor unexpected by those with battle experience, was that the big *Merrimack* drew all the enemy attention. All the Union guns were trained on her whenever possible. A veritable hail of shot and shell bounced off her greased sides, demolishing her smokestack, tearing off her flagstaff, wrecking her two boats in their davits. Her consorts, much smaller ships—hardly worth notice while the huge iron-plated casemate dominated the scene, though lightly armed and thinly armored (only in strategic spots)—were thereby enabled to come much closer to the enemy than they might otherwise have dared, and they took full advantage of the opportunity. Most of the damage suffered by the immobilized *Minnesota* on this day was done by the little *Patrick Henry* and the still smaller *Jamestown* after Jones had succeeded Buchanan in command of the *Merrimack*. Flames were leaping up the masts of the *Congress*, aground off Newport News Point near her sunken mate *Cumberland*, when Jones headed for the next ship on Buchanan's agenda, the fleet flagship herself.

Captain Van Brunt of the *Minnesota* had made it easy for her enemy, but the Confederate ironclad failed to take advantage of what, in retrospect, was her greatest opportunity. Traveling too close to the shallow-water line, Van Brunt had driven his ship firmly into the muck lining the bottom of Hampton Roads. She was totally immovable and presented an easy target. There were two hours of daylight left.

But *Merrimack*, built on the same hull and weighed down with armor, needed at least as much water as her former sister. Jones fired a few rounds at her from long range, struck her once, but dared not approach closer for fear of also sticking in the mud. His smokestack having been shot away, the draft for the fires under his boilers was now poor; steam pressure was low, good for only four knots speed. With the redoubtable Buchanan disabled, Jones was assailed by the nervous pilots, who feared the ebbing tide and the approach of darkness—and, it is almost redundant to say, the battle. Buchanan would have insisted on staying longer, probably would have approached the helpless *Minnesota* more closely, might have finished her off. His executive officer could not stand against the pilots' importunings and took the ship back to Sewell's Point. Other than the *Merrimack*'s single hit, all the damage to the *Minnesota* this first day was done by two rifled guns smaller than those in the ironclad. The *Patrick Henry* and *Jamestown* had chosen positions on *Minnesota*'s bow and stern quarters where the frigate's heavy broadside could not bear and pounded away with impunity until Van Brunt, realizing they presented a greater threat at that time than the monster he feared, shifted two of his big guns to positions where they could return the fire.

The day ended as a catastrophe for the North. Captain Van Brunt was making plans to destroy his ship and might have done so had the *Merrimack* shown more aggressiveness at the end. Had the fleet flagship been destroyed, or destroyed herself, a major portion of Mallory's and Buchanan's purpose might have been realized then and there. Marston, commanding the *Roanoke* and the senior officer present, would almost certainly have sent the *Monitor* up the Potomac to Washington in accordance with Welles's order and utilized all the tugs available to move *Roanoke* and *St. Lawrence* (they were not so hard aground as the *Minnesota* and had already been freed of the mud) as far away from the scene of battle as possible. This would have left the entire scene of the battle to Buchanan's James River squadron, undoubtedly with far-reaching results that can be only dimly suggested now.

As events later proved, Washington held a greatly exaggerated view of the prowess of the converted *Merrimack*. Had the flagship also become her victim, the panic in the nation's capital must inevitably have been many times worse. The orders to the *Monitor* to avoid battle would have been at least as firm as they became in fact, after the battle. Lower Chesapeake Bay would have become a Confederate inland sea, open to the Atlantic; and England, already angry over the Mason-Slidell affair,* might have taken some kind of action favorable to the Confederate cause.

---

*James Mason and John Slidell, two former U.S. senators, were sent to England by the Confederacy in 1861 to negotiate for assistance. Embarked in a blockade runner, along with family members and some staff, they reached Havana, Cuba, where they reembarked in the British steamer *Trent*. There had been no secret of their voyage, nor their mission. Charles Wilkes of the 1838–1842 "Exploring Expedition," now captain of the Union steam-powered sloop of war *San Jacinto*, had lost little of the hard initiative that brought success to that aberrant naval effort of two decades past. Acting in the absence of orders, he deliberately intercepted the *Trent*, forced her to heave to by firing across her bow, sent over a boarding party to search for the two emissaries, and forcibly brought them aboard his own ship (the boarding officer performed the protocol

None of this happened, but it was a very near thing. Jones anchored his big vessel at Sewell's Point, sent Buchanan and his aide, also injured, ashore to the hospital by boat, and prepared to get underway early the next day. And at midnight, the *Monitor* arrived.

The nearest big ship Worden saw was the *Roanoke*, so he reported aboard for information and instructions. As it happened, this was exactly where he should have gone, for John Marston made the biggest decision of his life, and it was the right one. He would disobey the categorical orders of Secretary of the Navy Welles, which Welles had gone to so much trouble to make explicit.

"Proceed immediately to Newport News and report to Van Brunt in the *Minnesota*," ordered Marston. "The flagship is aground there and in great danger from the *Merrimack* at first light this morning. That is where your ship is needed. The *Merrimack* will be out again for sure when it's light enough."

Marston said nothing about the secretary's instructions to send the *Monitor* to Washington. Since he was disregarding the direct order of his superior, he had best keep it to himself and take full responsibility. There would be no reason to burden Worden's mind, especially if there was to be a battle at daybreak.

Worden returned immediately to the *Monitor*, hove up the anchor, and moved her the few miles to where the *Minnesota* lay cradled in her bed of soft mud. The moment he stepped through her gangway he sensed that the atmosphere on board the flagship was very different from that in the *Roanoke*. Marston's ship had not been in combat. Tenseness there was, no doubt of it, for her turn might come with the new day. But the *Minnesota* had already met the enemy, and the wounds of the encounter were both visible in the ship and palpable in

---

of "laying hands forcibly on" the two men by formally touching the arm of each for a moment). British protests were instant, claiming that the flag of England over the *Trent* protected everyone and everything on board—forgetting that they themselves had been on the other side of this very issue during the years prior to the War of 1812. Now the situation was reversed, and feelings ran high. Our State Department, after much discussion, disavowed the act and provided the two commissioners with safe-conduct to England, but also seized the opportunity to point out that by her complaint England acknowledged her previous wrongdoing. The point was lost on the English public, but its government quietly accepted the rebuke. The two Confederate commissioners came far closer to getting England into the war on their side by being abducted from the *Trent* than they were able to once they arrived in London.

her crew. Great holes showed in her sides, surrounded by splinters where showers of broken timbers had maimed and killed crewmen in the vicinity of the hit. Some splinters were great spikes of wood, several feet in length, nearly a foot in cross-section at the big end, tapering to a lethal point at the other. In the days of wooden ships, more battle casualties occurred from flying splinters, which had something of the character of shrapnel, than directly from the projectiles themselves (even the newly invented explosive shells). *Minnesota* had had her share. Great bloodstains on her once white, holystoned decks, hastily mopped up but still visible where the blood had soaked into the absorbent planks, demonstrated the cost of battle. Her crew was still in a state of shock at the damage received and her inability to inflict any on the enemy. Preparations were going forward to abandon ship and scuttle her. Morale was low, particularly on the part of the captain.

Van Brunt had been hoping the arrival of the *Monitor* would change his situation for the better. Now he saw her: very low in the water, tiny, without a single mast or other extension, only a round box on deck and space for two guns—only two guns—to peep out. She was supposed to be the salvation of the Union fleet, but she was commanded by only a lieutenant. The Navy Department could hardly expect much from her. Her crew was only a tenth the size of his; what could they do if boarded in force by the *Merrimack*? Clearly that little thing was unseaworthy; waves would roll right up on her ridiculous flat deck, only a foot or so above the surface.

Van Brunt greeted Worden gravely. He was lightening the ship to the best of his ability. She was several feet into the muck, and neither the engine nor the tugs had been able to move her. If he could not get her off the shoal by the time the *Merrimack* came, he would destroy her. The feverish activity of his crew was proof of the urgency they felt. A number of smaller craft were alongside receiving ammunition, provisions, equipment of all sorts. Guns were being swayed out and into the largest of the boats. The spare anchors were already gone. Even personal equipment was being put overboard or jettisoned. As a final measure, the crew would also go aboard the boats and leave their ship, while a handpicked group would remain aboard to fire her.

Perhaps Worden was a little forward. A mere lieutenant does not commiserate with and offer solace to a senior captain. "I will stand by you to the last if I can help you, sir," said he, meaning the words in only the best sense, in the face of mortal danger. But they were not taken quite the same way by the embattled Van Brunt, already well aware that the best chance the Union ships had had against the *Merrimack* had been badly muffed: they should have all been anchored together, in that part of Hampton Roads that offered the deepest water and the greatest room for maneuver. Each ship lacking an engine should have had at least one tug moored alongside to assist her in getting into combat. Allowing the Confederate ironclad to take on each ship individually had showed total failure to understand the danger or how to handle it. There was no flag-officer present, no concerted plan of operations. Marston was senior, but he had not assumed command of the Union squadron. Each ship captain had been on his own, to seek his own salvation.

"No sir," said Van Brunt crisply, a little ungraciously. "You cannot help me."

Aboard the *Merrimack*, anchored under the guns at Sewell's Point, the wounded were sent ashore and provision made for appropriate disposition of the two dead men; the galley provided a hot meal, and then Jones directed all hands to get what rest they could at their quarters. A careful watch was kept in case the Union forces tried a surprise attack at night, though none was expected. All hands were called before sunrise, when Jones planned to up anchor and finish the job on the *Minnesota* that had been denied him the evening before. During the night he received word that a lookout had noted a water tank being brought into Hampton Roads, apparently to replenish the remaining Union ships in some way.

Aboard the *Monitor* there had been no sleep the night before because of the storm they had weathered with such anxiety. Now, the strenuous situation into which they had landed upon arrival in Chesapeake Bay precluded sleep again. Some members of the crew may have curled into corners for a few hours, but not many, and none of the officers. Everyone was keyed up, for dawn was to bring the biggest test of their ship's commission, perhaps the biggest of their lives as well. Having seen and heard what the *Merrimack* could do, they had no illusions about the morrow: they were going into battle with a new and as yet untried, unshaken-down, unproved, experimental ship. If she was not equal to the test—not the equal of the *Merrimack*—she might well be sunk. There was no escaping out of her little hull; once the hatches were shut over them, all hands inside were doomed to go down with her, exactly like the crew of a submarine of later years. As dawn broke, breakfast was ready; but at the same time lookouts in the towering *Minnesota* reported that the *Merrimack* was coming.

Sometime during this final period of preparation—the specifics are not clear because there was no record ever made of them—Executive Officer S. Dana Greene, who was also in charge of the turret,* reminded Worden that the navy had never rescinded its categorical instruction that "henceforth until further notice, no gun will be fired aboard any ship with more than half its intended weight of powder." This order was issued after the *Princeton* catastrophe of 1844, but now, eighteen years later, the causes of bursting guns had been largely identified and removed. Moreover, *Monitor* was about to enter upon the battle of her life, the fight she had been built for, with incalculable consequences riding upon the outcome. "May I have your permission to use full-weight charges tomorrow?" the twenty-three-year-old exec asked.

Worden refused. "We will carry out all department orders precisely," he announced. Whatever argument Greene made was of no avail against his strong-willed skipper. He could not convince him that special circumstances existed, warranting intelligent interpretation of ancient, no longer valid rules. The *Monitor* fought the Battle of the Ironclads, as it was called in some circles, with half-weight propellant charges in her guns. She never penetrated the iron casemate of the *Merrimack* and never depressed her guns to strike at the waterline, where her adversary's armor was lightest. Had she used full-weight

---

*Ericsson's concept of his "battery" was that the engines and armor were necessary only to bring the turret into action (he frequently referred to the *Monitor* as a "self-propelled battery"). Thereafter, the ship was expected only to support the turret, which was to do the fighting. Hence, the ship's organization he proposed gave the officer in charge of the turret a position second only to the captain. The Swede's engineering vision, unfortunately, did not extend into the problems involved with running and fighting a ship—but no one had the courage, or took the trouble, to face him down. One cannot but have at least some sympathy, at this point, with Robert Stockton.

charges or struck her enemy at a weak spot, her 11-inch shot would have penetrated through *Merrimack*'s shield, and no doubt she would have sunk the Confederate ironclad.

Jones, now in sole charge of the *Merrimack*, had directed the chief pilot to bring him as close as possible to the Union flagship. His last conversation with Buchanan before seeing him into the boat that would convey him to the hospital had impressed upon him the urgency and importance of destroying the *Minnesota*. "Burn her, Jones, as we did the *Congress*!" the pain-ridden flag-officer had croaked.

The *Merrimack* was showing many signs of the battle she had been in. All her boats were shot away; her smokestack no longer existed. She was leaking forward, where the iron ram had been wrenched off by *Cumberland*'s death-lurch. Two of her guns were damaged—one with a large section of the muzzle blown away by a shot from the *Cumberland*, the other still serviceable, with less of her muzzle gone. One anchor had been shot off; the chain, whipping inward, had injured two men. And the flagstaff was down, along with nearly all of the rail around the upper deck—of small concern. But she was still a very formidable warship. Jones had vowed to carry out Buchanan's parting demand, and the pilot had also promised. But as they took their ship away from Sewell's Point and into the main channel of Hampton Roads, the little water tank that had been reported the previous night lay between them and their target. No matter. He would simply avoid it. At his direction, the pilot ran the ship directly northward until past the Middle Ground Reef and then turned westward to approach the *Minnesota*, on the shoal north of the reef. But the water tank seemed to have some means of propulsion; smoke from an engine of some sort came out of the water in two places near the tank, and it remained between the *Merrimack* and her quarry. Catesby Jones quickly realized what it was. He had already tried one or two long-range shots at the Union flagship and had received a broadside back that had done no damage. But his ship was not handling well. Without her stack there was insufficient draft for the boilers to work properly; the old *Merrimack*'s weak engines had not benefited by their period of submergence following the capture of Norfolk Navy Yard. Despite Chief

Engineer Ramsay's optimistic report of the previous day, the highest speed he could depend on, which barely gave her steerageway, was four knots. The *Monitor*, for this he now knew was what he saw, could move twice as fast and could maintain her position between his ship and the immobile *Minnesota* with ease. He would have to deal with her first.

Jones fired two broadsides at the tanklike Union ironclad, and he saw at least two shots strike home on that strange round structure. And then he saw the round tank begin to rotate. Soon he knew exactly what it was, and why it looked like a stubby, round tower. No one had ever seen anything like it before. The ship that carried it had not turned, but that tower now held two huge guns, pointed directly at him. In a moment first one, then the other, fired. He saw the puffs of smoke, saw the two great balls as they sailed through the air, heard and felt the shock as they hit. They were heavier than anything the *Minnesota* carried, heavier than anything *Merrimack* had aboard. Her big iron casemate rang with the double blow. Jones could not see where the shot hit, nor observe what damage they might have done. But in a moment the reassuring report came up to him in his little armored pilothouse: "Two hits, sir! The planks are started a bit, but no penetration!"

The first battle between ironclad ships had begun. It lasted six hours by most reports. Neither ship was able to damage the other sufficiently to claim an outright victory. Both fought under what would today be described as the most appalling conditions, such as insufficient ventilation and extreme heat (it was fortunate the battle took place in March; had it been in the summer, there would have been deaths from heat prostration). The *Merrimack* was in such poor mechanical shape on her second day of fighting as to be virtually unmanageable. She lay so deep in the water that her movements were much restricted by the shoals all about. The *Monitor*, of shallower draft and in better condition, suffered from unforeseen design difficulties. Her skipper, Worden, in his tiny pilothouse on the bow, had no regular communication with Greene in the turret. Paymaster Keeler described his role as messenger, standing under the turret and shouting up when the opening in the turret's deck lined up with the access hatch from below. In both ships, the battle was against two enemies at once, the second, in each case, being the unfamiliar problems of difficult machinery.

During the course of the battle, Jones managed once to maneuver his unwieldy monster to ram Worden's much handier vessel. Historians sympathetic to the Confederacy have taken this success as proof that had the iron beak not been broken off in the *Cumberland*, the *Merrimack* would have sunk the *Monitor* then and there. Perhaps, but not likely, for measurements of both vessels indicate her ram did not extend sufficiently far forward under the surface to penetrate the *Monitor*'s unarmored lower hull; that, in other words, the *Monitor*'s iron deck, which Ericsson called her ''armored raft,'' extended beyond her hull in all directions far enough to have saved her. In fact, the *Monitor* took the blow on the side of her deck with no injury, whereas the *Merrimack* crushed some of her timbers in the area and worsened the already serious leak started there the day before.

Part of the time, the two ships lay actually in contact alongside each other. The much more heavily manned *Merrimack* might have boarded, though the boarders probably could not have gotten below. Had they been equipped with tarpaulins to cover the air intake pipes and the firebox exhausts, or wedges to jam under the turret to prevent it from rotating, conceivably they might have been able to capture her (all these schemes were planned for a subsequent meeting, which never took place). Ericsson had intended that the turret guns be reloaded with the gunport shutters closed, but this reduced ventilation and light and was quickly superseded by simply turning the turret away so that its broad round back was toward the enemy. But then it was inevitable that readiness to deliver another salvo would be telegraphed when the turret began to turn once more. Whenever the ships were close aboard, the *Merrimack* had sharpshooters with rifles ready to fire into the ports of the *Monitor* when they could be seen, which meant when turned in preparation for firing. But the steam rotating engine never stopped exactly on the bearing intended, so that considerable right-and-left motion was required to aim the guns as Greene, her combination executive officer and turret officer, wanted. During this time all the hand guns the Confederate ship possessed would fire into the *Monitor*'s open gunports. As a consequence of a few bullets zinging around inside her turret, the Union ironclad began to "fire on the fly," as Greene later wrote, not stopping the turret's rotation but pulling the firing lanyards as the enemy ship rumbled into view as the turret turned. In the process, everyone in it became totally disoriented. Not surprisingly, accuracy suffered also.

In the meantime, Jones became convinced his shells were not damaging his antagonist, despite the many direct hits that he personally observed. Surmising the function of the only other projection on her flat deck, he then directed his guns upon the *Monitor*'s pilothouse. It took a direct hit while Worden had his eyes to one of the slits— which, of course, was nearly all the time—and blinded him. Greene, summoned by the ship's doctor, arrived after some delay, occasioned by the need to train the turret to align the hatch in its deck with the hatch in the main deck beneath. He found Worden prostrate, in great pain, bleeding heavily and unable to see at all. (Fortunately for Worden, he later recovered the sight of one eye, but for the remainder of the battle and for some weeks and months later he was entirely unable to function.) Greene took command, which not only put a very young officer in charge of the ship but also deprived her of her turret officer in the middle of combat. Greene had to spend some little time orienting himself to the situation, because in the rotating turret he had not only been disoriented but also totally isolated from the ship's maneuvers.

On the injury to Worden, the helmsman had turned away from the *Merrimack*, for which he was later criticized as having acted without orders. This was totally unfair. It was an entirely normal reflex. So far as he knew his captain had been killed alongside him, and for long minutes no one came to take his place. Nonetheless, it did cause a hiatus in the action.

Seeing he could not hurt the *Monitor*, Jones resolved to ignore her and concentrate his efforts on the still grounded *Minnesota*. He directed William Parrish, the pilot, to bring him as close as possible to the helpless Union flagship. Fearful of coming under the gunfire of the

Minnesota, not able to make any judgment as to her ability to hurt the *Merrimack*, and no doubt already scared out of his wits by the *Monitor*, the pilot (according to an article published twenty-five years later by the *Merrimack*'s doctor) deliberately ran her into the mud bank two miles distant from her target instead of closing to half a mile in a place where there was plenty of deep water. The doctor wrote that Parrish himself confessed this after the fight.

Assistant Secretary of the Union Navy Gustavus Fox arrived at Old Point Comfort while the battle was in progress, and there was nothing he could do but observe. After the battle Fox congratulated Worden in the sick bay where he lay suffering, not knowing whether he would ever see again. Fox appointed Lieutenant Selfridge, late gunnery officer of the *Cumberland*, to relieve Worden—much to Greene's disgust, since he had hoped to succeed to the post himself (Fox felt Greene was too young, and in any case, after succeeding to command, he had not pressed the pursuit of the *Merrimack* to the degree he might have). And Fox took back with him to Washington the knowledge that, had Worden disobeyed the instruction regarding half-weight charges, the *Monitor* might have sunk the *Merrimack* on the spot. (Ericsson was greatly exercised over her failure to do so, averring—as was doubtless true—that had he been in command he would indeed have disobeyed the regulation and pressed the battle to a conclusion.) From his powerful post, Fox immediately set in motion a recision of the half-weight charge rule and put all the influence he could muster into a massive building program of more monitors. At the request of both army and navy officers conducting the campaign to capture control of the Mississippi River, he included a new class of very shallow draft river monitors in the program.

The first battle of the ironclads was a draw. Neither side won, but the dire consequences to the North of a decisive victory by the Confederate Navy, the situation at dusk on 8 March, had been averted by the events of the ninth. Inevitably, however, a controversy arose as to which ship ''won the fight.'' Nothing could be a less useful exercise so far as the realities were concerned. The Confederacy came within an ace of winning the battle, and thus possibly the war, but failed. The Union nearly lost it but staved off defeat. In the long historical run, the battle would go down as the first fight between ironclads, the debut of the revolving turret, and the first of many clashes between guns and armor. Naval professionals noted, however, that all technical results of the encounter had been anticipated, that there was in this sense nothing new. What was new was the sudden, overwhelming perception that a new day in navies had just dawned. Navies, and sea battles, would never be the same again.

Noteworthy, too, was that no one on 9 March was killed or injured on either side except for the skipper of the *Monitor*, who permanently lost the sight of one eye and bore a disfiguring scar on his face the rest of his long life. Hospitalized, Worden recovered to take command of the new monitor *Montauk*, in which he participated in several actions. He became superintendent of the Naval Academy in 1869, for five years, and finally retired in 1886. Congress voted him full sea pay as a rear admiral for the rest of his life, and he died in 1897.

Following the battle with the *Monitor*, the Norfolk Navy Yard took the *Merrimack* back into her dry dock, whence she had been only recently floated out. The ship had suffered heavily in her two days of combat, to the extent that some who saw her thought her nearly in a sinking condition, with plates badly dented and their wood backing cracked and splintered. There was, certainly, much superficial damage, and two of her guns had to be replaced. In addition, much uncompleted work related to the original conversion to ironclad remained to be done; and her old engine, unsatisfactory since the day the ship first went to sea in the old federal navy, required yet another thorough overhaul and repair. She was under overhaul a month and came out of the yard in April, much improved. Her new skipper, replacing the still disabled Buchanan (promoted to rear admiral), was Josiah "blood is thicker than water" Tattnall. Three times, during April and early May, the big ironclad sortied from the Elizabeth River to challenge the *Monitor*, but the orders from Washington were specific: the invitation to a second ship duel was not taken up, and *Monitor* remained safely under the guns of Fort Monroe.

During this period, *Merrimack* controlled the mouth of the James River and the access therefrom to Norfolk, but since the basic flaws of design that made her unseaworthy could not be corrected, she posed no threat to Union control of the entrance to Chesapeake Bay. Thus Confederate Navy Secretary Stephen Mallory's basic hope—that she could open Norfolk to Confederate commerce—was dashed. She did, however, cause Union General George McClellan to give up his plan of approaching the Southern capital, Richmond, by the direct route along the James and to settle instead for a more circuitous route—one of the factors, perhaps, that caused his failure.

Viewing the results of the battle between the *Monitor* and the *Merrimack* from long range, the ignorance of both sides regarding the actual capabilities of the ships involved can only be categorized as appalling. A few months later, the Union lost the *Monitor* at sea in a minor storm; the Confederacy would likewise have lost the *Merrimack* had she attempted to travel to New York, as Confederate Secretary of the Navy Mallory seriously suggested. Union Secretary of War Edwin Stanton infected Lincoln's cabinet with fear that she might come up the Potomac River to shell Washington, disregarding entirely the fact that her draft made such a trip impossible. And the Union embarked immediately upon a massive building program for more ships similar to Ericsson's extraordinary design—ignoring their basic lack of seakeeping capability.

The professionals in both navies addressed themselves to what had gone right and what wrong in the epic battle, as did the many observers from foreign navies. Political consequences aside, it was quickly apparent that the decision might have gone either way and that many incidental occurrences had had totally disproportionate effects. They set themselves to the remedies, some of which, in the material line, were things they could accomplish once the need was clear. But others had to do with the spirit, and these were far more difficult to understand.

According to Greene's account, after assuming command of the *Monitor* he turned once more toward the *Merrimack*, but found her in retreat. He fired a few more times, but without apparent effect, and despite his higher speed did not try to overtake her. According to Catesby Jones, after getting off the mud bank the ebbing tide forced him to heed his pilot's admonitions to return the *Merrimack* to base. In this inconclusive way did the first battle of ironclads come to a close. Technically it was a draw, but the fairest thing that can be said is that the Union fleet had not been destroyed and that the *Merrimack* had therefore failed in her first (and as it turned out, her only) mission. It is also noteworthy that both ships were at the end reduced to command by their executive officers who, for different reasons, found themselves unable to continue.

Final destruction of the *Merrimack* is of a piece with what we have heard about the pilot(s). In May, the Confederate defenders suddenly abandoned Norfolk in face of General McClellan's advance. This action, many thought, ought to have been preceded by far more warning to the *Merrimack*, for the ironclad's base was thereby destroyed, her regular refuge suddenly taken from her. Desperately seeking a solution for the dilemma, Josiah Tattnall received orders to take her up the James River for her own safety and to join the defenses before Richmond. The pilots stated she could be moved if she could be lightened to a draft of 18 feet or less. In the emergency, the crew worked all night, jettisoning guns, ammunition, and stores to bring her to the required level. Then, with the work accomplished and the ship rendered impotent for either attack or defense, the pilots announced they could not bring her up after all, and the anguished Tattnall was forced to destroy her. The destruction of the *Merrimack* is a matter of history; the motives of the pilots, in particular the chief pilot, purely speculation. But if the doctor's story about the ship having been deliberately grounded during the battle of 8 March can be believed (and Parrish's every action before and afterward attests its plausibility), then the apparently deliberate misinformation two months later that resulted in her premature destruction must be viewed not merely as cowardly acts by an untrustworthy civilian employee, or employees, but as a gross example of mismanagement on the highest level. To allow military decisions of such importance to hang upon the unknown abilities and courage of a single man not even a member of its military force bespeaks an incredible misorientation of priorities.

Nor was the North much better. Welles's and McCauley's dilatoriousness had caused the loss of Norfolk Navy Yard and the most valuable ship there. Finally understanding the threat *Merrimack* posed in her new guise, the Navy Department barely managed to ready one ship to meet her. But the *Monitor*, arguably the most important ship in the Union Navy at the moment, with the fate of the Union almost certainly depending on her, did not receive the backup support her tiny crew of fifty-eight officers and men needed. No careful consideration was given to her organization, to the means by which her commander might transmit his orders to the turret rotating above the armored deck behind his station, to the succession of command if he were to be injured. His second-in-command, on whom was to fall command of the ship and the responsibility for decisions affecting the fate of the nation, was still in his twenty-fourth year, not yet three years graduated from the newly formed Naval Academy. Yet it was this twenty-three-year-old youth whose request to use full powder charges might have made the battle a decisive victory for the North. And, so far as is known, no one in the Bureau of Ordnance and Hydrography, nominally in charge of proof-testing and certifying naval guns, bethought himself of the manifest need that the guns slated to go aboard the *Monitor* be proofed to the full designed charges, as so easily could have been done during the hundred days of her emergency construction.

The contest for control of the seaways available to the South—of which the battle of the ironclads was a part—was not the only naval strategy of the war. Histories are fond of mentioning the "Anaconda Policy" of the North, the strangling of the South by naval blockade combined with a relentless overland squeeze by encroaching armies. Little by little and one by one, Confederate seaports on the Atlantic were closed, the defending forts captured, entry and egress by blockade runners rendered more difficult and finally impossible. Another very important part of the naval campaign involved denial of the Mississippi waterway to Southern shipping and, by Union control of its entire length, splitting the Confederacy in half. This was a major portion of the grand strategy of the North, involving a slow and stumbling downstream move by forces from the north and an equally difficult move upstream from the Gulf of Mexico. In the process there was much desperate fighting on land as well as on the river, and feverish construction or conversion of armored boats by both sides. Not generally appreciated is that the campaign was probably the first in which full-scale cooperation with the army was a basic factor from the beginning. Army and navy coordination was an obvious necessity, given the special conditions existing with the broad Mississippi River—almost an inland sea, but long, narrow, and convoluted—and the requirement that control of the land go hand in hand with control of the waterway. The basic strategy of capturing the Mississippi was thus under control of the army, since it had to be in position, successively, to capture the strong points once Union naval forces had reduced the shore batteries controlling passage in the river. A very early understanding between the naval commander, Captain Andrew H. Foote (who received a wound midway in the campaign that eventually disabled him and caused his death), and the army commander, Brigadier General Ulysses S. Grant, contributed immensely to the success of the campaign and thus to Grant's extraordinary career.

With but few exceptions, mostly in the South, all of the effective gunboats on both sides were improvised from converted river steamers of very shallow draft. The North constructed shallow-draft river monitors, but pressure from the Union army and the cabinet for still further reduction in draft, combined with heavier armor (demands made in apparent ignorance of the relationship between displacement and the weight a hull can bear), caused Assistant Secretary Fox to turn Ericsson's original design over to Chief Engineer Alban C. Stimers with requirements for a reduction in maximum draft from 6 feet to 4 feet and the addition of considerably more armor. Stimers had been chief engineer of the *Merrimack* before her conversion, and later served as a volunteer in the *Monitor* during the famous battle. From these antecedents he set himself up as a design engineer, a post for which he appears to have been singularly unqualified. Among other items, he evidently did not allow adequately for the lesser buoyancy of fresh water as compared to salt.

Ericsson adamantly withdrew from participation in building these craft, giving as his opinion, after inspecting the plans, that they would sink upon being launched. Stimers went ahead anyway and his first river monitor—launched with neither turret, guns, stores, fuel, provisions, nor crew—nearly fulfilled Ericsson's contemptuous prediction; it floated, but with only three inches of freeboard. The shallow-draft river monitor program was a tremendous embarrassment to Fox and all others who had been involved. Massive design changes were required, their construction was tremendously delayed, and by consequence, they had little effect on the Mississippi River campaign.

The South, lacking enough suitable river steamers to convert, built a few new river ironclads as well; their design was more competently handled than that of the North's river monitors and buoyancy was not a problem, but providing them with dependable engines was always most difficult, because the South had no plants able to build them. The practice was to take working engines from other uses, but in every case such conversion resulted in a detriment to the war effort somewhere else.

The campaign to capture the Mississippi automatically divided itself into two parts: a downstream effort, originating in the north under Grant and Foote (after Foote's disablement, Charles Davis of the Ironclad Board), and an upstream drive, originating in New Orleans, under Captain David G. Farragut and supported by army forces under General Ben Butler and later General N. P. Banks (who seemed not to have Grant's drive). Commander David Dixon Porter, son of the David Porter of War of 1812 fame, was given command of Farragut's river gunboats, most of them hastily armored river craft.* Porter was dynamic and energetic, and, like his father, sometimes intemperate in thought and language. The command relationship between the two men would probably never have been successful, had it not been for the friendship

*Farragut was a very young midshipman aboard David Porter's *Essex* during the South Pacific cruise and the battle with the two British ships that ended it, having been virtually adopted by Porter in consequence of twin family tragedies (loss of Porter's father from sunstroke while visiting his good friend, Farragut senior, and of Farragut's mother of yellow fever while nursing her sick guest). His fondness for the Porters was a permanent factor in his life.

between their families. Porter, a friend and confidant of Assistant Secretary Fox, while privately corresponding with Fox and occasionally disparaging his superior, nevertheless turned in a fine performance cooperating with Grant, and is generally given most credit for the final success on the great river. He was, however, a disciplinary problem, principally because of his ungovernable tongue. He "broke swords" with Farragut in the south, antagonized Davis to the north, and earned the disapprobation of Welles, all of which resulted in his being called back to Washington, where he was temporarily relieved of all active service and sent home on recuperation leave. Fox was for a time his only friend in official naval circles but, as in the case of Grant, Lincoln was impressed and took the matter up with Welles, pointing out the need for action on the critical front where he seemed, like Grant, to be the only commander with enough energy to do everything that was necessary.

The upshot was Porter's promotion from commander to acting rear admiral, and his return to the Mississippi River to relieve Davis in command of the newly formed Mississippi Squadron to the north of Vicksburg. His private instructions were to cooperate to the utmost with General John A. McClernand of the Union Army, who was expected to move down the banks of the river while Porter held command of the water alongside. But McClernand proved to be slow and ineffective, like Banks to the south. The breakthrough came when Porter finally met a man of the same mold as he: Ulysses Grant.

"Blue-water" navy forces under Farragut made a decisive contribution to the combined campaign against Vicksburg. With heavy losses in a series of engagements, his deep-draft ocean-going steam-powered frigates and sloops of war fought their way up to Vicksburg, where junction was ultimately effected with the Union forces coming down river. Capture of Vicksburg, however, was difficult in the extreme. It finally fell to General Grant on 4 July 1863, and in a few days the entire river was in Union hands, after a campaign on land and water that had lasted a year and a half. It was a massive effort on the part of the Union and involved tremendous defense on the part of the Confederacy, which rightly viewed loss of the river as a first-magnitude disaster.

Commerce raiding was one strategy employed by the Confederate Navy that met with a great deal of success, although it has been argued that the resources thus expended might better have been used to strengthen the Mississippi River defenses. Great damage was nevertheless done the Union; the number of warships sent out by the North in search of the few raiders at sea at any one time was many times greater than the effort put out by the South. At the beginning of the Civil War, the Confederacy made an attempt to revive the old system of privateering (commerce-raiding by privately owned cruisers). This had its difficulties, however, in that the South had as yet no legal status except in its own eyes. Furthermore, privateering had been outlawed by the international privateering convention (the Declaration of Paris of 1856, but the United States had refused to become a signatory). Two privateers were relatively quickly captured, and federal authorities threatened to treat their crews as common pirates, an action that caused Jefferson Davis to order reprisals against Union officers who were Confederate prisoners. The potentially difficult situation was finally solved by a simple exchange of prisoners, and no executions took place. However, privateering seemed less profitable than blockade running, and for the South, beginning to feel the pinch of the Union blockade as early as November 1861, running the blockade was also a necessity.* As a result, privateering died out. But the Confederate government's need for commerce warfare against the North continued.

America had grown up on maritime commerce, and in 1861 seaborne commerce was one of the North's biggest industries. To Southern leaders it presented a big prize: an opportunity to damage the North severely, and, simultaneously, a source of much needed revenue. Since privateering could not do the job, the Confederate government began to fit out commerce raiders as part of its navy. Of these, the most famous was the *Alabama*, and the most famous of the raider skippers was her commander, Rafael Semmes, like Franklin Buchanan a Marylander who had "gone south" while his state did not. Of major significance was that a number of the Confederate raiders (the most

---

* Bermuda and the Bahamas became the principal blockade runner terminals. The Blockade Runners' Museum in St. George, Bermuda, is their permanent memorial.

successful ones) were built or purchased in England under the subterfuge of being ordinary merchant ships; their warship construction was covert, and only later were they armed and manned at hidden localities. The *Alabama*, for example, sailed forth from her building yard in Great Britain on her initial trial and never came back. In the Azores, she rendezvoused with a supply ship, also sent from England by the Confederate agent, James D. Bulloch, a former officer of the Union Navy who proved himself a master of intrigue in circumventing the British laws intended to prevent just what he was doing.

Semmes commissioned the *Alabama* as a unit of the Confederate Navy at sea in September 1862. She was finally caught in Cherbourg, France, in October 1864, having captured (and usually destroyed) seventy-one Union merchant ships and having tied up many Union warships in their search for her. Her end came when Semmes, a romantic of the Buchanan stamp, took *Alabama* to sea to meet the Union *Kearsarge* in what amounted to a challenge match. In a battle that lasted about an hour, *Alabama* was so badly damaged that she sank immediately after surrendering.*

In all, the South sent out nineteen commerce raiders, some of them hastily converted from vessels captured at sea and none so successful as the *Alabama*. The last of them, the *Shenandoah*, began operations late in 1864 and continued until August 1865, months after the end of the war, when the news of the surrender of the Confederacy finally came through to her.

Damage done to the Union cause by the raiders built, purchased, or outfitted in England was the subject of an international claim filed by the United States against that country after the war, on the ground that Great Britain had not adequately enforced her own laws to prevent construction and outfitting of the raiders. In 1871, by treaty, agreement was reached to submit the claims to an international court of arbitration, which met in Geneva. In 1872, after exhaustively examining the

---

*Semmes jumped into the sea and was picked up by the British yacht *Deerhound*, which had come out to see the battle. The *Deerhound* transported him to England instead of turning him over to the *Kearsarge*—thus creating an incident nearly the same, but on the opposite side of the fence, as the one that caused Southern historians so much heartburn, the escape of the two senior surviving officers of the *Congress* after surrendering to the *Merrimack*.

claims, the arbitrators awarded the United States $15,500,000 for direct losses, but disallowed all those considered to be indirect or "consequential." Payment for virtual destruction of the U.S. merchant marine—which, either by capture or by transfer of ships to foreign flags, suffered tremendous reduction from which it never recovered—was refused.

Despite these other campaigns, the big contribution to navies and seapower made by America and its awful Civil War was, as everyone understood, the first battle between the ironclads. Among other results, the original *Monitor* gave her name to the type of ship of which she was the first and the most illustrious. She caused what might be termed a "monitor fixation" on the part of the Union Navy, in which an excessive number of these self-propelled gun platforms, suitable for smooth-water combat but not much else, were built. The monitors did introduce rotating turrets into combat (although Captain Cowper Coles of the British navy may have been the first to suggest them), and they were innovative in that they deliberately had so little freeboard that the water itself armored them (another boast of Ericsson's). (But as a result, they had so little reserve of buoyancy that they sank extremely easily; and any attempt at speed drove their low, flat bows under the surface.)*

But the epic battle of the ironclads in Hampton Roads had left many unanswered questions. Did it, in fact, make all other types of warship obsolete and useless? Granted the *Merrimack* had made short work of *Congress* and *Cumberland*, and would most likely have done the same to the *Minnesota*; but none of her victims had been able to move. Could more aggressive tactics have made a difference? Could a

---

*Assistant Secretary Fox, enamored of monitors, embarked in the *Miantonomoh*, a two-turret monitor completed in 1865, on a cruise to Europe to demonstrate the ship was actually seaworthy. On arrival, she did create something of a sensation, principally that the voyage had been possible at all. *Miantonomoh* was one of the largest monitors, with a tall stack and the beginning of a deckhouse between her two turrets, where their arcs of fire were blocked. Although most of the voyage across the Atlantic was favored by calm seas, her deck was constantly swept by good-size waves; rigorous measures had been instituted to eliminate all leakage below, but it was nevertheless a wet, uncomfortable trip, clearly one that could not have been undertaken in anything but benign conditions. Even unnautically inclined individuals wondered, on seeing her, how she could perform her mission in face of bad weather.

fast-moving ship with a spoon-shaped bow ride up on top of a low-lying and unwieldy ironclad having little reserve buoyancy (as was the case with both the ironclads in Hampton Roads) and simply push it beneath the surface so that it filled and sank? Such questions were rife among all naval professionals, especially those of supposedly more advanced European navies. They looked for an answer in the only place where one would likely be forthcoming: the continuing civil war in America. And they found one, late in that war.

Franklin Buchanan, promoted to admiral for his service in the *Merrimack*, spent many months convalescing from his wound. In August 1863, he was ordered to Mobile to take charge of the port's defenses. Since the fall of New Orleans in April 1862, Mobile was the most important seaport on the Gulf of Mexico and correspondingly vital to the South. This automatically put him in command of the squadron being built there and nearby in Selma, Alabama, where Catesby Jones was now in charge of producing guns and iron plates for armor. The most powerful ship under construction was the ironclad ram *Tennessee*, much like the *Merrimack* but built for the purpose, not a makeshift conversion, and much more powerful as well as more seaworthy. She was put in commission in February 1864 under the command of James D. Johnston, and Buchanan hoisted his flag in her in May. In the event, she would be tested in battle against the entire Union fleet commanded by newly appointed Rear Admiral David Farragut.

Formidable as she was, the *Tennessee* had some serious faults. Her engines had been taken from a river steamer and were underpowered and undependable. Through a still unexplained design deficiency, the chains that operated her rudder lay partially exposed on her afterdeck, which, unlike the *Merrimack*, was above water. Last among her most serious deficiencies, her gunports had heavy iron shutters that were intended to close while the guns they served were being reloaded. As events were to show, they were excessively sensitive to being jammed by minor distortions when the nearby shield plating was hit by heavy shot.

The *Tennessee* was launched at Selma and completed at the city of Mobile. When ready for service, she drew far too much water to pass the bar at the mouth of the Mobile River, a fact well known to the Union (which was of course watching her carefully). Buchanan, always characterized by drive and ingenuity, built camels (large wooden barges weighted down with sand, then wedged on either side under heavy beams through *Tennessee*'s gunports, and the sand off-loaded) to lift her sufficiently to clear. He had her towed across the bar at night by two tugs, one of which carried coal and the other ammunition, with her crew rapidly loading the supplies into her as the water deepened. His intention was to take her to sea that very night to attack Farragut's blockading Union fleet by surprise. But the move took longer than expected, and the high tide he had counted on receded; *Tennessee* was again aground and had to wait for high water, which came after daylight frustrated the scheme by revealing her presence in the bay. A surprise attack being no longer possible, the ironclad with her consorts assumed the role of a fleet in being—a threat the enemy would have to deal with—anchored under the guns of Fort Morgan at the mouth of Mobile Bay, waiting for the anticipated attack by the Union fleet.

Unlike the Battle of Hampton Roads, Buchanan had two months in which to prepare his little Mobile Bay fleet for the battle. The time was well spent, the engineers and gun crews well exercised. When the test came, early on the morning of 5 August 1864, they were ready. Doctor Daniel B. Conrad, fleet surgeon, later described the situation: "We had been very uncomfortable for many weeks in our berths on board the *Tennessee*, in consequence of the prevailing heavy rains wetting the decks, and the terrible moist, hot atmosphere. We knew that the impending action would soon be determined one way or the other, and every one looked forward to it with a positive feeling of relief."

In addition to the *Tennessee*, believed to have been the most powerful and heavily armored of all the Confederate ironclads, Buchanan commanded three wooden gunboats, mounting in all 22 guns (including those in the flagship), with 470 men in all. In the Union fleet, Farragut had eighteen ships, 155 guns, and more than 3,000 officers and men. To the Confederate forces should be added 72 heavy guns in Fort Morgan, defending the bay but out of range during much of the action, and to the Union strength some 5,500 troops intended to land and capture the fort after the defending ships had been taken care of.

The disparity in strength was great, but both Buchanan and Farragut had thought carefully about it. Buchanan was once again in the position he had held two and a half years earlier, but in a much stronger ship. As before, he had deep water to maneuver in, with shallow water all around; but this time the draft of his ship was less than that of most of his antagonists, so it was he who could utilize the shallows to his advantage. He had also taken the precaution of assuring himself of the zeal of his pilot, and he believed the *Tennessee* the equal of the entire Union fleet. Even the monitors, of which there were now four with the recent arrival of the very heavily armed *Tecumseh*, would have difficulty penetrating the 6 inches of armor and 23 inches of yellow pine and white oak of which *Tennessee*'s shield was made. He would ram one ship after the other, blast them at short range with his powerful rifled guns. Loss of the *Merrimack* would be avenged, her solitary battle continued, this time to glorious victory. Typically, Buchanan concerned himself not at all with his ship's capacity to carry out his grandiose plans, and probably even less so with the possible schemes of his antagonist, whom he knew well.

Farragut, no less than Buchanan, had laid his plans for the battle. Foremost among them was that it would be a battle of movement. No one was to anchor, or run aground, under any circumstances. The fleet was to operate in close proximity, all units in action all the time, none moving into separate locations where individual actions, as at Hampton Roads, might take place. All ships were to ram the enemy as often as possible, for which some of them had been fitted with strong iron rams, but to ram in any case, if only with a wooden stem against an iron side. All ships were to seize every occasion to get alongside the *Tennessee* and fire every gun that would bear at point-blank range. It was not lost on the Union commander that the greatest damage suffered by the *Merrimack* in the entire two days' battle in Hampton Roads had come from the hotly served guns of the *Cumberland* as she sank alongside.

The Battle of Mobile Bay was no doubt the most dramatic of all the naval battles of the Civil War, with much credit going to both sides. Farragut, no less than the somewhat less stable Buchanan, fought like a tiger. Farragut's own ship, *Hartford*, suffered more casualties than any other, twenty-five killed, twenty-eight wounded—more than twice as many killed as the next highest, *Brooklyn*, with eleven dead in the action. The *Tennessee* fought the entire Union fleet alone with little assistance from her consorts (who were outclassed in any case), finally surrendering only when she lost her rudder and could no longer fire even a single gun (the exposed tiller chains were cut by continuous close range fire from the monitor *Chickasaw*, and her guns were disabled one by one by her gunport shutters being jammed closed from continuous battering, or by failure in the firing mechanism). When she gave up the fight, she was surrounded by Farragut's wooden ships, all vying with one another for the opportunity to ram or get alongside to blast her with their heaviest guns.

Surprisingly, with the exception of the *Chickasaw* the monitors had not done well. Four were present: *Manhattan* and *Tecumseh*, with two 15-inch guns each, fully qualified to fire full powder charges, and *Chickasaw* and *Winnebago*, lighter twin-turreted monitors mounting four 11-inch guns also proofed for full charges (the same size as had been installed in the original *Monitor*, now long submerged off Hatteras). But the *Tecumseh* had rashly passed to the wrong side of the buoy marking the limit of the Confederate minefield (called "torpedoes" at this time) and detonated one, which caused her to sink instantly and dramatically, in full view of everyone. The *Winnebago* had something wrong with her turrets, neither of which could be rotated, and the *Manhattan* was apparently reduced to only a single gun. But this was the biggest gun in the fight, and she fired it only six times, otherwise staying out of the thick of the melee. One of her huge 15-inch solid shots hit *Tennessee*'s casemate and did tremendous damage, throwing a shower of splinters inside and nearly penetrating the interior of the Confederate ram. The light monitor *Chickasaw* retrieved the honor of her class by sticking close to the *Tennessee*'s stern and pounding away at her casemate and rudder chains, with the decisive result already mentioned.

But the significant fact was that the most powerful ship the South ever had in its navy was beaten by a fleet of strong wooden ships powered by reliable steam engines, which simply overwhelmed her. So could it have been with the *Merrimack*, had the ships without engines had tugs moored alongside from the beginning, and had they all fought like the *Cumberland*, which is to say with the drive and determination of the Union ships under Farragut's command.

Several other things remain to be told about the Battle of Mobile Bay. Farragut originally intended to lead the attack in his flagship, *Hartford*, but this was unanimously opposed by his officers, who felt he should not expose himself to this risk. The *Brooklyn*, equal in size and strength to the *Hartford* and commanded by Captain James D. Alden, therefore was selected to lead the Union fleet, with *Hartford* in second place. This was the same James Alden who, three years earlier, had refused Chief Engineer Benjamin Isherwood's entreaties to take over the *Merrimack* and get her out of Norfolk. At Mobile, he ran true to form, for as he led the way into the bay, he saw on his port bow, to the west, the line of buoys marking the torpedoes placed by the defenders to force all incoming ships to pass close under the guns of Fort Morgan on the eastern side of the channel. The *Brooklyn* was as far from the fort as Alden could get her, on the western edge of the channel, so that the eastern end of the minefield appeared nearly directly ahead, as of course it should have. At this point he reversed his engine, in the process throwing the *Brooklyn* across the channel, and began signaling in army signal code (the big ships all carried army signal officers for communication with the troops after they had been landed, but there was no expectation of needing them prior to landing troops). Time was lost getting the *Hartford*'s army signal officers up on deck from their station below to receive and interpret the signals. Alden now sent several signals showing nothing so much as his own mental disarray under stress. Several messages from Farragut directing him to go on were not obeyed, and finally, in desperation, Farragut ordered the *Hartford* to take the lead. To do this he had to go around *Brooklyn* to the west, directly over the minefield that had so visibly and dramatically sunk the *Tecumseh*. It was then he bellowed his famous battle cry, "Damn the torpedoes!" And to his flag-captain in the *Hartford*,

"Four bells! Drayton! Go ahead! Full speed!" Farragut's son and biographer, Loyall, states that he mentally said a short prayer before giving the famous order. It was shouted in as loud a voice as he could muster (in those days when seamen prided themselves on their ability to give stentorian commands), and was rendered all the more remarkable because he was known as a most pious individual who held Wednesday night prayer meetings on board his flagship and had never been heard to utter an imprecation of any kind.

Once someone had shown the way, Alden straightened himself and his ship out and resumed his course past the fort. The confusion he had caused, however, bunched the entire fleet in front of the fort and gave its gunners a field day of which they took maximum advantage. Most of the casualties suffered by the Union ships (except for the *Tecumseh* crew) were inflicted during this period, and Alden must bear the responsibility.

The *Tennessee* and Fort Morgan offered the only opposition to passage of the Union fleet into the bay, for the other three vessels of Buchanan's squadron were too small and weakly armored to combat directly with the big seagoing steamers of the North. Inside the bay, however, one of them, the *Selma*, was credited with doing major damage to the *Hartford* by raking her from ahead (while *Hartford* was occupied with the *Tennessee*) until the speedy side-wheeler *Metacomet* was sent after her and captured her. The other two were not so aggressively handled and could not compare with the work done by the *Merrimack*'s consorts at Hampton Roads. The *Tennessee*, however, fought each ship of the Union line in turn as she came through the channel. There is evidence she may have intended to ram one or more of the Northern ships as they came by, for the reports of their commanders state she headed for them on a steady bearing and then, in effect, flinched away at the last moment. This is hardly believable, given the known character and previous history of Buchanan. It is far more likely that the *Tennessee* simply had insufficient speed with her old engine to retain the initiative—that is, to strike the enemy ship with her own ram bow, or beak. (Ramming, like any other naval maneuver, is difficult to do well, without practice. At Hampton Roads the *Cumberland* fought at anchor, with no means to move herself. At

Mobile Bay all the ships had steam, and even the slowest Union vessel was faster than the *Tennessee*.)

The facts are that *Tennessee* never used her own ram, but was herself rammed numerous times by the eager wooden ships of the North, who hurled themselves upon her with increasing abandon during the course of the battle—and incidentally did themselves far more damage than they did to the Confederate ironclad. Had this tactic been tried on the *Merrimack*, with her tiny amount of reserve buoyancy and her bow and stern already under water (thus she had no additional displacement if they were pushed deeper), she would almost certainly have been listed over and pressed down far enough to take in a fatal amount of water through her gunports. The *Tennessee*, however, was built with 18 inches of freeboard at both bow and stern; she lurched heavily when hit, but quickly righted herself without shipping water to any degree.

Farragut's plan had been to take the fleet into the bay and then land army troops for capture of the forts at its entrance, the largest of which was Fort Morgan. Once the forts had been taken, the city of Mobile, the last big port still open to the South, would be closed. It was a scheme that had been in the planning for months. After successfully forcing the entrance passage, he anchored his fleet in the deep-water portion of the bay and began preparations for the landing. Withal, he recognized that the *Tennessee* had not been beaten. Although she had not succeeded in frustrating his entry, or in seriously damaging any of his ships, she was still loose in Mobile Bay and would have to be accounted for in some way. For the time being, however, the *Tennessee* had retreated to the vicinity of Fort Morgan, whose heavy guns effectively protected her from assault by the Union force now in possession of the bay. Both sides celebrated the hiatus in battle by sending their crews to a long-delayed breakfast.

Farragut has been quoted as saying, "I didn't think old Buck was such a fool!" when the report came that the *Tennessee* was coming back. The two admirals had known each other during a lifetime of service in the same navy; and the truth is that Farragut expected he would be hearing somehow from Buchanan before the day was over. But it was nevertheless extraordinary, unprecedented, for a single ship, no matter how well armored, to come out from a place of safety to challenge a fleet of seventeen (having been reduced by one through loss of the heavy monitor *Tecumseh*). The Union fleet included eight screw-sloops, three of the most powerful class, and three surviving monitors, any of which was more than a match for the original *Monitor*. All hauled up their anchors with enthusiasm and a grand melee ensued, during which the *Tennessee* was rammed five times, struck on her shield fifty-three times, but penetrated only once, by a 15-inch 440-pound solid shot driven by 60 pounds of gunpowder from the monitor *Manhattan*.

Even so, she continued to take everything the Union fleet could throw at her, including themselves. (In the process, the *Lackawanna* crashed into the *Hartford*, knocking a large hole into the flagship's quarter, fortunately above the waterline, and very nearly hit her a second time a few minutes later.) The end came when Buchanan was wounded, in a manner that was evidently typical of him. *Tennessee*'s rudder chains were already severed and no guns could fire: she had been silent for some long minutes when Buchanan impetuously hurled himself into getting at least one gun back in action. Taking charge of the work at the scene, he sent below for a machinist to knock out a hinge pin and free a shutter, and according to some accounts was actually holding on to some part of the mechanism himself when a heavy shot, evidently aimed at the damaged shutter, struck on the other side of it at that precise spot. The machinist and a seaman were instantly killed (the only fatalities aboard the *Tennessee*), and Buchanan's leg was broken (the same one that had been wounded aboard the *Merrimack*), putting him out of action again. In this condition, when it was reported to him that resistance was out of the question and the ship unable to return enemy fire, maneuver, or even steam effectively because of the loss of her stack, he authorized surrender.

What Buchanan expected to prove by single-handedly taking on the entire Northern fleet has never been explained. He did demonstrate the tremendous strength of the *Tennessee* and the extraordinary bravery of her crew. He drew generous praise from all his enemies, including Farragut, who wrote in his report that the Battle of Mobile Bay "was the most desperate battle I ever fought since the days of the old

Essex.'' In Buchanan's own words, the example of the *Merrimack* being blown up by her own officers without a fight (which he did not mention because of his regard for Tattnall) determined him "by an unexpected dash into the fleet, to attack and do all the damage in my power; to expend all my ammunition and what little coal I had on board, only six hours' steaming, and then, having done all I could with what resources I had, to retire under the guns of the fort, and being without motive power, thus to lay and assist in repulsing the attacks and assaults on the fort.''

This may be deprecated as self-justification after the fact, as many of Buchanan's detractors have done, contending, like Pierre Bosquet writing about the Charge of the Light Brigade in 1854, that "it was magnificent, a sort of desperate beau geste, but it was not war.'' To be fair, it was much more than that. If he thought about it at all, in August 1864 Buchanan must have realized that minus some sort of miracle, defeat of the South could only be a matter of time. He had under him the best ship yet built by the South—in his biased view the best built by either side. In the face of a lost cause, the intangibles automatically assume far greater importance than otherwise. The only thing Franklin Buchanan could do for the South was to give it something to be proud of, and this he did, at very little cost in lives or injuries. Whether he thought all this through at the time is unlikely, for it is one of those deeply psychological emotions that affect a whole populace, not just a few individuals, and whose proof lies in the judgment of history, not in pragmatic reactions to problems of the immediate future. In the case of the *Tennessee*, both the South and the North are now proud of her, for she is part of the heritage of our reunited nation.

And, at the same time, Farragut proved that spirit, if applied with drive, determination, and careful planning, can be victorious over armor. The invulnerable warship with sides of iron was captured after the most desperate resistance. It took an entire fleet to do it, but it would have been foolhardy to try any other way.

12

The Post–Civil War Doldrums and the Beginning of Idealism

The Civil War was a tremendously difficult purification for our navy and our country, with everything the word implies: a purge, a cathartic, the destruction of an old order. A detestable institution, already long outmoded by the world of which we held ourselves members, was at last abolished. It had been maintained for one reason only: economic advantage, and it was destroyed amid a storm of fire and brimstone. Given time, perhaps the older order might have been set aside more easily—without a war, the death of millions of our nation's youth, and the martyrdom of a president. Perhaps, but not likely. Most probably the change was ordained to be bloody, regardless of when it came: given the power of the vested interests so deeply involved, it most likely could have happened no other way.

In any case, the loss in blood, treasure, social well-being, and national cohesiveness was immense. The nation was exhausted, its reservoirs of everything depleted. The Union Navy (now again the United States Navy), having been built up from the few score ships of 1860 to the several hundred of 1865—some of them the most modern in the world, uniquely tested in battle—was at the zenith of its power and prestige. But our nation's exhaustion kept us from consolidating and improving this position. Instead, we began to disband the navy, leaving all the wartime innovations to be picked up and employed by the nations on the other side of the Atlantic. The navies of Europe, in short, made full use of the War Between the States to check out their notions of ship construction and tactics. The United States did not, for in addition to its weariness its customary deep reaction against navies had set in.

Secretary of the Navy Welles, enjoying the country's plaudits for having led the Union fleet to victory in 1865, had nonetheless no concept of the underlying forces that were impacting upon the navy under his charge. Neither had his assistant, Gustavus Fox. From their point of view, the Union Navy had won its war at sea and that was all that mattered. To build on that victory, they would send a ship of the navy on an annual visit to every American port and they would station one wherever it seemed possible that an American merchant ship might be in need of assistance or protection. To prove their seaworthiness two of the big monitors, *Mondanock* and *Miantonomah*, made lengthy voyages: the former to California via the Straits of Magellan, the latter to Europe, with Fox on board in a sort of triumphal voyage. But that was the end of it. In their minds, nothing more needed to be done.

In truth, many naval officers, tired of the fighting and the endless privation, welcomed a return to the comfortable days of old. Cruising on a sailing ship was much easier on them—on everyone, in their opinion—than cruising in a stink pot, as steamers were derisively called. So the big majority of the monitors—awful things with engine- and boiler-room temperatures often nearing 150 degrees, the atmosphere of machinery spaces filthy with a mixture of fine coal dust and oil vapor that coated all surfaces, a noise level that made normal exchange of information next to impossible—were laid up in preservation for the next war. At that time, according to their advocates, they would again sweep the seas of our foes (so argued those who, like Ericsson—now riding the crest of national adulation—could neither conceive of any other type of warship, nor concede their obvious faults, like impossible working conditions and basic unseaworthiness).

Perhaps the greatest postwar naval dereliction lay in our inability to see that, in a time of important changes, large vacuums can be created. Our navy's failure to capitalize on its strength at the end of the Civil War, despite the huge changes created by the Industrial Revolution, immediately put it in the backwash of the other strong nations of the world. Part of the reason for our neglect, as compared to their instant grasp of the situation, no doubt lay in our insular position and our westward-turning attention. European nations had potential enemies on their borders, or across relatively narrow bodies of water; we did not. They had a heritage of war with rapacious neighbors; we had no such immediate heritage. We abdicated our lead. They seized upon a development they could not ignore.

The Civil War also had a long-term effect on our once far-flung merchant marine. The American merchant trade had been one of the country's biggest industries, stemming from early colonial times. It had suffered badly during the war from captures by Confederate raiders and from the resulting high insurance rates, which caused many shippers to transfer their cargoes, and the ships as well, to foreign registry. But its reversals had numerous causes, other than the war, so that those who believed the end of hostilities would set everything right found themselves unable to explain why our mercantile industry did not recover. Unwise laws contributed: for example, ships that had transferred to foreign registry during the Civil War were not permitted to return to American registry. Foreign crews were cheaper and, by and large, satisfactory. Once the patriotic impulse to renew U.S. registrations had been set aside by law, shipowners were free to accept the greater profits resulting from foreign crews to whom no national obligation was owed. In addition, we had no policy of government aid to shipping. We subsidized internal expansion by railroads, but did not follow the European custom of subsidizing our merchant marine as well. American investment capital went westward, following the path of least resistance and most immediate profit. The results to our national development were remarkable, but to our seaborne commerce they were, as well, a near death knell.

The period between 1860 and 1865 was, of course, seriously affected by the war and should be discounted. Nevertheless, during the following quarter century the proportion of our foreign commerce that was carried in U.S. bottoms dropped from two-thirds to less than a tenth. In the same period, the tonnage of our shipping engaged in foreign trade was reduced by two-thirds. Meanwhile, nonetheless, the dollar value of our foreign trade increased an estimated seven times. Obviously, other nations were carrying it and garnering not only the profits but the national security benefits as well.

The effect of the war was felt in other, less obvious ways. Our shipyards were poorly suited to the rapid transition from wooden ships powered by sails to much bigger ships of iron and steel that were powered by coal. Concentration on wartime building, in which the urgency of the moment required quick production with methods at hand, had permitted no orderly changeover to modern equipment. All resources, moreover, had gone into the sinews of war instead of into the industrial establishment. When the war was over, the shipyards of Europe, watching with business acumen and a hawk's eye for the big profits, were already well into the new production methods and techniques. Ours never caught up, and our merchant marine was never even in the race.

The Industrial Revolution, which had made such an impact on our navy in the early stages of the war, afterward simply bypassed both it and our merchant marine. Yet the impact of machinery on the navies of the world was to open a new age. Sails and wooden ships had been the norm for centuries. Now steam engines promised far greater maneuverability, changing forever the shape of battle; equally dramatically, steam radically changed even the appearance of ships on the sea. Moreover, iron and steel hulls changed shipbuilding methods at the same time that they made possible great increases in size. The very concept of the speed of ships at sea changed, and second only to this was the whole operational theory of endurance, which, initially limited to fuel, quickly extended to include provisions, replenishment of parts, and ammunition—a whole gamut of additional factors. Although the navy was so badly neglected in the United States at this time that the period was called "the doldrums" by everyone associated with it, it took no great discernment to recognize the extraordinary effect of the new technology. As the years went on, the fact that so little of it seemed to affect our navy became a source of embarrassment to the few dedicated persons serving in it or in charge of it.

It is even probable that the Industrial Revolution actually contributed to our doldrums, for events were moving so rapidly abroad in foreign navies that opponents to navy development in the United States could argue the advisability of awaiting some consensus before embarking on any expansionist program. So the great fleet of the Civil War slowly turned into rotten wood and rusty iron at its moorings. America's face turned away from the sea. Congress continually cut down funding. Neglect, corruption, and despair were nearly everywhere. The naval cycle of boom and bust, deeply reminiscent of the three up-and-down cycles between the Revolution and the War of 1812, was in full downswing again. By 1881, according to Dudley Knox, for many years curator of the archives of our Navy Department and its foremost historian, ''scarcely a single vessel was fit for warfare and only a few were in condition for normal cruising.''

Within our navy, nevertheless, the great questions of the time were still what sort of navy to have and how to employ it in furtherance of national policy. Little consensus existed, yet the stakes were high. As mundane a consideration as the location of jobs made nearly all decisions highly political. And, in those pre-Mahan days, the proper use of the sea for legitimate defense needs was far less clear than today. Dogmatic assertion by persons in authority too often took the place of real study and scholarship. By consequence, every move the navy made was perceived as political by naval officers and members of Congress alike—or could be made to seem so. Personal feuds were bitter. Partisanship reached deep. Politicians and high-ranking naval officers were passionate about their own ideas. Corruption was rampant. For all his fine personal integrity, President Grant's administration (1869–1877) is notorious in our history for the dishonesty and outright knavery of so many of his appointees to high public office—among them, it was freely reputed, the secretary of the navy. Grant's successor, Rutherford B. Hayes, served competently but colorlessly, with but little improvement in the terrible condition to which the navy had been allowed to sink.

The War of the Pacific, between Chile on the one side and Peru and

Bolivia on the other, broke out in 1879 and ended with a Chilean victory in 1884. Its impact on the United States came through the realization that the navy of either of the warring sides was superior to ours. But even before this war's end, there were some signs of change. The inactivity with which Hayes seemed afflicted was perhaps due to the confused circumstances of his election (the Hayes-Tilden contest resulted in a tie in the electoral college that was resolved by the House of Representatives in a deeply flawed partisan vote). All this finally changed when James A. Garfield became president in 1881. He appointed as secretary of the navy Federal Judge William H. Hunt, who happened to be the father of a young naval lieutenant. Hunt immediately appointed a board of naval officers to recommend what should be done, but the board had little time to act before Garfield was assassinated and Hunt left office. Fortunately, Chester Alan Arthur's secretary of the navy, William E. Chandler, also had a son in the navy and was, like Hunt, a man of integrity and action. Chandler fought vigorously for, and brought about, authorization by Congress of a second advisory board in 1882, with the same mandate.

Finally, in 1883, Congress approved the new board's recommendations and authorized construction of four new ships to be built of steel (instead of iron) to the most modern design. While steel is superficially similar to iron, its many different properties resulted in great differences in raw material production and ship fabrication technique. Making the basic decision to step forward into a relatively untried shipbuilding system required courage on the part of the board, for which its members were never adequately recognized. This was the beginning of what became known as the New Navy, the third naval era in our history to have that title. The ships—the cruisers *Atlanta*, *Boston*, and *Chicago*, and the gunboat or despatch boat *Dolphin*—were from their initials known as the ABCD ships. When completed they were first formed into a so-called squadron of evolution to work out tactics and combined operations.

The ships were not, of course, completed at the same time, but an apocryphal and amusing story has been told about their first day's trial outing (or, more likely, the trials of one of them). The yarn, like so many others, has its own hidden truths. The ship, or ships, had been fitted with a full suit of masts, spars, and sails. The trial board, wanting as little as possible to do with the newfangled engines and smokestacks that soiled their clothes and the ship's lovely decks, directed the first day's trials to be conducted under sail alone. So up went the sails, and the ships looked handsome indeed under their billowing clouds of new white canvas. But the men handling the taffrail logs shook their heads. Under sail the ships were slow, and made entirely too much leeway. Still the trial board kept on, until the message was brought to the admiral in charge that they might not get back to harbor in time for the reception scheduled for the end of that first day. Then the board saw things in a different light and authorized use of the engines, which performed as expected and got them back on time.

Not all was black and disheartening for the navy during the period of the doldrums, however. There were a few bright spots, among them Benjamin Isherwood, its engineer-in-chief from 1861 to 1869, the man who valiantly, if unsuccessfully, tried to get the *Merrimack* away from Norfolk Navy Yard in 1861. He was, unfortunately for himself and the navy, an irascible individual, prone to controversy and the creation of professional opponents who became personal enemies as well. Also, apparently, he was Jewish, a fact of which little written record is made but which, like so many other under-the-table matters in those difficult days, must have affected everyone with whom he dealt. No less a personage than David Dixon Porter, one of the highest-ranking officers of the navy and a loose cannon in his own right, at the height of his invective against Isherwood (whom he had liked and praised as a young officer, and much later liked again when they happened to be on the same side of something) wrote of him, ''When I have Isherwood shorn of his glory and sent back to the tribes of Israel where he belongs. . . .''

Isherwood also made the mistake of setting the science of engineering equal to, if not higher than, the science of commanding ships at sea. This, to line officers of the late 1860s, was unforgivable. Unwisely, he allied himself with politicians and involved himself in some of their arguments and concerns without the safety net of a political constituency to whom he could turn for ultimate support. (Robert Stockton had such a constituency, and it served him well.) In addition, the engineers themselves were divided according to the particular type of steam engine they had been trained in, or liked best. Almost as a matter of course, professional disputes in those days became personal hatreds. Thus, the Ericsson group hated the Isherwood group, and vice versa. The longtime editor of the *Army and Navy Journal*, William Conant Church (later a highly thought of biographer of Ericsson), was a devotee of the Swedish engineer, got many of his derogatory ideas about Isherwood from Ericsson (no mean antagonist himself), and spent much editorial time viciously attacking the engineer-in-chief.

The fundamental disagreement between steam engineers of the time was over the "expansive theory" of steam. Stated simply, Isherwood demonstrated by a series of experiments that theoretical calculations of the pressure steam could exert against a piston by pure expansion after "cut-off" (of the steam entry valve) did not allow for practical heat losses in the engine itself. Much loss was through cylinder walls and piping, and there was much lost elsewhere, too—as, for example, in the many tiny steam leaks all engines had in their operating valves and mechanisms. Thus, Isherwood's experiments proved, and he vociferously argued, the most satisfactory engines for service on board ship should have a late cut-off, as late as 75 percent of the piston stroke, as opposed to the very early steam inlet cut-off most designers advocated on the basis of theory (7 to 10 percent of stroke). His system also required more steam to run the engines, therefore more and larger boilers, always at the expense of living accommodations and all the other things: ammunition, provisions, water, stores, and fuel. Nevertheless, much to his rivals' dismay, he was able to show that his engines operated better, were more reliable and used less fuel than those with earlier cut-offs. He continued his experiments during his entire life, publishing the results in more than one hundred articles in the journal of the Franklin Institute in Philadelphia. The voluminous data he produced has ever since been one of the basic sources from which much of the science of steam engineering has been derived.

However, Isherwood's challenge to the theory of steam expansion ran exactly counter to all accepted engineering design since the first engines built by James Watt. Scientific theoreticians had written tomes about the properties of steam, but most of the men building engines were basically only skilled mechanics who worked by their own practical rules of thumb, much as did the early shipbuilders. Isherwood was the first man to investigate, scientifically and pragmatically, what actually happened when steam was let into the cylinder of a steam engine. His experiments were a landmark, not only in America but in the world; but they ran counter to so many shibboleths espoused by proud and jealous men that these men reacted by trying to destroy him. Ultimately, they succeeded in forcing him out of his post as engineer-in-chief of the navy, but he lived to see himself and his ideas totally vindicated.

In the process, Isherwood made an implacable enemy out of the man he ought most to have sought as a professional supporter and friend, a man almost his duplicate in so many ways: his contemporary John Ericsson. He did this by studying the engines Ericsson built for his monitors and proving that they were not as efficient as they should be. Characteristically, the Swedish inventor could accept no criticism and instantly declared all-out war on everything Isherwood stood for.

Yet, despite all the terrible controversy, which would have destroyed a lesser man, Isherwood persevered with his unpopular policies, and his unpopular ships and engines. The result, one of the last things he did for the navy, was a ship and engineering plant that some sixty years later was chosen as one of six historic vessels whose models were to be placed on the walls of the David Taylor Model Basin at the Washington Navy Yard. This was the *Wampanoag*, today recognized as a landmark of naval design.*

The *Wampanoag* was first proposed in 1863, during the Civil War, when it seemed the Union Navy might require very fast cruisers to counter any European nation intervening on the side of the South.

---

* Another idea introduced by Welles was to use New England Indian names for ships of the navy. The practice was unaccountably continued for years after the Civil War, resulting in ships with strange names that were comically mispronounced by their crews.

They were to have huge engines for high speed, full suits of sail for maximum endurance, and heavy armament. The war's end curtailed the immediate need, but five of the ships were well along, and Welles directed they be used to compare the various engineering schemes.

But no one understood the real nature of the controversy. At its base was opposition to what amounted to a far-reaching social change in the navy: admitting that engineers (mechanics, not sailors) could also be men of the sea. In psychological resistance to the encroachment of engineering, seamanship (or "sailormanship," to coin a term) was subconsciously elevated to an art form. Its highest expression was typified in the white sails that had driven ships for centuries (that they were really dirty gray did not reduce the romantic symbolism). For the line of the navy to surrender sails, with all they stood for in naval lore, to coal dust and oil, to filthy, noisy, and unbearably hot machinery, was like giving up its birthright. Instinctively its members fought it, and they hated everyone who carried the banner of the enemy.

Of the five ships, two were to have Isherwood propulsion plants and the three others were to have engines designed by his rivals. Isherwood's design embodied big boilers and huge wooden gears (of lignum vitae, an extraordinarily hard wood) to turn the propeller at a higher speed than the engine, contrary to present practice. He also gave his ships superheating boilers, now well accepted among boiler designers but innovative then. All their machinery was below the waterline, behind the coal bunkers for better protection, and four tremendous smokestacks projected between the three square-rigged masts. The ships were designed to sacrifice everything to speed, as had been the instructions of Congress when the appropriations were approved, and, as was already the accepted practice for monitors, with only minimal accommodations for officers and crew. At the outset, this fact alone brought violent criticism by those who did not share Isherwood's understanding of their purpose. The *Wampanoag* was the first of the two Isherwood ships: at 335 feet length, 44 feet beam, and 4,216 tons displacement, she was a veritable rapier of a high-speed cruiser, twice as fast as the comparably sized *Minnesota* and *Merrimack* of a decade before.

Of the three other ships, one was a complete failure and two were moderate successes, the best of these being *Madawaska*, the one powered by Ericsson engines. When the *Wampanoag* ran her initial trials, in February 1868, she clocked a sustained top speed of 17.75 knots. At one-quarter power, she logged a respectable half speed: 9 knots. None of the other vessels could approach these speeds, or, for that matter, her fuel economies. As might have been expected, the success of Isherwood's ships brought a storm of protests down upon him—the result in part of his propensity for antagonizing people, but more subtly because he so threatened the established order. Even some English engineering journals published critical reports, though in the end England began to build a competing warship.*

Wampanoag was without doubt the fastest ship in the world, equaled to a fraction of a knot only by the second Isherwood cruiser, the *Ammonoosuc*. Ericsson's *Madawaska* was third, with 15 knots top speed and 12.75 average. For eleven years *Wampanoag*'s speed was unmatched by any steamship, and not for twenty-one years by any other warship. But the navy showed Isherwood what it thought of him and his designs by almost immediately removing half the boilers from his ships and then, because of their narrow hulls and low speed, declaring them unfit for service. In justice to the first board Secretary Welles appointed to evaluate the five new cruisers, two of its three members reported she met the requirements ordered, needing only certain modifications in accommodations and habitability to make her more practicable as a peacetime cruising warship. The dissenter was the same James Alden who, in April of 1861, had refused to take the *Merrimack* out of the Norfolk Navy Yard on his own after Isherwood got the engines operating. Now, almost exactly seven years later, Alden had his opportunity to criticize the ship and engine designer severely, and did so. In this he enjoyed the full support of the navy line, for Isherwood had come to personify the upstart engineers who were the enemies of seamen.

A board during the administration of President Grant, chaired by

---

*This was HMS *Inconstant*, launched in 1868 and designed, in the words of the Admiralty's chief constructor, "expressly to compete with . . . a very powerful class of American vessels, then under construction." She was, however, considerably larger than the American ships, and not quite as fast.

Louis Goldsborough, the absent fleet commander at Hampton Roads in 1862, was even less kind than the first. It condemned the design of the new ships in unequivocal terms. Appreciation of Isherwood's engineering genius came late in life; the enmities he had nurtured struck immediately. Hardly were the *Wampanoag* trials over when he became embroiled in a bitter line-staff fight over the relative ranks and perquisites of engineers and line officers. This, actually an extension of the fight over engineering design, was a battle he was destined to lose at first and win, in a manner of speaking, only in the end.

In the process, these conflicts cost Isherwood his position as engineer-in-chief, for Admiral David Dixon Porter, appointed by President Grant to be the de facto operating head of the navy, resolved the controversy he had had a large part in fomenting by summarily removing Isherwood (years later he recommended he be reappointed, but nothing came of this). Isherwood undeniably was treated shabbily by the naval service. Jealousy and prejudice cut short much of what his eager mind was capable. But the legacy he left behind, of combative assertiveness in the cause of engineering excellence, lasted far beyond his long and productive life.

Several other bright spots developed during the doldrum years, five of them centered on individual officers, two on institutions.

During these years, Rear Admiral Stephen B. Luce made an enduring contribution by laying the groundwork for the continuing search for improvement that began to characterize our navy in the decades just before the turn of the century. In the same period, Alfred Thayer Mahan, the navy's first theorist on naval matters, delivered his seminal lectures and published them in bound form as *The Influence of Sea Power on History*. And Albert A. Michelson, recognized as a near genius by his classmates of the Naval Academy class of 1873 and, later, a Nobel Prize winner for calculating the speed of light (which he did while on duty at Annapolis), began his researches.

Michelson, however, was by nature a scientist and researcher, not a dedicated naval officer like Luce, Mahan, Isherwood, and the others. His accomplishments brought plaudits to the navy more for the support and assistance it gave than for the discoveries themselves, which were exclusively and innovatingly his. The fourth officer, well known within the navy for his many and continual contributions to its betterment but hardly known outside except to a special group of men of similar mechanical, electrical, and inventive bent, was Bradley A. Fiske. The fifth and chronologically the last, but by no means least in his accomplishment and contributions, became almost notorious in the navy, in which he was both idolized and hated. Outside it, he became probably the most admired officer it produced until World War II. This was William S. Sims, whose "Simian theories" alternately delighted and infuriated his superiors and engraved the U.S. Navy on the minds of his countrymen in ways no one else ever did, until very recent years.

The institutions were the Naval Institute, founded at the Naval Academy in 1873, and the Naval War College, founded at Newport, Rhode Island, by Rear Admiral Luce in 1884.

The Naval Institute fills a unique place in the U.S. Navy. There is no other organ like it in any of the armed services of any nation. It was chartered as a private society for anyone interested in naval and maritime affairs. A self-supporting, nonprofit organization in no way connected officially to the U.S. Navy, its headquarters are on the grounds of the Naval Academy and most of its senior staff members have been associated with the navy in some way. Its board of control is composed of active duty officers of the navy, marine corps, and coast guard, and traditionally its president is the chief of naval operations, the highest-ranking officer in the navy. In spite of this close tie and the innate loyalties of all its staff to our navy, it jealously guards its editorial independence. Its basic function, as it conceives it, is to provide a forum for free dissemination and discussion of ideas in some way connected to the maritime world. Almost exclusively, these are related to the navy's improvement.

To perform its functions it holds annual meetings open to all the membership and publishes a monthly magazine that it calls its *Proceedings (Naval Institute Proceedings)*, which is held in extraordinarily high regard in all maritime, naval, and yachting circles throughout the world. It also publishes quality books on naval subjects, functioning in this respect like a university press with a discriminating interest, and once a year publishes its annual *Naval Review*. It has, of course, gone through considerable development and growth since its founding, and notable in its history is that the man who has held its presidency longest of all—who was never chief of naval operations but who held the post of aide for operations to the secretary of the navy (which immediately preceded it)—was Rear Admiral Bradley A. Fiske, president from 1911 to 1923.

The Naval War College was almost entirely the child of Admiral Luce. During the Civil War, Luce served both at sea and at the Naval Academy (then in exile in Newport) where, as head of the seamanship department, he prepared one of its first seamanship textbooks. Thereafter, he was deeply involved in training new sailors and officers in one way or another, including command of the training squadron. All during his career, he never ceased urging the establishment of a postgraduate training and study center, and this effort was crowned in 1884 when a former home for indigents, located on a small island in Narragansett Bay just outside the city of Newport, was turned over to him as the nucleus for what is now the U.S. Naval War College. Luce's other great achievement, in importance actually rivaling establishment of the War College itself, was in inducing Alfred Thayer Mahan, then commanding a small ship in the Pacific, to come there to teach.

Professorial rather than a ship-captain type, Mahan became controversial simply becase he wrote and lectured instead of walking the quarterdeck. The chief of the Bureau of Navigation, responsible for all officer assignments, is on record as saying, "It is not the business of a naval officer to write books," and two months after the Cleveland administration returned to the White House, in 1893, Mahan was ordered to sea. He got a choice command, the new cruiser *Chicago*— best liked of the ABCD ships—but his request for a delay to continue his study of the War of 1812 was not granted. Three months following this, Cleveland's new secretary of the navy, Hilary Herbert, embarked in USS *Dolphin*, another of the ABCDs, for a trip to Newport to inspect the War College. He left Washington with every intention of closing it down, and actually was making the trip to announce his decision to its president and to Luce, now retired and living in Newport but still active in War College affairs. En route, the *Dolphin*'s skipper acted upon the suggestion of a friend of the War College that he hand Herbert a copy of Mahan's latest book to read during the short sea voyage. When Herbert arrived in Newport, he had so changed his mind as to be convinced that the institution must at all costs be maintained, and became thereafter one of its most ardent supporters.

The Naval War College is still very much in existence, although its imposing appearance—gray granite Luce Hall brooding over the entrance to Narragansett Bay—has been destroyed by a large bridge built across its facade. Probably its greatest contribution to the navy was its pre–World War II decision to study how a war against Japan might be fought. Japan, in those studies, was known simply as "Orange," and the many strategies considered became known, in the aggregate, as "Plan Orange." All our naval leaders of World War II were steeped in it.

Mahan's books initially received cool notice in America. In Europe, however, they struck a responsive chord that has never been duplicated by any book, or books, on the subject. In England, Mahan had managed at one stroke not only to express what every Englishman, albeit only intuitively and generally inarticulately, strongly believed; he had also given the Royal Navy and the British government the best possible argument in support of continuing, and strengthening, its big-navy policies. That this support came not from a creature of the British navy but from a foreigner who had no purpose save that of responsible scholarship, made its impact all the stronger.

Since England's history was in Mahan's view the embodiment of sea power, it was not unnatural that her use of her navy made up a large part of his book. Her principal enemy during most of the years of which Mahan wrote had been France. Thus it could have been expected that second to England's reaction might have been that of France. France indeed reacted rather forthrightly, but she nevertheless ranks third among the countries affected. Second, without question, was Germany. Kaiser Wilhelm II had always been a navy fan. He had spent time at sea and, like many naval officers, occasionally sketched out his ideas for a better warship. As kaiser, however, he had more influence over the German navy than other officers and occasionally took direct action, as by ordering design and construction of a ship to a plan he had sketched. Grand Admiral Alfred von Tirpitz and others were sometimes dismayed by these proclivities, but they can only have been pleased by his reaction to *The Influence of Sea Power on History*, as stated in a telegram that was copied for Mahan: "I am just now not reading but devouring Captain Mahan's book; and am trying to learn it by heart. . . . It is on board all my ships and constantly quoted by my Captains and Officers." It may fairly be stated that Mahan's contributions to German naval thought were heavily instrumental in creating the naval rivalry with England that was one of the principal root causes of World War I.

Mahan, of course, had his critics in the U.S. Navy who saw little benefit in studying how predecessors might have handled similar problems. The anti-intellectuals, if they may so be called, saw their chance with Cleveland's return to office. Moreover, Mahan's ship, the *Chicago*, was designated the flagship of Rear Admiral Henry Erben, who had never written anything in his life and was contemptuous of anyone who had. The ship was sent to Europe on a social mission, to return the visits of friendly European warships to the United States on the 400th anniversary of the discovery of America, and the cruise, with the constantly carping Erben always ready to find fault with Mahan, began badly.

The worst thing, so far as peace on board ship was concerned, was that when *Chicago* arrived in Europe it was her captain, rather than the admiral, who was lionized everywhere the ship went. More and more, Erben found himself grandly forgotten at the head of the table, while his flag-captain was surrounded by the celebrities of the hour, all of them virtually hanging on his every word. Illustrative of the manner in which this was frequently done, Mahan was toasted at one lavish dinner by a British naval officer with the words, "We owe to [his books] the three million pounds just voted for the increase of the navy"— while his superior officer fidgeted unnoticed on the fringes and was yet obliged to join in the congratulatory toast. London press correspondents for American newspapers quickly came to see that Mahan was having a triumphal progression through the ports of Europe and that most of the extraordinary hospitality shown the *Chicago* was due to her skipper, not to the admiral embarked. Erben, already opposed to Mahan as a writer and now jealous as well, could not stand being upstaged by his subordinate. At the first opportunity, he submitted an unsatisfactory fitness report on him.

Fitness reports are the life's blood of a naval officer's career. An "unsat" report is a sentence to virtually instant retirement, under a cloud that no explanation can dissipate inasmuch as there is no trial and no airing of charges. It is the gun leveled at the head of every officer, and woe to him whose initiative makes him shine above a superior; revenge, via the fitness report, for a real or fancied slight, or merely because of professional envy, can be devastating and final. In practical fact, an "acceptable" report, tersely worded, can be an underhanded instrument of vengeance far worse than one baldly characterizing an officer as "unsatisfactory." Naval regulations prescribe that a copy of an "unsat" report be sent to the subject with the requirement that he submit a written statement concerning it, whereas a report characterizing him as merely "acceptable" instead of superior or outstanding can lie in the official record like a time bomb, waiting to go off when promotion boards meet. Admiral Erben showed, at least, that he was not a sly person. He stated outright that Captain Mahan was unsatisfactory as commanding officer of his flagship.

Erben's report, accompanied by Mahan's reply, went to Navy Secretary Herbert, who read both papers carefully. As noted, Herbert had originally been aligned with the faction to whom Mahan was an embarrassment, but in the meantime he had made the trip to Newport. Not only did he then reverse his earlier intention to disestablish the Naval War College, he also totally changed his thinking about the value of Mahan to the naval service. He refused to allow the Bureau of Navigation, in charge of officer assignments, to take any notice of the Erben report, and saw to it that when Admiral Erben reached the statutory retirement age, a short time later, he was immediately retired instead of being allowed to complete the *Chicago*'s cruise. His replacement was fully conversant with the vicious envy behind the effort to bring the "naval writer" to heel and was delighted at the opportunity to set matters to rights. So the last six months of Mahan's command, in which he had the full support and confidence of his new chief, were pleasant ones.

When the *Chicago* returned to the United States, Mahan—who by this time counted Senator Henry Cabot Lodge and Theodore Roosevelt, soon to become assistant secretary of the navy, among his admirers—found that his fame had grown immensely. American appreciation of the plaudits thrown to him by a fascinated British public doubtless played as much a part in his newfound fame as appreciation of his theories, which were somewhat recondite for most citizens. To his thorough research and incisive analysis Mahan was able to bring a certain sonorous and felicitous style of expression that exactly suited the feelings of the people about whom it was written. One of his most famous passages, which aptly illustrates the point, appears in his second work, *The Influence of Sea Power on the French Revolution and Empire, 1793–1812*. Referring to Napoleon's campaign against England, he wrote:

> The world has never seen a more impressive demonstration of the influence of sea power upon its history. Those far distant, storm-beaten ships, upon which the Grand Army never looked, stood between it and the dominion of the world.

Bradley A. Fiske, a thin, nervous type, graduated second in the Naval Academy's class of 1874 and was distinguished among his classmates by his innovative mind and quick energy. Shortly after he was commissioned in the service, the many needs of the naval profession under the new strictures and capabilities of the Industrial Revolution so impressed themselves on him that he began a series of inventions aimed at one or another of those needs. He also developed a lucid writing style, which he exercised prolifically in letters to acquaintances (nearly all fellow naval officers), and in articles published by the United States Naval Institute, to which he became a regular contributor. As noted, he capped his extraordinarily useful career in the post of aide for operations to the secretary of the navy, a position he filled for three years. He is remembered for his great fight for a Navy General Staff and for his determined stand on principle against Secretary of the Navy Josephus Daniels on the subject of our naval preparedness prior to World War I. Fiske believed steps should be taken to ready the navy for our possible entry into World War I. Daniels, citing Woodrow Wilson's campaign slogan, "He kept us out of the war," adamantly refused any of the measures Fiske proposed. Unfortunately, issues of this nature can rarely be kept out of the political arena. Fiske found his officially expressed opinions and advice demanded by Congressional committees and by the press, not to mention numerous organizations that would, today, be described as lobbyist in purpose. Although he loyally supplied the navy secretary with his professional opinions, it became publicly known that his views in certain areas—notably that of naval preparedness—differed fundamentally from the secretary's. Finally, after considerable opposition and delay, Secretary Daniels approved the first step in Fiske's navy general staff proposal: creation of the office of chief of naval operations. But then, instead of appointing Fiske to the post that practically everyone in the navy felt he had well earned, Daniels selected an unknown, William S. Benson, then a captain commanding the Philadelphia Navy Yard. The fact was that Daniels, the civilian head of the navy, was not comfortable with Fiske, who was intellectually and professionally his superior. However, Benson was an outstanding officer who performed a difficult job in exemplary manner—and, no doubt to Daniels's approbation, with remarkably low profile.

The influence of Fiske on the navy has never been adequately evaluated. He was the first of the reformers (to separate them from the Luce-Mahan type, who were essentially students). The students looked essentially to the past for the lessons which could be applied to the present and future; the reformers looked directly into the future, feared the problems they saw coming upon them, and endeavored to prepare the navy to meet them. The impact of both groups upon the navy, up through World War I, was deep. It is only a statement of fact to say that they prepared us for World War II, the greatest conflict on the sea the world has ever seen—or probably ever will see.

That William Sowden Sims was different from all the naval officers of his time is an understatement. The navy was his vocation, his avocation, his hobby, and his whole life. He gave it his full time and attention and had practically no outside interests. He corresponded widely with an ever-enlarging circle of like-minded officers of the navy and friends outside of it, and never ceased writing full and interesting reports on everything pertaining to it from everywhere his ship happened to visit. One time he wrote to someone, "I go ashore now so seldom I pass for a freak or a crank." But more and more people—other naval officers, of course, but also many of the officials in its secretariat who landed in his distribution network—began to look forward to the latest communiqué from Sims. They were never disappointed.

Sims, no more than the other individualists of his day, could not, of course, understand what was really happening—people in the epicenter of change seldom can. But all of them, from Isherwood to Sims, shared an idealism and a dedication to the navy, and to their work in the navy, to the near total exclusion of all other emotions.

Sims probably did most of his work by mail. He was a lucky man, in that there was much that needed to be done and a new world context—the maturing phases of the Industrial Revolution—in which to do it. He never tired of comparing our navy with foreign navies, often to their praise and our discredit, and he never got over the habit of writing lengthy letters to the Navy Department and his friends, pointing up our weaknesses and their strengths. In those days all naval ships were required (they are still) to submit intelligence reports on anything of interest that happened to come to their observation. Sims read the directive slightly differently: ships were to report *everything* of naval or military interest to the United States that took place anywhere on their station, particularly if it was in some way comparable to a similar thing, or effort, or procedure, in our own navy. Thus, when he was sent to the China station in the cruiser *Charleston*, in 1895, he shattered all records for the length, completeness, and readability of his intelligence reports. They became preferred reading in Washington; the Navy Department literally pounced on the mail when it arrived from the Asiatic Station in hope, usually fulfilled even to overflowing, that it would contain yet another amusing report from the indefatigable Lieutenant Sims.

Nor was he without a sometimes savage sarcasm, most often humorously expressed, usually (but not always) employed with circumspection. One of the stories told about him involved a crotchety skipper who came on deck one day to find Sims, as officer of the deck, superintending the loading of some barrels of oil on board. "Why aren't these barrels buoyed according to the ship's orders?" demanded the captain.

"Sir," replied Sims, "that's for something that might sink if it falls overboard. These barrels of oil can't sink, so they don't need buoys."

The captain was not impressed. "By God, Lieutenant Sims, don't give me any of your Simian theories! How do you know they won't sink! The ship's orders specify buoys, and by thunderation I'll have a buoy on every barrel. Is that clear!"

"Yes, sir!" said Sims. He was a popular young officer, already known for wit, repartee, and daring. Everyone within earshot stopped whatever noise he might have been making to listen, and they all heard him call out, in a piercing voice that carried throughout the ship, "Quartermaster! Get me a box of toothpicks and a spool of thread!" When the two items arrived he began buoying each barrel—with a short length of thread and a toothpick for a buoy—in front of a swiftly purpling skipper.

Sims landed "in hack" for this act of lèse majesté: the furious captain confined him to his room for ten days, which didn't bother Sims at all. He was not in the habit of going ashore, and the confinement took him off the watch bill so that he could give more time to his voluminous reports. And besides, as an act of insubordination, he knew his toothpick and thread buoying scheme was more apt to backfire against his skipper than against himself, once the word got around. The upshot of the yarn is that a chastened skipper lifted the confinement as soon as he realized that a wooden barrel full of oil could under no circumstances sink—as Sims felt certain he would, for otherwise the reason for Sims's punishment would have swiftly traveled from ship to ship, and more people than only that ship's crew would soon enjoy the story.

Sims's extraordinary industry got him assigned to the post of naval attaché in Paris, a position he accepted with some trepidation since he

had no personal funds to help pay the high expenses of such an assign-
ent. Nevertheless, he went; and the high volume of reports he sent
back, on every conceivable subject of interest to him, which by this
time meant of interest to the Navy Department, brought him more
kudos, especially from Assistant Secretary of the Navy Theodore
Roosevelt. Two years at this job, according to his biographer, Elting
E. Morison, produced eleven thousand pages of reports, mainly devoted to comparisons of the American navy with the navies of England, France, and Russia. He had already covered Japan pretty
thoroughly during his time on the Asiatic station in the *Charleston*,
where the main burden of his comments had been that the Japanese had
applied the developments of the Industrial Revolution far better than
we. Now he went to tremendous lengths to point out that the principal
navies of Europe had not been sitting on their hands either during the
period 1865–1895. They were all far ahead of us in every particular,
and his reports, not content with the generality, spelled out the details
minutely. By this time the whole U.S. Navy knew of him and stood in
awe, and not a little fear, for no one knew where his indefatigable
pen—by this time replaced by his personal typewriter—would strike
next.

Sims's orders to Paris also included posting to the legation in
Spain, but soon afterward came difficulties with Spain that culminated
in our short war with that country, and that portion of his orders was
cancelled. He was, instead, requested to provide intelligence reports
about Spain, which he did with his customary verve and inciteful com-
mentary. The entire war, for him, was spent in Paris.

Only afterward were his observations on the efficiency of the Spanish navy to enter heavily into his life's work. He reported that the guns
in Spanish warships could hardly shoot at all, let alone shoot straight,
that the Spanish navy was more akin to a social organization than a
fighting force, that upkeep in its ships was a farce. When it was learned
that the *Cristobal Colon* had been added to the Spanish squadron en
route to the Caribbean in 1898, Sims reported that although she was a
new ship, her machinery was so defective she could not steam at full
power, and that, furthermore, her main battery guns has not been

mounted. The speedy outcome of the Spanish-American War was no surprise to Sims.

Two years later, he was making the same sort of report about our own gunnery and our own newest ships, which, although they had all their guns and could generally make the contract speed, he proved statistically were otherwise not much better than those of Spain. For some appreciable time, he made no impact at all on the Navy Department. Some of its members were becoming downright restive at the constant onslaught of critical memos he sent in. But there were many who agreed with him, who were delighted to see someone take up a cause they believed in, which, for whatever reason, they did not feel confident in taking up themselves—and they helped him when they could. Almost automatically, because he dared more greatly than the others, Sims became the accepted leader of the insurgents in our navy.

13

The Spanish-American War

The Spanish-American War began late in April 1898 and ended in early December of the same year with a treaty of peace signed in Paris (ratified by the U.S. Senate in February 1899). The fighting, however, was over by mid-July 1898. From the naval point of view there were two great fleet battles, Manila Bay and Santiago, on 1 May and 3 July, respectively.

Foremost among the causes of the war was the sympathy of the American public for Cuban revolutionaries against the inept and repressive Spanish colonial rule. This had been growing for years, whetted by the so-called yellow journalism of newspapers owned by William Randolph Hearst and Joseph Pulitzer. In October 1873 the merchant steamer *Virginius*, illegally running guns under the American flag to the insurgents in Cuba, was captured by a Spanish cruiser and brought into Havana. Her master, Joseph Fry, a former U.S. naval officer who had "gone south" in 1861, and fifty-three of her crew and passengers, many of them Americans, were declared pirates by the Spanish authorities. After lengthy protestations of personal regard and compassion, they were summarily executed. The affair was protested through diplomatic channels and finally settled by payment of an indemnity by Spain—and is historically important because its timing reflects the long duration of the origins of the Spanish-American War. In 1876 President Grant seriously considered intervening in Cuba on the side of the insurgents. In 1895 the most fierce rebellion to date broke out, and the initially severe Spanish reaction intensified the clamor in America. By 1897, however, a more moderate Spanish policy damped somewhat the fires of rebellion. There might have been no war at all had not the rebels found, or stolen, a private letter from the Spanish minister in Washington in which he castigated President William McKinley as "a small-time politician." This they promptly gave to the American press. It caused a sensation when it was published— and then, most important and dramatic, the battleship *Maine* was sunk while making a goodwill call in Havana harbor.

Numerous concessions had been offered to the revolting factions in 1897, including autonomy under lenient Spanish rule. The rebels scented victory, however, and refused to accept the proffered half-loaf. In January 1898 the American consul in Havana, concerned about local rioting, asked that an impressive U.S. warship make a friendly visit to show the flag and, in effect, provide protection should any be necessary. Spain had no objections to the *Maine*'s visit to Havana. Seeking to defuse the tense relations that existed between the two countries, her government reciprocated by sending a ship on a similar visit to New York. The ship Spain selected for the mission was the armored cruiser *Vizcaya*, one of her best, under command of one of her most popular officers, Captain Antonio Eulate. Local society had received him with open arms on a previous visit. On this occasion, however, he was greeted on arrival with the news that the *Maine* had been sunk in Havana harbor four days before, after having been moored there to a buoy for three weeks. The *Vizcaya* had four uncomfortable days in New York under careful guard by American authorities, but there were no untoward incidents.

It is difficult today to visualize how anyone could believe Spain was responsible for the loss of the *Maine*. She had nothing to gain and everything to lose by such an act. It was far more likely that Cuban insurgents might plan it with intent to increase the tension between

Spain and the United States—but very unlikely that either side would have considered the benefits of success worth the political risk of apprehension. Typically, however, in the American state of mind at the time, little if any thought was seriously given to the difficulties of blowing up an alert warship, which the *Maine* clearly was while in Havana. The press, already in the war-fomentation business, jumped to the conclusion that the disaster must be the work of Spain because it had happened in a harbor controlled by Spain. Unfortunately for Spain and the cause of peace, the proceedings of the court of inquiry immediately convened by our navy under the presidency of the most highly thought of naval officer on active duty at the time, Captain William T. Sampson, found that the ship's forward magazine had been detonated by an external mine or torpedo of great force, placed under her keel in an unknown manner by persons unknown. Spain, incidentally, also convened its own investigation, which reported there was no evidence whatsoever of an external explosion. The U.S. Navy court found there had been two explosions, the first by a mine under the ship and the second by explosion of the ship's forward magazine, but it adduced virtually no evidence supporting the first one.

No one questioned that the *Maine*'s magazine had exploded. Today, however, it is far less clear that an external explosion set it off. No evidence has ever come to light of a plot in any quarter to mine the ship or in any way to sabotage her. The technical difficulties of doing so would have been tremendous, even without the additional requirement of accomplishing the feat without detection. Almost certainly, the explosion originated from spontaneous combustion in an adjacent coal bunker, as later inquiry demonstrates. But none of this made any difference, because the press and the nation were already ripe for war with Spain. All need for a pretext vanished if the Spanish had blown up the *Maine*.

Assistant Secretary of the Navy Theodore Roosevelt and his superior, Navy Secretary John D. Long, were among those convinced war had been imminent for some time. The two worked well together. Months earlier, anticipating hostilities, Roosevelt had selected Commodore George Dewey for command of the Asiatic Squadron; Long approved, and Dewey was on his way in December 1897. He had had many conversations with Roosevelt and was thoroughly briefed on what was expected of him in the event of war. His own disclaimer states that "at that time, war with Spain seemed no more imminent than it had appeared for many years" (this meant that everyone regarded it as imminent). He and Roosevelt also saw to it that additional supplies of ammunition were sent to his prospective command, and, on arrival, Dewey put his new squadron on a full war footing. He took over on board the *Olympia* in Nagasaki, Japan, in January, as soon as possible made the obligatory official call on the Emperor of Japan, and then moved his squadron as near to the Philippines as he conveniently could: Hong Kong.

Dewey's flagship, *Olympia*, was due to return to the United States upon arrival of her relief, the *Baltimore*, a slightly smaller cruiser. When Dewey arrived in Hong Kong on 17 February, he was greeted with the news of the destruction of the *Maine* (which had occurred on the fifteenth). This was confirmed next day by cable from Secretary Long. On the twenty-sixth, an often quoted cable arrived from Roosevelt:

ORDER THE SQUADRON EXCEPT THE MONOCACY TO HONG KONG. KEEP FULL OF COAL. IN THE EVENT DECLARATION OF WAR WITH SPAIN, YOUR DUTY WILL BE TO SEE THAT THE SPANISH SQUADRON DOES NOT LEAVE THE ASIATIC COAST, AND THEN OFFENSIVE OPERATIONS IN PHILIPPINE ISLANDS. KEEP OLYMPIA UNTIL FURTHER ORDERS.

Dewey was, of course, already in Hong Kong, where in addition to the *Olympia*, a relatively new 6,000-ton cruiser, he had the smaller and older cruiser *Boston*, one of the original ABCD ships, 3,000 tons, and the 900-ton gunboat *Petrel*. The obsolete paddle-wheeler *Monocacy* had already been sent to Shanghai and laid up. Ordered to join Dewey as soon as possible were the 3,000-ton *Raleigh*, through the Suez Canal from the Mediterranean, the 1,700-ton gunboat *Concord* with an emergency load of ammunition from Mare Island Navy Yard in California, and the 4,600-ton *Baltimore*, cruising on the Hawaiian station. The latter ship was directed to await the arrival of another load of ammunition for Dewey and then proceed as quickly as possible to

Hong Kong. She arrived the day before declaration of war, was hurried into dry dock to clean her bottom, and got clear just before the British governor apologetically invoked his government's neutrality statute and required the American squadron to depart.

WASHINGTON, APRIL 21, 1898

DEWEY, HONG KONG:

THE NAVAL FORCE ON THE NORTH ATLANTIC STATION ARE BLOCKADING CUBA. WAR HAS NOT YET BEEN DECLARED. WAR MAY BE DECLARED AT ANY MOMENT. I WILL INFORM YOU. AWAIT ORDERS.

LONG

HONG KONG, APRIL 23, 1898

TO SECRETARY OF NAVY:

THE U.S. CONSUL WILL ARRIVE FROM MANILA TUESDAY MORNING WITH THE LATEST IMPORTANT INFORMATION OF THE DEFENSES. IT IS CONSIDERED VERY IMPORTANT TO KEEP IN COMMUNICATION WITH CONSUL BEFORE SAILING. IN THE EVENT OF DECLARATION OF WAR COULD GO TO MIRS BAY, CHINA, TO AWAIT ARRIVAL.

DEWEY

HONG KONG, APRIL 25, 1898

TO SECRETARY OF NAVY:

IN ACCORDANCE WITH THE PROCLAMATION OF THE GOVERNOR OF HONG KONG THE SQUADRON LEAVES TODAY FOR MIRS BAY, CHINA, TO AWAIT ORDERS. TELEGRAPHIC ADDRESS HONG KONG. I WILL COMMUNICATE BY TUG.

DEWEY

Ensign H. H. Caldwell, Dewey's secretary and aide, remained behind in Hong Kong, haunting the cable office, with a chartered tug standing by to bring him to Mirs Bay.

From Secretary of Navy, April 24, 1898;

[Received Hong Kong, 12:15 P.M., April 25]
[Received at Mirs Bay, 7:00 P.M., April 25]

WAR HAS COMMENCED BETWEEN THE UNITED STATES AND SPAIN. PROCEED AT ONCE TO PHILIPPINE ISLANDS. COMMENCE OP-

ERATIONS PARTICULARLY AGAINST THE SPANISH FLEET. YOU MUST
CAPTURE VESSELS OR DESTROY. USE UTMOST ENDEAVOR.

LONG

MIRS BAY, APRIL 25, 1898

TO SECRETARY OF NAVY:
THE SQUADRON WILL LEAVE FOR MANILA IMMEDIATELY UPON
ARRIVAL OF THE U.S. CONSUL FROM MANILA.

DEWEY

MIRS BAY, APRIL 27, 1898

TO SECRETARY OF NAVY:
THE U.S. CONSUL FROM MANILA ARRIVED TODAY. THE SQUAD-
RON SAILS IMMEDIATELY FOR PHILIPPINE ISLANDS.

DEWEY

The *Baltimore*, second in column behind the *Olympia*, was commanded by Captain Nehemiah Mayo Dyer, famous for his temper and
therefore known as Hot Foot. Aboard as a passenger was the recently
arrived U.S. Consul at Manila, Oscar F. Williams, who had stuck to
his post at great personal risk gathering critically important information for Dewey. The last and most useful information he delivered
personally, in obedience to Dewey's peremptory order to evacuate Manila, and now he was being brought back to his post aboard one of the
ships due soon to attack it. Also aboard was a passed assistant engineer
with the rank of lieutenant junior grade, who has favored us with a
description of the events of the next few days. Speaking of the *Baltimore* as she was about to enter Manila Bay, he wrote:

> On the day before the battle, with Dewey's little fleet steaming
> in column in battle readiness enroute to Manila Bay, the crew of the
> *Baltimore* was called to quarters, assembled on deck in the largest
> open space. Her captain mounted the low platform of a broadside
> deck gun carriage, the better to address them.
> It was an impressive moment. There stood our captain, his very
> person seeming to radiate force, power, confidence. An intense
> stillness prevailed, except for the splashing of seas against the bows
> and the subdued thunking of the engines. We were soon to go into
> battle, and our captain was to speak to us.

A copy of the famous "fanfaronade" of Captain General Basilio Augustín Dávila, issued in Manila on 23 April, had been brought to Dewey by Consul Williams. Dewey had it duplicated for every ship in his squadron and directed it be read to all hands.

"Men of the *Baltimore* [Dyer began], you are about to listen to the most shameful set of lies, the most abominable falsehoods, the most horrible statements ever made against Americans. You are denounced as thieves, scoundrels, murderers, violators of women, destroyers of religion. Listen! This is what the Spanish Governor General of the Philippine Islands has published. And this means me, and you, and you, and you!—and you!"

An electric shock seemed to go through me. Every man felt the "you!" was specially for him.

Then Dyer read the fanfaronade in full. It concluded, "Pretending to be inspired by a courage of which they are incapable, the North American seamen undertake to take your riches, and to kidnap those persons whom they consider useful to man their ships or to be exploited in agricultural or industrial labor.

"Vain design! Ridiculous boastings!

"The aggressors shall not profane the tombs of your fathers; they shall not gratify their lustful passions at the cost of your wives' and daughters' honor. No, your valor and patriotism will punish and abase the people, that, claiming to be civilized and cultivated, have exterminated the natives of North America, instead of bringing to them the life of civilization and progress.

"Your General, Basilio Augustín Dávila."

As Captain Dyer read, he became possessed of a mad fury that constantly augmented. His wonderful voice rolled over the deck and reached and roused every heart. With the last word he became a mass of passion. He threw the paper on the deck, jumped on it, cursed it—then broke into a most beautiful, though violent, statement of the soul of America, past and present.

A wild cry went up from the hearts of the Americans before him. He had stirred us as a body in a way I had never seen men stirred. The cry became a mighty roar. Then up went Dyer's arm: there was perfect silence.

"March divisions to their quarters! Pipe down!" he ordered.

The Battle of Manila Bay began at dawn on 1 May 1898 and ended shortly before noon. When it was over, eight Spanish warships were sunk or destroyed, 381 officers and men killed or wounded. The American squadron made 170 hits upon the enemy ships according to their postbattle survey, and received only fifteen. Six United States officers and men were wounded, none severely. Seldom has a major battle, with such far-reaching consequences, been decided with such a disparity of losses. But there was another, only two months later.

The passed assistant engineer previously mentioned had his own description of the famous battle. Previously he had had the opportunity to question Consul Williams relative to the defenses and had made his own interpretation of what he heard. In the *Baltimore* the night before the battle, the officers of her wardroom were somewhat nervously assessing what might be the results. Most expected to be victorious, but there were actually a few pessimists, and all thought one or two, even as many as three, of our ships would be lost or heavily damaged, with commensurate deaths and injuries to our personnel. Bets were laid, in the manner of men about to enter into mortal combat, and the passed assistant engineer covered them all with his declaration that we would lose neither any ship nor any man. As he wrote later:

> Events proved that I was wrong. On the revenue cutter *McCulloch* which, convoying two colliers, followed Commodore Dewey at a distance of three miles, was an officer who, it is said, drank a bottle of Old Rye during the battle and dropped dead. What the whole Spanish squadron, backed by forts, was unable to do, John Barleycorn accomplished with neatness and despatch.

Dewey opened the battle with his now famous order to the *Olympia*'s captain: "You may fire when ready, Gridley!"—and thereby hangs another not well-known tale, for there was one more, unknown, casualty: the *Olympia*'s own commanding officer.

As war appeared more and more likely, Captain Charles V. Gridley had been growing progressively debilitated with what was probably cancer of the liver, and in April received orders invaliding him home. The arrival of his relief, Commander Benjamin Lamberton, virtually coincided with the declaration of war. As chief of staff and flag-captain, Gridley had had much to do with preparing Dewey's squadron, and now he protested his detachment on the eve of battle. He argued that, although weak from his illness, he was thoroughly familiar with all the detailed plans and could carry out all his duties. Finally, Dewey gave in, appointed Lamberton chief of staff, and left Gridley in command of the *Olympia*. On the voyage from Hong Kong, Gridley could hardly drag himself around, but he carried on with granitelike determination.

His battle station was in the conning tower (Dewey remained on the flying bridge, as shown in a well-known painting of him). Like all ships of that time, *Olympia* had poor ventilation to her below-decks spaces, and the hot and humid climate of Manila in May caused her conning tower to be an unbearably hot steel box. Gridley stuck it out during the battle, but sometime during the four hours concerned he apparently struck his side on the edge of the chart table or some other obstruction. When it was over he had to be carried out. His last official act was to make the required report to Dewey at the close of the main part of the action, when the squadron was ordered to anchor for breakfast and commanding officers were directed to come aboard the flagship. The blow to Gridley's side and the terrible heat in the conning tower, added to his already weakened condition, produced the most serious injury suffered by anyone. Thereafter he never rose from his sickbed, and he died a month later, on the way home, in Kobe, Japan.

The battle began just after daybreak, with Dewey's order to Gridley. Admiral Patricio Montojo, the Spanish commander, had placed his hopelessly outclassed squadron behind heavy stone-filled barges off Cavite. His second largest ship, the *Castilla*, with broken-down engines, was immobile in any case, and all except the flagship *Reina Christina* fought from their moorings. Dewey, in the meantime, directed his ships to form a very close-order column, with two hundred yards between ships, and the battle was opened when the American flagship spoke with one of her twin 8-inch guns on the forecastle. Dewey then led his squadron in a series of close ellipses, back and forth before the anchored and moored Spanish ships, firing alternately from port and starboard sides. After two hours, however, he received an incorrect report that the *Olympia*'s supply of ammunition for her broadside 5-inch guns was down to only fifteen rounds per gun. Startled, he pulled his fleet out of the firing line to look into the situation. It was serious if true, for whatever their other deficiencies, he knew the Spanish had ample ammunition. Breakfast was ordered for the crews, and all skippers were directed to report on board the flagship with information as to the states of their own magazines. Dewey was considering reapportionment of the remaining stocks of ammunition as his captains made their reports, and very quickly made the twin happy discoveries that not only was the report of shortage erroneous, but casualties had been extraordinarily light—no one killed, only a few slightly wounded.

Up to this point there had been no definite information as to how the Spanish squadron had been faring, but careful observation through telescopes now indicated it had been hard hit. Some ships were afire, others listing and sinking. Some of the crews were abandoning ship. Still, the Spanish kept their flag flying; so, some time after 1100, four hours after having broken it off, the Americans hove up their anchors and returned to the attack. In about half an hour more, all Spanish forces had surrendered. The city of Manila was then completely at our mercy and could have been taken at any time, but Dewey wisely kept to the informal truce existing under the surrender terms until he had received reinforcements of sufficient troops to maintain order. Once these had arrived, an arranged "bombardment" was carried out on an abandoned fort; Spanish honor was thus saved, and the city immediately surrendered.

The Spanish fleet at Manila was extraordinarily inept. It fought at anchor or moored alongside piers because its admiral did not believe all of its units could get under way, and in this he was absolutely correct. The deficiency, however, must be laid at least partly at his door, for he was well aware of the strain that for years had existed in the relations between Spain and the United States. Some of the Spanish ships had been long under dilatory repair, and little or no effort had been made to get them "buttoned up" upon the news of the war. For the Americans, aside from Dewey's momentary scare about his ammunition reserves, the famous battle was a simple excursion. Not for the Spanish. Dewey was later quoted as saying it had "actually been won in Hong Kong." His greatest problems came afterward, in the administration and control of the bay with the great influx of foreign warships that came out of curiosity and, almost surely in the case of the Germans, from ideas of territorial aggrandizement.

The passed assistant engineer wrote that "there was much gossip among American officers to the effect that the Germans were officially impolite, and that Admiral Dewey had informed Admiral Diederichs of certain requirements of international law as to communications with a blockaded port. . . . The British were boisterously friendly to American officers. The Japanese were friendly in spirit. The French were courteous, and neutral in manner."

The yarn is told that when it came time for the American squadron to carry out the prearranged "assault" on Manila, Sir Edward Chichester got the British fleet under way first and anchored in a semicircle between the Germans and Dewey's squadron, thus preventing them from interfering. The story does not stand up on investigation, but it accurately reflects the mental situation at the time. On a diplomatic level, in fact doing everything except physically moving his ships, Chichester most definitely interposed himself between Diederichs and Dewey, and the Americans present never forgot it.

In contrast to the well-planned, even "orchestrated" Battle of Manila Bay, the other big sea fight of the Spanish-American War happened almost by accident, and was marred by controversy. By all measures, including the power of the ships involved and the proximity of Cuba to the mainland of the United States, the Battle of Santiago was of greater importance to our navy. In careful preparation and organization, and in long-range results of a political nature, Manila Bay ranks, however, much higher.

The controversy over the Battle of Santiago arose from the characters of the two principal American commanders, William T. Sampson and Winfield Scott Schley, and to this day not all the factors are thoroughly understood. Schley graduated eighth from the bottom of the

Naval Academy class of 1860, while Sampson stood first in the class of 1861. By the system of the time, Schley during his entire career was therefore eight numbers senior to Sampson on the navy list. Sampson, however, not only first in his class but also class adjutant, the highest ranking midshipman, was always a man marked for advancement. Even as a young naval cadet, as midshipmen were known in those days, he was noted among his classmates for his imposing demeanor and seriousness of purpose. As a young officer he was regularly given important assignments, which he invariably fulfilled with the highest possible credit to the navy and his superiors. He was widely known as the ideal junior officer. Everything he did was superlative. He was much sought after as a subordinate or aide, and as the years went on, was more and more admired by his seniors and more and more revered by the younger men ranked below him on the navy list of officers. He was superintendent of the Naval Academy as a commander, then chief of the Bureau of Ordnance and Gunnery (descended from the Bureau of Ordnance and Hydrography of pre–Civil War days). In 1897 he was designated to command the navy's newest and finest battleship, the 11,000-ton *Iowa*. In 1898 he was president of the court of inquiry ordered to investigate the loss of the *Maine*. He was always quiet and reserved, a man of unswerving judgment and complete courage of his convictions. He was also looked upon as cold and unfeeling, though believed to be fair, dispassionate, and even kindly inclined to less deserving persons.

Schley, apparently, was much the antithesis of Sampson. A popular social figure, he was actively disliked by many of his navy colleagues before outbreak of the war with Spain. He was considered vainglorious, boastful, given to exaggeration and hyperbole. He was said never to miss an opportunity to brag about himself or his career, though some of these criticisms were of the sort that arise whenever an individual marks a personal path somewhat different from the norm. Schley was, without doubt, a dramatically inclined person. In some ways he may be said to have resembled the old style of officer who took to himself as a matter of "glory" the adulation and praise resulting from the exploits in which he figured. Whatever the psychological reasons, he was a very different person from Sampson, and by and large, far less appreciated. Better suited to an earlier epoch, in 1898 he was sometimes a laughingstock behind his back. Many stories circulated among less than entranced junior officers about what would today be called, surely with greater charity, his public-relations activities. He was a born storyteller, a sought-after guest at dinner parties, a man of humor and wit able to charm civilian audiences, male or female. But to his contemporaries in the navy, he would have been well cast as the Gilbert and Sullivan character who "polished up the handle so carefullee, that now he was the ruler of the king's navee." *

In 1898 the Navy Department made three significant appointments: Dewey, the most senior of the three men concerned, was given the Asiatic Squadron, based in the Far East; Schley, junior to Dewey, was appointed to command the Flying Squadron, based in Hampton Roads, with the mission of blocking any possible Spanish attack on our lengthy east coast. Both Dewey and Schley were directed to assume command with the rank of commodore. The rank of rear admiral in command of the North Atlantic Squadron and in overall command of the fleet the Navy Secretary gave to the most junior of the trio, Sampson. Not all the senior officers of the navy received news of these appointments with complete grace, though Sampson's prominence

---

* Schley was not all bluster and brag. He led the Greely relief expedition in 1884 that found the survivors of the ill-fated U.S. Army Signal Corps Arctic exploring detachment after two previous efforts had failed. He also figured, somewhat less creditably, in the celebrated Chilean affair of 1891. A revolution against the government of Chile had just successfully been concluded, with Schley, in the new cruiser *Baltimore*, present in the harbor but otherwise not involved. The revolution over, Schley unwisely decided to give liberty to some of his crew. He accordingly landed more than a hundred men who had been confined to the ship for over three months and were tumultously eager for a drink ashore (the issuance of grog or any sort of spirituous liquors to U.S. Navy crews had been abolished in 1862, though private wine messes in officers' wardrooms were permitted until 1914). A wild drunken free-for-all ensued, in which two American sailors were knifed in the back and one of them, already unconscious from wounds, shot by a policeman. Both injured men died. Valparaíso police sided with the local mob, and some Chilean army and navy officers helped defend the U.S. sailors.

The situation of the *Baltimore* was very tense, but it was relieved by arrival of the gunboat *Yorktown*, under Robley D. Evans (who in 1861 had managed to have his "resignation," submitted for him by his Southern mother, annulled). The *Baltimore* was ordered north, and to Evans fell the job of maintaining dignity, decorum, and the national honor. In this he succeeded outstandingly, with a combination of tact, firmness, and bluster that Schley could never have matched. It was here and thus he earned for himself the nickname of "Fighting Bob" Evans.

caused all of his juniors to applaud his promotion as proper in the war emergency.*

The departure of a Spanish squadron consisting of four big and modern cruisers under her most highly regarded admiral, Pascual Cervera y Topete, from the Cape Verde Islands for the west side of the Atlantic caused something near to a panic along our eastern seaboard. Every seacoast city demanded some sort of naval protection from attack. Knowing little about naval possibilities or limitations, almost without exception they asked that some naval vessel be stationed offshore to protect them from Cervera. Little thought was given by the press or by the local authorities making such demands to what a single ship could do should the Spanish squadron of several ships happen to strike at the spot where it was stationed. However, to provide at least a semblance of acquiescence to the outcry, the navy was obliged hastily to recommission a number of old ships and station them about the coast. But its main effort was placed in two squadrons, which were kept ready to move at minimum notice: the Flying Squadron, under Commodore Schley, and the North Atlantic Squadron, under Rear Admiral Sampson. Sampson, with the more powerful group, was based at Key West, Florida, in the probability the Spanish admiral would head for the West Indies and ultimately Cuba.

False alarms of all sorts abounded. In contrast to the laconic and straightforward directive given to Dewey, Secretary of the Navy Long bombarded Sampson and Schley with bad information and poorly considered instructions. In the meantime Theodore Roosevelt resigned his post as assistant secretary, formed the Rough Rider cavalry regiment, and headed for Cuba; so Secretary Long was deprived of his assistant's clear grasp of military realities. Prior to leaving, however, Roosevelt and Long had correctly sized up the need for the battleship *Oregon.*

---

*Rear Admiral F. M. Bunce had had much to do with the training and readiness of the fleet, and had been highly commended by both seniors and juniors for its fine condition. When illness caused his immediate successor, Sicard, to retire on the eve of the Spanish-American War, Bunce lobbied to resume his former post, but was set aside in favor of Sampson. This caused him some bitterness, but he could not change Secretary Long's mind and finally accepted the situation.

Built in San Francisco, the ship had remained on the west coast since she was delivered by her builders, the Union Iron Works, in 1896, but she had already become noted for the excellence of her engineering performance and the pride of workmanship everywhere evident. Captain Charles E. Clark, who had been a member of her trial board less than two years earlier, had reported aboard as her new skipper on 17 March 1898. Her chief engineer, Robert W. Milligan, also had been a member of the trial board. Both could remember that though her "contract speed" was 15 knots, she had actually logged nearly 18 on that occasion and had developed 25 percent more horsepower in her boilers and main engines than the 9,000 called for by her building specifications.

Only two days after Clark became her skipper, he got the *Oregon* under way in one of the epochal voyages of all time, from San Francisco around South America, through the Straits of Magellan, up the coast of Argentina and Brazil into the Caribbean Sea to rendezvous with Sampson at Key West. The fifteen-thousand-mile trip, interrupted only for replenishing coal bunkers and occasionally slowing down for target practice, took sixty-seven days, during the latter portion of which the Navy Department was beset with worry that she might fall in with Cervera's big cruisers and be outmatched. Clark's own belief was that his single ship could handle all four of them, and for the information of his crew he announced the tactics he intended to use should the encounter take place. Briefly, he planned to turn his stern to them and run at gradually increasing speed to entice them to string out in hot pursuit. Having got the enemy ships somewhat separated, he would suddenly reverse course, close in fast, and knock them out one by one with his heavy main battery of 13-inch guns. His crew, now veterans of many days' steaming at high speed and incessant drill, proud of their big battleship and what they had proved to themselves they could make her do, cheered themselves hoarse. Had the contact actually taken place there is little doubt that one of the more famous battles of history would have ensued.

Cervera crossed the southern Caribbean, coaled at Curaçao, and from there went straight into Santiago, where he arrived on 19 May. *Oregon* coaled at Barbados, headed north and east around the Caribbean Sea, outboard of the Bahamas, and then turned west for the coast of Florida, touching finally at Jupiter Inlet on the twenty-fourth. The telegram Clark sent in by boat for transmission to the secretary of the navy was a model of conciseness. Knowing the general location of the two U.S. squadrons, he sent, "OREGON ARRIVED. HAVE COAL ENOUGH TO REACH DRY TORTUGAS IN 33 HOURS, HAMPTON ROADS IN 52 HOURS. BOAT LANDED THROUGH SURF AWAITS ANSWER."

Two days later, while *Oregon* was coaling at Key West, Clark learned from Admiral Sampson of his scheme to sink the collier *Merrimac* (named for the same New Hampshire river as the *Merrimack* that concluded her career as the *Virginia*, but always spelled without the concluding letter *k* in the river's name). The collier *Merrimac* was considered the least useful member of the fleet train because of her frequent machinery breakdowns, and it had been proposed in effect to solve two problems in one move by sinking her as a blockship in the Santiago channel. Some have it that the idea of making use of the decrepit old collier in this way had first been proposed by naval constructor Richmond Pearson Hobson, who held the rank of lieutenant; other versions say that Sampson himself conceived the idea and commissioned Hobson to work out the details. In any case, Hobson asked for command of the ship for the exploit, and for a crew of volunteers from the fleet as a whole. Sampson, extraordinarily, agreed. Hobson, first in his Annapolis class of 1889, had entered the Construction Corps at graduation. As a naval constructor he was, like Isherwood thirty-six years earlier, not eligible to command at sea. Moreover, he had had no experience in doing so, and only three of his volunteer crew were familiar with *Merrimac*'s mechanical peculiarities. The *Merrimac*'s regular skipper, Commander James M. Miller, expected the honor of sinking his own ship, helped by an effective number of the crew that had struggled with her all this time. Thunderstruck at the orders he had received, he petitioned Sampson, citing both naval regulations and tradition. He almost had Sampson persuaded, but lost his case when Hobson had the last audience with the admiral. In the upshot, there was ample time to have referred the matter to the Navy Department; so Sampson could not cite that pressure to justify his disregard of the proper form. Had it really been imperative, as Hobson argued, that he be present to ensure proper operation of the demolition charges, there was nothing to prevent both men from being on board, except that this would have given the lion's share of the credit to Miller, the regular commanding officer, instead of to Hobson, Sampson's favorite.

Maneuvers of Schley's and Sampson's separate squadrons, and of the two together when they were joined under Sampson, have also puzzled naval strategists. Sampson initially proposed capture of Havana by amphibious assault, but the plan was vetoed on the grounds the army was not yet ready and that it would be unwise in any case with the approaching Spanish fleet unaccounted for. On 12 May he attacked San Juan, Puerto Rico, thinking Cervera's squadron would probably put in there for coal, but found no sign of it and returned to Key West (Mahan called this "an eccentric movement"). On 19 May Sampson sent Schley to investigate the harbor of Cienfuegos, on the south coast of Cuba. Being connected by rail with Havana, Cienfuegos seemed another logical place for Cervera to put in. On the twentieth he learned of Cervera's arrival the previous day in Santiago and sent a despatch boat after Schley with orders first to check Cienfuegos and, if satisfied Cervera was not there, to proceed to blockade Santiago.

Sampson then dropped down to show the flag off Havana once more (another eccentric movement), came back to Key West to meet with the newly arrived *Oregon*, and finally started for Santiago, where he arrived on 1 June. In the meantime, Schley was still checking the harbor of Cienfuegos as late as 24 May and did not arrive off Santiago until the twenty-sixth, when he actually sighted one of the Spanish cruisers in the harbor. But he departed immediately because his ships were low on coal. Next day he stopped his squadron for several hours in midocean while he mulled over the situation. Unknowingly, "Fighting Bob" Evans—who had relieved Sampson in command of the new battleship *Iowa*—illuminated this peculiar proceeding well in his autobiography, which was everywhere else clear and insightful. Evans, one of the senior captains present, obviously could not understand what was going on and his generally straightforward language is not only obfuscatory at this point but actually devoid of meaning. In the meantime, after several hours of self-communion, Schley finally decided to return to the blockade off Santiago and reversed the course of his squadron. He arrived nine days after Cervera. Sampson himself, with the bulk of the U.S. fleet, did not arrive for three more days. During the time Cervera was in Santiago without observation or blockade, he could easily have coaled and provisioned his ships and then disappeared once more, causing havoc in the American press, if nowhere else. Any admiral with a mission other than to be a sacrificial goat, which Cervera considered himself, would not have missed that opportunity.

The American fleet was finally together off Santiago on 1 June. The *Merrimac*'s attempt was scheduled for twilight before dawn the next day. Hobson actually was under way heading for the entrance when Sampson recalled him because he felt it had become too light. A second attempt was made earlier the next morning, the third, and this time it was carried through to completion. But the Spanish fort, which might have been caught by surprise the previous morning, had now been alerted, a picket boat spotted the blockship during her approach, and shelling began from the shore. Only a few of the projectiles fired at the collier struck home, but apparently these were enough to disable the rudder, some of the firing circuits for the demolition charges, and the stern anchor. Her unfamiliar crew was unable to reverse her engines, she held too much way for the bow anchor chain, which parted, and finally, when less than half of the explosive charges intended to blow holes in her bottom had functioned as planned (according to Hobson's report, she was also holed by a Spanish mine that detonated under her bow), she grounded and sank parallel to the channel, not across it as planned. Hobson and his men were gallantly rescued by none other than Admiral Cervera himself, who came out in a boat for the purpose, and the Spanish admiral endeared himself to the American fleet that afternoon by sending out Captain Joaquín Bustamante, his chief of staff, under a flag of truce to say that all were safe and well, and held as honorable prisoners of war. (Only a few days later, Bustamante was seriously wounded in a skirmish on shore and died shortly afterward.)

Summary displacement of Miller, who merited no censure, in favor of an officially ineligible person, Hobson, was totally contrary to Sampson's whole character and to everything he had stood for during his entire career. Moreover, it was not logical, for no one could be better suited to cope with the old ship's peculiarities than her own skipper and crew. As it turned out, Hobson's inexperience, and the inability of his volunteers to handle the *Merrimac*'s recalcitrant machinery, caused the blockship to sink in the wrong place. The entire effort was thus wasted. However, despite his nearly complete failure, Hobson became a national hero anyway in a nation hungry for heroes; but no one has ever explained why Sampson ruled the way he did.

Once established, the blockade of Santiago was closely maintained. Sampson's ships kept steam up and remained under way in a semicircle around the entrance, ready to take off instantly in hot pursuit should the Spanish fleet make an effort to leave the harbor. Sampson's battle orders were simple in the extreme: if they come out, go at them full speed. No instructions were issued to prevent mutual interference. All were simply to fall upon the enemy with guns blazing. Nor were there instructions regarding the ships' own internal conditions. That was left to each captain, and all save one, desirous of being off station the least possible time so as not to miss what was regarded as the sure battle ahead, economized on coal by keeping only half their boilers in service. All the ships, save one, were thus restricted to half power, three-quarters of their maximum speed, for more than an hour, the time needed to get steam up in a cold boiler. The exception was the *Oregon*, whose captain and engineer had their own ideas about how to get the most out of their ship.

The odds against Cervera were prohibitive. He had four fine cruisers and two torpedo boats, but the newest of his cruisers had not yet received her main battery guns. Her turrets were empty. Another had an inoperative after turret, some reputedly had ammunition that did not fit their guns. Against him were four first-class U.S. battleships, one second-class battleship, two fine armored cruisers superior to any of his, and two converted yachts equal or superior to his two torpedo boats. There could be no escape.

Cervera himself had informed the Spanish government that sending his squadron to Cuba was dooming it to destruction or ignominious retreat. In Cervera's own letters to the authorities in Madrid there is a strong suggestion that he believed his cruisers had been sent as a sacrifice to uphold the national honor of Spain before she sued for peace. This defeatist attitude may at least partially explain why he took no advantage of the nine days' freedom before the arrival of the Flying Squadron to blockade him. A month slowly passed with no movement by Cervera, and but little by the U.S. fleet now concentrated off the entrance to Santiago. Finally, Governor General Ramón Blanco y Arenas, in Havana, adamantly ordered Cervera to sortie, perhaps in the knowledge that Santiago could not hold out much longer against the troops of General William Shafter, who were already ashore a few miles east of the city. In any case, on Sunday morning 3 July, while the *Massachusetts* was off the blockade line coaling in the just captured harbor of Guantánamo, Sampson made the tactical mistake of taking his flagship, the *New York*, also off the line to carry him to a meeting with General Shafter. He could have gone in the *Gloucester*, formerly J. P. Morgan's yacht *Corsair*, or any of a number of other smaller units of his squadron, thus not depriving it of a second important big ship that day.

Seizing the opportunity offered by the absence of two of the big ships blockading him, Cervera made his dash at 9:30 A.M. Within four hours he saw his whole force annihilated. All four cruisers were driven ashore, wrecked, and the two torpedo boats were sunk, one demolished by a 13-inch shell fired by the *Indiana*. Of the approximately 2,200 men in his squadron, 323 were killed, 151 wounded, and most of the rest captured. American losses were slightly more severe than at Manila Bay: one killed, two wounded.

It must be assumed that if the Spanish squadron had come out in the darkest of night they might have had a much better chance of escape. When they did come out, in broad daylight, described as "a magnificent sight," "as gaily as brides to the altar," "with flags enough flying for a celebration parade" (a ridiculous time for an opposed sortie by an inferior force), there was great confusion among the American ships. No plans had been made for how they would maneuver under the various possible contingencies. Schley directed his flagship, *Brooklyn*, to make a complete circle to starboard, away from the enemy, thinking this would give him more sea room. In the process of this totally unlooked-for maneuver, the *Brooklyn* crossed the bows of the *Texas* close aboard, causing that ship to back her engines frantically to avoid collision. Fortunately, the catastrophe was avoided. A moment later the *Oregon*, swinging to the west in the dense smoke from funnels and guns which covered the scene, nearly collided with both the *Iowa* and *Texas*. All these potential disasters were avoided by good luck and good seamanship, and the American fleet began stringing out to the west in a long stern chase of the fleeing Spaniards. But though smoke had been sighted the evening before inside the harbor, indicating some kind of movement on the enemy's part, only the *Oregon* had steam up on all her boilers. The other American ships had all been caught with half their power plants cold and off the line and were capable of only about 10 knots. Fortunately, the Americans had the tactical advantage, more than two-to-one superiority of force, and the magnificently steaming *Oregon*, as the Spanish ships one after the other came out of the harbor entrance and turned westward.

After the battle, it was not possible to determine which U.S. ships fired the shots that hit home. Clark, commanding the *Oregon*, claimed his ship "speedily gained a position nearest the enemy, held that position during the crisis of the battle, attacked in succession all four of the enemy's ships, and passed none until they turned for the beach." Naturally enough, all the American skippers spoke highly of the damage their own ships inflicted, but all except *Brooklyn*, the *Oregon*, and the old *Texas* (a near sister of the *Maine*) gave up the chase of the last two fleeing Spaniards and concentrated on the two that had been driven ashore near the harbor entrance. Soon, as Evans, skipper of *Iowa*, relates, their efforts turned from destruction to the saving of lives. One after the other, beginning with the flagship *Infanta Maria Teresa*, the Spanish cruisers were all driven ashore, three in flames, complete wrecks, and the fourth in the process of surrendering. The third of the burning cruisers, finally destroyed after a valiant fight against insuperable odds, was the *Vizcaya*. Her captain, the same Antonio Eulate so recently popular in New York City, was wounded.

It was, in a sense, Captain Clark's scenario for the potential encounter with Cervera's squadron for which he'd prepared his crew—except that it was the Americans who were strung out in chase and the Spanish fleeing, and none of Cervera's ships harbored any scheme to turn suddenly on her pursuers. At the last, *Cristobal Colon*, newest and supposedly fastest of the Spanish cruisers, the one that had not yet mounted her main battery 10-inch guns, was being hotly pursued by our equally fast *Brooklyn* and the supposedly slower *Oregon*. To everyone's surprise, the *Oregon* outdid even her famous trial board speed. Her chief engineer, Milligan, had helped build her. Her engines and boilers were beautiful pieces of machinery to him, and he gave them loving care. He and his crew had picked over all their coal, selecting the best pieces to be saved for battle, stowing them in a special coal bunker. Now, with the emergency of battle on him, he made the supreme effort of his and of his engines' lives. He boosted steam pressure far above the standard 160 pounds, lavishly expended the battle coal, and had double watches at every station: twice the firemen, twice the engine oilers, twice the coal passers. When her captain called for everything she had, the *Oregon* had it, with some to spare. Her enthusiastic engineering crew drove her faster than she had ever gone before, so fast that her low, blunt bows dipped under her enormous bow wave and scooped huge rollers upon her forecastle, to cascade and break on the base of her forward turret. Built for 15 knots, she touched 18 that day, overhauled both the *Brooklyn* and the *Cristobal Colon*, and finally got her big 13-inch guns in play. Of the several shots she fired, the last one splashed ahead of but close aboard the fleeing Spanish cruiser. This was too much for the *Cristobal Colon*. She turned toward the beach and ran herself aground. The battle was over.

The *New York*, with Admiral Sampson staring in consternation at the distant battle, of course came back at full speed. Like the *Brooklyn*, she had four engines, two in tandem on each propeller shaft, connected by a cumbersome clutch. For economy, she was in the habit of steaming with the forward engines disconnected when she had only half boiler power available, and this was her condition now. To connect up meant stopping the ship, stopping rotation of the shafts, and throwing in the clutches—after first thoroughly warming up the unused engines.

The *Brooklyn* was in the same situation, and neither Schley nor Sampson would permit this maneuver, fearing it would slow them still further, as it would undoubtedly have. So the *New York* ran after the receding battle at half engine power, still, however, building up to a very respectable speed as, one by one, she got her cold boilers on the line. Finally she joined the *Brooklyn* and *Oregon* in the vicinity of the stranded *Cristobal Colon*, but it was all finished. The American fleet had fired some nine thousand shots of various calibers; the *New York* but three, all at inconsequential targets.

Sampson was well aware of Schley's propensity to grab the limelight whenever possible. Already nettled by his own absence during what he knew must be the greatest battle of this war, the climactic moment of his career, he could not stand the thought of how Schley would undoubtedly capitalize upon having been in fact the senior officer present. In a moment, Schley confirmed Sampson's fears by sending the exuberant signal: "A glorious victory has been achieved. Details later."

Sampson could not bring himself to answer. Schley tried again: "This is a great day for our country!" Someone, probably Sampson's aide, directed the noncommittal reply, sent, in fact, to all ships: "Report your casualties." But in the context of the moment's euphoria, it was a dash of cold disdain when simple and honest congratulations to men but lately in battle were called for. "One dead, two wounded," curtly signaled Schley, indignant now.

The next development of the day is variously reported. One version has Schley reporting aboard the *New York*, where Sampson received him distantly and coldly. While he was aboard there came a report from the former passenger liner *Yorktown*, in naval service as the *Resolute*, that another Spanish man-of-war, a battleship, had hove in sight. After long minutes of silent cogitation, Sampson frostily directed the tired Schley to take his weary *Brooklyn* and "go after her," not thinking to go after her himself with his own as yet unbloodied ship. Schley took on the assignment in bad temper; but when the *Brooklyn* rounded on the new arrival, ready to open fire, she identified herself as the Austrian battleship *Infanta Maria Teresa*, ironically bearing the same name as Cervera's flagship but flying Austrian colors, which much resembled those of Spain. Another version, given by Robley Evans, states it was he, in the *Iowa*, who approached the stranger and was on the point of opening fire when she signaled her Austrian identity. Still a third account has the *Indiana* in this role. Perhaps the *Brooklyn*, *Indiana*, and *Iowa* accosted the Austrian ship at different times, though one would have thought the American warships, still busy with the aftermath of the morning's battle, would certainly have seen one another. In any case, Sampson missed a possible chance to participate significantly in the day's activity by not going himself, and it was out of character for him not to do so; he had previously always ordered the *New York* to investigate the strange ships his fleet occasionally sighted.

More significant, perhaps, is that with the *Brooklyn* off to deal with the not yet identified Austrian, Sampson directed the *Oregon* to tow the *Cristobal Colon*, a new, undamaged, and valuable prize of war, off the reef on which she had stranded herself. Water was seen in her hull, but her captain's statement that all her sea valves had been closed was taken at face value. The fact was, whether or not he knew it, they were all wide open. When towed off the reef, the *Colon* immediately sank, despite desperate sudden efforts to push her back into shallow water.

Commodore Schley had always been friendly with the press. In Norfolk, while his Flying Squadron waited for news of Cervera before joining with Sampson, he had had ample opportunity to cement his relationships. Sampson, on the other hand, was more aloof and taciturn—and in addition had been farther away, based at the more isolated Key West. The first news stories of the battle therefore gave all the credit to Schley, impelling him to send a cable, via Sampson, to the secretary of the navy with obvious intent that it be given wide publicity:

FEEL SOME MORTIFICATION THAT THE NEWSPAPER ACCOUNTS OF JULY 6TH HAVE ATTRIBUTED VICTORY ON JULY 3RD ALMOST ENTIRELY TO ME. VICTORY WAS SECURED BY THE FORCE UNDER

Sampson, on reading the message, said, "Schley, this is kind and generous. I will transmit it at once." But he accompanied it with a secret message of his own in which, for the first time, he complained about Schley's dilatory tactics in establishing the blockade at Santiago a month previously. Such a complaint, after a month during which Sampson gave no hint of displeasure with his subordinate commander and in which his own speed in closing the blockade was even slower, was then, and is today, as incomprehensible as it was reprehensible. It was totally foreign to Sampson's hitherto straightforward and honorable nature.

As a naval officer, Sampson was the paragon of his time. From his earliest service as a midshipman, he had been marked for greatness. His selection for the most important sea command of the war had been because of his eminent fitness for the job. Secretary Long said as much in announcing his appointment, which he followed with a statement to the effect that Sampson came from a family of modest circumstances and was the quintessence of the ideal naval officer, self-made all the way through capability and character only. One searches in vain for the clue to the strangely inept operations of the North Atlantic Squadron under his command, until one comes upon the tragic circumstances of his death.

Photographs taken of him in 1897 and 1898 show a striking change, most markedly between February and December of 1898. In the latter part of 1897 he is alert, confident, and in robust health. In February 1898, pictured as president of the court of inquiry into the sinking of the *Maine*, he looks still alert and intelligent, but there are signs of sudden change. His collar fits loosely. There is a frown of

---

*One of the first things General Shafter had done when his troops landed on Cuba's south shore was to set up an army cable station, located at Siboney, the beachhead he established a few miles east of the entrance to Santiago harbor. The cable station was thereafter used by all forces and, by permission, by the press. His first and largest beachhead was a few more miles eastward, at a place called Daiquiri. It was to Daiquiri that Sampson took the *New York* for the aborted meeting with Shafter just before the Spanish fleet came out.

uncertainty in his face. His full beard has turned white, but his mustache is still quite dark. In a photograph taken on the deck of the *New York*, evidently a few months after the Battle of Santiago, beard and mustache are both white; he looks positively shrunken, as though the vitality he radiated all his life had suddenly abandoned him. He has lost much weight. His brows are knit in a puzzled frown, his mouth is hanging slightly open, and there is bewilderment in his once serene countenance.

In the reports of this period there is occasional reference to "the Commander-in-Chief's illness," which several times confined him to his bed in the admiral's quarters of the *New York*. He was said to work much too hard. One tale has him spending hours pacing the deck, matching his eyes with those of the lookouts, to see whether any Spanish ships might be moving in the harbor behind the distant hills. Noted for leadership all his life, he showed none of it personally during those last weeks before the battle. Everything was done by his staff in his name. In August 1898 he was appointed commissioner to Cuba, but returned to the fleet in December. Within a year, now visibly failing mentally, he took over a sinecure post in Boston, which he held until he reached the statutory retirement age. He was too ill to testify before the court ordered by President Roosevelt to settle the long-standing argument over who was entitled to credit for the victory at Santiago, and he was placed on the retired list in February 1902. He died that May, only sixty-two years of age and totally senile, a victim, according to his obituary, of "degeneration of the arterial system and softening of the brain, from which he had suffered for nearly a year." The previous summer his doctor reported confidentially to Secretary Long that he was "suffering from a mental depression, the most constant symptom of which is a certain form of aphasia characterized by his mixing up words." The doctor also described his uncommon inability to function under stress. Need for even a small decision would put him into a near catatonic state—exactly his condition as described in the aftermath of the Battle of Santiago. Today it would be guessed he was suffering from Alzheimer's disease, or something very like it in its effects on memory and general mental condition.

These details are brought out not to discredit Sampson in any way. It is well understood that such illnesses must commonly be treated with a great deal of consideration for the afflicted persons. But it is a disservice to the country when an incapacitating illness affecting the ability of an important official person to perform his duties is concealed instead of given the attention it should receive. This is not, of course, confined only to people in high places; but it is here that damage can accrue to more than only the individual's immediate circle. One can imagine Sampson's devoted staff, initially refusing to believe that their revered chief could make mistakes or issue poorly thought out commands, then—unconsciously, later from compassionate habit and duty—compensating, interpreting, even changing commands and instructions when they could. One who has seen a similar affliction occur to a beloved parent can imagine the internal struggles of those who cared for Sampson, the lifting of spirits on the good days, the sad concealment on the bad, the slowly fading hope for recovery of the strong, competent mind they once knew. One must also sympathize with the victim himself, unable to cope with circumstances as he used to, determined to triumph over his body and mind by sheer force of will, but betrayed by physical changes over which mind and will could have no control. Or, merciful nature may have caused him to be entirely unaware of what was happening to him.

It is characteristic of this terrible illness that few of those owing loyalty to an afflicted person will admit, even to themselves, that all is no longer as it was, as it should be, with the person to whom one owes the best products of one's own mind. If there is a staff supporting an admired chief, group interaction may make this yet more difficult. Finally his most intimate adherents would be engaged in an all-out battle to support him, fearful of all circumstances and all nonintimates who might expose him, their first order of operation to prevent any idea of their secret travail to leak out. Even after his death, they would maintain an unofficial cabal to protect his memory.

One may wonder whether Schley, the next senior officer in the American fleet present at Santiago, could have had an inkling that something was perhaps happening to Sampson. In the ordinary course of affairs he would have had occasional private meetings with his superior, but the submerged differences between them would have held such conferences to a minimum and caused Sampson's staff to take strong protective precautions. There is no record that Schley suspected the true nature of Sampson's illness, nor did he give any orders before or during the battle except to his own flagship. In fact, no ship in our fleet assembled before Santiago received any direction of any kind. Theodore Roosevelt referred to it as "a captain's fight"—and in this judgment the verdict of history bears him out.

In 1901, Volume III of Edgar Maclay's *History of the United States Navy* appeared, initially slated to join Volumes I and II as textbooks at the Naval Academy at Annapolis. In it, Schley's actions before institution of the blockade and during the battle were recklessly criticized, even to the charge of cowardice for having caused the *Brooklyn* to turn away from the enemy at the outset of the battle. Schley demanded a court of inquiry, which met for forty days under the presidency of Admiral Dewey and took more than two thousand pages of testimony. The majority findings were unfavorable to Schley, but Dewey issued an opinion of his own in dissent from the majority, vigorously defending Schley. Although the court had been ordered to consider only Schley's actions, the basic consideration, and the one the public took for its charter, was to determine to whom should go the credit for the victory at Santiago. The court's opinion supported the Sampson image, and the navy wholeheartedly approved; but by the time the decision was released, in 1902, the newly confirmed victor at Santiago was near death and no longer possessed of his faculties.

Schley protested the findings to President Roosevelt, who had ordered the court at his request. But Roosevelt concluded, "There is no excuse whatever from either side for any further agitation on this unhappy controversy." Maclay's third volume was withdrawn from the Naval Academy curriculum (this was of course its death knell; few copies were printed and it can now scarcely be found anywhere)—and that was the end of it, except for Admiral Schley's continued bitterness over his treatment by Sampson's supporters. This is still expressed on Highway 15, northwest of Frederick, Maryland, where a large sign marks the tree-lined entrance to an imposing farmhouse. On it, where passing motorists can read them if not driving too fast, are these words: "The Home of Admiral Winfield Scott Schley, Victor over the Spanish Fleet at the Battle of Santiago, July 3, 1898." The unhappy "victor" authored an autobiography before his death in 1911, but he was never able to convince the U.S. Navy that he had been in charge at Santiago, for it knew well that no one had.

21

22

21. The *Boston*, of the ABCD fleet (our first steel warships), was built as a brig: two masts and a full suit of sails. However, she and the others were able to make only three to four knots under canvas. This was principally because their sail area was small compared to their displacement. *(From the Wm. H. Topley Collection)*

22. The *Atlanta* and *Boston* under full sail during one of their trials following completion in 1889. A handsome sight, but going nowhere.

23

24

23. USS *Baltimore* photographed shortly before the war with Spain. Personal laundry has been triced up to the foreyard. The 4,500-ton "protected cruiser," half the size and displacement of a modern destroyer, was the second-largest ship of Dewey's victorious squadron at Manila Bay.

24. Our favorite ship of the Spanish-American War, the inspired *Oregon*. Her descent from the *Miantonomoh* is obvious. Two other ships of this class were built, *Indiana* and *Massachusetts*, but only *Oregon* carried two old-fashioned anchors on each bow, on slanted "billboards" for quick release. Note that her armor belt is almost entirely submerged.

25. The ordeal of Rear Admiral William T. Sampson, one of our most admired naval officers: *Top Left:* Photograph published in 1898, identifying Sampson as president of the *Maine* court of inquiry, but probably taken in 1897 while he was captain of the *Iowa*. He is wearing full dress uniform with captain's insignia. *Top Right:* This photograph was labeled "commander-in-chief, North Atlantic Station," but Sampson is still wearing captain's insignia. Hence it was taken shortly before 26 March 1898, the date of his appointment to command the North Atlantic Squadron. *Lower Left:* Rear Admiral Sampson aboard his flagship, the *New York*, in the winter of 1898–1899.

26. Rear Admiral Bradley A. Fiske, taken in 1912 shortly before he became aide for operations to the secretary of the navy—in effect, chief of naval operations, although he never had the title. In this post he embarked on his politically doomed effort to get the navy ready for World War I.

27

28

27. Commander William S. Sims, naval aide to President Theodore Roosevelt, in 1907.

28. Rear Admiral Sims in 1919, with another Roosevelt, then assistant secretary of the navy and not yet a victim of poliomyelitis.

29. USS *Kearsarge*, exhibiting several of the design faults so severely criticized by Sims: her armor belt almost entirely submerged; oversize gunports in her turrets; main battery guns of different sizes and dissimilar ranges, with the turret for the smaller 8-inch guns fixed to that for the 12-inchers, so that both had to be trained no matter which was to shoot.

30. USS *Wisconsin*, completed in 1901, but still showing the ineffective, low armor belt.

30

31

32

31. USS *New York*, our thirty-fourth battleship, with most of Sims's complaints corrected but still insufficiently compartmented below decks to allow her crew to minimize disabling damage during battle. Her broadside battery would be swamped in a moderate to heavy sea and unable to shoot.

32. The "Cheer Up Ship," USS *Nevada*, called by *Jane's Fighting Ships* the "first to embody the everything-or-nothing idea in the matter of protection." In her, all Sims's deficiencies were corrected except the broadside guns, and these were already slated to be elevated one deck. Note the armor belt. The photograph is dated 1917: the camouflage paint job is intended to confound enemy range-finder observation.

33

33. Fleet Admiral Chester W. Nimitz in December 1944, having just received promotion to five-star rank. Probably the most admired naval officer our navy has ever had.

34. USS *Iowa*, in the middle of the war (November 1943), showing the literally hundreds of antiaircraft weapons our big ships carried after the lesson of air power had hit home. With all these rapid-fire guns, the amount of "flak" a desperate crew could put into the air to stop a kamikaze was unbelievable.

35. 24 October 1944: Battle of Sibuyan Sea, a part of the Battle of Leyte Gulf. A poor photograph but one of the very few extant of the big Japanese battleship *Musashi*. Taken by a Japanese cameraman, this shows her going down by the bow. Heavily damaged forward but never stopping her engines, in effect she did a form of battleship hara-kiri, or *seppuku*, by executing a near perfect submarine-type running dive. *(Courtesy of Tobei Shiraishi)*

34

35

36. Having lost tremendous face at Leyte Gulf by running away from the battle, *Yamato* performed another type of *seppuku*. On 7 April 1945, listing heavily and about to sink, with no ability left to contribute to Japan's now desperate war effort, she detonated the magazines she had intended to explode after running aground at Okinawa. Her stern, listing steeply toward the camera, can be seen to the right of the explosion's mushroom cloud. Of her crew of nearly 3,000, 2,500 were instantly immolated.

37. Destroyers today would most accurately be called "battle-force general-purpose escorts." This is the *Moosbrugger* of the *Spruance* class, the most numerous. A new class under design will be named the *Arleigh Burke* class, after the famed destroyer commander of World War II who was later chief of naval operations for an unprecedented six years. The new ships will be configured around the Aegis Anti-Air-Warfare system.

38. The most combat-efffective of our new surface ships is the *Ticonderoga* class Aegis cruiser. Designed on a destroyer hull with incremental improvements, these ships are filling an important role in our battle-group preparedness. Shown is USS *Yorktown*, second of the class.

37

38

39

39. USS *Nimitz*, named for our Pacific Fleet Commander of World War II. This nuclear-powered carrier is one of six near identical sisters, the last three not yet completed. About 1,100 feet long and 250 feet beam and displacing 95,000 tons, under certain conditions her total complement may approach 7,000. She represents the epitome of naval capabilities in the modern age, the combination of everything we have learned about air and surface power at sea.

14

Idealism and the Reformers

The United States Navy's formative period had lasted 125 years. Now it was 1900: our navy had become an established institution. Its cyclical ups and down were behind it, and it had assumed a bureaucratic life of its own. Its budgetary problems with the Congress were not finished, of course, nor would they—or should they—ever be; but the question of whether our country should have a strong navy had been resoundingly answered in the affirmative one more time, this time for the foreseeable future.

There were several operative reasons for this new outlook. The march across the continent had been completed. The United States now stretched across the North American continent, and had acquired, in the bargain, a sizable overseas empire in the Caribbean and in the far western Pacific. Whatever our ultimate intentions for them, these territorial acquisitions were now our responsibility. Willy-nilly, they and all their attendant problems now looked to the United States for administration and control. But in the meantime, the scale of the world map had become much smaller. The advent of steamships alone speeded communication; steel hulls and improved metallurgy gave the world much bigger, much faster ships; the telegraph and international cables meant transmission of thought and policy was independent of physical movement. It took no geographical analyst to see that while America had grown to include half a continent, that same continent had become much smaller. That where America had once only occupied one side of a new world and looked only back across the tremendously broad Atlantic to the Europe whence it had come, now the United States stretched from coast to coast, and had to look in both directions, across two oceans that had betimes themselves grown much smaller. While the United States was expanding from sea to sea it was also beginning to see itself as an island nation, larger in the absolute measure of square miles, but much smaller in the new scale of the world. As an island virtually surrounded by the sea, it was clear that the safety of the United States—and for that matter of the entire Western Hemisphere —depended upon the strength and ability of the naval forces that our nation, alone in that hemisphere, had the capacity to set forth.

If the war with Spain proved nothing else, it had shown that the United States required readily deployable sea forces on both coasts and an immediately available means of shifting them at need from one side to the other. Mahan had strongly argued that the fleet should always remain concentrated; otherwise it would surely fall victim to an enemy that did observe this principle. Yet the Spanish-American War had been in two oceans. We had needed two fleets—but two connected continents, spanning from Arctic to (nearly) Antarctic, separated them. In case of need they could not have joined, or even helped each other. It had taken the *Oregon* sixty-seven days to move at full sustained speed from our west coast to our east coast. As it turned out, her presence at Santiago had not made a decisive difference, for our Atlantic Fleet was strong enough to have defeated the Spanish squadron without her assistance; but we had not been sure of that before the battle. Next time the situation might well be much more urgent. No less a figure than Mahan made the point: "It is not likely that the United States will ever again be confronted with an enemy as inapt as Spain proved to be."

There was another lesson, too, in the insistence of nearly every town and city along our entire Atlantic coast that it should have some sort of naval protection against possible attack by the Spanish fleet. Never mind that poor Cervera had his own problems, the people of the United States demanded positive certainty of security; something that could be guaranteed only by a navy big enough to station a force bigger than Cervera's before each seacoast town. But while thinking persons clearly understood that stationing even one warship at every seaport was hardly the way to counter possible attack by a concentrated enemy force of several, they also recognized that much less so was the idea of having no naval force at all, as had been the case only a few years previously.

From the 1880 navy, which Dudley Knox said had "scarcely a single vessel fit for warfare and only a few in condition for normal cruising," in twenty years the nation had grown to demand a fleet able to function in two oceans and sufficient to protect both coasts from a far more effective naval power than Spain had proved herself to be. This idealized navy would be needed for another purpose also: to support our overseas possessions. In 1898 the country had seen what such a navy could do and had had time to consider, albeit very briefly, what might have happened if it had not existed.

By good fortune, the tools were at hand. The Industrial Revolution had given us the machinery, but first and outstandingly foremost among the tools was the Naval Academy at Annapolis. Its graduates served as junior officers during the Civil War; in the Spanish-American War they held all the high-ranking posts. But it was beginning in about 1900, when the first naval reform movement began to take hold, that the deep underlying idealism of the Naval Academy made its greatest impact.

College undergraduates are generally considered to be a cynical lot, paying little or no attention to the ostensible purposes for which they entered school, determined to enjoy themselves at the expense of everyone else for as long as possible. Yet everyone, looking into his own soul and those of his friends so far as he is able, will argue that such a perception is only surface deep, that underlying all the frivolity there is also a serious purpose. This was particularly true of the Naval Academy. If one looks back into the literature of the time, when the senior officers of the first three decades of the new century were midshipmen, this impression intensifies. The classes were small, the competition severe, the moral tone and ethical standards high. This is not to say that young men the world and ages over are not much the same in their youthful spirits, but to point out that at Annapolis the single-minded idealism the academy founders intended took firm root. The midshipmen of the final years of the nineteenth century were taken in at a young age. They were trained to be idealists, and idealists they became in a world where the machine—and in particular the machinery of war—was competing for the minds of men. Foremost among them was a group that saw its obligation as rising above the mechanics of the trade to which its members had been apprenticed; instead, they sought to learn how to use the new industrial sciences to further the business of naval science. As technological development drove the horizons of thought to fill vacuums undreamed of in the days of sail, they strove to harness their minds to improve the navy. They found much to work on.

The natural leader of the navy's Young Turks was William Sowden Sims. Probably no one, before or since, with the possible exception of Chester Nimitz years later, or Arleigh Burke later still, has had the charismatic personality of Sims. To begin with, he was extraordinarily handsome: tall, the picture of physical fitness, with a short, well-trimmed dark beard and mustache. He had a great sense of humor, often the saving grace in his never-ending push for naval reform. Many of his letters are today relished not because of the reforms there advocated but because of the hilarious way he presented them. One famous letter describes the old monitor *Monterey*, to which he had been temporarily exiled: "She has warped since she was built, and don't go straight. The compass is set with the lubber's point fifty-two degrees on the starboard bow, for that is the direction in which she goes." In addition, he was addicted to poetry as a means of expression; he put forth his ideas in rhyme whenever possible, sometimes to the despair of his more serious fellows—but others were occasionally thereby enticed to respond in kind. The war on paper could well be waged in poetry, he felt, for it at least kept the mind higher. The older and more senior he became, the more would he try to lighten the mood of his cohorts by humor in prose and poetry, though the latter, many said, became increasingly atrocious the more elevated its author's naval rank. Still, it served its purpose admirably. As a junior officer it was a way to cloak his ideas in a patina of genteel wardroom horseplay, with the barb of criticism perfunctorily covered. When he became admiral, he could insist his subordinates read his poetry, though he could not force them to like it; yet they understood that the implicit permission to laugh was a means of thawing resistance and drawing the sting—all the while, though sometimes in an elliptical way, their superior made clear his ideas.

Humor and poetry were not, of course, Sims's only method of achieving attention for his reforms, nor even his primary ones. Anything would do, for the written word was his great tool. He used sarcasm also, sometimes heavy-handedly, heedless of the resulting discomfiture. His enemies claimed he hit below the belt, yet he had his supporters, too, many of whom openly stated that he was the most valuable man in the navy.

Sims had been born at a good time: before the advent of entertainment machines geared to preempt every scrap of an individual's spare time. Reading was still a common pastime; writing letters to friends and family still an obligation not to be discharged by a quick telephone call. The U.S. Navy was Sims's hobby and his vocation. He rode it to the limit. In his obituary late in 1936, the *New York Herald Tribune* said, "He influenced our naval course more than any other man who ever wore the uniform."

He was not, of course, alone, but he was the preeminent figure. He did not possess the genius always to be right—but sometimes, looking back on it, it seems he very nearly did. Perhaps more importantly, he was the leader of an extraordinary group of reformers, most of them young officers, who worked unceasingly within the system to better it. Their effect was felt throughout the naval service. Though the most often repeated accolade given to him is that "he taught the navy how to shoot," there was much more to him than only that. Probably his biggest passions were the proper design of our most important ships of the time, the battleships, and the proper organization of the navy and the Navy Department to achieve effectiveness. He never ceased to criticize all three, with every weapon at his command. The results of his concerns are with us to this day.

A most important factor in the navy of reformers that grew up at the turn of the twentieth century was the President of the United States: Theodore Roosevelt—a name still to conjure with in the navy. It was he who, more than anyone, prepared Dewey for his great role at Manila Bay. While still a very young man, he had written what is even today considered one of the best histories of the naval war of 1812. He became enthralled with Mahan's lucid analyses of the uses and meaning of sea power, entered into correspondence with him, and placed reliance on his judgment that lasted the rest of their lives. Roosevelt had read many of Sims's reports in the intelligence files and had corresponded with him about them—often to clarify some point, once or twice with encouragement. With his tremendous personal energy, the extreme verve with which he did anything of even minor importance, Roosevelt was far from the unknown figure many presidents are when they enter the White House. Nevertheless, he entered it unexpectedly, the result of an assassin's bullet. Suddenly, a tremendous opportunity dawned before Sims.

Sims knew well with whom he was dealing and exactly how the cards were laid when he wrote a letter to the President of the United States that has become famous. Nor can it be said that he wrote heedlessly to a former correspondent. For a junior officer of the navy to write directly to the President, bypassing his own Secretary and all other officialdom as well, was unprecedented and totally improper. He thought long and hard about it, well realized the risk he took, and sought advice from brother officers in whom he had confidence. Long since, he had determined that when the time was right he would probably have to "go public" with his criticisms of naval ship design and target practice methods. The bullet that killed McKinley simply changed his method of getting the result he felt was imperative, giving him a much better opportunity, if he could but use it properly. Everything depended on getting Roosevelt's direct attention and confidence, and enlisting his support. If the White House mail clerk, exercising his bureaucratic initiative, were to send Sims's letter automatically to the Navy Department for assistance in drafting a reply, as he might well do, the same response as for Sims's previous reports might come: a nicely composed letter saying his ideas had been placed in the file, where they would be available when needed. But this was the least that might happen. Someone in the department would almost certainly take it on himself to chastise the writer, perhaps severely, for going out of channels. Worst of all, were Roosevelt to refer the letter to the secretary of the navy directly (as presidents almost always should do when in receipt of mail of this kind), Sims's career and his usefulness would be at an end. But Sims remembered how Assistant Secretary of the Navy Roosevelt had shown interest in his reports from Paris, even sending him a couple of personal notes of appreciation. If Roosevelt were somehow able to remain sufficiently free of the institutionalized bureaucracy of the presidency, he would read the letter himself first, would fully understand what the former naval attaché in whom he had once felt some confidence was trying to accomplish, and would ally himself with the effort. Sims also understood that the longer he delayed sending the letter, the more chance that the new president would become enmeshed in the details of the extraordinary job to which he had succeeded in such a traumatic way. Perhaps he would not even see it. After much thought, and many redrafts, Sims trusted his letter to the postal system. Its date was 16 November 1901. Sims was then serving in the obsolete monitor *Monterey*, assigned to the China station.

The letter has often been referred to as having begun a revolution in our navy. No less a character than Bradley Fiske, himself a revolutionary, says in his memoirs,

> Realizing the inertia of the department, and the straightforward character of President Roosevelt, Sims wrote to him direct, which was a most improper proceeding from the point of view of officialdom. Mr. Roosevelt took up the matter at once and with his accustomed force. Backed by this, Sims was able to bring about an

actual revolution in our methods of target practice, and in the matters of the construction of ordnance apparatus as applied to naval gunnery. . . . The action of Sims precipitated a crisis for the telescope-sight, which it passed successfully. After that the telescope-sight was taken up at once all over the world. Too much credit cannot be given to Sims for this, and neither can too much credit be given to President Roosevelt, who took his duties as commander-in-chief of the army and navy more conscientiously than any other President except George Washington.

In later years, Sims himself is said to have recalled Roosevelt's answer to the letter to be "a series of pyrotechnic explosions." It is certainly true that most of the navy, in retrospect, also recalled the results in this way. The facts are that the letter, quoted in full by Elting Morison in his fine biography of Sims, was noncontroversial and considered (in that it was couched in temperate language and cast no blame), and Roosevelt's answer, also quoted by Morison, was equally considered. But Roosevelt knew the navy well from his time as assistant secretary. Most important at this time was to protect Sims from discovery by the bureaucracy, and then to utilize his talents and drive to do the most good for the navy. Roosevelt therefore did nothing directly, beyond sending Sims a courteous and personal reply in which he invited him to write again at any time, and making arrangements within the White House that letters from Sims be brought to his personal attention.

The pyrotechnics were there, however, for as Fiske says, Roosevelt promptly took forthright action, as was his custom when convinced or exercised. A more apt simile would be to compare the results to an earthquake. Roosevelt had already been accustomed to shaking up the bureaucracy on his own, as evidenced by his selection of Dewey for the Asiatic Squadron on the eve of the Spanish-American War and by the instructions he sent him. Possibly he, too, had some ideas about how to make the navy more effective, having the experience of the Sampson-Schley controversy just behind him and probably some inkling of the less than outstanding results of the postbattle damage surveys of both Santiago and Manila as well. Suddenly Sims, an officer for whom he already bore respect and confidence, had volunteered to provide him with what he needed: the facts of the issues he vaguely sensed. Nothing could have been more valuable to an activist president. Without reference to Sims, he directed that every report on the subject (nearly all of which, he well knew, came from Sims) be printed and distributed to every officer on active duty in the navy. Of none of this did he inform Sims, but the latter knew of it through letters from friends who were in on the secret, and of course the letters and reports were themselves a time bomb of the highest order, needing only the spark of high-level interest to set off their fuses.

Surprisingly, despite the exchanges of letters between Sims and Roosevelt, the two men had not yet met personally. When Sims finally came to Washington, late in 1902, he avoided making the traditional social call at the White House which, for all officers assigned to the Navy Department, was still the custom. Partly, his biographer suggests, the omission was for fear of embarrassing the President and partly for fear of tipping his hand. But by this time, the source of all the turmoil and new ideas was far better known in the Navy Department than he himself appreciated. Ultimately it took the secretary of the navy himself to make the suggestion, and Roosevelt invited Sims to lunch at the White House to initiate the long and useful personal relationship that existed between them from that moment onward.

Lest it be thought that Sims's principal contribution was to the improvement of target practice, it should be noted that a point of at least equal strength made in the famous letter to the President was in criticism of the design of battleships. The operative sentence was:

> I have, in the last of these reports, been forced to the very serious conclusion that the protection and armament of even our most recent battleships are so glaringly inferior in principle as well as in details, to those of our possible enemies, including the Japanese, and that our marksmanship is so crushingly inferior to theirs, that one or more of our ships would, in their present condition, inevitably suffer humiliating defeat at the hands of an equal number of an enemy's vessels of the same class and displacement.

Sims had partly in mind the recently completed survey of the naval actions of the Spanish-American War. He had studied the data, as had

Alfred Thayer Mahan, and fully agreed with the historian's pithy judgment that our navy had won the Battles of Manila Bay and Santiago only because the Spaniards were more "inapt" than we. He was still more upset, however, by "a recent special target practice in the North Atlantic Squadron which shows much greater inefficiency in marksmanship than I have reported, or than I could have imagined possible. Five ships each fired during five minutes at a hulk at a range of about 2800 yards and made a *total of two hits*. The hulk was afterwards sunk at close range."

The statistics of the two battles of the war with Spain were distressing enough. At Manila, Dewey had expended some 6,000 shot of various calibers and hit the enemy 141 times that could be counted. This gave an approximate hitting effectiveness of 2.3 percent, exclusive, of course, of hits that could not be found because of damage or sinking of the targets. Santiago produced worse results: 122 hits found out of 9,433 shots fired, for 1.3 percent; but the fact that the enemy ships were under way and maneuvering, as opposed to the situation at Manila where they fought at anchor, caused the gunnery problem to be greater. Moreover, Dewey was able to steam with his ships in column in a large ellipse, slowly closing the range, whereas the individual American captains at Santiago mainly ran at maximum speed in pursuit of a fleeing foe, thus compounding the accuracy problem. Inasmuch as large-caliber guns were known to be more accurate at normal battle ranges than those of smaller caliber, probably a more representative calculation was that of some 1,300 large caliber shots, 42, or 3.25 percent, had struck their targets.

It was not as though Sims had suddenly come onto these conclusions about our battle readiness. He, like many of the younger officers, had been deeply concerned for years and had felt increasingly that the entrenched bureaucracy of the older officers would not, or could not, see the facts. Sims was simply the most outspoken of them, the most ready to risk all on the importance of getting his message across. His best and by far his most important collaborator was Theodore Roosevelt himself; but it is not fair to the many who were with Sims from the beginning to suggest that Sims alone was responsible for the great naval reform. At the very outset of his campaign, at a time probably more critical even than when he addressed his letter to Roosevelt, he had the unstinting support and excellent advice of Rear Admiral George C. Remey, commander-in-chief of the Asiatic Fleet, who always forwarded the increasingly critical reports and recommendations of his indefatigable subordinate with strong endorsements of his own. His supporters in the rank and file of the navy were legion, particularly among the younger officers who were also railing at immovable officialdom, and among the more thoughtful enlisted men.

On the other hand, however, there were many officers, principally high-ranking ones, who were adamantly opposed to Sims, who felt his methods were destructive, that the improvements he so ardently urged were surely coming (if more slowly than he wished), and that it was not necessary to destroy the honest effort of years merely to make an incremental improvement. Some, it must be admitted, were too set in their own ways, too emotionally involved, perhaps, to make a fair judgment. In one case in particular, the result was to put a bureau chief in a ridiculous position in which he would justly have been the laughingstock of the entire navy, had not his exalted rank and status shielded him from at least the open derision he deserved.

Sims had dwelt at length upon the remarkable target practice results of HMS *Terrible*, under the command of Captain Sir Percy Scott. (Sims had cultivated Scott's friendship and that of his officers, and was freely given information and shown equipment that Scott kept rigorously secret even from other officers of his own navy.) Like Sims, Scott was something of an iconoclast, accustomed to taking regulations and laws into his own hands. Doubtless he believed that alliance with the U.S. Navy was in the long-range interest of Great Britain, for he showed no hesitancy in contributing to it in this unorthodox way. Scott had instituted a system of ''continuous aim firing,'' in which the gun pointer kept his gun at all times aimed at the target, regardless of the ship's motion beneath it. He had also devised telescopes by which the targets were magnified for the pointers' benefit, with cross hairs in the prisms replacing the notched sights of the old-style guns. As a result, his ship had produced an extraordinary number of hits at target practice. Sims, backed to the hilt by Remey, reported all of this to the secretary of the navy and recommended the U.S. Navy develop a similar system. But the chief of the Bureau of Ordnance, to whom Sims's report was referred for comment, demonstrated, by using a gun mounted on the seawall of the Washington Navy Yard, that it was simply not possible for a pointer to overcome the resistance involved in raising and lowering a large gun even as much as five degrees in ten seconds—equivalent to a modest roll in a small sea. In his official endorsement placed upon Sims's report, he declared flatly that what was recommended was impossible, as proved by actual experiment.

Sims prepared his answer to this unfavorable endorsement with extreme care, and when it was received, again glowingly endorsed by Admiral Remey, it blew the chief of the bureau out of the water. In the first place, continuous aim could not be impossible because it was working well aboard the *Terrible*, as his report stated and as could easily be verified. In the second, the chief of the bureau had forgotten his high school physics (Sims more kindly wrote that he had "received inadequate information"). The situation on the seawall at the Navy Yard, he pointed out, was precisely opposite to that of a ship at sea. The seawall could not roll; therefore the gun had to be raised and lowered through an arc to simulate the normal rolling of the hypothetical ship beneath it. But on board ship the gun's own inertia, due to its mass, caused it to try to remain in the same plane with relation to the earth, whereas the pointer on the Navy Yard seawall was forcing it to change that plane rapidly back and forth. "Pointing" a gun at sea by the continuous aim method meant that the gun's own inertia helped it to stay steady. By contrast, simulating the roll of a ship by continuously cranking the massive extended weight of a gun on land to higher and lower elevations was fighting the force of inertia as well as the normal friction of the elevating gears. Discomfiture of the chief of the bureau was complete, and the navy dissolved in quiet amusement. But had it not already become generally known that Sims had the ear of the President of the United States, that would have been the end of him, for no admiral could accept such treatment at the hands of a mere lieutenant.

Sims's criticisms of the designs of our newest battleships were muted for a few years beginning in 1902, for in September of that year he suddenly received telegraphic orders to proceed from the China station to the Navy Department in Washington to become inspector of target practice. Taking the new post, he immediately visited all the ships of the fleet to explain the new ideas he was instituting. Basically these were training for gun pointers (the men who actually aimed a ship's guns) by attaching a specially designed small-caliber rifle to the barrel of the larger gun, exactly parallel with it, its trigger controlled by the firing key of the big gun. Drill involved setting up a small independently maneuvered target such that the pointer looked at it through the big gun's telescope, centered his cross hair by elevating or depressing his gun (and training right and left), and fired when "on." The sub-caliber rifle would shoot a tiny bullet through the little target as though it were a big gun firing at a distant one, and the men of the gun's crew would have an immediate indication of their proficiency.

There was of course much more to his entire system. The mechanisms controlling the guns required the most careful overhaul to be in smooth operating condition—a condition easy to establish for new guns, sometimes far more difficult for old or outmoded ones. Some of the older guns were not even in good balance: another difficulty. The objective was to institute the "continuous aim firing" principle, so that no time was ever lost "finding the target" after a reload. Another dividend was that the pointer and trainer became so accustomed to the motion of their gun as it related to the motion of the ship that keeping it accurately lined up on its target became second nature to them. In the meantime, the most extreme pressure was placed on the Bureau of Ordnance to improve the design of gunsight telescopes and the operating mechanisms, some of which were almost painfully ineffective. Sims's point here was that even though a ship might be old, it should still have the most modern guns possible, especially in the smaller types that could most easily be upgraded or replaced.

Warships being made to fight, their basic function was to get their weapons into combat range and protect their crews while serving them. But their work was accomplished by their weapons; therefore, extra pay was awarded to pointers and gun captains, and prizes to the most proficient. Sims created the motto "The only shots that count are the

ones that hit'' and promulgated the idea of ''hits per gun per minute.''
A gun able to put one shot per minute into a target was obviously only
half as good as two such guns, or one that could hit a target twice in
one minute. The idea of competition between gun crews in each ship,
and between ships themselves, was introduced. A devotee of physical
fitness himself, Sims was not an athletics buff; but he adopted and
introduced into the navy the concept of team spirit within ships. Prizes
were awarded to the ship turning in the best record in each category,
and in an effort to equalize the competition, various balancing factors
were devised so that older ships could compete with newer ones on
equal terms. Weather, being also an important factor, came in for consideration as well. The more a ship rolled and pitched, the more difficult to serve and aim her guns. But though history is full of instances
where commanders deliberately delayed battle waiting for an improvement in conditions, as a matter of principle warships must be ready at
any time. One could not guarantee that battles would be fought only in
smooth seas. A ''roll and pitch factor'' was therefore created by which
the firing ship's motion during practice was taken into account, so that
a good score when a ship was rolling heavily counted more than the
same score on smooth seas.

The old system of target practice involved putting out a pair of
buoys to represent an enemy ship of the same size; then the firing ship
would lie off at the prescribed range and fire shots between the buoys.
A boat with a ''raking party'' would lie out of the line of fire but in line
with the buoys so as to estimate the location where each shot landed;
when the shoot was over, beautiful diagrams were drawn showing
where each shot would have hit an enemy had there actually been
one there. Ships fired slowly and deliberately, taking as much time as
necessary. The diagrams were drawn with care and imagination.
Many a fine target practice score resulted from the ingenuity displayed on the drawing board. But as Manila Bay and Santiago both
showed, diagrams did not put shots into the target. Sims never tired
of describing what would have been the outcome of both of these
battles had Percy Scott's *Terrible* happened to be among the ships on
the other side.

For years many officers had complained about the lack of reality of the target practice procedure, which unfailingly put more importance on the report than on the results. When Sims came on board their ships as inspector of target practice and announced that all this was to be changed, their cheers were ready. It was what they had been hoping to hear for years. They enthusiastically adopted his idea of using an actual target on a raft, towed by a tug with a long towing hawser, and they gladly accepted his dictum that actual hits on the target were the only thing that counted. He visited every ship in the battle fleet, and later stated, "I cannot exaggerate the satisfaction with which all hands received this information."

It is no doubt apocryphal, but the story told in the navy about this period when new target practice procedures "taught the navy how to shoot straight" illustrates the way in which they were received. The story goes that Roosevelt assigned Sims a battleship, the old *Indiana*, which had fought at Santiago, to show what he could do. He and the ship disappeared for months. No one knew what the ship was doing. Her practices and drills were secret, and no crew member or officer would talk. Finally came the day when the squadron to which she belonged was to hold its annual target practice. The two buoys were moored, each ship organized her own raking party, and one by one each ship came abreast of the buoys, a thousand yards away, lay to, and fired each of her guns in the standard way. The raking parties gathered their data and prepared to draw their diagrams. But there was no sign of the *Indiana*. She was supposed to shoot at the same time as the other ships. Yet she had not appeared. She could not simply skip the practice—it was mandatory. What could have happened to her?

Then a nondescript tug to which no one had paid attention got under way and began to steam directly across between the two buoys representing the imaginary ship. The tug had had some strange thing alongside while it was lying to, a sort of raft, which it left drifting astern, now with a strange square sail on it. The flagship signaled the tug to keep clear, but no one aboard paid attention. Another tug was sent to intercept her, but she continued on her course regardless. Then it was noticed that the tug was towing the raft with the peculiarly marked sail—and about this time a cloud of smoke appeared on the horizon. The *Indiana* came belting from nowhere with speed cones and "I am about to fire" signal flags two-blocked (both at full hoist), roared at full speed across the firing position, by some accident got there just as the raft the tug was towing happened to be crossing the firing range, and suddenly her forward main battery turret, with its two 13-inch guns, trained out to port and she opened fire. Twelve times she fired, with unheard of rapidity, using only the right-hand gun of the turret, gun number one. Everyone with a telescope or pair of binoculars in the other ships was watching the sail on the raft. One after the other, with unbelievable speed, twelve holes appeared in the sail. The *Indiana* stopped shooting as suddenly as she had started, roared on past the slowly moving target, threw her helm over full, and came back. This time the forward turret was trained out to starboard, and the number-two gun fired. Twelve shots. Twelve more holes in the target. Again she reversed course, this time fired the after turret—again first one gun, then the other. Forty-eight shots in all, there were forty-eight holes in the target, and the tug and its tow were still moving!

According to the gunnery officer of the *Nevada*, who was present and watched the *Indiana*'s performance, "with the crash of the last shot, a great roar went up from every ship present." And then, with her turrets turned back to the normal centerline position, *Indiana* finally slowed, put her rudder over once more, and at a more normal speed approached the other ships of the practice squadron.

Her speed cones were at the one-third speed position, the firing flag gone. In its place was a signal: "Request inspection of target." Damage to the square "sail" was already evident, but when the inspection party reported that there were positively forty-eight holes in it, twelve for each of the old battleship's guns, the thrill permeated the entire squadron, officers and men alike, from admiral to the lowest coal passer in the firerooms, for they knew they had seen history made. Captains and gunnery officers of all the ships avidly studied the *Indiana*'s procedures, pored over her training methods, and vowed to copy them immediately. Gone were the "rakes," estimates of hits on an imaginary ship, and phony charts of "fall of shot." Here was concrete evidence of what many of them had been talking about. Here was the proof of what could be done!

The facts of the demonstration were somewhat more prosaic, despite its emotional and dramatic recollection in later years. But history had indeed been made. In the professional naval world, a spike of time and place had been erected that was fully comparable to any others from which great events flowed. Never had a ship, of any navy, fired so fast and so accurately as the *Indiana* in her first practice with Sims's new methods. Jubilation was widespread. It infected the entire navy. Writing about this period, the gunnery officer of the *Nevada*, formerly a passed assistant engineer in the *Baltimore*, had this to say:

> A new spirit had come into the fleet—one of helpful cooperation, with intense competition. Every officer was spurred to make improvements, to pass them on to others, and to try out whatever they passed on to him. There was feverish work on the gun mechanisms and in drilling gun crews, with many conferences and discussions.
>
> At this time, it is true, President Theodore Roosevelt was commander-in-chief; several rear admirals were flying their flags afloat; and seasoned captains, pacing the decks, were giving peremptory orders. But in spite of all this, it is equally true that a brown-bearded lieutenant dominated the hearts, minds and ambitions of the officers and men of the fleet.
>
> In reading military and naval history I had often seen references to the spirit of an admiral or general that pervaded an armed force and made victory inevitable. But, with Tolstoi, I had always doubted the truth of this.
>
> But now I realized the influence of one man. In every group I joined the first name spoken seemed to be "Sims." Sims had done or said this, had advised so and so. Sims had suggested this innovation, or worked out that new principle. Sims had ordered reports to be made. I feel sure that the spirit of Sims, even in his absence, controlled the activities of the fleet. Here was leadership—and leadership as effective as if this lieutenant had been Admiral of the Navy.
>
> The glorious naval victories of 1812 had created the impression that the methods of that day could not be surpassed. As late as 1901

I had given orders: "Away second riflemen!" "Away boarders!"
"Stand by for a raking broadside!" "Lie down!" "Repel boarders!" "Charge, pikemen!" "Cheer, my lads, cheer!"—all suited
to the days of Bainbridge and Decatur, but as out of date as their
smoothbore guns. Now Sims blew the Navy into the Twentieth
Century!

But there was a penalty, too, devastatingly inflicted within a year.
In the eyewitness report of the old *Nevada*'s gunnery officer,

> The *Nevada* was to take her turn on the range after the *Missouri*.
> We therefore anchored a little in the rear of the course to be fol-
> lowed by the *Missouri*. She fired several shots from her after
> 12-inch turret. Immediately after the last shot there was a great burst
> of yellow flame which completely enveloped the after part of the
> ship. It rose high, and was followed by a second burst, and a third.
>
> Our captain, Captain Howard, was one of a group on our quar-
> terdeck watching the practice. "Gentlemen," he said quietly,
> "there has been a terrible accident; up anchor; get the boats ready to
> lower; get the surgeon and his assistants on deck!"
>
> The *Missouri* now turned, heading at full speed across our bow
> for shallow water. The *Nevada* got under way and followed close
> under her starboard quarter. We all realized the danger to the *Mis-
> souri*'s magazines. If fire reached them, the ship would blow up.
> Captain Howard wanted to be well placed for rescue work in case
> that dread event happened. We saw men running aft with fire hose
> and dropping into the turret. Then we saw inanimate burdens lifted
> out. Five officers and thirty-one enlisted men had lost their lives.
>
> But most of the crew and the ship had been saved. With the
> special appliances fitted, the magazine doors had been promptly
> closed; and the magazines themselves had been flooded.

The *Missouri* explosion, which took place in 1904, was a severe
setback for Sims, inasmuch as the facile explanation was that it was
caused by his emphasis on rapid fire. Both Congress and the press
instantly demanded corrective action. Fortunately, years previously he
had laid the ground for his reply to this criticism in his voluminous
critiques of our battleship design, several of which concentrated on
what he called the criminal openness of the ammunition hoisting sys-

tem. During the first few seconds after a gun was fired there were, naturally enough, extremely hot gases in its bore. When a gun had to be fired into the wind, which occasionally was the case, and its breech was opened to reload for the next shot, these gases were often blown back into the turret in the form of a spear of flame called a "flare-back." Men at gun drill or action stations were consequently required to wear clothing completely covering their bodies—contrary to the traditional concept of their being bare to the waist—and they were always cautioned not to stand directly behind a gun when the breech was opened. Even so, they were sometimes singed by these flames. In his old reports, Sims had pointed out that because of the open design of the powder hoists in our turrets, there would be great danger of an explosion should a new powder charge for the next shot be coming up in the hoist at just the wrong time. Moreover, should an explosion occur, there was nothing to prevent the greatly augmented flame from going all the way down into the ammunition handling room, below the turret, where it might easily explode the entire magazine. Foreign warships did not have this danger, he had written, because their ammunition hoists were not open all the way to the bottom as ours were. It was a fault of design, not of speed of firing. And it was so important that if the ships had to be redesigned to permit the speed of which the guns were capable, it was simply something that could no longer be postponed, or pigeonholed, as had happened to his earlier reports.

By this time, Sims was neither conciliatory nor respectful to seniors whose complacency had bypassed the many citations of deficiencies made by himself and others. Had investigation been made and action taken when the problem was first pointed out, the accident could not have happened. Now, the ships would have to be virtually rebuilt in the danger areas. In the meantime, even though it would inevitably slow the speed of firing, he would institute the maximum possible safety precautions about having ammunition on an open hoist before all danger from flarebacks had been eliminated. And he strongly backed development of a compressed air "gas ejection system" to blow the gases out of the muzzle of the gun as an automatic part of the process of opening the breech-block. But battle efficiency was paramount, he held out, because that was what the navy had been built for. Foreign navies already had safer turrets than ours because their designers had been wiser; they had listened better to the needs of the men who would have to use the equipment, who would be risking their lives with it. The real problem lay in our system, which had no provision for factoring in the experience of the operating personnel, and now the bureaus were defensively protecting their own rears. He would have none of it. The absolute maximum of safety measures would be placed in effect, but he would not back down on his "hits per gun per minute" criterion. When Congress and the press became too hard to handle alone, he resorted—one of the very few times when he did this—to the forceful personality of the President for a decision that put the quietus on all the rest.

The *Missouri* disaster was not as bad as it might have been. A flareback had ignited an exposed powder charge in the turret, causing an intense flame that ignited two others in the hoist on the way up. There was no explosion in the strict sense. The men in the handling room beneath the turret managed to get the magazines closed off and the burning ammunition flooded, thus saving the ship. Congressional Medals of Honor were awarded to the three gunner's mates involved.

The accident also revived the controversy about battleship and cruiser design that, largely initiated by Sims with his earliest reports of comparative characteristics of American and foreign warships, had of recent years lain dormant. The *Missouri* and her sister ships were of faulty design, he held, and not only in the matter of the interior arrangement of their turrets. In fact, as compared to foreign design, they were terrible in nearly everything else. Sims had by this time lost restraint. He felt it was necessary to awaken the navy, Congress, and the nation to the errors being perpetrated by inadequate review of the pertinent operating considerations for ships. Their secondary batteries were too low; in any sort of sea, even moderate seas, green seawater would sweep into the open gun emplacements and make the guns impossible to serve. Their armor belts had been designed with the thought that battle would be joined with the fleet most likely nearly out of fuel, whereas, since future needs could never be perfectly anticipated, it was the practice of all fleet commanders always to keep coal bunkers full, refueling at every opportunity, long before actually necessary. Battles were therefore far more likely to be fought with deeply laden battleships, their armor belts mostly submerged, than in any other condition.

Likewise, gun sizes were illogical; the latest battleships carried 12-inch, 8-inch, 7-inch, and 3-inch guns; but any battle would be decided by the big guns at long range well before the smaller ones could come into action. Except for quick-firing torpedo-boat defense, therefore, what good were the small guns? Would it not be far more logical to devote the weight and space thus occupied to the bigger ones? Sims and several others, notably a classmate of his named Homer Poundstone, had long been advocating ships with only two calibers of guns: the maximum possible number of big guns for battle against enemy ships of the biggest class, and very small rapid-fire guns for defense against enemy torpedo-boat attack, expected to occur most likely by surprise, at night, or during low visibility. The plans he and Poundstone had painstakingly drawn in 1901 for the ship they proposed, which they had called the *Skeered o' Nuthin*, had lain in some pigeonhole in the Bureau of Construction and Repair for years. Nothing, of course, had been done with them.

Already mentioned were Sims's voluminous and prophetic complaints that the turrets of all U.S. warships were dangerously exposed to hazard of accidental explosion: sparks from combat damage, or from any sort of accident near the guns, such as had taken place aboard the *Missouri*, could fall all the way into the bowels of the ship, where they could too easily ignite the magazines. There were many other incidental deficiencies, too: some minor in nature, some far more esoteric and complicated than the few cited, some confined to only a few classes of ships; all had been thoroughly covered in the tremendous volume of reports, notes, recommendations, and personal letters that Sims, among others, had turned out over many years.

Now Sims had discovered that fighting City Hall was a battle with no quarter, so far as the navy was concerned, for victory by the group he represented meant the entrenched bureaucracy that was his target would be implicitly guilty of negligence. But he had given up all idea of being delicate. He attacked in the monthly *Naval Institute Proceedings*, in national magazines, in committees of the Congress. It would be nice to say he achieved the same immediate and outstanding success in this crusade as he had with his target practice reforms, but there was a tremendous difference in the conditions and, correspondingly, in perceived results.

Target practice was something done every year and in different phases; sometimes it was carried out more than once a year. Any improvement was immediately evident in improved scores or procedures. Sims and his increasingly large group of supporters could see the results of their efforts at improving the accuracy of gunnery almost from day to day. Ships, however, were a tremendous investment. They were there for the foreseeable future and changes could not easily be made in them, no matter what was said or done. Even the most important changes required months and years. Moreover, criticism of any ship design automatically brought forward its defenders: the men responsible for whatever was done or not done in her design, who had had to make the decisions regarding the details of her construction. Thus, the men responsible for the design of ammunition hoists held that there had never been an accident because of open hoists, that Sims's insistence on "reckless speed" was the sole cause. Those responsible for the low-lying locations of secondary battery guns defensively pointed out the structural considerations of weight, space, and armor protection that had dictated their placement. Even Congress became deeply defensive, since the House and Senate Naval Affairs Committees had also been intimately involved in many of the decisions.

Sims had at least the pleasure of knowing that he had entirely convinced President Roosevelt, who espoused his cause for bigger, faster, and better built battleships with enthusiasm. But even the support of a president as forceful as Theodore Roosevelt was not enough. Although our navy completed the design of an "all big gun" battleship in 1906, the two ships built to this plan (*South Carolina* and *Michigan*, laid down at the end of 1906) took four more years to build and were actually only warmed-over versions of our previous so-called pre-dreadnought class. They had the same speed (18 knots) and were almost exactly the same size. A different main armament (eight 12-inch guns instead of four) was the only real distinction. Meanwhile England, with utmost secrecy and spectacular speed, was constructing the much bigger, faster, and in general far more formidable *Dreadnought* herself, in less than one year from laying her keel to commissioning. This ship, mounting ten 12-inch guns in five turrets, turbine powered and capable of 21 knots, began a new era in warship design and construction. When completed in 1906 she electrified the world.

It was in fact Sims himself, through his private contacts with high-ranking officers of the Royal Navy, who was able to break the news of her imminent operational effectiveness to the Navy Department, at the same time providing our navy with its first accurate description of this epochal ship. Again, one must admire British sagacity in recognizing that breaking their inviolate rule for Sims was to their ultimate great benefit. It was not done with disregard for the consequences. A policy decision had been made to expose the ship to him in a thoroughly guided tour through all her spaces and a full explanation of her special qualities. The Royal Navy knew well that the impressions thus gained would be stored in a highly trained and retentive mind, and that everything Sims saw and heard would be transmitted directly to the secretary of the navy and the President himself—which it was. Perhaps someone, or some very high-level body in England—one suspects the latter—made the fundamental evaluation of America's role-to-be in the future salvation of Britain.

Suffice it to say, the thing was done and done well. Sims's and Poundstone's USS *Possible* and USS *Skeered o' Nuthin*, in blueprint form, may be seen at the U.S. Naval Academy Museum at Annapolis and compared to the actual *Dreadnought*. Great Britain had a several years' jump on the rest of the world's navies, but the navy she most valued as a rival and potential ally—that of the United States—was given a leg up on a new class of battleship that, at a single stroke, rendered all the major warships of all maritime nations obsolescent. And it should be noted in passing that one of the officers most influential in getting Sims aboard her, then Captain John Jellicoe, was later commander-in-chief of the British Grand Fleet at Jutland and, still later, held the post of First Sea Lord when America entered World War I.

Dreadnought's superiority to all other ships of war was not only in her great size; her principal characteristic was in her main battery: she had only a single caliber of big gun but she had ten of them, as compared to the previous standard of four supplemented by others of smaller calibers. In addition she was the first big ship powered by turbines, and was several knots faster (and considerably more vibration free) than any battleship had ever been. On her shakedown cruise she crossed the Atlantic Ocean at an average speed hitherto considered the province only of fast cruisers, and with attendant reliability totally foreign to them or any ship. Her protection, in thickness and strength of armor and in the thought given to prevention of the spread of damage—as, for instance, in the turret handling rooms—was of an extraordinarily high order. She was, in short, incomparably better than any other warship in the world, and instantly proved that everything Sims and his friends had been saying for all these years was absolutely true.

The United States Navy immediately began laying down all-big-gun battleships, as did Germany, France, Italy, and Japan (our first two, however, the *South Carolina* and *Michigan*, beyond doubling the number of big guns and reducing the number of smaller ones, were little improvement over previous ones—and, as noted, were not completed until four years later). In the meantime, the name of the original British dreadnought became the type-name of the entire class of heavily armored, fast, one-caliber big-gun battleships. It is no exaggeration to claim that the naval building race between Great Britain and Germany that culminated in World War I had its genesis in the *Dreadnought*; for from the moment she was revealed to the world, England's lead over Germany in the most formidable of ships was reduced from some thirty to only one, the *Dreadnought* herself. Perhaps England already thought of the United States fleet as a possible adjunct to her own in a time of great need, but that time was still many years in the future.

In effect, the introduction of England's *Dreadnought* enabled Sims and his insurgents to win their battle for at least some of the improvements they demanded in our battleships, but the American versions of the type contained many of the faults they had found with the earlier pre-dreadnoughts. In the meantime, Roosevelt, wishing to demonstrate the power and flexible capability of the fleet he had had so much to do with and in which he took such pride, directed the famous Cruise of the Great White Fleet around the world (1907–1909). But it was a fleet of pre-dreadnoughts that sailed forth on this voyage. The new ships desired by the insurgents were still in the blueprint stage, for there was already nearly a decade's gap between the first plans for the design of a new ship and her first cruise.

Sims, meanwhile, enjoyed tremendous prestige, both in and out of the navy. He had remained a bachelor until age forty-seven, devoting all his spare energies to his extracurricular activity on behalf of reforming the navy. He was all his life an extraordinarily handsome man, always in top physical condition. He was personally known by the leaders of all the world's navies, most specially so by the English. President Roosevelt appointed him his naval aide during his last two years in office, so that he was both inspector of target practice and naval aide at the same time. Late in 1905, he married Anne Hitchcock, daughter of Roosevelt's secretary of the interior, whom he had met when her father passed through Paris while he was naval attaché there, before the turn of the century. The wedding was attended by President Roosevelt and members of his cabinet, and took place at the most prestigious location in Washington: St. John's Church, across Lafayette Square from the White House. But marriage did not change Sims. He had long been associated with those advocating a stronger organization for the Navy Department, and in 1906 he took up the cudgels for this cause in addition to the others.

In essence the argument centered on the same old ground: the readiness of the navy for battle and the combat capabilities of the navy's newest battleships. Although they were indeed dreadnoughts, the insurgents found many faults with them. Basic to the entire argument was that they were staff-corps designed. The line officers and men who would have to fight them had had no hand in setting up their military characteristics, beyond establishing the principle of a main battery of single-size guns. At heart of the entire controversy was a rebellion against the bureau system that divided the navy into several separate fiefdoms independent of even the secretary. The reformers wanted to set up what they called a general staff for the navy, somewhat similar to the general staff already in use by the U.S. Army, channeling authority up through a strong chief of naval operations to the secretary. The conservatives wanted only to preserve the old system with autonomous bureaus, because that was what they were accustomed to.

The bureau system had been responsible for many of the deficiencies Sims and his cohorts had been inveighing against for years. Bradley Fiske, Sims, and the others held that the American navy was not as ready for war as it should be; that though it had improved mightily (especially in the accuracy and speed of its gunfire, in which it now led the world), it was still too satisfied with its laurels over the little war with Spain, too ready to believe in its own superiority. Its bureaus were still not ready to expend the necessary energy to compare the units, combat procedures, and protective features of the United States Navy with comparable components of the best of foreign navies.

The insurgents complained of inadequate compartmentation of its most important warships, the battleships, which were intended to be protected against the most powerful guns, the most destructive explosives that any enemy could hurl against them. The navy's lack of interest in aircraft, its officially expressed unconcern over the Fiske-demonstrated practicability of using "automobile torpedoes" launched from low-flying planes as a weapon of battle, its nearly automatic rejection of all new ideas, such as those for improving the protection of powder hoists in the turrets, came in for hot criticism. The insurgents demanded objective investigation into the areas of their concern: not by staff corps bureaucrats principally interested in defending what had been done before, but by men who had experienced the deficiencies in the ships at sea in weather good and bad.

Bureaucracy is invariably the result of the codification of rules of procedure. But if the rules are created in a changing situation, then the rules become clothed with meanings beyond their original intent, often with interpretations directly contrary thereto. No one was suggesting disloyalty or inefficiency on the part of any staff corps person, but only that such persons too frequently lacked the view of one whose life might depend on their products. The ships they designed were always based on those built before, improved only incrementally. Seldom were truly innovative ideas tried. No effort had been given, for example, to discover fully what submarines could do. In this potentially deadly weapon, even though our navy had led the world in its initial development, it now lagged woefully behind the navies of Europe and Japan.

The solution advocated by the reformers was establishment of a chief of staff for the navy, with a general staff of highly qualified seagoing officers working solely for him. This chief of staff was to be the president's principal adviser on naval operational matters and would normally pass his advice and recommendations through the secretary. The intent was to give the line of the navy a powerful voice in composition of the fleet as well as in its utilization.

To be fair, the navy did have a General Board, headed by the venerated Admiral Dewey, which might have been considered a halfway step toward a general staff. This board did recommend military characteristics of new ships, but its function was strictly advisory, and, without any real power, it was already drifting toward the moribund condition that was inevitable.

Naturally, the proposal for a general staff raised great controversy and much opposition, particularly from the entrenched staff officers of the navy's bureaus. Even though many of them were actually line officers and had experience in the fleet, they tended to come back always to the same bureau, where their shore expertise was founded. More formidable yet was the virulent opposition of chairman Eugene Hale of the Senate Naval Affairs Committee, who, through 30 years of seniority in the Senate (1881–1911) and years of unopposed control over the navy, assumed a degree of mastery over it approaching personal ownership. Creation of a chief of staff similar to what the army already had would directly threaten the chairman's control. He fought it viciously, ordered a complete hearing of the subject before his committee—and then so dominated and managed the procedures that the voices of the reformers were submerged, disparaged, and contradicted. Sims's great supporter, Theodore Roosevelt, was soon to be out of office, and in any case had no direct control over the Senate. By the end of his term of office, time had run out. With inauguration of a new president, in 1909, the bureaucrats and politicians had taken completely over.

Two large conferences and another set of Congressional hearings were held. But without a deeply involved president, the reformers were beaten. Fiske and Sims were unable to change the march of events. One of the unfortunate impressions gained by the public about the proposed general staff—indeed the impression held by many naval officers as well, and assiduously fostered by its opponents—was that it was somehow connected with a staff of generals, that it would therefore become too "Prussianized" to be truly representative of America.

Opponents even turned the argument into an issue of patriotism. It was made out to be virtually disloyal to our nation and our shipbuilding industry to complain about the ships built. They were as good as could be, the best warships in the world, because they had been built in America, and American-built ships had never lost a war.

The reformers weren't helped by the fact the ships were already designed and the contracts let—faulty hoists, insufficient compartmentalization, and low armor belts notwithstanding—and there was, in fact, no alternative to accepting them. In the course of debate, it didn't matter that the reformers had no intention of rejecting these ships, that they wanted only to make significant changes in new designs before construction of new ships began. The article of faith was that all the ships built were fine ships because they had been built by Americans. In short, because they *had* been invented here, not because of any objective evaluation. By good fortune, they were never tested.

But the mark of the reformers was nonetheless evident in the next class of battleships designed, the new oil-burning *Nevada* and *Oklahoma* (along with far greater convenience of fueling, oil gave more energy and therefore greater operating range). To the naval cognoscenti, they were the "first to employ the 'everything or nothing' idea in the matter of protection, thus marking a 'new era in naval construction.'" So stated the prestigious *Jane's Fighting Ships*, the "bible" of international warship design, published in England since 1898. Completed in 1916, their broadside battery of 5-inch guns was elevated one deck a year later and the gunports were permanently plated over—another tardy victory for the naval insurgents.*

---

* All U.S. battleships of this era, until the post–World War I *California* and *Tennessee*, show the strange angularities in an otherwise smooth outer hull form where the lower level guns were

So far as the administration of the Navy Department was concerned, the post of chief of naval operations, creation of which was sought by Fiske, Sims, and all the reformers, became a fact by act of Congress in 1915. But Woodrow Wilson's secretary of the navy, Josephus Daniels, completely misunderstanding the added strength the CNO would bring to his office, attempted to emasculate the position of its planned authority by restricting its freedom of action and by circumventing the ambition of Fiske to be the first officer so appointed. More important, he also firmly set himself against the war-preparedness measures Fiske, as his aide for operations, was pressing upon him. Fiske, as was his duty, continually pointed out the necessity of becoming prepared for the possibility of involvement in the European war that had been going on for a year. Daniels had the idea that by taking the steps Fiske proposed he was making war more certain, and that the proper way to avoid war was to take no precautions at all.

Here was illustrated one of the weaknesses of the old system—one from which the present is not immune. Ideally, military establishments are a form of insurance, just as fireproofing a building or inoculating oneself against disease may be called insurance against the possibility of such disasters. While it may not be possible totally to separate military preparations from their political or psychological effects upon our own or other nations, there are some obligations that fall automatically to any military organization. Accepted as primary among these is accumulation of necessary tools that cannot be improvised on the outbreak of war. For a navy, these include ships, personnel, provisions, and ammunition. But there are also other, less tangible ones such as training, organization, tactics, and contingency planning. Without commitment of the national policy in any manner, it seemed to Fiske beyond all question that, faced with a war engulfing nearly all of western Europe, the United States Navy should have been expected to prepare plans for our possible involvement. Were such concepts better understood, there would be less danger that simple professionalism might be misinterpreted by a public whose principal interests do not

---

removed. Illustrative of the slow pace of design change, the later ships never carried guns there, nor ever were intended to; but the angularities were built into the hulls all the same.

encompass military readiness. The theory that there was little likelihood, or intent, of the United States entering World War I had logically no bearing whatever on whether our armed forces, charged with preparedness for all contingencies, but not with determining national policy, did a bit of legitimate "what if-ing." The obligation was to be ready to execute the public will, whatever that will might be, and there could be no excuse for failure to be ready. So, at least, argued Fiske.

Daniels, a newspaperman and liberally inclined politician, had no knowledge of the navy before he became its secretary. He consequently had to rely on its professional officers for advice, but he constantly clothed himself in the often misinterpreted concept of civilian control upon which our country was founded, particularly when he felt a given proposal was a threat to him or his authority. When Congress was considering the bill creating the office of the chief of naval operations, he fought the original wording, got some of the language weakened, and then looked around for a chief who would personify the opposite of the characteristics of Fiske and Sims, the two leading contenders for the post. But if he hoped to set up a straw man totally submissive to his own ideas as secretary, he picked the wrong individual. His selection for the navy's first chief of naval operations, William S. Benson, had not the reforming drive of Sims nor the inventive mind of Fiske; but he was a solid naval officer, solidly grounded in the traditions of the service. And though he differed in detail from both Fiske and Sims, he slowly created in the office of the CNO, as it became known, the basis of the position as it exists today. Benson never got the fifteen assistants proposed by Fiske, nor did he get absolute control over the navy bureaus. But there are other ways of achieving objectives, something Benson may have at least partially learned from Daniels. He *was* able greatly to improve the navy's readiness for the war against Germany in 1917, though not to the level he (and Fiske and Sims) would have liked. And today's CNO, with his vice chief and deputies and the whole staff of OPNAV (the Naval Operations organization under him) to work with, has gone far beyond the highest ambitions of Bradley Fiske, who really created the job.

As the second decade of the new century drew to its end, the work of the reformers had borne fruit. Our navy was no longer the slapdash, quixotic, semisocial organization of the Spanish-American War days, but an idealistic, highly trained, highly professional group of men, dedicated to using their experienced sea knowledge for the betterment of their country. Nearly without exception, they acknowledged their debt to Sims and, to a lesser degree, Fiske—and likewise to the other thinkers and reformers, including writers like Mahan. There had been no war between 1865 and 1917, except for the hundred-day war with Spain, which was more an exercise in American naval power than a contest between equals. Even so, when the United States entered the war in Europe, in April 1917, the reformers could look to the prospect of becoming involved with some feeling of having at least gotten their house in order.

As so often happens, however, it was not vouchsafed to the men who got the navy ready to lead it in the war for which they had prepared. For one reason, the battles at sea were over before our entry. For another, many of these men were no longer on active duty. Fiske, psychologically debilitated by the depth of his personal battle with Secretary Daniels over the CNO issue and naval preparedness in general, had retired from active service in 1916. Early in April 1917, before our declaration of war against Germany, Sims was sent to England to coordinate U.S. Navy participation, but all England and France wanted was a continuous supply of the sinews of combat: munitions of all kinds and food for their armies and populace.

There was a large argument over the desirability of sending a contingent of U.S. battleships to form a part of the British Grand Fleet located at Scapa Flow, and a much bigger one over the combined strategy of the Allies. In November 1917 a division of five battleships was finally sent to form the so-called American Battle Squadron, the British Sixth Battle Squadron. (Later in the war, three more ships, the new oil burners *Nevada* and *Oklahoma*, and the older *Utah*, went to European waters, though not to Scapa Flow, the Grand Fleet base of operations.) But no battle ever occurred, and the major employment of American naval forces during this war was in convoying supplies of all sorts across the Atlantic. Much was made in America of the importance of this service, and it is indeed true that it was important. When Sims arrived in London in 1917, England's Admiral Jellicoe, First Sea Lord, had his old friend to his home for a private dinner, where he quietly handed him a paper outlining England's desperate situation at the hands of German submarines. Sims reacted with an immediate cable to the U.S. Navy Department for destroyers for antisubmarine work as an initial emergency measure. As a result, the first destroyer division was sent, under Commander Joseph K. Taussig, whose laconic response to British Admiral Bayly, when asked when he could be ready to begin patrolling, was the ever-after famous "We are ready now, as soon as fueled." The arrival of these destroyers has also been commemorated in the well-known and often reproduced sentimental painting by Bernard F. Gribble titled *The Return of the "Mayflower."* But convoy duty was only one of a navy's possible functions.

The rest of the fleet remained mostly in American waters, ready for the possible exigencies of an expanded war at sea. That also, however, was not to be. Instead, a tremendous controversy developed over naval strategy, reaching depths of significance far greater than mere fleet employment. The American view was that, as full partners in the war effort, we should be involved in all parts of the war strategy as they were developed and take part fully in the decision-making debates. The British view, unstated but finally clear enough, was that the United States should simply supply whatever England needed to prosecute the war and let her, the more experienced nation, go about winning it with the extra resources we provided at her command.

At the bottom of the issue was England's intent to remain the strongest naval power in the world, as against the growing desire of the United States to be considered a fully equal partner not only in the war but among the world's navies as well. The war came to an end without resolution of this fundamental disagreement.*

---

* It finally came to a head during the early 1920s, in the conferences leading to the Washington and London naval treaties. In 1916, with the slogan "a navy second to none" and some of the lessons of seapower and the types of ships needed for modern war at sea in mind, the U.S. Congress had enacted the biggest warship-building program in our history. When complete, our navy would have thirty-five modern dreadnought-type battleships, all superior to England's weary Grand Fleet. Only three years later, with many of the 1916 ships still unfinished, Wilson

Although it was not an American naval engagement, no discussion of this era can omit the Battle of Jutland, which occurred on 31 May–1 June 1916. This great action has been studied virtually ad infinitum everywhere naval officers look at the strategies and tactics of the past. It has been called "the last great battle between battleships," but, strictly speaking, this title is erroneous. It is true that it was the last battle of the old type: a fleet of huge warships maneuvering as a unit in the hope of bringing the opposing fleet to action as a unit. It was this faulty concept that had prevented the British fleet from beating the French de Grasse off the Virginia Capes in 1781, thus leaving Cornwallis no alternative but surrender to Washington. The idea was openly defied by Nelson in his entire career, with great demonstrated success, but was supported by Mahan with his dictum of the concentrated fleet. In any case, England had not had a general fleet engagement since Trafalgar; Jutland was the next one, 111 years later, and the British navy expected it to come to a Trafalgar-like conclusion. But Jutland did not result in the overwhelming victory England craved.

Despite all the resulting controversy, the basic lesson Jutland showed was not correctly read: with main battle units capable of (relatively) high speed, heavily armed with long-range weapons and also extraordinarily resistant to damage, the scope of the battle at sea had gone far beyond the old-style conceptual capabilities. Aircraft and submarines were only the beginnings of the changes in store. New tactics and new strategies of all sorts were in the making. In only another

---

asked Congress for a new building program literally double the earlier one. The 1916 legislation already planned a U.S. fleet far superior to that of Britain; the 1919 program, if enacted, would have been impossible for England to match. Her navy would have fallen to a distant second place—albeit to a recent ally—for the first time since the days of Horatio Nelson. Wilson's reasons for the huge building program have been ascribed to various possibilities, among them U.S. annoyance at Britain's attitude regarding war aims and planning. Perhaps he expected to use it for leverage on the League of Nations issue.

Whatever were Wilson's motives, the U.S. proposal for a disarmament conference met with great international approval—and concealed gratitude on the part of Great Britain. It resulted in limitations on the size of battleships and their total tonnage, with England and America fixed at the ratio of 5, Japan at 3, and France and Italy at 1.75. Other provisions concerned the number and size of cruisers, creating yet another category of that much confused type, the "treaty cruiser," so-called because of the upper limit on displacement (10,000 tons) and on size of guns (8-inch). Submarines also came in for their form of control, the British concept—that in most situations they must operate as surface ships—being written into the treaties.

generation there would be electronically guided missiles and electronic combat weapons of all types. Jutland was thought of as a great battle of the old school, between battleships. In fact, it was a demonstration of the futility of the old idea of seapower measured against the new on-coming technocracy. In an esoteric sense, it was also proof of the often stated principle that any system reaching its highest expression is already on its way downhill. So was it with naval warfare of the old style, and the Battle of Jutland is the perfect example, on a very large scale.

The only big ships that were actually in action during most of the fight, and received most casualties (three British, one German sunk), were of the battle-cruiser class. Battleships hardly fought at all, except for very short periods quickly broken off. The British had four ''fast battleships'' in action for a time, during which one, *Warspite*, came under concentrated fire because of a rudder casualty; one or two German battleships received several large-caliber hits. But there was no battle between battleships in the commonly understood sense of the word. The first day's fight, which ended after dark, did not resume at daybreak, as the English had expected. Instead, the Germans seized a fortuitous opportunity to disengage, leaving a frustrated British fleet commanding the sea but unable to do the Nelsonian thing, so commended by Mahan, of annihilating the enemy.

Hindsight now tells us the German battle cruisers were far better protected than their English counterparts, a deficiency that seems to have lasted with that class of major warship through World War II, when the English *Hood*, her finest and biggest warship, completed in 1920 and also rated as a battle cruiser, blew up and sank in circumstances appallingly similar to the loss of her three predecessors a quarter of a century earlier. In strong contrast, the only German battle cruiser lost at Jutland was so damage resistant that she finally had to be scuttled by her own forces when it was apparent she could not be carried back to base.

This gives rise to speculation as to what might have been the outcome if the battle both sides expected with daylight on 1 June had actually taken place. British superiority was as 8 to 5 in numbers, but there was a long June day in northern latitude ahead of them. The best American student of the battle, Commander Holloway H. Frost, concluded that the Germans might have been able to beat a British fleet that had a superiority of only 6 to 5—and Jellicoe, the British commander, is supposed to have said that he was "the only man in the world who could have lost the war in a day"—which means he believed the German fleet might conceivably have beaten his, and thereby won the war. More magazine explosions in the British fleet, especially early on, might have evened the odds. Had German battleships displayed the same superiority over their opponents as did their battle cruisers, history might have been rewritten. But that contest never took place.

On a far more limited level, that of navies and naval ships of war, the lack of a real struggle between battleships at Jutland means that these great ships, once thought to be the epitome of naval strength, have never met the test of battle in the manner in which their designers and naval pundits from Mahan on have expected. Manila Bay was a cruiser battle; at Santiago all the enemy ships were cruisers. In neither case did the Spaniards hit our ships often enough to give them a real test. (There was a naval battle at the Yalu River in 1894 between China and Japan, in which two ten-year-old Chinese battleships, built in Germany, showed just how hard it was to sink a well-protected ship. But this was hardly a representative fleet action.) The next occasion of battleships in action was during the Russo-Japanese War of 1904–1905, but the ineffectiveness of the Russian tactics and a sequence of disasters—not least of which was loss of their best admiral, Stepan Makarov—prevented full employment of their capabilities. The climax came with the dreadful Battle of Tsushima, in which the Russian Baltic Fleet, sent halfway around the world in an unbelievable condition of insufficiency and unreadiness, was wiped out by an efficient Japanese fleet ready and waiting for it.

In summary, battleships, defined as heavily armed, heavily armored, and slow (as compared to all other warships), were developed and steadily improved for some eighty years after the *Monitor*, but after our Civil War no battleship in the world was tested in the way naval doctrine had always supposed it would be.* It had been expected battleships, true to their heritage, would be maneuvered in a great fleet into some huge Armageddon-type battle against another great fleet, just as in the days of the King James Fighting Instructions of the Royal Navy, or the far more modern-seeming tactics of Horatio Nelson at the Nile or Trafalgar (in both of which he actually disregarded the fighting instructions). But in the entire history of battleships, this never happened. Jutland was the last time an attempt was made to use battleships in the concentrated fleet action for which they had been supposedly intended.

In World War II, battleships were used for shore bombardment with their big guns and, on one romanticized occasion, a squadron of the battlewagons salvaged from Pearl Harbor "crossed the T"** against a smaller enemy force attempting to exit Surigao Strait in the Philippines and destroyed them all. But this was not a fleet action of the type for which the slow, heavily armored, and minutely compartmented ships had been designed.

In the meantime a new sort of battleship had been devised: not only heavily armed and heavily armored, but fitted with engines of such tremendous power that it could outrun all other warships and carry an extraordinary battery of antiaircraft weapons. These new "fast battleships" had much more in common with the German battle cruisers at Jutland than they did with the outmoded fleet sunk at Pearl Harbor, and the manner of their projected employment was also like that theo-

---

* In this connection, Germany's *Bismarck* must not be forgotten. No ship ever showed the damage resistance she did. At the end of her hopeless battle against England's fleet, in May 1941, two of Britain's heaviest battleships were pounding her at point-blank range. She probably suffered more major-caliber hits than any ship in history—and the best available information is that when her own fighting capability had been totally destroyed, she scuttled herself rather than surrender. Therefore it can be said that she demonstrated the battleship's damage-resistance qualities to a new high level; but that was not the only function she was designed for. Theoretically, a fleet of such ships should have been victorious over any other fleet—but the fact is that she was built to refight a battle that had not quite happened, exactly a quarter of a century before.

** When two opposing columns of warships so maneuver that one lies at right angles to the other and across its projected line of advance, so that all the guns of the first can bear on all the ships of the second, but only part of the guns of the second can bear on the first, the first column is said to have "capped the T" on the second. The situation is analogous to the raking broadside of sailing ships, in which the ship being raked can fire but few of her guns in reply. The after turrets of the "crossed" fleet cannot train far enough forward to hit the "crossing" or "capping" fleet, and except in the case of the lead ship, even its forward turrets would be at least partially blocked by

rized for the big cruisers. But by the time they were on the scene there was a new "queen of battles," one developed from an entirely different need. Unlike the battleship, this new queen, the aircraft carrier, was instantly put to the most strenuous of tests in the role for which it had been designed. It had the inestimable advantage of a reach far beyond the limitations of the old-style weapons. And through the same means, the aircraft, it could see farther as well.

After World War I, the "war to end wars," the world embarked with some enthusiasm on its first attempts to limit arms. Since battleships were the biggest and most obvious military objects, as well as the most expensive, they logically became the first targets for reduction. But professional military persons are not the only ones with better vision backward than forward. At the time they fell under limitations, battleships of the World War I type were already obsolescent (although new and even bigger ones were being built), and navies were undergoing great hidden changes. Aircraft and submarines were beginning their rise to acceptance as first-line naval-weapons carriers. It was only a quarter century since Mahan, yet the speed of change was already outstripping the scope of his studies. He had looked backward in time nearly a hundred years, and what he saw was significant. His name will forever be illustrious as one who most clearly described what it was that had controlled the world of which he wrote. But in 1920, followers of Mahan who lacked his incisive understanding were stretching his theories beyond their limits to accommodate the new practicalities; so that they served in fact more to restrain than to advance the science of naval strategy.

Henry L. Stimson, President Taft's secretary of war, is credited with referring to "the peculiar psychology of the Navy Department, which frequently seemed to retire from the realm of logic into a dim religious world in which Neptune was god, Mahan his prophet, and the U.S. Navy the only true church." He was a partisan of the other side,

---

the friendly ship just ahead. This entire concept, however, was highly theoretical, and could easily be avoided in nearly all situations. At Jutland, Jellicoe twice capped the T on Scheer, but both times the German fleet simply reversed course—a maneuver it had practiced which the British did not believe possible. At Surigao Strait in 1944, the Americans lay across the mouth of the strait and the approaching Japanese could not avoid being capped.

---

of course, but he might have had a point—and it would have been more strongly stated if he had referred to the cult of the *battleship* as the only true church, instead of the U.S. Navy as a whole. The cult was not confined to our navy alone; in fact, it was stronger in the Royal Navy, where it had existed for centuries. Since earliest times, the line-of-battle ship has been the highest expression of the naval art. Some of the early ships of the line were worthy of any museum for the concentrated and often very artistic embellishments embodied in them and upon them. Naval aficionados have always loved them—and painted them, and modeled them. Hand in glove with a form of worshiping them as static art objects in themselves went making their working, as well as their structure, the highest possible expression of the naval art they symbolized.

Only to look at the extraordinary development that took place in these ultimate warships during the four decades around the turn of the century is to observe the greatest change in their entire history. Psychologically, the ships of the line of naval battle *were* the navy, and had always been. "Stay in the big ships, young man," the older officers counseled. "Work your way to the top in a big ship. That's where the real navy is. Don't waste your time in little ones. Stick with the big ships." So always spoke the old *Nevada*'s onetime gunnery officer to his eager, growing son.

The advice was sincere and well intentioned. There always has been a mystique involving the self-contained little world of a large, well-found ship, combating the far greater elements of wind and sky and the huge, trackless, sometimes malevolent sea. It was not lessened when the lovely square-riggers with their clouds of gray-brown canvas gave way, unwillingly, unavoidably, to steel behemoths powered by steam engines. There has always been something mysterious, and beautiful, about a ship on the bosom of the sea, something which makes men fall in love with her, call her by a personal pronoun, even invest her with a living personality. But not only did a big ship become a living, sentient being to those who served her, she was also a community of kindred souls, of men who thought alike and worshiped at the same shrine. Never, even to the youngest sailor, has a ship been only a mechanism. To men who have devoted their lives to ships, any ship—but principally their own ship—becomes their reason for life itself. Perfection of the ship becomes its own objective. Battle has nothing to do with it, although one always talks of battle. Battle is harmful to the ship, and should be avoided if possible, though not so one can notice. To sailors of the old time, enlisted men and officers, their ship was their home and their religion.

So was it with the fleet so much created by President Theodore Roosevelt. But this fleet, strong and fine though it was, contained some egregious flaws. All its personnel were dedicated to the effort toward perfection, but in that effort it was not surprising that the reformers, who were not content with slow and simple growth, who insisted on overturning old forms of worship to institute new ones they felt were better, were not popular. In ancient days they might have been sacrificed on the altars they had profaned. In more civilized times, they were merely ostracized, fought against, turned aside whenever possible, accepted when they had to be. No one in the U.S. Navy believes Sims would have gone as far as he did had he not had the support and protection of the president. Isherwood was shattered by the navy that now reveres his memory. Mahan's initial recognition came not from the U.S. Navy, but from the British navy, for he explained better than anyone why their worship of the ship was right for their time. Bradley Fiske, the most innovative of the unbelievers, who spent his career trying to reorganize the navy—the religion of the ship—into something more akin to the modern age, was cast aside. Only Sims, and years later, a gnome-faced individual named Rickover, were able to beat the coterie of high priests at their own game.

To the men who, at the turn of the century, had fought to bring the navy to its highest possible effectiveness, the cynosure of naval capability was the greatest ship that could be built, operated in the most efficient way it could be operated. This had always been their single-minded objective—even though the speed of modern industrialization caused achievement of this end to recede much faster than any man's ability to pursue it. They had largely succeeded in creating a navy of such ships during their time. It must also be believed that, had they been blessed with more years, the new conditions of an expanding industrial capacity, with new devices and new ways of using them, would undoubtedly have caused them to change and improve their ideas accordingly. As is sometimes apparently the case, however, the inventors and iconoclasts, the reformers and dreamers, come all at once. Such a combination created the United States, slightly more than two hundred years ago, as historians have never tired of remarking. In the navy, such a combination came with Isherwood, Luce, Mahan, Fiske, and Sims—and created a new navy out of the old; but when they were gone, the impetus for improvement was replaced by a natural return to the old way.

Our fleet after World War I, strong and good of itself, was feeding on itself, becoming ever more efficient at less and less. Administration of the paperwork empires we had created in each ship, based on everyone's attempt to improve his own small area, engulfed it. Reputations rose and fell on how well the mystic ritual was carried out, how well the papers were handled, how neatly the inspections were performed. And yet, there was a great pride in what one did and what one's ship did. Even the enlisted men of the ships felt it, though not as strongly as the officers to whom service to their ship was a dedication. Whenever their boat left its side, whether a liberty party bound ashore or a work detail for some more mundane purpose, the people in it would turn and look back at their ship. Always it was with curiosity as to how she looked to others, and almost always with a feeling of ownership, even though they might not have understood why, or by what right.

For pride—static pride—in one's home, or one's ship, as she is, the refusal to allow change in the old ways, the inability to recognize the need for change when it is there, can only give the advantage to someone else. This was what Sims, Fiske, and the rest fought against. But they had had their day and had done their work and were now gone. Our wonderful fleet of great World War I battleships, all commissioned during or immediately after that war—which, to our navy, anyway, was a nonwar—was to discover it all over again on 7 December 1941.

15

World War I to Pearl and Midway

In the old days, time moved very slowly, or so it was said. What one really meant was that the speed of change was slow in comparison to the allotted time span of a human life. Britain's *Victory* was forty years old before she became Horatio Nelson's flagship at Trafalgar. Our *Constitution* fought her best battles between the ages of fifteen and eighteen, and was still a first-line ship when, like *Victory*, she was also forty. By comparison, the famous *Oregon* of the Spanish-American War, one hundred years newer than Old Ironsides, was obsolete in only ten years. Things began to speed up as the nineteenth century neared its end; today, they move even faster. Contemporaries of Isaac Hull and Stephen Decatur could aspire to command the same ships upon which they served as young officers, and in most cases the very ships were waiting for them. But by 1900, such were the advances of design that no warship could be assured of modernity for more than a few years; certainly not for the normal lifetime of her crew.

The ships of the Spanish-American War were obsolescent by 1904, replaced by new and far better warships of all classes from torpedo-boat destroyers to battleships. Units of this new "Great White Fleet" went around the world, from 1907 to 1909—and returned to Norfolk to find themselves also obsolete, no longer first line. None of these ships ever engaged in combat, but the contribution they made to our navy was massive all the same, for they provided the environment, and the opportunity, for professionalism to take hold in the navy, and for the reformers to do their vitally important work.

True professional enthusiasm for the navy, naval science, the tactics of ships at sea, and the study of naval strategy was one of the results of the movements led by Luce, Mahan, Fiske, and Sims, each in his own time contributing a portion of the drive toward betterment. Each sought to improve that portion of the whole complex that most touched his own personal psyche, and the end result was that they swept up everyone else in their earnestness. As President of the United States, Theodore Roosevelt also deserves a place in this pantheon; for although he could not give the navy his full time, he gave it a very great deal, becoming in the process very nearly a navy god, worshiped by all, followed with delight wherever he led. He embraced the cause of the navy reformers with alacrity and ebullience, wholeheartedly in agreement with their drive to keep the navy at the front of contemporary technology. Until passage of the National Defense Reorganization Act in 1947, sometimes called the Unification Act, his birthday was celebrated as Navy Day, a near national holiday in many parts of the country.

Roosevelt is variously said either to have "inherited" or to have "built" a navy. Both judgments are in fact correct, for the fleet he inherited from the war with Spain was not the same as the one he "built." Roosevelt and Sims worked to perfect the abilities of the navy that was in existence when they came on the scene, but though they appreciated its strengths and tried mightily to make improvements in them, they were also aware of serious flaws, ranging from failure to keep up with obvious advances in the technology of aiming and firing guns—relatively easily corrected—to illogically mixed armaments, dangerously open ammunition hoists, and badly placed armor—all of which could be corrected only in the design of new ships.

There were, in fact, two such groups of new-design ships that came about in quick succession during the decade before World War I. The first set consisted of the ships, beginning with the *South Carolina* and *Michigan*, we built in response to Britain's "all-one-caliber-big-gun" *Dreadnought*. They emphasized innovations in armament and steady improvement in engineering, but to the American navy reformers our own dreadnoughts were far less than they should have been. Their design had retained many of the old deficiencies in protection against catastrophic damage. The fact that no one else seemed worried about their shortcomings did not, so far as the insurgents were concerned, make them any less real. To Sims, Fiske, and their adherents, the deficiencies of our dreadnoughts were as significant as the instantly obvious advantages of their many great guns.

The advent of the dreadnought thus did not fully satisfy the reformers' demand for better warships in the U.S. Navy. Except for their main battery guns, our first dreadnoughts were little different from their immediate predecessors; and the near disaster to one of those, the *Missouri*, had brought the dangers close to home. In battle, a single hit in the vulnerable area might well sink any one of them. So said the reformers, and they said it in front of every official body that could be prevailed on to pay attention.

Naturally, they encountered entrenched opposition. It was easy to say, "Build a better ship," quite something else to do it within the size, weight, and budgetary limits imposed by Congress—to say nothing of the anguished cries of builders who attacked the proposed new standards as too severe. Furthermore, by their criticisms the insurgents also attacked all those who had honestly given the best that was in them, who were convinced the ships they had built were the best that could be built anywhere. There were thousands of such people, ranging from members of the Navy General Board, which passed on all designs of new ships, to the professional designers and draftsmen and to workmen in the shipyards. All felt themselves threatened, on the defensive, and therefore in league against "Simian theories." Had it not been for the president, Sims would have figuratively been tarred and feathered for taking the stance he did.

The traditional proof of a design was in the test of battle. Antireformers argued that the present designs had not yet been tested in combat, that radical change should await proof by actual use. But Sims and his followers had already strenuously pointed out the dangers of the new big guns with which ships were being fitted. Why wait for a test in battle if many men might thereby die needlessly, especially when disasters like the *Missouri* turret explosion—and others similar in nature—had already made it clear that a shell exploding in the right place could easily sink the ship?

Another point of disagreement was over the type and location of armor on the new battleships, presumably the best protected of all ships. Modern guns had great range, achieved by new slow-burning propellants, gun barrels built with "shrunk-on" hoops like those Ericsson had put on his Orator gun, and metallurgical advances that made possible much higher pressures than previously. They consequently fired their huge projectiles with very high initial velocities. But to achieve the longer ranges of which they were capable, the new guns arched their shells into the heavens in a high trajectory, and therefore they struck their targets at a sharply downward angle.

As a result, the old concept of how to protect a ship's vitals from damage in combat—a belt of armor along its side—was much less useful. A battleship 100 feet wide carried on her sides an extremely heavy armor belt of the hardest steel, 12 to 16 inches in thickness, 10 to 20 feet in the vertical dimension. In the days when naval battles were fought at close range—so that guns were fired almost horizontally—the armor belt protected everything behind it, to the full width of the ship. Even so, at point-blank range the latest big guns could defeat all but the heaviest armor; but more to the point, at the long ranges of modern battles, with shells plunging at, say, thirty degrees off the horizontal, the armor belt could protect a ship only to a geometric function of the angle of impact: a shell that grazed the top of her armor belt in its descending trajectory would continue to angle downward into her machinery spaces and magazines. Obviously, deck armor of some sort was necessary; but no ship could carry deck armor of sufficient thickness to protect her from such plunging major-caliber fire. Another system of protection was needed: deck armor as thick as the ship could stand; two armored decks some distance apart above the ship's vitals, to contain between them the explosive force of armor-piercing shells penetrating the upper armored deck; and extreme internal subdivision, so that opening one or more small compartments to the sea, or even several in the same general location, would neither sink nor disable the ship.

As the argument waxed, the opposition to change grew virulent. Roosevelt, trying to help achieve a consensus, directed a top-level conference to meet at the Naval War College at Newport. But senators and representatives, fearing invasion of their prerogatives in the Congressional committees, had by this time completely lost sight of the basic objective. To them, the insurgent naval officers were interested only in trying to dictate their own way, contrary to the hallowed principle of civilian control of the military, and the disputations began to resemble personal vendettas instead of the professional discussions Sims and those who believed in him intended. It took many years of bitter battles before the reformers made their point at last.

The second group of ships, thus, although also known as dreadnoughts (some called them ''super-dreadnoughts''), were the first ships finally designed to satisfy the criticisms of the reform group. The first two were laid down at the end of Theodore Roosevelt's administration, launched in 1914, commissioned into service in 1916, and immediately received high professional praise for their design improvements. The point was not lost on naval persons that these first two ''super-dreadnoughts'' remained in the first-line category, first-line ships of the Pacific Fleet for many years, whereas all ships of the earlier group, dreadnoughts though they may have been, had long been relegated to the second line. The very first of the new ''everything or nothing'' ships was the *Nevada* (which took the place of the older ship of the same name that had witnessed the *Missouri* disaster in 1904), and her first skipper was Captain William S. Sims. He had been through a lot, but he had at last got what he wanted in a ship of war, and he thought it was worth all the effort. He called her the ''cheer-up ship.'' The new *Nevada* was everything he had fought for in ship design for more than ten years.

Largely thanks to Sims, the offensive power of our naval ships had been developed until it was second to none in the world. But the parallel requirement, for which he had fought an even harder battle than that of teaching the navy to shoot straight, was the ability to remain an effective unit of the fleet after receiving major battle damage. This ability *Nevada* and her sister ship, *Oklahoma*, had in greater measure than any other battleships yet built. Immediately following them were two slightly improved versions, somewhat bigger, carrying two more major-caliber guns, but otherwise the same: *Pennyslvania* and *Arizona*. For the first time since the monitors of the Civil War, our navy had ships of the battle line that could take it as well as dish it out.

Twenty-five years later, all four big wagons, obsolescent by then but still in service because of the hiatus in battleship construction after the naval treaties of the early 1920s, were present at Pearl Harbor when Japan attacked. Two of the four, along with two still later (1922) models, were sunk by multiple torpedo and bomb hits, and of the eight battleships caught at their moorings, only *Nevada* was able to get under way. It was an exhibition of coordinated nerve, fighting spirit, and damage control that is remembered with awe and admiration by all who witnessed it.

Among the final gifts of the reformers who had produced the new spirit of naval professionalism was director-fire: a system of fire control in which the individual gun pointers in each turret were replaced by a single director, aimed by a single operator. With guns able to shoot well beyond the horizon, greatest effectiveness could be had if they were aimed by someone other than individual gun pointers looking through telescopes alongside their guns—men who, at the ranges of modern battle, would not even see their targets. To maximize damage to the enemy, moreover, all guns should ideally strike the same spot. Were even a few shells from a salvo of 2,500-pound projectiles to hit home, no ship on earth could withstand the blow. But the guns were in turrets, in different locations; each had its own special set of idiosyncratic corrections, compounded from slight differences in the number of times each gun had been previously fired, tiny variation in propellant charges, microscopic imperfections or tilt in the turret roller-paths (tremendously heavy steel rings that bore the weight of an entire turret as it rotated). Corrections were even set in to allow for a gun's being exposed to the direct rays of a hot sun, or its being shaded by masts, superstructure, or stack smoke. To combine all these corrections and allow for the target's own motion during the time of flight of the projectiles, one of the earliest computers, known as the fire-control director, was invented.

This was an extremely complex instrument, a forerunner of the modern electronic computer but using motors, vacuum tubes, odd-shaped cams, and synchronous generators. England and the United States shared in its development. The first to suggest it was Bradley Fiske, in about 1890. Shortly after the turn of the century Percy Scott of the Royal Navy, who had cooperated with Sims in improving target-practice techniques, became intrigued with the idea as he began to extend his interest to accuracy at long ranges. Sims, pursuing the same problem, was able to call upon the personal interest of the President of the United States. Exchange of information between the two navies was at its height, the development of a satisfactory system was pursued with energy, and the British ''step by step'' fire-control director was installed in U.S. warships at virtually the same time as in British ships, shortly after the end of World War I.

Naval gunnery was now referred to as a science in its own right, and the entire U.S. Navy had by this time become so convinced of the vital importance of steady improvement in gunnery systems that everyone in the Bureau of Ordnance, and all gunnery officers on board ship, were thoroughly ready for the introduction of director-fire.

The early directors, of rudimentary design, were first placed high in the ships, alongside the person controlling them; but their weight, complexity, and vulnerability to damage led to their being moved deep inside the bigger ships, protected to the greatest possible extent within the ''armored citadel.'' There they were fed data from all sensors, including ''spotting'' corrections from the top of the highest mast.

By 1920, naval guns could shoot nearly twenty miles with extremely good accuracy. Ideally, at that range a properly handled director could land an entire salvo of 14- or 16-inch shells within a radius of about 100 yards, straddling the target. As soon as the spotter observed a straddle, he would announce, depending on the ship's procedure, some version of ''On in deflection! On in range! Fire for effect! Rapid fire!'' and he would lock closed his firing key.

Operations within the turrets and handling rooms would become automatic, each man in his own tiny sphere moving with greased precision. Three 16-inch shells would slam upward on three identical hoists into each turret, tilt downward, slide into their loading trays (articulated, curved at the bottom to match the inner diameter of the gun, automatically positioned at exactly the right place). Instantly three rammer operators would lean into their control levers, smoothly and quickly ram the 2,500-pound shells home into the yawning gun breeches all the way to the top, or end, of the firing chamber. They would feel the copper "rotating band" around the base of each shell engage the spiral rifling of the gun, then swiftly withdraw the rammer. Moments later four tightly packed, cylindrical-shaped cloth bags of smokeless powder for each gun would come up the powder hoists, alongside the shell hoists. These, too, would be gently rolled into the loading trays, then also rammed, very gently indeed, into the empty powder chambers behind the seated shells. After a quick inspection of the bags, to ensure their proper placement in the chamber, the massive breeches would be swung shut and closed tightly with a quarter turn of the huge, beautifully machined "interrupted thread" (so that a quarter of a complete rotation of the breech plug would firmly engage and seat it). The gun captain would insert a primer cartridge, resembling an ordinary shotgun shell, into a small hole in the center of the breech plug and carefully place the cap, with its electrical connections, over it. "Ready," he would announce.

In the meantime the loading trays would have been lifted by their hydraulic mechanism and folded out of the way. The turret officer would have been watching all three tremendous cannon from his command station, seeing that the turret was still trained to precisely the proper bearing ("matched in train"). The moment the three great guns were ready he would order, "Match in elevation!" and the huge pieces of ordnance would solemnly rotate upward, their long breeches descending deeply into the pit beneath them. Watching a phalanx of dials in front of him, the turret officer would already have dropped his hand to his firing key, and would squeeze it when everyone in the turret crew was in his designated positions, all proper procedures had, to his certain knowledge been complied with, and his instruments showed his guns to be exactly matched in both train and elevation. Perhaps twenty seconds would have elapsed since the previous salvo was fired.

In the director tower, on top of the mast, the ship's gunnery officer would know that elevation of a turret's guns meant they were about ready to fire. He would be ready for their abrupt recoil, the awful belch of smoke and flame from the three tremendous muzzles. Before their thunderous crash reached him, he might even catch a glimpse of three huge shells hurled on their way, glinting in the sunlight. Inside the turret, three monstrous polished steel tubes, with breeches tightly closed, would begin their recoil backward and downward a nanosecond before the sound of the explosion that impelled them could be heard. But then the massive roaring would overwhelm everything, persisting long after all recoil movement stopped and the counter-recoil mechanism had shoved the gargantuan guns back to firing position.

As the sound of firing died away, gradually converting to a loud hiss of compressed air, that comforting noise would inform the turret crew that the gas-ejection system was functioning. This had been invented to force red-hot gases of exploded gunpowder out the muzzle of the guns instead of allowing them to blow back into the turret when the breeches of the guns were opened: the cause of the *Missouri* disaster. The guns were then swiftly lowered back to the loading position. When they were horizontal once more, their long polished rears extending straight back into the turret behind their tremendously thick armored faceplates, the breech plugs were spun open. "Bore clear!" from the gun captains, to signify there was nothing visible to impede loading. No hot gases, no pieces of soft rotating band that might have split off at firing. The loading trays would be unfolded, returned to the loading attitude. Another huge shell to the top of each hoist, slamming with seeming carelessness into the trays, rammed into the gun, to the far end of the powder chamber. Then the cylindrical bags of smokeless powder, just fitting the diameter of the powder chamber, handled with great respect, gently eased into it. Again a final quick check; then close the breech, check the handle in the proper place, insert the primer. "Ready!"

A well-trained, smoothly operating turret crew in a three-gun turret could load and fire nine 2,500-pound shells a minute.

For a column of battleships firing at another column, it was also necessary to distinguish between the salvos of each ship, and many systems and devices were arranged for that purpose, ranging from dye markers in each shell to color each ship's splashes differently (good only during daylight) to minute differences in timing of the salvos of the different ships at night. Officers were trained to be spotters, estimating the correction necessary to cause their own ship's salvos to straddle the target. Nothing was more career enhancing than to be known as a good spotter. The gunnery officer of a new battleship, one of the most prestigious of posts, normally earned his position through prior expertise in this capacity; he would quietly revel in the sobriquet Spot One that went with it. Battle practice at long range, where all the arts of fire control were employed, was the top practice of the fleet: more stock was placed in it and the scores counted more than any others in the annual fleet competition.

But gun-laying at extreme range was difficult. As ranges increased, spotting on became progressively more uncertain in daylight, impossible at night. This led to spotting by aircraft, a use of airpower that battleship skippers heartily supported. Obviously, spotting from an orbiting airplane would be more accurate than the best eyes and most powerful telescope in a ship's fighting top. Each battleship was outfitted with small planes for this purpose and much drill was undertaken. But the aviators were less than enthusiastic over this duty. It was boring and to their minds not the best use of their time and capabilities. Once catapulted into the air, they had first to clear away enemy spotting planes (this, involving air combat, was exciting and acceptable), but from then on they felt they could do more damage to enemy battleships with their own bombs and torpedoes, delivered with precision where they would hurt the most, instead of anxiously staying clear of whizzing 16-inch trajectories and radioing in corrections to the fall of shot.

In sum, they had insufficient support for their peculiar needs on board a ship devoted to its great guns and held insufficient rank to make their arguments felt. Their prestige came nowhere near rivaling that of Spot One, even though they knew they could give better results than he. Their liking for their job was not enhanced by the knowledge that when their mission was completed, or their fuel exhausted, they had to land in the sea, with ultimate pickup uncertain at best if a long and debilitating battle had taken place. And in the meantime, while technology marched onward with ever-increasing speed, the science of artillery in ships at sea had reached its highest expression. As is not unusual in man's development, improvement of the battle line continued to be pursued by its devotees long after time and events had passed it by.

The idea of a ship devoted solely to handling wheeled aircraft on a long flat deck received little encouragement. That such a ship could somehow participate in the ultimate fleet engagement was not worth considering. How could an aircraft carrier, unarmored, big and vulnerable, remain afloat after being hit by a salvo of 16-inch shells? A carrier might be useful for scouting, but it had no business in the battle line. More and more defensively, so thought the men whose lives and careers had followed a path whose dead end was now looming inexorably in front of them.

Only aviators asked the newly pertinent question: What use was a battle line with weapons of twenty-mile range if aircraft carriers could send weapons with greater accuracy ten times as far? Or the antagonistic, ambitiously cynical one: Why was a twentieth-century navy still enamored of the eighteenth-century line of battle? Did the psychological appeal of a line of great gray ships, with glorious heritage from the days of sail, somehow affect the strategic thinking of the fleet commanders of the 1930s?

Similar questions were being asked by those acquainted with the tremendous threat posed by submarine warfare.

Had there been a counterpart to Sims during the 1930s, conceivably the debacle in naval warfare that took place at the outset of World War II might have been prevented. But Sims, with his thunderous denunciations of things useless or contrived, was gone from the scene. So was Bradley Fiske, who had, among so many other things, spent much of his energy working on and advocating a torpedo-carrying plane, which everyone knew could never be made to work.* And so were such other contributors to our navy's improved effectiveness as Theodore Roosevelt, Luce, and Mahan.

In an exercise carried out before the war, Pearl Harbor was "attacked" by carrier-based planes one Sunday morning. The base was ruled "out of action" by the war-game umpires. But no other action was taken, for it was only a game, with little relevance to the Pacific Fleet. Admiral J. O. Richardson, commander-in-chief of the Pacific Fleet, paid attention, however. He complained almost continually to President Franklin Roosevelt that the great fleet of battleships for which he was responsible was too exposed, could not defend itself against air attack, had insufficient facilities for training, and, in sum, should be moved back to California. Roosevelt, doubtless getting better advice somewhere else, found Richardson's persistence uncomfortable and finally, early in 1941, had him relieved. Reading Richardson's memoirs, one is forced to the conclusion that the matter had become an obsession with him, and virtually everything he said and did was conditioned by it; maybe by that time he had indeed become annoying, and Roosevelt was right in looking on him as being in basic disagreement with his own policies as commander-in-chief of the armed forces. Yet the highest-ranking officer of the Pacific Fleet was so concerned that he put his career on the line over it—and lost. The fact remains that had the fleet been moved back, four aging battleships would not have been sunk ten months later, some three thousand American sailors would not have died, and it is conceivable we might not have hated Japan enough to use an atom bomb on two of her cities.

Our submarine force would also have been well served had it had someone like Sims to look into its torpedoes, the design problems of which so closely paralleled the ones he had corrected in the guns and

---

*Fiske lived long enough to learn of the tremendous damage done by Japanese torpedo planes at Pearl Harbor. But he was nearing the end of his life (he died in 1942, aged eighty-six) and it is doubtful whether he ever received full information of what had happened that fateful day. That half of our Pacific Fleet battle line had been sunk and the rest immobilized was, of course, kept secret throughout the war.

ammunition handling of surface warships. When World War II began, the submariners found their torpedoes running so deep that even a zero depth setting was often not shallow enough to hit an enemy ship; or the torpedoes detonated harmlessly before reaching it. Compounding the fault, when these deficiencies were finally eliminated, nearly two years after the war began, it was for the first time discovered that the torpedoes were duds if they struck the hull of an enemy ship squarely (i.e., a perfect shot). And throughout the war, they occasionally ran in a circle, sometimes with fatal results to the submarine that had fired them.

Since all four things did not go wrong every time, and some were obscured by others, reports of malfunction were not consistent. In the Bureau of Ordnance in Washington, far from the scene, it was easy to deny deficiency when every report of apparent malfunction seemed to differ in detail from every other. In the eyes of the men who risked their lives with defective weapons, Washington's failure even to investigate their repeated and passionate complaints was inexplicable, and their anger increased when the frequent failures were almost casually blamed on the commanders of our submarines and their crews. The debacle attending our defense of the Philippines was an example.

In December 1941, when Japan began its long-planned landing in the Philippines, our Asiatic Fleet had twenty-nine submarines, all of which were deployed to oppose the invasion armada. These twenty-nine submarines could have made an important impact on the enemy landing attempt. Had their torpedoes worked properly, they might conceivably even have totally frustrated it. For comparison, at the start of both world wars the effective German submarine forces were fewer than twenty-nine and generally less well equipped than ours, with inferior boats. They did, however, have a torpedo that worked. In both cases, they laid hundreds of England's vital merchant ships on the ocean floor during the first months of war. Had our submarine force of 1941 been as effective as the German submarine force of 1939, many units of Japan's invasion armada in the Philippines would have been sunk—very likely enough of them to have totally defeated the invasion: certainly, enough to have greatly delayed the easy conquest. Bataan might not have become the debacle it was, the death march might not have happened, and Corregidor might have been able to hold out long enough for an orderly evacuation. The American public would not have been fed pap about how our submarines brought gold, a few nurses, and other refugees out at night (true enough, but of no consequence to the war effort), in place of the real story that our armed forces had utterly failed in the purpose for which they had been created.

During the whole invasion campaign, our submarines were able to sink only one ship of Japan's invasion force. It was not from lack of trying, for the stories of their efforts were all over the submarine force. The failure rate of their torpedoes was nearly 100 percent.

In a sense, the fault lay partly with our navy's interest in competition. Under the spur of intership competition, with many carefully constructed procedures devised to improve gunnery and to give all ships and crews an equal chance to earn the public rewards going to high-scoring crews and winning ships, the whole navy had been able to observe and vicariously share in the great improvements Sims's methods had brought about. But officers attuned to gamesmanship instead of to the navy's primary mission had applied the same rules to torpedoes that Sims had prescribed for gunnery practice, without reckoning with the very different situation. Wasted shots from guns were acceptable in practice because of their low individual cost; but torpedoes were so expensive that no losses could be accepted. All torpedo firings were converted into competitive scoring affairs, placing maximum pressure upon having a flawlessly performing "fish." Torpedo failures of any nature were counted as the fault of the submarine shooting it. A single malfunctioning torpedo destroyed a ship's standing in the never-ending competition, and losing one was cause for more official reproof than missing the target. Faced with a situation where apparent results seemed wanted more than true ones, and competition more important than reality, ships, skippers, and crews all played the same game. The thing was to have the torpedoes run well and come to the surface afterward so that they could be recovered. Seldom did anyone inquire whether they actually worked as designed.

For the few proof-firings, the "fish" were invariably completely overhauled just prior to being launched, because any kind of failure, malfunction, or miss—in short, anything other than hitting the target hulk and blowing it up—was unacceptable. Such firings were always conducted on a U.S. torpedo firing range, without concern as to the strength of the earth's magnetism, upon which the functioning of the "influence" exploder depended. (The earth's magnetic field causes sympathetic magnetism in the steel hull of a ship that triggers the detonator when a torpedo passes beneath it—but the magnetic field in the Far East is much stronger than at Newport, where detonators were built and tested. Hence, detonators functioned in the Far East just before the torpedoes arrived at their targets, giving all the appearance of hits, but causing no damage.) Wartime conditions, when a torpedo might have to be fired with minimum preparation time and in a different part of the world with a different magnetic field, were never simulated. Proper functioning of the detonating mechanism under all the conceivable possibilities, including actual contact with the target's hull, was never tested. The depth at which torpedoes really ran was never looked into. And while destroyer torpedoes making a circular run were designed to self-destruct before returning to the ship that had fired them, the same was not so for submarine torpedoes. But that difference was neither investigated nor even known.

The other side of this equation also operated to the disadvantage of effectiveness. During annual war games, submarines acted both as scouts for the battle fleet and as enemy submarines attacking it. Only theoretical results ensued from the scouting line, but the psychological obligation of the big ships was to prove their invulnerability. Thus, aggressively inclined submarine commanders who closed to within periscope range (for better aiming) were routinely deemed "reckless" and judged to have been sunk by the forces that would theoretically have been sent against them. Torpedoes were to be fired at great range and on sonar bearings only—but the long-range shots produced long white wakes of exhaust bubbles that were easily spotted and gave the lumbering wagons time to avoid, while speedy destroyers raced down the tracks to their source to make depth-charge attacks that were almost invariably declared successful. All submarines thought to be within "lethal range" of a depth-charge attack (determined exclusively on the basis of how far it could move—at creeping speed—away from the position from which it fired the torpedoes) were declared "sunk" on the basis of a carefully drawn plot by the depth chargers. Submarine skippers who decried these procedures and tactics as unrealistic were rated irresponsible and marked down in command ability.

Our most successful wartime submarine commanders now say the combination of these factors caused the successful peacetime skippers, by and large, to be unsuccessful in war. Shortly after the war began, however, a new group of skippers began to emerge, the bellwether of which was Lieutenant Commander Dudley W. Morton, unabashedly aggressive where the older men were overly cautious. Already painfully aware of torpedo malfunctions, from which there appeared to be no recourse, Morton refused the conservatively recommended solution of waiting for "perfect" conditions. Instead, he attacked with abandon under all conditions and, purely through the law of averages if for no other reason, had far greater success than any other skipper.

Morton's method of handling the torpedo problems was simple: hit the targets more often. With few exceptions, he fired all his torpedoes to strike the target (instead of in a doctrinal "spread" which aimed two-thirds of the "fish" to miss either ahead or astern), and he aimed each with extreme deliberation. The results were dramatic. In the process he became known as the perfect fighting submarine skipper, and his submarine, the *Wahoo*, a living legend to her mates. Naturally, other skippers began to follow where Morton was so outstandingly leading, but then disaster, in the form of a yet unexplained sequence of bad torpedoes, struck him. After three brilliant patrols during which Morton's stock had risen to the pinnacle of the Submarine Force escutcheon, his fourth, in the land-locked Sea of Japan, was a fiasco. He made attack after attack, but all his torpedoes, without exception, failed to function, and finally, in desperation, he returned to Pearl Harbor with a few samples which he demanded be subjected to thorough investigation. But before the results could be evaluated, he resumed patrolling in the Sea of Japan and there, in October 1943 and in a way still not known, *Wahoo* became a casualty of the war.

Morton had at least some success on his final patrol, sinking four ships, and was still by a large margin the ranking skipper in terms of damage to the enemy. But his most important contribution to the war effort was not in the number of ships put on the bottom. He had shown the way to the entire submarine force. Its effectiveness in hurting the enemy was due in greater measure to him than to any other man, and his disappearance in action, because of its timing and circumstances, was the most grievous loss suffered by our submarine force during the entire conflict. Almost of psychological necessity, his memory was nearly deified by the submarine force of the time, and is still; but his worth to this day has not been adequately recognized by our navy as a whole.

Alfred Mahan died in 1914; he never had the opportunity to consider what aircraft, submarines, and radar might mean to the fleet charged to achieve the objective he held should be the purpose of any navy: control of the sea.

Throughout history, the sea has been thought of as a surface over which ships could move, but to which they were confined. What small incursions were attempted above and below the air-water interface mattered little. In the days of sail, the immutable laws of wind and sea affected all sides equally and were equally understood by all. Thus, if England's sailing admirals could overcome the enemy fleet, they could reap the benefit of total domination of everything passing upon the sea. This was Mahan's lesson. It had been true for centuries. It was no longer true.

Things began to be different as early as World War I, in which, in a totally unanticipated way, Germany's submarines showed that England's control of the sea did not apply to them. The great orderly English armada found to its dismay that mastery of the surface of the sea did not bring with it mastery of the infinite waters beneath.

In saving England from defeat in 1917, however, America also saved her from the monumentally depressing appreciation that her old naval policies had finally come to a natural termination. Meanwhile, in the wake of the war, the United States had begun a naval building program that would have made our country far and away the strongest naval power in the world. England had tremendous psychological resistance to relinquishing her putative hold on the balance of power on the sea. It was part of her heritage. For centuries her superiority on the sea had protected her, saved her, made the crucial difference in her survival. For two generations, her naval policy had held to the "two power" standard: a navy superior to the combined navies of the two next strongest naval powers. It was unthinkable to give up the superiority that had made England what she was—even to an ally, and even to the United States, a direct descendant with the same culture and language. At the Washington Naval Conference of 1921, Great Britain held fervidly to her idea that naval preeminence was a right she had somehow earned. It was not until she realized she could in no way match the huge U.S. building program already under way that she accepted equality with America. Japan, basically for reasons of national pride but also because she was already looking at the possibility of a war with the United States, had similar difficulty accepting her 60 percent status. Finally she did so with the determination to give it lip service only. She would pretend to carry out her commitment to the resulting treaty and fulfill its provisions in all outwardly observable ways. But, in the meantime, she would secretly build the ships and bases she needed to accomplish her long-range objectives.

A few years after World War I, the aircraft carrier made it possible for high-performance airplanes to operate far at sea, well within the domain preempted by Mahan's battle fleets, and thus struck the second blow at the time-tested sea-control concept. No vessel with a strike-speed of 20 or 30 knots—i.e., no vessel bound to the surface of the sea—could compete for instant control at a given point with vehicles not so bound—vehicles, moreover, possessing a strike-speed of 200 knots or more. This was clear to everyone after 7 December 1941.

As for the submarine, it used the sea itself for concealment and protection in a way foreshadowed by John Ericsson's own arguments for the invulnerability of his monitors. He had designed those innovative ships to be as low as possible to the water, to lie principally under and protected by the sea. A warship able to operate entirely beneath the surface was merely a logical extension of the same idea.

German submarines delivered this message with stunning impact in World War I.

Despite all the changes, however, the Allied navies between the wars acted as though time had stood still. The minds of the men in control were not attuned to the changes being wrought by advancing technology. Mahan's nearly mystical pronouncements had taken the place of reality for men who truly did not understand but were comfortable in not understanding.

Officers and men with doubts were dismissed as ignorant and disloyal. The occasional demands for realistic operational tests were almost never fulfilled. It is hard to understand how a navy so at the peak of ambition, innovation, training, and enthusiasm as ours was in 1910 should have so withered by 1941; but it is fairly easy to show the route. Fundamentally, it had lost its iconoclasts and had gradually become converted into a holding operation in which reality had been forgotten.

Nevertheless, all was not lost. Deep inside the psyche of the naval officers of 1941 was the knowledge that our navy had several times led the world in efficiency and development. It could again, once it found the right combination. At the same time, however, unacceptable conditions bring on their own corrections: either slow reform, like the gunnery and ship-design improvements instituted by Sims and his fellows; or radical and rapid change under the impetus of a war emergency, like our improved frigates after the Revolution and our adoption of ironclad warships under the stress of the Civil War; or a catastrophe which destroys the old structure and brings in a new one. In the U.S. Navy of 1941, a minority of its leaders felt its deficiencies, but there was no Sims to galvanize reform, nor yet enough general dissatisfaction to start a grass-roots movement to upgrade itself. Most important, there was no time. By 1941, the only thing that would serve was a catastrophe, and this Japan supplied.

There is no proof of the loose talk that President Franklin Roosevelt deliberately exposed our Pacific Fleet in 1941 in order to entice Japan to attack and thus precipitate the country into World War II. Logic argues against any such construction, for the attack presented Adolf Hitler with the greatest opportunity of his career, and he did not see it. It is highly unlikely that American reaction to the overwhelmingly successful Japanese raid on Pearl Harbor would have been war against Germany, had Germany not immediately associated herself with it. Had Hitler not declared war on the United States—which he did without direct provocation on 11 December 1941 (in contrast to his forbearance under many provocations during the two years preceding)—Congress would have thought long and hard before declaring war on Germany simply because Japan had initiated war on us, on the other side of the world; particularly when Japan had so dramatically shown herself to be an enemy of important stature, and most particularly, when the populations of California, Oregon, and Washington were convinced of the imminent invasion of our west coast.

There is little doubt that sometime near the beginning of Franklin Roosevelt's third term he came to believe it would be necessary for the United States to enter the war on the Allied side, and that war with Japan, probably during the same time frame, was not unlikely. The "ABC–1 Staff Agreement" of January 1941 set the priorities: defeat of Germany was primary; Japan, in the event of a war with that nation, was to come second. This, however, was contingent on a low profile for Japan, not the all-out explosion she created. But although Japan made a grievous mistake in "awakening a sleeping giant" (in the words of Admiral Isoruku Yamamoto, her naval commander-in-chief), Germany made an even greater one by seizing on Pearl Harbor as the occasion for her own declaration of war on 11 December. Whatever misgivings our leaders might have entertained four days earlier about the direction of our war effort, this restored the original priority.

To the U.S. Navy, deprived of the time and opportunity for needed improvement, Japan's attack might be described by a military sociologist as a net gain despite the high cost in lives and obsolete battleships. At a stroke, the dead weight of our useless battle line was eliminated. Chester Nimitz, who took over command of the Pacific Fleet a few days after the Pearl Harbor debacle, immediately recognized this by relegating its survivors to west coast ports, not to be brought out until needed for support of amphibious landings. On the other hand, he put the new, much faster battleships to use as they arrived, as he might have a group of very fast, very heavily armored cruisers.

Not quite a year after Pearl Harbor, the new *Washington* achieved a first for American battleships in a ship-to-ship engagement with the Japanese *Kirishima*. It was the first time an American battlewagon had engaged and defeated an enemy of the same class since the classic battle between the *Monitor* and *Merrimack*. For a comparison of the opposing ships, however, it is only fair to note that *Kirishima* mounted eight 14-inch guns and had been built in 1915 (with extensive modernization later upping her speed to a reported 30 knots), and that she had within the hour put our very newest battleship, the *South Dakota*, out of action with disabling, though superficial, damage.

Her initial antagonists were two: *Washington* and *South Dakota*, completed in 1941 and 1942 respectively, each with nine 16-inch guns and 27 knots speed. *Kirishima*, supported by two heavy cruisers and two destroyers, came upon the *South Dakota*, which had become separated from her consort, and achieved early hits. Unfortunately, the injuries were to *South Dakota*'s fire-control equipment, without which she could not aim her guns accurately, and this forced her to leave the combat area. The *Washington*, however, superbly trained and thoroughly shaken down, was arguably the most efficient surface warship in our navy at that moment. She had recently been fitted with a new radar fire-control set in which her crew and the admiral on board, Willis A. Lee, had great confidence. Now bereft of supporting cruisers or destroyers (which had retired with the *South Dakota*), *Washington* determined to press the action to a decision and took on the entire Japanese force. Her guns flamed with speed and precision, and within seven minutes she pumped out 72 rounds of 16-inch shells aimed at *Kirishima* and 107 rounds of 5-inch aimed at the vessels accompanying her. How many hits the *Kirishima* received is unknown, for she was so badly damaged that she could no longer maneuver, and the Japanese admiral ordered her sunk by her remaining consorts.

But these battles in the Guadalcanal area, where most of the early ship-to-ship fighting took place, were not fleet actions of the traditional kind. They were individual single-ship or small-squadron actions, more reminiscent of the Civil War sea fights or those of 1812 than of Jutland or any other of the famous battles of past epochs. On this point it is worth noting that, with the exceptions of Tsushima (1905), Jutland

(1916), and the Surigao Strait (1944), no such traditional action took place during the entire history of battleships, and each of these had its own special unorthodoxies: At Tsushima, battleships and cruisers were intermixed and traditional battle lines were not formed; the battle was one of maneuver. At Jutland, decisive engagement between main forces did not take place; the battle-cruiser action, highlight of the engagement, was also a maneuvering battle. At Surigao Strait, in the last year of the war, inferior Japanese forces moved in single file through narrow seas almost as a willing sacrifice toward waiting disaster.

Battleships were great ships: handsome, strong, seaworthy. By their very appearance they brooked no nonsense; they contained—and expressed—the very essence of brute power at sea. All seamen, even the most jaded, reacted to the embodiment of raw force in the low, rakish lines, the tremendous mobile stability of the great hulls, and the self-sufficient impregnability each exemplified. Like Theodore Roosevelt's round-the-world fleet, however, their contribution to the navy of the United States was as training ships for a new type of naval warfare, different in all respects from the heritage of sea power and "control of the sea" we thought we were serving. In World War II, they finally came into their own but, because of their low speed, not in the great fleet action they had been theoretically designed for. Instead, their big battleship rifles proved to be exactly what was needed for shore bombardment in support of amphibious landings. The new fast battleships, likewise, never were in battle with like ships (*Washington* excepted), but were ideally suited to be powerful fleet escorts for the great numbers of aircraft carriers we turned out in the wake of the terrible lesson of Pearl Harbor.

The Queen of Battles of the Pacific War, lifting the crown from the battleship (which had never worn it in combat), was the aircraft carrier. In contrast to the long peacetime gestation of the battleship, the carrier leaped almost at birth into relentless combat. For years, naval aviators had stressed the superiority of three-dimensional combat over two-dimensional strategy tied to the surface of the sea. Suddenly, instantly, war at sea in three dimensions took over from war in two, and sea-air power dominated naval tactics. Surprise became the basic ingredient of naval combat. The slow inexorable confrontation of all available forces that lay at the bedrock of Mahan's ideas was no longer germane to the ability to carry out a naval mission quickly. To strike where needed and with stunning speed was the new way of war on the sea. In this outlook, naval aviators and submariners were joined, for both groups had shared the three-dimensional concept from the beginning.

Counting time from the instant an enemy might become aware of danger, aviators and submariners could attack almost without warning. A plane came from nowhere in only minutes, did heavy damage, and disappeared. A submarine did not reveal its presence until its torpedoes were on their way (assuming it had not been detected during the approach phase). All the old ways of bringing ships into battle were outmoded: they now fought from places of invisibility, over the horizon, widely dispersed, or submerged. Only the weapons (or the last-stage weapons carriers)—the aircraft or the torpedoes—were visible, and then only after they had entered the attack phase.

During the war, submariners and aviators alike often called the Japanese attack on Pearl Harbor a hard lesson but one we needed, for it catapulted our navy out of static old-line thinking into a new age of technology. Absent the carriers from Pearl Harbor, the next most important target of the Japanese attackers should have been the navy fuel farm in the hills behind Pearl City. Had that been wiped out, all ships, carriers included, would have been immobilized for a lengthy period. Probably the fleet and its task forces would have had to retreat to operable bases at Bremerton, San Francisco, Long Beach, or San Diego, at least until the tanks and pumping stations had been rebuilt and the necessary tankers assembled to replenish them.

According to the common wisdom, after the oil tanks, the Japanese should have attacked the submarine base and the submarines located there, for elimination of these would have greatly set back the submarine campaign that eventually hurt Japan so grievously.

Perhaps. But, truth to tell, whatever damage Japanese planes might have been able to inflict on the five submarines at Pearl Harbor that day would have been nothing compared to the damage inflicted on all of them by the Americans who built and tested their torpedoes. The debacle of our submarine weapons during the first half of World War II is a disgraceful chapter in our history. It is true that by the time the war was ended, American submarines had accomplished against Japan what German submarines two times nearly did to England—Japan's home islands were cut off from support of any kind beyond their own physical borders—but the war was nearly half over before our subs became effective.

The Battle of Midway has rightly been called four things, for the four different impacts it has made on the history of our times. First, it is only fair to call it a continuation of the attack on Pearl Harbor with which the war began. The purpose of that first raid had been to persuade the United States to allow Japan a free hand in the southwest Pacific—what it termed the Far East Asia Co-Prosperity Sphere. This it had not achieved. Japan's high command believed administering the lesson a second time, by capturing Midway Island and thus establishing a nearby and very credible threat to Hawaii, might accomplish what the hit-and-run raid six months earlier had failed to do.

Second, since Japan was overwhelmingly defeated, Midway has been called one of the most decisive battles of naval history, ranking with Lepanto, Tsushima, and Trafalgar in both short- and long-range results. Had Japan won, this writer, at least, does not believe the battle would have ranked so high, for Japanese occupation of a coral atoll only a thousand miles from Hawaii would have called forth the most vigorous and quickest response our nation was capable of. Sooner rather than later, Japan would have been ejected from Midway. But the war might well have lasted longer, and we might have reversed the priority given to the defeat of Germany—an imponderable upon which speculation cannot proceed much further.

In the third instance, Japan's attempt on Midway marked the high point of her success in the war she so dramatically began the previous December. Only six months into the conflict, from that moment on she was on the defensive, slowly being driven back from the farthest reaches of her conquests. Little more than three years later, after a series of terrible defeats at sea, on land, and in the air, her emperor took unprecedented charge of the government and accepted the unconditional surrender terms decreed by the victorious Allies.

Midway has also been called a battle won by intelligence, for there was no way Nimitz's meager forces could have met the Japanese fleet without the advantage of foreknowledge of Yamamoto's plan. The disparity in strength of forces is actually beyond belief. Yamamoto had a total of 190 ships under his command, including 4 first-line aircraft carriers and 2 smaller ones, plus 2 more committed to a diversionary Aleutian invasion, and 11 battleships (his flagship was the still secret *Yamato*, except for her sister ship, the yet uncompleted *Musashi*, the biggest battleship ever built anywhere). He also brought with him 22 cruisers, 65 destroyers, and 21 submarines, plus seaplane tenders, minesweepers, troop transports, and supply ships to the number of 63 more. He had about 700 combat aircraft embarked. His American opponent by extraordinary effort was able to assemble only 38 ships: the carriers *Enterprise*, *Yorktown*, and *Hornet*, 8 cruisers, 15 destroyers, and 12 submarines. On board the U.S. carriers were 232 planes, and the American commander had operational control of 121 Midway-based planes.

Nimitz's intelligence advisers, notably Commander Joseph John Rochefort, pinpointed the time and place of the next enemy offensive and correctly gauged it as an all-out major effort. Rochefort did this by deep knowledge of the Japanese psychology, intuitive reading of their collective mind, and probably the biggest emergency code-breaking operation our navy—and perhaps any navy, anywhere—has ever conducted. It was a day and night chore. Rochefort, as "non-reg" (non-regulation) an individual as ever wore the uniform of a U.S. naval officer, hardly slept, changed clothes, shaved, or ate—sometimes apparently for weeks at a time. He and a few top assistants lived and worked in the basement beneath the Pearl Harbor headquarters of the Commander-in-Chief Pacific Fleet (CINCPAC) for days on end when they were on to something. It was a good thing they did so, for there came the day when Rochefort informed Nimitz that Midway Island was the target of the next Japanese offensive, and that the date for the landing had been set for 4 June 1942. By his inspired performance of his duty—there is no other way to describe it—Joe Rochefort gave our side an inestimable advantage, which Nimitz used with matchless skill and daring.

Getting the three available carriers back into the Central Pacific was Nimitz's first priority, upon which hung all else. Japanese observers had reported all three carriers in the South Pacific as late as 15 May. The Japanese naval high command knew *Lexington* had been sunk and *Yorktown* severely damaged in the Battle of the Coral Sea on 8 May, and that *Enterprise* and *Hornet* had also been in the area, though too distant to participate in the battle; but its intelligence did not report the return of the three surviving carriers to Pearl the last week in May. Repair to *Yorktown*'s damage was estimated as a three-month job; a herculean effort by the navy yard at Pearl Harbor got her ready for action in three days. In contrast, the Japanese took *Shokaku* and *Zuikaku*, also at the Battle of the Coral Sea and also originally scheduled for Midway, out of the operation because of battle damage and losses to their air wings. They had no idea *Yorktown* could by any stretch of effort be made ready and assumed the others would be out of action as well.

It was a disappointment to Yamamoto that no U.S. carriers were to oppose him at Midway. His entire purpose was to draw the U.S. Pacific Fleet into battle and defeat it decisively.

He was defeated by one man, whose special genius enabled him to give Admiral Nimitz the invaluable background that made all the difference between fighting blindly and fighting with full awareness of the enemy's plans. To Commander Joe Rochefort must forever go the acclaim for having made more difference, at a more important time, than any other naval officer in history.

16

The Armageddon at Sea

If it can be said that our navy had only about fifty-six hours of combat experience prior to World War II, it can also be said that World War II was one long gigantic battle with almost unrelieved stress on all participants. Respites in harbor were conspicuously few (unless a ship sustained serious damage). In the Atlantic, it was a long, torturous, weather-traumatized war against German submarines. There was little action against surface raiders, particularly warships, since the British navy had eliminated most of these before our entry or immobilized them in port (the notable exception being the powerful *Scharnhorst*, finally run down and sunk in the far North Atlantic on Christmas Eve 1943). The war against submarines in the inhospitable waters of the North Atlantic became one of sheer desperation, and the fantastic convoy battles, in some cases against combinations of submarines, surface warships, and air power—as in the terribly difficult Murmansk runs— made history.

As the weight of our superior resources became felt, the Battle of the Atlantic came to include action against Vichy French—controlled warships at Casablanca, the amphibious landing in Morocco, armed entry into the Mediterranean and amphibious assaults on Sicily and on Italy at Salerno—and, finally, the greatest amphibious assault landing ever made: the Normandy landings on the beaches of France. This effort involved millions of English and American soldiers and sailors and all services—army, navy, marine corps, army air corps. After a year of ground and air fighting, the German forces were decisively defeated and victory in Europe became a reality.

Meanwhile, in the Pacific, the initial reaction of most of the men serving in the ships and air wings was to wonder if they would ever see the promised industrial backup of America. They felt as if they were fighting alone, without help. They had been led to expect an outpouring of new equipment, ships, and personnel the moment war was declared; on the contrary, there was very little, for first priority went to the war against Germany. Even ammunition was scarce. Despite the trumpeted upsurge of support from America's factories, during the first critical months of the war very little found its way to the ships and aircraft carrying the brunt of the struggle against Japan. For eighteen months, for example, torpedoes for submarines going on patrol were in short supply. In some categories, stocks of aircraft bombs were low as well. How Admiral Nimitz managed to accumulate the ammunition with which to meet Yamamoto's immensely superior force at Midway was one of the wonderful mysteries of the battle. Those professing to know about such things stated categorically that he had stripped every depot, every ship, and every aircraft not directly engaged to find the essentials for his fighting men.

From the American point of view there were many things about the Battle of Midway that went our way. First and foremost, before the battle the American side had the sort of intelligence information that should have been available when the Japanese carriers were approaching Pearl Harbor six months previously. Second, as the engagement developed, the Japanese carriers' Zero fighters, acknowledged to be the best shipborne combat aircraft on either side, were drawn down to low altitude by the American torpedo-squadron attacks. Our torpedo-planes, nowhere up to the performance of the Zeros and through inadvertence bereft of the fighter-escort scheduled, achieved no hits and were nearly all shot down; but the American dive-bombers had practically no opposition—and it was this circumstance that decided the battle in favor of the American fleet. They caught all four big Japanese carriers in their most vulnerable situation: refueling their planes, fire hazard at its maximum. All four were sunk. Significantly for the proponents of naval air, who were quick to point out the tremendous disparity between forces attacking and results achieved, all the lethal damage was inflicted by only about forty planes, in dive-bombing attacks that resulted in a total of thirteen hits (by Japanese accounts) in the four carriers.

Had the Japanese carriers been attacked at almost any other time, however, less serious damage would have been inflicted—and this was another fortuitous circumstance. Had the American attack come earlier or later, the damage it inflicted on the first three Japanese carriers attacked—all three were immediately put out of action and ultimately sank (hours later the fourth shared their fate)—would almost surely have been less. The result of the battle might even have been reversed, for deficiencies in the supply of armor-piercing bombs with delayed-action fuses had forced the American planes to attack with smaller instant-fused bombs. However, these ignited exposed ammunition and gasoline, causing raging fires that engulfed all four ships.

The Japanese version of events also indicates how great a factor was pure chance. The first strike on American defense installations on Midway, made by all available planes save those held back in case of unexpected retaliatory attack, had reported much damage and many fires on the atoll's two principal islands. Nevertheless, the damage observed did not appear conclusive. The defenders were not out of action; the airstrips, though hurt, were still usable. As his flight was returning from Midway to the location of the Japanese carrier force, the leader of the attackers radioed his recommendation that another strike be organized and sent as quickly as possible. Admiral Chuichi Nagumo, in overall charge of the attack force from his flagship, *Akagi*, had been expecting such a recommendation. Accordingly, he directed the torpedo-bombers that had been held back for use against possible United States aircraft carriers be rearmed with bombs suitable for the proposed second strike. This was done with tremendous urgency, in order to be ready to take the returning Midway strike back aboard the Japanese carriers as soon as they came into sight.

A short time later, with his returning planes almost in sight of his anxious lookouts, Nagumo received a delayed scouting plane's report of the discovery of "what appears to be a carrier." * Like Yamamoto, Nagumo had been disappointed that there were apparently no American carriers likely to be encountered, for more important to Japan than anything else was a decisive victory at sea in which American naval power was convincingly destroyed. Even more than the Americans at this stage of the war, the Japanese had determined that aircraft were the principal weapons of naval warfare, and the carriers the most important warships. Thus, discovery of a single aircraft carrier was a welcome surprise. He believed his four could easily handle her, and her destruction would make the capture of Midway an even greater blow to the United States. How the single unknown American carrier could have suddenly appeared on the scene made little difference. From the information he had at hand, she could hardly have come from the Coral Sea area. Perhaps she was a newly built ship, or one hurriedly transferred from the Atlantic. In any case, sinking her would be a tremendous addition to the damage inflicted by the Midway task force.

At this juncture Nagumo had thirty-six dive-bombers ready in *Hiryu* and *Soryu* for immediate attack on ememy ships, and he received an urgent recommendation from the rear admiral in *Hiryu*, in charge of that echelon, that the newly discovered carrier be immediately attacked with the planes then available. After thinking over the

---

*The search plane had been delayed by catapult trouble aboard the cruiser *Tone*. As it happened, the sector assigned to it was one of the most important. There is no explanation why that sector was not covered by one of the other search planes—except that in complex things something always goes wrong. Probably no one thought of it. The carrier sighted was almost certainly the *Yorktown*. Presence of the other two, *Enterprise* and *Hornet*, was as yet unsuspected. At his headquarters at Pearl Harbor, Nimitz, of course, had full information as to the composition of all of Yamamoto's forces, including specifically those in Nagumo's Mobile Force, the principal striking force.

situation, however, Nagumo decided first to take aboard the returning flight from the Midway strike, which were already coming over the horizon, and in the meantime seize the opportunity once again to rearm his torpedo-bombers. At the cost of a moderate delay, he would strike the lone American carrier with greater force. The torpedo-bombers initially held in reserve had by now been loaded with bombs intended for Midway, and were already lined up on the flight decks of *Akagi* and *Kaga*, the two biggest carriers. The flight decks of *Hiryu* and *Soryu*, however, still held planes armed with antiship bombs. Landing the returning Midway attack flight required that all planes on all four decks be struck below, the torpedo-bombers being rearmed with armor-piercing ammunition in the process. Then the returning planes had to be shifted out of the takeoff area, or moved below, while the hastily rearmed torpedo-bombing planes and the temporarily delayed *Hiryu* and *Soryu* dive-bombing squadrons were brought up once more, along with such fighters as could be quickly prepared for their escort. Despite all possible effort, an inevitable delay of two hours or more was in sight. Feverish effort in changing the bomb loads caused careless but unavoidable stacking of bombs on the hangar and flight decks. Tremendous haste in gassing up the returning planes for a quick turn-around resulted in numerous small spills. All aircraft fuel lines were employed; none were drained back to the gasoline storage tanks. There was no time for the regular fire precautions. Gasoline, most dangerous of all, was everywhere, in myriad rubber and fabric hoses crisscrossing hangar and flight decks. There could not have been a worse fire hazard. But everyone realized a great battle was in progress; although no enemy ship or plane of any kind had been sighted, except off Midway itself, anything might happen at any time. Urgent cutting of corners was the order of the day.

Reports vary as to the critical moment when Nagumo realized he was facing three enemy carriers. The scouting plane report had indicated there was a single (probable) carrier opposing him. According to one dramatic version, it was then reported that a flight of more than one hundred enemy planes was approaching his task force. Realizing this was more than a single carrier could launch, he demanded confirmation of the number, was gratified to be informed that a somewhat smaller flight was approaching, but infuriated that the new report had it coming from a different direction. Only minutes before the first wave of American planes began its attack, an amplifying report made it clear for the first time that there were two flights totaling more than two hundred planes in all, that no less than three American aircraft carriers of the largest and most effective class were on the scene—and Nagumo realized that he had allowed himself to be caught in the most dangerous of conditions: no ready flight decks, fire hazard at an untenable high, his ships temporarily unable to respond to the attack that was coming. In a way, it was the same situation as faced our battleships in Pearl Harbor on the day the Japanese began the war—except that there was no excuse for Nagumo's mistaken conduct of those crucially important two hours.

The Japanese crews watched with fear as the first American attackers, clumsy torpedo-bombers, lined up for the steady run in to launching range that was obligatory for torpedo-planes, which for successful launch had to get down low to the surface of the gently heaving sea. They had become separated from the fighters designated to protect them during this critical and greatly exposed moment, however, and were therefore totally defenseless. They chose to attack all the same, well knowing it was suicidal, and the Zeros, for whom they were like so many sitting ducks, picked them off one by one. None got through. Of the forty-one torpedo-bombers launched from the three American carriers, only six returned. No hits at all were scored. Japanese crewmen topside in the carriers, and thus able to see this overwhelming victory in the air battle, cheered themselves hoarse, until suddenly they realized someone was not cheering but screaming.

One of the lookouts had his hands straight up, pointing into the heavens. "Dive-bombers!" he was yelling.

The horrified watchers on the bridge of *Akagi* saw three black silhouettes directly overhead, coming straight down. Their fuselages were mere discs, with a whirling propeller in the center, their wings pencil thin. Their engines were roaring at full throttle, and they were already on the point of dropping when sighted. Everyone on *Akagi*'s bridge instinctively ducked for cover, the captain shouted for full rudder and full speed, but there was no time for anything. Three bombs were dropped; one struck close alongside, a near miss, but two struck the center of *Akagi*'s loaded flight deck, jammed with bomb-laden aircraft full of gasoline.

The result was holocaust. Fuel tanks exploded, sending sheets of flame in all directions. Ammunition—bombs and torpedoes—"cooked off" and exploded also. The flames leapt to the hangar deck, which quickly became a second mass of red-hot flame. The crew fought the fires courageously, but unsuccessfully. *Akagi* was doomed from the moment the first bomb hit.

So were *Kaga* and *Soryu*, the former hit by four bombs, the latter by three. Only *Hiryu* was undamaged, having been a few miles to the northward and, for the time being, unnoticed by the attackers. The sequence of events aboard *Kaga* and *Soryu* was exactly the same as in *Akagi*. Nothing could be done for them. *Kaga* and *Soryu* ultimately sank from the damage received, and *Akagi*, the favorite ship of the Japanese naval air arm, Yamamoto's own flagship in years past, had to be scuttled.

This climactic attack, which changed the course of the Pacific war and therefore the course of history, lasted less than five minutes.

There was a U.S. submarine also on the scene, the *Nautilus*, and although handicapped, as were all subs, by her slowness submerged, she was finally able to fire a salvo of three torpedoes at the damaged and drifting *Kaga* (under the impression that she was attacking *Soryu*) and claimed three hits. Japanese records confirm that the ship attacked was actually the *Kaga* and state that two of the three torpedoes missed. The third torpedo struck the damaged carrier but broke in two instead of exploding. Japanese personnel aboard *Kaga* saw *Nautilus*'s torpedo strike the already sinking *Kaga*'s side, break in half, and drift away with men in the water clinging to the torpedo's floating air flask. *Nautilus* had taken all her risks for nothing. It is perhaps understandable that her skipper might have mistaken some other explosions, of which there were certainly many in the area, as those of his torpedoes; but the erroneous claim, fully credited by our side and carefully not denied by

Japan until after the war, only helped to obscure the torpedo fiasco that existed.*

Hiryu, as yet undamaged, was the only Japanese carrier able to respond to the surprise American attack. She launched immediately, found *Yorktown*, and struck her with two heavy bombs, leaving her, according to reports by the returning fliers, disabled and emitting clouds of black smoke. *Yorktown*'s damage control was so effective, however, that when *Hiryu*'s second strike found her again, about two hours later, she had the fires out and her injuries temporarily repaired, and was taken for an entirely different carrier. This time she received two torpedo hits, which ultimately proved lethal; but *Hiryu* believed she had put two American carriers, of the three now known to be present, out of action. Her crew was at their battle stations preparatory to launching her remaining planes in search of the third American carrier when a lookout suddenly sounded the alarm: "Dive-bombers! Overhead!" Thirteen planes had come in with the sun behind them so that they had not been seen; when discovered, they were already in their attack dives. *Hiryu* maneuvered desperately, avoided some of the bombs, but was struck on her flight deck by four. Knocked out of action, she experienced the same devastating progressive fires that had doomed her sister carriers, finally losing all power and becoming unmanageable. She was accordingly scuttled next morning, shortly after the *Akagi* hulk was similarly disposed of.

Naval battles had changed mightily, nowhere better demonstrated than at the Battle of Midway. There, superiority of force meant nothing in the balance against strategic surprise. Not until the American attacks were under way was Admiral Yamamoto, hundreds of miles away in the *Yamato* but in overall charge, made aware of the presence

---

*The reason for the Japanese concealment was to prevent our discovering how defective the torpedoes really were, since we would then correct the problem. In the early years of the war, Japanese skippers estimated their chances of escaping undamaged, even from a torpedo about to strike their ship, as better than two to one. Apparently there was only one break in this policy of silence: one of our intelligence officers, interrogating a Japanese officer captured from a sunken Japanese submarine, asked, "Did Japanese submarines have difficulty with torpedoes that exploded prematurely?" "We don't, but you do," the Japanese answered with a knowing smirk on his face. But even with this report, our Bureau of Ordnance was unconvinced.

of the three unexpected American carriers. He endeavored to change his plans accordingly, but within minutes three of his four striking force carriers were burning furiously and clearly doomed, and the fourth, *Hiryu*, was knocked out shortly afterward.

As to other aspects of the Midway battle, army air corps B-17s made several high-level bombing attacks on various units of the Japanese fleet, among them the carriers, but not one of their bombs hit their targets. A highly alert and rapidly maneuvering ship under such circumstances is extremely difficult to hit, for it can maneuver out of the way while the bombs are dropping.

There was some submarine success at Midway, but it was not by our side. The Japanese submarine I-168, after creating a diversion by shelling Midway Island, had been ordered to search for the damaged *Yorktown*, whose position had been reported by a search plane. *Yorktown* was under tow, with a protective screen of four destroyers and a fifth, secured alongside, providing power for the repair parties. Two days after the battle, the I-168 found the damaged carrier and hit her with three out of four torpedoes fired; all exploded, sinking both *Yorktown* and the destroyer *Hammann* with the same salvo. We claimed sinking I-168 immediately afterward, but in fact she escaped all countermeasures and returned to port undamaged.

Because Japan had lost so much of her naval air power, measured in loss of qualified aviators as well as in ships, Midway became one of the most decisive battles of world history. It ended with Japan's navy in headlong retreat from the farthest extension of its power, a retreat from which it never recovered. At the same time, the U.S. fleet, in spite of still unsolved problems with its weapons, had seized the initiative and never relinquished it. Though there was still much hard fighting—and some heartbreaking defeats ahead—we knew we had taken the measure of the enemy and were as good as they were. Seen from this angle alone, the battle made an extremely important difference.

From the point of view of the participants, prosecution of the war can be divided into three basic fields: air, submarine, and amphibious. And there was a fourth field, of a totally different type, technical instead of operational, cerebral instead of merely physical, that looked resolutely toward the future and its promise instead of to the here and now of combat. It was so different that it cannot be listed in the same breath as the three fields of warfare mentioned, and yet it pervaded all of them and ultimately had a greater effect on the outcome of the war than any of them: radar.

It was radar (the acronym of radio detection and ranging), not even a weapon in the true sense, that made the biggest difference in the war. Merely an electronic device, yet it could unfailingly see objects at night, in fog, even under certain conditions beyond the curvature of the earth. Not only see, but measure exact distance and precise direction continuously, and constantly remeasure, so that direction of movement and speed, plus altitude if aircraft, were all instantly detectable.

Radar had been discovered before the war and developed with urgent secrecy. During the Battle of Britain it saw German bombers as they approached England and permitted controllers to vector defending Spitfires and Hurricanes into position. Had it not been for radar, German bombing might have been decisive in the war, for it was nearly so, anyway—though in this respect second to the U-boat.

First priority naturally went into England's defense. But ships and aircraft also needed radar, and as the war threw electronic engineering into high gear there were ever more exotic uses developed for it. Radar came slower to the Pacific, but probably the first evidence that the Pacific war was not in truth a "forgotten" war came with the beginning of a steady influx of newer and better radar and the technical people to install the sets. Simple search radar came first. In short order, there was radar gun-control equipment for antiaircraft batteries, which did away with antiquated methods of aiming guns at speedy aircraft and made hits a high probability instead of the matter of pure chance they had been.

The main batteries of cruisers and battleships also received radar fire control. Electronic certainty was substituted for increasingly difficult long-range spotting of the fall of shot. It was this that enabled the *Washington* to demolish the *Kirishima* off Savo Island with the war not quite a year old.

Submarines came in for their share of radar development with anti-aircraft and antiship radars that could be taken underwater (though they would work only with their antenna heads above the surface). Late in the war, our subs received a periscope with a built-in radar that greatly improved submarine approach techniques.

Aircraft also acquired radar for detection of targets in the air or on the ground and for accurate aim of both guns and bombs. Identification of an approaching plane became of so much moment—with only seconds available in which to decide whether or not to open fire—that an IFF (Identification, Friend or Foe) system was invented by which the detecting radar triggered off a specially coded answering signal in the aircraft. Radar was developed to assist planes to land aboard their carriers and to detect objects on the surface of the sea as small as a snorkel or even as tiny as the tip of a submarine's periscope.

There was only one apparent limit to the capability of radar: it would not penetrate through seawater. Extensive laboratory work only confirmed that it could not be made to. Air, space, and clouds, however, were transparent to radar's electronic emissions. Toward the end of the war, tiny radar sets were even put into antiaircraft ammunition, just in time to be used against the kamikaze attacks. Many a ship and sailor survived the war because of the phenomenal lethality of the "VT" (Variable Time) fuse against the fanatically heroic suiciders.

Japan and Germany were both completely outclassed by the Allied electronic revolution. The production of ever newer and more capable radar sets, followed by radar-detection sets and precise electronic-navigation sets, might have been almost more than the fighting men could assimilate—except that every improvement added to their combat capability and survivability, and there was no dearth of enthusiastic young men to become devotees of the new and exotic equipment. Pushed by the urgencies of war, electronics, with all its manifestations, made fundamental and far-reaching changes in it: long-range gunfire, for example, was virtually certain to be correctly aimed and, within the variations in projectile trajectory, much more likely than ever before to hit its target. And this was true whether the target was stationary ashore, moving at sea like a ship, or flying through the air at ten times the speed of a ship. The element of chance was replaced by one of sureness. The new naval art, as it developed, needed only adroit use of the unseen particles of matter, followed by judgmental employment of the information thus derived. Traditional risks of combat were converted to the risk of superior enemy electronics—and in the early 1940s the United States and her allies held all the advantage. It was a situation the reformers of the early 1900s would have loved, for it removed the greatest imponderable of naval operations and replaced it with something they would have understood and used with gusto and finesse.

The urgencies of war, however, do not ordinarily march in time with technical development (unless there is deliberate intent to profit by temporary ascendancy). Neither side had effective radar at Midway, though some U.S. ships possessed rudimentary air-warning sets that emitted a signal detectable by radio direction-finders (and were therefore distrusted). The night surface actions immediately following in the Solomon Islands were likewise without benefit of this extraordinary new development. The Japanese navy had trained assiduously for these forms of battle and had developed considerable expertise. The Americans, who had also trained in combat at night, were nonetheless far less expert and tried to make up for their fundamental feeling of inferiority by intensified alertness. Unfortunately, this worked exactly opposite to the way intended. American crews were kept in condition watches (condition two, half the crew on their battle stations, or one, regular action stations), for days on end, but without adequate modification in normal routine. They were thus up for general quarters during morning and evening twilight, required to do ship's maintenance during working hours, in general deprived of adequate rest. (Not for nothing had the British navy derisively said of ours that in the event of war with the United States they would keep their fleet safely in harbor for a couple of weeks, after which we would collapse from the unremitting strain of indiscriminate and unrealistic readiness at all times.) During the period after Midway, that was precisely what happened.

The Battle of Savo Island, in August, proved the point. Recognizing the threat posed to Australia by the Japanese advance to the Solomons, as well as the opportunity resulting from Midway, U.S. strategists focused our immediate effort on blocking enemy occupation of Guadalcanal, which had already begun. Our landing began on 7 August 1942, and on the night of 8–9 August a combined U.S. and Australian force of five fine cruisers (our *Quincy*, *Astoria*, *Vincennes*, and *Chicago*, and Australia's *Canberra*) was caught totally by surprise in the vicinity of Savo Island, off Guadalcanal, by a superior Japanese force. All hands in the American squadron, including those on watch, were exhausted from days on end without rest. Although technically in alert status, they were so tired as to be literally asleep on their feet. Neither picket destroyers nor the rudimentary radar carried by some ships gave them warning. The first word of approaching battle was the frantic radio message in plain language from a nearby destroyer: "Strange ships entering harbor!" Moments later, a fusillade of shell fire began falling upon the unfortunate cruisers.

Adrenaline at low ebb, not alert (although they had honestly tried to stay alert), bewildered by the savagery of the onslaught, their condition-watch people struggling hopelessly to get generators started, loading gear operating, ammunition hoists running, unable even to train out their turrets toward the source of the pitiless flashes of gunfire—so close aboard—the Allied ships stood no chance at all. Only *Chicago*, with her bow nearly blown off, survived. The other four were almost instantly sunk, some actually before they had been able to close up battle stations. The Japanese were damaged only by one lucky shot into the chart house of their flagship. Postwar investigation has credited this injury—by good luck in the spot where the Japanese admiral's principal tactical planning was concentrated—with dissuading him from carrying out his original intention to proceed into the transport area with his seven big cruisers. Had he done so, the result would have been horrendous for the landing forces; as it was, more than a thousand Allied sailors were killed in the five cruisers he handled so roughly.

American reaction ran the gamut: at one extreme enemy capability was elevated to an unrealistic stature; at the other, the Australian and

U.S. admirals were blamed for improper early-warning dispositions. In addition, the commanders of the ships involved were castigated for their individual lack of alertness. Yet to the officers and men who had suddenly found themselves subjected to murderous fire at close range, the fault lay in unrealistic demands for readiness at all times, with the inevitable result that although awake and on their stations, their crews were not truly alert.

The immediate analysis of the debacle brought out two long-range causes: low readiness had resulted from the effort to maintain an artificially high state of readiness at all times, even when it was not necessary. It would have been far better to establish carefully thought out patrols and let the crews turn in for the rest they so greatly needed. The second cause was the lack of radar, which could so greatly have extended the range of even the best lookouts. In this instance, the policy of "Europe first" had gone too far. Ships in the Pacific combat areas needed radar too—in many cases to a far greater extent than those in the European theater. Steps were immediately taken to resolve both problems. The latest surface-search and fire-control radar sets began to appear very quickly, diverted from less urgent destinations in ships en route to Europe. And commanders in the Pacific began to think more about the human demands being made on their eagerly willing crews.

It is an axiom of naval warfare that the entire purpose of navies and sea power is to influence the land. Mere possession of acreage of seawater has little intrinsic benefit. Man will fight to protect something of value to him; but with few exceptions, like fishing rights, what he fights over is located ashore. Yet, one of the oldest lessons is that the contiguous sea nonetheless often contains the key to accomplishment of objectives that are themselves far from it: objectives that are deep inshore, hundreds of miles away—yet unfailingly affected by remote events happening on the sea. It has always been so, and many have been the demonstrations thereof. Generally this has been by relatively subtle pressures, though Englishmen remembering the threat of Germany's two submarine campaigns may not agree with their characterization as subtle.

History is also full of the more direct form of influence: the landing of troops. In early days, debarkation almost anywhere was possible, but as the equipment brought in with the men grew in complexity and weight, it became desirable whenever possible to capture a harbor city and then debark the armies at suitable quays. Rarely in Western military history, until recent years, has a landing been attempted in which the troops had to fight their way ashore. This was true even if a battle was expected immediately thereafter. When the Persians landed at Marathon in 490 B.C., the Athenians did not attack until the Persian army was ashore and drawn up in battle array. In the Punic Wars, the Romans and Carthaginians fought battles at sea as well as on land, but none while either side was in the process of putting troops ashore. William the Conqueror encountered no opposition when he landed his army and horses at Hastings on the far side of the English Channel (the decisive battle took place at a spot, appropriately named Battle, that is 14 miles inland). Perhaps, had Napoleon actually attempted a landing against England, he might have tried a true amphibious assault, but more likely he would have taken a seaport through which to land his army, as he did by capturing Alexandria for the invasion of Egypt in 1798.

The bellwether of the modern amphibious landing was Gallipoli, in 1915, which became a British disaster through a sequence of unfortunate occurrences and some extremely ill-advised decisions by commanders on the scene. By all odds, the campaign should have succeeded. That it did not gave rise to the common wisdom of the time: in case of a landing under fire, the advantage always lies with the defenders. The U.S. Marine Corps, however, made a thorough study of Gallipoli. Its commandant from 1920 to 1929, John A. Lejeune, searching for a unique role for the Marine Corps, had convinced himself through his own personal study that Gallipoli failed through incompetence of execution and not because it violated some arcane and immutable principle. Even so, it had very nearly succeeded. Once in command of the Marine Corps, Lejeune required all his officers to become intimately familiar with every facet of the debacle. Nowhere in the world has Gallipoli been so thoroughly covered, and by so many professionals in that very sort of business.

Lejeune probably ranks as high among marines as Mahan ranks among admirals, but he was a very different type, having first established himself, in the words of Rudyard Kipling, as "a first class fighting man" (he commanded one of Pershing's U.S. Army divisions in France during World War I). As Marine Corps commandant, he pressed his convictions. The result was the establishment of the amphibious assault landing as one of the corps' principal specialties.

Commanders of a military force conducting an amphibious landing on a hostile shore will always endeavor to select the least costly method of doing so; but in its most difficult example, the amphibious assault force lands on heavily defended enemy beaches with nothing but the weapons in their hands. It must immediately fight its way inland and establish a beachhead for the receipt and immediate storage of all the combat equipment it needs. Much specialized gear and equipment is of course necessary, not to mention medical facilities for the wounded and food for the troops. When the war with Japan began, our marines had already spent years working on what they recognized would be a new form of the age-old requirement of bringing force from sea to shore: the frontal assault against determined opposition.

It was well they were ready, for the history of that war in the Pacific is a succession of amphibious landings as our forces inexorably leapfrogged their way across the ocean. But in the beginning of their island-hopping campaign, in spite of all their preliminary study and preparation, they still had much to learn.

The landing on Guadalcanal Island, on 7 August 1942, was the first of several actions for which the U.S. Marines became justly famous during the war. The campaign for conquest of that strategic island, begun actually to frustrate Japanese attempts to establish an air base there, led to one of the longest and most difficult series of land battles of the entire conflict. Covered in detail by the press, it can be said to have been the first instance in which the terrible trauma of war was brought home to our population. The enemy threw everything they had into the effort to take back the island and its airfield (which had, since the initial landing, been completed by U.S. forces) and were met by as determined resistance. In the end, the Japanese failed, and Guadalcanal remained in American hands, a legend of jungle combat under extraordinary difficulties. For the navy, it was a land campaign that brought in its train a sequence of fierce naval engagements as both sides sent supplies and reinforcements to the troops slogging it out ashore. So many ships of both sides were sunk in "the slot" off Guadalcanal that the name our navy gave to the area has stuck: Iron-bottom Sound.

Guadalcanal, however, was not an assault landing in the accepted sense. The marines went ashore unopposed, although the fighting became fierce and unremitting thereafter. The first full-fledged amphibious assault landing, part of the island-hopping campaign initiated by Admiral Nimitz, took place at Tarawa in November 1943. The war was just two years old.

Tarawa was a dreadful, enervating battle with mistakes made by both sides. The measure of the Japanese fighting man had already been taken at Guadalcanal and we knew he was a dedicated soldier who expected to die for his emperor and who had yet to learn the meaning of surrender, even when further resistance was patently useless. Most Japanese units on Guadalcanal had died nearly to the last man; at the end, their objective was only to do as much damage as possible to our side, regardless of the cost to themselves. This had also been the experience at Attu, at the end of the Aleutian chain, occupied as a diversion at the same time that Yamamoto had made his main thrust at Midway.* At Tarawa, despite a tremendous bombardment—U.S. production of ammunition had finally begun to reach the fleet in the Pacific—more than half of the Japanese defenders were still effective, thanks to an excellent and imaginative system of trenches and dugouts. The fighting was fierce; casualties on our side exceeded anything yet encountered. It was a textbook case of both attack and defense—and when it was all

---

*In May 1943, faced with a greatly superior force of U.S. Army troops recently landed on the island, the Japanese troops on Attu carried out a desperate banzai charge, at the end of which many of them committed suicide. Only 28 were captured. American army forces on the island amounted to 11,000; the Japanese numbered only 2,600. Casualties among our forces, in total killed and wounded, approximated the entire number of Japanese involved.

over, the mopping up completed, only 17 Japanese defenders out of an initial force of nearly 5,000 were still alive. There were 1,000 American dead and 2,000 wounded, most of them among the 6,500 initial assault troops. When the island was finally secured, some 18,000 marines were tramping its devastated terrain.

Marine Corps doctrine has always differed from that of our army in the matter of attack and casualties. Where the army moves forward slowly and surely, minimizing its casualties every step of the way because it knows it is there for the long haul, our marines try to get it all over quickly, believing an all-out attack in the beginning will result in fewer casualties in the long run. Where the army pushes the enemy back with irresistible force, the marines try to annihilate him from the outset. There is, manifestly, a place for both concepts; but in the island-hopping campaign, there was nowhere either side could retreat to. The battle, once joined, was to the death.

The lessons of Tarawa were that halfway measures could not be employed; that mistakes or misconceptions in the beginning would inevitably be paid for in the lives of our men in the landing forces; that shore bombardment of a massive nature was a prerequisite, that it had to be fired from a distance sufficient for the big battleship shells to land in a steeply descending arc and cover every bit of land where defenses could be erected or defenders hide. Close-in flat-trajectory fire might sink a ship, but not an island; survivors were still dangerous. A determined enemy expecting to be the target of an assault landing could be expected to set up all sorts of obstacles, not only on the shore but also in the water. If he were really clever, he would set them up in such a way that certain clearly defined open spaces might be visible from the direction where an assault force could be expected to come, and these apparently careless openings in the defenses would be zeroed in for a murderous cross fire. All of these stratagems, and more, were employed by the Japanese commander at Tarawa. Afterward, every one was thoroughly studied by ours.

The next marine invasion was at Kwajalein, the stronghold of the Japanese Marshall Islands defense system. Nimitz had made the considered decision to bypass a number of lesser enemy bases, and the lessons learned from Tarawa paid off superlatively. Reports from witnesses of the air attacks and shore bombardments told how not a single square foot of any of the islets in the atoll escaped either bombing or battleship long-range fire. Then, as the hour of the landing neared, the big ships approached close and simply leveled the landscape. Published photographs of the doomed atoll showed it literally flattened—not a tree still standing, not a single object projecting above the desolate terrain of what had once been a green and fertile vista.

For this landing, U.S. Army as well as Marine Corps troops were employed, with vastly improved boats and vehicles, among them the later well-known Amtracs (amphibious tanks with tractor treads). Many were brought to the scene in the bellies of LSTs (Landing Ship, Tank) and smaller landing craft, from which they were disgorged after the mother ship beached herself and dropped her bow ramp. The figures once again tell their own story. Kwajalein had nearly 9,000 defending troops; the assault landing force numbered over 40,000 army and marine soldiers. When it was over, all but 300 of the defenders were dead. American losses were 400 killed and four times that number wounded.

At the same time as Admiral Nimitz in the Central Pacific was driving westward toward Japan, a separate and parallel effort, based in Australia under General MacArthur, was aimed first at blocking the Japanese march into their designated Southeast Asia sphere, and second, at fulfilling MacArthur's promise as the Philippines fell to the Japanese: "I shall return!" The battle for Guadalcanal and ensuing associated operations were a part of this. For the return to the Philippines, however, experience had by now shown that much more than isolated theater action would be necessary. First, it would be necessary to capture or neutralize those island bases through which Japan could stage assistance to her forces in the Philippines. These included the islands of Guam, Saipan, and Tinian in the Southern Marianas. The former American possession of Guam was by far the most heavily fortified and it drew the heaviest preassault softening-up. But the experience already gained stood the assault forces in good stead. Overwhelming forces attacked each island and, although the Japanese troops as usual fought virtually to the last man, they were, except for isolated bands, completely wiped out. One of the traumatic things seen by our men was hundreds of civilian suicides. At Saipan, which, unlike Guam, had not been American before the war, the civilian population had been thoroughly indoctrinated with Japanese values. Many of them were Japanese. And fearing what they did not know, whole families hurled themselves off the cliffs, the parents first flinging their children, then jumping themselves to certain death. Our forces, observing from a distance, were powerless to intervene. The Southern Marianas were declared secure to our side in August 1944. (But small bands that had taken to the hills and caves hid there for years, occasionally making forays, in some cases long after the termination of the war.)

The tempo of the Pacific war was speeding up. The successful invasion of Normandy meant that the emphasis of the war against Germany had moved to the land. Thereafter, except for combating the diminishing German submarine threat, resources for naval action could go almost exclusively to the Pacific. New long-range bombers, the B-29s, had been specifically designed to bomb Japan from distant overseas bases: Guam and Saipan. The enemy's homeland began to come under increasingly heavy assault from the air. For the navy, conquest of Guam and its neighbors meant (except for the submarines) looking away from Japan for a time. The objective was now twofold: to sink the Japanese fleet and to support MacArthur's return to the Philippines.

To everyone serving in the U.S. Navy, Chester Nimitz was the consummately right naval officer in the right place at the right time. Not only was he magnificent as commander-in-chief of the Pacific Fleet, he was always supremely alert to the best interests of the country and the navy. As a commander, he was brilliant; as a leader, without a peer. He never shirked responsibility when things went badly, and he always exhibited a form of good-humored self-deprecation when they went well. He was a student of naval affairs, and had thoroughly grounded himself in Plan Orange at the Naval War College. On top of this, he was invariably considerate of those serving with or under him. He loved ships, sailors, and submarines (as a young officer he had been a submariner, a background he never forgot). No sentimentalist, he understood the capabilities and shortcomings of his men and always did his best to improve conditions or compensate for them as the situation might require. He had been greatly influenced by Fiske and Sims, as were nearly all the junior officers in his time. To the Lieutenant Nimitz of the pre–World War I era, Fiske, Sims, and Theodore Roosevelt were the best thing that could have happened to the navy.

Except for their contributions in improving the functioning of the navy, none of those three exerted any influence on World War II—but suddenly Nimitz found himself in charge of the magnificent weapon they had helped so mightily to forge. They had bequeathed him a tool beyond compare, and in a figurative sense, it was their banner he was flying. He used this tool daringly, with full appreciation of its abilities. The Battle of Midway is only one example, but it was the beginning. Its strategy was not accidental. It was the outgrowth of Nimitz's makeup, which he showed in the way he led his forces across the ocean, bypassing most of the garrisons on outlying islands, leaping deep into waters Japan had thought hers since, in some cases, the mandates resulting from World War I. It was an audacious strategy, perfectly suited to the conditions under which the war was being fought. U.S. forces would suddenly move into a target area and assert total control by the combined force of aircraft, surface ships, and submarines. The principal base would be isolated, cut off, and overwhelmed. Thereafter, all other bases depending on it were left to wither, without planes or ships, supplied haphazardly by slow-moving submarines that had to stay submerged all day. Mahan had never envisioned control of the sea of this nature. Instead of being a control by influence—in that no enemy ship dared to move for fear of being intercepted by opposing cruisers—it was a control in deadly fact: to appear meant to be sunk or, if an aircraft, shot down.

Our navy had well learned the lessons of Pearl Harbor, the Coral Sea, Midway, and the nearly continuous battles in "the slot" off Guadalcanal. The march across the Pacific was irresistible, and everyone who participated in it gloried in the part he played. Most dramatic to our naval aviators was the Battle of the Philippine Sea, otherwise known as the Marianas Turkey Shoot, in late June 1944. Submarines sank two big Japanese carriers, while carrier aircraft sank one and heavily damaged two more, as well as several other ships. Great numbers of the new and precious carrier-qualified pilots Japan had trained after Midway were lost. The improved navy fighter planes now used by our carriers were superb, their pilots confident.* The judgment of history is that from this moment Japan had no further chance of winning the war, or even of being able to ask for peace on any sort of favorable terms. Any such hope would, in any case, have had little chance. There was neither pity nor compassion in the attitude of our Pearl Harbor survivors—or anyone else of our 1941 navy.

The commanders of Nimitz's principal task forces shared his outlook and never ceased to press their advantage. The submariners, accustomed to the idea that only a ship able to submerge in the face of superior forces could survive in the far western Pacific, particularly marveled at the surface fleet's entrance into areas they had heretofore thought accessible only to them. And they marveled also at the huge fleet of aircraft carriers—so big that even from the air only a part of it could be seen at any one time—their country had created. The next move, directed at the highest level, was to redeem MacArthur's historic promise. All forces were gathered together: ships of all types, more than 200,000 army troops, all the Marine Corps amphibious forces, and virtually all of the naval surface and air forces, turned their faces to the south, toward the Philippines. Japan knew they were coming, prepared herself as best she might—and invented the kamikazes.

American troops under General MacArthur landed in the Philippines on the island of Leyte late in October 1944. Previously, all lo-

---

*Toward the conclusion of this battle, begun at extreme range, our returning planes began to run out of fuel. In the annals of our navy it will always be remembered how Admiral Marc Mitscher, in command of the U.S. task force, directed ship lights be turned on, searchlights beamed into the sky, star shells fired to maximum height to help the struggling aviators find their way back. This, in violation of every principle of naval air warfare except that of succoring one's own warriors—an attitude never learned by the Japanese command—enabled most of our fliers to land safely. Some eighty planes landed in the water, but three-fourths of the men in them were saved by destroyers and seaplanes sent along their return flight path to search for them.

catable defense installations had been pounded with bombs and naval gunfire. There was no opposition to the landing worth noticing, but all hands knew this was only the respite before the storm, for the pattern of last-ditch defense was by this time well established. During the softening-up operations, American fighter planes and bombers had destroyed nearly every Japanese aircraft in the area, including those based in Formosa. The Battle of the Philippine Sea had already virtually destroyed Japan's naval air warfare capability. Her army in the Philippines was bereft of logistics support and soon would be in equally dire straits. Japan accordingly invoked the weapon of desperation by which her conduct of this war will always be typified: the Kamikaze (in Japanese, "divine wind") Special Attack Forces—the suicide divers.

No enemy tactic could have so taken hold of the imagination of the Americans. Our men hated and feared the kamikazes, seeing them as crazed fanatics who were utterly impervious to anything but total personal destruction. They did one good thing for us, however: ships in the attack zone kept themselves in a higher state of preparedness against air threat than any warships had ever done the world over. Nor was this through orders from higher authority; it was the normal self-generated reaction of crew members who found themselves subject to terror from the air that surpassed their understanding, to which the only possible reaction was the full-bore fusillade of all weapons. It is safe to state that never in history was so much ammunition flung into the air as by our ships under kamikaze attack.

Only later did we begin to think about the tremendous sacrifice made by the thousands of young men who flew the suicide missions, who gave their lives in the faint and vain hope of thereby ameliorating the holocaust descending on their country.

There have always been instances where the fury of battle resulted in self-immolation in one way or another. Midway itself was no exception—on both sides. But never before had suicide been organized and planned by a government on a large scale as a part of a campaign. Off Leyte, during the landings, the first instances noted were thought of as aberrant actions taken by fliers whose aircraft had been fatally damaged, as some, indeed, may have been. But soon it became apparent that more than combat madness lay behind the increasing numbers of suicide dives. The first U.S. man-of-war casualty to the kamikazes took place on 2 October 1944, when a division of four small aircraft carriers came under attack. According to reports, planes dived upon them that, unlike normal dive bombers, made no effort to drop bombs and swoop out of their dives. Instead, they flew directly into their targets, carrying fully armed bombs with them.* Nor were they dissuaded by injuries to themselves or their planes, even by raging flames, by anything short of total destruction. USS *St. Lo*, hit by two suiciders in quick succession, was sunk, and *Kalinin Bay*, *Kitkun Bay*, and *White Plains* were severely damaged. All four were so-called escort carriers, designed on merchant ship hulls and hence far less resistant to damage than regular first-line carriers.

The Battle for Leyte Gulf has been called "the largest naval battle ever fought," comprising four very large actions, any one of which was a bigger battle (more ships, more men) than any other battle of the war except Midway. There were also innumerable smaller ones. All segments of the navy were involved, and in complexity and magnitude the sum of all the different battles was without parallel in naval history. Some battles were between surface forces without the involvement of air power, others were with the admixture of aircraft; but there was no Japanese combat air power worthy of the name, since most of what remained after the Battle of the Philippine Sea had been destroyed on the ground even before the landing. U.S. carriers controlled the air and took on targets of opportunity whenever they appeared. Mostly these were on land, but important targets still roamed the sea as well.

Dramatic action occurred. The Japanese super-battleship *Musashi*, sister to *Yamato*, Yamamoto's flagship at Midway, was attacked by U.S. torpedo-carrying aircraft in the Sibuyan Sea; she received by some accounts more than twenty torpedoes equally divided on both sides, finally dipped her bow under and, engines still running, sub-

---

*For safety reasons, aircraft bombs normally cannot detonate until after being released ("dropped") from the aircraft. The fact that the kamikaze bombs were armed in place was, of course, proof of the premeditated character of the crashes.

merged almost like a huge submarine making a normal dive. And during the night of 24–25 October, a powerful Japanese surface task force attempted a sortie through Surigao Strait, where it met the rejuvenated and largely rebuilt Pearl Harbor battle line, which shot it to bits by radar-controlled main-battery gunfire. Standing opposite to this, on the morning of 25 October the remnants of the *Musashi*'s task force, still including the *Yamato*, caught a division of so-called baby flattops within range of their guns. The carriers, handicapped by insufficient speed to outrun the big Japanese wagons, came under main-battery fire. The situation was saved by a torpedo attack made by a division of destroyers and destroyer escorts, in the course of which a Japanese cruiser was sunk and the main body driven off. Three of the U.S. destroyers (they received Presidential Unit Citations, and at least one of their skippers received the Congressional Medal of Honor) and one escort carrier were sunk as well.

Far to the north, the Japanese aircraft carriers, reduced to but thirty-five operable combat planes, were employed as a decoy to lure Admiral William Halsey's squadron of fast battleships away from the scene of action. They succeeded beautifully, resulting in what the press, with delight, called the Battle of Bull's Run. All of them, however, were sitting ducks to our own carriers and, unable to fight back, were sunk with ease.

Paradoxically, had Halsey stayed where he should have been, *Iowa* and *New Jersey*, with their accompanying carriers, might have found themselves in action against *Yamato*, *Nagato*, *Kongo*, and *Haruna*. With his air power, Halsey would most likely have sunk all four. This, of course, might have happened before he got into gun range of his own battleships—but it is also possible that the great test denied at Jutland might have taken place off Samar. As it was, he saw nothing, and for once in his career, did nothing (except throw one of our navy's more famous tantrums).

After the battle, when Nimitz's staff experts began to analyze what had happened, one of the big unanswered questions was why Japan had used her fleet in the reckless, self-destructive way she had. She had sacrificed her most valuable fleet units—carriers, battleships, cruisers, and destroyers—in ways that even her most chauvinistic planners must have known could benefit her war effort but little. Perhaps this, too, was a sort of naval kamikazelike suicide; to a samurai, only glorious death in battle, fighting against insuperable odds, could expiate defeat. It was as good an explanation as any, but too foreign to American minds to be more than an idea thrown into the air. To paraphrase Pierre Bosquet once again, it might be enemy psychology, but it was not war.

The Battle of Leyte Gulf was so widespread that no one—not even Admiral Nimitz in his headquarters, with a staff of experts to evaluate all messages and great wall-hung maps on which to display their import—could possibly have kept track of it all. To most of the participants the only thing visible was the portion in which they figured; the rest of the sea and sky simply could not be seen. What went on elsewhere was beyond their ken. But when it was over, Japan had lost four carriers, three battleships (including the great *Musashi*), ten big cruisers, and eleven destroyers. It was incomparably the greatest naval victory of all time. By comparison, U.S. losses were slight: one light carrier, two escort or "jeep" carriers, three destroyers, and two destroyer escorts, including those sunk by continuing kamikaze attacks immediately after the battle. No naval battle had ever been fought with so much determination and desperation, been so far-flung, and lasted so long. None had ever had such far-reaching and immediate results. Liberation of the Philippines was assured. The total defeat of Japan was a foregone conclusion which even her diehards had to face. To all intents and purposes, her navy had ceased to exist.

During and following the gargantuan battle, a strange aberration took place in Japan. Her information ministry began to issue communiqués claiming extraordinary destruction of American warships. Nearly every day saw the broadcast of these greatly inflated claims. "Our fliers yesterday sank four carriers, seven cruisers, and sixteen landing craft of various types. The day previous, two fleet carriers, three cruisers, and an even dozen destroyers were destroyed. The American navy cannot much longer stand losses like this. The self-sacrificing forces of the Emperor are everywhere showing their superiority to the enemy.'' Announcements of this nature found their way into the American press and American radio broadcasts, albeit accompanied by disclaimers that they consisted only of unsupported enemy claims. They were picked up by troops ashore and sailors at sea, some of whom could tune in Tokyo's own broadcasts for confirmation. Despite their own personal observations that the claims must be greatly exaggerated, the gnawing doubt could not be put down that some worrisome losses to our forces might nevertheless have occurred.

Controversy developed at Nimitz's headquarters as to the degree of notice to be taken of enemy claims that were on the surface so preposterous. However, Nimitz took the view that the morale of his fighting men—many of whom were isolated from all news except radio—was of primary importance. The upshot was a message addressed to all ships and stations from Nimitz himself, giving the true statistics of losses on both sides and advising that no credence whatever be given to Japan's claims. So far as the navy was concerned, this ended all doubts, for the word of the commander-in-chief was beyond mistrust; but the question of Japan's purpose in floating the patently false reports still persisted. The most obvious answer, finally generally believed, was that acceptance at face value of the claims of kamikaze successes was obligatory, inasmuch as in each case a dedicated and patriotic young man had given his life in the process. Accurate evaluation, moreover, was difficult. Action assessments were perforce made by the escorting fighters, for there were no other sources. Their function was to deliver the kamikazes to the vicinity of enemy ships and watch from a distance as clouds of smoke signaled termination of their last dives. But from a distance, one cloud of black smoke looked much like any other—whether it was from slight or heavy damage, or none at all, could not be determined. Perhaps more significant was the judgment of some of our intelligence officers that Japan's military and samurai traditions, in which self-destruction held a high place as the ultimate expression of loyalty, would force its high command to accept whatever claims were made for the kamikazes. On a more cynical speculation, any doubts as to their effectiveness could only dilute the determination of the young members of the Special Attack Force.

Nimitz's single message on the subject was enough. Thereafter the Japanese were allowed to believe all kamikazes struck their targets, as they apparently wished to, and the actual percentage of hits, more on the order of 10 percent, was kept classified. So were the figures on sinkings and serious damage.

After Leyte, the Pacific Fleet turned north again, and the watchword became "unremitting pressure" upon the enemy. It was now clear to Japan that the ultimate objective of the United States was actual invasion of the mainland of Japan, the home islands. B-29s were arriving in great numbers in Saipan and Guam; massive air raids were being staged on Tokyo and other cities in the mainland. Japan correctly anticipated a U.S. requirement for a halfway station to provide fighter escort and emergency refueling, among other services, and also correctly picked Iwo Jima as the most likely target for attempted takeover. One of Japan's ablest generals was put in charge, with a heavy garrison, and as American intentions became increasingly clear, so did the fervor of his defense preparations. The expected amphibious assault landing was made on 19 February 1945. It was preceded by three days of nearly continuous shore bombardment in which Sims's old *Nevada* endeared herself forever to the marines by selectively knocking out the strong points holding them down. Carrier aircraft also participated by spotting and bombing, and the marines crunched steadily forward, foot by foot, against the most desperate resistance ever put forward by the troops of any nation. The disparity of forces on land alone, without counting the support and bombardment forces in the ships at sea, was three to one. Yet the Japanese fought fanatically, and, as fully expected, almost to the death of the last man. Of the 23,000 troops opposing the landing, all but 200 died.

It was by far the most heavily contested and deadliest amphibious operation yet conducted anywhere. The defenders had burrowed extensively throughout the island, constructing a network of interconnecting tunnels through which large bodies of men could infiltrate behind our lines, and by which unexpected attacks could be—and were—made at any time. Complete capture of the island took a month, but it was being used in support of the B-29 bombing raids on Japan's home islands long before the last of the Japanese defenders had been found and wiped out.

Nor were the ships at sea surrounding Iwo left out. Several kamikaze attacks on them took place, particularly against the carriers in the area, and one escort carrier was sunk, while the venerable *Saratoga* was badly damaged. By this time, U.S. forces recognized the suicide crash as an accepted battle tactic on the part of Japan. Our fleet units, in their turn, doubled and redoubled their antiaircraft defenses, adding heavy rapid-fire weapons wherever they could be installed, gearing air defense to physically destroying oncoming aircraft. Bitter experience had proved that a dying pilot in a flaming plane might still retain enough control to dive into a ship instead of falling helplessly into the sea. It was additionally suspected that some of them might have taken some drug to reduce any debilitation from injuries during their Valkyrie-like ride to Yasukuni Shrine, the Japanese monument to fallen warriors. Only total destruction before he came near could stop a kamikaze, and no quarter was given or expected.

U.S. commanders, fully ready for kamikazes at Iwo Jima, were actually slightly surprised that only a few such attacks developed. Having by this time had more than adequate opportunity to estimate the Japanese character, they guessed that the suiciders were being held back against prospect of greater need elsewhere. This proved to be the case, for the invasion of Okinawa—a much bigger island than Iwo and considerably closer to the home islands—brought them forth in great numbers.

The timetable of "unremitting pressure" called for the invasion of Okinawa immediately after the takeover of Iwo Jima, and indeed it did take place less than a month after Iwo was secure, in April. The timetable also called for full exploitation of Okinawa as the major staging base for an all-out assault on the mainland of Japan planned for the fall of the year. It took no Japanese genius to recognize the inevitable import of the gradual encroachment of American power from across the Pacific. Nor could the nation that had initiated war by surprise air attack by major forces have any illusions about the intent of the jugger-naut headed her way. Japan's high command pulled out all the stops they had left. By this time they had realistically lost expectation of winning the war, or even of America's agreement to any sort of terms. They were fighting for the salvation of their country and their way of life, in the hope that a demonstration of the high cost of invading Japan's home islands might finally predispose the United States to ac-cept something short of unconditional surrender. They failed to per-ceive that if national perfidy results in war, there can be no recovery of trust should defeat eventuate. Surrender is the only alternative. Noth-ing will be trusted by the victor, nor will he be in the mood to compro-mise. By perpetrating Pearl Harbor on the one hand and refusing to surrender in the face of obvious defeat on the other—even going to awesome pain in the defense of her Pacific islands to demonstrate the cost in lives of landing in her home islands—Japan made it inevitable that a nuclear weapon, if developed, would be used against her.

In the event, the battle for Okinawa was furious, and costly for both sides. For Japan it was the penultimate disaster. She had nothing left: only a few bombs and an ill-assorted group of aircraft. Her indus-tries had been largely destroyed, her sources of raw materials cut off, most of her warships sunk. Aside from the determined and even in-spired resistance of the land troops on Okinawa, the only weapons she had were her kamikazes, and these she expended prodigally and uselessly.

American power was crushing. The amphibious force alone com-prised more than 1,200 ships of various types. Huge carrier task forces cruised off the beleaguered island, itching for the chance to wreak even more vengeance for Pearl Harbor. Submarines prowled the area and both coasts of the enemy mainland islands, searching for the few ships Japan could still send to sea, confident at last in a torpedo that worked as it should. Japan, which had begun the war in cold blood, was reel-ing in defeat, and in the U.S. Navy the blood-lust was up.

The battle for possession of Okinawa was fought on land by both the army and the marine corps. Each executed an amphibious landing, and each had its terrain mapped out in advance for conquest. The navy's role was to deliver the landing troops to the places selected, bombard shore fortifications as requested (either by carrier aircraft or from the big guns of battleships), and maintain total command of the air above and the sea around the beleaguered island. As at Iwo Jima, the Japanese defense was inspired but futile, and as always, they fought to the death. The island had about 110,000 troops and Okinawan draftees in its garrison; all but 11,000 died, as did 24,000 Okinawan civilians. American troops killed numbered about 8,000, and there were 32,000 wounded, of an invading force approximating 200,000 assault troops. Nearly 5,000 sailors died in their ships, mostly from kamikaze attacks. The battle on shore lasted from 1 April to 21 June. As it ended, plans were already well along for the final stage of the war: an all-out assault landing on the shores of the home islands of Japan, scheduled to begin on 1 November.

One of the first kamikazes at Okinawa was a ship, the *Yamato*, one of the few remaining operational ships of the Japanese navy, thus confirming the theory that self-immolation may have been one of the operative motives at Leyte. Along with the paltry few accompanying vessels Japan could assemble, she was loaded with what little fuel was still available in the home islands and sent south, toward Okinawa. She was, in fact, being given the opportunity to retrieve the honor she had lost through her survival at Leyte. As was later learned, her intention was to beach herself in the midst of the U.S. landing force and fight until her ammunition was exhausted and she was overwhelmed, at which point she would blow herself up to avoid capture. It was, pure and simple, a suicide mission, a form of naval hara-kiri, or *seppuku*, to which all the members of her crew were bound, not by their own will but by their commander's orders. To men of the persuasion of the Japanese officer corps, this may have come as a sort of relief from the disaster staring them in the face. Their spirits could come to the sacred Yasukuni Shrine and face the other dead warrior spirits with heads held high, for by dying in battle they divested themselves of responsibility for the coming debacle.

No one knows what the doomed men felt about it in the machinery spaces, behind tightly closed watertight doors, as the great ship to which they had devoted their lives absorbed bomb after bomb and torpedo after torpedo, until bulkheads were converted to decks, and decks became bulkheads—and she could take no more.

To the fliers of the U.S. task force, however, *Yamato* epitomized the earlier arrogance of the Japanese navy. She had been planned in 1934 in violation of the 1922 London Naval Treaty. Her construction was one of the destructive forces that brought that early effort at disarmament to naught. She had become Yamamoto's flagship immediately after the Pearl Harbor attack, had been at Midway, and had been the fleet flagship ever since. At the Battle for Leyte Gulf, she and her consorts had surprised the small task force of "jeep" carriers, sinking one of them, and then been bluffed into turning away by the heroic attack of the relatively tiny destroyers. She was, in simple fact, the most famous ship in the Japanese navy, and by April 1945, one of the very few Japan had left.

To the American aviators under Admiral Raymond Spruance, she was the prize par excellence, the embodiment of everything they hated. Until now she had escaped them, but at last they would destroy her. Now came their chance for retribution. That the Japanese task force's sortie to certain destruction was pitiful, as well as heroic, struck them not at all. Nor could it have, for they had been totally conditioned in the opposite direction, as always happens in war. Under the circumstances, we would not have wanted them any different. But it was sad, in retrospect, for *Yamato*'s sacrifice, like everything Japan tried at this stage of the war she had started, was totally useless.

The U.S. naval aviators had considered the problem carefully. *Musashi*, *Yamato*'s sister ship, had taken nineteen or twenty torpedoes and had gone down by the bow but otherwise on an even keel. She had shown an extraordinary ability to accept damage and still function. *Yamato*, they determined, would not be given that chance. They would put their torpedoes only into her port side, flood only port-side compartments, and thus cause her to capsize even though her hull might not be as severely damaged as that of her sister.

Yamato had no air cover. She and her nine consorts were detected by our submarines as they exited from the Bungo Suido, and they were tracked the entire length of their short, one-way voyage. On the after-noon of 7 April 1945, they were attacked by an air armada of some 300 carrier aircraft (more than had struck Pearl Harbor), each one individually eager to deal the tiny Japanese task force a telling blow. Struck by at least five bombs and eleven torpedoes during a sustained two-hour pounding, the great battleship lost power, listed to port, and finally wearily rolled over and sank. A dramatic explosion took place within her stricken hull as she went down, another hara-kiri for a nation whose culture saw self-destruction as a warrior's final act of supreme loyalty. It sent an enormous column of smoke thousands of feet into the air, bulging at the top like the mushroom cloud that a few months later was to write finis to the war.*

All the same, for our navy, defense against airborne kamizazes was the principal issue of the Okinawa campaign. To detect incoming raids, picket destroyers were sent out to distant stations around the island, charged to report when their radars detected aircraft coming in. Soon aware of the function of these lonely ships, the kamikazes took to attacking them first, and it was here that the bloodiest fighting took place, in each case literally one small desperate ship madly shooting back against a murderous onslaught suddenly flung out of the air.

Under the stress of wartime necessity, radar was well advanced by June 1945. The American ships were covered with antiaircraft weapons of all kinds, most of them radar controlled, the larger ones firing the newly invented "VT" fuse ammunition containing a small radar. The radar exploded a heavy charge of high explosive when it passed within lethal range of a target, so that detonation by time or a direct hit was not necessary and effectiveness was greatly enhanced. The fusillade thrown up against the half-crazed suiciders knocked most of them

---

*The men and officers manning Japan's final naval sortie had been told that one of their purposes was to be a decoy mission so that a full-scale kamikaze attack on Okinawa, scheduled for the same time, would be able to achieve extraordinary results: the criterion was one warship sunk by each heroic Special Attack Force pilot. Although there were several ships sunk by kamikazes on 6 April, the day *Yamato* sortied, the supreme irony is that, on the day of her sacrifice, air attack damaged only three U.S. ships, none seriously. The total of it all was far less than the sacrifice itself. But this was not unusual for Japan.

out of the air before they could accomplish their mission, but even so, occasionally kamikazes got all the way to the landing forces standing by off the invasion beaches—especially when more than one kamikaze attacked at the same time.

At this juncture in the constant war between surface and air, the greatest difficulty faced by U.S. forces was coordination of weapons. Air warfare, and the defense against it, had developed to the point where the delay required to transmit instructions or ideas by voice could no longer be tolerated. With suicidal air raids coming in from several points of the compass, coverage had to be over all, all the time. But all available weapons were also required to augment the wall of flak aimed at the nearest kamikaze. A quicker, more capable control than the frenetic speaking voice of an air-defense coordinator was needed, and thus was born the first stated requirement for some kind of electronic antiaircraft (later broadened to include antimissile) coordination control.

But this was for the future. At Okinawa, coordination was by good sense and the seat of the pants. Had it not been for radar, it is not likely our fleet could have stayed. But stay on station it did, though it paid a price. Of the 4,000 kamikaze attacks Japan's navy and army air forces mounted during the war, 3,000 took place at Okinawa. Many of the poorly trained young zealots did not succeed in coming within range of their objectives, but nevertheless, during the eleven-week-long Okinawa battle, the U.S. Navy had 368 ships damaged and 32 sunk, mostly by suicide attack. During the battle, 4,900 navy men were killed, an equal number wounded.

By any system of measurement, Okinawa was the bloodiest and longest-lasting battle in the history of any navy, rivaled in size, though not in duration or casualties, only by the fantastic four-day Battle of Leyte Gulf. Only Japan could have put up such extraordinary resistance against such overwhelming odds.

Very much to the credit of our commanders in the Pacific, our conduct of the war became increasingly well coordinated as it went on. At the end, all forces were operating in unison, with a single exception. At

Okinawa, we achieved the epitome of cooperation and coordination of all wartime efforts: land-based air, carrier air power, amphibious assault, army and marine ground troops, surface ships, logistic support. It was, as well, a dress rehearsal for Operation Olympic, the amphibious assault landing on Kyushu, the southernmost of the home islands of Japan, which was planned to become the staging area for Operation Coronet, a jump across Japan's Inland Sea to the biggest island, Honshu.

The exception was our submarines. Everyone agreed they would be best employed by continuing their already very successful campaign against enemy seaborne supply lines. The torpedo problem had at last been solved, or nearly so. No one had yet zeroed in on the propensity of torpedoes to run in a circle, which caused extreme danger to the firing submarine, but all other difficulties had at last been found and eliminated. Torpedo production had caught up with torpedo expenditure sometime in 1943, and in 1945 enemy ships were becoming scarce. Many submarines were now returning from patrol without a single sighting to report. After Okinawa, this was the case for most.

At the beginning of the war, the far western Pacific was divided into submarine patrol areas surrounding the islands of Japan and the Philippines and bordering the coasts of Indonesia and China up to the Asian mainland. Each area was assigned to a single submarine. The principal concern of the operational planners was to keep all areas covered, to the limit of the available subs and weapons. Some submarines had to be sent out "short loaded," or with mines instead of unavailable torpedoes.*

For the first thirty months of the war, the submarine patrol areas were inviolate, traveled only by Japanese naval and merchant ships and the American submarine designated to prey upon them. But obviously some adjustment had to be made when U.S. surface task forces

---

*During the early patrols, skippers were given an order signed by Admiral Nimitz directing them to "execute unrestricted warfare" against enemy merchant ships. The idea was that a captured skipper could produce this document in his defense if charged with violating the old cruiser rules of World War I, which, at this juncture, were still technically in effect. It was another case of Admiral Nimitz accepting responsibility he felt rightfully should rest on him. But as the war developed, this bit of paperwork was soon forgotten.

began to move into waters hitherto considered entirely under Japanese control (and hence entered only by our submarines). The result was a rigidly enforced overlay of submarine-free zones where any submarine discovered would be subject to instant and unremitting attack, submarine areas where no U.S. ships could enter until given unequivocal clearance by the submarine force commander, passage lanes where no submarine could be attacked unless positively identified as enemy, and so-called moving havens surrounding subs in transit, in the center of which they were required to remain. The simple patrol areas became things of the past. The new rules made navigation more complicated for the subs, but they also made it unquestionably clear that the war was going well for our side, very badly for Japan.

Absent the atomic bombs on Hiroshima and Nagasaki, whether Japan would, or could, have surrendered without the planned invasion of the home islands will never be known. All experience to that time had been that her military forces would fight to the bitter end. Some Americans now feel a dramatic demonstration, perhaps dropping the bomb into Fujiyama's yawning crater, might have given the peace faction the political strength required to initiate a cease-fire. Probably not, however, and such thoughts long after the fact are academic. In August 1945, the bombs were welcomed by our forces and our people as being just retribution to the nation responsible for Pearl Harbor and for the war atrocities, particularly those visited on our troops defending Bataan and Corregidor.

That the people inhabiting Hiroshima and Nagasaki—and firebombed Tokyo, too—were no more responsible for Pearl Harbor than the population of New York City or San Francisco did not occur to us then. Praise be, it does now.

May this be the great and only gift of the atomic bomb: that by the way it brought World War II to an end, it converted it into the Armageddon predicted in one form or another by nearly all the religions of the world.

Even a former military man may hope that those two bombs will forever prevent such a war from ever happening again.

Epilogue: A Few Ideas About Our Postwar Navy

Since World War II there has been no time for peaceful consolidation of our accomplishment. We thought we had made the world safer, but it remained deeply unsettled. In the war's aftermath, as our navy radically reduced its size, its ships had to be driven harder than ever before. Crews spent more time at sea and had less time for upkeep for their ships or, in a manner of speaking, for themselves. The pressures of exercises increased, and, because of rapidly changing technology, so did the demands of proficiency. Although the war was over for the nation at large, for the sailors manning our navy's ships the demands upon them were much the same as always, except for the shooting.

Beginning with the *Nautilus* in 1955, nuclear power revolutionized submarines, divorcing them from dependence on the earth's atmosphere and giving them fabulous speed and endurance. The result was a quantum jump in capability, literally beyond the comprehension of submariners of the war days. Next to benefit have been our big carriers, whose overall military value has been increased half again by replacement of many tons of fuel with a few pounds of enriched uranium. For all other ships, massive improvements in under-way reprovisioning techniques, pioneered between the wars and perfected in World War II, are now a matter of course. Hence, today, a battle group can stay at sea for periods comparable to those in the old days of sail—in other words for months—without even smelling the shore. Someday soon, as soon as necessary, a nuclear-powered ship will stay at sea for a full year: this is a record still to be set but we have the capability, and it will be done when the need arises.

For navies, no less than for the world as a whole, nuclear power and nuclear weapons have brought with them far-reaching changes in design, tactics, and operations. Submarines may already be the most important type of warship in the world. Not many years ago the author was called on the carpet by members of the old guard for telling the president this was inevitable—but it is an accepted fact today.

There is a psychology in the affairs of men that wants always to preserve things in the mold to which they have become accustomed—which is why some men resist innovation even though they themselves may boast of their participation in earlier changes. Many of the older submariners, who had had much to do with the development of the grand diesel-powered boats with which we fought the war, refused to accept their demise—and closed their minds to nuclear power's extraordinary increase in capability. They fought—some of them—with underhanded weapons. Some were not above using vicious personal tactics reminiscent of the onslaught against Isherwood. Today that battle is over, the short-sighted old guard and the casualties they caused gone from the scene. Our largest submarines today are more than ten times the size and displacement of the standard World War II sub, three times as fast, and have a thousand times the endurance. Their counterparts in the Soviet navy are bigger yet. Both are larger than the battleship that became the archetype of naval power, shortly before World War I: HMS *Dreadnought* herself. And, still more significant, U.S. and U.S.S.R. submarines can unleash many thousand times the destructive power, to several hundred times the range, any battleship ever could—and from under the sea, with nearly absolute accuracy, besides.

There are several individuals who contributed to this fantastic change. One, Hyman G. Rickover, has been highly spotlighted and has not lacked for honors, in the navy and out of it. Another should be better known in this connection, for he did for Rickover what Theodore Roosevelt did for William Sims. This was Senator Henry "Scoop" Jackson, of Washington State. Jackson was Rickover's original source of power in Congress; he marshaled the strength that prevented the navy from retiring Rickover instead of promoting him and was one of the admiral's principal advisers in terms of his relations with Capitol Hill. (Jackson died suddenly in 1983 and is appropriately memorialized by the navy in the new *Ohio*-class Trident submarine *Henry M. Jackson*, so-named by order of President Reagan.) Rickover is well known for the nuclear power plant, the first successful one in the world being his design for the USS *Nautilus*. Whether there would have been nuclear power without him is hardly debatable; there would have been. But he pushed it forward harder and faster and with greater success than anyone else would have, or could have. One may argue whether the world would be better or worse off today had nuclear power for submarines been slower in development, but there is full agreement that the USS *Nautilus* (SSN 571), successor to the impotent *Nautilus* at Midway, is Rickover's monument for all time.

The list of others who share credit for the Polaris-Poseidon-Trident deterrent program must begin with President Eisenhower himself, who ordered the in-depth study of technology and requirements that resulted in formation of the Navy Special Project Office to design the submarine and missile and to oversee the work. In charge of the project were Rear Admiral William F. Raborn and his assistant, Captain Levering Smith. There were in addition, as might be expected, a host of others: in the Special Project Office, in Rickover's own Nuclear Reactor Branch of the Navy Bureau of Ships, and in the line of the navy, most particularly some of the younger officers of its submarine branch. It was far from a one-man effort.

Rickover was, and is, the true inconoclast, and as such bears real comparison to William Sims. There are more points of similarity than there are differences between them. Both dedicated themselves to improving the navy in ways they thought were needed, and both had a massive impact on it. Both developed strong enmities among their brother officers. (Sims's supporters, however, were enthusiastic about him personally, not only about his work.) Each man decided, early on, that if he was to accomplish anything against the massed forces of the navy bureaucracy, he must be constantly on the offensive—and on the defensive as well. It is undoubtedly true that both survived in the navy for one reason only: each had a friend high in the political realm where the basic decisions that mattered were made.

Coincident with the spawning of nuclear weapons, World War II produced an extraordinary development of electronic marvels, beginning with radar. We are seeing the beginning of a new age of man, already presaged by the movement of computers into nearly every aspect of society. For obvious reasons, one of the foremost of such aspects is our armed forces. An example in point is the missile, a computer-controlled, robotic kamikaze. Its computer-memory-chip brain is immune to the tremendous stresses that must have impacted on those sacrificial young men, the real kamikazes, as they hurtled to their extraordinary doom. It goes without saying that its success rate is much better than theirs was.

To a sailor of any earlier navy, today's warships would be veritable palaces, with excellent working and living conditions. With our ubiquitous replenishment system replacing consumables virtually as fast as used, today's ships can stay at sea indefinitely—and the nation's needs are such that all too often we must operate them accordingly. The nuclear-powered *Eisenhower* not long ago remained under way (except for a four-day port call at Singapore) for nine consecutive months. Sometime during that lengthy period, every man of her crew was issued two cans of beer by special order of the secretary of the navy, authorized by the president. More recently yet, the newly recommissioned but forty-year-old World War II fast battleship *New Jersey*, still on her shakedown cruise in the Pacific, was urgently ordered through the Panama Canal and across the Atlantic to the coast of Lebanon, where she cruised for months. Time after time our navy has demonstrated its unique ability to protect our national concerns wherever decided by our national leadership. It is wonderful to have a mobile force so able to go anywhere there is deep water, but sometimes the country loses sight of the demands thereby placed upon the ships and their crews.

It has been over a century since our sailors were subjected to such long-at-sea schedules. It is true that, today, their mail is delivered almost weekly by helicopter or replenishment ship, and in emergency, individuals can be airlifted off their ships on very short notice. During off hours they can patronize their ship's "geedunk stand" (soda fountain) and see movies or television on one of a number of TV sets. Big ships carry chaplains who perform religious services and provide basic counseling at need. Nearly all ships generally carry good-sized libraries (but, sad to say, these are no longer as popular as before the proliferation of TV and movies on demand). No matter how big the ship, conscientious commanders do their utmost to provide for the human needs of their crews. But a ship at sea inhabits a world totally unlike the land. A big ship is a city in itself, yet inescapably austere. It cannot provide everything. Its crews cannot have beer or wine or liquor of any kind. Women, to them, have to be pushed into fantasy. Even in the few cruising ships with women in their crews, it is not the same as "on the beach." Thoughtful persons should understand this when they rail against the exuberant behavior of young men on shore leave for the first time in months. Their needs are very different from those of ordinary civilians.

Along with its newfound capabilities and the problems they bring with them, the navy also has a few long-standing old concerns that should be resolved. Prominent among these is the promotion and retirement system. Of recent years there has been rising Congressional discontent at its high annual cost, now approaching $19 billion. Too many officers and men, it is said, retire to a lifetime pension at the twenty-year mark, thereby excessively inflating the pension budget.

The fact is that a large majority of these are career men who would not retire if there were any other option. Whatever reason they may give for their decision to leave active service, with twenty years of their youth invested in the navy, they cannot be other than career-oriented. But only about 5 percent of personnel with twenty or more

years of service can be continued. The remaining 95 percent, men—
and now women, too—still in the prime of their productivity, are
forced out to make room for a new crop of soon also to be 95 percent
pensioners.

The system under which the navy had developed promoted *everyone*, regardless of capability, when a vacancy occurred in a higher
grade. In effect it assured everyone of high rank if he lived long
enough and avoided serious derelictions. It was thanks to this that Stephen Decatur's killer, by law a murderer (though he was never arraigned), remained on active duty for twenty-eight more years. A half
century later, the same system caused Sims to remain a lieutenant until
well into his forties. It resulted in a minimal retired list, but it also
caused the navy's leadership posts to be held by superannuated officers
and men who could by no stretch be effective in war, and in some
cases were discredited or known incompetents because of drink or
other disabilities. The indefatigable Sims became one of the strong
advocates of a system of selecting and promoting the best fitted while
still in their prime.

Pioneered with only the highest motives, however, the new system
had a serious flaw: controls were exercised only at the top. There were
but minimal restrictions over entry into the service, and inevitably
these increased out of all proportion to the actual need. Taking the
officer corps as a bellwether, and bearing in mind that entry into it
today is from many sources, nevertheless Naval Academy statistics
give an inkling of the parameters of the problem: prior to World War
II, Annapolis provided nearly all the regular officers in the naval service. In the hundred years from the academy's inception in 1845 to the
end of World War II, it produced a total of 17,513 graduates. In the
forty years since 1945, it has supplied twice as many, but there have
also been other sources of young officers, numerically far more prolific
(for example, inputs from NROTC and Officer Candidate Schools during this same period have been three to four times as numerous as those
from the Naval Academy). By consequence, a conservative estimate of
new officers from all sources since 1945 must approach—or even ex-
ceed—100,000.

In spite of the navy's expressed desire that they opt for a full career, most of these newly commissioned postwar officers had no real chance of achieving one. Their eyes opened to the true facts, many left the service when their obligations were completed; but of those who honestly strove for a career in the navy, nearly all were forced into premature retirement while still in their productive years and still fully competent to perform their duties.

In time of war there is a great need for officers and men. In time of peace there must of course be retrenchment—but the retrenchment, illogically, comes at the wrong end of the personnel pyramid. Well-performing assets are wasted, and the country must pay for them at least twice over: earned pensions for upward of thirty years more for those put aside, and costly training of unnecessary replacements.

Despite his earlier strong support, Sims became a critic of the selection system as it developed. Although by then retired himself, he wrote innumerable letters and articles suggesting corrections to the faults he saw; nothing came of these efforts. Known to the navy as a proponent of the new system, Sims ended his career in deep opposition to the unbalanced results produced by the manner of its implementation, and virtually predicted the present unacceptable condition.

As might be expected, most of the testimony heard by Congress on this subject has been supportive of the present "up or out" system, as in earlier days it supported the moribund seniority system: those testifying are active-duty officers who have benefited personally from it. The forced retirees (nearly all of whom once aspired to many more years of service than they were allocated) will, if asked the same questions, respectfully disagree.

The navy needs to return to the basic principle on which the original system was founded: retention of as many as possible—instead of only an illogical few—of those fully qualified to do the jobs it needs done. We are, after all, talking about maintaining an effective peacetime navy, not maintaining a burgeoning wartime one. To do this it will be necessary first to reduce the numbers of young persons offered entry, second to restructure the assignment allocations in each rank or grade to more fully utilize the qualifications and experience of the older personnel thus retained, and third combine the retired and reserve components of the navy into a single unified organization, so that needs for augmented personnel can be met in the most economical way. If done properly, this will greatly reduce total costs of salaries and pensions, thus satisfying Congressional concerns without reducing any presently authorized (and richly earned) benefits. The result can only be greater efficiency of personnel utilization, greater retention of both officers and men, and therefore higher morale at much lower cost.

If this cannot be done by the navy, Congress will soon do it as a cost-cutting measure; and any such legislation will inevitably be less palatable than what the navy can and should do of itself.

Another problem of ever-growing proportions is our merchant marine. Our navy does not create national objectives. It only accomplishes the tasks laid upon it to the best of its ability, and by law must ask for the tools it needs for whatever the country says it must be prepared to do. Thus, while the North Atlantic Treaty remains in effect, it must remain prepared to carry out our national commitments for the succor of Western Europe. In any scenario of future war this will involve a "bridge of ships" across the Atlantic Ocean (and elsewhere for similar emergencies, perhaps in lesser amount). It is, however, a given fact of modern international conflict that never again will there be time to build the requisite fleet of ships.

The professional term is adequate "sea-lift" (a basic part of sea-power, defined as the capability to transport men and materiel by ship). We can do a lot with air lift, as witness the Berlin Air Lift; but to contemplate that means of supporting the rest of Europe is to look at an impossibility. For that, this country requires a viable merchant marine and the shipbuilding and repair facilities that go with it. As noted earlier, since the Civil War we have not had such a merchant marine, except in time of war, when we hurriedly built one. In World War III, however, we may find ourselves facing the choice between initiating the use of nuclear weapons or accepting a rapidly developing fait accompli—unless the merchant fleet we shall need is already in existence, and readily available.

When we entered World War I a massive shipbuilding program was begun to create the merchant fleet required to support our European Allies—but the war ended before the full effect was felt. In World War II, with more time, our shipbuilders performed prodigies. But then our regular postwar pattern reasserted itself. Causes of the continuing debacle are numerous and complicated, in fairness only partly the result of unrealistic union demands, although the latter have been among the more serious problems. For years the navy has been very much concerned over the deterioration of our merchant marine, and only recently has it shown some signs of bottoming out at last. It is high time, for it cannot go much farther down the drain.

Our mobilizable merchant fleet is in three categories: the small operating fleet still sailing under the American flag, the committed NATO ships, of which at least the mobile ones, it is hoped, will move immediately toward the west if their homelands are threatened, and the "ready reserve" of ships maintained by the U.S. Maritime Commission. A fourth category is the so-called "reserve fleet," obsolescent ships kept at minimum upkeep levels in various reserve-fleet anchorages, but these are of negligible value. The "ready reserve," consisting of more than 100 good ships, is regularly exercised, has union crews assigned, and is kept in a condition of five to ten days readiness. Our operating fleet and the committed NATO ships are of course under way nearly continuously—so that, in all, we have a potential of some 600 ships with which to exercise sea-lift in the event of war. Except for the ready reserve, all are in full competitive service today. Too, our maritime unions have finally understood that they must be competitive if they are to survive. It is, in short, probably entirely true that our merchant marine is in the midst of the most radical improvement since the end of World War II. This is an encouraging sign, but it is not enough.

While we could not logically expect to carry *all* our foreign trade in our own ships, we still carry far too little. Despite remarkable improvement in recent years, American ships handle but a quarter of our containership cargoes, and only a tiny 3–4 percent of our dry bulk cargoes. Cost-wise, our crews still cannot compete with the crews of foreign nations. Our shipbuilders cannot compete with foreign shipyards in terms of cost and quality of the ships they produce. The net result is that instead of the several thousand ships our experience over two centuries has taught us we must have, we have barely 600 we think we can count on.

Despite the improvement of recent years, in this author's opinion very strong and innovative measures are yet required, of a scope sufficient to reverse the trend of twelve decades and change a moribund industry into the vibrant part of our overall national defense complex that the maritime interests of our country so obviously must have.

Since big wars by definition cannot be fought with the "regular" armed forces, it becomes necessary to create some form of military-industrial cooperation that can operate in the peacetime environment and at the same time serve the nation's wartime needs without delay. Our solution to this problem may predetermine the fate of Europe.

In the long range, the purpose of a navy is to use the sea to influence the decisions on the land by which we live. For slightly over two hundred years this has been the reason we have maintained a navy. But the world has not stopped changing, and because of electronics it is changing now faster than ever before. Mahan's ideas about control of the sea were correct for his time and for the past centuries that he studied. He made an immense contribution, but today many of his ideas no longer apply. While, for example, he stressed the necessity for concentration of forces, today we cannot concentrate them in the face of homing weapons and nuclear warheads. His arguments about meeting and defeating the enemy fleet presupposed that a strong enemy would also seek battle, and that a weak one would keep his fleet units together for mutual support, thus providing the opponent with a clear objective.

But, instead, as all the sea battles of 1939–1945 showed (and so did the battles on land), the strategy of choice by both sides was the war of speed, mobility, and surprise. Superiority in any one of these categories was more important than mere strength. By judicious use of its advantages, a weaker fleet could defeat a stronger one less imaginatively led. Applying this appreciation to today, the new strategy of war at sea is different from that of Mahan, although it sounds similar. Briefly, no one can control the sea in the old sense; but one may plan to use it for one's own needs and deny its use to the enemy, even in his own home waters. This is, in effect, what we did in the war against Japan, and the concept is more valid today, after four decades of development. The vehicles of the new strategy are aircraft, missiles, and submarines, and its most important tool is electronics. It is effective regardless of whether or not a sea area is under the enemy's nominal control, and it does not require a visible presence—only a perceived threat.

The speed of aircraft and missiles, the ability of submarines to remain undetected for long periods in enemy home waters, and the ubiquity of electronics that can pervade everything mean that today control of the sea can be asserted only temporarily. A battle group can sweep in from over the horizon, take charge of the sea in a determined area, and there carry out its mission, but at no time can it be immune to surprise attack; thus it cannot freely control the sea, if by control is meant exclusive ownership in the old sense. It can only occupy it temporarily, generally by locally superior force, brought in by surprise. If a confrontation develops, the side using all its advantages with the most skill will win. In the Falkland Islands War, England was able, despite massive difficulties, to project her sea power far across the sea and take control of the waters near the disputed islands. She thereby brought the dispute to the conclusion she wanted, despite Argentina's manifestly greater available strength. Had Argentina used the factors of time and force with greater awareness, the final decision might have gone the other way.

As a far more sophisticated nation than in 1941, and certainly than in 1918, we need to do more than simply say we must employ our navy in the ways best suited to modern needs and conditions. Yet this is still a true syllogism, and the present years are critical. The determinative issues are in many ways reminiscent of the controversies over the proper employment of naval airpower before World War II. Technological sophistication has outstripped all other forms of growth, and the individual has become tiny in comparison with the destructive capabilities that seize mankind today.

Since the end of World War II, our navy has continued to grow in capability and technical quality, even as its physical size has diminished. It has remained in the forefront of our national policy as it affects the world—not as the creator of the policy but as its first and most flexible instrument. It has maintained its traditions of service, adaptability, and capability. It has remained true to its oath, now two hundred years old, to stand always ready to do what the nation requires of it.

In the largest sense, a navy need not be built solely to fight. It must be able to do that, of course, but ideally it should be built in the hope that it will not have to. Such has always been the rationale behind our ballistic-missile submarines, now upgraded to Trident, and it is indeed the hope and prayer of all navies everywhere. Nothing is quite so clear in history as that a nation well prepared may never have to fight, whereas one unprepared is not only much more likely to find itself in battle—it could lose everything it has. This homily is far more true now than in the past, for now there will not be time to build a navy after the fighting begins.

It is this writer's belief that the Armageddon of our navy was its battle with the mystical samurai navy of Japan, a conflict it had unwittingly prepared for during all the years of its existence. World War II was the first and only time our navy was put fully to the test of all its abilities, the only time it was stretched to the uttermost. All unknowingly, this was what our navy had been built for, and our ships and men did their job admirably. Forty years have passed since then, and all that is now behind us. It is instructive to note that the time since the close of World War II has been twice as long as between World Wars I and II. Forty more years may pass, or a hundred, before mankind may be able to believe that was the last world war, but there is ever-growing hope that someday it will.

I personally believe that nuclear weapons, the doomsday weapons, will never be used again, even though it is obvious that the battle for the minds of men will not thereby end. In their place will be the weapons of economy, of propaganda (both the truth and what is today called ''disinformation''), of guerrilla warfare, and of mindless terrorism—and of things and technologies only dreamed about today.

As for the aspirations of mankind, when it is clear that conflict with weapons of death and destruction is no longer tenable or thinkable, then and only then can navies of electronic-capable ships, fitted with fantastic missiles and extraordinary guidance systems for them, be put aside. Then and only then can other means of settling clashes of national purpose be devised. Yet, this is the silent, deep hope of mankind, to which all of us subscribe—except those who would use our institutions of freedom as weapons against us.

Until then, with the intent and conviction that they may never—and prayerfully will never—have to be used again, America has no other choice than to keep her weapons ready. To do otherwise is to invite disaster in a world that, full of hope as well as despair, is still not sure of the direction in which it is about to move.

Appendix: Author's Notes

What follows is a loose compilation of miscellaneous information probably useful only to people deeply interested in the details of our naval history, or desiring to know more about the processes by which the author came by some of his conclusions. An extensive bibliography of primary and secondary sources follows, compiled with the assistance of William M. P. Dunne. This appendix is supplementary thereto, and intended only as a vehicle for comments on some of them. Most of the tracts Dunne and I have read have been both lengthy and dull, only occasionally relieved by the nugget of hitherto unknown information, the witty description, or the satisfaction of having squeezed just a little bit more out of an old account. We have had these rewards, spread out here and there over the years of our research; but the purpose of this section is to describe the most useful, pointed, or generally interesting reading. These, in short, are the books or articles it was fun to read, noted for those who enjoy reading naval history as much as I do.

Interspersed among such references I have strewn some criticisms where I felt them justified, and have waxed philosophical about the navy where I thought it appropriate. Were I a poet, like Kipling or (heaven forbid) William S. Sims, I might even have tried to do some of it in verse—for the sea and the sky and the gentle roll of your ship as the power speeds out astern bring forth the poet in most men whose life has been spent at sea. You may, however, count yourselves fortunate.

On the majority of the books referenced I feel no need to comment at all, since the information is clearly conveyed and self-explanatory. I have also deliberately eschewed footnotes as obstructive to the free flow of the navy story I am trying to tell. Those desiring to follow in greater depth any of the subjects or anecdotes alluded to in these pages will find ample field in the bibliography.

1: TREES, THE ESTABLISHMENT, AND OUR REVOLUTION

Virginia Steele Wood's thoroughly researched and very informative treatise on live oak timber, *Live Oaking*, provided much valuable insight not only into the source of the wonderful wood used for our early navy but also into the many problems encountered in getting it out of the Southern wilderness where it grew. She also went into ship construction techniques, supplying many careful drawings to illustrate how the pieces were used.

Another useful book was *Forests and Sea Power* by Robert Greenhalgh Albion. Dr. Albion gives a rather more complete exposition than Wood does of the role of English shipwrights in denigrating live oak in favor of their own native English oak. By the time of the American Revolution, nearly all the available English oak had been harvested already, even to the second and third generations of some trees. He also describes some of the shenanigans of the early American shipwrights.

Detailed plans of some of the Revolutionary War ships herein discussed have been found in the primary documents listed in the bibliography at the end of this book. Generally speaking, the few in America are located at the Peabody Museum of Salem, Massachusetts, the New-York Historical Society, and the National Maritime Museum, Greenwich, England. Most are in Greenwich, by virtue of the British practice of "taking off the lines" of captured ships, which was the fate of nearly all of them. Unfortunately, the plans of our most successful Continental frigate, *Alliance*, are kept from us by that very fact, for she was never captured. Richard Dale, in a merchant cruise to India, mentions having seen her in her merchant role, but little is known about her actual construction or subsequent career.

The most useful history of these early times is doubtless James Fenimore Cooper's 1839 *History of the Navy of the United States of America*, which I read and reread as a child, to the point where Dad's old volume (an 1847 edition) fell apart under my eager but unheeding fingers (now professionally rebound, it is again a thing of beauty). Cooper must be read with discrimination, however, for he was a captive of his sources in the navy, chief among them Isaac Chauncey, and is therefore subject to many of the old ideas and prejudices of the times about which he writes. His history is entirely operational (except for the chapters devoted to Chauncey) and he attempts no evaluation or balance. Indeed, some of the facts he recites are so denuded of analysis that one suspects they may have been reduced in impact to avoid possible challenge to a duel by anyone considering himself criticized (a hazard of authorship in those days).

William M. Fowler, Jr., in *Rebels Under Sail*, attempts an analytic type of history and by and large succeeds, but his book is seriously flawed by errors of simple and easily ascertainable fact, some so obvious as to suggest proofreading carelessness. The reader must beware of details found here that are not corroborated elsewhere.

Howard I. Chapelle, of the Smithsonian Institution and a naval architect by training, has made a significant contribution to our overall knowledge of the design of our early wooden ships. His *History of the American Sailing Navy*, originally published in 1949, has been reissued and is therefore still in print. Chapelle, a skilled draftsman, has given us many well-constructed drawings of our early warships. Unfortunately, however, some of his work contains errors that have been carried forward by historians and researchers dependent on his seminal product. Hopefully, corrections will be made in due course; in the meantime, until a better compendium is available, Chapelle is the most authoritative source of information on those now somewhat mysterious vessels, so vitally important to the early days of our country.

For much of the information about Nicholas Biddle of the *Randolph* and John Young of the *Saratoga*, as well as background about our privateers, I am indebted to William Bell Clark of the Louisiana State University, whose careful research has earned him preeminent rank among the historians of our early navy. It was not from him, however, that I received the hint about *Randolph*'s wet powder, but from the South Carolina Historical Society, located in Charleston, where original papers or first generation printed copies thereof relating to the early history of the state can be found. Such an accusation, about an event more than two hundred years in the past, would hold only passing interest today had it not had such a long-range effect on our early naval history.

A thorough account of Admiral de Grasse's expedition from the Caribbean to Chesapeake Bay can be found in relatively few sources—partly, perhaps, because the credit goes not to an American (except to Washington for conceiving of the idea) but to a Frenchman. Sadly for de Grasse, he soon afterward suffered a disastrous defeat by the British navy, which then claimed it had "avenged the inconclusive Battle of the Virginia Capes"—as if any battle that resulted in the surrender of a British army in the field and separation from England of the most valuable portion of the New World could be called "inconclusive." De Grasse's contribution of sea power at this critically important moment ought never to be forgotten by any student of our early history. Foremost among accounts influencing my rendition of the story is that of Dr. William J. Morgan of the Center for Naval History: *The Pivot upon Which Everything Turned: French Naval Superiority That Ensured Victory at Yorktown*. The title is a quotation from George Washington. Dr. Morgan's monograph was first published by the *Ironworker* magazine in spring 1958 and has been republished by the Naval History Foundation, from which it is still available. For the few biographical details I needed about the admiral, I have used *Admiral de Grasse and American Independence*, by Professor Charles Lee Lewis. The United States has named three naval ships *De Grasse*, the latest being a new and powerful *Spruance*-class destroyer.

And finally, no account of these early days of our history would be complete without credit to Commodore Dudley W. Knox, who, forced to retire from active duty by a physical disability, made the study of naval history his life and contributed more than any other man to its appreciation. *A History of the United States Navy* was sent to me at Annapolis by my father upon its publication in 1936. Unfortunately, Knox was sparse with his acknowledgments as to sources, though it is also true that in most cases he himself was the best source there could be. In addition, his book contains some passages that, in my view of modern readers' needs, could stand more life. There were places, too, where I thought he seemed to know more than he was willing to commit to the printed page (no thought of duels, here, but in any bureaucracy, especially one so closely knit as the navy, criticisms of peers or superiors is bound to bring unpleasant reaction). Nonetheless, I have now had Knox on my shelves for half a century, and his influence will be seen on every page of this book.

An Aside, for Model Buffs and Old Ship Aficionados

A word about that last ship of the Continental Navy. Despite disappointing results, the Continental Congress and its Marine Committee continued to build ships until 1778. *Alliance*, *Confederacy*, and *Bourbon* were the last ones ordered. *Bourbon* never served and has been lost to history. As with so many others, capture of *Confederacy* gives us her plans. Since the *Alliance* was built to satisfy identical specifications, it must be surmised (unavoidable differences of local design practices aside) that *Alliance* and *Confederacy* were probably much alike. *Alliance* was reputed, however, to be slightly shorter, with slightly greater draft, and not as beautifully finished as her sister ship. But she was fast on a wind, especially after John Paul Jones rerigged her at l'Orient, and it may be that some accident of form or layout contributed to her superiority in this important characteristic.

No one has ever found the building plans for *Alliance*, or anything that can give us an accurate idea of her design. However, from inspection of her British-drawn "lines," the *Confederacy* might be called an enlarged and improved *Hancock*, and *Alliance* was almost certainly one also. *Alliance*, in fact, was built in Salisbury, Massachusetts, not far from Newburyport, *Hancock*'s birthplace, and there were frequent meetings and discussions between the respective builders, Greenleaf of Newburyport and the Hacketts of Salisbury. One can also easily imagine the conferences (one must, for there are no records) where they undoubtedly debated the specifications of the new ships.

After her merchant service and final ignominy as a towed barge (a fate not unusual for strong ships past economical repair), the hulk of the old *Alliance* is supposed to have lain half buried somewhere along the muddy banks of the Delaware River, where according to one account the remains of her timbers could be seen as recently as 1909. Even at that late date a determined effort could have taken some of her measurements and reconstructed others. Live oak actually grows stronger in mud and water (timbers submerged more than one hundred years in a bog near Portsmouth, New Hampshire, were found and used finally for their original purpose in the early part of this century: rebuilding *Constitution*'s age-ravaged hull). *Alliance*, could she be found, might even be worth the extravagant excavation her resurrection would undoubtedly entail. With *Vasa* of 1638 raised and on exhibit in Stockholm, and the even older *Mary Rose* of 1545 now rescued from her grave in The Solent, it is evident that the equipment and techniques required are available today, and possibly even the necessary interest. Not so in 1909, and our history is the worse for it. It would be significant indeed if *Alliance* turned out to be the progenitor of the six fine frigates Congress authorized in 1794—for then *Hancock* would be, too; and we would know more clearly the process by which the ships we designed for our reconstituted navy of 1794 took their very special shape.

We should at this point, however, take note of a divergent view. One of the frustrations of John Paul Jones's career was his failure to get command of the *Indien*—or *L'Indien* as her name was written in French. Built in Amsterdam to the order of the American comissioners headed by Benjamin Franklin, she was a very powerful ship, with a battery of heavy Swedish guns, long 36-pounders, on her gundeck. But the British knew of her, and that Franklin wanted her for Jones. (What he might have done with her as the *Bonhomme Richard*, instead of the barely seaworthy *Duc de Duras* he did get!) The British were able to prevent Holland from passing *Indien* over to Franklin, and finally she fell into the hands of the French, who gave her to the South Carolina navy. As the *South Carolina* she made two cruises and captured a few merchantmen, then was inactive at Philadelphia for six months before finally getting under way and sailing right into the hands of an alerted British squadron. While she was in Philadelphia she must have been noticed by Joshua Humphreys, and historian Samuel E. Morison speculates that "in design she was the parent of U.S.S. *Constitution* and *Constellation*." This, of course, is perfectly possible; and it is equally possible that Humphreys merely fit her into the pantheon of ships that influenced his designs for the 1794 program.

2: THE YANKEE RACE HORSE, TRUXTUN, AND FINALLY PREBLE

One of the very useful books for this chapter was Eugene S. Ferguson's *Truxtun of the "Constellation."* Ferguson goes deeply into the motivations behind Truxtun's somewhat illogical actions in twice resigning from the navy, and I may be a bit beyond him in suggesting his final resignation could have been merely a poor choice of words.

The *Constellation* is still afloat, moored near her place of birth at Baltimore. Late in life she became the subject of controversy, in that (so it is said) when "administratively rebuilt" in Norfolk in 1853–1855, the term "rebuild" was a subterfuge to circumvent Congressional prohibition against expenditures for new construction. In fact, this story goes, the old ship was done away with and an entirely new one built. This is the position supported by Howard Chapelle, who goes on to argue that whether or not portions of the wood of the old ship were in fact used in the new one has no bearing, inasmuch as the 24-gun spar-decked corvette turned out in 1855 has no similarity to the 38-gun frigate Truxtun commanded.

Like all arguments, this one has another side. It is true that the ship at Baltimore is larger than the 44-gun *Constitution*, now similarly preserved at Boston, and she has the later design round stern instead of the square one with which she was originally built. Demonstrably, however, her original live oak frames and keel, the most important structural elements of a wooden ship—are still in her hull. The *Constitution* and Nelson's flagship *Victory* in Portsmouth, England, have both also been thoroughly rebuilt, and as this is written *Victory* is undergoing another massive restoration to return her as nearly as possible to her exact configuration at the time of Trafalgar. Understandably, this has taken considerable research, since the ship was already forty years old, underwent much repair after that battle, and served many years longer as well. The propensity of navies to improve their aging ships is well known and indeed a practical necessity; but it runs counter to the needs of historical preservationists, who would return things to their appearance at the time of greatest interest.

Although new research indicates certain changes may be appropriate, of the three ships, *Constitution* is today perhaps nearest to the configuration of her greatest moment, the War of 1812. When the British have finished with the *Victory*, however, she will be as close as historians can make her to the ship Nelson knew in 1805. As for *Constellation*, the 1853–1855 rebuilding involved lengthening her keel some 13 feet, adding new frames in the gap thus created, greatly strengthening her decks to carry the much heavier cannon coming into vogue at that time, replacing the flat stern with the more efficient round stern, and doing away with her spar deck battery. These changes increased her measured tonnage by about a quarter. She is not supported by the U.S. government, as is the *Constitution* (and the *Victory* by England), but even if she were it is questionable whether a useful purpose would be served by total restoration to the time of Truxtun. The fact is the ship was active in our navy from 1797 until about 1915. Thereafter, she served as a receiving ship for many years at the Naval Station at Newport, Rhode Island, and during World War II she was designated as a relief flagship and communication center. More than two-thirds of her total life span, now approaching two hundred years, has been in the present configuration.

The patriotic citizens' group now in charge of *Constellation* is endeavoring to restore her spar deck to its appearance in 1800, and has modified the bow and stern to more nearly approximate those Truxtun knew. But there are no plans to dismantle her to remove the spliced-in section of her keel or the additional frames. We shall have to be content to see her towering masts and massive spars against the Baltimore skyline and know that here, in her final harbor, lies as authentic a piece of American naval history as exists anywhere.

Regarding the ships she fought in 1799 and 1800: *L'Insurgente*, her first capture, was 15 feet shorter on the gundeck and 3 feet narrower, and was measured at 925 tons (not displacement, but a complicated formula combining length, breadth, and depth of hold that each navy made up for its own comparative purposes). By the same formula, *Constellation* was calculated at 1,266 tons, or one-third larger. The comparative broadside weights were 396 pounds to 282, 114 pounds difference in favor of the American frigate.

La Vengeance, the one that got away, was 1,182 tons by British measurement after capture by that navy. By a very rough extrapolation, this figure would be about 1,175 on the same scale as *Constellation*'s 1,266, which would make her 91 measurement tons smaller than her American adversary. Her weight of broadside, however, comes to an impressive 583 pounds against *Constellation*'s then revised broadside of 372, or 211 pounds in favor of *La Vengeance*. Of all the sea fights of our early history, those between *Constellation* and *La Vengeance* in 1800 and *Chesapeake* and *Shannon* in

1813 were the only ones between antagonists nominally equal in force. *Vengeance*, fractionally smaller than our frigate, had considerably heavier weight of metal in her broadside but was poorly fought by comparison with the tiger she encountered. In case of the *Chesapeake*, fractionally bigger than *Shannon* but nearly equal in weight of broadside, the *Shannon* was the tiger.

The best biography of Edward Preble is by Christopher McKee. Much has been written about Preble, but until McKee, little authoritative research on his life had been done. Almost surely he suffered from abdominal cancer, which was in remission during his service in the Barbary Wars. Thereafter, despite tremendous effort of will, he was gradually driven to the sickbed from which he could not recover. He died in 1807, aged only forty-six, not long after hearing with violent indignation of the *Leopard*'s attack upon the unprepared *Chesapeake*.

Preble's Boys, by Fletcher Pratt, a popular historian but excellent, too, for all that being popular rendered him somewhat unacceptable to the fraternity of historians, is an inspiring account of Preble's influence on the young officers under his command before Tripoli and Algiers. It does what history ought to do: explain and incite emulation, instead of merely recite actions and statistics. Occasionally guilty of overblown language, Pratt tells an excellent story and draws the right inferences.

A surprising thing about this period in our history is that despite the acrimony and bitter feelings there was actually a basis for professional respect and even friendship between officers of the rival British and United States navies. As noted, during the quasi-war with France the American navy depended on use of British bases overseas. Among the senior officers, mutual professional interests wove a bond of friendship, producing the reputed wager of a hat on the outcome of a contest at arms. There are records of American and British ships sailing in company on coordinated operations against pirates or slavers. Both naval services held merchantmen, even their own, in a sort of benevolent disdain. But among American merchant ships, some of which had tiny hiding places built into their structure for concealment of a part of their crews, the British navy was hated and feared.

3: THE BEGINNING OF THE WAR OF 1812

Because this war was so important to the development of our navy, I felt it necessary to treat it in three chapters, and the references for all three are of course the same. By all odds, the best account of this period of our navy's history is to be found in Leonard Guttridge and Jay Smith's magnificent volume, *The Commodores*, published in 1969, and very properly a choice for the Naval Institute's Naval Classics series. It is easy to see where Guttridge and Smith got their inspiration for the major thread running through their book, for I, too, have read with fascination the record of James Barron's court-martial and totally agree with their appreciation of its significance. Much lies between the lines in that record, but most significant, as the authors show, is that the lack of confidence most naval officers of the time had in Barron really existed long before the terrible affair with the *Leopard*. Barron was probably a good seaman and a fair subordinate officer, but he was not the sort of man who should be assigned important duties of trust and responsibility. The officers of the *Chesapeake* felt this instinctively. Once the terrible insult happened, all the cards were stacked against him. He was the obvious man to blame, and by doing so the navy could clear itself of deserved criticism for customarily sending ships out in *Chesapeake*'s condition. Barron, on the other hand, had not an inkling of the psychological emotions that were impelling the course of events.

John Rodgers is another case in point. Through the accident of being first lieutenant for Truxtun in the action with *L'Insurgente*, in which he had distinguished himself, he had been advanced to captain, first of the lieutenants so to be promoted. Senioritywise, this put him far ahead of his contemporaries (he was, for example, much senior to Preble in the Mediterranean, although also much younger). Being at the top of the naval heap intensified his naturally overbearing personality. Saturnine, aloof, strong in mind and body but cold and calculating, he was a man to beware of in all dealings. Yet he had two great deficiencies. First, for all his strength of personality, he had no fighting spirit. He may not have been a coward, but he was certainly a man of great circumspection. By his own logs, he had at least as many opportunities to bring *President* into combat—and on similar terms—as were successfully seized by Hull, Decatur, and Bainbridge. Yet he avoided them all, and by the force of his commanding presence overawed all incipient criticism. His second deficiency was an inadequate understanding of the principles of war at sea, as he showed by his insistence on coordinated operations when individual cruises were bringing the results the country needed.

The recognized authority on Rodgers is Charles Oscar Paullin, whose biography of him was originally published in 1910, and has since been republished by the Naval Institute. Although Paullin has difficulty explaining some of Rodgers's slow-moving failures, the reader will generally find Paullin more sympathetic to Rodgers than I. Today, Rodgers would be called a very complex character, but I believe that had he held high rank in the Pacific during World War II, Nimitz would have had to replace him with someone with a more active and aggressive view of his responsibilities. And had he been the senior officer on active duty in 1941, as he was in 1812, Roosevelt would have been well advised to do the same.

Among the writings that explain much about the age of fighting sail are those of C. S. Forester, creator of Horatio Hornblower. He was a master at the art of telling history in the guise of a novel, and correspondingly had no difficulty shifting into direct history. *The Age of Fighting Sail* comes closer to telling the dramatic, deeply romantic story of the history of that time than any other book I know. But it is in his novels about Hornblower that he tells best how the men of those days coped with the sea on the one hand, a difficult ship to handle on another, and the most cumbersome weapons the mind of man could devise on yet a third. For good history in novel form, read Forester.

Finally, I may be criticized for the inordinate amount of space given to the *Chesapeake*, but the response is that everyone knows how the other five of these first ships of the "new navy" of 1794 were built, and the genesis of their plans. But the unfortunate *Chesapeake* deserves more explanation than she has ever received. Why was she always unlucky? The answer, I think, goes all the way back to her beginning.

Born under the sign of bad luck, nothing went right for her; not her initial building, when her best timbers were picked over for another ship; not her launching, during which she stuck twice on the ways and had to be pried free with huge jacks; not her sailing qualities, always described as poor. Ships are more susceptible to such derogatory labels than any other of man's inanimate structures, no doubt partly because sailors feel the necessity to endow them with human characteristics. Thus, everything they do or that happens to them is somehow ascribed to the living spirits with which they are invested. To explain all this might take a new field of study, The Parapsychology of Material Things, and a thoughtful dissertation.

Chesapeake's reported dull sailing was no doubt in comparison to the fine turn of speed shown by her mates of the 1794 program (of whom the *President* was the fastest of all), for she was not a bad sailer and was even once stated to sail well. Fox, who apparently had a free hand in designing and building the ship, had been trained in England and had a propensity for the more compact British form of shorter, beamier vessels. The frigate he turned out in 1800 was the only one of the original six not built to the Humphreys design—easily noticed because *Chesapeake* had a length-to-beam ratio substantially less than the other five and had to carry more sail to keep up with them. Though a handsome ship, roomy in her flag and officers' quarters, she was the smallest of the six, the runt of the litter, always the last choice for everything, and especially the last choice of the proud skippers of the time.

For a very biased account of her battle with *Shannon* from the British side, showing that America had no monopoly on insensitive chauvinism, read *Guns off Cape Ann* by Kenneth Poolman. For a more balanced version, the *American Heritage Magazine* issues of April 1956 and December 1968 are recommended.

4: VICTORIES ON THE HIGH SEAS

Our histories have been full of the glorious victories of our frigates during the War of 1812, and rightly so. It was through them that we created our first naval traditions of excellence. However, other tides were running as well, and it has been my purpose to give them some notice so that the full story of what took place and the public reaction to it can have immediacy for the reader. Bare recital of events does not tell a story. Causes and results do, and sometimes speculation on what might have been.

The news of the *Chesapeake*'s overwhelming defeat and capture, coming on the heels of an unbroken series of five victories by our other ships, was a devastating surprise to a navy and a country that had begun to think of itself as somehow magically invincible at sea. From this point of view, it was a good thing. Apologists sprang up to explain it away as due to a mutinous crew, cowardice among some of them—a bugler who could not be found at a critical moment or a very junior officer, barely twenty years old, who failed to take command when everyone of higher rank had been put out of action—but the facts do not support this easy analysis. On the contrary, the entire sequence of events takes on the subtle nuances of a Götterdämmerung, for which we struggle to find answers in human scale. Lawrence fills the part of the central character: he whom the gods would destroy they first make mad.

In the sense of preparedness, the *Chesapeake* did more for the United States Navy than any other ship of her time: twice, she demonstrated to the highest degree the cost of unreadiness—once made to look woefully inept when caught by surprise, later in the finer point of preparing for battle in a routine way instead of a special way. After 1807, no United States man-of-war ever again sailed for a foreign station with capabilities impaired through extra cargo. Six years later, her defeat by the *Shannon*, England's top frigate, showed that preparedness is not only routine readiness but, as in athletic teams, a high condition of being up for a contest. While he commanded the ship, Decatur had the right combination, and one can even regret that the fantasy of an unofficial reprise of the uneven contest with *Leopard* could not take place. The unlucky *Chesapeake*, at the very least, would forevermore have had a new character.

5: THE WAR ON THE LAKES AND FINALE ON THE SEAS

In Washington, D.C., a huge painting depicting the moment in the Battle of Lake Erie when Perry transferred his flag to the *Niagara* can be seen hanging in the principal stairway of the U.S. Senate. It has been many times reproduced, but viewers should be warned that except for a close-up portrayal of the port quarter of the *Lawrence*, the ships shown resemble real seagoing ships instead of the small shallow-draft craft that actually fought the epochal battle. For example, *Niagara*, though correctly shown in the middle distance with two masts and the right number of gunports, sports a hull worthy of Old Ironsides! Extensively restored, the old ship survives in Erie, Pennsylvania, mounted on concrete blocks not far from where Adam and Noah Brown built her, and the difference can easily be seen.

Almost exactly a year later, in 1814, the ships that fought on Lake Champlain were far more evenly matched than contemporary American accounts would lead one to believe. The *Confiance*, the British flagship, was rated as a frigate of 36 guns and indeed carried a few of her smaller guns on forecastle and poop, a deck above the main gundeck. Her opposite number, the American *Saratoga*, was rated as a 26-gun sloop of war because she had no elevated forecastle or poop, therefore had all her guns on the gundeck. Frigates were usually more powerful than sloops, and thus the British fleet sounds nominally superior. In fact, *Confiance* measured 147 feet in length on the gundeck, 37 feet beam, and had an extraordinarily small depth of hold: 7 feet, according to Howard Chapelle, while *Saratoga* was 143 feet by 36½, with 12½ feet depth in hold. The flagships were thus nearly exactly comparable in size. Similar comparisons could be drawn for the other ships engaged, although the British seem to have had more and better guns while the Americans were probably the better sailers with their deeper-draft hulls—but the battle was fought at anchor.

Finally, to emphasize a point already made, Congress and the administration placed the greatest importance on securing our northern border and went to any length necessary to make it safe (although some of the dispositions of troops ordered from Washington can be greatly faulted from the distance of a century and a half). The greatest naval force assembled under our flag up to that time was on Lake Ontario.

Both fleet actions that our navy fought in the War of 1812 were on the lakes (and Chauncey had some fleet skirmishes). Our greatest anxiety over a possible military reversal was directed there.

All history books describe the Battle of Lake Champlain, though most of them speak only of the battle and give little time to the important consequences. In the December 1963 issue of *American Heritage Magazine*, C. S. Forester takes the opposite tack: the battle is outlined briefly, but its effect upon the peace commissioners sitting in Ghent is dramatically described.

6: THE SLOW ADVENT OF STEAM

Four times during the first forty years of its existence the navy of the American states faced the question of continuance or extinction. Three times the decision was adverse (abolition in 1785, the great reduction of 1801, and the gunboat mania of 1806); but at the end of the War of 1812 the national decision was overwhelmingly in favor of a permanent and professional navy capable of carrying out the nation's will at sea—and just at this time, the Industrial Revolution entered its most influential phase.

An entire series of sources provided the background for the short summary of technological experiments given in this chapter, none exclusively. William Conant Church, publisher of the *Army and Navy Journal* for many years and later author of the definitive biography of John Ericsson, supplied many of the anecdotes cited. Others were culled from periodicals of the period, generally in extremely short notations or references. Most useful have been the hundred years of the United States Naval Institute and its magazine, the *Proceedings*, and the beautifully done volumes of the *American Heritage Magazine*. Both are profusely indexed. Any item of special individual interest can be studied to much greater depth in almost any technical library.

7: MUTINY?

I grew up implicitly accepting the judgment of my personal source of naval information that our navy had once had a mutiny but the guilty ones had been caught and punished just in time. Looking back on it now, I think even then I sensed some kernel of doubt in my father's mind, but I paid scant attention to this bit of ESP. When I became a midshipman, however, the first doubts began to assail me. It was, of course, clear that no mutiny had actually occurred, though the common wisdom was that it was about to. Later on, as I read about the many courts-martial held in the early days— Esek Hopkins, the first commander-in-chief; Pierre Landais, when he was cashiered from command of the *Alliance*; James Barron of the *Chesapeake*; David Porter, in 1825, for the overreaction to what he considered an insult to the U.S. flag—I was impressed with how meticulously careful all the courts were in their detailed procedures; but aboard the *Somers* there had been no evidence of any such concern for the rules. Little by little, my doubts grew, and then a book titled *The Captain Called It Mutiny*, by Frederic F. Van de Water, crossed my path.

Van de Water was an accomplished writer, author of many books, but this one was something special, for his great-uncle was one of the young sailors also manacled, though not executed, by Mackenzie. A 20-year-old apprentice seaman, George Warner completed the last two and a half weeks of the *Somers*'s cruise in irons on the little brig's quarterdeck, the final week exposed to gradually worsening mid-December weather as she plowed northward to New York. Thereafter held in a cell for four months in the Brooklyn Navy Yard in anticipation of trial for mutiny, he was finally, like all the other surviving "mutineers," simply released and allowed to leave the naval service as though he had never been in it. No charges were ever placed against any of them, and none was sophisticated enough to sue for false arrest or even to wonder what had become of their sworn obligation to serve in the navy for the term of an enlistment. But young George Warner had done one thing that now, many years later, has helped to put a different light on the entire episode. He passed the time of his incarceration by writing a private account of his ordeal, and this first-person report passed down into the hands of his grand-nephew, Van de Water.

The story of the mutiny on the *Somers* has been mentioned countless times in the published histories of our navy; but since most histories are devoted to wars, campaigns, and battles, the incident understandably was treated only briefly, generally followed by the comment that though it was a sad affair, the sentences were deserved—and anyway, good resulted through founding of the Naval Academy at Annapolis. With the notable exception of Professor E. B. Potter's excellent tome, *The United States and World Sea Power* (he served as editor), every version I have read took Commander Mackenzie's story at face value, and uncritically accepted the verdicts of the two courts held on Mackenzie as official exoneration, without considering the underlying pressures that might have lain upon the membership thereof and the naval establishment as a whole, or even recognizing the equivocal character of the simple acquittal. Potter simply says, "The evidence suggests to a thoughtful reader that Spencer was mentally unbalanced and that Mackenzie was not much more stable himself [so that he] managed to convince himself, on the basis of some curious evidence, that [hanging the three men] was necessary."

I do not say Philip Spencer was an attractive youth—only that he and two other members of the naval service were hanged illegally, that the evidence condemning the three was ridiculously inadequate, and that Alexander Mackenzie behaved in the most irresponsible fashion. At the time, however, except for the relatives of the slain men and two notable editorialists, hardly anyone bothered to question the decisions of the courts on Mackenzie. The three men killed were unimportant; public interest had moved onward. But it is clear that the navy of 1843 was in uneasy agreement with Potter's later analysis, at the same time as it found itself forced to support the legal whitewash applied to the case.

Not long after the events recounted in this chapter, Daniel Webster resigned as secretary of state, and Navy Secretary Abel P. Upshur was elevated to that post. Within a year, Upshur was lying dead on the deck of the *Princeton*.

8: THE GUN AND THE SHIP

The *Princeton* catastrophe was a sensation of its time. Beginning with the first highly colored news reports, it has been written up extensively, nearly always in an emotional way. The practice of printing verbatim the excited and emotional accounts of witnesses added verisimilitude to the facts, but tended to obscure them as well. To this must also be added the great sensitivity of the situation: not only the high rank of the dead, but the President of the United States involved in a direct way; a high-ranking, aristocratic, authoritarian naval officer, uneasily aware that his own dereliction was a principal cause of the tragedy; a navy not sure that its own systems and procedures were not seriously wanting.

Not for some years did the public and the press begin to feel that determined investigation might have turned up other areas where prejudice to the public good was routinely done in the name of the personal honor of naval officers, or their sometimes excessive ambitions. It was more and more clear that ineffective performance by nearly everyone charged with responsibility had contributed to the catastrophe of the *Princeton*. There came a growing awareness that there had been a massive cover-up, that the duly constituted investigative bodies had rigorously pursued what they had been directed to pursue and not one iota more.

The facts are clear but deeply obscured, far more deeply than usual. Nearly everyone involved endeavored to avoid taking a position on the merits of the various elements of the incident. The code duello was still in force. Anyone who felt even the slightest twinge of guilt ran for cover. The only safe attitude was to concentrate on the emotion and the tragedy.

The most thoroughly researched account is that by Lee M. Pearson, historian for the Bureau of Naval Weapons, found in *Technology and Culture*, a quarterly journal. He cites all the pertinent primary sources for a careful recital of the events and avoids taking sides on any of the issues involved. This, as the reader already has seen, has not been my approach, but I found Mr. Pearson's research invaluable.

The Franklin Institute report of its investigation of the fragment of Peacemaker's breech is contained in its *Journal* for 1844.

President Tyler's description of Mrs. Gilmer's premonition is given in a letter quoted in the U.S. Naval Institute *Proceedings*, in an article titled "The *Princeton* Explosion," by Commander A. H. Miles. This is, however, one of the emotional accounts.

The *Iron Worker* for Spring 1957 (Vol. XXI, No. 2), house organ of the Lynchburg (Virginia) Foundry, contains a rewritten version of Commander (by then Captain) Miles's article. It embodies several intriguing sketches and photographs, by far the most interesting (to this former submarine engineer-officer) being a transverse section of the *Princeton* taken from a drawing by Ericsson showing his "semicircular piston engine" fitting neatly into the bottom of the ship. The nearest modern counterpart for this extraordinary engine is the familiar vacuum-powered windshield wipers with which automobiles were fitted during the 1930–1950 era. Maintenance of an adequate seal in the semicircular pistons as they swept to and fro must have been one of their foremost difficulties.

The American Neptune for July 1946 contains an informative article by Thomas Hornsby, titled "Oregon and Peacemaker." Pearson's article, mentioned above, covers the same ground with more detail and maintains a somewhat more objective outlook.

9: IRON SHIPS AND SHELL GUNS

For a much fuller appreciation of the matters alluded to in this chapter, the reader is referred to Bernard Brodie, *Sea Power in the Machine Age*. This is a scholarly and thoroughly researched study of exactly what its apt title describes. A thoughtful comment on the debate between guns and armor is his observation that at 1,000 yards range in 1812 our *Constitution* essentially was invulnerable to enemy ships of comparable class, and that the new ships and guns of 1860, at the same range, likewise could not hurt each other much. But if one of the new armored ships with heavy guns came up against an unarmored one with identical or even stronger gun power, the new ship would close the range with impunity, to where she could indeed sink the other. Only if the older ship could keep the range open could she hope to survive. Brodie makes a very strong point of the sweeping winds of change during the last half of the nineteenth century and the beginning of the twentieth.

A second source of much fruitful contemplation is Oscar Parkes's monumental *British Battleships*, covering the period from 1860 to 1950. Not only are the various ships' types fully described—their genesis, the arguments pro and con—their histories and final fates are likewise outlined, albeit briefly. Of particular interest is the description of the considerations attending birth of the *Warrior* and the similar ships that came after. Perusal of this book emphasizes Brodie's comment about the acceleration of change in the past hundred years as compared with the more static condition of all centuries before.

10: THE RACE BETWEEN THE IRONCLADS

The world has generally treated the arrival of the *Monitor* in the nick of time at Hampton Roads as one of the great coincidences of history. It was that, of course, but it was not an accidental coincidence. Both sides knew well what the other was doing and both strove mightily to win the race. A dead heat would be a better description.

There was, however, a coincidence of another sort. Had the *Merrimack/Virginia* had only one more day against only ships of wood, the Union Fleet blockading Norfolk at Hampton Roads would have been destroyed or driven off in disarray. The cause of the Confederacy would have been immeasurably helped, and the history of the Civil War might have been different. On the other hand, had the *Monitor* arrived one day sooner, Secretary Welles's order to send her up the Potomac to protect Washington— away from the scene of battle—would probably have been obeyed, and she would not have been present on the crucial second day.

In either case, the *Merrimack* would have had a clear field in Hampton Roads, and only the factor of pure chance caused the *Monitor* to arrive at precisely the window in history that was waiting for her. The battle was a dramatic thing, but so was the struggle to get the two ships ready. And by the evening of 7 March, both sides must have been well acquainted with whatever in those years passed for the equivalent of the modern Murphy's Law.

The letters and telegrams quoted in this chapter are only a few of the many to be found in the *Official Records of the Union and Confederate Navies*, published by the Government Printing Office. I decided to let these documents speak for themselves in telling the tense story of the *Monitor*—not usually a desirable device, but in this case I felt it was an effective one.

For a thorough exposition of the Confederate side of both the Hampton Roads and Mobile Bay battles, the *History of the Confederate States Navy*, by J. Thomas Scharf, is recommended. The work is not without strong bias, but Scharf can give a whole new dimension to the outlook and descriptions of operations. Scharf was a Confederate naval officer. What he wrote came from firsthand knowledge, or nearly so, but being largely written from memory (his own or those of others), it may not be absolutely reliable as to objective facts or their interpretation. It is, however, an extremely valuable source of opinion and reaction, and it stands nearly alone on the side of the South.

In the same vein is William H. Parker's *Recollections of a Naval Officer*. Like Scharf a Confederate naval officer, but also previously of the Union Navy, Parker was a more skilled writer, with a lively and engaging style that brings wit and humor to his narrative. His *Recollections* do not, however, pretend to give us the history of the Confederate States Navy; they tell us what Parker saw and felt. He finished the war in charge of the Confederate Naval Academy, and one of his anecdotes of interest concerns the Confederate treasury, which the Confederate midshipmen transported and guarded under his immediate command until they could turn it over to Jefferson Davis.

11: BATTLES BETWEEN IRONCLAD SHIPS; WAR IN THE INLAND WATERS AND AT SEA

In 1957 Henry Steele Commager wrote the introduction for a little book by William C. and Ruth White titled *Tin Can on a Shingle*. With pardonable flair, he begins:

> March 9, 1862, was surely the most dramatic day of the American Civil War, and perhaps the most important as well. It was dramatic because it combined, in a unique degree, coincidence, chance, heroism, and beauty; it was important because, after one momentary glimpse of triumph it dropped the curtain on Confederate victory, and then lifted it to reveal not so much victory as a new chapter in the history of warfare.

Two pages later, he says:

> We need not beguile ourselves with speculations about what might have happened (had the *Monitor* not arrived just when it did); it is enough to note what did happen. Other battles of the Civil War—Vicksburg, Gettysburg,

the Wilderness—might have been more consequential for the outcome of that war, but none had such far reaching consequences for warfare in general. It is hackneyed but still valid to say that the Battle in Hampton Roads revolutionized naval warfare. Granted that the ironclad was already on the way, that Napoleon III boasted *La Gloire* and Queen Victoria *The Warrior*, and that the United States Navy was already brooding over the potentialities of ironclads, yet it was this battle that dramatized the whole thing and that enormously hastened new navies and new naval races everywhere.

William Chapman White died before his book was complete; his talented wife, Ruth, finished it for him and saw it through publication. It is a thin book, only 176 pages including bibliography and index, and it has a particular interest for me in that I had been writing a manuscript on the same subject during the same period and was forced to lay it aside because of greater demands on my spare time by the naval profession. Mr. and Mrs. White impressed me with their product because they saw the same things in that battle that I did, and that Mr. Commager did.

But of course we were not unique in that; as Commager points out, virtually the entire maritime world was waiting for the first battle between ships of the Industrial Revolution, with steam power and armored iron hulls. As it happened, the two-day Battle of Hampton Roads contained all the ingredients needed to give it significance far beyond the single ship combat it was in fact. Like the *Constitution-Guerriere* and *Chesapeake-Shannon* fights, it overturned the common perception. By the events of the first day it demonstrated beyond all cavil that, despite their history and romance, handsome wooden sailing ships were simply not in the same league with ugly iron ships of steam, and no amount of nostalgic rhetoric could alter that fact. All arguments were precipitately hushed; the proof was incontrovertible, and the very concept of how wars would be fought at sea was revised. It was, of course, high time this was so.

Similar historical watersheds have occurred since: at Pearl Harbor, nearly eighty years later, where those still favoring the battle line of armored behemoths saw them helpless against the lethal wasps sent by aircraft carriers out of sight and out of reach. The pattern continues to repeat: nearly a century after the Battle of Hampton Roads, nuclear-powered submarines began to do wondrous things, confounding our antisubmarine forces in exercises, making a playground of the Arctic, circumnavigating the world. The nature of warfare at sea changed as a result—and it will change again under the impetus of the explosion of electronic capabilities that is happening at this very moment.

Many aspects of modern culture had their beginnings in our Civil War, not least of them being the transmission and reportage of news immediately after it happened. *Harper's Weekly* and *Frank Leslie's Illustrated Newspaper* for the period are collector's items now because of the tremendous number of illustrations, most of them done by the steel engraving process and many of them veritable works of art. The text of the articles accompanying the pictures is of excellent quality, though subject to reporting errors and partisan pressures. There have been articles and books written about this war ever since it happened, and they are still being produced. So far as this conflict is concerned, the historian's only difficulty—but it is a mammoth one—is to select and discard from the mountain of material.

12: THE POST–CIVIL WAR DOLDRUMS AND THE BEGINNING OF IDEALISM

This chapter attempts to relate the combined effect of the Civil War and its devastation of spirit, as well as of material things, to the sweeping aura of change ushered in by the Industrial Revolution that had been going on for a century. Add to this the call of the empty lands to the west and the absence of rivals on our own continent, and we can get some inkling why the United States, once it had been reunited, felt no call to stay on top of military and defense issues. Speaking only of the navy, there were nevertheless some efforts made, the first of note being by Benjamin Franklin Isherwood, as related. It was not for nothing that the Naval Academy for many years taught marine engineering (which the midshipmen called simply "Steam") in a building known as Isherwood Hall. Finally shot down in flames by the navy's bureaucracy, Isherwood lived to see his ideas accepted and his thorough research even bragged about by the very navy that had denied him either understanding or recognition while he was leading it into new technology. His biographer, Edward William Sloan, provides chapter and verse of his conflicts, his experiments, his defeat, and his final vindication many years after he had retired from naval service. Later day comparison with Admiral Rickover is inevitable—but Rickover outmaneuvered the navy at every turn.

The stories of Luce and Mahan had happier endings. Stephen B. Luce, intellectual, highly thought of, devoted his later life to establishing the Naval War College at Newport. Mahan was his protégé, in that it was Luce who persuaded Mahan to give up the life at sea, come to Newport, and try to express in lectures and writing the deep-set feelings about sea power that naval officers have felt stirring within them since the Spanish Armada.

Fiske wrote an autobiography, in the latter pages of which he shows his deep disappointment at the outcome (as he saw it) of his reform efforts. Sims left us a tremendous amount of written works, and Elting E. Morison has provided a fine biography, written with the help and cooperation of the Sims family and many of his "band of brothers." A simple perusal of the index to the Naval Institute *Proceedings*, now just one hundred years old, will show the tremendous number of writings both men contributed to it. It was their principal instrument for communicating ideas to the naval service at large.

13: THE SPANISH-AMERICAN WAR

Little can be written about our naval war with Spain that has not already been said or printed. The question of how the *Maine* was sunk was never settled to anyone's satisfaction, except those who wanted a war. Admiral Rickover, who cannot be accused of lack of thoroughness, applied his naval engineer's mind to the question in 1975. Like many, he had never been reconciled to the facile explanation that there must have been an external mine, nor the even less supportable idea that the Spanish must have planted it. A careful reading of his *How the Battleship "Maine" Was Destroyed* can lead only to the conclusion that at last we have a definitive answer that neither the Spanish nor the Cuban insurgents were responsible. It was a pure accident, not the result of a nefarious plot, similar to other accidents that had already taken place aboard the new steel warships of seafaring nations.

Beginning with wooden steamship days, design practice had been to locate the coal bunkers around engines, boilers, and magazines for additional protection. These were the vulnerable parts; the coal could add to the armor normally placed around them. But with the additional protection came another hazard, only imperfectly understood by the early designers: spontaneous combustion. Fires in coal bunkers were not unknown; temperature sensing devices were among the safety features installed in all of them, as were systems for circulating cooled air through them. But not everything worked perfectly all the time. Late in 1897, Assistant Secretary of the Navy Theodore Roosevelt recommended institution of better measures for prevention of spontaneous combustion—particularly in ships, like the *Maine*, that had coal in bunkers directly adjacent to their magazines. It is now clear that by far the most likely cause of the disaster to the *Maine* was undetected spontaneous combustion in the coal bunker alongside the forward magazine. Smoldering in the limited oxygen in the sealed bunker, the fire could have heated the steel bulkhead separating it from the explosives to the point where one of the ammunition charges on the other side ignited, flashed into a flame of intense heat, detonated the entire forward magazine, and destroyed the ship.

The *Oregon*, carried on the navy list as battleship number 3, had been built on the west coast, and rumors about her extraordinary performance were rife before her commissioning. Even before the Spanish-American War, in knowledgeable quarters she was already the most famous ship in our navy, and her performance in that conflict justified all the praise and confidence lavished on her. Not for years was her high-speed run from San Francisco Bay through the Straits of Magellan to the coast of Florida duplicated. During the battle off Santiago de Cuba, she outsped all the other ships present. For an excellent account of her construction and early tests, see Rear Admiral George van Deurs's article *"Oregon's Builders Trials"* in *Shipmate* (the U.S. Naval Academy alumni magazine) for July–August 1976. Commander John D. Alden, one of our navy's inveterate lovers of fine old ships, contributed *"Whatever Happened to the Battleship Oregon?"* to the Naval Institute *Proceedings* for September 1968. Ralph E. Shaffer described *"The Race of the Oregon"*—in the Oregon Historical Quarterly for September 1975. Captain Charles E. Clark's own description of *Oregon's* service is contained in his autobiography, *My Fifty Years in the Navy*, republished by the Naval Institute Press as one of its Classics of Naval Literature series.

In addition to the *Oregon* article, Commander Alden has published a fine picture book of the old ships of the Spanish War period, titled *The American Steel Navy*, which gives an excellent verbal and photographic portrait of what the ships and their crews that fought in that war were like. Robley D. ("Fighting Bob") Evans gave us his autobiography, *A Sailor's Log*, and Commander Nathan Sargent contributed the definitive account of the Manila Bay actions in *Admiral Dewey and the Manila Campaign*. In *The Splendid Little War*, Frank Freidel presents in words and pictures more of the army action than the navy combat, but does touch lightly on the simmering conflict between Sampson and Schley. It remained for a retired army officer, A. C. M. Azoy in *Signal 250!*, to try to put all that together.

The report of the court of inquiry presided over by Admiral Dewey was voluminous and virtually incomprehensible to anyone not deeply involved. Hardly anyone has read its 2,300 pages of turgid repetition in their entirety. Everything in it must be viewed with appreciation that the war had ended gloriously victorious for our side, so that there was little incentive for the inquiry, except for Schley's wounded pride. Sampson's failure to appear is fully explained in his doctor's report, contained in the papers of Secretary of the Navy John Davis Long. This is a poignant description of Sampson's affliction. It is no exaggeration to suggest that the loss of the highly regarded Sampson, just at this important juncture, set the navy's development back many years. The court's report contains both nuggets of information and flashes of insight for the researcher willing to tackle it. A copy is available at the Navy Department Library.

As to Admiral Cervera's analysis of the actual purpose of his mission and his own despondency at being sent forth to sacrifice himself and his squadron, there is ample proof in the letters he sent back to Spain upon being ordered to head for the war zone. These also may be found at the Navy Department Library, some of them in translation from the Spanish. It appears that virtually no one in the Spanish government held any real illusions about the war with America. Spain knew she could not win, knew Cuba was lost, and wanted only to keep her national honor intact. When it was all over, America honored Admiral Cervera as a gentleman and naval officer who had done his duty to the best of his ability against odds he could not overcome. He is recorded as having been the most popular prisoner ever held captive in the United States, where he was treated more like an honored guest than anything else.

Through it all, the underpinning to understanding has, as before, been Bernard Brodie and *Sea Power in the Machine Age*, now joined by Harold and Margaret Sprout, *The Rise of American Naval Power 1776–1918*.

14: IDEALISM AND THE REFORMERS

It is evident from Bradley Fiske's autobiography (*From Midshipman to Rear Admiral*) that inventions for the betterment of the navy were the early passion of his life. Later on, new naval tactics utilizing them became his obsession, the thread of innovation still running strong, and finally reform of the naval bureaucracy itself, particularly creation of a strong naval staff headed by a chief of naval operations. His final effort began after World War I broke out in Europe, over getting our navy prepared for possible involvement. This was the issue over which he broke his lance against Secretary Daniels, who, to support President Wilson in his political stand that "He kept us out of the war,'' refused to consider even the most basic contingency planning. Only one month after Wilson began his second term, nonetheless, he asked Congress to declare war against Germany.

Another book that provided much background material for this chapter is Elting Morison's biography of Sims, fittingly dedicated "To the insurgent spirit, and to those officers who have maintained it within the United States Navy in time of Peace." Although the book is devoted entirely to Sims, it is also, in a real sense, the biography of the reform movement, which he typified, and led, all his adult life.

As the reader will discern, it is with this chapter that I have shifted my target slightly to conform with what I conceive to be the most useful way of presenting coherent modern history. In considering the history of our navy, I feel it is abundantly clear that the gun explosion in the *Princeton* and the nonmutiny aboard the *Somers* rank in importance with, for example, the battle between the *Monitor* and the *Merrimack*. As we get into modern times, however, it is much more difficult to make such evaluations. By far the safest measure is to confine oneself to operations, which is what most historical writers do. Combat will always be exciting, but it is my thesis that equally important to an appreciation of the navy are the personal pressures that caused it to be the way it was. Thus the target of these concluding chapters has been to describe the navy's reaction to events instead of merely reciting them. I am not trying to compete with the eminent historians cited at the end of this text in retelling the old stories, but, instead, hope to give them a different, more personal, dimension.

15: WORLD WAR I TO PEARL AND MIDWAY

Historians have always been intrigued with the "might have been" of World War I. If America had not entered it, despite our overt and even blatant aid to the Allied Powers, the general consensus is that the Central Powers, Germany and her allies, would have won. Had Admiral Scheer, the German commander at Jutland, stayed at sea and sought a decision on the second day (as the British expected), instead of seizing the opportunity for a retreat to Helgoland and Wilhelmshaven, there was at least the possibility he might have pulled off the naval long-shot upset of all time (judging from the disparity in damage resistance, his ships were individually superior to those of his enemy; whether they were enough superior to have made up for England's superiority in numbers will, of course, never be known). But it *is* known that the British navy was never satisfied with the results of Jutland. It wanted to destroy the enemy in the style of Horatio Nelson, and in this it failed. During the entire remainder of the war it lived in the hope and belief there would be another chance, which never came.

For the German High Seas Fleet, less can be said. At Jutland, Kaiser Wilhelm's prideful creation gave up whatever chance it might have had to bring World War I to a victorious termination. U-boats excepted, the German navy from that moment onward lived in the shadow of defeat and steadily decreasing morale, culminated ten days after the armistice by formal surrender at Scapa Flow, the British wartime base. The most thorough study of the battle and its aftermath can be found in Commander Holloway H. Frost's expertly written book *The Battle of Jutland*. For a very personal account of the surrender and subsequent scuttling of the German fleet, see Admiral Friedrich Ruge, *Scapa Flow 1919: The End of the German Fleet*, published in Germany in 1969 and in translation in London in 1973. Another of his books listed in our bibliography, *Der Seekrieg, The German Navy's Story: 1939–1945*, begins with a short, thoughtful recapitulation of the High Seas Fleet experience and its effect on the new German navy of 1939.

It is probably legitimate to state that the failure to fight to a finish at Jutland in 1916, and the subsequent supine surrender at Scapa Flow in 1918, affected the 1939 German navy far more profoundly than they did the British. When the interned German fleet scuttled itself in 1919, the remnants of that navy viewed the act as being loyal to its traditions (the commander of the scuttled fleet, von Reuter, said to the British admiral in charge, "I have done nothing that any British admiral would not have done in my place"). But when the "pocket battleship" *Admiral Graf von Spee* blew herself up at Montevideo twenty years later, rather than face a purportedly superior force of English warships, Hitler and the world at large put the worst possible interpretation on the desperate action. The ship bore the name of a much admired admiral who had heroically gone down with his outclassed squadron in World War I. Suicide without a fight was cowardly, dishonorable, something he would never have done—and from that moment anathema to the German navy of 1939. It can be only a matter of conjecture as to how much influence the incident had on subsequent actions by the German navy, but the record shows that from then on all its units fought to the bitter end, and except in the cases of one or two submarines driven to the surface by vastly superior forces, refused to surrender, even against hopeless odds.

It is even more useless to speculate as to whether the Japanese navy was likewise influenced by these events in the history of war at sea. The samurai way was to fight to the death in honor of their lord or their emperor. Japanese naval officers were samurai to the core, and they forced their nonsamurai crews to observe the same strict tradition. All the warships of Japan fought until they could fight no more—most of them until the waters of the sea closed over them—and in the end it took direct orders from the Japanese emperor himself to cause the remaining few to lower their colors.

16: THE ARMAGEDDON AT SEA

The reader will already have observed that there has been no attempt to recount the events of World War II at sea in this final chapter. As noted, this is not a "proper" history, and I refer those requiring more detail to the rich lode of materials on World War II, such as Samuel Eliot Morison's fifteen-volume operational history, written virtually on the spot, as well as any of hundreds of other worthwhile books, only a representative sampling of which is listed in my bibliography. My purpose is to find the one clear thread that explains what went on. In the Atlantic the thread was an extension of our intent a quarter of a century previous: to support England in her fight for national life. It was a rerun of World War I, but more ferocious because of the viciousness to which Germany had succumbed. The war against submarines was more bitterly fought, the losses heavier on both sides, but the stakes were the same. In the

Pacific, the thread was the legacy of Pearl Harbor. That unexpected attack, like the unexpected onslaught on our frigate *Chesapeake* in 1807, but so much more, produced a sense of national outrage never before experienced in our country. It set our goals, controlled our thinking, conditioned everything we did. It fixed our minds on only one purpose: the utter destruction of the system responsible. It made the war against Japan into a blood feud to which there could be only one outcome.

EPILOGUE: A FEW IDEAS ABOUT OUR POSTWAR NAVY

This chapter, which I've not labeled as such because it is a personal view of our postwar navy rather than a description of events, does not rely heavily on published materials. More distance in time is necessary. Just as the last few chapters of the text proper drift away from a simple recital of events in an attempt to draw insights from the war as a whole, this final section strays from any effort to describe our postwar navy battles—most of which, anyway, occurred in a House or Senate hearing room. Instead, I've tried to direct attention to areas and things that need to be fixed. For this I shall get little thanks from most of the navy, because it is in the nature of large organizations always to support the existing condition.

The reader, therefore, has here my own deeply felt ideas and opinions and has full right to disagree with them—just as I have the right, having thought about them for years, to hold them. Correction of the problems suggested will not convert the world, or our navy, into utopia; but they will improve serious conditions that today cry out for resolution, and which, one way or another, inevitably will be resolved. It is my hope, as a person loyal to the memory of all that our navy has done for our country, that it will work out solutions to improve its ability to perform the functions for which it was created, instead of the reverse; that it will not ultimately be forced, because of its own inaction, to accept solutions imposed from above by authority less thoughtfully attuned to its needs.

Bibliography

PRIMARY SOURCES

Published Documents, Narratives, Letters, and Memoirs

Allen, Gardner W. *The Papers of Isaac Hull*. Boston: The Boston Athenaeum, 1929.

American State Papers. *Naval Affairs*. 2 vols. Washington, D.C.: Gales and Seaton, 1832–1861.

Civil War Chronology 1861–1865. Washington, D.C.: Government Printing Office, n.d.

Clark, William Bell, and Morgan, William J. *Naval Documents of the American Revolution*. 8 vols. Washington, D.C.: Government Printing Office, 1966–82.

Commander Submarine Forces, U.S. Pacific Fleet. *U.S. Submarine Losses, World War II*. NavPers 15,784, 1949. Washington, D.C.: Government Printing Office, 1949 (first published 1946).

Dickerson, Edward N. *The Navy of the United States, An Exposure of Its Condition, and the Causes of Its Failure*. New York: John A. Gray & Green, 1864.

Ellicott, John M. (Lieutenant, U.S.N.). *Effect of the Gun Fire of the United States Vessels in the Battle of Manila Bay, May 1, 1898*. Washington, D.C.: Office of Naval Intelligence, 1899.

Glasstone, Samuel, and Dolan, Philip J. *The Effects of Nuclear Weapons*. Washington, D.C.: U.S. Department of Defense and U.S. Department of Energy, 1977.

Hibben, Henry A., A.M. (Chaplain, U.S.N.). *Washington Navy-Yard, History from Organization, 1799 to Present.* Washington, D.C.: Government Printing Office, 1890.

Humphreys, Joshua. Letter to Robert Morris dated 6 January 1793. U.S. Navy Department Operational Archives.

Knox, Dudley W. *Naval Documents Related to the Quasi-War Between the United States and France.* 7 vols. Washington, D.C.: Government Printing Office, 1935–38.

————. *Naval Documents Related to the War with the Barbary Powers.* 7 vols. Washington, D.C.: Government Printing Office, 1936–45.

Neesor, R. W. *Letters and Papers Relating to the Cruises of Gustavus Conyngham.* New York: Naval History Society, 1915.

Official Records of the Union and Confederate Navies in the War of the Rebellion. Series 1, vols. 6 and 7. Washington, D.C.: Government Printing Office, 1898.

Paullin, Charles Oscar. *Out-Letters of the Continental Marine Committee and Board of Admiralty, August, 1776–September, 1780.* 2 vols. New York: Naval History Society, 1914.

Record of Proceedings of a Court of Inquiry in the Case of Rear Admiral Winfield Scott Schley, U.S. Navy, Convened at the Navy Yard, Washington, D.C. September 12, 1901. 3 vols. Washington, D.C.: Government Printing Office, 1902.

The Ship Registers of Newburyport, Massachusetts, 1789–1870. Salem, Mass.: Essex Institute, 1937.

U.S. Congress. House. *Report of the Committee on Naval Affairs on H.R. 244* [a bill for the relief of officers and crew of the USS *Monitor* who participated in the action on 9 March 1862]. 48th Cong., 1st session, 1884. H. repts. 335, 1725.

United States Office of Naval Intelligence. *Information From Abroad. War Notes.* 1899–1900. VI The Spanish-American War, Blockades and Coast Defense. Nunez, Severo G. VII The Spanish-American War, A Collection of Documents Relative to the Squadron Operations in the West Indies. Arranged by Admiral Pascual Cervera y Topete. VIII The Squadron of Admiral Cervera. Concas, Victor M. y Palau.

Wilkes, Charles. *Autobiography of Rear Admiral Charles Wilkes, 1798–1877.* Edited by William J. Morgan, David B. Tyler, Joye L. Leonhart, and Mary F. Loughlin. Washington, D.C.: Government Printing Office, 1978.

Government Documents and Correspondence

U.S. National Archives, Washington, D.C.
  Navy & Old Army Branch, Record Group 45:
    Miscellaneous entries, bound 1822–1859
    Miscellaneous entries, loose 1815–1842
National Maritime Museum, Greenwich, London, England
  Admiralty draughts:
    Chesapeake—Negative 7343/34

 Confederacy—Negatives 6174/35, 6175/35, 6176/35, 6177/35, 6178/36, 8255, 8256, 8257

  Frolic—Negative 3085/46

  Hancock—Negatives 2285, 2285A/38

  President—Negative 1305/25

  Providence—Negative 4110

  Raleigh—Negatives 2400/40, 2400A/40

  Virginia—Negatives 2351/39, 2352/39, 2353/39, 2354/39

Public Records Office, Kew, London, England

 Admiralty captain's log collection:

  ADM51/2102-*Acasta*, Alexander Kerr

  ADM51/2110-*Arab*, Henry Jane

  ADM51/2236-*Chesapeake*, Alexander Gordon

  ADM51/2236-*Chesapeake*, George Burdett

  ADM51/2236-*Chesapeake*, Francis Newcombe

  ADM51/2465-*Junon*, Clotworthy Upton

  ADM51/2524-*Leander*, Sir George Ralph Collier

  ADM51/2516-*Loire*, James Nash

  ADM51/2543-*Majestic*, John Hayes

  ADM51/2589-*Newcastle*, Lord George Stuart

  ADM51/2609-*Narcissus*, John Richard Lumley

  ADM51/2695-*Pique*, Honourable Anthony Maitland

  ADM51/2681-*Shannon*, Philip B. V. Broke

  ADM51/2909-*Tenedos*, Hyde Parker

  ADM51/2958-*Venerable*, James Andrew Worth

Manuscript Collections

G. W. Blunt-White Library, Mystic Seaport, Conn.

 Officer's journals:

  Captain John Rodgers, 1802–1803

  Master Commandant A. S. Wadsworth, 1820–1821

  Master Commandant James Renshaw, 1822–1822

 Manuscript collections:

  Silas Talbot Papers, Log of *Constitution*

Constitution Museum, Charlestown, Mass.

 Officer's journal:

  Captain Samuel Nicholson, *Constitution*, 1797–1799

Historical Society of Pennsylvania, Philadelphia, Pa.

 Truxtun Collection:

  Am. 6795—Truxtun LB, 1798–1799

  Am. 679—USF *Constellation* Orders, Muster Rolls, Stores

  Am. 680—Truxtun LB, 1798–1800

Am. 681—Truxtun LB, 1800–1801
Historical Society of Old Newburyport, Newburyport, Mass.
    Officer's journal:
        Captain Moses Brown, *Merrimack*, 1799–1801
Library of Congress, Washington, D.C.
    Officer's journals:
        Commodore Edward Preble Papers, 1797–1807
        Commodore James Sever Papers, 1794–1801
        Captain Thomas Tingey Papers, 1798–1801
Mariner's Museum, Newport News, Va.
    Officer's journal:
        Commodore O. H. Perry, Journal of Squadron Dimensions, 1815
National Maritime Museum, Greenwich, London, England
    RUSI/NM/64—Royal Navy List through 31 December 1816
New-York Historical Society, New York, N.Y.
    Officer's journals:
        Commodore Stephen Decatur, Jr., Papers
        Rufus King Papers
        Captain James Lawrence Papers
        Commodore Richard Valentine Morris Papers
        Commodore Edward Preble Diaries, 1802–1804
        Commodore John Rodgers's Letters, 1813
        Commodore Silas Talbot Journal, *Constitution*, 1799–1801
Peabody Museum, Salem, Mass.
    Josiah Fox Papers
    Nathaniel Spooner letter, 2 June 1813
U.S. Customs House Museum, Newburyport, Mass.
    Nicholas Johnson Papers, 1790–1814
United States National Archives, Washington, D.C.
    Officer's journals:
        Captain Stephen Decatur, Sr., *Philadelphia*
        Midshipman Frederick Cornelius deKrafft, *Siren*
        Midshipman Charles Morris, Jr., *Siren*
        Lieutenant John Mullowny, Journal, *United States*
        Captain Alexander Murray, Letter Book
        Midshipman James Pity, Journal, *Constitution*
        Commodore Edward Preble, Papers
        Captain Thomas Tingey, Letter Book
United States Naval Academy, Annapolis, Md.
    Officer's journals:
        Commodore Richard Dale, Letter Book, *President*
        Captain Moses Tryon, Journal, *Connecticut*
Private Collection of Captain Bladen Dulany Claggett (Ret.)

Officer's journals:
  Commodore Bladen Dulany, Letter Book, *Boston*

Newspapers and Periodicals

Charleston Library Society, Charleston, S.C.
  City Gazette & Daily Advertiser (Charleston, S.C.). 1798–1801
South Carolina Historical Society, Charleston, S.C.
  South-Carolina State Gazette & Timothy's Daily Advertiser (Charleston, S.C.),
  1798–1801
Library of Congress, Washington, D.C.
  Claypoole's American Daily Advertiser (Philadelphia, Pa.), 1794–1800
  Coliseum Museum & Savannah Daily Advertiser (Savannah, Ga.), 1798–1799
  Columbian Centinel (Boston, Mass.), 1799–1800, 1809
  Commercial Advertiser (New York, N.Y.), 1800
  Connecticut Courant (Hartford, Conn.), 1799–1800
  Connecticut Journal (New Haven, Conn.), 1800
  Daily Advertiser (New York, N.Y.), 1800
  Federal Gazette & Baltimore Daily Advertiser (Baltimore, Md.), 1797–1801
  Georgia Gazette (Savannah, Ga.), 1799
  Harper's Weekly (New York, N.Y.), 1861–1870
  Leslie's Illustrated Newspaper (New York, N.Y.), 1861–1864
  Leslie's Pictorial History of the War of 1861 (New York, N.Y.), 1862
  Massachusetts Mercury (Boston, Mass.), 1799–1800
  Mercury & New England Palladium (Newport, R.I.), 1801
  New Hampshire Gazette (Portsmouth, N.H.), 1799
  Norfolk Herald (Norfolk, Va.), 1799–1800, 1807, 1812–1815, 1853
  Poulson's Daily Advertiser (Philadelphia, Pa.), 1800
  Salem Gazette (Salem, Mass.), 1800
  Southern Daily Argus (Norfolk, Va.), 1853–1854
Newburyport Public Library, Newburyport, Mass.
  Herald and County Gazette (Newburyport, Mass.), 1805–1806, 1813, 1863

SECONDARY SOURCES

Books

Abbot, Willis J. *Bluejackets of 1812.* New York: Dodd, Mead, and Company, 1887.
———. *Bluejackets of '76.* New York: Dodd, Mead, and Company, 1888.
———. *Bluejackets of '61.* New York: Dodd, Mead, and Company, 1886.
Ackworth, Barnard (Captain, R.N., D.S.O. Retired). *The Navies of Today and To-morrow.* London: Eyre and Spottiswoode, 1930.

Agawa, Hiroyuki. *The Reluctant Admiral: Yamamoto and the Imperial Navy.* Tr. by John Bester. Tokyo: Kodansha International, 1979.

Albion, Robert Greenhalgh. *Forests and Sea Power: The Timber Problem of the Royal Navy, 1652–1862.* Cambridge, Mass.: Harvard University Press, 1926.

Alden, John (Commander, U.S.N.). *The American Steel Navy.* Annapolis: U.S. Naval Institute Press, 1972.

Allen, Gardner W. *A Naval History of the American Revolution.* 2 vols. Boston: Houghton Mifflin and Company, 1913.

———. *Our Naval War with France.* Boston: Houghton Mifflin and Company, 1919.

———. *Our Navy and the Barbary Corsairs.* Boston: Houghton Mifflin and Company, 1905.

———. *Our Navy and the West Indian Pirates.* Salem, Mass.: Essex Institute, 1929.

———. *The Papers of John Davis Long 1897–1904.* Boston: Massachusetts Historical Society, 1939.

Anderson, William R. (Commander, U.S.N.), with Blair, Clay, Jr. *Nautilus 90 North.* New York: World Publishing Company, 1959.

Anthony, Irvin. *Decatur.* New York: Charles Scribner's Sons, 1931.

———. *Revolt at Sea.* New York: G. P. Putnam's Sons, 1937.

Archibald, E. H. H. *The Fighting Wooden Ship, 897–1860.* Poole, England: Blandford Press, 1968.

Auchinleck, Gilbert. *History of the War of 1812.* London: Arms and Armour Press, 1856.

Auer, James E. *The Postwar Rearmament of Japanese Maritime Forces, 1945–1971.* New York: Praeger Publishers, 1973.

Azoy, A.C.M. *Signal 250! The Fight off Santiago Bay.* New York: David McKay Company, 1964.

Bailey, Thomas A., and Ryan, Paul B. *Hitler vs. Roosevelt: The Undeclared Naval War.* New York: Free Press, 1979.

Barnes, J. S. (Lieutenant Commander, U.S.N.). *Submarine Warfare, Offensive and Defensive.* New York: D. Van Nostrand, 1869.

Barney, Mary. *A Biographical Memoir of the Late Commodore Joshua Barney from Autographical Notes and Journals in Possession of His Family, and Other Authentic Sources.* Boston: Gray and Bowen, 1832.

Bass, B. and E. *"Constitution," Super Frigate of Many Faces, Phase 2.* Melbourne, Fla.: Self-published, 1981.

Baxter, James P. *The Introduction of the Ironclad Warship.* Cambridge, Mass.: Harvard University Press, 1933.

Beach, Edward L. (Captain, U.S.N.). *Around the World Submerged.* New York: Henry Holt and Company, 1962.

———. (Commander, U.S.N.). *Submarine!* New York: Henry Holt and Company, 1952.

Beach, Edward L., and Maroon, Fred J. *Keepers of the Sea.* Annapolis: U.S. Naval Institute Press, 1983.

Beesly, Patrick. *Room 40.* London: Harcourt Brace Jovanovich, 1982.

Beirne, Francis F. *The War of 1812*. New York: E. P. Dutton and Company, 1949.

Blair, Clay, Jr. *The Atomic Submarine and Admiral Rickover*. New York: Henry Holt and Company, 1954.

———. *Silent Victory*. New York: J. P. Lippincott Co., 1975.

Bloch, Marc. *The Historian's Craft*. Manchester: Manchester University Press, 1954.

Bowen, A. *The Naval Monument*. Philadelphia: self-published, 1816.

Bowen, Frank C. *Men of Wooden Walls*. London: Staples Press, 1952.

Braisted, William R. *The United States Navy in the Pacific*. Austin: University of Texas Press, 1958.

Brewington, M. V. *Shipcarvers of North America*. New York: Dover Publications, 1972 (first published 1962).

Breyer, Siegfried. *Battleships and Battlecruisers, 1905–1970*. Garden City, N.Y.: Doubleday and Company, 1973.

Brodie, Bernard. *Sea Power in the Machine Age*. Princeton, N.J.: Princeton University Press, 1941.

Brookes, R., M.D. *Brookes' Gazetteer*. London: J. Richardson and Company, 1823.

Brown, D. K., RCNC. *A Century of Naval Construction*. Greenwich, England: Conway Maritime Press, 1983.

Buenzle, Fred J. *Bluejacket*. New York: W. W. Norton and Company, 1939.

Butow, Robert J. C. *Japan's Decision to Surrender*. Stanford, Calif.: Stanford University Press, 1954.

Butow, Robert J. C. *Tojo and the Coming of War*. Princeton, N.J.: Princeton University Press, 1961.

Calvert, James (Rear Admiral, U.S.N.). *The Naval Profession*. New York: McGraw-Hill Book Company, 1965.

Carter, Worrall Reed (Rear Admiral, U.S.N.). *Beans, Bullets and Black Oil*. Washington, D.C.: Government Printing Office, 1953.

The Century Magazine. Battles and Leaders of the Civil War. New York: Thomas Yoseloff, 1956 (first published 1887).

Chadwick, F. E. *The Relations of the United States and Spain*. 2 vols. New York: Charles Scribner's Sons, 1911.

Chapelle, Howard I. *The Baltimore Clipper: Its Origin and Development*. Hatboro, Pa.: Tradition Press, 1965 (first published 1930).

———. *History of American Sailing Ships*. New York: W. W. Norton and Company, 1935.

———. *History of the American Sailing Navy*. New York: W. W. Norton and Company, 1949. Reprinted by Bonanza, 1949.

Church, William C. *The Life of John Ericsson*. New York: C. Scribner's Sons, 1890.

Clark, Charles E. (Rear Admiral, U.S.N.). *My Fifty Years in the Navy*. Boston: Little, Brown and Company, 1917. Reissued in 1984 by U.S. Naval Institute Press, Annapolis, with Introduction and Notes by Jack Sweetman.

Clark, George R. (Rear Admiral, U.S.N.); Stevens, William O., Ph.D. Litt.D.; Alden, Carroll S., Ph.D.; Krafft, Herman F., LL.B. *A Short History of the United States Navy*. Philadelphia: J. B. Lippincott Company, 1910.

Clark, J. J. (Admiral, U.S.N.), and Barnes, Dwight H. (Captain, U.S.N.R.). *Seapower and Its Meaning*. New York: Franklin Watts, 1966.

Clark, J. J. (Admiral, U.S.N.), with Reynolds, Clark G. *Carrier Admiral*. New York: David McKay Company, 1967.

Clark, Thomas. *Naval History of the United States*. Philadelphia: M. Carey, 1814.

Clark, William Bell. *Ben Franklin's Privateers*. Baton Rouge, La.: Louisiana State University Press, 1956.

―――. *Captain Dauntless: The Story of Nicholas Biddle of the Continental Navy*. Baton Rouge, La.: Louisiana State University Press, 1949.

―――. *The First "Saratoga."* Baton Rouge, La.: Louisiana State University Press, 1953.

―――. *Gallant John Barry, 1745–1803*. New York: Macmillan Company, 1938.

Clowes, William Laird. *The History of the Royal Navy: From the Earliest Times to the Present*. 6 vols. London: Sampson Low, Marston and Company, 1900–1901.

Coggeshall, George. *The History of the American Privateers and Letters-of Marque During Our War with England in the Years 1812, 1813 and 1814*. New York: self-published, 1856.

Coletta, Paolo E. *The American Naval Heritage in Brief*. Washington, D.C.: University Press of America, 1978.

Colledge, J. J. *Ships of the Royal Navy*. 2 vols. Newton Abbot, England: David and Charles, 1969–1970.

Cooper, J. Fenimore. *The History of the Navy of the United States of America*. 2 vols. Philadelphia: Lea and Blanchard, 1839 (with subsequent revisions and abridgements).

―――. *Lives of Distinguished American Naval Officers*. Philadelphia: Carey and Hart, 1846.

―――. *Ned Myers*. 2 vols. New York: G. P. Putnam's Sons, 1899.

Costello, John. *The Pacific War, 1941–1945*. New York: Quill, 1982.

Costello, John, and Hughes, Terry. *The Battle of the Atlantic*. New York: Dial Press, 1977.

―――. *Jutland, 1916*. New York: Holt, Rinehart and Winston, 1976.

Courtemanche, Regis A. *No Need of Glory*. Annapolis: U.S. Naval Institute Press, 1977.

Cremer, Peter. *U-Boat Commander*. Annapolis: U.S. Naval Institute Press, 1982.

Cunningham, Viscount of Hyndhope (Admiral of the Fleet, R.N., K.B., C.G.B., O.M., D.S.O.). *A Sailor's Odyssey*. New York: E. P. Dutton and Company, 1951.

Currier, John J. *History of Newburyport*. 2 vols. 1906–1909. Newburyport, Mass.: self-published.

D'Albas, Andrieu (Captain, French Naval Reserve). *Death of a Navy*. New York: Devin-Adair Company, 1957.

Daly, John J., ed. *Diaries and Letters of William F. Keeler: Aboard the U.S.S. "Monitor": 1862*. Annapolis: U.S. Naval Institute Press, 1964.

Davis, Charles G. *Ships of the Past*. New York: Rudder Publishing Company, 1929.

Davis, Vincent. *The Admiral's Lobby*. Chapel Hill, N.C.: University of North Carolina Press, 1967.

————. *Postwar Defense Policy and the U.S. Navy*. Chapel Hill, N.C.: University of North Carolina Press, 1962.

Dearborn, H. A. S. *The Life of William Bainbridge, Esq.* Princeton, N.J.: Princeton University Press, 1931 (first published 1816).

Denton, Jeremiah A., Jr. (Rear Admiral, U.S.N.), with Brandt, Edward. *When Hell Was in Session*. Clover, S.C.: Commission Press, 1976.

Doenitz, Karl (Admiral of the Fleet, Third Reich, German Navy). *Memoirs, Ten Years and Twenty Days*. New York: World Publishing Company, 1958.

Donovan, Frank. *The Odyssey of the "Essex."* New York: David McKay Company, 1969.

Douglas, Sir Howard (General, R.A.). *Naval Gunnery*. London: J. Murray, 1851 (first published 1829).

Drummond, John D. *H.M. U-Boat*. New York: British Book Centre, 1958.

Dudley, William S. *Going South: U.S. Navy Officer Resignations and Dismissals on the Eve of the Civil War*. Washington, D.C.: U.S. Naval Historical Foundation, 1981.

Dugan, James. *The Great Iron Ship*. New York: Harper and Brothers, 1953.

Dull, Paul S. *The Imperial Japanese Navy (1941–1945)*. Annapolis: U.S. Naval Institute Press, 1978.

Edwards, Kenneth (Lieutenant Commander, R.N.). *We Dive at Dawn*. Chicago: Reilly and Lee Company, 1941.

Eliot, George Fielding. *The Ramparts We Watch*. New York: Reynal and Hitchcock, 1938.

Eller, E. M. (Admiral, U.S.N.); Morgan, William J., Ph.D.; and Basoco, R. M. (Lieutenant, U.S.N.). *Sea Power and the Battle of New Orleans*. New Orleans: 150th Anniversary Committee of Louisiana, 1965.

Emmons, George F. (Lieutenant, U.S.N.). *The United States Navy, 1775–1853*. Washington, D.C.: Gideon, 1854.

Evans, Robley D. *A Sailor's Log*. New York: D. Appleton and Company, 1901.

Fairburn, William Armstrong. *Ships of the American Merchant Marine* (vols. 2, 5, and 6). Center Lovell, Maine: Fairburn Marine Educational Foundation, 1947–1955.

Falk, Edward A. *From Perry to Pearl Harbor*. Garden City, N.Y.: Doubleday, Doran and Company, 1943.

Ferguson, Eugene S. *Truxtun of the "Constellation": The Life of Commodore Thomas Truxtun, U.S. Navy, 1755–1822*. Baltimore: Johns Hopkins University Press, 1956.

Fincham, John. *History of Naval Architecture*. London: Scolar Press, 1979 (first published 1851).

Fiske, Bradley A. *From Midshipman to Rear Admiral*. New York: Century Company, 1919.

Flexner, James Thomas. *Washington, the Indispensable Man*. Boston: Little, Brown and Company, 1969.

Forester, C. S. *The Age of Fighting Sail*. Garden City, N.Y.: Doubleday, Doran and Company, 1957.

Fowler, William M., Jr. *Rebels Under Sail*. New York: Charles Scribner's Sons, 1976.

Frank, Wolfgang. *Enemy Submarine*. London: William Kimber and Company, 1954.

Freidel, Frank. *The Splendid Little War*. Boston: Little, Brown and Company, 1958.

Frost, John. *Book of the Navy*. New York: D. Appleton and Company, 1842.

Frost, Holloway H. (Commander, U.S.N.). *The Battle of Jutland*. Annapolis: U.S. Naval Institute Press, 1936.

————. (Lieutenant Commander, U.S.N.). *We Build a Navy*. Annapolis: U.S. Naval Institute Press, 1929.

Fuchida, Mitsuo (Captain, Imperial Japanese Navy), and Okumiya, Masatake (Commander, Imperial Japanese Navy). Edited by Clarke H. Kawakami and Roger Pineau. *Midway, the Battle That Doomed Japan*. Annapolis: U.S. Naval Institute Press, 1955 (first published in Japan, 1951).

Fukui, Shizuo. *Naval Vessels 1887–1945, Mitsubishi Zosen Built* (in Japanese). Tokyo: Mitsubishi Shipbuilding and Engineering Company, 1956.

Gleaves, Albert (Rear Admiral, U.S.N.). *The Life and Letters of Rear Admiral Stephen B. Luce, U.S.N.* New York: G. P. Putnam's Sons, 1925.

Goldsborough, Charles W. *The Naval Chronicle* (vol. 1). Washington, D.C.: James Wilson, 1824.

Goode, W. A. M. *With Sampson Through the War*. New York: Doubleday and McClure, 1899.

Grant, Bruce. *Isaac Hull, Captain of Old Ironsides*. Chicago: Pellegrini and Cudahy, 1947.

Grenfell, Russell (Captain, R.N.). *The "Bismarck" Episode*. New York: Macmillan Company, 1949.

————. *Main Fleet to Singapore*. New York: Macmillan Company, 1952.

————. *Nelson, the Sailor*. New York: Macmillan Company, 1950.

————. *Unconditional Hatred*. New York: Devin-Adair Company, 1953.

Griffin, Martin, I. J. *Commodore John Barry*. Philadelphia: self-published, 1903.

Guttridge, Leonard F., and Smith, Jay D. *The Commodores*. New York: Harper and Row, 1969.

Hackett, Sir John (General, R.A.). *The Profession of Arms*. New York: Macmillan Company, 1983.

Halsey, William F. (Admiral, U.S.N.), and Bryan, J., III (Lieutenant Commander, U.S.N.R.). *Admiral Halsey's Story*. New York: McGraw-Hill Book Company, 1947.

Hara, Tameichi; with Saito, Fred, and Pineau, Roger. *Japanese Destroyer Captain*. New York: Ballantine Books, 1961 (first published in Japan, 1955, under the title *Teikoku Kaigun no Saigo*).

Hastings, Max, and Jenkins, Simon. *The Battle for the Falklands*. London: Michael Joseph and Company, 1983. New York: W. W. Norton, 1983.

Hattendorf, John B., and Hayes, John D. *The Writings of Stephen B. Luce*. Newport, R.I.: Naval War College Press, 1975.

Hattendorf, John B.; Simpson, B. Mitchell, III; and Wadleigh, John R. *Sailors and Scholars*. Newport, R.I.: Naval War College Press, 1941.

Hay, David and Joan. *The Last of the Confederate Privateers*. New York: Crescent Books, 1977.

Heinl, Robert Debs, Jr. (Colonel, U.S.M.C.). *Soldiers of the Sea*. Annapolis: U.S. Naval Institute Press, 1962.

Henderson, James. *The Frigates*. New York: Dodd, Mead, and Company, 1971.

————. *Sloops and Brigs*. Annapolis: U.S. Naval Institute Proceedings, 1972.

Hendrick, Burton J. *The Life and Letters of Walter H. Page, 1855–1918*. 2 vols. Garden City, N.Y.: Garden City Publishing Company, 1927.

Hezlet, Sir Arthur (Vice Admiral, R.N.). *The Submarine and Sea Power*. London: Peter Davies, 1967.

Hewlett, Richard G., and Duncan, Francis. *Nuclear Navy, 1946–1962*. Chicago: University of Chicago Press, 1974.

Hoehling, A. A. *Thunder at Hampton Roads*. Englewood Cliffs, N.J.: Prentice-Hall, 1976.

Holmes, W. J. (Captain, U.S.N.). *Double-Edged Secrets: U.S. Naval Intelligence Operations in the Pacific During World War II*. Annapolis: U.S. Naval Institute Press, 1979.

————. *Undersea Victory*. Garden City, N.Y.: Doubleday and Company, 1966.

Hooper, Edwin Bickford (Vice Admiral, U.S.N.). *Mobility, Support, Endurance: A Story of Naval Operational Logistics in the Vietnam War, 1965–1968*. Washington, D.C.: Department of the Navy, Navy History Department, 1972.

————. (Vice Admiral, U.S.N.); Allard, Dean C.; and Fitzgerald, Oscar P. *The United States Navy and the Vietnam Conflict*. Vol. 1, *The Setting of the Stage to 1959*. Washington, D.C.: U.S. Naval History Division, Government Printing Office, 1976.

Horsman, Reginald. *The Causes of the War of 1812*. Cranbury, N.J.: A. S. Barnes and Company, 1962.

Hough, Richard. *Death of the Battleship*. New York: Macmillan Company, 1963.

————. *Fighting Ships*. New York: G. P. Putnam's Sons, 1969.

Humble, Richard, ed. *Naval Warfare: An Illustrated History*. London: Orbis Publishing, 1957.

Inoguchi, Rikihei, and Nakajima, Tadashi, with Pineau, Roger. *The Divine Wind*. Annapolis: U.S. Naval Institute Press, 1958.

Jackson, Melvin H. *Privateers in Charleston, 1793–1796*. Washington, D.C.: The Smithsonian Institution Press, 1969.

James, William. *Naval History of Great Britain* (vol. 6). London: Harding, Lepard and Company, 1826.

————. *Naval Occurrences in the Late War Between Great Britain and the United States*. London: T. Egerton, 1817.

Jane's Fighting Ships. London, 1898, 1919, 1941, 1945.

Jentschura, H.; Jung, D.; and Mickel, P., tr. by Antony Preston and J. D. Brown. *Warships of the Imperial Japanese Navy (in German)*. Frankfurt: J. F. Lehmans Verlag, 1970 (U.S. edition, Annapolis: U.S. Naval Institute Press, 1977).

Johnson, Robert Erwin. *Thence Round Cape Horn: The Story of the United States Naval Forces on the Pacific Station, 1818–1923*. Annapolis: U.S. Naval Institute Press, 1967.

Jones, Virgil Carrington. *The Civil War at Sea*. Vol. 1, *The Blockaders*. New York: Holt, Rinehart and Winston, 1960.

————. *The Civil War at Sea*. Vol. 2, *The River War*. New York: Holt, Rinehart and Winston, 1961.

————. *The Civil War at Sea*. Vol. 3. *The Final Effort*. New York: Holt, Rinehart and Winston, 1962.

Karig, Walter (Commander, U.S.N.R.), and Kelly, Welbourn (Lieutenant, U.S.N.R.). *Battle Report*. New York: Farrar and Rinehart, 1944.

Karsten, Peter. *The Naval Aristocracy: The Golden Age of Annapolis and the Emergence of Modern American Navalism*. New York: Free Press, 1972.

Kemp, Peter. *Oxford Companion to Ships and the Sea*. London: Oxford University Press, 1976.

Keunne, Robert E. *The Attack Submarine*. London: Yale University Press, 1965.

Keyes, Sir Roger (Admiral of the Fleet, R.N.). *The Naval Memoirs of the Admiral of the Fleet, Sir Roger Keyes*. Vol. 1, *The Narrow Seas to the Dardanelles, 1910–1915*. New York: E. P. Dutton and Company, 1934.

————. *The Naval Memoirs of the Admiral of the Fleet, Sir Roger Keyes*. Vol. 2, *Scapa Flow to the Dover Straits, 1916–1918*. New York: E. P. Dutton and Company, 1935.

Kimball, Horace. *Naval Battles of the United States in Different Wars with Foreign Nations, from the Commencement of the Revolution to the Present Including Privateering*. Boston: Higgins and Bradley, 1857 (first published 1831).

Kimmel, Husband E. (Rear Admiral, U.S.N.). *Admiral Kimmel's Story*. Chicago: Henry Regnery Company, 1955.

King, Ernest J. (Fleet Admiral, U.S.N.). *U.S. Navy at War 1941–1945*. Washington, D.C.: U.S. Navy Department, 1946.

Knox, Donald. *Death March*. New York: Harcourt Brace Jovanovich, 1981.

Knox, Dudley W. *A History of the United States Navy*. New York: Van Rees Press, 1936.

Labaree, Benjamin Woods. *Patriots and Partisans: The Merchants of Newburyport*. New York: W. W. Norton and Company, 1962.

Lake, Simon. *The Submarine in War and Peace*. Philadelphia: J. B. Lippincott Company, 1918.

Langley, Harold D. *Social Reform in the United States Navy, 1798–1862*. Urbana, Ill.: University of Illinois Press, 1967.

Larrabee, Harold A. *Decision at the Chesapeake*. New York: Clarkson N. Potter, 1964.

Layton, Edwin T. (Rear Admiral, U.S.N. Ret.), with Captain Roger Pineau, U.S.N.R. (Ret.) and John Costello. *"And I Was There."* New York: William Morrow and Company, 1985.

Leather, John. *World Warships in Review 1860–1906*. Annapolis: U.S. Naval Institute Press, 1976.

Lewis, Charles Lee. *Admiral de Grasse and American Independence*. Annapolis: U.S. Naval Institute Press, 1945.

———. *Admiral Franklin Buchanan: Fearless Man of Action*. Baltimore: Norman, Remington Company, 1929.

———. *David Glasgow Farragut*. Vol. 1, *Admiral in the Making*. Annapolis: U.S. Naval Institute Press, 1941.

———. *David Glasgow Farragut*. Vol. 2, *Our First Admiral*. Annapolis: U.S. Naval Institute Press, 1943.

———. *Famous American Naval Officers*. New York: L. C. Page and Company, 1924.

———. *Matthew Fontaine Maury: The Pathfinder of the Seas*. Annapolis: U.S. Naval Institute Press, 1927.

———. *The Romantic Decatur*. Philadelphia: University of Pennsylvania Press, 1937.

Lloyd, Christopher. *The British Seaman*. London: Collins, 1968.

Lockwood, Charles A. (Vice Admiral, U.S.N.). *Sink 'Em All*. New York: E. P. Dutton and Company, 1951.

Long, David F. *Nothing Too Daring: A Biography of Commodore David Porter, 1780–1843*. Annapolis: U.S. Naval Institute Press, 1970.

———. *Sailor-Diplomat: A Biography of Commodore James Biddle*. Boston: Northeastern University Press, 1983.

Lord, Walter. *Day of Infamy*. New York: Henry Holt and Company, 1957.

———. *Incredible Victory*. New York: Harper and Row, 1967.

Lorenz, Lincoln. *John Paul Jones*. Annapolis: U.S. Naval Institute Press, 1943.

Macartner, Clarence Edward. *Mr. Lincoln's Admirals*. New York: Funk and Wagnalls Company, 1956.

MacBride, Robert. *Cival War Ironclads*. Philadelphia: Chilton Company, 1962.

McCordick, Robert Stanley. *The Yankee Cheese Box*. Philadelphia: Darrance and Company, 1938.

McGregor, David W. *Merchant Sailing Ships, 1775–1815*. Watford, England: Argus Books, 1980.

MacIntyre, Donald (Captain, R.N.). *Jutland*. New York: W. W. Norton and Company, 1958.

———. *U-Boat Killer*. London: Weidenfeld and Nicholson, 1956.

McKee, Christopher. *Edward Preble: A Naval Biography 1761–1807*. Annapolis: U.S. Naval Institute Press, 1972.

Mackenzie, Alexander Slidell. *The Life of Commodore Oliver H. Perry*. New York: Harper and Brothers, 1840.

————. *The Life of Paul Jones*. New York: Harper and Brothers, 1845.

————. *The Life of Stephen Decatur*. Boston: Charles C. Little and James Brown, 1846.

Maclay, Edgar Stanton. *A History of American Privateers*. New York: D. Appleton and Company, 1899.

————. *The History of the United States Navy*. 3 vols. New York: D. Appleton and Company, 1894.

Mahan, Alfred Thayer (Captain, U.S.N.). *The Influence of Seapower on History*. Boston: Little, Brown and Company, 1890.

————. *The Influence of Seapower on the French Revolution and Empire, 1783–1812*. Boston: Little, Brown and Company, 1892.

————. *The Life of Nelson: The Embodiment of the Sea Power of Great Britain*. Boston: Little, Brown and Company, 1897.

————. *Major Operations of the Navies in the American Revolution*. Boston: Little, Brown and Company, 1913.

————. *Seapower in Its Relation to the War of 1812*. 2 vols. Boston: Little, Brown and Company, 1905.

Manus, Max. *Underwater Saboteur*. London: William Kimber and Company, 1953.

Maroon, Fred J., and Beach, Edward L. *Keepers of the Sea*. Annapolis: U.S. Naval Institute Press, 1983.

Mars, Alastair. *British Submarines at War 1939–1945*. Annapolis: U.S. Naval Institute Press, 1977.

Martin, Tyrone G. *A Most Fortunate Ship*. Chester, Conn.: Globe-Pequot Press, 1980.

Marvin, Winthrop L. *The American Merchant Marine*. Cambridge, Mass.: Charles Scribner's Sons, 1902.

Masefield, John. *Sea Life in Nelson's Time*. London: Conway Maritime Press, 1972 (first published 1905).

Mason, Theodore C. *Battleship Sailor*. Annapolis: U.S. Naval Institute Press, 1982.

Middlebrook, Louis F. *The Frigate "South Carolina."* Salem, Mass.: The Essex Institute, 1929.

Middleton, Drew. *Submarine: The Ultimate Naval Weapon—Its Past, Present and Future*. Chicago: Playboy Press, 1976.

Miller, Nathan. *The U.S. Navy: An Illustrated History*. Annapolis: U.S. Naval Institute Press, 1977.

Millington-Drake, Sir Eugene, K.C.M.G. *The Drama of the "Graf Spee" and the Battle of the Plate*. London: Peter Davies, 1964.

Millot, Bernard. *Divine Thunder: The Life and Death of the Kamikazes*. New York: McCall Publishing Company, 1970.

Mitchell, Mairin, F.R.G.S. *The Maritime History of Russia, 848–1948*. London: Sidgwick and Jackson, 1949.

Morgenstern, George. *Pearl Harbor: The Story of the Secret War*. New York: Devin-Adair Company, 1947.

Morison, Elting E. *Admiral Sims and the Modern American Navy*. Cambridge, Mass.: Riverside Press, 1942.

Morison, Samuel E. *History of United States Naval Operations in World War II*. 15 vols. Boston: Little, Brown and Company, 1947–1962.

———. *John Paul Jones: A Sailor's Biography*. Boston: Little, Brown and Company, 1959.

———. *The Maritime History of Massachusetts, 1783–1860*. Boston: Houghton Mifflin and Company, 1921.

———. *"Old Bruin": Commodore Matthew Calbraith Perry, 1794–1858*. Boston: Little, Brown and Company, 1967.

———. *The Two Ocean War*. Boston: Little, Brown and Company, 1963.

Morris, Richard Knowles. *John P. Holland*. Annapolis: U.S. Naval Institute Press, 1966.

Nash, Howard P. *The Forgotten Wars*. Cranbury, N.J.: A. S. Barnes and Company, 1968.

———. *A Naval History of the Civil War*. Cranbury, N.J.: A. S. Barnes and Company, 1972.

Neesor, R. W. *Statistical and Chronological History of the U.S.N., 1775–1907*. 2 vols. New York: Macmillan Company, 1909.

Nevins, Allan. *The Emergence of Lincoln*. 2 vols. New York: Charles Scribner's Sons, 1950.

Noel, John V., Jr. (Captain, U.S.N.), and Beach, Edward L. (Captain, U.S.N.). *Naval Terms Dictionary*. 3rd and 4th eds. Annapolis: U.S. Naval Institute Press, 1971, 1978.

Okumiya, Masatake, and Horikoshi, Jiro, with Caidin, Martin. *Zero!* New York: Ballantine Books, 1956.

Ollard, Richard. *Pepys*. New York: Holt, Rinehart and Winston, 1974.

Pacific War Research Society. *Japan's Longest Day*. New York: Ballantine Books, 1972 (originally published in Japanese as *Nihon no Ichiban Nagai Hi*. 1965, by Bungei Shunju).

Paine, Ralph D. *Joshua Barney: A Forgotten Hero of Blue Water*. New York: Century Company, 1924.

Parker, William Harwar (Captain, C.S.N.). *Recollections of a Naval Officer, 1841–1865*. New York: Charles Scribner's Sons, 1883.

Parkes, Oscar. *British Battleships*. London: Seeley, Service and Company, 1957.

Parkinson, Cyril Northcote, ed. *Trade Winds: A Study of British Overseas Trade During the French Wars, 1793–1815*. London: George Allen and Unwin, 1948.

Parsons, William Barclay. *Robert Fulton and the Submarine*. New York: Columbia University Press, 1922.

Paullin, Charles Oscar. *Commodore John Rodgers: A Biography*. Cleveland: Arthur H. Clarke, 1910 (reissued in 1966 by U.S. Naval Institute Press).

———. *The Navy of the American Revolution*. New York: Haskell House Publishers, 1973 (first published 1906).

Peillard, Leonce. *The "Laconia" Affair*. New York: G. P. Putnam's Sons, 1963.

Perry, Milton F. *Infernal Machines*. Baton Rouge, La.: Louisiana State University Press, 1965.

Pinckney, Pauline A. *American Figureheads and Their Carvers*. New York: W. W. Norton and Company, 1940.

Pineau, Roger, ed. *The Personal Journal of Commodore Matthew C. Perry*. Washington, D.C.: The Smithsonian Institution Press, 1968.

Polmar, Norman. *The Ships and Aircraft of the U.S. Fleet*. 12th ed. Annapolis: U.S. Naval Institute Press, 1984.

————, and Allen, Thomas B. *Rickover*. New York: Simon and Schuster, 1981.

Poolman, Kenneth. *Guns off Cape Ann*. Chicago: Rand McNally, 1961.

————. *Periscope Depth*. Chicago: Sphere Books, 1981.

Pope, Dudley. *The Black Ship*. Philadelphia: J. B. Lippincott Company, 1964.

Porter, David Dixon. *The Naval History of the Civil War*. New York: Sherman, 1886.

Potter, E. B. *Illustrated History of the United States Navy*. New York: Thomas Y. Crowell Company, 1971.

————. *Nimitz*. Annapolis: U.S. Naval Institute Press, 1976.

Potter, E. B., ed. *The United States and World Sea Power*. Englewood Cliffs, N.J.: Prentice-Hall, 1955.

Potter, E. B., and Nimitz, Chester W. (Admiral of the Fleet, U.S.N.). *The Great Sea War*. New York: Bramhall House, 1960.

Powell, Edward Alexander. *Gentlemen Rovers*. New York: Charles Scribner's Sons, 1913.

Prange, Gordon W. *At Dawn We Slept*. New York: McGraw-Hill Book Company, 1983.

Pratt, Fletcher. *The Civil War in Pictures*. New York: Henry Holt and Company, 1955.

————. *Civil War on Western Waters*. New York: Henry Holt and Company, 1956.

————. *The "Monitor" and the "Merrimack."* New York: William Sloan Associates, 1951.

————. *The Navy: A History*. Garden City, N.Y.: Doubleday, Doran and Company, 1938.

————. *Preble's Boys*. New York: Wiliam Sloan Associates, 1950.

Puleston, W. D. (Captain, U.S.N.). *Mahan*. New Haven, Conn.: Yale University Press, 1939.

Pullen, H. F. *The "Shannon" and the "Chesapeake."* Toronto: McClelland and Stewart, 1970.

Raeder, Erich (Grand Admiral, German Navy). *My Life*. Tr. by Henry W. Drexel. Annapolis: U.S. Naval Institute Press, 1960.

Raymond, Jack. *Power at the Pentagon*. New York: Harper and Row, 1964.

Rayner, D. A. (Commander, D.S.C. and Bar, V.R.D., R.N.V.R.). *Escort*. London: William Kimber and Company, 1955.

Reed, Rowena. *Combined Operations in the Civil War*. Annapolis: U.S. Naval Institute Press, 1978.

Reynolds, Francis J. *The United States Navy from the Revolution to Date*. New York: P. F. Collier and Sons, 1917.

Richardson, James O. (Admiral, U.S.N.), as told to Dyer, George C. (Vice Admiral, U.S.N.). *On the Treadmill to Pearl Harbor*. Washington, D.C.: U.S. Navy Department, Naval History Division, 1973.

Rickover, Hyman G. *How the Battleship "Maine" Was Destroyed*. Washington, D.C.: Government Printing Office, 1976.

Roberts, W. Adolphe. *Semmes of the "Alabama."* New York: Bobbs Merrill Company, 1938.

Robison, S. S. (Rear Admiral, U.S.N.), and Robison, Mary L. *A History of Naval Tactics from 1530 to 1930*. Annapolis: U.S. Naval Institute Press, 1942.

Rogge, Bernhard. *Under Ten Flags*. London: Weidenfeld and Nicholson, 1955.

Roosevelt, Theodore. *The Naval War of 1812: Or, The History of the United States Navy During the Last War with Great Britain*. New York: G. P. Putnam's Sons, 1882.

Roskil, S. W. (Captain, D.S.C., R.N.). *White Ensign: The British Navy at War 1939–1945*. Annapolis: U.S. Naval Institute Press, 1950.

Roskil, S. W. (Captain, D.S.C., R.N.). *White Ensign*. Annapolis: U.S. Naval Institute Press, 1960.

Ruge, Friedrich (Vice Admiral, Federal German Navy). *Der Seekrieg, The German Navy's Story: 1939–1945*. Tr. by M. G. Saunders. Annapolis: U.S. Naval Institute Press, 1957.

———. *Scapa Flow 1919: The End of the German Fleet*. Tr. by Derek Masters. London: Allan, 1973 (originally published in Oldenburg, Germany, 1969).

———. *Sea Warfare 1939–1945; A German Viewpoint*. Tr. by M. G. Saunders, London: Cassell and Company, 1957.

Ryan, Paul B. *The First Line of Defense: The U.S. Navy Since 1945*. Stanford, Calif.: Hoover Institution Press, 1981.

Sandler, Stanley. *The Emergence of the Modern Capital Ship*. Newark, Del.: Delaware University Press, 1979.

Sargent, Nathan (Commander, U.S.N.). *Admiral Dewey and the Manila Campaign*. Washington, D.C.: U.S. Naval Historical Foundation, 1947.

Scharf, J. Thomas. *History of the Confederate States Navy*. New York: Rogers and Sherwood, 1887.

Schlesinger, Arthur M., Jr., ed. *The Almanac of American History*. New York: G. P. Putnam's Sons, 1983.

Schofield, William G. (Captain, U.S.N.R.). *Destroyers—60 Years*. Boston: Burdette and Company, 1962.

Sherburne, John Henry. *Life and Character of the Chevalier John Paul Jones, a Captain in the Navy of the United States During the Revolutionary War*. Washington, D.C., and New York: Wilder and Campbell, 1825.

Shomette, Donald. *The Flotilla*. Annapolis: U.S. Naval Institute Press, 1981.

Sims, Williams Sowden (Rear Admiral, U.S.N.). *The Victory at Sea*. Annapolis: U.S. Naval Institute Press, 1984.

Sloan, Edward William III. *Benjamin Franklin Isherwood, Naval Engineer: The Years as Engineer-in-Chief, 1861–1869*. Annapolis: U.S. Naval Institute Press, 1965.

Sloane, Eric. *A Reverence for Wood*. New York: Ballantine Books, 1974 (first published 1965).

Smith, Moses. *Naval Scenes in the Last War*. Boston: Gleason's Publishing Hall, 1846.

Smith, Philip F. C. *Captain Samuel Tucker (1747–1833), Continental Navy*. Salem, Mass.: Essex Institute, 1976.

———. *The Empress of China*. Philadelphia: Philadelphia Maritime Museum, 1984.

———. *Fired by Manley Zeal*. Salem, Mass.: Peabody Museum, 1977.

———. *Frigate "Essex" Papers: Building the Salem Frigate, 1798–1799*. Salem, Mass.: Peabody Museum, 1974.

Smith, S. E., ed. *The United States Navy in World War II*. New York: William Morrow and Company, 1966.

Snider, C. H. J. *The Glorious "Shannon's" Old Blue Duster*. Toronto: McClelland and Stewart, 1923.

Snow, Elliot. *Life in a Man of War*. Cambridge, Mass.: Riverside Press, 1927.

Soley, James Russell. *The Blockade and the Cruisers*. New York: D. Appleton and Company, 1895.

———. *Historical Sketch of the United States Naval Academy*. Washington, D.C.: Government Printing Office, 1976.

Spector, Ronald. *Admiral of the New Empire: The Life and Career of George Dewey*. Baton Rouge, La.: Louisiana State University Press, 1974.

———. *Eagle Against the Sun: The American War with Japan*. New York: Free Press/Macmillan, 1985.

Sprout, Harold and Margaret. *The Rise of American Naval Power 1776–1918*. Princeton, N.J.: Princeton University Press, 1967 (first published 1939).

Stafford, Edward P. (Commander, U.S.N.). *The Big E: The Story of the USS "Enterprise."* New York: Random House, 1962.

———. *The Far and the Deep*. New York: G. P. Putnam's Sons, 1966.

———. *Little Ship, Big War: The Saga of DE 343*. New York: William Morrow and Company, 1984.

Stevens, William Oliver, and Westcott, Allan. *A History of Sea Power*. Garden City, N.Y.: Doubleday, Doran and Company, 1935.

Stevenson, William. *A Man Called Intrepid*. New York: Harcourt Brace Jovanovich, 1976.

Stewart, Charles W. (Superintendent, Library and War Records). *John Paul Jones Commemoration at Annapolis, April 24, 1906*. Washington, D.C.: Government Printing Office, 1906 (reprinted 1966).

Stinchcombe, William. *The XYZ Affair*. Westport, Conn.: The Greenwood Press, 1980.

Swann, Leonard Alexander, Jr. *John Roach, Maritime Entrepreneur*. Annapolis: U.S. Naval Institute Press, 1965.

Sweetman, Jack. *An Illustrated Chronology of American Naval History, 1775–1983*. Annapolis: U.S. Naval Institute Press, 1984.

————. *The Landing at Vera Cruz, 1914*. Annapolis: U.S. Naval Institute Press, 1978.

————. *The U.S. Naval Academy: An Illustrated History*. Annapolis: U.S. Naval Institute Press, 1979.

Theiss, Frank. *The Voyage of Forgotten Men*. New York: Bobbs Merrill Company, 1937.

Thomas, Emory M. *The Confederate Nation*. The New American Nation Series, edited by Henry Steele Commager and Richard B. Morris. New York: Harper and Row, 1979.

Thomas, Lowell. *Count Luckner: The Sea Devil*. Garden City, N.Y.: Doubleday, Page and Company, 1927.

Toland, John. *Infamy*. New York: Berkeley Books, 1972.

Truxtun, Thomas. *Instructions, Signals and Explanations for the United States Fleet*. Baltimore: J. Hayes, 1797.

————. *Remarks, Instructions and Examples Relating to Latitude and Longitude*. Philadelphia: Dobson, 1794.

Tucker, Glenn. *Dawn Like Thunder: The Barbary Wars and the Birth of the U.S. Navy*. New York: Bobbs-Merrill Company, 1963.

Tuleja, T. V. *Twilight of the Sea Gods*. New York: W. W. Norton and Company, 1958.

Turnbull, Archibald D. *Commodore David Porter*. New York: Century Company, 1929.

Valle, James E. *Rocks and Shoals*. Annapolis: U.S. Naval Institute Press, 1980.

Van de Water, Frederic F. *The Captain Called It Mutiny*. New York: Ives Washburn, 1954.

Van Powell, Noland. *American Navies of the Revolutionary War*. New York: G. P. Putnam's Sons, 1974.

Villiers, Alan. *Captain James Cook*. New York: Charles Scribner's Sons, 1967.

Von Mullenheim-Rechburg, Baron Burkhard. *Battleship "Bismarck": A Survivor's Story*. Annapolis: U.S. Naval Institute Press, 1980.

Von Pivka, Otto. *Navies of the Napoleonic Era*. Newton Abbot, England: David and Charles, 1980.

Waldo, S. Putnam. *Biographical Sketches of Distinguished American Heroes in the War of the Revolution*. Hartford, Conn.: Silas Andrus, 1923.

Wallach, Sidney, ed. *Narrative of the Expedition of an American Squadron to the China Seas and Japan*. New York: Coward-McCann, 1952.

Ward, Christopher. *The War of the Revolution*. 2 vols. New York: Macmillan Company, 1952.

Weems, John Edward. *The Fate of the "Maine."* New York: Henry Holt and Company, 1958.

Welch, Gordon. *The Hut Six Story*. New York: McGraw-Hill Book Company, 1982.

West, Richard S. *The Second Admiral: A Life of David Dixon Porter*. New York: Coward-McCann, 1937.

Wheeler, Gerald E. *Admiral William Veazie Pratt, U.S. Navy*. Washington, D.C.:

U.S. Navy Department, Naval History Division, U.S. Government Printing Office, 1974.

Wheeler, Harold. *Stirring Deeds of Britain's Sea Dogs*. London: Robert M. McBride and Company, 1916.

White, William Chapman and Ruth. *Tin Can on a Shingle*. New York: E. P. Dutton and Company, 1957.

Wilcox, L. A. *Mr. Pepys' Navy*. London: G. Bell and Sons, 1966.

Wood, Virginia Steele. *Live Oaking: Southern Timber for Tall Ships*. Annapolis: U.S. Naval Institute Press, 1981.

Woodward, W. E. *George Washington: The Image and the Man*. New York: Boni and Liveright, 1926.

Yokota, Yutaka, with Joseph D. Harrington. *Suicide Submarine* (formerly *The Kaiten Weapon*). New York: Ballantine Books, 1962.

Zumwalt, Elmo R. Jr. *On Watch*. New York: Quadrangle, 1976.

Essays and Articles

Alden, John D. "Whatever Happened to the Battleship *Oregon*?" *U.S. Naval Institute Proceedings* (September 1968): 146–49.

Anderson, William G. "John Adams, the Navy, and the Quasi-War with France." *The American Neptune* 30, no. 2 (April 1940): 117–32.

Augur, Helen. "Ben Franklin and the French Alliance." *American Heritage Magazine* (April 1956): pp. 66–88.

Beach, Edward L. "Rickover." *The Washington Post*, 27 May 1977.

Bolander, Louis H. "The Introduction of Shells and Shell Guns in the United States Navy." *The Mariner's Mirror* 17, no. 1 (February 1931): 105–112.

Buhl, Lance C. "Mariners and Machines, Resistance to Technological Change in the U.S. Navy, 1865–1869." *The Journal of American History* (1924): 703–27.

Butow, Robert J. C. "The Hull–Nomura Conversations: A Fundamental Misconception." *The American Historical Review* 65, no. 4 (July 1860): 822–36.

Chapelle, Howard I. "Ships of the American Navy in the War of 1812." *The Mariner's Mirror* 18, no. 3 (July 1932): 287–302.

Daly, John J. "Truxtun of the United States Navy." *The Washington Post*, 21 October 1928.

Dunne, W. M. P. "The *Constellation* and the *Hermione*." *The Mariner's Mirror* 70, no. 1 (February 1984): 82–84.

Eller, Ernest M. "Truxtun, the Builder." *U.S. Naval Institute Proceedings* 63, no. 10 (October 1937): 1445–52.

Forester, Cecil Scott. "Bloodshed at Dawn." *American Heritage Magazine*, October 1964.

———. "Victory on Lake Champlain." *American Heritage Magazine*, December 1963.

Greene, Samuel Dana. "The Fight Between the *Monitor* and the *Merrimack*." *United Services Magazine* 12 (April 1885): 350.

———. "In the *Monitor*'s Turret." *Century Magazine* 29 (1885): 754–63.

Hornsby, Thomas. "Oregon and Peacemaker: 12 Inch Wrought Iron Guns." *The American Neptune* 6, no. 3 (July 1946): 212–22.

Luce, Stephen B. "The Story of the *Monitor*." *Papers of the Military History Society* (Boston) 12 (1914): 127–54.

Miles, A. H. (Comdr. U.S.N.). "The *Princeton* Explosion." *U.S. Naval Institute Proceedings* 52, no. 11 (November 1926): 2226–45.

———. (Captain, U.S.N.). "The *Princeton* Explosion." *The Iron Worker* 21, no. 2 (Spring 1957): 1–11.

Miller, Jonathan. "Hyman Rickover, the Ancient Submariner." *The New Republic*, 12 November, 1977.

Morgan, William J. "The Pivot Upon Which Everything Turned: French Naval Superiority That Ensured Victory at Yorktown." *The Ironworker* 2, no. 2 (Spring 1958).

Palmer, Michael A. "The Dismission of Captain Isaac Phillips." *The American Neptune* 45, no. 2.

Pearson, Lee M. "The *Princeton* and the Peacemaker." *Technology and Culture* 7, no. 2 (Spring 1966): 163–83.

Rodger, N. A. M. "The Design of the *Inconstant*." *The Mariner's Mirror* 61, no. 1 (February 1975): 9–22.

Shaffer, Ralph E. "The Race of the *Oregon*." *Oregon Historical Quarterly* 76, no. 3 (September 1975): 268–94.

Van Deurs, George. "The *Oregon*'s Builder's Trials." *Shipmate Magazine* (Annapolis) 39, no. 6 (July–August 1976): 27–30.

Watts, Harry C. (Ensign, U.S.N.). "Ericsson, Stockton and the U.S.S. *Princeton*." *U.S. Naval Institute Proceedings* 82, no. 9 (September 1956): 961–67.

Novels

Beach, E. L. (Lt. Cdr., U.S.N.). *An Annapolis Plebe*. Philadelphia: Penn Publishing Company, 1907.

———. (Lt. Cdr., U.S.N.). *An Annapolis Youngster*. Philadelphia: Penn Publishing Company, 1908.

———. (Lt. Cdr., U.S.N.). *An Annapolis Second Classman*. Philadelphia: Penn Publishing Company, 1909.

———. (Lt. Cdr., U.S.N.). *An Annapolis First Classman*. Philadelphia: Penn Publishing Company, 1910.

———. (Lt. Cdr., U.S.N.). *Ralph Osborn, Midshipman at Annapolis*. Boston: H. A. Wilde Company, 1909.

———. (Commander, U.S.N.). *Midshipman Ralph Osborn at Sea*. Boston: H. A. Wilde Company, 1910.

———. (Commander, U.S.N.). *Ensign Ralph Osborn*. Boston: H. A. Wilde Company, 1911.

———. (Commander, U.S.N.). *Lieutenant Ralph Osborn Aboard a Torpedo Boat Destroyer*. Boston: H. A. Wilde Company, 1912.

———. (Commander, U.S.N.). *Roger Paulding, Apprentice Seaman*. Philadelphia: Penn Publishing Company, 1911.

———. (Commander, U.S.N.). *Roger Paulding, Gunner's Mate*. Philadelphia: Penn Publishing Company, 1912.

———. (Commander, U.S.N.). *Roger Paulding, Gunner*. Philadelphia: Penn Publishing Company, 1913.

———. (Commander, U.S.N.). *Roger Paulding, Ensign*. Philadelphia: Penn Publishing Company, 1914.

———. (Captain, U.S.N.). *Dan Quin of the Navy*. New York: Macmillan Company, 1922.

Beach, Edward L. (Commander, U.S.N.). *Run Silent, Run Deep*. New York: Holt, Rinehart and Winston, 1955.

———. (Captain U.S.N.). *Cold Is the Sea*. New York: Holt, Rinehart and Winston, 1978.

———. (Captain U.S.N.). *Dust on the Sea*. New York: Holt, Rinehart and Winston, 1972.

Buchheim, Lothar-Gunnar. *Das Boot*. Munich: R. Piper and Company, 1973.

Carlisle, Henry. *Voyage to the First of December*. New York: G. P. Putnam's Sons, 1972.

Coppel, Alfred. *The Burning Mountain: A Novel of the Invasion of Japan*. San Diego: Harcourt Brace Jovanovich, 1983.

Divine, David. *The Iron Ladies*. London: Hutchinson and Company, 1961.

Dodson, Kenneth. *Away All Boats*. Boston: Little, Brown and Company, 1954.

Exum, Wallace Louis. *Battle-Ship! Pearl Harbor, 1941*. Virginia Beach, Va.: The Donning Company, 1974.

Eyster, Warren. *Far from Customary Skies*. New York: Random House, 1953.

Marryat, Frederick (Captain, R.N.). *Frank Mildmay, or The Naval Officer*. London: Saunders and Otley, 1829.

———. *Masterman Ready*. London: Henry Colburn, 1841.

———. *Mr. Midshipman Easy*. London: Saunders and Otley, 1836.

———. *Percival Keene*. London: Henry Colburn, 1842.

———. *Peter Simple*. London: Saunders and Otley, 1834.

Unpublished Materials

Beach, E. L. (Captain, U.S.N.). "From Annapolis to Scapa Flow: The Autobiography of a Naval Officer."

Dent, Keith S. "The British Navy and the Anglo-American War of 1812–1815." M.A. diss., University of Leeds, Leeds, England, 1949.

Klachko, Mary. "The First Chief of Naval Operations" (a biography of Admiral W. S. Benson). U.S. Navy Department, Naval History Division, 1984.

Index

545